The Money Book of Personal Finance

The Money® Book of Personal Finance

by Richard Eisenberg

and the editors of Money magazine

WARNER BOOKS

A Time Warner Company

Warner Books, Inc., 1271 Avenue of the Americas, New York, NY 10020

 A Time Warner Company

Printed in the United States of America
First Printing: January 1996
10   9   8   7   6   5   4   3   2   1

Library of Congress Cataloging-in-Publication Data
Eisenberg, Richard
   The money book of personal finance / Richard Eisenberg.
     p. cm.
   Includes index.
   ISBN 0-446-52429-8 (hc)
   1. Finance, Personal.   I. Title
HG179.E395   1996
332.024—dc20   95–31462
                                     CIP

Book design by Giorgetta Bell McRee

Acknowledgments

This book was truly a collaborative effort. Numerous **MONEY** writers and editors wrote chapters. Specifically:

Elizabeth Fenner wrote Chapters 2 and 13

Mary Sprouse wrote Chapter 4

Vanessa O'Connell wrote Chapters 5 and 6

Carla Fried wrote Chapters 7 and 8

Shelly Branch wrote Chapters 9 and 18

Joseph S. Coyle wrote Chapters 10 and 12

Lani Luciano wrote Chapters 11 and 21

Eric Schurenberg wrote Chapter 14

Ruth Simon wrote Chapter 15

Gary Belsky wrote Chapters 16 and 17

Marguerite Smith wrote Chapters 19 and 20

Susan Berger wrote the Appendix

In addition, many experts offered advice, information, and data. They are: Lewis J. Altfest of L. J. Altfest & Co., Inc.; Joseph Anderson, president of Capital Research Associates; John W. Barnhill, M.D.; Thomas Benson of Opus/Portfolio Concepts; Adriane Berg; Jim Blue of the U.S. Department of Veterans Affairs; Budget and Credit Counseling Service of New York; D. J. Caulfield and Mike Stamler of the U.S. Small Business Administration; *Consumers Union;* Bob Coyle of the Federal Housing Administration; Ken and Daria Dolan; Kenneth Doyle; Larry Elkin; Susan Forward; Echo Montgomery Garrett; Ruth Hayden; Ibbotson Associates; David W. Krueger, M.D.; Richard Lehman of the Bond Investors Association; Herman

Max Leibowitz; Jules Levine, Boston University Law School; Annette Lieberman; James Lynch of Lynch Municipal Bond Advisory; Rebecca Maddox; Ray Madoff, Boston College assistant professor of law; Tom Margenau of the Social Security Administration; John Markese of the American Association of Individual Investors; Stuart Kessler of Goldstein Golub Kessler; Jerry Mason; Arlene Matthews; Katherine McGee; Olivia Mellan; Merrill Lynch; Marcia Millman; Morningstar Inc.; Donna Naftalis; Gary Naftalis; National Insurance Consumer Organization; John O'Leary of Lifecycle Testing; Earl Osborn of Bingham Osborn and Scarborough; J. Boyd Page of Page & Bacek; Population Reference Bureau; Norman Powell of Grant Thornton; Susan L. Repetti of Nutter, McClennen & Fish; Mike Shuster; Thomas J. Sitzmann of Goulston & Storrs; Deborah Stead; Phyllis Jackson Stegall; Laurence Steinberg; Teenage Research Unlimited; James Wilson, president Consumer Financial Education Foundation; Young Americans Bank; and the Securities and Exchange Commission.

At **MONEY,** thanks to Frank Lalli for giving me the time to work on this book. Thanks also to Genevieve Fernandez; Malcolm Fitch; Dan Green; Simon Green; Jude Hayes; Mark Hernandez; Susan Lehman; Rosalyn McDavid; Pat McManus; Patti Straus; Mike Terry; Teresa Tritch; Walter Updegrave; and David White.

I'd like to offer special gratitude to my agent, Stuart Krichevsky, and my editor, Rick Wolff.

Finally, my sincerest appreciation to my wife, Elizabeth Sporkin, and my sons, Aaron and Will.

My apologies if any names of people who contributed to this book were unintentionally omitted.

Table of Contents

Introduction

Welcome to *The **MONEY** Book of Personal Finance.* You have just taken the first step on your journey toward financial independence. In today's complicated and busy world, it's difficult to find the time to educate yourself about money matters. It's harder still to keep current, what with all the changes in the tax laws, new mutual funds opening daily for business, government programs that get adjusted (sometimes eliminated) routinely, and many financial-services companies coming out with new—and they claim improved—offerings ranging from life insurance invested in stocks to credit cards that pay you for being a frequent buyer. This book will help you make sense of personal finances and make you wiser about money.

Covering the entire range of personal finance topics, this book walks you through the basics of everything from taxes to home-equity loans to investing in mutual funds. It has been updated to reflect all the changes brought by the 1997 tax law. Unlike other personal finance guides, however, the book takes you to another level. After explaining the key terms and techniques you need to know, it tells you how to put them to best use so you can reach your financial goals. Throughout the book you'll find clear and easy checklists, worksheets, phone numbers, Web sites, and questions to assist you in understanding how you're doing and how you can do even better.

The best way to use this book is *not* to sit and read it cover to cover. Admittedly, *The **MONEY** Book of Personal Finance* won't rock you with the suspense of a John Grisham novel or the plot twists of a Tom Clancy thriller. What it will do for you, however, is provide pointers in the parts of your financial life that could stand improvement. We all have them. You might need an introduction to disability insurance, for instance, or a refresher course in taxes. You can get either—plus the lowdown on dozens of other topics—by reading the chapter or chapter section dedicated to the subject.

First, though, take the time to read the three chapters that constitute Section One: "Getting Started."

Chapter 1: "How Are You Doing?" will show you exactly where you stand today financially and how you compare with other people with similar incomes or others about your age. You will also learn how to determine your assets, liabilities, and net worth, set financial priorities and goals and learn some secrets for saving money. The financial-planning checklist at the end of the chapter will show you where to begin concentrating your efforts.

Chapter 2: "The Basics" walks you through the essentials of record keeping, using a bank wisely, and getting the insurance protection you and your family need. You'll also see what kind of insurance you *don't* need.

Chapter 3: "Getting Help You Can Trust" starts with the premise that no one has to handle his or her finances alone. So if you're in the market for a tax preparer, a lawyer, an insurance agent, a stockbroker, a financial planner, or a money manager, you will find solid advice on how to find one you can trust—and afford. At the end of the chapter you will see how your computer can become a trusted financial adviser, too.

Review the Table of Contents to find the chapters in the rest of the book that will help you most. Section Two: "Reaching Your Financial Goals" provides information and advice about taxes (Chapter 4), boosting your savings (Chapter 5), managing your debt (Chapter 6), buying a home (Chapter 7), getting the most out of your home (Chapter 8), getting the most out of your career (Chapter 9), affording college for your children (Chapter 10), retiring comfortably (Chapter 11), and managing your estate (Chapter 12).

If you're looking to improve your investing prowess, turn to Section Three: "Investing Your Money." There you'll learn the basics of investing wisely (Chapter 13), how to invest in stocks and stock mutual funds (Chapter 14), how to invest in bonds and bond mutual funds (Chapter 15), how to invest in real estate (Chapter 16), and how to invest in other ways (Chapter 17).

You can read about money topics that come up in everyday life in Section Four: "Your Family Finances." Here's where you will learn how to get the best deals when you spend (Chapter 18), how men and women manage money (Chapter 19), how to teach your kids about money (Chapter 20), and how to help your aging parents with their finances (Chapter 21).

Ever wondered if there is a government agency or program out there that could help you get ahead? Turn to the Appendix for an exclusive guide to federal benefits. You will see what's available, who can get what the government offers, and whom to call to receive more information. Odds are you will flip back to the Appendix from time to time when the need arises. For example, if you're about to buy a car and wonder how safe it is, you can find the agency that will tell you. If you wonder about the safety of a country you plan to visit on vacation, the Appendix will show you how to get the skinny. If you're looking for federal finan-

cial aid to pay for your child's college education or would like to learn how much you are due to receive from Social Security, you can turn to the Appendix for assistance there, too.

To help you increase your money knowledge even further, the book is filled with addresses and phone numbers of organizations offering free or inexpensive specialized advice on topics. In addition, whenever financial software or computer on-line services might be instructive, their names are noted. It's all part of the goal of *The MONEY Book of Personal Finance:* to help you get all you want out of life.

Richard Eisenberg
New York, New York
January 1998

SECTION ONE

GETTING STARTED

CHAPTER 1

How Are You Doing?

Taking control of your finances. The very sound of it delivers a jolt of self-confidence. Once you're in control of your finances, after all, you can do what it takes to reach your most important money goals. But don't be in a hurry. Many people mistakenly think that the way to become financially independent is to plunge into stocks or mutual funds and hope for some winners. Actually, however, the secret to financial success is educating yourself about all the key areas of personal finance—from taxes to investing to debt management to estate planning—and then taking the right steps in each.

Before you make any moves to improve your financial lot in life, you need to know how you're doing currently. By putting down on paper the true numbers representing your finances—your assets, your liabilities, and your net worth—you'll see where you need to get started improving your situation. Then, after you have sorted through your own money, you can treat yourself to an eye-opening experience and see in the tables later in this chapter how your finances compare with those of others like you.

Determining Your Assets, Liabilities, and Net Worth

So, do you know how you're doing, really? Chances are, you have a vague notion. For instance, you may be pretty certain that your debts are higher than they ought to be. Or that you could be investing a bit more. Perhaps you've been squirreling away money for years and have amassed a substantial amount. By filling in the following worksheets, you'll know for sure.

Sizing yourself up means looking at three important financial indicators: your **assets,** your **liabilities,** and your **net worth.** Your assets are all the things you own: the money you have in the bank, your furniture, your home, your investments. Your liabilities are the debts you owe. Your net worth is what you get when you subtract your liabilities from your assets. In some cases, particularly if you are young and haven't accumulated much yet, your net worth is a negative figure.

Complete the following worksheet and the one on page 8 and you'll learn exactly how much you have in assets and liabilities and, ultimately, your current net worth. In order to fill in the blanks, you will need to pull together your financial records. This could take a few hours, and admittedly, it's not a lot of fun to do. Once you've completed the exercise, however, you'll have all the data you need to help you make some important calculations, such as the amount you'll need to save and invest to retire comfortably or to send your children to college. What's more, you'll be able to tell which types of assets you should build up and which

types of liabilities you should whittle down. You'll learn more about investing and debt management later in the book.

YOUR ASSETS

To tote up your assets, first collect all your year-end bank, brokerage, mutual fund, mortgage, and employee benefits statements. Then sort out the investment accounts by the particular type of investment. Under each asset listed on the worksheet, write down the total dollar amount. Then match the investments to their particular asset classes and write the correct amount there, too. If you have doubts about which asset class to select, see Chapters 14 and 15.

A few pointers: Any money in the four subcategories of cash belongs under Liquid Assets. The asset class known as Income Stocks is for stocks and stock mutual funds yielding 4.5% or more. For Real Estate, just write in the current market value of the property. For Personal Assets and Collectibles, include only belongings that you think are likely to appreciate in value.

After you've totaled each of the nine asset class columns, write in the sums on the line called Asset Totals by Class. Add those totals to get your Grand Total of Assets. If you divide the asset class totals by your total assets, you'll learn what percent of your portfolio is in each asset class.

	BLUE-CHIP STOCKS	INCOME STOCKS	AGGRESSIVE GROWTH STOCKS	FOREIGN STOCKS	HIGH-GRADE BONDS	HIGH-YIELD BONDS	LIQUID ASSETS	REAL ESTATE	OTHER

Cash
Checking
account
$
Money-
market
account
$
Money-
market fund
$
Certificates
of deposit
$

Securities
Individual
stocks
$
Individual
bonds
$
Mutual funds
$
Unit trusts
and
partnerships
$

	BLUE-CHIP STOCKS	INCOME STOCKS	AGGRESSIVE GROWTH STOCKS	FOREIGN STOCKS	HIGH-GRADE BONDS	HIGH-YIELD BONDS	LIQUID ASSETS	REAL ESTATE	OTHER
Retirement accounts									
401(k) or 403(b) plans $									
IRAs and Keoghs $									
Annuities $									
Profit-sharing plan $									
Life insurance									
Variable life $									
Whole life and universal $									
Real Estate									
Primary residence $									
Vacation home $									
Investment property $									

	BLUE-CHIP STOCKS	INCOME STOCKS	AGGRESSIVE GROWTH STOCKS	FOREIGN STOCKS	HIGH-GRADE BONDS	HIGH-YIELD BONDS	LIQUID ASSETS	REAL ESTATE	OTHER
Personal assets and collectibles Jewelry $									
Collections (stamps, coins) $									
Miscellaneous $									
Business equity $									
Trust funds $									
Asset totals by class	$	$	$	$	$	$	$	$	$
Grand total of assets					Total $				
Asset classes as percentage of total portfolio	%	%	%	%	%	%	%	%	%

YOUR DEBTS AND NET WORTH

Now you're ready to figure out what you owe, what you're paying on all your debts, and what you're truly worth. Get out your December 31 statements for all mortgages, loans, and revolving credit cards. Add up their outstanding balances, subtract that amount from your Grand Total of Assets from the preceding worksheet, and you will get your net worth. You can make your net worth grow by controlling your spending, reducing your debts, and increasing savings and investments.

TYPE OF DEBT	OUTSTANDING BALANCE	INTEREST RATE
Housing loans		
Primary residence mortgage	$	%
Second mortgage/home-equity loan		
Home-equity line of credit		
Vacation home mortgage		
Investment-property loan		
Installment loans		
Car loan	$	%
Education loan		
Unsecured bank loan		
Other debt		
Charge card 1		
Charge card 2		
Charge card 3		
Charge card 4		
Charge card 5		
Margin loan		
Insurance policy loan		
401(k) loan		
Family loan		
Total debt	$	
Net worth	$	

How You Compare with Your Neighbors

Now that you know how you're doing, take a look at the next tables and see how you're doing versus your fellow Americans with similar incomes. Notice the huge jump in net worth and net financial assets once income tops $20,000.

NET WORTH, HOME EQUITY, AND FINANCIAL ASSETS

FAMILY INCOME	NET WORTH	NET FINANCIAL ASSETS
Less than $10,000	$416	$0
$10,000–$19,999	$500	$500
$20,000–$29,999	$45,964	$3,700
$30,000–$39,999	$62,462	$7,570
$40,000–$49,999	$85,978	$12,772
$50,000–$59,999	$120,472	$23,024
$60,000–$74,999	$136,723	$21,011
$75,000 and up	$204,724	$50,148
U.S. MEDIAN	**$23,520**	**$970**

Notes: The figures are medians. Net financial assets represents savings and investments. It does not include home equity, business equity, or the value of automobiles. **Source:** Capital Research Associates Analysis of Survey of Income and Program Participation Data.

WHERE THE MONEY IS

Increasingly, Americans are socking away money in retirement accounts such as IRAs, Keogh plans, and employer-sponsored savings programs. Consequently, retirement accounts constitute the largest percent of all family assets: 22.7%, followed closely by stocks.

FINANCIAL ASSET	PERCENT OF ALL FAMILY ASSETS
Retirement accounts	22.7%
Stocks	21.0%
Checking, savings, money-market accounts	16.4%
Certificates of deposit	7.9%
Bonds	7.7%
Mutual funds (excluding money–market mutual funds)	7.2%
Other managed assets	6.4%
Cash value of life insurance	5.7%
Other	3.9%
Savings bonds	1.1%
Financial assets as a percentage of total assets	**32.3%**

THE PERCENTAGE OF FAMILIES HOLDING KEY ASSETS

Most people have checking accounts, and the majority of upper-income Americans have money stashed in retirement accounts. Less than a third of Americans, however, have money in bank CDs, mutual funds, stocks, bonds, or savings bonds. The more income you have, the more likely you are to own financial assets. For example, while only 14% of people with incomes of $25,000 to $49,999 have stocks, 45% of those with incomes of $100,000 and up are shareholders.

	CHECKING, SAVINGS ACCOUNTS	BANK CDs	MUTUAL FUNDS	STOCKS	BONDS	RETIREMENT ACCOUNTS	SAVINGS BONDS	LIFE INSURANCE
All Families	**87%**	**14%**	**12%**	**15%**	**3%**	**43%**	**23%**	**31%**
Income								
Under $10,000	61%	7%	2%	3%	1%	6%	6%	16%
$10,000–$24,999	82%	16%	5%	9%	1%	24%	12%	22%
$25,000–$49,999	95%	14%	12%	14%	3%	53%	27%	33%
$50,000–$99,999	99%	16%	21%	26%	5%	70%	40%	43%
$100,000 and up	100%	21%	38%	45%	15%	85%	36%	54%

THE MEDIAN VALUE OF HOLDINGS FOR FAMILIES WHO HAVE THESE ASSETS

This may be one of the most interesting tables you'll ever see. It shows you exactly how much people who own particular financial assets have in them. For instance, people who own mutual funds have a median value of $19,000 in those funds, but mutual fund owners with incomes of $100,000 and up have $48,000 worth of fund shares.

	CHECKING, SAVINGS ACCOUNTS	BANK CDs	MUTUAL FUNDS	STOCKS	BONDS	RETIREMENT ACCOUNTS	SAVINGS BONDS	LIFE INSURANCE
All Families	**$2,100**	**$10,000**	**$19,000**	**$8,000**	**$26,200**	**$15,600**	**$1,000**	**$5,000**
Income								
Under $10,000	$700	$7,000	$25,000	$2,000	——	$3,500	$400	$1,500
$10,000–$24,999	$1,400	$10,000	$8,000	$6,000	——	$6,000	$800	$3,000
$25,000–$49,999	$2,000	$10,000	$12,500	$7,000	$29,000	$10,000	$700	$5,000
$50,000–$99,999	$4,500	$13,000	$15,000	$6,000	$9,400	$23,000	$1,200	$7,000
$100,000 and up	$15,800	$15,600	$48,000	$30,000	$58,000	$85,000	$1,500	$12,000

MEDIAN VALUE OF DEBTS FOR FAMILIES WHO HAVE SUCH DEBTS

As with financial assets, the higher your income, the higher your debt load, in general. For example, Americans with incomes of $10,000 to $24,999 who owe money on their credit cards owe $900 on their cards, while those with incomes of $100,000 and up have median outstanding credit card balances of $2,700. Inter-

estingly, however, debt loads tend to start falling once people hit their mid-fifties. While Americans with debt in their late thirties and early forties owe a total of $39,100, those aged 65 to 74 owe just $5,400. In addition, although the table doesn't show this, debt represents 18.2% of family income for people age 35 to 44, but only 3.8% of family income for people 75 and up. Overall, debt represents 16.7% of U.S. family income.

	MORTGAGE, HOME EQUITY	INSTALLMENT DEBT	CREDIT CARD	OTHER LINES OF CREDIT	OTHER DEBT	ALL DEBT
All Families	**$47,400**	**$5,000**	**$1,100**	**$2,200**	**$2,700**	**$19,500**
Income						
Under $10,000	$15,200	$2,100	$500	——	$1,600	$2,500
$10,000–$24,999	$20,600	$3,100	$900	$2,900	$1,100	$6,300
$25,000–$49,999	$42,300	$5,700	$1,200	$1,500	$2,200	$19,300
$50,000–$99,999	$60,800	$8,100	$1,600	$2,000	$3,300	$59,300
$100,000 and up	$99,700	$11,200	$2,700	$4,300	$6,500	$120,100
Age of Family Head						
Under 35	$55,300	$5,000	$1,000	$1,300	$1,500	$11,500
35–44	$59,700	$5,400	$1,300	$2,000	$3,300	$39,100
45–54	$43,400	$5,100	$1,600	$5,400	$3,300	$31,300
55–64	$32,600	$4,800	$1,100	$4,300	$3,300	$22,600
65–74	$18,400	$4,300	$900	$4,300	$1,600	$5,400
75 and up	$30,400	$3,400	$600	——	$2,900	$2,600

BUDGETING AND CASH FLOW

Now that you know how you're doing and how you're faring versus your neigh-

bors, you can begin looking for ways to do better. Start by getting a handle on where your money goes every month. This way you can start plugging your money leaks and find ways to spend less, save more, and boost your net worth.

Nobody likes to keep a running budget of expenses. The process is a pain and generally winds up as an annoyance. That said, jotting down how and where you spend your money can be an eye-opening experience. How often have you said to yourself: "I just don't know where the money goes. I make a decent living, but there's nothing left at the end of the month." By keeping tabs on your expenses, you'll be able to solve America's greatest unsolved mystery: the case of the vanishing paycheck.

So, try this mini-budgeting program and think of it as cash-flow management. For two months, starting the first day of next month, keep a written record of every time you spend money. (Yes, one month would be easier, but some expenses such as clothes don't show up monthly; by giving yourself two months, you're more likely to end up including the full range of your spending.) Jot down exactly how much you spent and what you spent it on. In addition, make note of every time you take cash from the bank or your automated teller machine and write down the amount.

When the two months are over, get a blank piece of paper. At the top of the page, write down your gross income for the two months. Underneath, create a table divided into the following expense categories: Housing and Utilities; Taxes, Savings, and Investments; Food (break this down into groceries and eating out); Debt Payments;

Vacations, Entertainment, and Hobbies; Transportation (both for pleasure and for work); Insurance; Clothing and Personal Care; Gifts and Contributions Made; Medical Expenses; Child Care and Education; Unreimbursed Business Expenses; Mystery Cash; and Alimony and Child Support (if you pay any). Then, add up your spending in each category. Estimate where you must and include as Mystery Cash the difference between your income and all your other expenses. Finally, get out your calculator and determine the percentage of your gross income that you spent in each category.

You could instead create your budget using helpful computer software such as *Quicken 98* or Microsoft's *Money 98,* which sell for $30 to $90. Both programs have a computerized ledger for entering purchases. *Quicken 98* and *Money 98* also let you connect to their related Web sites (www.qfn.com and investor.msn.com, respectively), where you can get stock market updates and business news and do research on stocks and mutual funds.

Chances are, you'll be astounded to see where your money actually went. You might find that you spent an exorbitant amount on food, particularly for restaurants or workday lunches. You could also be surprised to see how much it cost to clothe your family or drive them around. The cost of upkeep for your home and your utility bills may also be sky high.

Similarly, you may be shocked to see how little you saved or invested. Continue on such a path and you'll have a devil of a time meeting your long-term financial goals, such as paying for your child's college education or retiring before age 65.

Take a look at the table on page 15 to get a sense of how your spending compares with the amount financial planners recommend for average households and affluent households.

Reining in your spending isn't easy, but it's not impossible, either. Some fixed expenses are largely unbudgeable, such as your health, disability, and life insurance premiums. Largely, but not entirely. You'll find advice in Chapter 2 about cutting insurance premiums. Most of your other expenses, however, are what economists call discretionary. That means you could spend more or less on them if you choose. Ask yourself the following 20 questions and odds are you'll find at least one expense that you can snip without feeling much pain:

20 QUESTIONS TO TURN SPENDERS INTO SAVERS

1. How can I eat out less often?
2. How can I spend less money when I eat out?
3. How can I cut back on my vacation spending this year?
4. How can I reduce my entertainment expenses and still have some fun in my life?
5. How can I get my boss to pick up more of my business expenses?
6. Can I lower the cost of child care and education without harming my kid in any way?
7. What can I do to cut my household's medical expenses without endangering my family's health?
8. How can I spend less shopping? (Hint: Try less expensive stores, more sales, fewer trips to the mall, and hand-me-downs for your kids.)
9. How can I lower the cost of commuting to work?
10. What can I do to reduce my car expenses? (One idea: Do more work on your car instead of taking it in. Another: Wash it yourself and save the car wash fee.)
11. What can I do to reduce the cost of upkeep for my home?
12. How can I pay less in debt? (Consider charging less on your credit cards or trading in a loan or a card for one with a lower interest rate.)
13. How can I lower my home heating and cooling, telephone bill, and cable TV bills?
14. What can I do to pay less to the IRS and the state tax man and keep more for myself?
15. Could I fight my property tax bill and get it lowered?
16. How can I reduce my dry-cleaning bill? (How about laundering and ironing more clothes yourself?)

17. Can I cut the fees I pay to my bank, mutual fund, or stockbroker? (Try consolidating accounts so you're not hit with so many different fees.)
18. Could I lower my mortgage payments by refinancing?
19. Are there discounts I could receive to cut my homeowners and car insurance premiums?
20. Can I buy less expensive gifts without looking stingy?

WHERE AMERICANS' MONEY REALLY GOES

Comparing the results of a *Money* magazine poll with comprehensive Bureau of Labor Statistics data shows that average and affluent Americans alike spend more than they realize on transportation and clothing, among other things. They need to cut back on those items and divert more dollars to saving.

Spending category	What we say we spend (%)[1]		What we really spend (%)		What we should spend (%)[8]	
	Average[2]	Affluent[3]	Average[4]	Affluent[6]	Average	Affluent
HOUSING	22.7	22.6	19.1	19.9	25.0	20.0
SAVINGS AND INVESTMENTS	14.7	16.0	4.9[5]	8.5[7]	10.0	15.0
FOOD	13.8	13.1	13.6	11.0	13.0	13.0
TRANSPORTATION	11.6	12.5	17.8	16.6	16.0	13.0
HOUSEHOLD MAINTENANCE, UTILITIES	11.1	9.8	14.5	14.1	11.0	10.0
ENTERTAINMENT, VACATIONS	9.3	9.5	8.5	9.2	4.5	8.5
HEALTH CARE	5.1	4.1	5.1	3.9	5.0	3.0
MISCELLANEOUS	4.9	5.4	9.0	8.7	6.0	7.5
CLOTHING	3.4	3.2	5.4	5.3	5.0	4.0
EDUCATION, CHILD CARE	3.4	3.8	2.1	2.8	4.5	6.0

Notes: [1]As a percentage of after-tax income throughout. [2]Assumes that the average household (annual gross income of $42,300) has an annual after-tax income of $38,581. [3]Assumes that the average affluent American household (annual gross income of $50,000 or more; average of $75,650) has an annual after-tax income of $64,724. [4]Based on Bureau of Labor Statistics' Consumer Expenditure Survey (CES) annual after-tax income of $38,520. [5]According to the U.S. Department of Commerce. [6]Based on CES annual after-tax income of $59,194. [7]**MONEY** estimate. [8]According to several financial planners and credit counselors. **Sources: MONEY** poll, Bureau of Labor Statistics' CES, U.S. Department of Commerce's Bureau of Economic Analysis; financial planners.

Throughout this book you'll find budget-cutting ideas that will answer many of those questions. Chapter 18, for instance, is devoted to making you a wiser consumer. But only you know for sure what you can give up or scale back. Only you know the alternatives in your area to your favorite restaurants and stores.

If you're truly serious about spending less and having more cash to save and invest, set monthly or annual limits for certain expenses. For instance, you might force yourself not to spend more than, say, $50 a month on telephone bills or $200 a month on clothes. Or you could limit your annual vacation spending to, say $2,000. That might require you to give up a vacation altogether. Alternatively, you could just find a less expensive way to relax. Make sure you let yourself have *some* pleasures, though. Otherwise you'll eventually get so fed up with your budget constraints that you'll bust loose and spend wildly to compensate.

You may find it easier to put yourself on a budget by deciding in advance what you will do with the savings. This means converting your budgeting into a specific financial goal. It might be using the savings to pay down your debt or to invest for your child's looming college bills. Whatever the goal, give yourself something to shoot for. That way you won't feel as though you're simply punishing yourself.

After you have a spending plan you can live with, stick with it for three months. Then, repeat your initial exercise and see how you're doing. Find out exactly how much you are spending in every category again. You may even be able to kick in for a luxury or two that you've done without. After 12 months you ought to be so used to this spending regimen that you'll no longer mind the cutbacks you have made.

A final budgeting tip: Don't carry around too much cash, since you may be tempted to spend the money. If you normally take out $100 from the bank each week for spending money, try withdrawing $80 for a few weeks and see how you manage. If you're in the habit of yanking cash out of your bank's automated teller machines constantly, cut your visits in half. If you must, change your routine so you're not anywhere near your bank's ATMs. If you can't see the machine, you can't take money out of it.

YOUR FINANCES BY YOUR AGE

A useful way both to see how you're doing financially and to figure out what you ought to be doing with your money is to compare yourself with other people about your age. So take a look at the following tables, in which the American public's income and assets are shown according to their age. Then you'll learn a bit about what you should be focusing on financially today, depending on your age.

Incidentally, if you're one of the 76 million baby boomers born between 1946 and 1964, there's a strong chance that you're not saving enough for retirement. According to a recent Merrill Lynch survey, baby boomers are saving only 38% of the amount they'll need to retire at age 65 without cutting into their lifestyles.

WHAT AMERICANS MAKE

Think you're earning less than you deserve? Wonder whether other people your age or in your field are making more than you? Then estimate your household's annual income before taxes and take a look at the table below to see how your income stacks up against the competition. Remember to add in your earnings from work, any income from investments, and any other outside income such as alimony, child support, or regular income from trust funds.

	MEDIAN FAMILY INCOME (BEFORE TAXES)
U.S.	**$27,900**
Age of Family Head	
Under 35	$25,300
35–44	$36,300
45–54	$43,100
55–64	$32,100
65–74	$18,300
75 and up	$13,500

Source: Federal Reserve Board Survey of Consumer Finances 1992.

NET WORTH AND HOME EQUITY

The older people get, the bigger their net worth and home equity—until retire-

ment. Then net worth and home equity reverse course and shrink, because many older people sell their homes.

AGE	NET WORTH (INCLUDING HOME EQUITY)	HOME EQUITY
25–34	$3,800	$0
35–44	$22,679	$1,373
45–54	$51,602	$22,345
55–64	$82,733	$41,142
65–74	$82,282	$48,000
75 and up	$61,438	$34,927
U.S.	**$23,520**	**$4,000**

Note: The figures are medians. **Source:** Capital Research Associates Analysis of Survey of Income and Program Participation data.

THE PERCENTAGE OF FAMILIES HOLDING KEY ASSETS (BY INCOME)

Asset holdings tend to rise as people age, too, though this rule doesn't always hold

true. Middle-aged people are the ones most likely to own stocks, retirement accounts, and life insurance, while people over 65 are the prime candidates for bank CDs.

	CHECKING, SAVINGS ACCOUNTS	BANK CDs	MUTUAL FUNDS	STOCKS	BONDS	RETIREMENT ACCOUNTS	SAVINGS BONDS	LIFE INSURANCE
Age of Family Head								
Under 35	83%	7%	6%	11%	1%	30%	23%	26%
35–44	87%	9%	11%	21%	3%	47%	29%	36%
45–54	89%	15%	11%	19%	7%	53%	25%	40%
55–64	91%	21%	17%	23%	5%	53%	21%	44%
65–74	90%	32%	17%	19%	9%	37%	14%	39%
75 and up	92%	37%	13%	18%	8%	6%	15%	34%

THE MEDIAN VALUE OF HOLDINGS FOR FAMILIES WHO HAVE THESE ASSETS (BY AGE)

Not surprisingly, the amount people have in various financial assets rises as they get older. Holdings in mutual funds, bonds, savings bonds, and life insurance start getting smaller, however, once people hit age 65—the typical retirement age; mutual funds holdings rise again for people 75 and up. The amount of money held in checking accounts, savings accounts, and bank certificates of deposit continues rising, though. Stockholdings begin falling only once people are 75 and older. Retirement accounts rise by age until Americans are 65 to 74, when they start pulling money out.

	CHECKING, SAVINGS ACCOUNTS	BANK CDs	MUTUAL FUNDS	STOCKS	BONDS	RETIREMENT ACCOUNTS	SAVINGS BONDS	LIFE INSURANCE
Age of Family Head								
Under 35	$1,300	$4,500	$1,300	$3,400	$7,800	$4,500	$500	$2,200
35–44	$2,500	$7,800	$4,500	$3,900	$13,000	$10,100	$600	$3,600
45–54	$2,900	$11,200	$11,200	$5,600	$11,200	$14,500	$600	$4,500
55–64	$3,400	$15,100	$22,300	$20,400	$39,100	$26,800	$1,800	$5,600
65–74	$3,600	$19,500	$19,000	$31,300	$38,000	$13,400	$1,700	$2,200
75 and up	$4,900	$30,200	$33,500	$19,000	$31,300	$27,900	$3,400	$2,200

Now to put it all together, take a look at the financial profile of the average American by age, and see how yours compares. Then find the appropriate advice for your age group and try to follow it.

■ PEOPLE UNDER AGE 35: THE STARTING OUTS. Just getting off the ground financially, these young people have a median gross income of about $25,000 and no net worth to speak of. Most have checking or savings accounts, and about a third of them have retirement accounts. But few own stocks, bonds, mutual funds, or life insurance.

Other interesting stats for Americans 25 to 34:

- 58% are married
- 56% have children under 18
- 44% own homes
- Median income of affluent households: $49,100

ADVICE:

1. Stop living paycheck to paycheck and start saving regularly. Ideally, you'll want to salt away 10% of your income. Then you can start investing in the stock market, through mutual funds.

2. Start investing as early as you can. Put aside $2,000 a year in an Individual Retirement Account earning 8% for just the 10 years from ages 25 to 34 and you'll have nearly $315,000 by the time you're 65. If you wait to age 35, however, and then start investing $2,000 a year in the IRA for a full *30 years,* you'll have only about $245,000.

■ **PEOPLE 35 TO 44: THE CLIMBERS.** This group is starting to make some serious money, with median gross income of roughly $36,000. They're beginning to build up assets, too, with a net worth of approximately $23,000. By now, virtually half have retirement accounts and a third own life insurance. But most still aren't investing much.

Other interesting stats:

- 70% are married
- 65% have children under 18
- 66% own homes
- Median affluent-household income: $63,200

ADVICE:

1. Get serious about cutting your spending and debt. This is the time of your life to break bad spending and debt habits. Otherwise you'll likely be stuck with them for life and you'll find yourself struggling to reach your financial goals.

2. Don't forget about insurance. It's easy to put off buying life and disability insurance. Don't. You want to be certain that if something happens to you, the people you care most about won't be hurt financially.

■ **PEOPLE 45 TO 54: THE PEAK EARNERS.** Income levels are hitting their heights here, with median gross income of just over $43,000. Net worth is rising, also, to nearly $52,000. Interest in bank certificates of deposit is heightening; 15% of these people own bank CDs.

Other interesting stats:

- 74% are married
- 33% have children under 18
- 76% own homes
- Median affluent-household income: $73,000

ADVICE:

1. Don't let looming college bills prevent you from saving for retire-

ment. When tuition payments approach, it's easy to decide to forgo contributions to employer-sponsored retirement savings plans, IRAs, and Keoghs. That would be a mistake, however. Borrow more for college, if you must. But you need to look out for yourself as well as your kids.

2. Meet with your aging parents to discuss their finances. Your parents may need some help with the likes of investing wisely, dealing with Medicare or Social Security, holding down medical bills, or simply making ends meet. You may even want to try to save a bit for their potential nursing home bills.

■ **PEOPLE 55 TO 64: THE PRE-RETIREES.** Now income is starting to trail off. The median gross income has slipped to about $32,000. But these people are feathering their nests nicely. The median net worth has shot up to roughly $83,000. Investing in mutual funds and stocks is catching on among this crowd, as well; roughly one in five owns mutual funds or stocks.

Interesting stats:

- 73% are married
- 7% have children under 18
- 80% own homes
- Median affluent-household income: $61,000

ADVICE:

1. Meet with a financial adviser to discuss how to handle a pension payout. You might want to take all the money at once. Instead, you might prefer to get the pension in monthly installments for the rest of your life. Whichever way you go, there will be tax and investment implications.

2. Wise up about Social Security, particularly as you approach 60. You'll need to decide when to start getting your first checks. Plus, you should determine how much of your benefits will be taxable and whether income you earn in retirement might reduce the size of your Social Security checks. For more on these topics, see Chapter 10.

■ **PEOPLE 65 AND UP: THE RE-TIREDS.** Income has taken a nosedive; the median gross income for people 65 to 74 is just about $18,000, even below the incomes for people under 35. Net worth for this age group remains steady at approximately $82,000, though. Now, a full one-third own bank CDs. For those 75 and up, income has plunged farther to a median of $13,500. Net worth has dropped, too; the median net worth now hovers around $61,000, which is about three times the U.S. average. Bank CDs are more popular than at any younger age, though holdings of mutual funds, stocks, bonds, and retirement accounts have shrunk.

Other interesting stats:

- 51% are married
- Less than 1% have children under 18
- 75% own homes
- Median affluent-household income: $38,500
- 5% are in nursing homes

ADVICE:

1. Don't buy a home for retirement in another part of the country until you've fully checked out the area. It's smart to rent for a year or so before you buy. That way you'll have time to see whether you like the climate, the setting, the people, and the attractions.

2. Focus on preserving your assets and preventing them from losing value to inflation. That means keeping about half of your investments in stocks or mutual funds that buy stocks. You can put the rest in safe bonds, mutual funds that buy bonds, or the bank.

SETTING YOUR FINANCIAL GOALS

No matter how old you are or how much you make, you'll want to zero in on the key financial goals you hope to achieve. Too often, people have just vague notions about what they want financially. Their goals are things like "I want to have a lot of money." Or "I don't want to die poor."

Or "I want to be comfortable." Or "I want mutual funds that will go up." Trouble is, these goals are too squishy to help you much.

Instead, you ought to get more precise and decide exactly what it is you want to have and when you want to have it. For instance, your goal might be "I want to be able to retire at 65 and live as well as I did before retirement." Or "I want to buy a house in my city within three years." Or "I want to have enough saved to pay for 75% of my son's college education when he is a freshman."

The best way to make the right goals is to figure out what's important, what isn't, and when you want to achieve your goals. Once you've placed priorities on your financial goals, you can start adopting appropriate strategies to hit your marks. For example, if reducing debt is much more important to you now than goals requiring you to save and invest— such as buying a house or financing education—you'll want to focus on your credit cards and loan payments. If you've been negligent in properly insuring yourself and your family, you'll want to make that a top priority and concentrate on building up protection. Similarly, it's crucial to divide your goals into short-term, medium-term, and long-term commitments. That will help you see how quickly you need to work. For instance, if you have teenagers, paying for college is a short-term goal. So you'll need to find ways to increase your savings, borrow wisely, find scholarship or grant money, or some combination of all of these.

Complete the following two work-sheets by checking off the appropriate money goals and you'll get a clear idea of both your true financial goals and your timetable for reaching them.

MAKING PRIORITIES FOR MY MONEY GOALS

OBJECTIVE	NOT IMPORTANT	SOMEWHAT IMPORTANT	VERY IMPORTANT
Reduce debt			
Build an emergency reserve fund			
Increase insurance coverage			
Buy a house			
Make home improvements			
Buy a vacation house			
Buy a car			
Make another big purchase			
Have children			
Finance children's education			
Live more luxuriously			
Take an expensive vacation			
Take an unpaid leave from work			
Start a business			
Take early retirement			
Live well after retirement			
Other			

TIMING MY MONEY GOALS

OBJECTIVE	SHORT TERM	MEDIUM TERM	LONG TERM
Reduce debt			
Build an emergency reserve fund			
Increase insurance coverage			
Buy a house			
Make home improvements			
Buy a vacation house			
Buy a car			
Make another big purchase			
Have children			
Finance children's education			
Live more luxuriously			
Take an expensive vacation			
Take an unpaid leave from work			
Start a business			
Take early retirement			
Live well after retirement			
Other			

After you've created these master goal lists, remember to return to them from time to time. After all, your goals may change, or—with any luck—you'll be able to cross some off your list over time. At the very least, draw up new goals worksheets once a year. Be certain to make revisions when you have dramatic life changes, such as the birth of a child, a marriage, a divorce, a new job, a layoff, a move, or the purchase of a home.

YOUR FINANCIAL-PLANNING CHECKLIST

One last way to get a read on how you're doing financially: a financial-planning checklist. The Consumer Financial Education Foundation, a nonprofit group in Chicago (312-201-0101), has created this helpful list that will clue you in to your current financial status. The group also has a brochure called *The ABC's of Planning* that's handy if you're just starting to get serious about your money ($2; CFEF, 11 South LaSalle St., Suite 1400, Chicago, Ill. 60603). In this checklist you'll find 25 questions about your finances. Circle the YES or NO answer for each and see how you score when you finish:

1. Are you saving money? **YES NO**

2. Do you know how much you spend each month? **YES NO**

3. Do you pay all of your bills each month on time? **YES NO**

4. Is your net worth improving over time? **YES NO**

5. Do you have a satisfactory credit rating? **YES NO**

6. Do you have enough life insurance? **YES NO**

7. Do you have adequate medical coverage? **YES NO**

8. Do you carry disability income insurance? **YES NO**

9. Are your investments diversified? **YES NO**

10. Do you invest according to your own tolerance for risk? **YES NO**

11. Do you have a growth component (such as stocks or stock mutual funds) in your investment portfolio? **YES NO**

12. Do you rely on financial information from an objective source? **YES NO**

13. Do you learn as much as you can before you invest? **YES NO**

14. Do you review your investments regularly? **YES NO**

15. Do you take taxes into account when you spend and invest? **YES NO**

16. Do you file tax returns on time? **YES NO**

17. Do you know how much money you'll need to live on when you retire? **YES NO**

18. Do you know how much you'll receive in Social Security benefits when you retire? **YES NO**

19. Do you contribute to your employer's 401(k) or other pension plan? **YES NO**

20. Do you know how much you'll need in personal savings to fund a comfortable retirement? **YES NO**

21. Do you have a will? **YES NO**

22. Have you considered ways to minimize estate taxes that may be due on your death? **YES NO**

23. Do you have a file for your important documents? **YES NO**

24. Have you recorded the location of all your assets? **YES NO**

25. Have you prepared so-called advance directives such as a durable power of attorney, living will, and health care proxy? **YES NO**

Score (one point for each YES):
20–25 points: You have taken solid steps toward establishing financial security—keep working.
15–19 points: You have begun the journey to financial stability—continue and focus.
Less than 15 points: You need to get started—use this to take control of your financial life.

CHAPTER 2

The Basics

Now that you know how well you're doing financially, you're ready to learn the basics about personal finances. One mistake people often make is skipping over the basics and plunging headlong into investing. Bad idea. It's essential, first, to learn how to keep good financial records, use a bank wisely, and purchase the insurance protection you need for yourself and your family. Once you have these bases covered, you can move to the next stage: managing your money and making it grow.

Keeping Good Financial Records

It's a drag to see all those papers taking over the desk by your bed. But it's even more of a drag to be audited by the Internal Revenue Service and suddenly realize that the crucial receipts you need to prove that mammoth tax deduction are now mingling with the landfill on the other side of town.

Think of it this way: The moderate amount of discipline that smart record keeping requires is good practice for moving on in your financial life. If you don't have the discipline to file away crucial bills and chuck useless ones, for instance, how will you have the discipline for the far more demanding task of saving large chunks of your money for retirement?

Let's start with documents you probably already have lying around in boxes. If you're like most people, you can safely toss many of them. Here are the ones to keep and store in a fireproof file cabinet or in a safe-deposit box:

■ **Real estate documents.** These include the title to your home, the deed of purchase, your mortgage contract, and your sales contract. (It's best to keep these in a bank safe-deposit box.) Also save any receipts for capital improvements or property repairs you have made, such as reroofing or adding a deck. You'll need these records to minimize the taxes you might owe someday after selling your home for a profit.

■ **Receipts for valuable items such as furniture, silverware, furs, and jewelry.** If you lack a receipt for, say, those diamond brooches your grandmother left you, have the jewelry appraised and save the appraisal forms. You'll need them to fill out an insurance claim if your house burns down or is burglarized.

■ **Records of all personal property you own.** It's best to keep photographs or a videotape of these items, along with written estimates of their value. Your homeowners or renters insurer will be far more willing to accept your insistence that you owned four mint-condition Hepplewhite chairs if you can show him or her recent photos of them in your dining room. (It's a good idea to keep copies of all this at your office or in a bank safe-deposit box as well as at home, just in case.)

■ **Warranty statements covering your major appliances or electronics, along with a receipt proving the date of purchase.** Write down the make, model, and serial number for all items, if applicable.

■ **Old tax returns.** It's crucial to keep copies of your income tax returns for the past three years. That's because the IRS can typically probe that far back if it chooses to audit you. But it's a good idea to keep *all* your tax returns: they can be helpful reminders of previous financial moves you made. For more information about the IRS and record keeping, get IRS Publication No. 552, *Record Keeping for Individuals* (800-829-3676).

■ **Old tax-related documents.** The three-year holding period also applies to documents that substantiate claims you made on your tax returns. In a tax audit, if you cannot document an expense you deducted, you may lose the write-off. So save receipts or canceled checks that prove your deductible expenses. Save your annual pay stubs; you can toss them after three years.

■ **Insurance policies.** Keep all policies you still hold, from life to liability, at home. But it's a good idea to create a list of all your policies and your agents and keep it in your safe-deposit box.

■ **Legal documents.** You also need to keep copies indefinitely of your will and, if you have them, your living will and power of attorney. Have your lawyer keep the originals; you should retain your copies at home. And be sure to get rid of old wills. Otherwise, after you die there could be confusion about which will is the one you wanted.

■ **Credit-card statements.** Save these for a year or so. That way, if a charge erroneously appears on your bill more than once, you'll be able to prove you already paid it. Also, if a product you bought breaks and needs to be returned, you'll remember where you bought it. The statements can also come in handy at tax time.

■ **Bank checking and savings account statements, including canceled checks.** Holding on to your checks helps you keep track of where your money goes. The checks can also work as proof of a payment if necessary. For instance, it helps to have a check if your landlord says you didn't pay last September's rent and you know you did. Keep these statements and checks for three years, indefinitely for home improvements.

■ **Investment records.** Save monthly statements from your mutual fund companies and your brokerage firm. These statements will establish what you paid for an investment, so you'll have the information to compute the taxes when you sell it. After you get your annual summary statement, you can toss the monthly statements—as long as the annual statement shows all your transactions for the past 12 months. Exception: Save all trade confirmations and divi-

dend-reinvestment statements for three years after you file a tax return declaring a gain or loss from selling securities. Save your annual statements indefinitely. If you have certificates of ownership for stocks, bonds, or other investments, keep them in a safe-deposit box at the bank.

■ **Retirement accounts.** Hold on to all annual statements from tax-advantaged retirement accounts such as Individual Retirement Accounts (IRAs), Keogh retirement accounts, and Simplified Employee Pensions (SEPs). The statements will document your contributions and your earnings.

It's especially important to keep annual statements from any nondeductible IRAs you may have. Reason: You'll need them to show the IRS which part of any future withdrawal was funded with after-tax money. Otherwise you'll wind up being taxed twice. And if you make a nondeductible IRA contribution, be sure to keep a copy of your IRS form for it, No. 8606.

■ **Debts.** Aside from your mortgage contract, you'll also want to save records for your student loans, home-equity loans, car loans, bank loans, and other large debts. Then, when they're paid off, just keep the statement that says so.

■ **Miscellaneous documents.** Also keep in your safe-deposit box the following: the title to your car, your birth and marriage certificates, your children's birth certificates, and deeds to cemetery plots you own.

Records You Can Toss

Here are the types of records you don't need to keep:

Old, expired insurance policies
Receipts for cars you don't own anymore
Pay stubs from earlier years
Expired product warranties
Old annual reports and proxy statements

Records You Should Start Keeping

Now it's time to get organized with the financial documents that will come rolling in this year. Doing so will make end-of-the-year tax moves much easier. For instance, if you maintain careful records of your family's medical expenses every month, toward the end of the year you'll be able to see if they'll exceed 7.5% of your adjusted gross income—the level at which they become deductible on your tax return. If they do, you can, say, shift upcoming January medical appointments to December in order to deduct them.

Don't worry. You needn't create a whole room or some fancy system for these records. Just pick up a large accordion file or a handful of individual manila folders and spend a few minutes labeling them by their deductible category. (Refer to Schedule A of last year's tax return to see what all these categories should be.) Don't forget to create a folder to stow your old tax returns, too. Here are a few tips to be sure you don't miss anything important:

■ **Medical expenses.** Keep all receipts for health insurance premiums, prescription drugs, eyeglasses, and contact lenses, and for fees to your doctors, dentists, psychotherapists, and hospitals.

■ **Charitable donations.** Remember to hang on to canceled checks for your cash contributions plus receipts for used clothing and other property donations. If you throw a $10 bill in the collection plate at church every Sunday, keep a log of that, too. Also keep a record of trips you make to perform volunteer work. You can deduct those travel expenses at the rate of 14¢ a mile.

■ **Miscellaneous expenses.** These expenses become deductible only once they exceed 2% of your adjusted gross income. So be sure to keep receipts and canceled checks documenting fees to financial planners and tax advisers; subscriptions to trade and professional journals; costs related to looking for another job in your current profession; and safe-deposit box rental fees.

■ **Your income.** In this folder toss in your pay stubs, of course. But be sure also to throw in records of all other earnings from any other sources of employment, such as freelance work or consulting. Otherwise you might wind up forgetting about the work at tax time. Guarantee: The IRS won't forget.

After you've completed your tax return for the previous year, you can junk any records of expenses that you couldn't deduct, such as medical receipts if the expenses didn't exceed 7.5% of adjusted gross income. Put the papers you did use in preparing your return into a file labeled by the tax year.

A bonus. If you use a tax preparer, organizing your records this way before sending them to him or her should save so much time that you may be able to save as much as 50% off last year's bill. That should have you smiling all the way to the bank.

Banking Smart with Your Checking and Savings

A bank was probably your first connection to the world of personal finance. Remember that childhood savings passbook, stamped by a teller every time you deposited $5 from your paper route? Things have changed since then, but banks still provide a host of basic—and crucial—

services, from checking to savings to borrowing. Surprisingly, however, many people fail to get the most out of their banks.

If you are already a customer of a small, friendly bank where the staff knows your name and responds quickly to your needs, consider yourself lucky. But while good service is important, so is getting the most for your money. So don't feel you have to do *all* your bank business—from your checking to your credit cards to your mortgage—with the same institution. A dedicated relationship with one bank *can* sometimes work in your favor; for example, if you have your checking and savings accounts at one bank, that institution may lower or even waive its annual credit-card fee for you as gratitude. That said, you usually come out ahead if you shop around for the best deal on the individual services you need.

Let's start with the most basic bank service: the **checking account.** The purpose of a checking account is to give you a place to park your cash safely and let you spend it (via writing checks or making withdrawals) whenever you like. The bank with the best checking account for you is one that's conveniently located, has automated teller machines (ATMs) near where you live and work, and has the lowest possible fees.

More than ever, it's essential to check out a bank's fees before opening a checking account—and review fees on the account you already have. In the past few years banks have been hiking their fees on checking accounts like mad. They've also become increasingly creative in finding new ways to charge. For instance, some banks actually hit customers with a fee of 35¢ every time they make a deposit if their average monthly checking balance falls below $2,000. Nowadays, unless you keep a balance of at least $1,000 or so in your checking account, your bank will probably charge you a monthly fee of $5 to $8 and maybe an additional fee of 25¢ for each check you write. Balances are figured in different ways, so be sure to ask a bank officer about the institution's method before opening an account.

A word to the wise: Some banks charge service fees according to your lowest balance during the month. That way, fees kick in if your bank requires a minimum monthly balance of $1,000 for free checking and your account, which averages $2,000, dips to $900 for a single day. Look instead for a bank that bases its fees on your *average* daily balance.

Also, ask any bank you're considering for a list of all fees associated with checking accounts. You may find that the bank is making up for a low monthly account fee by socking customers with big charges for bouncing checks (typically $18 or more), confirming account balances, stopping payment on checks, transferring funds by telephone and—most insidious of all—using ATMs. According to a study by the Consumer Federation of America and the

U.S. Public Interest Research Group, ATM levies have risen by more than 50% since 1990. Most banks charge you 75¢ to $2 for making withdrawals from ATMs that are owned by another institution, but about half of all banks now also charge you 25¢ to $1 or so each time you use their *own* ATMs. (Three times as many banks impose surcharges as in 1995.) If you're a regular ATM user, insist on a bank that doesn't charge you extra. To find one, call the No-Surcharge ATM Alliance at 888-748-2667 or log on to its Web site at www.theco-op.org. You can get a more complete list of no-surcharge institutions by visiting the *Bank Rate Monitor* Web site (www.bankrate.com).

On the positive side, most banks will pay interest on your checking account (well, not much interest, actually), provided you maintain a minimum balance of around $1,000 to $2,500 or more. Such accounts are often called NOW ("negotiable order of withdrawal") accounts. Interest rates are normally pegged to your balance: the higher your balance, the higher the rate. In recent years the average interest-paying checking account has yielded around 1.5%.

If it's interest you're after, another alternative is to open a linked savings account at the same bank that supplies you with checking. As long as you maintain a minimum savings balance of around $1,000 to $3,000, many banks will waive all their checking account fees.

There are also three safe alternatives to checking accounts that will pay you more in interest:

Alternative 1: A Money-Market Mutual Fund. This is a pool of money managed by an investment firm; you actually become a shareholder when you get into a money-market mutual fund. The money is typically invested in short-term IOUs from government agencies and corporations. Money funds, as they're often called, generally yield a few percentage points more than bank checking accounts and at least one percentage point more than bank money-market deposit accounts. They aren't federally insured, but the managers of the funds work to ensure that no shareholder ever loses money. Most money funds make you keep a $5,000 minimum balance or let you write checks only for amounts of $250 or more. But there are a few exceptions. For instance, a few let you write unlimited checks if your balance is at least $1,000. Some even have no minimum balance and let you write checks as small as $100. You typically make deposits into the money funds by writing a check and sending it through the mail to the fund trustee, although some money funds have local walk-in offices. There are taxable money funds and, for people in the upper tax brackets, tax-exempt money funds, whose interest is not taxed by the feds. Taxable money funds tend to yield a little more than one percentage point over tax-exempt funds.

Alternative 2: A Credit Union Share Draft Account. This kind of account is a lot like a bank checking account, except it generally pays more interest while charging no, or low, fees. In fact, the average credit union's checking fees are about half those of the typical bank. Best of all, most credit unions will give you free checking with interest no matter what your balance is. You don't belong to a credit union? No big problem. It's becoming easier and easier to get into one. Ask your friends or business associates if they're a member of a credit union you could join. Another place to look is your alumni association. Or you can ask the Credit Union National Association (P.O. Box 431, Madison, Wis. 53701) how to locate your state credit union association, which can refer you to local credit unions you may be able to join. Just make sure that the credit union you choose is covered by the U.S. government's Federal Deposit Insurance Corporation (FDIC) insurance.

Alternative 3: A Brokerage or Bank Cash-Management Account. Also known as an asset-management account, this may be the perfect arrangement for you if you own stocks or bonds and make at least a few trades every year. A cash-management account is a combination money fund, brokerage account, and checking account. As a rule, you need to keep at least $10,000 in cash or securities in the account. Also, you may be asked to pay an annual fee of $50 to $125.

A **savings account,** of course, keeps your money safe but readily available for withdrawal, either at the teller's window or through an ATM. Deposits of up to $100,000 are insured by the FDIC. In other words, in the unlikely event that the bank or savings and loan fails, the feds will pony up your missing cash. (If you'd like to deposit more than $100,000, divide your money among different banks so you'll get full FDIC coverage on all of it.)

Oh, yeah—a savings account also pays interest, recently averaging a bit above 2%. If you keep enough money on deposit, that is. Once your balance dips below $200 to $500 or so, some banks stop paying interest and even start charging account-maintenance fees. (Banks often waive these penalties for kids; alas, grown-ups have no such luck.)

When shopping for a savings account, be sure to analyze the way it calculates its yields, because methods of compounding interest vary. Try to use a bank that pays interest on the balance accumulated in your savings account every day, rather than on your average monthly balance or (even worse) on your lowest balance each month. And it's best to use a bank that compounds interest daily: All things being equal, the more often your interest is compounded, the more money you make. A quick way to cut through interest rate double-talk: ask an officer at three differ-

ent banks you're considering what $1,000 deposited today would be worth in a year if you leave all your interest on deposit. Go with the bank whose answer is highest.

If you've got at least several thousand dollars to sock away, consider stepping up to a bank **money-market deposit account.** Such accounts often require minimum deposits of $1,000 or more but normally pay slightly higher rates than those on traditional savings accounts. Yields rise and fall with short-term interest rates; the accounts often pay about two percentage points less than those of money-market mutual funds. You're not limited to the banks in your hometown or even in your home state, however. So to get the highest possible yield, consider opening an out-of-state money-market account (for a monthly list of the highest-yielding money-market accounts from safe institutions, see **MONEY** magazine's "Your Money Monitor" department). The difference can be substantial: when the national average money-market rate is, say, 2.6%, you might be able to find a bank or S&L paying 4.4%. Institutions that court out-of-state depositors often have toll-free numbers; call to request application forms.

If you're willing to lock up your cash for a period of time in exchange for a higher rate of interest than you would get from a savings account, ponder a bank or savings and loan **certificate of deposit (CD).** A CD has a fixed maturity, commonly three months to 10 years. You promise to leave the money on deposit until maturity, and generally the longer you commit your money, the higher the interest rate. For instance, if a six-month CD is yielding 4%, a five-year CD might well yield about 6%. If you withdraw the money before the CD matures, you'll pay a penalty equal to roughly three to six months' interest. So CDs are appropriate only if you're confident you won't need to raid the account soon.

Some of the best-yielding CDs are sold by brokerage firms. The CDs you purchase from a firm like Merrill Lynch or Charles Schwab are actually ones that have been issued by banks. So they're insured up to $100,000. And, as at a bank, you pay no commission to get them. Brokers tend to require minimum investments of $1,000. You can get a CD as short as three months or as long as five years. There's just one catch: It can be a little tricky if you want to pull your money out before the CD matures. You'll then have to ask your broker to try to find a buyer for you. Assuming he finds a buyer, you'll have to accept whatever price the purchaser is willing to pay.

For a list of the highest-yielding bank CDs (plus the lowest rates on bank loans), check out the Web site of the *Bank Rate Monitor* (www.bankrate.com). Every week, the site surveys more than 3,000 banks, credit unions, and other financial institutions and then lists the best deals in the U.S. on its site. Typically, you must call the institution to get an application for a CD (or loan), but some let you download an application to your computer directly from the site.

Getting the Right Insurance

Spending money on insurance policies is an act of faith: you are buying promises that you hope will never have to be kept. But because none of us can predict the future, it's crucial that you protect your assets (and therefore your family's well-being) from risks. Insurance is the way to do it. What follows is a guide to getting the insurance you need for the price you can afford.

BUYING HEALTH INSURANCE

It's amazing how many people think they can do without health insurance. They're making a big mistake. If you're uninsured, a serious accident or debilitating illness can wipe out you and your family financially. And yes, young people get sick, too. In short, insurance that protects you against major health catastrophes is absolutely crucial.

If you're like most working Americans, your employer supplies you with group health insurance coverage. The kind of health insurance plan that corporations have traditionally offered is a so-called **fee-for-service plan.** Such a plan covers visits to any doctor you choose. For an annual **premium** (sometimes paid by the employer, sometimes paid by the employee, and sometimes shared between them), group plans typically pay about 80% of your medical expenses after you pay an annual **deductible** of, say, $150 for a single person or $400 for a family of four. (A deductible is the amount you must pay toward your bills each year before your insurance kicks in. Once it does kick in, the small percentage of your medical expenses that insurance doesn't cover—and that you must pay for—is called your **co-payment.**) Luckily, many group plans limit your annual share of the bills to $2,500 or so, meaning that $2,500 is the most you should have to pay toward medical care in any year. Of course, if your plan excludes certain treatments, such as dentistry or drug abuse counseling, you'll have to pay the entire cost yourself.

Trouble is, employer-provided health coverage is getting less generous. Fully one-tenth of the 633 employers surveyed by the Watson Wyatt human resources consulting firm upped medical deductibles for their employees in 1996. Translation: More of the cost of medical care is coming out of employees' pockets. What's more, a growing number of companies want you to kick in for the cost of the insurance itself. Some 15% of em-

ployers raised employee coinsurance or copayments in 1996 and 12% planned to do so in 1997. Even once generous IBM has scuttled free health care for its 124,000 employees and their families, charging them $23 to $50 a month instead.

There's not much you can do about such increasingly Scrooge-like behavior, short of banding co-workers together and lobbying for better coverage. But you can increase your chances of getting the right coverage at the right price by taking advantage of another trend: the growing tendency of employers to offer more than one type of health care plan.

The alternative to a traditional fee-for-service plan is a **managed-care plan** that restricts your choice of doctors. There are two main types of managed-care plans: **health maintenance organizations (HMOs)** and **preferred-provider organizations (PPOs).** HMOs are the strictest: typically, only visits to doctors who are members of their network are covered automatically; you must get approval to see outside specialists. (For information on Medicare HMOs see Chapter 21.) By contrast, PPOs allow you to see specialists who are in their network and go out of network, paying 20% of the bill. In general, HMOs don't require you to pay a deductible; HMOs and PPOs cover preventive care, physical exams, and often extras like eyeglasses that insurers don't cover; and you need not fill in those annoying claim forms that traditional insurers demand. When all is said and done, managed-care plans are usually cheaper than fee-for-service plans. Moreover, most studies show that the quality of care that patients get is just as good with a managed-care plan as with a fee-for-service plan.

A new type of managed-care plan is called **point of service,** or **POS.** Run by insurers and HMOs, POS plans let you go out of network—for a higher price. You usually need a referral in order to see a specialist.

Which should you choose? If you care less about cost cutting and more about the ability to see whichever hot specialist you've heard about—or if you're devoted to a current doctor who does not belong to your company's managed-care network—stick with your old fee-for-service plan. But understand that going with a managed-care plan will probably be cheaper. Even though the monthly premiums you pay may be $6 to $20 higher, such plans usually charge copayments of just $5 to $15 for doctor visits, prescription drugs, and laboratory tests.

Among managed-care plans, PPOs and POSs tend to spell slightly higher out-of-pocket costs to you than HMOs. It's a simple trade-off: extra flexibility equals extra cost. So if you don't have any tricky medical conditions or you have young kids and will thus likely take them in for lots of potentially costly checkups, an HMO is probably your best choice.

Sizing up a Managed-Care Plan

If your employer offers a managed-care plan and you need to decide whether to join it, ask the following four questions:

1. How good are the doctors? First, get the plan's doctor directory and see if there's a doctor in it you know. If so, call the physician and ask his or her opinion of the other doctors in the plan. That will give you a clue about the quality of the group.
2. What kind of preventive services are offered? Some plans figure you'll get preventive care if you want. Others are more proactive, keeping records on patients and letting you know if, for instance, you're due for a mammogram. The more the HMO or PPO watches out for you in advance, the more you can feel sure the group cares about your health.
3. What kind of accreditation does the group have? Two voluntary accrediting agencies have started to certify managed-care plans based on strict measures of quality. They are the National Committee for Quality Assurance (for HMOs) and the American Accreditation Program (for PPOs). This isn't to say that a plan without accreditation isn't a good one. But one that has ponied up the fee to get accredited and then passed the standards demonstrates a quality plan.
4. What's it really like to be a member? Ask the plan's representative what

kind of wait you might expect for an appointment. The average for a routine visit to an HMO is about four weeks. Find out, too, how old most of the patients are. If you're about the typical age, that means the doctors will be focused on the kinds of medical issues that matter most to you. Finally, ask about doctor turnover. The average turnover for fee-based doctors, like the kind in PPOs, is 5% a year. It's about 10% for salaried physicians, who tend to work at HMOs. If you learn that the plan's turnover rate is much higher than those percentages, that could be a signal that the doctors in the group aren't very happy.

Buying Coverage On Your Own

What if you work for a company that does not provide group health insurance? Or you're self-employed? Or unemployed? There's no way around it: buying health insurance on your own means you'll face some hefty bills. Sadly, there is simply no such thing as a bargain individual health policy. At least not yet.

When it comes to forking over cash for your own individual health insurance policy, the first thing you must do is figure out how much coverage you truly need. When buying health insurance, as with any kind of insurance, you should insure only against losses that you couldn't absorb without derailing your family's finances. Remember: there's a seesaw effect between deductibles and premiums. The higher the deductible you choose—meaning the more you're willing to pay out of pocket—the lower your premium will be. The lower the deductible, the higher the premium. It's a waste of money to pay high insurance premiums for costs you could handle yourself without too much pain.

Your primary concern, then, should be **catastrophic coverage.** That is, if you're hit by a car or develop cancer and rack up total medical costs of $500,000, you want to make sure that your insurance will pick up as much of that staggering amount as possible. So buy a health insurance policy that has a maximum annual payout of at least $500,000 or (preferably) $1 million. It should cover the full cost of basic hospital services and surgery as well as most doctor bills and prescription drug costs. Also make sure never to buy a policy without a ceiling on your out-of-pocket expenses ($2,500 per year is typical). After you reach the ceiling amount, your insurer should pick up 100% of remaining bills. Finally, make sure the policy you buy is guaranteed to be renewable. That way the insurer can't cancel your policy just because your health deteriorates.

If you're turned down by a number of insurers because you have a preexisting condition such as diabetes or heart disease, check out your local Blue Cross/Blue Shield. These nonprofit insurers often have open enrollment periods when they take all applicants, regardless of their health. And they charge pretty much the same rates for everyone of the same age and sex in the same area. Another possibility is a health insurance pool for the "uninsurable," available in about half the states. The downside: you'll probably pay premiums about 50% higher than normal, with a deductible running into thousands of dollars. But at least you'll be covered.

One of the scariest experiences for people changing jobs or leaving the corporate world is the prospect of losing health coverage. If you are unsure whether you'll have health insurance in your new position, tell the benefits department of the company you're about to leave that you'd like to extend your old coverage under the terms of the **Consolidated Omnibus Reconciliation Act (COBRA).** As long as the company you are leaving has 20 or more employees, COBRA guarantees you the right to continue your health insurance coverage for up to 18 months, at the same group rate. That will give you plenty of time to shop for an affordable, longer-term policy. Unfortunately, although your employer probably paid for much of the premium while you worked there, under COBRA you must pay the total cost of the premium yourself. Still, it's almost certainly cheaper than any plan you could buy on your own. Even if your new job offers health insurance, extend your coverage under COBRA for a few months anyway. Reason: Many employers' health coverage doesn't go into effect until you've been working there for three months or so.

If you're about to retire, you have different concerns. Once you reach age 65, the federal government's Medicare health insurance program kicks in. Medicare comes in two parts: Part A, which you get automatically and for free, covers bills for hospital stays and care in hospices and skilled nursing homes. Part B, for which you must sign up (and pay $36.60 a month extra), covers 80% of doctor bills, outpatient surgery, lab tests, X-rays, certain drugs, and other costs that don't exceed the "approved" amounts—those that Medicare has decreed are standard in your area.

If you're retired, check with your former employer to see whether its health plan will continue to give you and your family the care you need. If not, sign up for Medicare Part B. If you have an individual health insurance plan, definitely sign up for Part B when you turn 65. Your existing individual plan will metamorphose into a so-called Medigap policy, which pays only certain medical bills that Medicare doesn't.

Choosing a Medigap Plan

It has become much easier than it used to be for people 65 and older to find a health insurance policy that fills in Medicare's gaps—that is, a Medigap policy. The reason: A recent federal law has created 10 different types of standardized Medigap policies; the plans don't apply to policies sold in Massachusetts, Minnesota, or Wisconsin, however. All you need to do is find the one that's right for you and then find the insurer selling it for the least amount of money. It's important to shop around among insurers because studies by United Seniors Health Cooperative show that premiums can vary by as much as 100% for the same plan. (States may allow only some of the 10 plans to be sold to their residents, however.) Here are the 10 different plans, which go by alphabet names, and their benefits marked with X's. The more benefits you want, the more you'll pay, so plan A is the least expensive and plan J is the priciest:

MEDIGAP PLANS HEAD TO HEAD

MEDIGAP BENEFITS	A	B	C	D	E	F	G	H	I	J
Basic benefits	X	X	X	X	X	X	X	X	X	X
Part A: Hospital deductible		X	X	X	X	X	X	X	X	X
Part A: Skilled nursing home coinsurance			X	X	X	X	X	X	X	X
Part B: Deductible			X			X				X
Foreign travel emergency			X	X	X	X	X	X	X	X
At-home recovery				X			X		X	X
Part B: Excess doctor charges						100%	80%		100%	100%
Preventive screening					X					X
Outpatient prescription drugs								Basic	Basic	Extended

Key: *Basic benefits* means that the plan pays the coinsurance of Medicare Part A of $174/day for hospital days 61 to 90 and $348/day up to day 150 and 100% of up to 365 extra days per lifetime. Also, basic benefits cover the 20% coinsurance of Medicare Part B's allowable amounts and for the first three pints of blood yearly. *Part A: Hospital deductible* pays the $696 deductible for hospital stays. *Part A: Skilled nursing home coinsurance* pays $87 per day for days 21 to 100 of daily skilled care in a nursing home. *Part B: Deductible* pays for the first $100 of Medicare covered medical services per year. *Foreign travel emergency* covers necessary emergency care beginning during the first two months per trip outside the United States. After you pay the $250 annual deductible, the benefit covers 80% of emergency care, with a lifetime maximum of $50,000. *At-home recovery* pays for short-term personal care services when Medicare pays for home health care services after an illness, injury, or surgery. The benefit pays up to $40 per visit for no more than seven visits per week, with a maximum annual benefit of $1,600. *Part B: Excess doctor charges* pays the difference between the doctor's actual charge and the Medicare approved amount. *Preventive screening* covers $120 per year for health care screening ordered by your physician. *Outpatient prescription drugs* has basic coverage of 50% of outpatient prescription drug charges up to $1,250 per year, after you pay a $250 annual deductible. The extended coverage pays 50% of charges up to $3,000 per year, after the $250 deductible.

Six Ways You Can Lower Your Medical Costs

1. Ask professional, fraternal, alumni, or religious groups you belong to whether they sell group health insurance to members. Group coverage is often—but not always—less expensive than individual coverage. If you don't belong to any such group, look into joining up.

2. Consult an independent insurance agent who sells comprehensive major medical policies for individuals from a variety of companies. He or she may be able to turn up a policy that you couldn't. Tell the agent you want policies only from financially sound companies.

3. Consider joining an HMO rather than buying an individual policy from an insurance company. You may have to give up a little freedom in your choice of docs, but you'll help keep your medical costs down.

4. Choose the highest deductible that you can afford. If you figure you can probably afford $1,000 in medical bills this year, take a $1,000 deductible; it might be 25% cheaper than a similar policy with a $100 deductible.

5. Become a smarter medical consumer. Actually, this is sound advice for everyone these days. The more you understand about your own health, the more you can save. According to studies by the actuarial consulting firm Milliman & Robertson, at least 10% of doctor visits are wholly unnecessary. Speaking of doctors, you may be surprised to know how much doctor fees can vary in the same area. Studies show that charges for the same service can differ by more than 700% among local doctors. Lately it's been getting a little easier—though not too easy—to compare prices, since some local consumer and business groups have been putting together price guides.

6. Get healthier, too. You might be able to slash your health premiums by as much as 50% by stopping smoking or losing weight or taking action to lower your blood pressure or cholesterol level. Don't expect your insurance agent to tell you about such discounts. It's up to you to ask.

BUYING DISABILITY INSURANCE

What, you may think, *me become disabled?* Unfortunately, chances aren't as slim as you may think. If you're 35, your chance of becoming disabled for three months or more over the next 30 years—as a result of contracting cancer, suffering a stroke, or being hit by a car, for example—is three times greater than your chance of dying. Think of it this way: a disability policy is the way to insure what's likely your largest asset—your earning power. Here's how to get the coverage you need:

Generally speaking, you should have enough disability coverage to replace at least 60% of your gross income while a long illness or injury prevents you from working. In fact, that's usually the most coverage that insurers will sell you (though some will sell as much as 70%). If they provide much more coverage, they figure, you'll have little incentive to return to work. The best policies start paying benefits no more than 90 days after your disability occurs and continue to pay until you can work full-time again or reach age 65.

Large corporations often offer their employees a group long-term disability plan (typical percentage of pretax salary replaced: 40% to 60%, up to a specified ceiling). If you don't own such a policy, ask your benefits department if one is available. Your employer may also offer short-term disability coverage to bridge the gap between when your sick leave runs out and a long-term disability policy kicks in. Some states, including New York and California, require that most employers provide short-term disability benefits (usually for 26 weeks).

But if you work for one of the two-thirds of U.S. companies that don't offer disability coverage, you're self-employed, or you work for an employer whose benefits fall below the 60% threshold, look for an individual disability policy sold by a life insurance company. Buy the highest-quality coverage you can get and be prepared to pay a bundle for the policy; the cost for women especially is rising because fewer and fewer insurers offer unisex policies. Provisions to hold out for, if you can afford them:

■ **Own-occupation coverage.** This means that the policy will pay in the event that you develop any disability that prevents you from performing your own occupation, even if you are still able to do other kinds of work. For example, with such coverage, an airline pilot who went blind would collect benefits even though blindness wouldn't prevent him from being, say, a deskbound administrator. You can keep receiving benefits even if you earn money doing something else, as long as you are under a doctor's care. This coverage costs big time: 10% more, on average, than a policy that will pay benefits only if you are unable to work at any occupation suitable to your training and experience. And this feature is becoming harder and harder to find.

■ **Residual benefits.** This mouthful simply means that you can return to work part-time while you are recuperating and still collect partial benefits. If your policy doesn't have residual benefits built in, pay the extra 25% or so and have it added as a rider.

■ **Annual cost-of-living adjustments.** With this feature, your benefit

42

payments will rise with inflation every year.

■ **A noncancelable contract.** This feature means that the company must insure you without raising premiums or lowering benefits as long as you continue to pay the premiums. Like own-occupation coverage, noncancelable contracts have been becoming scarcer.

■ **Guaranteed increase.** This is simply the option of buying more coverage later without having to undergo a medical exam.

■ **Guaranteed level premiums.** By getting guaranteed level premiums, you'll prevent the insurer from raising your premiums later. Again, this coverage is getting scarcer.

The size of your annual disability premium will depend on your age, occupation, how much income you want replaced, and how many months you're willing to wait before benefits kick in. Take a 40-year-old, nonsmoking, $80,000-a-year professional man. At large disability insurer UNUM, premiums for his policy, which begins paying 90 days after he becomes disabled, total roughly $1,800 a year. Many policies sell for $2,500 a year or so, however.

The best way to trim your premiums is to accept the longest waiting period (also known as "elimination period") you can. That's the length of time you must be disabled before the insurance company starts paying benefits. Accepting a 180-day rather than the standard 90-day waiting period, for example, can save you several hundred dollars a year.

If you automatically get employer-provided long-term disability coverage, your employer sometimes lets you buy more. But the insurer it uses may not offer the lowest available rates, so it pays to compare premiums among several insurers. At the very least, check with any professional organizations to which you belong, such as the American Institute of Certified Public Accountants or the National Association for Female Executives. Such groups often can negotiate cheaper rates than a large company.

If you plan to leave the corporate world to strike out on your own, you may not qualify for disability insurance anymore—at least at first. Because people starting their own businesses don't have any income yet, they can't insure it against disability. Homemakers, with no earned income, have the same problem. One solution: Buy an individual policy before you quit your job.

Many people don't realize that the Social Security system provides disability benefits, too. But you must be in pretty bad shape to qualify: you've got to prove that your disability will keep you from working at any kind of job for more than a year or is fatal. Furthermore, these payments don't kick in until five months after your disability sets in. Your salary and the number of years you've worked determine your benefit amount.

BUYING LONG-TERM-CARE INSURANCE

If you're concerned about the high cost of staying in a nursing home (upward of $100 a day), or having home health care for a long period of time and you have a family history of longevity, you might consider purchasing a long-term-care insurance policy. These policies have been around since the late 1980s, and the truth is that at first they were often pretty much of a rip-off. Not only were the policies extremely expensive, their coverage was fairly limited. But long-term-care policies have improved a great deal recently, and now many financial planners often recommend them to their clients in their fifties and older. In a few states—California, Connecticut, Indiana, and New York—the state governments now offer long-term-care policies that protect policyholder assets.

Nowadays, the typical long-term-care policy will pay for all types of care—nursing home care, at-home care, aid in an adult day care center, and assisted living. Previously, many policies demanded a doctor's certification before they would pay any benefits. Today, you'll be covered if you can get a physical therapist or another professional health care provider to tell the insurer that you need help with either one or two daily functions or are mentally impaired.

One thing that hasn't changed, however, is the high cost of long-term-care insurance. Premiums often run about $1,500 a year and up. And the older you are, the more the insurance will cost. For instance, someone buying a policy at age 70 might wind up paying close to $3,000 annually for the same coverage that would cost $1,500 for a 55-year-old. That's the chief reason it's best to buy long-term-care insurance in your fifties, rather than waiting. Another reason: If you delay purchasing the coverage, you increase the odds that you'll be rejected by insurers for having a medical condition.

Shopping for a long-term-care policy is somewhat like hunting for disability coverage: you want to find a policy that can't be canceled unless you don't pay your premiums. And, like disability insurance, if you lengthen the waiting period before benefits kick in, you'll lower your premiums. Ask for a waiting period of somewhere between 20 days and 100 days. Also, look for a policy that is renewable for life and whose premiums are level over the life of the policy. Finally, buy three to five years' worth of long-term-care coverage; a longer period will just raise your premiums.

BUYING HOMEOWNERS OR RENTERS INSURANCE

No matter where you live or whether you own your home or rent, you need to have insurance to protect your belongings against loss from theft and against damage by fire and other hazards. Homeowners insurance also covers the value of the home itself. In addition, property insurance on your home provides personal-liability protection for members of your household, covering you for claims against you involving injuries to people on or off your property. Many renters think they can get away without buying insurance for their apartment. They think differently after a burglary or other disaster, though. Don't be chintzy about paying to cover what you own.

For homeowners, the amount of coverage you should buy is whatever would be enough to pay for rebuilding your house if it were leveled by disaster. (Standard homeowners policies cover your home's contents for half the dollar limit you place on the house.) Your insurance agent can help you figure rebuilding costs, or you can hire a real estate appraiser for about $150. Essentially, you'll be multiplying the square footage of your house by the building cost per square foot in your area. If you have fancy add-ons like a Jacuzzi, factor those in.

Your annual premium depends on many different factors, among them the value of your house; its age; whether your area is prone to natural hazards such as hurricanes or earthquakes; the crime rate in your neighborhood; and what materials your house is made of (fire-vulnerable wooden houses cost more to insure than stone ones, for example). Annual premiums might run $500 to $1,000 for a $150,000 house.

The best kind of coverage to get is known as HO-3, or "special form," insurance. It protects your house against all perils not specifically excluded by the policy. (So-called HO-1 and HO-2 policies are 15% to 20% cheaper, but they cover fewer risks.) Depending on where you live, common exclusions are damage from floods, earthquakes, sewer and drain backups, war, and nuclear accidents. Your insurer may cover you for some of the excluded perils—at extra cost, of course. For instance, earthquake insurance—advisable for all Californians—runs about $400 to $900 a year for a $200,000 house.

If you want to buy flood insurance, ask someone at your town hall whether your community is among the 18,000 or so that participates in the federal government's National Flood Insurance Program. That list includes almost every place with a serious risk of floods. To better gauge your vulnerability, ask your homeowners insurance agent to show you a flood insurance rate map; that will show you if you live in a minimal, moderate, or "special" hazard area. If your risk is high, buy (think Mississippi River in 1993). Cost: about $300 a year for a $100,000 house. The coverage is available through your regular homeowners insurance agent; for insurers, call 800-427-4661.

Make sure you purchase **guaranteed replacement cost** coverage for your home, if you can. This simply means that you're insured for the full cost of replacing your house, even if the amount exceeds the dollar limit set in your policy. Your coverage will rise yearly with inflation, but the provision adds just $5 to $30 or so to your annual premium. Not every home is eligible for guaranteed replacement cost coverage, though. Some insurers won't provide it for properties built more than 40 or so years ago. One reason: The intricate moldings and other detail work common in old houses can be very expensive to replace.

If guaranteed replacement cost is not an option, go for the second-best type of coverage: **replacement cost.** It covers the full cost of replacing your house, but with a price cap. If you buy one of these policies, it's important that you're covered for 100% of your rebuilding costs. *Never* let that amount fall below 80%. If your coverage is at or above the 80% mark, your policy may not pay the entire cost to rebuild your house if it's completely destroyed—but it will pay the entire repair

cost if a *portion* of your home is damaged, such as after a fire. If your house is insured for less than 80% of its replacement cost, insurers will reimburse you for only that percentage of what is lost. For instance, if you've insured your house for only 60% of its value and your roof blows off, your insurance will pay only 60% of the cost of replacing the roof. **Cash-value** coverage is the cheapest way to go. Avoid it, since such policies pay only the current value of any part of the house you lose.

Another feature to insist on is **replacement-value coverage on the contents** of your home. That means if a tree falls into your living room and reduces your 10-year-old couch to a pile of twigs, your insurance will pay the entire cost of a new one. Otherwise you may get only the cash value of the old couch at the time it was destroyed. Ouch. A replacement-value feature adds just 10% or so to the cost of coverage. If you don't have replacement-value coverage and the entire contents of your house are destroyed, the insurer will generally pay you no more than half the face value of your policy.

What if you have lots of expensive jewelry, silverware, or furs or a valuable stamp collection? You're right to ask, because most policies have a low $1,000 to $2,500 limit for these items. Hardly enough for such valuables. The solution: Buy a so-called floater, or rider, to make up the difference. Floaters cost about $4 per $1,000 for furs, $5 per $1,000 for silverware, and $30 per $1,000 for jewelry. Another advantage of a jewelry rider: it covers you for losses that occur on or off your property. So if a mugger takes off with your $10,000 engagement ring, you're covered.

In the past few years a number of homeowners insurers have jacked up their premiums or stopped offering coverage altogether in certain areas around the country. If you find that your insurer has announced a giant rate hike, call your state insurance commissioner to see if the proposal is likely to go through.

If you can't find private homeowners or renters insurance at any price, you may be able to get coverage by joining your state's "risk pool." Premiums are steep, though. Often they go for 10% to 100% more than those on the open market. Similarly, if you live in a high-crime area and have been turned down for a policy, you may be able to buy federal crime insurance. It covers losses due to robberies and burglaries and is available in California, Florida, Illinois, Kansas, Maryland, New Jersey, New York, Pennsylvania, Tennessee, and Washington, D.C. The crime insurance pays losses up to $10,000 after a deductible of $100, or 5%, whichever is greater.

Eight Ways to Cut Your Homeowners Insurance Costs

1. Equip your home with smoke detectors, deadbolts, and burglar alarms, and tell your insurance company about them. These steps can reduce your homeowners premiums by 5% to 20%.

2. If you own a new home, ask about special breaks. Some insurers lower premiums by 5% to 25% for customers whose homes are less than five years old.

3. Raise your annual deductible. Hiking it from the standard $250 to $1,000, for instance, can save you as much as 15% to 20% per year.

4. Check to make sure the facts on your policy statement are correct. If the stated square footage is bigger than your house's actual square footage, say, or if the policy says your home has wood-frame construction when it's really concrete, you're being overcharged. Call your insurer to correct the problem.

5. Phone agents representing six insurers to find the cheapest policy with the coverage you want. This advice is especially crucial now that major disasters such as Florida's Hurricane Andrew have hiked rates as much as 30% over the past few years in some areas. The agents you call can be independents who represent a number of companies, or salesmen who work for a single insurer.

You're likely to get the best price from a company like American Express or Amica that sells directly through toll-free telephone numbers, because its costs are lower. Your next best bet is likely an insurer such as State Farm or Allstate that sells via its own in-house sales force. Companies represented by independent insurance agents are almost always more expensive, mainly because your premium must cover their commissions.

Don't sacrifice safety for savings, though. A cheap policy won't be worth much if your insurer has gone under by the time you need to make a claim. Stick only with an insurer rated A+ or better from the insurance ratings service A. M. Best or AA- from Standard & Poor's. You can find these reports in most libraries.

6. Don't pay for floaters you don't need. If you bought a floater for a $5,000 fur coat you got five years ago, for instance, but have since given the coat to charity, be sure the insurer isn't still charging you for the coverage.

7. Ask agents about insuring your home and your car with the same company. Some insurers snip homeowners premiums by 5% to 15% if you double up this way. But don't go this route until you check to be sure the insurer's car insurance premium is fairly priced.

8. Finally, if you have guaranteed replacement cost coverage, keep a close watch over your annual premium adjustments. The company will raise your rates each year to keep pace with inflation. If the price hikes are getting too hefty, look for a better deal elsewhere.

BUYING AUTO INSURANCE

Are auto insurance premiums costlier than ever? Is a car alarm noisy? Unfortunately, auto insurance premiums will continue to soar along with the costs of lawsuits, medical care, and car repairs. That's why it's crucial to become a smart auto insurance shopper. Annual premiums in big cities such as New York and Los Angeles often climb into the thousands of dollars, especially if you are under 25, own more than one car, or have a teenager in the house.

To find a suitable, affordable auto policy, first decide what level of coverage you want. Car insurance comes in a package that consists of the following provisions:

■ **Liability protection.** Like homeowners insurance, auto insurance protects you against liability. Here, the coverage protects you against claims for injury and property damage brought by other drivers, pedestrians, or property owners who allege that you caused an accident. Your auto insurer will defend you in or out of court against any claims. The insurance company pays the legal expenses and, if necessary, the damages, up to the dollar limit specified in your policy.

Most policies have three separate dollar limits for each of the following: (1) each person injured in an accident; (2) all people injured in the same accident; and (3) property damage, typically damage to the other driver's car. Most states require drivers to take a minimum of between $20,000 and $30,000 of coverage per person in an accident, with a cap of between $40,000 and $60,000 per accident. (This gets complicated; hang in there.)

A typical bare-bones policy covers $25,000 of liability per person, $50,000 per accident, and $10,000 for property damage; the shorthand name for the insurance would be 25/50/10 coverage. But that's not enough coverage for most people. Unless you have virtually no assets, be sure to purchase at least $100,000 of liability per person, $300,000 per accident, and $100,000 for property damage, or 100/300/100. This enhanced level of coverage will cost you about 20% to 30% more per year, but the protection is worth it.

■ **Collision and comprehensive coverage.** If you carry collision coverage, your insurer will pay for the repairs to your car in the wake of a smash-up. Comprehensive coverage takes care of damages from fire, storm, vandalism, or theft. Few banks and finance companies will approve you for a car loan unless you buy both kinds. Together, collision and comprehensive coverage can get expensive: they typically represent at least 30% to 40% of your total premium.

Both of these coverages are subject to a deductible, the amount you must pay out of your own pocket before the insurance kicks in. Beefing up your deductible can really cut your car insurance premiums. By raising your deductible from $100 to $500, for example, you can cut your collision premium by about a third; raise it to $1,000, and you'll cut this part of your premium in half. A tip: Deposit in the bank the money you're saving by upping your deductible, earmarking it to pay for fender-benders that don't reach the new deductible level.

If your car is more than five years old and on the decline, consider skipping collision and comprehensive coverage altogether. The reason: Your insurer will pay you no more than the car's market value if it's totaled or stolen. When the annual cost of your collision and comprehensive insurance exceeds 10% of your car's "blue-book" value—the amount you'd get if you sold the auto—drop the coverage. Your insurance agent can tell you the current blue-book value of your car.

■ **Uninsured/underinsured motorist coverage.** It has become a fact of modern American life: in many places, the streets are thick with drivers cruising blissfully without car insurance—or without enough insurance. The provision known as uninsured/underinsured motorist coverage means that if you have a close encounter with an uninsured, underinsured, or hit-and-run driver, your insurer will pay for injuries to your passengers, your own "pain and suffering," and other expenses that health plans don't pick up. If you don't buy this coverage and get hit by one of these scofflaws, you'll have to pay for everything your medical insurance doesn't cover plus other expenses resulting from the accident. Clearly this is protection you want to have. You can buy as much coverage as you carry under the liability section of your policy, but it's a good idea to fork over the $40 or so a year that $100,000 of uninsured/underinsured coverage will cost.

■ **Personal injury protection (PIP).** You must purchase this type of coverage if you live in a state with no-fault insurance laws, which generally require your insurer to pick up medical costs for your injuries regardless of whether you or someone else caused the accident. Your agent can tell you whether you need PIP.

Just as with homeowners insurers, there are three main kinds of auto insurers: those like Allstate and State Farm that sell policies through their own agents in local offices nationwide; those like Aetna and Travelers that sell policies through independent agents who earn a

commission for each policy sold; and those like Amica and GEICO that sell policies through toll-free telephone numbers. It's impossible to say which insurer will offer you the best deal. Premiums for identical policies in the same city often vary by hundreds of dollars a year, so compare price quotes from a minimum of five insurers.

In general, though, if you have a pristine driving record, you may have the best luck with an 800-number insurer: they choose only better-than-average risks, and they pass on to you the economies of noncommission telephone selling. If you've had a few speeding tickets or accidents in the past three years, try Allstate or State Farm: they cover a much broader range of drivers, and their premiums are generally not outrageous.

Be sure to ask for any and all discounts you might be entitled to receive. The discounts might save you 5% to 25% of your premiums. Get the conversation started by telling your agent if any of the following factors apply to you:

- You'll insure more than one family car with the same company.
- Your car has safety features such as air bags, automatic seat belts, or an antitheft device.
- Your car isn't a racy high-performance vehicle.
- You've taken a state-approved defensive-driving course.

- You're a senior citizen.
- You're a middle-aged woman and are the only driver in your household.
- You participate in a carpool.
- You park in a garage rather than on the street.

If you have a teenager—which can double your insurance costs—look for discounts that he or she can help you get. Examples: completing a high school driver's education course and getting good grades in school. Be sure to tell the insurer if your teen is not the principal driver of the car but only pilots it occasionally, since occasional-driver status is often cheaper.

BUYING UMBRELLA LIABILITY INSURANCE

If you own a car or a home, of course, your homeowners and auto policies provide some liability coverage—typically $100,000 to $300,000 for your homeowners policy and about $50,000 for your auto policy. (Renters insurance policies provide some liability coverage, too). But if you can afford it, you ought to buy additional liability coverage—known as umbrella liability insurance—from a homeowners or auto insurance agent. After all if, say, you or a member of your household cripples a bigwig executive by plowing into him on a ski slope, you

could be the target of a massive lawsuit that far exceeds those limits. Or if your teenager throws a party in your basement while you're away and a friend breaks a leg on the stairs, you could be held responsible and your liability could be enormous.

An umbrella liability policy covers any claims that come because you or members of your household have damaged others out of negligence—or libeled, slandered, or defamed them—in excess of the limits on your other policies. Buying such insurance is especially important if you fit one or more of the following profiles:

- You have substantial assets and are thus a prime target for a big lawsuit.
- You employ hired help who are not licensed or bonded, such as a cleaning woman, baby-sitter, or gardener.
- You often have people house-sit for you.
- You rent out a room in your home.
- You have a home-based business.

To be safe, if you have as little as $200,000 in assets, it's wise to purchase a total of $1 million in liability coverage (the minimum for umbrella policies). If you have, say, $500,000 in assets, you're better off with $2 million or more. The cost of the coverage depends on where you live and how many cars, boats, and homes you own. Generally, a $1 million policy might cost $150 to $200 a year. The next million dollars would cost an added $75 annually; you'll pay about $50 for every million thereafter. (Umbrella liability coverage on a home-based business will cost about $30 extra a year.)

To shave the cost of an umbrella liability policy, see about raising your liability coverage to the highest allowable levels on your homeowners and auto insurance policies. Then buy an umbrella policy for just the remainder you'd like covered. Also, look into buying your umbrella policy from the same insurer that provides your auto and/or homeowners coverage. In return for all this business, many companies will knock about 15% off your umbrella policy premium.

BUYING LIFE INSURANCE

Amazing but true: buying life insurance is one of the most important moves you can make to solidify your personal finances, yet it is also one of the most complicated. It's extremely difficult to compare life insurance policies. On top of that, life insurance has its own jargon that is enough to make anyone head for the aspirin bottle. It doesn't help, of course, that buying life insurance means coming to terms with your own mortality. Great.

Nevertheless, if you have dependents but your assets wouldn't provide for them adequately after you die, you need life in-

surance. By contrast, if you're single and have no dependents, you probably don't need to buy life insurance since no one is relying on your financial support. A life insurance agent may argue that you should buy a life insurance policy to cover the cost of burial when you die. But you should have enough in savings for this expense.

How much life insurance do you need? The simple answer: Enough to sustain your family's present standard of living and let them meet their financial goals in the event that you're no longer around. If you're married and the only breadwinner, your life policy's **death benefit**—the face amount of the policy, collected by your beneficiaries after you die—together with your other assets should be large enough to deliver lifetime income for your spouse. If you have kids, you'll need to provide income for them, too, until they leave home, as well as a tuition fund if you intend to pay their way through college. If both you and your spouse work and earn income that the family relies on, both of you need coverage.

But putting a dollar figure on the exact amount you need is trickier than you may think. The rule of thumb that says you should insure yourself for five to seven times your annual gross income is far too simplistic. Instead, meet with a life insurance agent or a financial planner who can do the calculations to match your situation. Many personal finance software packages can also handle the calculations right on your personal computer—with no salesman in the room!

FIGURING OUT HOW MUCH LIFE INSURANCE YOU NEED

This worksheet can help you estimate the size of the minimum death benefit you need.

Add up the following:

1. Your family's annual living expenses for the number of years you want coverage (remember that these will rise with inflation)

2. Any extras that are important to you, such as the inflation-adjusted cost to: send your kids to college; pay off your mortgage; pay your funeral expenses (about $8,000 today, including cemetery plot); pay estate taxes or leave your children an inheritance

Then subtract the following (all for the total number of years you want insurance coverage):

1. Your spouse's estimated annual after-tax income

2. Estimated income on your investments

3. Social Security income (call 800-772-1213 for an estimate)

4. Pension income (ask your employee benefits department for an estimate)

Voilà! The approximate total death benefit you need. You may have some of this covered already through a policy provided by your employer at work. You can trim the amount by cutting back on certain goals (for example, maybe you don't want to leave each of your kids a $100,000 inheritance after all). Still, the basic amount of coverage a family of four needs can easily reach into the millions.

To decide which kind of life insurance policy is best for you, the first thing to understand is the difference between the two major types: **term insurance** and **cash-value insurance.**

Term insurance is pure insurance: your premium payments go toward the guaranteed death benefit for your survivors. Well, almost exclusively. A portion also pays the agent's commission and the insurance company's overhead and profit. The term policy is good—in insurance terms "stays in force"—as long as you keep paying the premiums. When you stop paying, you're no longer insured.

Cash-value insurance, on the other hand, is a hybrid. It's life insurance combined with a savings fund. Part of the premium you pay goes toward the death benefit, the commission, and so forth, just as with term insurance. But a large piece of your premium goes into a tax-deferred investment fund. The balance you build up in this investment fund is known as the policy's **cash value.** The cash value has a guaranteed interest rate, typically 4% to 5%; but the policy is likely to earn more than that for you. Depending on the policy, you can eventually borrow against your cash value or even withdraw it. Insurance agents sometimes like to call cash-value coverage "permanent insurance."

So which kind of insurance is best: term or cash value? For most people, term is the clear winner. If you're young or money is tight, opting for a cash-value policy is downright foolish. That's because for the same death benefit, term insurance is far less expensive, especially in the early years. And the commissions are far less steep (commissions on cash-value policies generally run five to 10 times higher than those on term policies). If you're 35 and want to buy $500,000 worth of life insurance, your annual term premiums will run about $850 to $1,500. A cash-value policy might cost you three times as much in that first year.

The most common type of term insurance is called **annual renewable term.** Its premium rises each year as you age. Male nonsmokers can buy $250,000 worth for as little as $275 a year at age 30, $325 at age 40, and $875 at age 50.

Women pay less; smokers pay much more. You generally cannot renew the policy after age 70, at which point you probably won't need life insurance anymore anyway. If you go with an annual renewable term policy, make sure the contract guarantees that you'll be able to keep it regardless of changes in your health. Another kind of term: level-premium term, which has premiums that remain constant for a period of years, then spike up.

Price hikes for annual renewable term are not as scary as they may sound. While the premium rate keeps rising, the amount of coverage the typical family needs will likely level off and then decline. That's because as your children grow up and your savings and investments accumulate, you typically need to own less insurance, not more. And cutting back on the death benefit amount means lowering the premiums.

If you're shopping for a term policy, don't be taken in by one just because it has the cheapest first-year premium. Instead, make sure the agent shows you its projected annual cost five, 10, and 20 years into the contract (through what's known as a policy illustration) and the maximum premium charge in each case. A policy with the lowest initial premium may cost more as the policy ages than a similar policy with a higher initial charge. Your agent may recommend a level-term policy with set premiums for an extended period, such as 10 years. Since the premium is basically an average of the cost for the entire period, you'll pay more in the early years of a level policy than with a traditional annual renewable term. That's fine, but go for level term only if you expect to keep the coverage for the entire period.

The typical cash-value policy carries a much higher premium than a term policy because that premium must cover two things: insurance plus savings. That high premium ordinarily stays the same each year. But unlike term, cash-value insurance can be kept until you're at least 95. If you decide to purchase a cash-value policy, be sure you'll hang on to it for at least 10 years. Otherwise the policy's fees and agent commissions will eat up far too much of your cash-value fund.

There are many different types of cash-value policies. Among the most common are **whole life, universal life,** and **variable life** policies. Here's how they differ:

■ **A whole life policy, the traditional form of cash-value insurance, invests mostly in bonds and earns a fixed, modest rate of return.**

■ **Universal life policies let you adjust your premium and death benefit every year to suit your changing circumstances.** Part of your premiums are invested in short-term securities similar to those in money-market mutual

funds, paying money-market rates of interest. Premiums are flexible: you may even be able to skip adding to the cash value if money is tight—though you'll probably be forced to pay higher charges later on.

■ **Variable life invests your cash value in your choice of stock, bond, or money-market funds.** Returns fluctuate according to the markets and the fund manager's investing skill. Variable life policies generally deduct sales charges and other annual expenses that can cut their cash-value returns in half over the first 10 years you own them.

If you're shopping for a cash-value policy, be especially careful: such policies are so complex that it's extremely difficult to compare the costs and benefits of different insurers' offerings. At a minimum, ask each agent what assumptions he or she is using to calculate policy illustrations. Some illustrations assume that cash-value accounts will earn an average of 8% a year for 20 years, for example, even though the kinds of things they invest in may now yield only 6%. Also ask the agent to verify that the interest rate figures are net of expenses, since that's what you'll really earn. Tell the agent to show you what would happen to your cash value if the insurer earned two percentage points less than anticipated, just to be sure. Also get a worst-case scenario—what the cash-value buildup would be if the insurer ends up paying the mere guaranteed rate, typically 4% to 5%.

No matter which type of life insurance policy you want, don't sacrifice safety for price. If your life insurer goes belly up, your coverage will be worthless. So stick with an insurer that gets a safety grade of no lower than A+ from rating agency A. M. Best or AA- from Standard & Poor's. Books detailing both agencies' ratings are available at most public libraries.

THREE WAYS TO LOWER YOUR LIFE INSURANCE COSTS

Follow these suggestions to help save money on your life insurance premiums:

1. Get healthier. Quitting smoking can cut your life premium in half; losing excess weight can save almost as much.

2. Call a price comparison-shopping service or use one on-line. Several companies exist that will report the lowest rates available to you from a variety of different insurers. Price quotes are free; you can usually buy the policy you want directly from the company offering the price quote. Three such firms: Quotesmith (800-556-9393; it scans more than 150 insurers); SelectQuote (800-343-1985; 16 insurers); and TermQuote (800-444-8376; 75 insurers). On-line services can also help you buy life insurance wisely, by advising you on how much coverage you need, the most appropriate type of policy, and the least expensive one. To get a second opinion on the right coverage, try *QuickQuote Insurance Agency's Term Life Estimator* (www.quickquote.com). If you want tips on choosing the right type of policy and finding the least expensive choices for term insurance, check out *InstantQuote* (www.instantquote.com), *QuickQuote,* and *Quotesmith* (www.quotesmith.com).

3. Make sure to get some quotes from low-load insurance companies. Ten low-load insurers such as Ameritas and USAA, both of whom sell by telephone, charge sales fees that amount to just 10% to 20% of your first-year premium and perhaps 2% of subsequent premiums. If you work with a fee-only financial planner, that pro can locate low-load policies for you, too. If you don't know how much insurance you want, a planner or an insurance consultant can help you figure out the right amount. You'll pay a flat fee of perhaps $200 to $500 or a rate of something like $100 to $150 an hour.

INSURANCE YOU DON'T NEED

You may well be thinking, *Gee—I sure need a lot more insurance than I have now!* Well, maybe you do. And maybe you don't. According to the National Insurance Consumer Organization (NICO), a nonprofit group, fully 10% of the $180 billion or so that Americans spend on insurance is unnecessary.

Remember, the purpose of insurance is to protect your family against financial catastrophe. So you should insure only against losses you can't absorb without serious pain—not against small losses that you can meet by tapping your savings. Nor should you buy policies that insure you against just one risk, such as dying in an airplane crash or contracting one specific illness. Such narrow policies are usually very expensive for what you get back in benefits.

Among the policies you should spurn—or dump if you already have them:

■ **Life insurance for your kids.** It's amazing how many people take out policies on their young children's lives considering how little reason there is to do it. You should insure a person's life only in order to protect his or her dependents against the loss of that person's income stream. So unless your kid is supporting you, save your money.

■ **Dread-disease insurance.** Policies that pay only if you get cancer, for example, cost a whopping $250 or so a year—about the same as your cost for an employer-sponsored health policy that covers virtually every malady.

■ **Hospital indemnity insurance.** Such heavily advertised policies promise to pay you, say, $75 a day for every day you spend hospitalized. But the typical hospital stay costs $750 a day. And any decent comprehensive health insurance policy should cover hospitalizations adequately. Besides, you may have other medical expenses outside the hospital. What's more, these policies don't protect you against medical-cost inflation, because their dollar limit is locked in place.

■ **Credit life and credit disability insurance.** It's a rare person who hasn't heard the credit insurance pitch from car dealerships, finance companies, or banks offering loans. "This policy will make your loan payments if you die or become disabled. And won't you feel better with that peace of mind?" Probably not—once you realize that credit insurance is usually a crashingly bad buy, costing perhaps $300 on a $10,000, four-year car loan.

About half of all credit-card issuers offer such insurance, too, usually pushed in fliers included with your monthly bill (cost: about 60¢ on every $100 of your credit-card balance each month). The insurance generally pays off revolving credit-card debt if you die, become disabled, or lose your job. But there's one big problem: The policies generally pay off your entire debt only if you kick the bucket. If you're disabled or laid off, they'll pay just the monthly minimum on your card—typically a puny 2.5% of your balance—usually for no more than a year.

Meanwhile interest keeps accruing on the balance.

Instead of buying such insurance, simply beef up your personal emergency savings fund to cover small debts. As for large debts, make sure your life and disability coverage is adequate to cover them.

■ **Mortgage protection insurance.** Similar to credit life, this type of policy would make your house payments for six to 12 months if you were laid off. But it's too overpriced to be appealing: premiums usually amount to 3% to 4% of your annual mortgage payment.

■ **Home warranties.** Builders or real estate agents offer these contracts, which protect you against major defects in your home. Such warranties are expensive, though. Most cost $300 to $500 a year, plus $50 to $100 whenever the company's contractor visits your house. And they are usually filled with exclusions. Another risk: The builder selling you the warranty will go out of business, as more than 12,000 have since 1988, rendering your "insurance" useless. If you're worried about defects in a house you're looking at, have a home inspector check it out instead.

■ **Extended-service contracts on cars.** These complex and overpriced policies (costing about $600 to $2,000 for two to five years of coverage) simply aren't worth it. They pay if certain big-ticket components in your car break

down, which is unlikely during the first few years of ownership.

The same goes for extended-service contracts on appliances and consumer electronics. Such a contract might cost anywhere from $20 to $500 and promise free repairs or replacement if the product breaks within one to five years. But you're duplicating coverage for at least part of the time: the manufacturer's warranty usually lasts from three months to two years. Fact is, more than 80% of service contracts go unused.

■ **Towing insurance.** Typically piggy-backed onto your auto insurance policy, this coverage pays, say, $75 for getting your sick car to a repair shop. But if you belong to an auto club such as AAA, you almost certainly have towing coverage already. Many luxury-car makers also throw in free towing for the first few years of ownership.

■ **Collision-damage waivers for rental cars.** These waivers, costing from $10 to $15 or so a day, can add 50% to the cost of your car rental. But for most people, accepting the coverage is completely unnecessary: your own auto policy probably covers any car you rent (check to make sure). And some gold credit cards, as well as most American Express cards, automatically provide such protection when you charge your rental car.

■ **Flight insurance.** You've heard it before, and it's true: You're 56 times more likely to be killed in a car accident than in a plane crash. So if you don't buy an insurance policy every time you step into your Ford Escort, don't do it before you enter that 747. That way you'll save the roughly $16.75 per flight it costs for, say, $500,000 of Mutual of Omaha life coverage. Moreover, credit-card issuers often throw in free life insurance when you charge an air ticket (at least $100,000 in coverage when you charge your ticket to American Express, for example).

■ **Trip-cancellation insurance.** If your sciatica flared up just in time to force you to cancel your prepaid vacation last year, you might be intrigued by such a policy, which your travel agent can generally sell you for $5.50 or so per $100 of coverage. Not so fast. The policies usually won't pay if your cancellation is due to recurrence of an old ailment. And these days most airlines will let you change the dates of your ticket for a low $25 fee anyway.

■ **Rain insurance.** Worried about a drizzle dampening your guests' spirits at an outdoor reception? Worry about this instead: The premium for a rain insurance policy can cost fully 10% of your party's tab. Better to spend a few dollars on a housecleaner in the event that you have to move the revelers inside.

■ **Wedding insurance.** The main offerings of these policies, which cost up to $600 or so, are up to $500,000 in personal liability protection (which you should have already under your umbrella liability policy) and as much as $20,000 for non-refundable expenses incurred by a sudden wedding cancellation caused by, say, the bride's breaking her leg. Unfortunately, the policies won't pay out in the event that the bride or groom gets cold feet. There are some things in life you just can't insure against.

CHAPTER 3

Getting Help You Can Trust

Fortunately, managing your finances isn't something you need to do alone. In fact, you will probably be more likely to reach your financial goals if you hire some crackerjack advisers: a tax preparer, insurance agents, one or more lawyers, perhaps a stockbroker, financial planner, or even a money manager. A sharp real estate agent can help you get the best price when selling your home and direct you to suitable shelter if you're buying (more about finding and using one in Chapter 7). Electronic helpers—in the form of computer software and on-line services—can guide you, too.

You don't have to be rich to hire advisers, either. The key is finding the right pro for your needs and your wallet. For instance, although you could pay a CPA $1,000 or so to fill out your federal and state tax returns, you might do just as well with a storefront preparer charging between $50 and $100. A helpful rule: To find an appropriate, honest adviser, start by asking your friends or business associates whom they use and begin interviewing them. What follows is kind of an annotated Yellow Pages to help you turn up the financial advisers you need.

Choosing a Tax Preparer

Face it: filling out your tax return is no fun. First there are the hours of sorting through your records, statements, and receipts to see what you need for your return. Then there is the time it takes to actually sit down and complete the tricky forms, made more complicated by the 1997 tax laws. Once you're done, you may very well think to yourself, *Could I be paying less somehow?* A top tax preparer can save you not only some time and aggravation, but probably some taxes, too. That's why paid preparers complete two-thirds of the nation's 1040 long forms. In the next chapter you'll learn how to best use a tax adviser and tax software.

Which type of preparer to hire and how much you'll pay depend on the complexity of your tax return and your financial life. You have three basic options: **storefront preparers, certified public accountants (CPAs),** and **enrolled agents.** You needn't hire a tax lawyer just to fill out your return or to get sensible tax-planning advice. A tax lawyer is worth a call, however, once you arrive at the intersection of taxes and the legal system—for instance, if you are about to get a divorce or buy or sell a business.

Try *not* to look for a tax pro in the heart of tax season, during March or April. By that time most of the better preparers are already booked. You'll also have a tough time getting one to sit with you for a free consultation. The best time to seek out a tax adviser who will provide tax-planning advice is in June or July;

many take well-deserved vacations in May. If you want someone only to fill out your returns, start your search in January, once you have the necessary data for last year's finances. The skinny on your tax adviser choices:

■ **Storefront preparers.** These are the people at places such as H&R Block, Jackson Hewitt Tax Service, and Triple Check Income Tax Service. Some are part-timers, some work full-time year round preparing tax returns. Nearly all are conservative about the write-offs they'll let you claim. Storefront preparers are the least expensive way to go. Figure on spending between $50 and $100 for a basic tax form, maybe $150 or so for one that's a bit more complicated. A knowledgeable storefront preparer can certainly fill out a 1040 with ease (you ought to be able to fill out the simple 1040EZ or 1040A by yourself), along with Schedule A and Schedule B for itemized deductions, interest, and dividends. However, once you get into more complicated areas, such as home offices, small businesses, rental real estate, and the sale of stocks, bonds, or mutual funds, you might consider stepping up to either a CPA or an enrolled agent.

A storefront preparer has two drawbacks: First, you won't get any tax-planning advice. This type of preparer might tell you about ways you could have reduced your taxes after he or she completes your return. You won't have a session discussing how to cut next year's taxes, however. In fact, you probably won't even talk with the preparer throughout the year until tax season rolls around again. The second drawback comes if the IRS starts asking questions about your return. Commercial preparers aren't allowed to represent you in dealing with the IRS. So if the tax man starts snooping, you'll either have to defend yourself or hire an accountant or an enrolled agent to act on your behalf.

■ **Certified public accountants (CPAs) and enrolled agents (EAs).** These are the pros to consider when you're looking for help with a complicated tax return, year-round tax-planning advice, and someone who might be able to help you if you need to do battle with the IRS. In fact, a CPA or EA can become one of your trusted allies throughout your life. This pro may turn into the sounding board you need when deciding things such as: Should I get a home-equity loan? Does it make sense to borrow from my 401(k) savings plan? Would I be better off in a tax-free municipal bond mutual fund or a fund that invests in U.S. Treasury securities?

Certified public accountants who specialize in taxes (not all 400,000 CPAs do) and enrolled agents are similar in many respects. Both have received rigorous training. A CPA must pass a state accountancy exam and then take continuing ed-

ucation classes to keep up. An EA has either worked at the IRS and earned a special license or passed a stiff two-day IRS test. Both can represent you in front of the IRS. You'll pay either one more than a storefront preparer, because of their training. Figure on spending $200 to $1,000; enrolled agents often charge a little less than tax partners at big-city accounting firms. Many charge by the hour—$75 and up. If that's how yours gets paid, do whatever you can to bring your accountant or enrolled agent organized records. Otherwise you'll be throwing money away paying the adviser to sort through your receipts and determine which ones are important.

As noted earlier, it's a good idea to ask friends or business associates for the names of advisers they use. Since there are only about 30,000 enrolled agents in the country, however, you may not know of anyone using one. To get names of enrolled agents in your area, call the National Association of Enrolled Agents at 800-424-4339 or write to the group at 200 Orchard Ridge Dr., Suite 302, Gaithersburg, Md. 20878.

Ideally, you want a CPA or EA whose clients have incomes and jobs similar to yours. For instance, some know small-business taxes backward and forward; others don't. You also want to find a tax pro who will be just as aggressive about claiming write-offs as you would yourself—no more, no less. The tax code has many gray areas, particularly when it comes to things such as home offices and business expenses. Some preparers are willing to take chances and claim iffy deductions, figuring the IRS won't notice or that they will have a decent chance of defending them in an audit. Others favor a safer letter-of-the-law approach that could cost you more in taxes. When interviewing prospective tax advisers, find out how aggressive they are and see how you feel about their stances.

Ask, too, who will actually be preparing your return. At many accounting firms, low-level preparers and even temps make the first run filling out returns. They then pass their work up to the experienced CPAs, who sign the returns. There's nothing necessarily wrong with this approach; you just don't want to be surprised to find out that the person you thought was your preparer has farmed out your 1040.

Don't become wholly ignorant about taxes once you hire a tax adviser, however. The more you know about the tax code, the better the questions you can ask your preparer. It's worth picking up an annual tax guide sold in bookstores. You might also want to subscribe to a tax newsletter written for laymen. One excellent candidate: *Write-Off,* a monthly with smart tax-planning strategies for professionals and small-business owners,

edited by James Seidel and Robert Trinz ($119 a year; ProPub Inc., 201-447-6485).

Choosing Insurance Agents

It's hard to think of anything more important than protecting yourself and the people you love. That's why buying insurance is so important and why you need to have trustworthy insurance agents. The preceding chapter told you how to shop for life, health, disability, auto, and homeowners insurance policies. Now a few words about getting the right agents who will sell you the policies. There are two types of agents: **independent agents,** who sell policies for a variety of companies; and **exclusive agents** or **captive agents,** who work for just one insurer. Theoretically, an independent agent should be better for you, since he or she can search among different companies for the least expensive policies with the broadest coverage from the safest insurers. Real life doesn't always work that way, however. An independent might be tempted to sell you the policy paying him or her the highest commission. Also, a captive agent's policy might be better than any policy sold by an independent. So don't rule out any agent because he or she works for too many or too few insurers. Instead, when interviewing agents, talk with both independents and exclusives. Some specifics for particular types of policies:

■ **Life insurance.** In recent years the news about the honesty of life insurance agents has been less than comforting. Metropolitan Life, the second biggest life insurer in the country, was hit with $20 million in fines for possibly deceiving thousands of customers into buying life insurance policies disguised as retirement plans and investments. The New York State Department of Insurance levied a $500,000 fine against National Benefit Life, a Travelers subsidiary, after customers complained about potentially misleading sales materials. Indeed, regulators in a handful of big states have been investigating life insurers for deceptive sales practices. While most life insurance agents are honest, the rash of problems with policy salesmen suggests that you need to be extremely cautious before choosing an agent. Five tips in finding a scrupulous agent:

1. Be sure the agent represents one or more insurers with top safety grades from independent analysts. It won't matter how kindly your agent was if your insurer goes out of business. You'll want to get a policy from an insurer rated no lower than A+ from A. M. Best or AA- from Standard & Poor's.

2. Ask the agent to explain clearly how much insurance you need, why you need that much, and why he or she recommends a particular insurer and its policy. If you don't get straight answers that you can understand, move on to another agent.

3. Look for someone who is a chartered life underwriter (CLU) or a chartered financial consultant (ChFC). These designations are no definitive defense against moral turpitude, but they do suggest that the agent was serious enough about the profession to take the courses necessary for the moniker. The American College, an insurance school in Bryn Mawr, Pa., awards both the CLU and the ChFC.

4. Don't buy from someone pitching insurance as an investment. Remember: The reason to buy life insurance is to replace a lost income, not to get rich.

5. Consider hiring an independent insurance adviser, not an agent, to help you choose a policy. For instance, the National Insurance Consumer Organization (P.O. Box 15492, Alexandria, Va. 22309) will evaluate any cash-value policy for $40. Glenn Daily of the Life Insurance Advisers Association (800-521-4578) will both review policies and offer alternatives for a fee of $175 an hour. Figure on a two-hour review. For general life insurance questions, you can call the National Insurance Consumer Helpline

(800-942-4242) of the American Council of Life Insurance.

■ **Health and disability insurance.** Many of the same agents who sell life insurance offer health and disability policies. So the first two life insurance tips apply here, too. In addition, however, when buying a health or disability policy, stick with agents who represent larger insurers. The bigger the policyholder base, the easier it is for the insurer to spread its risks and thus keep your premiums down. If you're looking for a health policy and have a medical problem, be sure to meet with an independent agent. This type of agent is more likely to find you an insurer who will sell you coverage.

■ **Homeowners insurance.** With homeowners insurers dropping customers or going out of business about as often as they take on new policyholders, these days you really need an agent on your side. The agent is the person who will go to bat for you if you need to file a claim after a casualty loss. Interview a half dozen agents. You're likely to find that in many cases you'll get the best price from a captive agent working for a single insurer with its own in-house sales force. As with life, health, and disability policies, buy homeowners coverage from a financially solid company. So make sure the agents you call sell policies from insurers rated no lower than A+ from A. M. Best or AA- from Standard & Poor's.

While many states have so-called guaranty funds to protect customers if their insurers fold, many limit reimbursement to $100,000 to $300,000.

■ **Car insurance.** The advice here echoes that of finding a decent homeowners agent, since both types of policies are sold by casualty insurers. You may be able to get the cheapest price quote from a direct seller such as Amica or GEICO, proffering policies through toll-free numbers. However, you may want to spring for a little more to have an agent you know who will help you collect if your car is in an accident or gets stolen.

One indicator of a helpful agent: When calling around for premium prices, see if the agent volunteers information about policy discounts. If you don't hear any, ask what discounts are available and watch what happens. A decent agent will either tell you without prompting about insurers' discounts for, say, policyholders with antitheft devices, or at least explain the discounts when asked. Nearly all insurers offer some kind of discounts today, so a cagey agent is one to be avoided.

Choosing a Stockbroker

The word "stockbroker" has almost gone into extinction on Wall Street. Today, brokerage firms like to call their employees "account executives" or "account specialists" or "financial consultants" or nearly anything other than stockbrokers. Somehow, "stockbroker" has taken on a connotation of a narrowly focused, money-grubbing, cold-calling salesman whose sole interest is in making money for himself, not his clients. While some stockbrokers out there may be like that—actually, there are undoubtedly quite a few like that—many of the nation's 94,000 brokers truly want to make money for themselves and their clients. That's the kind of stockbroker you want to find.

Sadly, recent studies suggest that the stereotype is all too true, particularly if you don't have much money to invest, you're young, or you're a woman. Many brokers, it seems, prefer to deal with older, male customers who are loaded. One example of broker bias: In a recent **MONEY** survey of 21 leading full-service brokerage firms, brokers failed to ask about the investment history of 25% of their female customers versus just 10% of the men. Another **MONEY** brokers' survey found that when men and women walked in off the street with the same amount of cash to invest, the men got an average of 47 minutes with brokers while the women got only 38 minutes. More distressingly, in these surveys the brokers frequently failed to ask key questions of many potential clients regardless of their age, sex, or income. For instance, 42% of-

fered advice without asking customers about their tax brackets, and 39% forgot to inquire about household income. Roughly a third failed to find out about their customers' tolerance for investment risk or their financial goals. The surveys also showed a fair number of brokers pushing investments that generated higher commissions for them. One reason: In-house offerings such as the brokerage's own mutual funds often give brokers 2% to 5% more in commissions than others. These surveys, incidentally, showed no clear difference between salesmen at big brokerages and ones at smaller firms. Clearly, when looking for a broker, you need to do a fair amount of weeding before you can plant your dollars.

After getting the names of brokers recommended by people you know, do a little research on them—even before you meet any face-to-face. You'll want to be sure that the broker hasn't done his customers wrong. The best way to do this is by calling your state securities administrator (the phone number is in your phone book) and the National Association of Securities Dealers (800-289-9999). Ask both if the broker is licensed in your state and if there have been any complaints or disciplinary actions against him. The state agency should give you a copy of the broker's **Central Registration Directory (CRD) file,** listing any complaints or disciplinary actions taken against the broker.

Once you've found several brokers with clean records, make appointments to meet with them. At these free sessions, you'll want to see both how knowledgeable the brokers are about investing and how much the brokers want to know about you. As with an accountant or enrolled agent, you're looking for someone whose temperament and tolerance for risk matches yours. Tell the broker up front about your investing goals, financial status, and risk tolerance, since this is the only way your broker can get a true sense of what you should be investing in. Then ask this key question: What kinds of investments would you recommend for me and why? If the investments seem too risky for you or too safe, you need to find a better match.

Unlike, say, tax preparers or lawyers, stockbrokers have quantifiable performance records you can review. By checking out how well the broker's recommended stocks, bonds, and mutual funds have done, you'll be able to see whether you're likely to make money with him or her. And that, after all, is the bottom line. Ask the broker for 12 months' worth of performance for three clients whose objectives are like yours. Then have your broker compare those returns with the appropriate yardsticks. For instance, if you want to invest in stocks or stock mutual funds, stack up his returns against the Standard & Poor's 500 stock index.

Another way to eliminate inappropri-ate brokers is by discussing compensation. Now and after you've hired a broker, ask what kind of commission he or she would make from the recommended investments. You're not looking to cheat the broker out of a decent livelihood; you just want an explanation that will tell you whether the fees are reasonable. Brokers tend to keep about 60% of the commissions they receive; their firms get the rest. Ordinarily, brokers collect the highest commissions on complicated and risky investments that require some effort to sell, such as limited partnerships (typical commission: 6%). If your broker recommends any investment paying a commission of more than 5%, ask whether a less costly alternative could help you achieve the same financial goal.

Find out too about additional charges you might get socked with by the brokerage firm. Some firms charge $40 a year to maintain an account, $50 to keep the account open if the brokerage considers it inactive, and $100 just to set up an IRA. You might also pay extra to get and keep your stock certificates. Brokerages have been piling up these junk fees in recent years, so you'll want to check out the charges before you select a broker.

Once you have found a broker you like, fill out the Investment Profile form on pages 68 and 69 and give a copy to him or her. This way, you'll both know exactly what you want out of the relationship.

MY INVESTMENT PROFILE

This disclosure form, created with assistance from Thomas Benson of Opus/Portfolio Concepts of Naples, Fla., and J. Boyd Page of Atlanta's Page & Bacek, will help ensure that you and your broker are on the same wavelength. By filling in the worksheet, your broker will know your risk tolerance, objectives, investment knowledge and experience, and financial goals. Make a copy of this and give it to your broker.

My name _____

Brokerage firm _____

My account number _____

Risk tolerance (circle appropriate level)

Low (CDs and bonds)   High (options, margin trading)

| 1 | 2 | 3 | 4 | 5 | 6 | 7 | 8 | 9 | 10 |

My objectives (don't rate any two classifications the same):

Capital preservation					Growth				
1	2	3	4	5	1	2	3	4	5
Less Important			**Important**		**Less Important**			**Important**	

Income					Tax savings				
1	2	3	4	5	1	2	3	4	5
Less Important			**Important**		**Less Important**			**Important**	

Liquidity				
1	2	3	4	5
Less Important			**Important**	

Value of my investments:

Stocks	$_____	Bonds	$_____
Pensions	$_____	Cash	$_____
Real estate	$_____	(money funds, CDs)	
(other than residence)		Other	$_____

My investment knowledge and experience:
Extensive   Moderate   Minimal   None

Investments I've made (circle if applicable):
Stocks   Taxable bonds   Tax-free bonds   Junk bonds
CDs   Mutual funds   Partnerships   Penny stocks
Short sales   Preferred/warrants   Options   Futures

I am relying on my broker for investment ideas . . .
Not at all   Partially   Totally

In any year, I'm willing to lose no more than $_____

I consider myself to be generally a . . .
Long-term investor   Short-term investor

I do not wish to pay more than _____**% of my account in commissions
in any year.**

Broker's name and how we met _____
_____

Expected role and function of broker _____
_____

My big upcoming expenses (include estimated amount and date): _____
_____

**Other instructions (when to sell securities; maximum
sales charges I'll pay)** _____
_____
                                        _____
                                        _____
                                        _____
_____   _____
Broker's signature, date   **My signature, age,
                                        address,
                                        date**

Once you've hired a broker, keep an eye on him or her. When the broker recommends an investment, find out why. You want to be sure that the investment fits your needs and isn't just one the broker is touting to earn a fatter commission. From time to time, some brokerages offer sales incentives such as contests with prizes if their brokers sell a certain amount of a particular investment, such as a specific stock, mutual fund, limited partnership, or annuity. Most firms also increase brokers' commissions if they sell stocks that their firm is eager to clear out of inventory or if they sell their own in-house mutual funds rather than other funds. (A few brokerages, prodded by the Securities and Exchange Commission, are moving away from such practices.)

When your broker recommends an investment or you have one you want to buy, be sure to ask whether you're eligible for a discount. For example, if you invest at least $25,000 in a single mutual fund, you may qualify for a so-called break point that lowers the commission you pay by 1 to 1½ percentage points. When buying stocks, ask if your brokerage firm can shop around various dealers who make a market in given securities in order to get you the best price. Most full-service brokerages also authorize salespeople to slice trading commissions for their best customers by 20% to 50%.

Make sure you get your money's worth from your broker, too. If you're paying for the services of a full-service broker, you ought to be receiving research reports on investments that interest you—from the brokerage's own analysts or from outside firms such as Standard & Poor's, Value Line, and Morningstar. Feel free to ask your broker questions about the outlook for the economy and the securities markets, if you trust his or her judgment. Always discuss your investment strategies and concerns. At least once a quarter, review your portfolio with your broker, identifying investment winners and losers and plotting future moves.

When your broker suggests a particular investment, ask if it could be especially difficult or costly to unload later. If it could, that may well be an investment you can do without. For example, you might be stuck with a limited partnership for life. With annuities and some mutual funds, your problem could be the cost of selling your holding. For example, if you sell shares of some mutual funds within five years, you'll get hit with a fee of 1% to 5%.

Resist efforts by a broker to trade too often. Because brokers earn a commission on every sale, they have an incentive to encourage trading. But you're almost always better with a buy-and-hold strategy. If you sell an investment within a year or so, brokerage commissions may eat up any profits. To discourage your broker from **churning** your account—that is, trading actively simply to rack up commissions—ask him how long he expects you to hold

70

any investment and why. Being so conscientious will convince a broker that if he has any churning impulses, you're not interested. One last point: Never let your broker trade without your approval.

What should you do if you have a dispute with your broker? First, take a deep breath, since getting brokerage wrongs righted is not easy. Don't sit and stew. Federal law says claims against brokers must be filed within three years of buying a security or one year of discovering a problem, whichever is less. Some states give you more time, however. Start your battle by complaining to your broker directly. If that strategy doesn't work, meet with the brokerage's branch manager and write a letter to the firm's regulatory compliance department, spelling out your problem. The more precise your complaint, the better. Merely saying that you lost money or you don't like your broker won't get you anywhere. But if you can demonstrate that your broker took your money and put it into investments that weren't suitable for you or churned your account, you may have a solid case. If your complaint remains unresolved two months later, escalate by consulting a securities lawyer. For details about going to arbitration or through mediation, usually your only recourse under a standard brokerage agreement, call the National Association of Securities Dealers at 212-858-4400. One arbitration tip: Be sure to insist on a face-to-face hearing. You're more likely to win when arbitrators con-

duct a formal hearing rather than merely review documents submitted by both sides.

Choosing a Financial Planner

Do you need a financial planner? Maybe. A planner can be an invaluable playmaker for you, keeping a wide focus on your finances and instructing you on how to reach your goals. A talented planner may, in fact, act as the quarterback for your team of financial advisers, working closely with your specialists in taxes, insurance, investing, and the law. It's worth hiring a financial planner once your household income approaches $75,000 or so. At that point you could probably use—and can probably afford—a little help keeping your financial house in order. Some people instead hire financial planners only when they need advice about a particular issue such as evaluating an early retirement offer, paying for college, or budgeting better. That's a smart strategy, too.

The trouble with financial planners, however, is that anyone can call himself one. By some accounts as many as 250,000 people say they are financial planners. Unlike a CPA or a lawyer, a financial planner is not required to undergo any specific training. In fact, some planners are little more than glorified insurance agents or stockbrokers, hoping to bring in business by adding a lofty title. The federal Securities and Exchange Commission ostensibly regulates registered investment advisers, but many planners don't even bother to register with the agency. What's more, SEC staffers are so busy, they rarely monitor financial planners until one gets into trouble. States regulate financial planners a bit more, but even their regulators don't do regular inspections of planning firms. So it falls to you to do some due diligence before hiring a planner.

The financial-planning field is divided three ways, based on compensation practices. There are **fee-only planners,** who earn their living either by charging customers a flat fee or a percentage of their assets under management. There are **fee-and-commission** or **fee-based planners,** who charge fees and also earn commissions based on the investments and insurance policies they sell. Both types of planners will charge you for creating a written, comprehensive plan that looks at your whole financial picture from taxes to investments to estate planning. Figure on paying around $1,000 to $2,000 for such a plan and perhaps as much as $5,000. You may be able to get a shortened version for $300 or so. Some will manage your investments for about 1.4% of the amount under management, or for an hourly rate of $80 to $400. Finally, there are **commission-**

only planners, who get paid only from the commissions they earn on what they sell you.

If you can afford one, a fee-only planner often is the best kind to hire. By not accepting commissions, the planner—possibly a CPA—can be unbiased in his or her advice. To find a fee-only planner near you, call the trade group known as the National Association of Personal Financial Advisors or NAPFA (888-333-6659; it's also reachable through the computer on-line service CompuServe). NAPFA's membership directory includes names, addresses, and phone numbers of fee-only planners around the country, as well as the number of years they have been in the financial-services industry and any professional designations.

If you can't find a fee-only planner you like or can afford, try a fee-and-commission planner. It's best to avoid commission-only planners; they have too much temptation to stick you in high-fee investments. Should you wind up hiring a fee-and-commission planner, don't be shy about asking for advice whenever you need it, whether it's what to do about the fact that the manager of a mutual fund you own just quit or how to establish a college saving strategy. If you're not satisfied with his or her responsiveness, take your business elsewhere.

One way to narrow the field of planners in your area is by meeting only with ones who have legitimate professional designations. As with the CLU and ChFC initials, these don't guarantee Solomonic wisdom or pristine ethical behavior. However, there is some comfort in knowing that the planner is serious enough about his or her profession to have some technical schooling. There are three meaningful designations other than ChFC to look for when choosing a planner: A **CFP** is a certified financial planner who passed an exam administered by the College for Financial Planning in Denver; for names of CFPs in your area, call the Institute of Certified Financial Planners at 800-282-7526. Any planner you choose should be a CFP. A **CFA** is a chartered financial analyst, which is a title given to someone who passed an exam about investments and finance given by the Financial Analysts Federation. And a **PFS** is a personal financial specialist, a title given to CPAs who have several years of financial planning for individuals under their belts.

You'll also want to check out the history of any planner before interviewing him or her. Follow the same steps mentioned earlier about researching the employment records of a stockbroker. In addition, write to the Securities and Exchange Commission (Public Reference Department, 450 Fifth St. N.W., Washington, D.C. 20549) and ask for its report on your planner.

Before going to interview any planner, get a copy of the free interview form published by the International Association for Financial Planning (800-945-4237), a national trade group for planners. It offers a checklist to help you ask the right questions of all the planners you consider. Ask any planner you're meeting the following questions:

■ **Do you specialize, and if so, how?** Many planners try to be a jack-of-all-trades and take any client who can pay the freight. Some, however, work primarily with a particular type of client such as small-business owners or widows. Others tend to focus on one area of financial planning such as retirement planning or college funding. Be sure the planner has experience working with people whose financial lives are similar to yours.

■ **How are you compensated?** Any reputable planner won't flinch when you ask this important question. It's imperative to find out ahead of time both how you'll be charged and how much.

■ **Can I have a copy of your ADV, Part II?** This is a report (the name is short for Adviser) the planner files with regulators noting his or her experience, investment strategies, and potential conflicts of interest.

■ **Who are three of your clients similar to me?** You'll want to talk to them about their opinion of the planner. Tell the planner you'd also like to see at least one recent written financial plan; the planner can block out the name of the client for privacy protection.

Getting action against a financial planner who defrauded or looted you is even tougher than fighting a bad broker. No formal body censures wrongdoers. The best advice: Try to work out a settlement with the planner or with his or her firm. If that doesn't work, you'll have to go to arbitration or sue. That's when good record keeping becomes critical. You'll bolster the chances of winning your case if you have kept notes about the planner's promise that a certain dicey investment is low-risk, for example. If you win, you might even consider putting that chunk of money into an investment you select all by yourself.

Choosing a Money Manager

If all you need is an adviser to help you invest and you've got plenty of bucks, you might want to hire a **money manager.** Usually, money managers require at least $100,000 (sometimes far more) to invest, though some will take $50,000. The advantage of using one of the nation's 8,000 money managers rather than just buying professionally managed mutual funds on your own is that you have more control over how your cash is invested. For instance, you could tell the money manager not to buy certain types of stocks for you, such as tobacco companies. This brain

won't come cheaply, though. Many money managers charge 3% of the amount you invest, which is more than twice the fee of an average stock mutual fund.

Brokerage and financial-planning firms will find a money manager for you, if you like. Instead, get an independent specialist known as an investment management consultant or talent scout to find one for you. Chances are you'll wind up paying less in fees and have more personal contact this way. For the names of talent scouts near you, call the Institute for Investment Management Consultants (602-265-6114). Once you have the names of a few money managers, read through their ADV forms and ask them to supply you with performance figures going back at least five years for portfolios similar to the one you would like. After you have hired a money manager, monitor his or her performance quarterly. If, after a year, the manager hasn't beaten the appropriate market averages, you may want to make a switch.

A **wrap account** is an increasingly popular way for people who can't afford a money manager to buy the services of one. Most brokerage firms now offer wraps. They work like this: You hand over a chunk of money—typically $25,000 and up—and the money manager selected by the brokerage firm decides which stocks, bonds, or sometimes mutual funds to buy for you and moves your money around at will. Cost: up to 3% of the assets you invest. You needn't pay 3%, however, and shouldn't. Instead, negotiate the fee with your broker. You may well be able to get it down to 1.5% or so. The average brokerage annual wrap fee is 2.3%; mutual fund wrap accounts tend to charge 1% to 1.5% plus annual expenses of 0.5% to 2%. Your broker must give you a brochure explaining the compensation arrangement for the wrap and how the manager's track record is calculated (these brochures aren't required for wraps that invest exclusively in mutual funds).

Should you take the wrap? That depends on how much money you have to invest. Wrap accounts make the most sense for people investing $250,000 or more. Once you have that amount of money, you have the best chance of cutting down the fee. What's more, you can then diversify among two or three wrap managers.

If you decide to get a wrap account, be sure you can select among managers with different investing styles. Be sure each manager's performance record has been verified and calculated according to the standards of the Association for Investment Management and Research, a trade group for money managers. You'll also want to find out how much personal attention you can expect to receive from the manager.

Choosing Lawyers

Sooner or later, you'll need a lawyer. In fact, you'll most likely wind up needing more than one lawyer—one for your real estate closings and routine matters such as reviewing contracts and another for estate matters like wills and trusts. If your marriage sours, you may need a divorce lawyer. You might even hire a tax lawyer if you find yourself in a serious fight with the IRS or you're about to sign a business deal with significant tax implications.

The cost of hiring a lawyer can vary enormously, depending on the expertise of the pro and the amount of time you'll demand. Lately, growing numbers of people have turned to **prepaid legal plans** as a way to save on legal fees. These plans, often offered through employers and credit-card companies, are kind of like legal HMOs. You pay a set annual fee of $200 or thereabouts, which entitles you to a specified amount of service from lawyers in the prepaid plan's network. These plans can be handy if you need a lawyer for fairly mundane matters such as a real estate closing or a simple will. They're not terrific, however, if your legal needs are more complex. Being limited to using just the lawyers in the group is also restricting, particularly if you would prefer to hire specialists who don't belong to the plan.

When hunting to hire a lawyer on your own, start the way you would look for any adviser: ask your friends and business associates for pros they've used. Find out whether they thought the lawyer's fee was reasonable and if the attorney did everything he or she promised. You might also tap into Court TV's Law Center on the Internet and on America Online. This electronic aid offers advice about shopping for a lawyer from its *Cradle to Grave Legal Survival Guide* book. Court TV's free on-line service, called *Try Out Your Lawyer,* lets you post on-line the kind of lawyer you need. Then interested lawyers respond and Court TV forwards their names to you. The Web site address: 205.181.114.35/legalhelp/lawyer. Another resource: the *Martindale-Hubbell Law Directory.* This book, actually a shelfful of books, lists attorneys throughout the United States and notes their specialties. You can find *Martindale-Hubbell* in the public library or a law library or on the Internet at www.martindale.com. The American Bar Association's guide, *The American Lawyer: When and How to Use One,* is also useful ($4.50; 312-988-5522). Don't waste your time getting referrals from the local bar association, however. Lawyers pay to get listed with such groups, so you're really getting nothing more than a bunch of names of lawyers who've paid to advertise their services.

When interviewing lawyers you might want to hire—the first consultation is usually free—check out their experience, aggressiveness, and fees. Don't use a lawyer fresh out of law school; let someone else be the guinea pig. Instead, work with lawyers who have been practicing at least five years. Choosing a suitable lawyer is much like finding the right tax preparer: you're looking for someone who is as much of a tiger as you prefer. For instance, some lawyers are extremely tough in real estate negotiations, demanding extraordinary concessions from buyers or sellers, even if that means walking away from a deal. Others are more willing to bargain a bit and cut a quick contract. Before taking on a lawyer, have a discussion about how tough he or she plans to be. Ask, too, for names of several clients and call them to find out how satisfied they were.

Most lawyers charge by the hour. You might pay as little as $50 an hour or as much as $400, depending on the firm. For simple matters such as a house closing or reviewing a lease, you may be cited a flat fee of $500 or so. A will could run about $1,500. Some lawyers ask clients for a **retainer;** this is an up-front deposit that might range from $500 to $5,000. If yours does, make sure to get in writing exactly what the retainer covers. For a personal injury case, expect the lawyer to charge a **contingency fee.** This means he or she will collect a portion of any amount you receive, generally 30% to 40%.

Divorce lawyers are a special breed.

Most are tough and expensive. The Coalition for Family Justice (821 North Broadway, Irvington, N.Y. 10533), a self-help group for divorcees, can help you locate a lawyer in your area. Before hiring any divorce lawyer, however, get a rough estimate of what the total bill will be. Also, make sure the lawyer agrees in writing not to file any motions or papers before you have had enough time to review them.

You may be able to avoid hiring a divorce lawyer altogether or at least save on some legal fees by ending your marriage through either a **mediation** or **arbitration specialist.** When you hire a mediator (cost: about $500 to $3,000), this expert meets with you and your soon-to-be ex and works out terms of the divorce. Often, the mediator is a lawyer or a family therapist. Once your lawyer and your spouse's lawyer agree to the mediator's agreement, the divorce is final and binding. For the names of mediators near you, write to the Academy of Family Mediators (1500 South Hwy., Suite 355, Golden Valley, Minn. 55416). Arbitration, which runs a little more (figure $750 to $4,000), entails hiring a pro to listen to both sides of the marital dissolution and then determine the terms for the divorce. For names of arbitrators, write to the American Arbitration Association (140 West 51st St., New York, N.Y. 10020).

Using a Computer As Your Adviser

These days, your blinking electronic terminal can be one of your best financial advisers. By purchasing the right computer software, subscribing to an on-line service, or surfing the Internet, you can get assistance in practically every topic in the world of personal finances. Throughout this book you'll find references to particular software programs or on-line services that can help you on specialized matters from finding stocks and mutual funds to figuring out how much money you'll need to retire comfortably.

If you've never used your computer to help you manage your money, start simply. Drop by a software store and pick up an electronic banking program such as *Quicken 98* or Microsoft's *Money 98* (cost: about $30 to $90), which will make paying your bills practically painless. After typing in the names of those delightful businesses that routinely send you bills—your credit-card issuer, your mortgage lender, your utility companies—*Quicken* will see to it that your bills get paid on time electronically. You'll pay an extra $9.95 a month for 20 "checks." What's more, the software program will balance your checkbook in five minutes and sort your transactions into categories that will come in quite handy at tax time. It's especially useful as a way of getting control of your spending. A few taps on the keyboard and you'll see a pie chart showing you precisely where your money went over the past month or year. Then you can start looking to find a way to make a more appetizing financial pie.

Once you feel comfortable making your computer your financial friend, you can advance to the next category of personal finance software, the broad money-management programs that track your investments, organize your taxes, and show you your current net worth. These programs, such as *Managing Your Money, Microsoft Money, Kiplinger's Simply Money,* and *Wealth-Builder,* cost between $15 and $50. Just be sure to get the version that matches your computer: Windows, DOS, or Mac.

The on-line services, most notably America Online and CompuServe, offer a wealth of information about personal finances, including business news flashes. Cost: about $10 a month plus hourly fees of roughly $2 to $35. You can set up your own investment portfolio on them, too. This way, any time you want to check to see how your stocks are faring, just call up your portfolio and find out. Perhaps their best feature: the bulletin board, which lets you chat with other people about money. You can use these message rooms to find out, for instance, what people think about a particular mutual fund or whether a certain deal is a rip-off. The on-line services also bring in experts from time to time who will answer

questions from subscribers for free. In addition, you can go on-line to read back issues of articles from publications ranging from *Business Week* to *Consumer Reports* plus the latest editions of the business pages of newspapers such as the *New York Times* and the *Chicago Tribune.*

The next dimension in computerized financial planning is the World Wide Web on the Internet. By landing on the Web, most easily done through a connection from one of the major on-line services, you can browse among a nearly never-ending library of financial data and chat groups comprising people who want to gab about money. Two useful Web sites for all kinds of financial data and calculations are maintained by **Money** magazine (www.money.com) and FinanCenter (www.financenter.com). Some mutual fund companies and other financial services firms, such as Fidelity and Vanguard, have their own Web sites. These can be especially useful if you want to find out more about a particular fund from that company or need a basic course in investing in mutual funds.

A word to the wise: Once you start playing around on-line, it's easy to get hooked. If you're using a commercial on-line service, you can find yourself looking at a monthly phone bill of $100 without breaking a sweat. So be careful. These services, while fun, can wind up being harmful to your wealth.

REACHING YOUR FINANCIAL GOALS

CHAPTER 4

How to Lower Your Taxes

By some estimates, the average American household now pays 40% of its income in federal, state, and local taxes. This means should you fit that description:

- If you're granted a $1,000 raise, you'll take home $600.
- A money-market mutual fund paying 3% nets you only 1.8%.
- A tax-exempt bond paying 6% earns you the equivalent of a taxable bond yielding 10%.
- You must earn $1.67 to recoup every $1.00 you spend. Put another way, you would have to make $125 in order to earn enough money to pay a $75 restaurant tab.

Clearly, taxes make it tougher to reach your financial goals, although the 1997 tax law eased the pain a bit with reductions in the taxes owed on investments and home sales as well as new tax breaks to help you save for both retirement and college. Nevertheless, coupled with inflation, taxes steadily eat away at your wages and investment gains. So in order to build up your net worth, you have to bring your taxes down. That means getting a basic understanding of the tax rules and then putting together a well-thought-out, carefully implemented tax plan. It's easier than you might think.

Determining Your Tax Bracket

The key to shrewd tax planning is knowing your **tax bracket.** This number is essential because it tells you how much of any extra earnings—from investments or moonlighting—you actually get to keep. Furthermore, only by knowing your tax bracket can you pinpoint what your home mortgage interest or business driving costs you after taking tax savings into account.

Under the present graduated U.S. tax system, as income rises, so does the percentage of income that goes to the government. In theory, the federal tax law has only seven rates: 15%, 28%, 31%, 36%, and 39.6% for employment earnings and interest earned; and the 1997 tax law's new additional 10% and 20% rates for profits on your investments, known as **capital gains.** (There will also be an 8% and 18% tax rate on capital gains in the future, but more about that in a moment.) With exemption and itemized deduction phaseouts, however, your federal tax bracket can rise even higher than 39.6%.

The tax you pay is an *average* of the rates on your earned income. For example, in 1997 married couples with a **taxable income** between $41,201 and $99,600 fell into the 28% federal income

tax bracket. (Your taxable income is the amount of income your taxes are based on, after subtracting so-called adjustments, deductions, and exemptions.) But this doesn't mean that if you make $55,000, 28% of it (or $15,400) would go to the Internal Revenue Service. In the first place, part of your earnings aren't taxed at all. If you claim three exemptions on your return, that lops $7,950 off your taxable income, since exemptions are worth $2,650 apiece. You could also reduce your taxable income by at least the **standard deduction** amount of $6,900 (for 1997 joint returns). If you itemize deductions, even more of your income escapes taxation. So, assuming you take the standard deduction, your $55,000 of earnings would be pared down to $40,150. The government wouldn't even get 28%—or $11,242—of that amount. On a joint return, the tax bill on $40,150 of taxable income is roughly $6,026. That's about 15% of $40,150 and a hair over 11% of $55,000.

The reason? Some of that income is taxed at a 15% rate and some is taxed at a 28% rate. Your *top* tax rate—not your average rate—is still the number to keep in mind for tax-planning purposes, though. In the preceding example, 28% of any extra taxable earnings would go to the IRS because that's the **marginal rate.** Conversely, extra deductions—such as for an IRA contribution or a charitable donation—would produce tax savings at a rate of 28%. For example, a $2,000 deductible Individual Retirement Account contribution would knock $560 (28% of $2,000) off a tax bill for someone in the 28% bracket.

To determine your own federal tax bracket, you need the latest IRS tax rate schedules. The current tax rates are shown in the table on page 85. Find the taxable income range in column 1 of the tax rate schedule for your marital status that includes your taxable income (line 37, Form 1040). Then move across to column 2; the percentage shown is the marginal tax rate for your income. For example, if your taxable income on a joint return is $35,000, your tax bracket is 15%.

If you are a high-income taxpayer, the tax rate schedules may not tell the whole story, however. Hidden federal income tax rate increases take away the benefit of exemptions and itemized deductions in the upper-income ranges. The result: "bubble brackets" that can hike your tax bracket. The phaseout of exemptions that begins at **adjusted gross incomes** of roughly $182,000 for joint returns (or about $121,000 for singles) boosts your effective marginal rate by .79% for each exemption. That means a jump of 3.16% for a family of four. (Your adjusted gross income is your total income minus what are known as adjustments, such as IRA deductions and alimony that you paid.) The phaseout for itemized deductions begins at approximately $121,000 of adjusted gross income, whether married or single, and adds as much as 1.19% to your marginal rate.

Of course, federal income tax is merely the most notorious levy. For a complete picture of your tax bite, you'll need to add in the percentage of state and local income taxes you pay as well. For instance, if your federal tax rate is 31% and your state tax rate is 9%, your combined marginal tax rate is 40%.

The tax rates and rules for sales of your investments changed dramatically with the 1997 tax law, too. So it's now become essential to understand which investments are taxed at which rates. It used to be that figuring out your capital gains tax rate was fairly simple. Before the 1997 tax law, if you had owned the investment for more than 12 months, it was a long-term capital gain and was taxed at a lower rate than if you had owned it for a shorter time (when the asset would be treated as a short-term gain and taxed at your income tax bracket). The 1997 law, however, complicated life for investors. Now how much you'll pay in tax depends on whether you sold the investment before July 29, 1997; whether you hung on to it for more than 12 months, between 12 and 18 months, or over 18 months; and what income tax bracket you were in when you unloaded it. As if that wasn't messy enough, there are additional rules for investments you sell after the year 2000. Specifically, here are the new rules:

CAPITAL GAINS TAX RATES

For assets sold after May 6, 1997, but before July 29, 1997

If held more than 12 months 20%
    For filers in the 15% bracket.........10%

For assets sold on or after July 29, 1997

If held more than 18 months 20%
    For filers in the 15% bracket.........10%
If held more than 12 months but not more than 18 months 28%
    For filers in the 15% bracket.........15%

For assets sold after Dec. 31, 2000

If held for five-year gain 18%
    For filers in the 15% bracket 8%

Smart Federal Income-Tax-Saving Strategies

Funny thing about taxes: most people approach them backward. They sit down between January 1 and April 15 and start sifting through the records of things they've already done, looking for ways to save.

The problem is, by then it's too late to take advantage of many of the tax-saving opportunities that do exist. A smarter way to approach the task would be to look ahead, not behind. You should chart a year-round tax strategy that will yield the lowest possible tax bill come next April 15. Sitting down and filling out your return is only the last step in such a strategy.

The Tax Reform Act of 1986 severely limited the range of tax-saving techniques. But the 1997 tax law created some new ones, and smart tax planning can still pay handsome rewards. Run through this list of 32 tax-saving ideas to make sure you're taking advantage of the opportunities that remain.

1. Don't wait until it's too late. Begin tax planning early. This gives you time to take advantage of strategies that may not be available later in the year because of law changes. Also, it sometimes takes several months to realize maximum benefits or implement the strategy. For example, wait until July to look for a new home and you probably won't reap any tax benefits until at least October—count on a month or so for house hunting and around two months to close. That will give you only two or three months of mortgage interest to deduct, costing you thousands of dollars in write-offs.

2. Don't overwithhold. One of the biggest tax mistakes people make is having the wrong amount of taxes withheld from their paychecks during the year. Having too much money withheld can be a kind of forced savings plan that transforms into a hefty refund at tax time. But think about it: Why should the IRS have its hands on your money all

1997 FEDERAL INCOME TAX RATES

TAXABLE INCOME	TAX RATE
Married Couples Filing Jointly and Surviving Spouses	
Up to $41,200	15%
$41,201 to $99,600	28%
$99,601 to $151,750	31%
$151,751 to $271,050	36%
Over $271,050	39.6%

Note: A surviving spouse or qualifying widow or widower is someone whose spouse died in either of the previous two tax years, has a dependent child who lived with him or her throughout the year, and who paid for more than half the costs of keeping up the home.

Singles	
Up to $24,650	15%
$24,651 to $59,750	28%
$59,751 to $124,650	31%
$124,651 to $271,050	36%
Over $271,050	39.6%

Note: You qualify for head of household if you are unmarried and have provided more than half the costs of maintaining the principal home of a qualifying relative—a home you lived in for part of the year. (Your parents don't need to live with you.) You can also file as head of household if you are married but you and your spouse don't live together, you file separately, pay more than half the cost to keep up your home, your spouse didn't live in the home during the last six months of the year, and for more than six months your home was the principal residence of your child, whom you claim as a dependent or could.

Married People Filing Separately	
Up to $20,600	15%
$20,601 to $49,800	28%
$49,801 to $75,875	31%
$75,876 to $135,525	36%
Over $135,525	39.6%

year long instead of you? If you got a big refund after you filed your last tax return or recently had a baby or bought a house (two occasions that produce tax savings—and joy), fill out a new W-4 form at work and revise your withholding allowances on the Deductions and Adjustments Worksheet.

Here's how doing so can help: Take a married couple earning $75,000 who have no house and don't itemize. They might plan to take two withholding allowances. If they have a child and buy a house costing $12,000 in annual mortgage interest and $2,000 in property taxes, however, they'll be able to raise the number of allowances from two to eight. As a result, they will be able to up their biweekly paycheck by about $110.

3. Maintain tax-smart records. Keeping track of your deductible expenses can save you a shoebox full of tax dollars. If you use your car for business, for example, the IRS lets you deduct either a flat 31.5 cents per mile or—if you keep careful records—write off your actual operating expenses. The business portion of your gasoline, auto insurance, repairs, and other costs may net you hundreds of dollars more in tax savings than the government's standard mileage rate.

Nowhere is poor record keeping more costly than in an audit. Without records, the IRS may disallow your write-offs. Audit-proofing your records means paying by check or credit card (and keeping a receipt) or requesting cash receipts. If you entertain for business, back up restaurant stubs with notations or diary entries showing the date, place, amount, name of person entertained, and business purpose.

You might think that when Congress in 1997 all but eliminated taxes on the sale of homes, this meant you no longer needed to keep records related to your house for tax purposes. But you'd be wrong. It's true that the 1997 law says that you won't owe taxes on gains on your principal residence of up to $500,000 if you're married or $250,000 if you're single for sales after May 6, 1997. However, if you're audited and the IRS wants you to prove that your gains didn't exceed these thresholds, you'll need to come up with the documentation. What's more, you might be lucky enough to have a profit over those amounts when you sell—especially if you bought a fancy home before the 1970s and have held on to it. So when you do sell, you'll still want to reduce any taxable gain by adding to your original purchase price the amount you've spent on improvements over the years (and have the records to verify). You may also need the records to deduct the interest on a refinanced loan. Bona fide improvements include remodeling your kitchen, adding central air-conditioning, refurbishing a basement, landscaping, and installing a spa. Repairs, painting, and routine maintenance work do not qualify as improvements, though. Sorry.

4. Prepare for the worst. You never know when disaster may strike, but you can be prepared if it happens. Inventory your valuable possessions, take photographs, or make videotapes and keep them together with purchase records and appraisals in a secure place outside your home, such as in a safe-deposit box or your office. This way you'll have proof if a deductible casualty or theft loss occurs.

5. Shift your profitable investments to your kids. If you are ready to sell shares that have appreciated in value, make a gift of them to your child instead. Your child can then sell the stock, paying tax at his or her rate on the **capital gain** (the profit from an investment), which is likely to be 10% or 15%—rather than your rate of 20% or higher. Under the new capital gains rules, you are taxed on long-term capital gains at either the 20% or 28% tax rate, even if you're in the 31%, 36%, or 39.6% bracket. Short-term gains (those under 12 months) are still taxed at your income tax bracket. One exception to these rules: Collectibles such as art, antiques, and coins aren't eligible for the new, lower capital gains rates; they're still taxed up to 28% for long-term gains. Red alert: If your children are under age 14, their investment income above $1,300 will be subject to the so-called **kiddie tax.** In other words, that amount of income will be taxed at your top rate.

If your investment drops in value, you can sell it for a **capital loss** and offset up to $3,000 in losses against your capital gains. This move effectively reduces your capital gains taxes. If it turns out you don't have any capital gains, you can offset up to $3,000 in losses against your regular income, known as **ordinary income.** You can carry over to future years losses exceeding $3,000.

6. Don't pay taxes on income that isn't taxable. Among the types of income you don't have to report for taxes: gifts, inheritances, life insurance proceeds, child support payments, personal injury damages, disability benefits, rental security deposits (unless you don't refund the money), new-car rebates, and utility company rebates for buying energy-conservation devices.

7. Defer taxes. Certain kind of investments let you postpone paying taxes on earnings to a later year, when you may be in a lower bracket. One sure advantage of tax deferral is tax-free compounding. Series EE U.S. savings bonds offer this feature, as do annuities. You can defer paying taxes on the interest on savings bonds until the bonds are cashed. With an annuity, taxes aren't due until the income is actually paid out. Another tax-delaying tactic: Buy Treasury bills that mature next year. Although you get your T-bill interest when you buy the security, you don't need to report the income on your federal tax return until the T-bill matures.

Every rule has its exception, so here's this one's. Quite a few of the changes in the 1997 tax law provide tax breaks only if your income is below certain levels during the year. So you may find that in order to claim them you'll want to push income into the current tax year in order to keep your income lower next year, when you'll then be able to grab these new tax breaks. For instance, say you're a married couple with two children under 17 and your adjusted gross income will be $126,000. If your income will be the same next year, you won't be able to claim the full $400-per-child tax credit created by the 1997 law, since it phases out for couples with incomes over $110,000. But if you can push $16,000 of next year's income into this year (or just find new ways to keep the tax man away from $16,000 of your income next year), you'll get that credit after all. One way to do this: Increase your pretax contributions to your employer-sponsored retirement plan and flexible savings account next year, which will lower your adjusted gross income.

8. Bunch your deductions if you will have trouble itemizing. You may find that you don't have quite enough write-offs to exceed the standard deduction ($7,100 in 1998 for married couples filing jointly; $4,250 for singles) and itemize on your tax return. In that case, see whether there are some deductible expenses you expect to incur next year that you could

make this year to let you itemize and get some extra write-offs. (Some often overlooked deductions: legal fees relating to the production, collection, or advice about taxable income and investment expenses such as financial planner fees, IRA custodian fees, subscriptions to investment publications, or the cost of safe-deposit boxes in which you store securities or tax documents.) Conversely, if it's pretty clear you won't be able to itemize, try to postpone to next year expenses that you could write off if you itemize. That's because next year you might just have enough deductions to itemize.

By the way, make sure you understand the difference between a tax deduction and a **tax credit.** A deduction isn't as valuable as a credit. That's because a deduction reduces the amount of your income subject to tax, so that only a percentage of the expense gets recouped as tax savings. A credit, however, reduces your tax liability dollar for dollar. Put another way, if you owe $5,000 in taxes but have a tax credit of $500, you would owe only $4,500 in taxes.

The 1997 tax law created three new tax credits:

■ The $400-a-child tax credit for children under 17, which rises to $500 in 1999; maximum income to claim the full credit: $119,000 in 1998 for a couple with one child.

■ The Hope scholarship credit of up to $1,500 a year for tuition paid during the first two years of college (100% of the first $1,000 in costs and 50% of the next $1,000); maximum income to take the full credit: $100,000 for couples and $50,000 for singles.

■ The Lifetime Learning credit of up to $1,000 a year for tuition and related expenses paid after June 30, 1998. This credit is available for undergrads, grad students, and even people taking a class to improve their job skills through a training program. You can claim 20% of up to $5,000 in tuition costs; up to $10,000 starting in 2002. You can't take this credit and the Hope credit in the same year, though.

9. Make sure to claim a child care tax credit for all your costs that count. If both you and your spouse work and you pay someone to take care of any children under age 13, you're entitled to a child care credit equal to as much as $720 a year for one child and $1,440 for two or more. What you may not realize, however, is that the IRS lets you include the cost of summer day camp, nursery school, and the extra cost of having a nanny live with you.

10. Fund higher education without higher tax. Look for investments for your child's college fund that avoid the kiddie tax. Consider buying investments that pay no interest until maturity—ideally after the child turns 14—such as Series EE U.S. savings bonds and tax-free municipal bonds or bond funds. Growth stocks or growth stock mutual funds unlikely to pay more than $1,300 in dividends are a sensible option, too. You won't owe any taxes on their capital gains until you sell the stocks or funds.

11. Keep wages all in the family. One of the best substitutes for an allowance, if you have self-employment income, is to put your child on the payroll. Because the salary is deductible as a business expense, you not only succeed in having your earnings taxed at a lower rate, you also reduce your net profit subject to self-employment (FICA) tax. Furthermore, your child can earn up to $4,150 a year or so and pay no federal tax. The next $25,350 (in 1998) of earned income is taxed at just the 15% rate. Wages paid to a child under the age of 18 are exempt from employment taxes. Just be sure that the salary you pay is reasonable for the services rendered.

12. Don't file jointly with your child. As a convenience, you may decide to avoid filing the kiddie tax return (Form 8615) for your child under age 14 by reporting his or her investment income on your own Form 1040. This election can be a mixed tax blessing, however. By effectively raising your income on your tax return, you may lose deductions for medical expenses, casualty losses, for miscellaneous expenses, which all become tougher to claim as your adjusted income goes up.

Also conceivably affected by increasing your income this way: the phaseout of itemized deductions and exemptions for wealthy people (deductions are reduced by 3% of the amount your adjusted gross income exceeds $124,500 in 1998; exemptions are phased out for couples with incomes between $186,800 and $311,800 and for singles with incomes between $124,500 and $249,500).

Finally, this ploy could backfire on your state taxes. In 36 states and the District of Columbia, your state tax liability is pegged to your federal income or tax. Adding your child's income to your own can, therefore, wind up boosting your state tax. Moreover, if you instead file separately for your son or daughter, the child's standard deduction and exemption could wipe out his or her state tax.

13. Pad your nest egg with a retirement savings plan. With Social Security benefits being increasingly taxed, you can rely on them less and less for your retirement. If you are an employee, your best single tax-slashing move is to contribute the maximum to an employer-sponsored **401(k) savings plan.** Your contributions, as well as their earnings, escape federal and most state and local taxes until withdrawn. If you can't afford the annual maximum contribution ($10,000 in 1998), try to invest at least enough to get your employer's full matching funds, usually 50 cents for every dollar you kick in, up to 6% of your pretax pay. A bonus: You won't owe Social Security or FICA tax on the money your employer donates. (For more on Social Security and retirement plans, see Chapter 11.)

14. Contribute to an IRA or Keogh plan early in the year. If, like so many taxpayers, you wait until April 15 to claim an IRA or Keogh deduction for the previous year, you're passing up 15½ months of compounding. That's a big loss. Just watch: If you invest $2,000 on January 1 of every year into an IRA earning 9% a year, you will have $297,150 at the end of 30 years. Wait until April 15 of the following year to invest your $2,000, however, and in 30 years you'll have only $264,098—a difference of $33,052. Merely contributing the same amount in the same investment 15½ months apart makes a difference of over $1,000 a year. Think how great the difference would be in a Keogh plan for self-employed people where you can invest up to $30,000 a year. Even if you can't make the full contribution on January 1, invest as much as you can as early as possible. You must open a Keogh plan by December 31 to deduct your contribution for the year; you can wait until tax time to open the IRA for the write-off, though you shouldn't.

15. Strike tax gold with job benefits. Next to 401(k)s, **flexible spending accounts,** or **FSAs,** are an employee's roomiest shelter, enabling you to pay dependent-care costs and unreimbursed medical expenses with money taken out of your paycheck before federal income tax—and before Social Security tax if you earned less than about $61,000. (Money in FSAs is also free of state and local income taxes, except in New Jersey and Pennsylvania.) You and your spouse can each fund a medical care FSA up to the limits set by your employers, generally $2,000 to $4,000; the tax code caps a couple's contribution to a dependent-care FSA at $5,000, though your employer may set a lower limit. The savings: By paying $5,000 of medical bills from an FSA, you could cut your tax bill by nearly $1,800, assuming you are in the 28% bracket.

Working parents with joint incomes of $24,000 or more can come out ahead by forgoing the child-care tax credit and instead paying child-care expenses from an FSA. That's because the tax credit scales down as your income goes up, while the FSA's tax-cutting power goes up as your income rises. In the 28% bracket, a couple with one child would save $1,400 in taxes by paying $3,000 for care from an FSA, but they would get only a $480 write-off by claiming the child-care credit.

16. Don't foot the bill yourself. Persuade your boss to reimburse you for business expenses, even if it means taking an offsetting cut in salary. Why? In order to claim unreimbursed business expenses, their total—plus any other so-called miscellaneous expenses—must exceed 2% of your adjusted gross income. That's a tough hurdle to jump. For instance, if your income is $60,000, your miscellaneous expenses have to top $1,200. Don't ask your employer to reimburse you for a car you drive for pleasure, however, or any other expenses that could be judged personal. If you do, your reimbursement will be taxable.

17. Moonlight and rake in some extra tax breaks. Freelancing can open the window to a host of tax breaks. You may suddenly be able to write off expenses that would otherwise have been personal. For instance, if you start doing some consulting or freelance writing from home, you can write off a portion of your residence, property taxes, and some utility bills. Plus you can deduct as much as $18,500 a year for the cost of business equipment you purchase. In addition, once you have self-employment income, you can open a tax-deferred Keogh retirement plan. (For the details about this arrangement, see Chapter 11.)

18. Share the cost of a move with Uncle Sam. If you move for work and the distance between your new employment and your old home is at least 50 miles more than the distance between your old job and former home, you can deduct the unreimbursed costs of moving your household goods and your travel expenses, aside from meals. Best of all, you don't have to be able to itemize deductions to claim moving expenses.

19. Write off business equipment in one year. The law allows you to write off up to $18,500 of the cost of business equipment in a year. You can put this tax break to maximum advantage if you make your business purchases late in the year. For example, if you invest in a $12,000 computer system in November, you can **depreciate** the system (translation: deduct some or all of its value) and write off $554 for the whole first year, saving $172 in taxes if you are in the 31% bracket. Or you can elect to **expense** the full $12,000 (that is, claim the full deduction at one time) and save $3,720 in taxes.

20. Consider tax-exempt securities. Income from municipal bonds is free from federal taxes. Better still, invest in municipal bonds issued in your own state and you can save state and perhaps local taxes as well as federal taxes. Focus on after-tax yield when comparing the returns on different income investments. For example, if you are in the 31% bracket, a municipal bond paying 5% is equivalent to a taxable investment earning 7.25% (see Chapter 5). Seniors may pocket even more tax savings from municipals. Although tax-free interest counts when figuring how much of your Social Security benefits are taxable, the lower yields on tax-exempts will hold down the extra tax.

21. Round up all mutual fund transactions. To avoid getting socked by the IRS with a negligence penalty, carefully review all the Forms 1099-B you received from your mutual funds during the year. You may have more gains or losses than you think. You also incur gains or losses each time you pick up the phone and switch from, say, a stock fund to a bond fund in the same fund family.

22. Don't overstate mutual fund capital gains. If you calculate the **tax basis** (the cost on which your capital gain or loss is based) of your mutual fund shares and come up with a round number like $10,000, you've probably erred in Uncle Sam's favor. You likely forgot that your dividends and capital gains distributions were automatically reinvested in new shares. Because you have reported those amounts as income in prior years, you will wind up paying taxes on them twice if you don't add the reinvestments to your basis. Here's how to figure your taxable gain: First, start with your original purchase price. Then, add together any amounts the fund reported to you during the year as undistributed capital gains and ordinary income dividends. Next, subtract any nontaxable dividends that represented a return of your investment. The result is your basis. Subtract that figure from the sale price. Voilà! Your taxable gain.

23. Unload your most expensive shares first. When selling stocks, bonds, or mutual funds you've bought over time, cut your taxable gains by identifying the shares you want to sell—that is, the ones that cost you the most. This strategy works best when fund prices have fluctuated dramatically. Review your brokerage or mutual fund statements to find the dates when you paid the most for each share or bond. Then write a letter of redemption to your broker or mutual fund, specifying which shares you're selling according to the date you paid. Keep a copy for your records and ask your broker or fund for confirmation in writing. If you don't specify which block you are selling, the IRS will use what's known as the **first in, first out** method. That simply means the first shares you bought will be presumed to be the first shares you sold, which could force you to pay more in taxes than necessary.

24. Look for mutual funds that are tax-efficient. These are the ones that produce the highest returns for investors, net of taxes on income, and capital gains distributions. The average diversified stock fund had a tax-efficiency ranging from 84% to 88% over three, five, and ten years, according to the Morningstar mutual fund service. Translation: Shareholders returned to Uncle Sam 12% to 16% of the annual gains they received from their funds. (You can find a fund's tax-efficiency rating in *Morningstar Mutual Funds* at your library.) There are now about 15 so-called tax-managed mutual funds that are specifically designed to increase your after-tax returns by, for example, limiting trading in their portfolios.

25. Consider a home-equity loan or credit line instead of a car loan or

401(k) loan. Interest on up to $100,000 of a home-equity loan is generally tax-deductible; interest on those other kinds of debt is not.

26. Don't forget about the exclusion from taxes on the sale of your home. In the past, many homesellers felt trapped by the IRS because they knew that if they didn't buy another home costing as much or more, they'd owe taxes on their home-sale profits. (There had been one exception to this rule, too: If you were 55 or over, you could exclude from taxes once in your lifetime up to $125,000 in capital gains on the sale of your principal residence, as long as you had lived there for at least three of the past five years.) But the 1997 tax law changed all that. Now a couple can exclude from taxes up to $500,000 in profits ($250,000 if you're single) from selling a home, and you can take this exclusion once every two years. The age-55 special exclusion has disappeared, though.

27. Write off points when you refinance. Usually, points you pay to refinance a mortgage must be written off over the life of your new loan. But refinance a principal residence a second time before all the points are written off on the first refinance and you can typically deduct the entire remaining balance in that year. That could produce an instant write-off worth several thousand dollars.

28. Count the days if you plan to roll over a pension. You have just 60 days to deposit a pension distribution into an IRA account without paying tax. Neglect can cost you a bundle. For example, if you are under age 59½, missing the deadline on a $10,000 lump sum distribution will raise your tax bill by $4,100 if you're in the 31% bracket ($3,100 income tax and a $1,000 penalty for premature distribution). Caution: There is a 20% withholding tax on lump-sum distributions. Take $10,000 out of your pension plan and you will get only $8,000 ($10,000 minus $2,000 withholding). You must roll over the full $10,000, however, to avoid tax and penalty. That means you'd have to come up with an extra $2,000 out of your own pocket. You can avoid the 20% withholding trap by instructing your employer to transfer your pension distribution directly to your IRA trustee.

29. Swap, don't sell. If you are thinking of selling rental real estate you own, consider a nontaxable **like-kind exchange** instead. If you sell, you may well have a huge capital gain because of the depreciation you have claimed over the years. For example, if you sell for $1 million a building with an adjusted basis (its cost minus depreciation) of $100,000, you would pay a 28% capital gains tax, or $252,000, on your $900,000 gain; any gain attributed to earlier depreciation deductions may qualify for a 25% maximum tax rate. But if you intend to reinvest in a similar property, you can avoid paying the tax now by having the buyer deposit the money with an inde-

pendent third party, usually an escrow company. You then identify another building, purchased with the money in escrow. As long as you don't get any cash or other property out of escrow and your new mortgage balance equals or exceeds the balance on your old one, you will defer the capital gains taxes until the new building is sold. To make sure the complex requirements of the tax law are met, hire a real estate or tax pro who specializes in like-kind exchanges to arrange the transaction.

30. Spend insurance earnings tax-free. Unlike annuities and traditional deductible IRAs, which tax your withdrawals and often penalize them, cash-value life insurance policies let you pull out earnings without paying a penny in tax. Within limits, you simply borrow the money from your policy. No payback is required; the amount of any unpaid principal and interest will be subtracted from your death benefit. If you choose to pay the interest, you can do so whenever you wish.

31. Take advantage of the new IRAs. The 1997 tax law created two types of IRAs, described in more detail elsewhere in the book. A brief rundown: The new **Roth IRA** doesn't let you deduct your annual contribution of up to $2,000. But your earnings are tax-deferred while they grow in the account, just like a traditional deductible IRA. And, best of all, your withdrawals are fully tax-free as long as you have had the IRA for at least five years and you are 59½ or older, are disabled, or will use the cash to buy a first home. To open a Roth IRA, your income cannot exceed $110,000 if you're single or $160,000 if you're married. The **Education IRA** (yes, that's a contradiction in terms; blame it on Congress) lets you put aside up to $500 a year per child in a nondeductible but tax-free account whose proceeds will be used to pay for college. Maximum income to open an Education IRA: $160,000 for married couples and $110,000 for singles.

32. Deduct long-term care costs if you can. A little-known 1996 law now lets some of the premiums or fees you pay for long-term care insurance or services qualify as a tax-deductible itemized expense. Only the expenses combined with other medical outlays that exceed 7.5% of your adjusted gross income can be written off, though. The amount you can deduct rises with your age and the medical-cost inflation rate. Lately, people 61 to 70 could write off up to $2,000, while those 71 and older could claim up to $2,500.

Smart State Income-Tax-Saving Strategies

You can't do serious tax planning unless you take state and local taxes into account, too. States and municipalities, forced by Congress to shoulder more and more of the burden of social programs, have been hiking levies dramatically in recent years. The result? State and local taxes can no longer be ignored. Fortunately, you can fight back. In some cases you can do so just by making the federal income-tax-saving moves previously mentioned. That's because federal and state tax returns often piggyback on one another. Most states exact a percentage of what you pay to the feds or use your federal return as a starting point in computing your state tax. Lower your federal tax and you then automatically chip away at your state tax, too.

That's just the first step, though. Now comes the hard part: sifting through your state's tax code for any odd twists and turns you can exploit. For instance, some expenses that aren't federally deductible are allowed as write-offs by many states. A few examples are political contributions, a portion of your rent, and medical expenses that fall below the federal deductibility threshold of 7.5% of adjusted gross income. Some states also offer their own tax credits not available from the federal government, such as a renter's credit in Hawaii and, in several states, credits for installing energy-saving equipment. Ask your tax pro or consult a state tax handbook, available in most libraries, for a listing of your state's deductions, exemptions, and credits.

Here are ten ways to fight back against steep state taxes:

1. Invest in municipal bonds. Most municipal bonds issued by your state pay interest that is exempt from federal, state, and local taxes. This can be especially valuable in states that tax interest at a high rate, such as California, Connecticut, and New York. For instance, a California couple in the 36% federal bracket and the 9.3% state bracket who buy municipals yielding 6% would have to find a taxable investment paying 10.97% to make as much money after tax.

2. Buy Treasury securities. Not only are they the safest investments, their interest is exempt from state and local taxes. That lets you pocket up to seven-tenths of a percentage point in extra yield if you live in a high-tax state. For the same reason, look at money-market funds that hold only Treasuries; such funds offer yields very close to those on the best-performing nongovernment money funds. After taxes, however, the government money funds pay nearly a point more in high-tax states. *Caution:* The words "U.S. Government" in a mutual fund name don't necessarily mean all of its earnings are tax-free in your state. For example, many states tax interest earned on U.S. government-backed mortgage securities known as Ginnie Maes. The fund will usually enclose a list with its year-end statement, showing the percentage of its income that is exempt from tax in your state.

3. Don't pay tax on tax-exempt income. Social Security benefits are fully exempt from state taxes in California, Illinois, New York, Pennsylvania, and 22 other states. Pension income is also exempted, or at least partially exempted, in 16 states. The pensions of specific employees (usually military personnel) are not taxed in 14 states. Lottery winnings—you should be so lucky—are also tax-free in many states.

4. Benefit from favored capital-gains treatment. Four states currently protect a percentage of capital gains: Kentucky (60%), Maryland (30%), Massachusetts (50%), and Wisconsin (60%).

5. Take full advantage of your federal deductions for state and local taxes. If you itemize deductions on your federal return, remember to write off the state and local income tax withholding shown on your Form W-2, as well as your real estate tax and any personal property tax. Don't overlook such items as the state estimated tax payment for the previous year that you made last January and taxes for a prior year that you paid as a result of an audit or because you filed an amended or late return. State disability insurance withheld in California, New Jersey, New York, and Rhode Island is also deductible. Finally, ask your tax adviser or local tax agency what local charges, such as water or sewage fees, may be federally deductible.

6. Know where your state is stricter than the feds. Don't assume that the federal rules automatically apply to your state. Among the snares: 10 states and the District of Columbia will *not* grant an extension for filing your state income tax return simply because you requested a federal extension. Also, the estimated tax penalty may be different in your state from the one the feds use. Under federal law, if you make **estimated tax payments** (quarterly taxes due if you don't have enough withheld) and underpay your federal liability by $1,000, you're hit with a tax penalty. The cutoff can be much lower at the state level, however. The feds say that you must make quarterly estimated tax payments to the IRS if you expect to come up with a tax due of $1,000 or more at the end of the year and your withholding won't cover 90% of your tax or 100% of last year's tax, whichever is less.

7. See whether it pays to file separate state returns for you and your spouse. To ease the tax bite on two-earner couples, 11 states let married persons file separately, even if they file a joint federal return.

8. Research the taxes of a locale before you move. Don't jump from the frying pan into the tax fire. For example, only the District of Columbia and five states exempt interest on out-of-state municipal bonds from income tax: Indiana, New Mexico, and Utah and, in certain cases, North Dakota and Vermont. A full 20 states refuse you the right to special five- or ten-year averaging on lump-sum distributions (for more on the advantage of averaging pension distributions, see Chapter 11). But six states (Hawaii, Illinois, Louisiana, Michigan, Missouri, and West Virginia) don't tax lump-sum distributions at all if you elect special averaging on your federal return.

9. Plan your estate. Half the states impose estate or inheritance taxes independent of federal estate taxes. The result: Even a modest estate may be exposed to death taxes. Consult an estate-planning lawyer for ways to reduce or eliminate death duties through charitable gifts, trusts, and other strategies.

10. Move to a no- or low-tax state. If you are blessed with economic freedom of choice, you can always take tax flight. Six states have no income tax at all. They are Alaska, Wyoming, South Dakota, Nevada, Texas, and Washington. Florida has no personal income tax but does levy an annual .1% wealth tax on portfolios above $20,000. New Hampshire and Tennessee impose a flat tax on interest and dividends only. Other states that take a smallish income tax bite include Alabama, Delaware, Louisiana, Mississippi, Missouri, New Mexico, and North Dakota.

Smart Property-Tax-Saving Strategies

Americans are up in arms against property taxes. In recent years, California, Colorado, Illinois, New Jersey, and Oregon, to name a few, have been swept up in anti–property tax sentiment. And little wonder: property taxes have risen by as much as 37% a year since 1989. You do not have to mount a widescale taxpayer revolt to cut your own property taxes, though. By following the five tips below, you may be able to stage your own personal tax protest and save money, too.

1. Find out whether you qualify for any special property tax breaks. Many states reduce property taxes for being 65 or older, a veteran, or disabled. Make sure you take advantage of any general homeowner's exemption as well.

2. Check the accuracy of your home's assessed value. Review your property record card on file at your local assessor's office. This card lists such characteristics as lot size and number of rooms. If you find an error on the card—the assessor overstated your home's square footage, for example—a visit to the assessor can usually win you a tax reduction.

3. If you do not spot an obvious error, determine whether your home's value has been overstated. Maybe your house has suffered damage or housing prices have plunged in your area. To find out if your property tax bill is inflated, ask your local tax assessor for your home's official assessed value. Compare that number with the result you get when you multiply your property's fair market value by your town's residential assessment ratio. That figure, which is also available from your assessor, is the percentage of fair market value subject to tax. To estimate your home's fair market value, ask a real estate agent or your assessor for recent sales prices of comparable homes in your neighborhood. If the assessed value you computed is less than the official assessed value, it's time to appeal. Roughly half of homeowners who do so are successful, often cutting their bills by 10% or more.

4. Document your case. No tax official is going to take your word for it when you plead for a reduction. If you're fighting your assessment, you will need written verification of the sales prices of three to five comparable homes. Drive by those houses to make sure they are similar to yours. Then photograph the exteriors to strengthen your claim. If your home has deteriorated or been damaged since the last assessment, take pictures of it, too.

5. Appeal an unfair assessment. Make sure you follow your local appeals procedure to the letter. The first step is usually an oral plea before the local assessor. If that does not succeed, you must fill out an appeals form and request a hearing before the local, county, or regional board. Ask for the board's schedule and try to attend one meeting to get a feel for the process before your appeal is heard. When it's your turn, bring the documents and photographs you have assembled to back up your oral testimony. If the appeals board rejects your challenge, you can go to court or the state review board, but you will probably need to hire a lawyer.

don't overlook any tax-saving deductions or credits.
2. Double-check your math.
3. If you're married, include your spouse's Social Security number.
4. Check the "65 and over/blind" boxes if you are claiming the extra standard deduction for being elderly or blind.
5. Claim the earned income credit if you are eligible.
6. Attach explanations of any item you think might be questioned.
7. Report the Social Security number of any dependent you will claim.

Seven Tax-Return Filing Tips

Knowing the tax law is only half the battle. Your tax planning will pay off only if you know how to present the results to the IRS. Observing the correct mechanics for filing your tax return will speed up your refund, save you interest and penalties, and keep you out of the clutches of an IRS audit. Before you drop your return irretrievably in the mailbox, make sure to do the following:

1. Use the long form 1040 instead of the 1040A or 1040EZ to be certain you

Using Tax Software

Tax software does away with the tedious calculations and math errors that can make April so taxing. It also lets you experiment with different combinations of depreciation, expensing, and Keogh or IRA contributions to save the most tax. Preparing your return electronically lets you correct your return in seconds if you discover overlooked deductions or income just as you are ready to mail the completed return, too. If you do your return by hand, the thought of redoing the entire return from scratch could be enough to keep you from claiming additional tax savings. Finally, tax software can help you gauge the answers to key tax questions such as: What are the tax effects of buying or leasing a car? How much can I save in taxes by investing in rental property? What taxes will I owe when I get my pension plan distribution?

Before you rush out to buy software (typical cost: $20 to $40 for federal returns; perhaps $25 to $30 more for state returns), remember that you still have to gather all the information about your income, deductions, and credits. Sadly, you cannot escape this scut work whether you do your return with a pencil, use a computer, or turn the whole mess over to a tax preparer. Another piece of friendly advice: If you've never used tax software before, it will take a while to get the hang of the program.

Tax software performs two functions. It stores and organizes your income and expense records and uses this information to prepare your return or analyze tax strategies. Although the major tax programs are far from being clones, they all offer certain basic features:

■ **Selecting the right forms.** If you don't know a Schedule E from a Form 2106, one of the brightest benefits of tax software is its ability to tell you which forms you will need. The software asks you a series of questions and from your answers lists the forms to be completed. When you are done, the program checks

to see if you have been thorough and tells you when a form seems incomplete.

■ **Matching the right number to the right line.** The program lets you select a tax item from a list, such as church contributions, and carries the dollar amount you enter to the correct line of the correct form.

■ **Mathematical accuracy.** With tax software, you can usually avoid worrying about any math errors. The exception: when there's a bug in the software, as happened to many users during the 1995 tax-filing season. Fortunately, software makers tend to be extremely apologetic when bugs are discovered and go out of their way to help customers resolve any problems.

■ **Internal consistency.** That $2,532 capital gain on Schedule D will show up where it's supposed to—on line 13 of the Form 1040—and as $2,532, not $2,352 or some other transposed figure.

■ **Spotting omissions.** You don't have to worry about forgetting to include a critical piece of information to make your return complete. Case in point: To claim a child care credit, it's not enough to enter the amount you spent, you also need to include the name and identification number of the child care provider. If you forget, your software will remind you so that no form is left undone.

■ **Technical advice.** At a minimum, you get the IRS instruction booklet online, with specific form and line instructions keyed to those places on the screen. The amount of additional advice you get depends on the software.

■ **Tax forms.** No more last-minute trips to the library for forms the IRS never sent. They're all in your computer; at least they are if your software includes your state's forms, too. If you have a laser printer, you can print forms that look just like the IRS versions, with your tax information already typed in.

■ **Importing financial data.** You will save hours at tax time if your tax information is already stored in a banking software program. The tax program then can read your income and deductions from your checkbook files and transfer the data directly to your tax return. Make sure the tax program you choose supports your banking program. For example, *TurboTax* imports data from *Quicken* and *Managing Your Money.*

■ **Auditing.** When you have finished your taxes, the program checks for inconsistent or incomplete items, which could draw unwanted attention from the IRS.

The leading tax programs are Intuit's *TurboTax* (Windows or Macintosh, $39.95; deluxe edition, $49.95) and Block Financial's *Kiplinger Taxcut* (Windows or Macintosh, $19.95; deluxe, $39.95). You can also now file your taxes electronically on-line with *TurboTax Online* ($9.95; www.turbotax.com). In a 1998 review of the software programs, **Money** rated *TurboTax* deluxe best. The magazine said that this software, produced by the maker of the popular *Quicken* financial management software, was especially good at offering tax planning advice. But if your tax return is simple and you're looking for a good, quick, cheap way to fill it out and get it to the IRS, the *TurboTax Online* site is worth a shot.

Electronic Filing

If the IRS has its way, we will all be filing our returns electronically within five years. Electronic filing—the system that zaps your tax information almost instantly to IRS computers over telephone wires—is now available nationwide. The government hype is enormous: electronic filing is convenient, accurate, and quick. Your refund will arrive in three weeks or less (compared to five to eight weeks the old paper way). The money can be deposited directly into your bank account.

One thing the IRS doesn't tell you: Electronic filing will cost you. The fact is, you cannot file electronically without the help of a person or company approved by the IRS. The cost varies from $25 to $100. (To find an authorized transmitter in your area, call the IRS at 800-424-1041.) If you use one of the leading tax software packages, you can send your return information via modem or on a disk to an authorized service, which, for a fee, will file your return electronically with the IRS.

Is electronic filing worth the cost? Generally, if you compare the cost versus the financial benefit of a speedy refund, the answer is no. Electronic filing is simply not economical for small refunds. Although $25 may seem like a modest fee, if you figure how much your money could earn in the bank during the extra two to five weeks you have the use of your money, you need a refund of $4,000 or more to break even on the cost. Paying to file electronically makes no sense at all if you *owe* tax. You still have to *mail* a check for the balance due to the IRS by April 15, along with a statement showing that the return data was sent electronically. About the only reason to file electronically is to do the IRS a good turn. The process saves the agency money on processing and storing returns and is less error prone than conventional proper returns.

Electronic filing has led to a booming business in loans against your tax refund. The tax preparer will give you a check for your refund amount minus fees within a couple of days if you file electronically. Unless you desperately need the money, though, do not bite. These quick refunds are really short-term, very expensive loans. The fees, which range from about $30 to $65, get you the use of your money only for an extra two to five weeks. If you pay $40 to get a $400 refund loan, for example, you're paying more than 100% interest on what amounts to a three-week loan. Even if you need the money immediately, you should be able to find a cheaper source of credit.

Dealing with the IRS

Over 1 million individual tax returns are audited every year, a figure that's on the rise. About 80% of the unfortunate taxpayers wind up owing additional tax. What combination of tidal forces or plain bad luck subjects you to audit in the first place? No one outside of the IRS knows exactly, but this much is for sure:

■ **The higher your income, the more likely you are to be audited.** Statistics indicate that just 3% of returns showing income between $25,000 and $50,000 are likely to be examined. But some 6% of those reporting $50,000 and up are audited.

■ **Deductions larger than the national norm often are scrutinized,**

too. If, for instance, you report charitable contributions or employee business expenses that are far higher than what most people with your income claim, the IRS is likely to want to know why.

Lately, the IRS has begun focusing more on returns through what it calls an "economic reality" approach to auditing. If the IRS thinks that your write-offs seem unusual based on your lifestyle or occupation, your return may be flagged for an audit. Particular targets of economic reality audits are self-employed people and owners of small corporations. IRS agents lately have received special training in economic reality investigating, defined by the agency as "the process of gathering information about a taxpayer which is a reflection of the individual's financial status." So the IRS might try to figure out whether someone with your reported income should be able to afford those possessions. If the IRS thinks you're living more lavishly than your income would normally allow, you may be called in on the assumption that you haven't been reporting all your income. Similarly, IRS agents might look at your prior tax returns to see how much investment income you reported. If they spot a huge increase on your current return, you may be asked to explain where the money came from to produce that extra income. Once you come face-to-face with an IRS auditor, you may be asked about everything from your country club member-

ships to the vacations you take to how much you spent on your daughter's wedding.

Another fairly new wrinkle: audits based on your occupation through its Market Segment Specialization Program. The IRS is in the process of focusing its sights on particular businesses, preparing audit manuals for agents specifically about the likes of every category from lawyers to Laundromat operators. In these manuals, agents learn the tricks some wily taxpayers use to hide income based on their occupation.

■ **Math mistakes are likely to be caught by the IRS computers.** In these instances, your audit is likely to be little more than a letter from the IRS saying that you screwed up in your calculations and you owe some extra bucks.

■ **Where you live may make you more or less susceptible to an audit.** A **MONEY** investigation revealed that certain IRS districts—that's the way the IRS divides up the United States—have far higher audit rates than others. People living in the 10 toughest target districts, on average, face double the risk of being audited as taxpayers in the other 53.

■ **You may be the target of an IRS special project.** In recent years, these projects have focused on tax shelters, home office deductions, direct-sales businesses (such as being an Amway or Shaklee distributor), and the "underground economy"—unreported income by persons who moonlight for cash or barter.

Every three years or so, the IRS has unloaded its big-gun project: the **Taxpayer Compliance Measurement Program,** or the **TCMP audit.** This is an excruciating line-by-line audit of randomly selected taxpayers; 153,000 people were selected for their '94 returns. It was postponed in '95.

Many people believe that if the IRS does not call them in for an audit within six months after their return is filed, they are home free. Receiving your refund check does not mean you are immune from audit, however. The IRS has three years from the date your return was filed or due, whichever is later, to audit your return. (There is no statute of limitations for fraud, however. If your reported income is overstated by 25% or more, the IRS has six years to audit.)

There are three types of audits:

■ **Correspondence audits** originate at your IRS Service Center (where you sent your return) and are handled entirely through the mail. For this reason, they generally involve only minor matters requiring a letter of explanation or simple documentation. You are most likely to face a correspondence audit if the income on your return doesn't match the amounts reported to the IRS on W-2 and 1099 forms.

■ **Field audits** usually target businesses, and for these an IRS agent comes to your home or business to review your records.
■ **Office audits** are the most common type, and for these an individual gets a personal invitation to come down to the local IRS office. The audit notice will tell you to call for an appointment or to come in at a specified date and time. Read this notice closely. It contains valuable information about who may represent you at the audit and outlines your appeal rights. It also tells you the items on your return that are being questioned—usually broad categories, such as medical or employee business expenses. Included with the notice will be information guides noting the types of records you'll need to verify the items being audited. Office audits are usually limited to two or three issues, so you won't be expected to haul in all your records and prove every entry on your return.

An exception is the TCMP audit. If you're unlucky enough to get tapped for this one, you can expect an IRS agent to grill you on every single line of your return. That's because you are being used as a laboratory animal. By studying returns like yours so closely, the IRS believes it can get a better idea of where taxpayers in general are fooling around on their returns or at least getting confused. The data from these audits also is used to determine the average amount of exemptions, deductions, losses, and credits claimed by taxpayers at all income levels. The results of this survey then get compiled to form a picture of the typical tax return, which the IRS computers will later use to judge whether a taxpayer's return looks like good audit material.

If you are called in for a standard office audit, you will probably have at least two weeks after being notified to get your records and arguments together. However, if you need more time, you generally can get at least one reasonable extension.

If you are unable or unwilling to appear in person, you may mail in your records. A word of warning, though: An audit conducted by mail can be much more costly than one done in person. Unless your records are perfect and self-explanatory, you stand a good chance of losing the deduction, because you won't be present to answer the auditor's questions.

Usually, once an audit is started, it cannot be stopped. There is one exception, though: the **repetitive audit.** If you went through a non-business audit for the same issues in either of the two preceding tax years, emerged without owing tax, and still get audited again on them, you can alert the IRS and tell the agency that it can't audit you about these write-offs this time.

Assuming there's no way out, though, you need to prepare. First, get a copy of the tax return under audit and pull together all the documents that support the

items being questioned. Try to reconstruct any missing records. Get copies of canceled checks from your bank, duplicate receipts from your credit-card company, church, synagogue, or doctor, for example, or letters from people who can back up your claims. For instance, if you deducted business expenses, get your boss to write a letter verifying their legitimacy.

Your records do not have to be perfect. If you cannot dig up proof, try to prepare a convincing argument. The auditor usually must give weight to your oral testimony, except for disputes over business entertainment expenses.

If record keeping fails, the following guidelines may save the day:

■ **Don't volunteer information.** What you do not know about the tax law can hurt you. Answer the auditor's questions, but do not feel compelled to elaborate.

■ **Leave your emotions and hostility at home.** Be courteous and cooperative. That does not mean you have to automatically give in when the auditor disallows your donation to Goodwill or your trip to Miami. In fact, being too eager to agree can raise suspicions.

■ **Look for areas of compromise.** The auditor will probably be willing to bargain in order to close your case. If you are flexible and know when to give a little, both you and the auditor may come away from the audit satisfied with the final bill.

Should you brave the IRS by yourself or, if you hired a tax pro to prepare your return, have him or her do the talking? It all depends on what the IRS wants to know. If you had a preparer fill out your return, when you get an audit letter from the IRS, show it to your adviser. Then ask for his or her guidance. If the issue is a simple one, you may be able to handle it on your own and save another fee to your tax preparer, either by sending back a letter to the IRS or meeting with the auditor. However, if the IRS wants to ask a lot of questions, you're being audited on a gray area of the tax law, or you took a write-off you shouldn't, it's best to let your tax adviser handle the audit for you. In fact, you'll probably be better off not even going to the audit, since you could inadvertently say something to the auditor that could be held against you.

After all the evidence has been presented, the auditor will make a decision. This judgment may come at the end of the audit or after you have provided more information at the auditor's request. If you are in the IRS office, the auditor will give you his or her ruling and explain any proposed changes to your tax liability. Otherwise you will get an audit report by mail. Call the auditor if there is something you do not understand.

Three outcomes are possible: (1) no extra tax due; (2) additional tax due; or (3) a refund. In four out of five cases, the wheel of fortune lands on more tax due.

If you agree, fine. What if you don't have the cash to pay the extra taxes? The IRS says that if your audit bill is $10,000 or less, you can get a three-year installment payment plan. Figure on owing annual interest and penalties at about 14%, however. You'll need to fill out Form 433 to get the installment plan. If, however, you think you'll never be able to pay the full amount, try to work out a settlement with the IRS. Fill out Form 656, known as the **Offer in Compromise** form, and type in: "Doubt as to collectibility of the full amount of tax, penalty, and interest." On average, the IRS accepts 15¢ on the dollar from people who get such offers. It can take six months to a year to find out what kind of deal the IRS will make, however.

But bear in mind that the auditor's findings are not necessarily final; you don't have to accept them. You have 30 days after you receive the audit report to decide what action to take. During this period, you may submit additional information you believe might change the auditor's mind.

If you have no other information to help your cause, you may either agree or disagree with the audit report. If you decide to agree, sign a copy of the report and mail it back. Keep the other copy for your records. You may send the IRS a check for the tax due with the signed report or wait for a bill for the extra tax, plus interest and penalties, from the IRS Service Center.

If you decide the audit report is unfair or incorrect, tell the auditor within the 30-day period that you want to appeal. The IRS gives you several choices if you want to keep fighting. You can ask for an informal appeal to the auditor's supervisor. If you go that route and are still unhappy or you prefer to skip this stage, you can go to the IRS Appellate Division. This is called a **formal appeal.** Then, if you lose at the appellate level, you can take your case to court. This decision should be made with the help of an experienced tax professional, however, since going to court can be extremely expensive and time-consuming.

Most tax disputes are settled in the U.S. Tax Court, although you can also take your case to the U.S. District Court in your area or the U.S. Court of Claims in Washington, D.C. The tax court, which hears cases at sites around the country, has a special procedure for so-called small cases, in which the disputed amount is $10,000 or less. With relatively informal procedures, you can represent yourself in these suits. Unlike regular tax court cases and those in the district courts and court of claims, however, the ruling in a small tax case cannot be appealed.

Getting the Most Out of Your Tax Pro

In Chapter 3 you learned about how to choose a tax adviser. Now a few words about using him or her to greatest effect. Plan on seeing your preparer at least twice a year—once to have your return prepared and once to explore ways to reduce next year's taxes. A good time for your planning session is May or June, to give you enough time to implement your preparer's suggestions during the rest of the year. A second planning meeting in early November may be warranted if you are active in the stock market, own a business or rental properties, have income over $100,000, or had unexpectedly large earnings or capital gains during the year. If you fit any of those descriptions, you may want this session for some last-minute tax tips to shave your bill to the IRS and your state.

Just meeting with your tax pro is not enough, however. You need to arrive prepared. If you are dealing with a new preparer, give him or her copies of your last two or three returns. Besides painting a fairly complete picture of your tax situation, your returns may contain valuable information about property you are depreciating and about losses or credits you can carry over into future years.

Be sure your records are complete and up-to-date. Your preparer cannot invent numbers to put on your return. Unless you supply accurate information, money you spent on deductible items will be lost. Remember that your income is even more important to the IRS than your deductions. So make sure your professional has copies of all of your Forms W-2 and 1099 when preparing your return.

If you are coming in for tax-planning advice, bring an estimate of your year-to-date income, federal and state tax withholding, and deductible expenses. Also carry along the latest monthly or quarterly statement from each of your investments; a summary of year-to-date capital gains and losses; a record of estimated taxes paid; and a record of deductible pension or savings plan contributions you made.

Write down any questions you have before coming in, such as whether there are any changes in the tax law that affect you or whether you will be subject to the **alternative minimum tax** (a special tax system with a flat tax rate levied on some wealthy people to ensure that they pay their fair share of taxes). Always ask if there is anything you should be doing to save taxes.

Use a tax manual to bone up on any areas of the tax law that affect you. This is especially true when you come in during the filing season, because your busy preparer will have only a limited time to question you. If you do not know that the cost of removing trees killed by southern pine beetles may be deductible, it is unlikely your preparer will uncover it unless you get around to chatting about your landscaping.

Mention changes in your family situation, too. Unless you send your preparer a baby announcement, he or she will not know you have a new exemption to declare. Keep your preparer informed of any marriage, divorce, births, or deaths in your family, children who leave home, and changes of address.

Unless you quake at the thought of an audit, make it clear that you want all the deductions you are entitled to receive. Once your return is prepared, feel free to question any decisions you do not understand or challenge. Ask for a reference to the tax law supporting his or her opinion if you are still unconvinced.

Remember that your preparer is only a phone call away. Seek his or her advice before making any major financial move, such as buying a house or funding your child's education. Just give your pro enough time to research the tax angles.

Finally, act on your professional's advice. Don't ignore it. After all, in the long run, how much you save in taxes is up to you.

CHAPTER 5

How to Boost Your Savings

Wouldn't it feel great to kiss your biggest money worries good-bye? Imagine being able to pay off all of your credit-card debt, buy a second home, afford your kids' college tuition bills, and know that you will be able to retire in comfort. It's not impossible if you get into the savings habit early. By setting aside money regularly, you will be able to solve most of your financial problems—and afford the good stuff in life. What's more, a monthly savings program will give you confidence in your ability to handle an unexpected financial emergency and help lower your stress.

Of course, it could take you a decade or longer to finance life's biggest expenses, such as four years at a private college or your eventual retirement. But you can amass thousands of dollars—even hundreds of thousands of dollars—over time by setting aside just a few dollars a day and letting that money earn money (see the table on page 111). For example, you can build up $10,000 in cash in five years by saving and investing only $133 each month if the money earns 7% on average. That's less than $34 a week or the cost of a nice dinner for two.

Thanks to the beauty of compound interest—when your interest earns its own interest—the earlier you start saving, the less you'll have to set aside each month or year to reach your goals. To save $100,000 for, say, a child's college fund 15 years from today, you'd have to save $316 a month, assuming your money earns 7% a year on average. But if you

109

waited 10 years before starting to stash funds away, you would have to save $1,397 a month ($16,764 a year!) to meet that goal. Trouble is, you probably have a number of humongous financial headaches coming at you in the future. You may need a seven-figure nest egg to get you through retirement and a six-figure stash to afford a young child's future tuition, to cite just two. That's why financial advisers often say you should start saving for retirement as soon as you start working and you ought to begin putting money away for college right after your child is born. Easier said than done.

The first way to begin boosting your savings is finding more cash to save. The best way to do that is to get rid of all or most of your high-interest rate debt. The reason is simple: You will never get rich earning 3% on your savings while you are paying creditors 17%. Turn to the net worth statement you filled out in Chapter 1. (You might want to mark the page with a paper clip, since there will be more references to it throughout this chapter.) Do you have any double-digit debts other than a mortgage on your home? If so, list the loans (excluding your mortgage) or credit-card balances in the worksheet at the bottom of page 111 and estimate the extra amount you could put toward paying off each of these debts each month. Then, try to fully pay off your loans and credit cards with the highest interest rates as quickly as you can.

In general, try to avoid using your plastic unless it's absolutely necessary. If you carry a balance on a number of credit cards, you might consider purchasing the Debt Zapper kit from the nonprofit group Bank Card Holders of America (524 Branch Drive, Salem, Va. 24153). For $15, the kit will help you figure out how much to put toward each outstanding balance each month in order to pay them all off as quickly as possible.

HOW SMALL SAVINGS CAN ADD UP

This table will show you how much your savings can build, depending on the amount you salt away weekly and how long you do it. Choose the amount you think you can save from the row across the top. Then, determine how many years you think you could continue saving. The intersection of those two boxes will show you how much you'll have at the end of your chosen time period—before taxes.

	AMOUNT YOU SAVE EACH WEEK				
EARNING 7% FOR . . .	$1	$5	$10	$15	$20
5 years	$319	$1,597	$3,194	$4,791	$6,388
10 years	$796	$3,979	$7,957	$11,936	$15,914
15 years	$1,506	$7,530	$15,061	$22,591	$30,122
20 years	$2,566	$12,828	$25,655	$38,483	$51,310
25 years	$4,146	$20,728	$41,455	$62,183	$82,910
30 years	$6,502	$32,509	$65,091	$97,528	$130,037
40 years	$15,257	$76,285	$152,570	$228,855	$305,140
50 years	$34,730	$173,649	$347,299	$520,948	$694,598

CANDIDATES TO REDUCE YOUR HIGH-COST DEBTS

Call your lenders or look at your latest statements to find the interest rates and monthly payment information you'll need in order to fill out this simple work-sheet.

CREDIT CARD OR LOAN	AMOUNT YOU OWE	ANNUAL INTEREST RATE	MINIMUM REQUIRED MONTHLY PAYMENT	TARGET MONTHLY PAYMENT

CREATING A CASH CUSHION

Before you start figuring out how much to save for the future, you'll want to squirrel away some money for the present. It's extremely important to have an emergency reserve fund just in case you suffer an illness, unemployment, or any other financial setback. As a rule, it's best to keep an amount equal to three to six months' living expenses in this fund, either in a bank account or a money-market mutual fund. Use the worksheet below to figure out roughly what size emergency fund you should keep. To fill in the blanks, you may want to refer back to the table on page 15.

1. **Add up your total annual expenditures.** (You should have totted up those figures in Chapter 1.) $\underline{\hspace{2cm}}$

2. **Add up the amount you spent last year on vacations, gifts, savings, and investments.** (This figure represents outlays you could forgo in the event of a financial crisis.) $\underline{\hspace{2cm}}$

3. **Subtract line 2 from line 1.** $\underline{\hspace{2cm}}$

4. **Divide line 3 by 4.** (This will give you an estimate of your necessary expenditures for three months.) $\underline{\hspace{2cm}}$

5. **Divide line 3 by 2.** (This will give you an estimate of your necessary expenditures for six months.) $\underline{\hspace{2cm}}$

Fine-tune your emergency savings to fit your own circumstances. For example, you'll need to consider your job safety and any misfortunes that could occur that would not be covered by your health and disability insurance. Your emergency fund should be large enough to cover living expenses until your long-term disability insurance kicks in, which might take from two to six months. The reserve also should carry you through any periods of unemployment, so you'll have to make some assumptions about your employability. If you are a highly paid executive in a slow-growth industry, you may want to keep cash reserves equal to a year's worth of living expenses. But if your skills are in demand and you have ample insurance, just two months' worth of expenses may be sufficient.

After you have decided how large your cash cushion should be, use your net worth statement on page 8 to add up the balances you now have in cash and cash equivalents, such as checking accounts, savings accounts, credit union accounts, money-market mutual funds, Treasury bills, and CDs with maturities of a year or less. The total ought to be at least enough to cover the minimum emergency fund needs you listed on the worksheet above. If not, start growing your cash reserves to cover the shortfall before you begin putting away so-called discretionary savings—money for buying a house, paying for a child's education, or funding your retirement.

FIGURING HOW MUCH YOU NEED TO SAVE

One of the most common financial questions people have is: Am I saving enough? That's a tough question to answer, since the amount you need to save depends on so many factors; your age, your goals, whether you expect to borrow to reach your goals, your income, and the rate of return on your savings, for starters. A general guideline is that you should try to save at least 10% of your gross income each year. That may sound impossible. If so, don't just throw up your hands. Instead, try a strategy of saving 4% to 8% of your gross income in your twenties and doubling that percentage in your thirties and forties. In your fifties, when your children's college bills have been paid off and thus your expenses have dropped but retirement looms, you should attempt to squirrel away 20% of your pay.

But rather than rely on general rules,

you'll help safeguard your future by plugging in some real numbers for your financial situation. The key is to determine what your financial goals are and when you want to pay for them. The worksheet on page 115 will show you how much you should save each month to meet a specific goal. Here's what you need to know to fill in the rows:

Column 1: When you make a list of your objectives, include your short-term and long-term goals plus some that are just for fun, like spending two weeks at a spa or buying that shiny Harley-Davidson. You'll see that there's a special place at the bottom of the worksheet for you to list the amount you think you need to save for college and retirement; you'll find specific advice about figuring out how much to set aside for your golden years and your kids' college educations in the respective chapters in this book. If you're planning to buy a new home, assume that the amount required for a down payment and closing costs will equal roughly 16% of the price of the home.

Column 4: A car that sells for $12,000 today may cost $14,000 in three or four years. So you'll need to consider how inflation will raise the cost of whatever you plan to buy in future years. It's impossible to determine exactly just how much inflation will add to the price of a new car or a new home, since no one knows exactly how the economy will fare. But you can use the factors shown here for a quick-and-dirty estimate of the future cost of goals that are a year or more away. They assume that prices will increase by 5% a year, close to the historical average inflation rate.

Column 6: Subtract any savings you already have from the amount you think you'll need. For example, if you already have $5,000 to put toward a $25,000 down payment in 1998, list just the $20,000 shortfall. Don't plan to use any of the cash you have earmarked for your emergency fund, since you shouldn't tap that reserve for any purpose other than a true financial crisis.

Column 7: Here's where you need to forecast the interest rate your savings will earn after taxes. You can make an educated guess for the average rate of return on your investments by using the average annual returns for the types of investments you expect to use. Historically, stocks have earned about 10% a year on average, while taxable bonds have returned 5% and Treasury bills roughly 3%.

Unless you plan to keep your savings in a tax-deferred savings plan like an IRA, Keogh, or 401(k), you'll have to reduce your return by the rate at which you pay federal income taxes each year. (The tax brackets appear in Chapter 4.) For example, if you are in the 28% tax bracket, your after-tax return on an investment that pays an average of 10% a year would be about 7.2%, which is calculated like so:

$$10 - (10 \times 0.28) = 7.2\%$$

This method may exaggerate the amount you'll lose to taxes if you're in a high tax bracket and decide to keep your savings in growth-type investments, however. That's because growth stocks and growth mutual funds often pay out little by way of taxable income each year. Instead, most of their gains consist of an increase in their share price. That price appreciation is taxed at the long-term capital-gains rate—the maximum rate is 28%—only when you sell the stock or mutual fund. So you would lose less of your return to taxes if you bought a growth stock or growth stock mutual fund and held on to it for at least a few years.

You'll also have to adjust your return for inflation. You can do this by subtracting an expected rate of inflation from your expected after-tax return. For example, if you think your savings will earn 7.2% after taxes and you think inflation may average 5% or so, your real return is about 2.2%. To find a more accurate real return, get a calculator and use the following formula:

$$\frac{1 + \text{after-tax return}}{1 + \text{inflation rate}} - 1 \times 100$$

So, for example, if you think inflation will average 5%, your real after-tax return on an investment that pays 7.2% a year after taxes would be 2.1%:

$$1.072/1.05 - 1 \times 100$$

Columns 8 and 9: Once you have an estimate of your return after taxes and inflation, use the divisor table to look up the appropriate divisor for your time horizon. Divide it into your savings shortfall. The result is the amount you need to set aside each month in order to meet that goal.

Now for the moment of truth: Add up all of the amounts in column 9 to figure out the total amount you need to set aside each month to meet your goals. You can then multiply by 12 to find the total amount you need to save each year.

YOUR SAVINGS WORKSHEET

1	2	3	4	5	6	7	8	9
SAVINGS GOAL	COST TODAY	YEARS TO GOAL	INFLATION FACTOR (FROM BELOW)	AMOUNT NEEDED (COL. 2 X COL. 4)	SHORTFALL (AMOUNT NEEDED MINUS READY SAVINGS)	RATE OF RETURN AFTER TAXES AND INFLATION	DIVISOR (FROM TABLE BELOW)	COL. 6/COL. 8 (AMOUNT YOU NEED TO SAVE EACH MONTH)

Monthly retirement savings (see Chapter 10)	+ $_____
Monthly college savings (see Chapter 11)	+ $_____
Total monthly savings needed:	= $_____
Annual savings needed:	x 12 = $_____

INFLATION ADJUSTMENTS FOR WORKSHEET

To estimate the future cost of an item, assuming inflation of 5% a year, multiply its current cost by the appropriate factor below:

IF YOUR GOAL IS THIS MANY YEARS AWAY . . .	USE THIS INFLATION FACTOR.	IF YOUR GOAL IS THIS MANY YEARS AWAY . . .	USE THIS INFLATION FACTOR.
1	1.06	16	2.54
2	1.12	17	2.69
3	1.19	18	2.85
4	1.26	19	3.03
5	1.34	20	3.21
6	1.42	21	3.40
7	1.50	22	3.60
8	1.59	23	3.82
9	1.69	24	4.05
10	1.79	25	4.30
11	1.89	26	4.55
12	2.01	27	4.82
13	2.13	28	5.11
14	2.26	29	5.42
15	2.40	30	5.75

(continued)

INFLATION ADJUSTMENTS FOR WORKSHEET (continued)

Divisors (by Real Estate After-Tax Rate of Return)

YEARS TO GOAL	2%	4%	6%	8%
1	12.1	12.2	12.3	12.4
2	24.5	24.9	25.4	25.9
3	37.1	38.2	39.3	40.6
4	49.9	51.9	54.1	56.4
5	63.1	66.2	69.8	73.6
6	76.5	81.1	86.4	92.1
7	90.2	96.6	104.1	112.3
8	104.2	112.7	122.8	134.1
9	118.4	129.5	142.7	157.7
10	133.0	146.9	163.9	183.4
11	147.8	165.1	186.3	211.1
12	163.0	184.0	210.1	241.2
13	178.5	203.6	235.4	273.7
14	194.2	224.0	262.3	309.0
15	210.4	245.3	290.8	347.3
16	226.8	267.4	321.1	388.7
17	243.6	290.4	353.2	433.6
18	260.7	314.3	387.3	482.2
19	278.2	339.2	423.6	534.9
20	296.1	365.1	462.0	592.0
21	314.2	392.1	502.9	653.8
22	332.8	420.1	546.2	720.8
23	351.8	449.3	592.2	793.4
24	371.2	479.6	641.1	872.0
25	390.9	511.2	693.0	957.2

A Guide to Your Savings Alternatives

Once you know how much you need to save, the next step is deciding where exactly to put your savings. And don't think you have to keep all your savings in the same place. In fact, you probably will want to spread it around a bit by keeping your emergency reserve fund in a super-safe, if low-yielding, account and your long-term savings in something a little racier with a higher return.

The rate of return on your savings will play a big role in how much you need to save. The best evidence of this is something called the **Rule of 72.** You divide 72 by the interest rate you expect to earn and that will tell you how long it will take to double your money. If you earn 5% a year, you'll have twice as much in fewer than 15 years. If you earn just 3% a year, however, it will take 24 years before your savings doubles.

The following is a quickie run-through of the best savings alternatives for every one of your goals. Most of the choices described here are the safe, traditional savings vehicles most appropriate for short-term savings needs; some already have been discussed a bit in Chapter 2: "The Basics." Stocks and bonds, which are an important component in any long-term savings plan, are discussed in greater detail in Chapters

13, 14, and 15. The goals and the appropriate ways to save for them:

YOUR EMERGENCY FUND AND SAVINGS GOALS ARE LESS THAN TWO YEARS AWAY

If you are planning to spend your savings on, say, a new car or home in the coming year or two, safety should be your biggest concern. You need to keep your savings in a safe place where you can get to it quickly without paying a stiff withdrawal penalty. You could go with a plain old **savings account** at a bank, savings and loan, or credit union. These accounts pay interest, but usually not much. The average savings account has been paying out a little more than 2% in interest in recent years. That rate assumes you keep enough in the account to earn interest at all. Some banks stop paying interest and even begin socking you with account-maintenance fees if your balance dips below $200 or $500 or so. True, your money is insured by the Federal Deposit Insurance Corporation. (Credit unions are insured by the National Credit Union Insurance Association; look for the NCUIA sticker in your credit union's window.) Should your bank, S&L, or credit union fail, you'll be covered against a loss of up to $100,000. That limit applies to all accounts in your name, so be sure your total balances in all accounts at any one institution are less than $100,000.

It's also true that you can take money out of these accounts without cost or penalty.

But you can earn more money without giving up much and by staying at the same bank, S&L, or credit union. You do so by stepping up to a **money-market deposit account.** When savings accounts were yielding 2%, money-market accounts were paying 2.6%. No great shakes, but a better deal nonetheless. You need to keep more money in these accounts to get the best returns, however. Money-market accounts typically demand minimum deposits of $1,000 or more. They also somewhat restrict your ability to retrieve your money. The accounts limit your withdrawals to a maximum of just six a month. Money-market accounts, however, do permit checkwriting, but you can write no more than three checks a month (other than ones made out to yourself or to "Cash"). Don't limit yourself to local institutions, however. You can frequently earn two percentage points more on your savings by opening a money-market account at one of the nation's top-paying, federally insured banks or S&Ls.

If you're willing to sacrifice federal deposit insurance in exchange for a higher return, by all means look into opening a **money-market mutual fund** account instead. These funds, which invest in short-term corporate and government IOUs such as Treasury bills, often pay two percentage points more than the average rate on money-market deposit ac-

counts. The funds usually demand you keep a balance of $5,000 or more, but you can write checks with them. Like other types of mutual funds, money funds are made up of shareholders. But unlike stock and bond funds, whose share prices fluctuate, the price of money funds generally remains constant at $1 a share. So if you deposit $5,000 in a money fund, you are buying 5,000 shares at $1 apiece.

There's really no need to lose sleep about not having federal deposit insurance on a money fund since the last thing a money fund manager wants to do is cause his shareholders to *lose* money. Until recently, money-market mutual funds had a near perfect track record: no one had ever lost a dime in one of these funds. In 1994, however, one money fund that was open only to institutional investors (such as banks) did suffer a drop in its share price. To boost its yield, the money fund had invested heavily in complex financial instruments known as derivatives, which backfired when interest rates rose throughout the year.

Derivatives are financial products whose value is based on, or "derived" from, yet another financial product or benchmark, such as long-term interest rates or a commodity price index. Although individual money-market fund customers generally haven't lost any principal because of derivatives, rising interest rates sparked wholesale carnage in the derivatives markets in early 1994 and severely cut into yields of some money funds. Roughly a dozen money funds, including Pacific Horizon Prime Fund and Zweig Cash Fund, were bushwhacked by derivatives-related losses. In every case but one, investors in such money funds were made whole, as fund and plan managers dug into their own pockets for cash to keep net asset value from falling below the $1 standard.

When choosing a money fund, do your best to avoid any that own complex derivatives. It's up to you to watch out for potential land mines. One red flag: If your money-market fund is yielding a quarter of one percentage point more than its competitors holding similar investments and its expenses are about average, there's a pretty good chance the manager owns some derivatives to boost his yield. To better assess the potential risks in a money fund, call its toll-free 800-number and get answers to these two questions:

1. What percentage of the fund's assets are exposed to structured notes, floaters, strips, and other exotic derivatives? If a money-market fund has more than 5% of its assets in these derivatives, you should be skeptical.
2. Why is the fund using derivatives, and can it achieve the same goals through simpler means? Some funds—including many of the money-market funds that ran into trouble—have used derivatives to circumvent restrictions limiting the maturity of the securities they own. If the

fund you're considering is doing this, you may want to find another one. At the very least, you should ask the money fund telephone sales rep what could go wrong with its strategy.

The ultra–safety conscious might want to put short-term savings in a **U.S. government-only money fund.** Government money funds are composed solely of T-bills or other government obligations that mature within a year and can be easily identified from their names, which usually include the word "government." Government money funds that invest strictly in U.S. Treasuries are exempt from state and local income taxes, like all direct obligations of Uncle Sam. They are, however, still subject to federal income tax.

If you're in a high income tax bracket, you might want to consider keeping your short-term savings in a **tax-free money-market fund.** These funds buy short-term municipal securities whose interest is free from federal income taxes. To figure out if tax-frees are right for you, check the list of the month's top performing taxable and tax-free money funds and their toll-free phone numbers in the "Monitor" column of a recent issue of **MONEY.** Subtract your income tax bracket from 100 and divide the remainder into the tax-free yield you are considering. For example, suppose the average tax-free money fund yield is 3.5% and you are in the 31% bracket. You would have to find a taxable money fund yielding at least 5% to earn more than the tax-free fund (100 minus 31 equals 69; that divided into 3.5 equals 5). If you live in a high-tax state, you can increase your after-tax yield even more by choosing a money-market fund that sticks to tax-free securities issued in your state.

If you're willing to tie up your money for a few months or years in exchange for a higher yield, then you want a **short-term certificate of deposit (CD).** CDs are simply deposits that you agree to keep at a bank or S&L for a certain time period in exchange for a set rate of return. Generally the return, or yield, you earn depends on how long you'll leave the money with the institution, how much you'll deposit, the general level of interest rates, and the competitiveness of the bank.

CDs come in a variety of time periods—or terms. The most common types are for three months, six months, one year, 2½ years, and five years. At the end of the term, you can either withdraw your principal and interest, or roll over the proceeds into a new CD for another term earning whatever yields are at the time. As long as you stick with institutions backed by the Federal Deposit Insurance Corporation and limit your deposits to less than $100,000 at any one institution, you will be completely protected against loss of principal. If you withdraw your money before the CD matures, however, you'll pay a penalty

and lose one month's to one year's worth of interest. Some of the top CD yields are available at brokerage houses, of all places. That's because the brokerage firms can buy CDs in massive quantities and scour the country for the best rates around.

CDs look marvelously simple. But don't be fooled. Banks and S&Ls play lots of games with these certificates and you need to know the rules before you put a penny into any. Watch out for these two CD traps:

1. Interest rates that don't reflect your true return. There are almost as many ways to compound interest as there are banks. Some compound your interest (or pay interest on your interest) each day. Some do it each month, each quarter, or each year. And others pay so-called simple interest, which means they don't compound at all. A simple-interest CD isn't necessarily a bad one; it all depends what rate the institution is paying. You could wind up earning more on a simple-interest CD than on one compounding quarterly, for example. To compare apples with apples, when you're shopping around for a CD, ask the bank or S&L for the certificate's **annual percentage yield,** which shows what really matters. The annual percentage yield will tell you the precise percentage increase you'd earn on your investment if you kept the CD for 12 months. Another way to compare CDs is to ask one simple question: How much money will I have at the end of the term of the certificate? That way, if you're planning to deposit, say, $10,000 in a CD, you'll see who will have paid you the most interest by the time the CD comes due.

2. Excessive penalties. Early withdrawal penalties are all over the map these days. And you can be sure that the penalty isn't something you'll find trumpeted boldly in any ad trying to lure your CD money. Some penalties are based on the cost to the bank to replace the funds you withdraw and can be calculated in a number of ways. One example: If you want to cash in a three-year, 4.5% CD after one year and the bank's current interest rate for two-year CDs is 5.5%, then its replacement cost would be 2% of the face value (or 1% times two years). That kind of penalty can be extremely costly if interest rates have risen since you bought the CD.

Aside from asking about withdrawal penalties before you make a CD deposit, you can minimize the bite of a withdrawal penalty by spreading your stash among several CDs. Then, if you have to cash out a portion of your money early, you won't pay a penalty on the entire principal; you can just take out a little from each of your CDs.

Another popular short-term savings alternative is **U.S. Treasury Bills.** T-bills are issued and backed by the U.S. government and are always sold at a discount. That means you purchase them for an amount less than their face value. They come in maturities of three, six, or 12 months and with face values in increments of $5,000, starting with a minimum of $10,000. As with CDs, typically the longer the maturity of the T-bill, the higher its yield; one-year Treasuries often yield about half a percentage point more than three-month T-bills. You'll often find T-bills yielding one to one and a half percentage points more than what you'd get on the average bank CD with the same maturity. Best of all, the interest on T-bills is exempt from state and local taxes, which can boost your after-tax yield.

You can buy newly issued Treasury securities through a bank or brokerage for a commission of $50 or more. To save that expense, you can send your money directly to the Treasury with a form that you can pick up at Federal Reserve Banks and branches. You'll need to open what's called a Treasury Direct account. For more information, get a copy of the booklet *Buying Treasury Securities at the Federal Reserve Banks* (send a check for $4.50 to *Buying Treasury Securities,* The Federal Reserve Bank of Richmond, P.O. Box 27471, Richmond, Va. 23261, or call the U.S. Bureau of the Public Debt at 202-874-4000). Three-month and six-month T-bills are auctioned every Monday; one-year T-bills are auctioned every fourth Thursday.

T-bill rates rarely change dramatically from day to day, so you can get an idea of what the new bills will pay by checking yields of similar securities under the "Money Rates" heading inside the *Wall Street Journal.* You will get the full face value of your T-bills as long as you hold them until maturity, but if you need to sell them earlier, you'll be at the mercy of whatever price someone will pay for them.

YOUR SAVINGS GOALS ARE TWO TO THREE YEARS AWAY

Because some time will pass before you'll need *your* stash, you can afford to subject your savings to slightly more risk in order to get beefier returns. For example, if you want a federally insured bank CD, you could get one that matures in up to three years. Other choices:

Take a step up the Treasury ladder and, for a $5,000 minimum investment, buy **two- or three-year Treasury notes.** They pay more than bank CDs of the same maturities, and their interest is exempt from state and local taxes. If you live in a high-tax state such as California or New York, that tax break can effectively add half a percentage point or more to your yield. You buy Treasury notes through the same channels as T-bills. But unlike Treasury bills, whose interest is deducted from your purchase price, your T-note accrues interest twice a year.

For a yield that's about one to two percentage points higher than a money fund but with little added risk, check out

ultra-short-term bond funds. These mutual funds invest in high-quality corporate and government debt with maturities of three to 12 months vs. money funds' average maturity of 42 days. The share value of ultras moves with interest rates, however, making them more volatile than money funds. Because ultras stick with very short-term debt, they can weather rising rates pretty well. In the first 10 months of 1994, for example, the average ultra returned an annualized 2.4%, vs. losses of 1.4%, 3.7%, and 5.1%, respectively, for short-, intermediate-, and long-term U.S. government bond funds.

Short-term taxable and tax-free bond mutual funds—with average maturities of one to three years—carry minimal risks but pay yields about two percentage points higher than money funds. Bear in mind, though, that as you start moving out along the maturity spectrum, you start upping the odds that you could lose some of your principal if interest rates shoot up. Still, the chance of taking a loss on such a short-term bond fund is small. For more on how to choose a bond fund that's right for you, turn to Chapter 15.

YOUR SAVINGS GOALS ARE THREE TO SEVEN YEARS AWAY

With a number of years to go before you need to get your hands on your savings, you can be a bit more bold. That means investing in longer-term Treasuries, bond funds, or even stocks, where you put your principal on the line. (For fuller descriptions on investing in bonds and bond funds, see Chapter 15; for more on buying stocks and stock funds, see Chapter 14.) You can earn handsome returns for your valor, however. Aim for total return—a low-volatility combination of income and capital gains—with a mixture of stocks and bonds or with high-quality, dividend-paying stocks and so-called convertibles (see page 330) or the funds that buy them. By purchasing these kinds of investments for your savings, you stand a better chance of outpacing inflation over the years. Total-return investing offers another key benefit: It reduces your overall risk. Between 1982 and 1994, the highest-yielding 20% of the S&P 500 stocks outperformed the index as a whole around 80% of the time when the market fell for stretches of one, three, or six months.

A few smart choices:

Intermediate-term bonds and Treasury notes and the **intermediate-term bond funds** are a smart way to get a yield boost for your savings. Five-year Treasury notes, for example, often pay a percentage point more than what you'd earn on a six-month Treasury bill. And they require a minimum investment of only $1,000. You'll want to stay with the bonds and bond funds whose issuers are least likely to default. That means sticking with either U.S. government bonds and bond funds or corporate or tax-free bonds rated A or better for financial safety. You don't want to be buying so-called junk bonds—which are bonds rated Ba, BB, or lower—or junk bond funds for your crucial savings. Although the yield is likely to be higher than on other bonds with similar maturities, you're opening yourself up to a bigger possibility that the issuer won't pay you the interest you're counting on. Bond funds have one big advantage and one big drawback compared with bonds themselves. If you buy a bond fund, you get automatic diversification by owning pieces of many different bonds. That can be especially useful if you want to own corporate or municipal bonds, whose interest is not backed by the U.S. government. The drawback, however, is that you can't be 100% sure of getting your principal back, even with a U.S. Treasury bond fund. That's because the value of the bond fund shares changes daily, and if you want to sell your shares after interest rates have risen, you could take a loss. By buying high-quality individual bonds and holding them to maturity, you can feel secure about getting your principal back and interest.

U.S. savings bonds are a handy place to save—if your goal is more than five years away. Pass on them if you'll need the money in three or four years, since the savings bond rules will require you to take a cut in your yield. One of the attractions of savings bonds, beyond the fact that the interest is exempt from state and local taxes, is that you can also defer paying federal taxes until you redeem the bonds. Parents who need to save for upcoming college bills may qualify for a special tax break with savings bonds, too. You'll escape owing any federal income tax on savings bonds redeemed to pay for college expenses if your adjusted gross income when you redeem the bonds does not exceed $50,850 for single parents or $76,250 for married couples. These thresholds are adjusted for inflation each year. (For information about the current interest rates on U.S. savings bonds, call the government's toll-free number: 800-487-2663.) You can learn more about how savings bonds work in Chapter 2.

Intermediate-term mortgage-backed securities are kind of a cousin to U.S. Treasury notes and short-term bonds. When you buy these bonds, you're owning part of a package of mortgage loans. The bonds are usually issued or guaranteed by government agencies such as the Government National Mortgage Association (known as Ginnie Mae), the Federal Home Loan Mortgage Corporation (known as Freddie Mac), and the Federal National Mortgage Association (or Fannie Mae). But unlike the interest on Treasuries, interest on these bonds is not exempt from state income tax. And except for Ginnie Maes, the bonds aren't backed by the full faith and credit of the U.S. government. Because you're taking on slightly more risk with mortgage-backed securities than with Treasuries, you get rewarded by receiving slightly higher yields. If you'd like to diversify with these securities, you can buy a mortgage-backed securities mutual fund.

Income-paying stocks like certain blue chips and utilities stocks as well as the mutual funds that own them can give you steady returns plus a kick if their stocks rise in value. A popular breed of income-paying stocks are **real estate investment trusts,** also known as REITs. These are stocks of companies that buy, develop, and manage all kinds of real estate—from apartment buildings to hotels to nursing homes.

If you're comfortable investing in both the stock and bond markets, you might want to buy so-called **convertibles.** These are bonds or a type of stock known as preferred stock that can be converted at the owner's option into a fixed number of the issuer's common shares. There are also a number of convertible mutual funds, if you're looking for broader diversification.

YOUR SAVINGS GOALS ARE EIGHT OR MORE YEARS AWAY

Because you won't be needing your savings for quite a while, you can afford to save primarily in investments with the highest yields, such as top-quality **intermediate-term** and **long-term bonds** or **bond funds.** Don't get greedy and grab for the highest yields around with long-term, low-quality junk bonds; these bonds, usually issued by financially shaky companies, just raise the likelihood that you won't get the interest payments you expect. For a long-term goal, you can also put some of your savings into investments with capital growth potential, such as **growth stocks** and **growth mutual funds.** The growth investments should outpace inflation if you hold on to them for at least a few years. The trade-off with these types of investments, however, is volatility over shorter time periods.

To lock in a return, you could buy a 10-year Treasury note (minimum investment: $1,000) or even a 30-year Treasury bond (also $1,000 minimum) for the highest yield of all Treasuries. If you want to buy Treasury bonds through a broker and will invest any multiple of $5,000, you can get the best prices and lowest fees on them by purchasing the Treasuries through a broker who uses a fairly new trading system offered by the American Stock Exchange. Alternatively, you could go with an intermediate-term bond fund, as long as you're willing to live with a share price that fluctuates daily.

Fifteen Painless Ways to Save

One of the most effective ways to boost your savings is simply to cut your spending—and this book is loaded with ideas for ways to do that. For example, you may be able to free up some savings by raising the deductibles on your auto insurance policies, choosing a less expensive broker or mutual fund, or refinancing your mortgage. But trimming your spending gets you only so far. Most people also need some sort of incentive to help them save for the future. If you're one of them, try out one or more of the following 15 painless savings tactics:

1. Put your savings on autopilot. The most effective way to build savings is to have the money removed from your paycheck or bank account before you can get your hands on it. By siphoning funds into your savings stash automatically, you are making saving mechanical—which means you'll never miss a payment. And since you don't see these funds or have the option to spend them easily, you won't miss them much. You can sign up for an automatic investing plan just by filling out a simple form at work or by mail from home. The following five automatic saving programs let you invest as little as $25 a month:

■ **Employee benefit savings plans.** They go by a variety of names—401(k)s at private companies, 403(b)s at nonprofits, 457 plans at government agencies—but regardless of their titles, these popular programs are unbeatable for long-term savings. You invest a percentage of your pretax salary in stock, fixed-income, or money-market funds and your earnings grow tax-deferred until you withdraw them. The pretax angle is a beaut: for example, if you are in the 28% tax bracket and contribute $5,000 of your pretax salary to a 401(k) account, you'll save $1,400 in taxes for the year. Think of it as the equivalent of a $1,400 pay raise.

Perhaps the greatest plus of a company plan is that more than 80% of the 175,000 firms offering 401(k)s match some or all of employee contributions, typically kicking in $1 for every $2 invested up to a certain percentage of pay. Your employer's matching contribution, if any, will produce an automatic return on your savings. A 401(k) contribution earning 9% a year with a 50% match will return a whopping 63.5% annually, after tax benefits are taken into account. For that reason, you should strain to invest as much of your pretax salary as the plan allows.

To start saving through your employer's savings plan, ask your benefits department for the forms you need to specify the amount to be withheld from your paycheck. If you can't afford to set aside the maximum, try to invest enough to qualify for 100% of whatever match the company is offering. You'll have to specify how you want the money invested. For advice in figuring out the best mix for you, see Chapter 11.

■ **U.S. savings bond payroll deduction plans.** At more than 48,000 companies, including nearly every one with at least 100 workers, you can ask your employer to withhold $25 or more from every paycheck and invest the cash in a Series EE savings bond (maximum: $15,000 a year). Because you don't get the interest until you redeem the bonds, you're forced to save the earnings, too. Your payroll department can give you the enrollment form specifying how much to withhold.

One clever strategy: After your baby is born, fill out a new W-4 federal income tax withholding form at work, to adjust your withholding for an additional exemption for a dependent. The reduction in withholding will leave you with about $65 more a month in your paychecks. Instruct your payroll department to use that $65 to buy you savings bonds. By doing so, you'll ensure that your bundle of joy will have more than $20,000 to put toward tuition when he or she is ready for college.

■ **Mutual fund automatic savings plans.** Based on your instructions, a fund company will automatically transfer a set amount each month—usually at least $25—from your checking account to one of its mutual funds. These programs are a great way to make you save for a future goal, such as your child's college education. You can withdraw the money whenever you want for whatever reason.

But you don't have to remember to write the checks to invest.

By signing up for an automatic investing plan, you can sometimes avoid having to meet a mutual fund's minimum initial investment of $1,000 to $3,000. To get started, simply fill out a form authorizing the fund to deduct a set amount from your bank account or paycheck at regular intervals, typically either monthly or quarterly. You can ensure that the fund gets your correct bank account number by returning the form with a blank personal check and writing "void" across it. A number of fund groups, including Twentieth Century and Dreyfus, even let you have money shunted directly from your Social Security check into their funds. At any time, you can switch off the flow without penalty by calling the fund. If you set up an automatic investing program with a fund group that levies up-front sales charges known as loads, however, you will still have to pay the normal sales charge on your periodic investments.

FIVE MUTUAL FUND SAVINGS PROGRAMS

To give you an idea of how these automatic savings programs tend to work, here are details for the arrangements at five of the most popular low or no-load fund families.

FUND GROUP	MINIMUM INITIAL INVESTMENT	MINIMUM INVESTMENT PER PERIOD	TRANSFERS AVAILABLE FROM . . .	TELEPHONE (800)
Fidelity	$2,500	$100	All bank accounts; payroll	544-8888
Janus	$500	$100	All bank accounts	525-8983
T. Rowe Price	None[1]	$50	Checking accounts; payroll; Social Security checks	541-8832
Twentieth Century	$2,500[2]	$50	All bank accounts; payroll; Social Security checks	345-2021
Vanguard	$3,000	$50	All bank accounts	662-7447

Notes: [1] Customary $2,500 minimum waived for automatic investment plan.
[2] Waived for stock funds.

■ **Mutual fund reinvestment plans.** If you automatically reinvest the dividends and capital gains paid to you by a mutual fund, your profits can mount. For example, had you invested $10,000 in the Fidelity Equity-Income Fund in 1980 and plowed back the $50,269 in dividends and capital gains paid out to you over the years, your holdings would now total over $70,000—4½ times more than if you had spent your earnings. Watch out for hidden fees on reinvestments, however. For instance, Franklin and Smith Barney funds, sold by brokers for a sales commission, keep 4% of your reinvestments. To get your earnings reinvested automatically, call your mutual fund company and request an application.

■ **Stock dividend-reinvestment plans.** Approximately 1,100 publicly traded companies offer dividend-reinvestment plans (DRIPs). As their name suggests, these plans take your stock dividends and use them to buy even more stock for you. Better still, about 100 companies let you use your dividends to buy their stock at a discount of 3% to 5%. While most companies with DRIPs reinvest a shareholder's dividends for free, some charge fees. For example, IBM assesses a 2% fee on reinvested dividends, up to $3 per quarter, while Bristol-Myers Squibb imposes a 4% fee, up to $5 a quarter. Setting up a DRIP will add to your record keeping, however; you must usually hold the shares in your name, rather than at a brokerage in so-called street

name. To get started, ask the DRIP company or your stockbroker for a DRIP form.

2. Skip one big expense a year. You might be able to realize some meaty savings simply by skipping your winter vacation, trading in your turbocharged sports car for an econo-box, or ditching your chichi health club membership and switching to the YMCA.

3. Hold a garage sale to raise cash. By getting rid of an old computer, TV, stereo, dining set, or exercise machine, you could earn $300 to $3,000 more in just a day or two.

4. Use your flexible spending account (FSA), if you have one. Don't pass up the opportunity to pay medical and dependent-care expenses with pretax dollars through these accounts (see Chapter 9). A family of four is almost certain to spend $1,000 a year on doctors, dentists, and prescription medicines. Your tax savings if you pay these bills from an FSA can be at least $280.

5. Make higher down payments. When financing your next major purchase—a new car, new kitchen, whatever—put up as much money as you can and keep your borrowing down. By *not* financing $500 at 12% over three years, you can keep $98 jingling in your pocket; not financing $5,000 saves you $979.

6. Use a home-equity loan to pay off high-rate debts. Replace consumer debts at, say, 18% with a home-equity loan at 12%, and you'll cut your interest costs by a third. In addition, the interest on a home-equity loan can be fully deductible on your income tax return. Let's say you consolidate $10,000 in car payments and credit-card cash advances with a home-equity loan. Counting the tax break, a taxpayer in the 28% bracket will save $936.

7. Pay in cash. This high-discipline technique will teach you a lot about the difference between what you want and what you really need. Moreover, by paying in cash, you avoid paying finance charges. For example, trimming your credit-card balances by $500 this year can save you almost $100 in interest if your card issuer charges 18.6% interest.

8. Don't pay for financial services you could get for free. Using only no-fee checking accounts, no-fee credit cards, and no-load mutual funds can save you $100 a year or more. For instance, checking accounts often run $60 a year; annual fees for credit cards typically range from $15 to $50.

9. Squirrel away your next raise. This tip is an example of the rule financial planners love to tout: Pay yourself first. To squeeze out money for your savings, earmark your next raise as savings toward a specific goal. If you earn $40,000, for instance, a 5% raise will give you $2,000 to set aside toward your baby's college fund.

10. Keep paying for debts you've already paid off. When you come to the end of your payments on a student loan, car loan, or credit-card balance, don't jump for joy and start spending those would-be payments. Instead, send the same amount each month to a mutual fund that you have chosen for a particular savings goal. Because the payment was already factored into your budget, you won't miss it. Smart, huh?

11. Give yourself an incentive. When you meet your targeted savings goal for the month, reward yourself and your family by spending any leftover savings on a treat.

12. Pay yourself back—with interest. If you have to tap your savings, aim to pay yourself back with interest. For instance, say you need to withdraw $250 of your savings and you figure it will take you two months to pay it back. At the end of two months, throw into your savings another $40 or so.

13. Moonlight for moolah. Figure out what you could do in your spare time to bring in some extra cash. Then take some or all of that found money and save it toward an important financial goal. Here are five moonlighting jobs and what they typically pay: kid's party clown ($75 an hour and up); housepainter ($13 an hour); word processor ($8.45 an hour); pet- or house-sitter ($5.50 an hour); and baby-sitter ($5.25 an hour).

14. Earn a higher return on your savings. The higher the interest rate on your savings, the less you have to salt away each month to meet your goals. Remember that Rule of 72? One way to earn more interest on your savings is to put your money in a CD or bond with a longer term than you had originally planned. Another idea: Make your annual IRA contribution every January instead of at the start of the following year. That way your savings will earn an extra 12 months' interest tax-deferred.

15. Deposit your stash where you can't easily get at it. The biggest enemy of savers may very well be the automated teller machine, or ATM. Sure it's convenient and easy to use. But that's just the problem. Your ATM lets you have instant access to your money any time of the day or night, and the more you withdraw, the less you have left in your savings. So try to limit your ATM visits to one a week.

If you are saving for a short-term goal and like the idea of keeping your money at a federally insured institution, consider CDs, which carry penalties of up to six months' interest on early withdrawals. Those lock-up penalties actually serve as a useful deterrent against unnecessary savings withdrawals. If you are saving for a longer-term goal, take advantage of a tax-deferred savings plan. It will also discourage you from pulling money out by slapping you with a 10% penalty for withdrawals before age 59½; in some cases you won't be able to withdraw cash at all unless you can prove financial hardship.

Making the Most of Tax-Deferred Savings Plans

These gems will also speed you along the road to wealth. Not only can you get an immediate federal income tax deduction or its equivalent for your contribution, but over the years the effects of tax-deferred compounding can be awesome. For instance, if a 35-year-old earning $60,000 a year annually routinely contributes 6% of his salary to a taxable account earning 8% a year, he would have $185,744 by age 65, assuming a 30% tax rate. Not bad. If he were to invest that money in a tax-deferred account, however, he would amass a hefty $407,820—more than twice as much. And even if he then withdrew the entire amount and paid taxes at a 30% rate on the proceeds, he would still be ahead by 54%. You can read about these retirement plans in greater detail in Chapter 11, but here are the most important things you should know:

■ **Employee savings plans.** Mentioned earlier in this chapter, these programs siphon off a percentage of your salary into your employer's retirement savings plan. These are simply the best savings deals available today. Because you save the money before it's taxed, the size of your contribution is effectively a deduction from your federal (and often state) income taxes.

■ **Individual Retirement Accounts.** If you have no tax-deferred saving plan at your workplace, you ought to do some disciplined tax-deferred saving on your own. Don't overlook the humble IRA. Even though Congress has limited the deductibility of IRA deposits (raising the bar a bit in 1997), you can still write off some or all of your contribution if you're not covered by a retirement plan at work or if you're married and have an adjusted gross income of less than $60,000 ($40,000 for singles). And the 1997 tax law created a new type of IRA, known as the Roth, whose withdrawals are fully tax-free if you've had the IRA for at least five years and you're 59½ or older at the time. The Roth IRA is not deductible, however. If you don't qualify for an IRA deduction and your income is too high to open a Roth, you can still contribute up to $2,000 annually in a **nondeductible IRA** and watch those earnings grow tax-deferred.

Since tax rates on upper-income people were raised in 1993, nondeductible IRAs have become much better deals for people in tax brackets of 31% or higher. But before you make a nondeductible IRA contribution, first contribute the maximum allowed to an employer-provided plan such as your 401(k), if you have one. Then aim to set aside the maximum $2,000 or $2,250 in an IRA account each year.

■ **Retirement plans for the self-employed.** If you own a small business or are self-employed, you can use a Simplified Employee Pension (SEP) that lets you write off as much as 13.0435% of your annual income, up to $30,000, and defer taxes on the earnings. (If you're an employee and your firm offers a SEP, you can fund it with up to 15% of your income.) SEPs are pretty simple to set up and require little record keeping.

A business owner can also set up a so-called Keogh plan, which allows you to contribute anywhere from 15% of annual gross income to $118,000. Keoghs can be kept at almost any institution that offers qualified plans such as IRAs. With a defined-contribution Keogh, you can contribute—and deduct from your taxable income—either as much as $30,000 a year or 20% of your net self-employment income, whichever is smaller. With a **defined-benefit Keogh,** you decide how much income you want to receive each year in retirement, within federal limits, and then contribute the right amount each year to achieve that benefit. Say you are 55 and haven't saved a lick. You can begin saving and deducting whatever it takes (up to $90,000 a year if you earn that much) to give yourself a retirement income equal to the average of your earnings in your three consecutive highest paid years. Every year you must submit to the IRS a form on which an enrolled actuary has made the official calculation for your defined-benefit Keogh plan.

■ **Deferred compensation plans.** Another form of forced savings, these plans are designed for highly paid executives who can afford to put aside a portion of their earnings. You make an election to defer a bonus or part of your salary until a stated time and you are not taxed on the income until you actually receive it. By deferring part of your compensation, you hope to avoid a current tax of, say, 36% or 39.6%, and ultimately pay tax at a lower rate on funds that have appreciated tax-free in the meantime. To set up a deferred compensation plan, you must enter a written arrangement with your employer.

The problem with a deferred compensation plan is that there's no guarantee the employer will actually deliver on its promise. One type of arrangement that provides more security for an employee is a so-called **rabbi trust,** so named because this arrangement was approved by the IRS for a synagogue and its rabbi. Your employer sets up an irrevocable trust in your name and stashes part of your salary in it every year. Of course, postponing your pay still involves some risk. For instance, you have no control over your trust, which could be seized by creditors to pay your employer's debts should the firm go bankrupt.

TAX-DEFERRED PLANS HEAD TO HEAD

The following table summarizes the important features of the most common tax-deferred retirement accounts. Except for nondeductible and Roth IRAs and deferred compensation plans, all allow a tax break or its equivalent for your contributions as well as your earnings. Loans, if permitted, are taken out against the amount in your account. All plans are subject to a 10% income tax penalty on withdrawals made before age 59½, except in the case of death or disability.

NAME OF PLAN	AVAILABLE TO . . .	BEST FOR . . .	MAXIMUM ANNUAL CONTRIBUTION	LOANS ALLOWED?	EARLY WITHDRAWALS?	NUMBER OF INVESTMENT OPTIONS
IRA	Anyone with earned income	Those who don't have pension plans or have put the maximum into their employer's savings plan	$2,000 a year	No	Always permitted	Nearly unlimited (excluded: real estate, collectibles, or most hard assets)

(continued)

133

NAME OF PLAN	AVAILABLE TO . . .	BEST FOR . . .	MAXIMUM ANNUAL CONTRIBUTION	LOANS ALLOWED?	EARLY WITHDRAWALS?	NUMBER OF INVESTMENT OPTIONS
401(k)	Employees of for-profit businesses	Everyone who qualifies	15% of compensation up to $150,000 or $9,500, whichever is less	Yes[4]	Only in hardship cases	One to 10, typically, depending on the plan
403(b)	Employees of schools and charitable organizations	Everyone who qualifies	16⅔% of compensation or roughly $9,500, whichever is less	Yes	Only in hardship cases	Three to 10, typically, depending on the plan
457	Employees of schools, charitable organizations, and government agencies	Everyone who qualifies	33⅓% of compensation or roughly $7,500, whichever is less	Yes	Only in hardship cases	One to 10, typically, depending on the plan
SEP	Self-employed people and employees of small businesses	A sole proprietor	The lesser of either 15% of taxable compensation or $22,500 for employees. If you're self-employed, it's the lesser of $22,500 or 13.04% of compensation for sole proprietors[1]	Yes	Always permitted	Same as an IRA

Profit-sharing Keogh	Self-employed people and employees of small unincorporated businesses	A small-business owner funding a plan for himself and employees	Same as SEP[2]	No	Generally permitted after full vesting	Unlimited
Money-purchase Keogh	Self-employed people and employees of small unincorporated businesses	A small business owner who wants to shelter more than allowed by a profit-sharing plan	25% of compensation for employees or $30,000, whichever is less; for self-employed, 20% or $30,000, whichever is less[1]	Yes[4]	Not permitted until you leave or the job is terminated	Unlimited
Defined-benefit Keogh	Self-employed people and employees of small unincorporated businesses	A self-employed person nearing retirement who needs to set aside a large percentage of income	100% of earned income[3] or the maximum needed to fund a $118,800 annuity, whichever is less[1]	Yes[4]	Same as a money-purchase plan	Unlimited
Non-qualified deferred compensation plan	Employees	Highly paid executives who expect to be in a lower tax bracket in the future	None	No	You typically must meet the terms of the agreement	Unlimited

Notes: [1]Small-business owners make contributions to SEPs or Keoghs for their employees.
[2]To get the maximum benefit, the plan must be in combination with a money-purchase plan.
[3]Calculated on a three-year-average basis.
[4]Unless you are self-employed or more than 10% owner of an S corporation.

CHAPTER 6

How to Manage Your Debt

The classic Jimmy Stewart movie *It's a Wonderful Life* has a touching scene where George Bailey, an ambitious dreamer, describes how loans improved the lives of folks in Bedford Falls. Henry Potter, the resident Scrooge, grouses that loans fill the heads of the "discontented, lazy rabble . . . with a lot of impossible ideas." Residents of Bedford Falls should be a "thrifty working class" and wait and save money before buying a house, he cracks. "Wait for what?" Bailey asks. "Until their children grow up and leave them? Until they're old and broken down? Do you know how long it takes a working man to save $5,000?"

Sadly, you would need 21 times that amount, or $106,000, to purchase the average home in America today. But Bailey's argument is still true: debt is a powerful tool that can improve your lifestyle. When you take out a loan or buy something on credit, you are able gradually to pay for things you want to use or enjoy now. You can have what you want when you want it—a new car, a college education, or a home for your family.

Fortunately, borrowers have many more choices today than they did during the '20s, when Potter and Bailey debated the pros and cons of debt. Credit-card issuers, retail stores, mortgage companies, banks, savings and loans, credit unions, auto dealers, and consumer finance companies are scrambling to lend you money. Anyone with a credit card can now finance even the most routine expenditures—groceries, prescription drugs, and newspaper subscriptions. Not surprisingly, Americans have come to live by the mantra: Buy Now, Pay Later. The public currently owes more than $900 billion, not including mortgages or loans against home equity, which add up to another $3.14 trillion.

From a balance sheet standpoint, the less debt you have, the better. That's because the money you spend on interest charges is cash that could otherwise be saved or invested for your future. What's more, if you one day can't manage your debt payments, you may have to declare bankruptcy, which could cripple your ability to borrow, rent an apartment, or get a job for as long as seven years. So go ahead and borrow—but do it wisely.

How Much Debt You Can Afford

Fill out the following worksheet to calculate your **debt-to-income ratio,** which will tell you how much debt you can realistically afford to carry. Generally, your total debts excluding your mortgage should eat up no more than 10% to 15% of your take-home pay. You may be able to handle a 20% debt level if you make a healthy living and are not likely to incur new debts anytime soon. Including a mortgage, your debt payments shouldn't exceed 36% of your gross monthly income. When you're at or beyond your debt limit, you'll need to get your debt-to-income ratio down. That means: refuse future invitations to borrow, put your credit cards in a drawer, and look for ways to reduce your current debt load.

YOUR DEBT WORKSHEET

To fill out this worksheet, you'll need to assemble your latest month's bills and statements from lenders, credit-card companies, and stores where you have charge accounts. (Ignore first mortgages on your home and credit-card accounts that you habitually pay in full.) Also, turn back to your cash-flow statement in Chapter 1 to find your annual disposable income for line 2. It's the amount you had last year after taxes.

LOANS AND CHARGE ACCOUNTS (EXCLUDING MORTGAGES AND CREDIT CARDS PAID IN FULL)	LAST MONTH'S PAYMENT
_____	$_____
_____	$_____
_____	$_____
_____	$_____
_____	$_____
_____	$_____

_____	$_____
_____	$_____
_____	$_____
_____	$_____
_____	$_____

1. Your total monthly payments $_____

2. Your total annual disposable income divided by 12. Do not include bonuses, since you can't depend on them. Unless you are living on investment income, exclude dividends, interest, and capital gains, too. $_____

3. Total monthly payments you can safely handle. If you are over 65 or the sole wage earner in your family, enter 10% of line 2. If you are married and you and your spouse work or you are under 35, enter 15% or 20% of line 2. $_____

4. Amount of room in your budget for additional debt (line 3 minus line 1). If the figure is negative, it's the amount of your current debt over the danger limit. $_____

Are You Too Deep in Debt?

For another way to see if you've got more debts than you should, take the following quiz. If you answer yes to three or more of these questions, you're in trouble:

- Do your monthly credit-card and loan payments (excluding mortgages and car loans) exceed 20% of your pay after taxes?
- Have you ever borrowed from one lender to pay another?
- Have you ever been forced to ask a friend or relative to co-sign a loan?
- Do you hold more than 10 credit cards, including cards issued by gasoline companies and department stores?
- Are you making only minimum monthly payments on credit cards?
- Are you unable to say how much money you owe?

Choosing and Using Credit Cards

Credit cards can be a big convenience. You can charge a purchase when you don't have the cash and don't want to pay by check. Many credit cards also let you pay off purchases over time. Indeed, fully 70% of the nation's 100 million cardholders carry balances from month to month. Like snowflakes, however, no two cards are exactly alike. And the cards you're holding right now may not be the best ones for you. Odds are you probably own more cards than you need. So here's a short course in how to choose and use credit cards.

The first thing to know is the difference between **credit cards** and **travel and entertainment cards.** Credit cards, like Visa, MasterCard, department store cards, and gasoline cards, let you make monthly payments of less than the amount you've charged. But you'll pay interest on your unpaid balance, perhaps as much as 18% to 21%. You may be surprised to learn that Visa and MasterCard are umbrella organizations comprising independent financial institutions that issue so-called bank cards and set their own terms for borrowers. So the Visa card from the bank on the corner could be much different from the one issued by the bank across town. Generally, there are bank credit cards with high interest rates but no or low annual fees and bank cards with high annual fees but low interest rates. If you tend to carry a balance, you'll want to look for a card with a low interest rate. If you never or rarely carry a balance, look for a card with no annual fee, possibly one that offers a bonus or perk

for every dollar you charge. (Each month, **MONEY**'s "Monitor" section lists the best credit cards with and without annual fees.)

Many credit-card issuers offer so-called **gold cards,** which typically come with higher credit limits, higher annual fees, and extras like free traveler's checks and purchase-protection insurance. The additional cost of a gold card is probably not justified unless you expect to use the card's extra services, such as discounts on selected hotels and rental cars. If an issuer offers you these perks on a card with a low interest rate and a low or no annual fee, however, don't hesitate to go for the gold.

In addition to financing purchases, you can also use a Visa or MasterCard to get a loan in a flash. You can go inside a bank to get a $200 to $500 credit-card **cash advance,** or get the same advance through many automated teller machines, for a fee of 2% to 4% of the amount you're taking out (minimum fee: $2 to $5). It's best to take out a cash advance only when you're truly desperate for quick dough, though, since the cost of this type of borrowing is so high. Furthermore, you'll probably owe the credit card's standard interest rate from the day you take out the cash advance. According to BankCard Holders of America, a nonprofit group in Salem, Va., someone who takes a $300 cash advance and pays a $2.50 cash advance fee and one month's interest at 18.5% will pay an effective interest rate of 32.94%!

Travel and entertainment cards, like American Express, Diner's Club, and Carte Blanche, require you to pay your entire balance every month. As a result, you don't owe interest on these cards unless you're late with your payments. They typically have no present credit limit and charge an annual fee of $55 to $300. American Express sells three types of cards: green ($55 a year), gold ($75), and platinum ($300). The gold card offers access to a 24-hour travel service and sends you a summary of charges at the end of the year. The platinum card, available to wealthy people, gives you free traveler's checks, free air miles in American Express's Membership Miles program, and memberships in both the Hertz #1 Club and the Northwest Airlines World Club. Although you can't get a cash advance against the American Express card, you can use the card to get cash from a bank account at an ATM machine that accepts American Express cards. Green-card holders can use their cards to get up to $1,000 every seven days; gold-card holders can take out as much as $2,500 every seven days; and platinum-card holders can withdraw up to $10,000 every 30 days.

Are travel and entertainment cards worth their relatively steep annual fees? Probably not, unless you think you'll use a lot of their perks or can't live with your credit cards' predetermined spending limits. These days most merchants that accept plastic honor all the major brands. In fact, Visa and MasterCard are accepted at three times as many locations as American Express, which isn't as widely recognized outside the United States.

Debit cards look like regular MasterCard and Visa cards but are linked to your bank checking account instead of a line of credit. They work like an electronic check. When you use one, the amount you spend is withdrawn directly from your account, usually after one to three business days. Banks that are part of the Visa or MasterCard associations issue debit cards with their logos that can be used at any store that accepts those credit cards. So if you're at a restaurant, short on cash, and don't want to rack up charges on your credit card, you don't have to excuse yourself for a run to the nearest ATM. Simply whip out your debit card, and voilà! the meal is paid for. Bear in mind that you can't build a credit history with a debit card, since you aren't actually borrowing money. Before getting a debit card, however, find out if your bank charges an annual fee or any transaction fees when you use the card. Many do. And at $10 a year or $1 a pop, the convenience of a debit card is less of a deal.

The latest wrinkle in the world of plastic is the **bonus** or **rebate card.** Issuers linking up with manufacturers, airlines, oil companies, and the like have been handing out rewards in the form of rebates to customers charging all manner of goods and services. There now are more than 950 rebate cards, and consumers are snapping them up: Americans now carry nearly 50 million rebate cards from Visa and MasterCard alone.

The rebate marketing war has touched off a guerrilla counterattack by clever people who've learned to manipulate the system to maximize their bonuses. Among card issuers, such people are known as "gamers," because they treat rebates like a game. To win the rebate game, you need to charge a lot. Even more important, you need the means and self-discipline to pay off your credit-card bills in full each month. Otherwise the interest rate on rebate cards, which can run as high as 19.8% compared with 9% for a typical low-rate card, will undermine any profits.

If you hanker to play the rebate game like a pro or just improve your weekend game, follow these five rules:

1. Get the right cheap rebate card for you. Send $4 to BankCard Holders of America (524 Branch Drive, Salem, Va. 24153) for its list of low-rate and no-fee cards. Then switch to one or call your card issuer's 800 number and threaten to transfer your balance to a card charging less. It will probably match the deal.

2. Charge nearly everything—even purchases you wouldn't normally put on a card. You can rack up bonuses by using rebate cards to pay for things like groceries, day care, college tuition, and medical bills. Just try to pay off your balances each month to avoid incurring finance charges.

3. Keep track of your charges and retire each card as you reach its maximum annual rebate. With the GM card, for example, you get a credit equal to 5% of your charges toward the purchase of most GM cars. But you can't build up more than a $500 credit in any single year or more than $3,500 over seven years. So if you manage to put $10,000 on your GM MasterCard this year, you will have maxed out (5% of $10,000 is $500). Then, start using another rebate card for purchases during the rest of the year.

4. Use one card to pay off another and thus double your rebates, as long as the rules permit it. Some cards—Volkswagen's and GM's among them—award you rebates for using the convenience checks that you often get when you first open a credit-card account. These checks are linked to your credit-card account, so you can use them to pay off charges accumulated on some other rebate card. In effect, you simply transfer your balance from one card to the other and get two rebates for one set of purchases.

5. Don't take the game too seriously. Remember that credit-card companies have the upper hand; they can change the rules whenever they please. American and several other airlines, for instance, raised the frequent flier miles required for a free domestic round-trip ticket from 20,000 to 25,000 in 1995. So play the game strictly for fun.

Secured cards are generally a sensible choice for people who can't get regular credit cards because of a bad credit history. A secured card looks and works just like a regular credit card, but to get one you must make a collateral deposit of a few hundred dollars in an interest-bearing savings account. You can then get a Visa or MasterCard from the bank *as long as you leave your deposit there.* If you fail to pay your bills, the bank will snatch your deposit. However, if you close the secured card account in good standing, you will get back your full deposit. Beware issuers who ply their secured card on TV or through 900 numbers, however. Their cards tend to come with high fees and rates. Shop for a better deal using BankCard Holders of America's list of secured card issuers ($4; same address as before).

Whether you're looking for or have a standard card, a gold card, a rebate card, or a secured card, scrutinize the following:

■ **The annual percentage rate.** The annual percentage rate (APR) is the total cost of credit expressed on an annual basis. You can find a credit card's APR on an application or its monthly billing statement. Most credit cards today have variable interest rates, usually pegged to 10 percentage points or so above the **prime rate** (the rate banks charge their best customers). Be careful: many cards that advertise rock-bottom, single-digit APRs have rates designed to last for only a few months before they soar by as much as 10 points. If you wind up taking one of these "deals," cancel your card before the initial rate expires.

Variable-rate cards sometimes masquerade as cost savers, since they purport to charge APRs that rise and fall with interest rates. But some of these cards sport a *minimum* interest rate that's actually a maximum rip-off. For instance, one bank recently offered a secured MasterCard rate of prime plus 10.5%. That might sound as though it amounts to roughly 18%. But the fine print says that the bank has a minimum rate of 18.9%, which is what cardholders actually pay unless the prime rate is 8.4% or higher.

■ **The annual fee.** Many bank card issuers charge an annual fee of $20 to $35 for standard cards and from $50 to $100 for premium or gold cards. Here's a secret: If you have a decent credit rating, you might be able to get this fee waived. When it shows up on your bill, call your card's issuer and, as politely yet fervently as you can, demand that the issuer stop assessing the fee. The issuer may waive it to keep your business. You may even be able to get American Express or another travel and entertainment card to do the same, especially if you threaten to cancel.

■ **The grace period.** A card's grace period lets you avoid its finance charge if you pay the balance in full before the due date. Usually the due date is about two weeks after you have received your monthly statement. Most cards offer a grace period that annoyingly vanishes whenever you carry a balance. So, if you charged your kids' fall wardrobes last month, for instance, but didn't pay the entire balance at the end of the month, you'll start accruing finance charges on whatever you buy today almost as soon as you leave the store.

American Express decided to capitalize on the grace period shell game in 1994, when it launched its True Grace card. The no-fee, low-interest rate card comes with a rare perk: a 25-day interest-free period on all your charges, whether you carry a balance or not. But a closer inspection of True Grace reveals that this card comes with several hidden costs. For one thing, although its interest rate starts at a low 7.9%, after six months the rate leaps to the prime rate plus a hefty 8.75 percentage points—that could easily land you a rate of 18% or so. Second, if you make three payments more than 30 days late, you'll pay prime plus 12.9 points—which could easily approach 22%. And

although True Grace comes with no annual fee for the first year, you'll pay $25 thereafter if you don't use the card at least three times a year. Then there's this: Like its AmEx siblings—the green, gold, and platinum cards—True Grace is accepted at only about a third of the number of merchants that accept Visa and Master-Card. So if you tend to carry a balance on your cards, you'd be better off sticking with a bank credit card with a rock-bottom rate. If you're worried that you'll happen to go to some hoity-toity restaurant that takes AmEx but not Visa or MasterCard, however, True Grace may be your ticket.

■ **The junk fees.** Most card issuers charge you a fee when you make a late payment (average fee: $12.50), exceed your credit limit (average: $12.75), or take out a cash advance (usually a fee of 2% to 4%). Watch out for cards that spare you an annual fee, then sock it to you with other steep charges.

■ **The minimum payment.** In recent years, three of the top ten credit-card issuers—Citibank, MBNA, and Chase—lowered their required minimum monthly payments from 2.8% or 2.5% of your monthly balance to around 2%. But if, like the average cardholder, you carry a balance of $1,100, paying off just 2% a month instead of 2.8% will add $120 to $400 to your annual interest bill. Unless you're strapped, reject this new offer. If possible, send in a payment that's at least double what your issuer requires.

■ **The balance-computation method.**
Here's a riddle: When is 18% not 18%?
The answer: When two credit-card issuers
calculate their interest rates differently.
There are basically four ways card issuers
can compute a balance: (1) the **average
daily balance (excluding new purchases) method,** in which the issuer totals the balances for each day in the
billing period without counting your
new purchases; (2) the **average daily
balance (including new purchases)
method,** in which an issuer figures your
average balance after counting your most
recent purchases; (3) the **two-cycle average daily balance (excluding new
purchase) method,** which totals your
average balances for two billing cycles not
including new purchases; and (4) the
**two-cycle average daily balance (in-
cluding new purchases) method,** figured the same way after taking your
recent purchases into account.

If you occasionally carry a balance,
you'll usually pay the least amount of interest when an issuer uses the average
daily balance (excluding new purchases)
method. Consider this example from
BankCard Holders of America: Suppose
that four times a year you charged $1,000
on a credit card with a 19.8% interest rate
and made the minimum payment of $28
when the charges appeared on your bill.
The following month you charged another $1,000 and paid off the entire bal-

ance when your next bill arrived. The interest you owe over a year could vary by
as much as $70:

TYPE OF BALANCE	INTEREST
Average daily balance (excluding new purchases)	$66
Average daily balance (including new purchases)	$132
Two-cycle average daily balance (excluding new purchases)	$131
Two-cycle average daily balance (including new purchases)	$196

Shopping for a Car Loan

The car-buying experience can be so aggravating that when it comes time to finance the purchase, you may be tempted
to go with the dealer's loan just to get it
over with. (For advice about car leasing,
see Chapter 18.) Nearly 80% of all car
buyers arrange financing through the
dealer. Jumping at the dealer's financing
isn't wise, though. You may be able to
borrow elsewhere at far better terms.
Dealers often stack two percentage points
on top of the APR (annual percentage
rate) that a bank would charge. So before
you walk into the showroom, check with

at least three local lenders, including the institution where you have a checking or savings account, to see what kind of deal you can swing. Then you'll know whether the car dealer's loan is best for you.

Sometimes car dealers dangle enticing loans with ridiculously low interest rates. These loans, however, often come with three strings: they are available only on certain models; you cannot qualify for any cash rebate if you accept the financing; and you can usually get the lowest rate only by signing up for a loan of no more than two years or so. That could make your monthly payments higher than you can afford, since shortening up the term of a loan raises the size of the monthly payments. Here are a few alternatives:

■ **Credit unions.** Car loan rates at the nation's 12,800 credit unions are nearly a percentage point less, on average, than rates at banks and S&Ls. Besides cheaper rates, major credit unions also offer Car Facts, a free car-buying advisory service developed by the Credit Union National Association. It provides car-quality ratings, rebate information, and dealer costs for various options.

■ **Your bank or S&L.** Sometimes banks and S&Ls give their depositors a slight break on car loan rates if they agree to have their payments deducted directly from their accounts.

■ **Home-equity loans.** More than 10% of all home-equity loans today are used to buy cars. Surprised? Actually, it's quite understandable once you look at the tax side of the car-financing equation. Interest payments on a home-equity loan are tax-deductible no matter what the money is used for; interest on a car loan is not deductible. If the interest rate on a home-equity loan is 8.6%, say, your after-tax rate might wind up being 6.2%, far lower than the rate on a typical car loan.

Before applying for a car loan, decide on the length of the term that you want. The shortest term is two years, but you may be able to stretch out your payments for as long as 10 years. Stay away from auto loans with terms longer than five years, despite their low monthly payments. By the fifth year, the amount you still owe could be more than the depreciation value of the car, putting you in what's known as an upside-down position. If you sell the car, you might have to come up with additional cash to pay off the loan.

Other car-financing tips:

■ **Ask if there will be any penalties for paying off the loan early.** If you can choose between two loans with similar rates, go with the one that most easily lets you get rid of the loan ahead of schedule.

■ **Mention your credit history if it's spotless, especially if you borrow from a car dealer.** According to the Consumer Bankers Association, about a third of lenders offer slightly lower rates for borrowers who never or rarely make late payments on their other loans. Typically, they'll knock 1% or so off their standard interest rate.

■ **Try to make a down payment of at least 20%.** Lenders often add a quarter of a point to their rates for borrowers who put down less.

■ **If you're a young, first-time car buyer, tell your car dealer.** Some dealers try to help people like you by using less stringent guidelines in deciding if you qualify for a loan. You may also be allowed to make a smaller down payment than normal.

Shopping for a Mortgage

For many people, the search for a mortgage can be overwhelming. You often must compare a variety of loans with different interest rates and terms to find the best mortgage for you. Miss out on the best deal and you could be stuck paying thousands of dollars in extra interest over the next 15 or 30 years. Bear in mind that in the early years of a mortgage, the bulk of your mortgage payment is going toward interest. In successive years, more and more of your payment goes to pay the principal. How much do one or two percentage points of interest or a difference of $50,000 matter for a mortgage? Check out the table on page 147.

The Internet can help you figure out how large a mortgage you can afford and where to get a loan. For instance, the sites www.internet.com and www.mortgagenet.com are great for learning what your monthly payments would be for different types of mortgages. You can get timely data on mortgage rates in your area at the Web sites www.hsh.com and at www.bankrate.com. Such services may also notify you if mortgage rates have risen or fallen since you last checked in. These days, roughly 80% of lenders with Web sites will let you know how large a mortgage you are likely to qualify for; these prequalification programs don't guarantee that you'll actually get the loans, though.

MONTHLY PAYMENTS FOR A 30-YEAR FIXED MORTGAGE

MORTGAGE AMOUNT	7%	8%	9%	10%	11%	12%
$50,000	$333	$367	$402	$439	$476	$514
$100,000	$665	$734	$805	$878	$952	$1,029
$150,000	$998	$1,101	$1,207	$1,316	$1,428	$1,543
$200,000	$1,331	$1,468	$1,609	$1,755	$1,905	$2,057
$250,000	$1,665	$1,835	$2,013	$2,195	$2,381	$2,573
$300,000	$1,997	$2,203	$2,415	$2,633	$2,857	$3,087
$350,000	$2,329	$2,568	$2,817	$3,073	$3,335	$3,601
$400,000	$2,663	$2,937	$3,219	$3,511	$3,811	$4,115

To begin the mortgage process, ask your real estate agent to recommend some lenders and see if your friends have used local lenders. Your agent might also be able to direct you to a mortgage broker, a kind of clearinghouse for home loans (for more on this, see Chapter 7). Also, find out from your agent if any firms publish lists with data on mortgages offered by lenders in the same area. For example, every week HSH Associates puts together surveys of loans offered by 25 to 80 lenders in most states (800-873-2837). Cost: $18 for two surveys. If you can't find such a list, check your local paper's real estate section for advertisements to give you a sense of the mortgage market in your area. Then call a half dozen or so lenders to find out their current rates and terms.

Most lenders are reputable and honest. Still, before you go with any, it's a good idea to make sure the firm is on the up-and-up. Beware lenders or mortgage brokers who ask you to pay stiff fees up front. Call your state banking department as well as the local Better Business Bureau to find out if any of the lender's customers have filed complaints. When an honest lender goes out of business, it will hand off its mortgages to another firm. However, if you are dealing with a fraudulent lender, your chances of getting money back depend on what's left when the scamsters are caught.

The type of mortgage you should choose generally depends on how long you plan to remain in the home and how you feel about your payment changing from month to month. There are two basic varieties: (1) **fixed-rate loans,** which have interest rates that do not change over the life of the loan and generally run for 15 to 30 years; and (2) **variable-** or **adjustable-rate mortgages (ARMs),** whose rates can rise or fall along with other interest rates. Most ARMs have 15-year or 30-year terms. An ARM's rate generally cannot rise by more than two percentage points a year or six points over the life of the loan, however. A 15-year mortgage has two attractions: your interest rate on a 15-year mortgage will probably be about a quarter of a percentage point lower than that of a comparable 30-year loan; and your total interest payments will be cut in half. The drawback is that 15-year loans have higher monthly payments. At recent rates, you would face a $1,010 monthly nut on the average $100,000 15-year mortgage, compared with $823 on a 30-year fixed-rate loan—a 23% difference. All in all, if you can afford a 15-year mortgage, go for it.

Adjustable-rate loans typically have initial interest rates that are about two percentage points lower than fixed loans plus lower initial monthly payments. At recent rates, for example, the initial monthly payment on a $100,000 ARM was about 20% lower than the payments on comparable 30-year fixed-rate mortgages, or $659 versus $823. Payments on adjustable-rate mortgages can increase substantially, though, if interest rates rise. Typically, you lock in the initial interest rate on an ARM for six months or a year. Then every year or so the lender will raise or lower the rate

in tandem with an index, such as the one-year Treasury bill rate.

The first-year ARM rate is set at a discount from the index, so even if interest rates remain flat, a borrower's ARM would go up in a year. That's right: after the first year of your ARM, your interest rate and monthly payments will rise even if other interest rates haven't increased.

You may have to sign up for an ARM if your income is too low to qualify for a fixed rate. (As a rule, you can qualify for a mortgage on a home that costs up to about 2½ times your gross income. Also, your monthly debt payments cannot exceed 36% of your gross monthly income.) If you do not expect to own the house for more than five years, an ARM can be especially appealing, since there is little risk that your rate will rise substantially over that short time. Before you commit to any adjustable mortgage, see whether you can live with it under the worst-case scenario. With a 6% ARM that maxes out each year—jumping to 8% in year two, 10% in year three, and 12% in year four—you still end up with a four-year average rate of 9%, which would beat a 30-year fixed-rate average of 9.2%.

A few other mortgage variations are worth considering. If you think mortgage rates might be heading down in a few years, check out a **convertible loan,** which starts out as an ARM but gives you the option of switching to a fixed rate between the second and fifth years of the loan. The interest rate is initially about one percentage point higher than that of a comparable ARM, though still lower than what you would pay for a fixed-rate mortgage. At conversion, you will owe a fee of about $250. Another type of convertible loan that makes sense is the fixed-to-adjustable variety. The initial rate is fixed for the first few years, then the rate adjusts annually.

If you plan to be in your house for five to seven years or so, a **two-step** or **balloon-reset mortgage** might be the call. The monthly payments stay at the same level for the first five or seven years, then are reset for the duration of the loan. Typically, the new rate is the yield of the 10-year U.S. Treasury constant maturity plus 2.5 percentage points. The rate on a balloon-reset mortgage is often one-half to three-quarters of a percentage point less than that of a 30-year fixed. For example, if a 30-year fixed rate is 8.61%, a balloon reset might charge 8.07%.

If you would rather lock in a discounted interest rate for a longer period than two-step loans offer, check out a comparatively new loan called a **10/1 adjustable-rate mortgage**. A 10/1 ARM can be a smart choice if you plan to move within 10 years. It locks in a rate for 10 years, but generally at a lower rate than the traditional fixed-rate loan. After 10 years, the rate adjusts annually as if it were a one-year ARM.

A **biweekly loan** is another way to slash your interest costs. It requires that you make half your monthly payment every two weeks. Because most months are longer than four full weeks, or 28 days,

you'll end up making two extra half payments a year. These extra payments will shave up to 12 years off the life of a 30-year loan. Problem is, most banks don't offer biweekly mortgages as such. Those that do may charge a higher interest rate that could offset your savings, making it essential to compare your lender's rate on biweekly loans and standard loans. Avoid third-party firms that will convert your standard mortgage to a biweekly for a fee of a few hundred bucks.

If you want to pay less in interest and unload your mortgage ahead of time, you can shorten the life of your loan on your own simply by tacking on more to your monthly payments. For example, if you added $25 to your regular monthly payments of $805 on a $100,000 30-year 9% fixed rate loan, you could save $29,440 in total interest and shorten your loan by almost four years. Most lenders will let you make these extra payments, although some will impose a **prepayment penalty** if you do so during the first few years of your mortgage. That's why you'll need to check with your lender before making extra payments. If there is a penalty, ask to have it waived. Then explain how much more you'd like to pay and how often, finding out the way the lender will want you to submit your extra payments.

WHAT'S THE BEST MORTGAGE FOR YOU?

The table below provides a brief description of a sampling of mortgages. Find the one that suits you best.

TYPE OF LOAN	COMMENTS
15-year fixed 20-year fixed 30-year fixed	**Fixed-rate loans** have interest rates that remain unchanged during the life of the loan. The shorter the term, the less costly the loan, since you pay lower total interest. Longer-term loans require smaller monthly payments, so it's easier to qualify for, say, a 30-year loan than a 15-year loan.
Five-year balloon Seven-year balloon Five-year balloon-reset Seven-year balloon-reset	**Balloon** and **balloon-reset loans** are worth considering if you intend to sell your home or refinance within seven years. You make fixed monthly payments for a set period, usually five or seven years, at which point the loan balance comes due. Consider a balloon mortgage if you plan to sell your home before the onerous lump sum is due. Balloon-reset loans offer low initial rates. At the end of five or seven years, you have the option of paying off the balance or renewing the loan for 25 or 23 years, normally at a rate that's slightly higher than the prevailing fixed-rate loan.
One-year adjustable Three-year adjustable 3/1 adjustable 5/1 adjustable 10/1 adjustable	**Adjustable-rate mortgages,** or **ARMs,** typically have rates that change every one, three, or five years. Your monthly payments start low since ARMs' initial rates are usually two percentage points or so below those on fixed-rate loans. But your rate and payments then rise or fall depending on changes in other interest rates. 3/1, 5/1, or 10/1 ARMs adjust once after the first three, five, or ten years, then change annually.

Minimum down payments are typically 5% to 10% for fixed-rate loans and 10% to 20% for adjustable loans and balloons. If you put down less than 20%, however, you'll need to buy **mortgage insurance.** That usually means paying the first year's insurance premium at closing—up to $950 on a $100,000 loan with 5% down—plus coughing up a few extra bucks each month as part of your mortgage payment.

Some financial professionals recommend putting down as much as possible and getting the shortest-term loan you can afford to save on interest. The alternate argument is that you should borrow as much as possible and invest the money you save. To make this strategy successful, however, you need the self-discipline to actually invest the extra cash in a way that will generate an after-tax return higher than the after-tax cost of your mortgage. (To figure your after-tax cost, subtract your marginal tax rate from 1 and multiply the result by your interest rate.)

Getting a mortgage is never easy, but first-time buyers have it roughest of all. They don't have cash from selling a previous residence to help them come up with the down payment or other mortgage closing costs. In fact, first-time buyers often find that it's the down payment and closing costs, not the monthly payment, that is the biggest obstacle to getting a mortgage. For solutions to problems faced by first-time home buyers, see the following table:

HELP FOR FIRST-TIME MORTGAGE BORROWERS

PROBLEM	SOLUTION
You can't come up with enough cash for the down payment	**Find a lender that will approve you for a loan with a lower down payment.** Many banks accept down payments as low as 5%. Lowering the down payment, however, means increasing the size of the mortgage, which could make it harder for you to qualify. If so, check out the 5% down, Fannie-Neighbors/ Community Homebuyer's, which allows a debt-to-income ratio of up to 40%. Fannie Mae has other low down payment programs for first-time buyers whose household income is less than the local median. One features monthly payments that start out less than normal and increase gradually over two to eight years. For more information, call Fannie Mae at 800-732-6643.

HELP FOR FIRST-TIME MORTGAGE BORROWERS (continued)

PROBLEM	SOLUTION
You can't come up with enough cash for the down payment (*continued*)	**Consider Federal Housing Administration–insured mortgages made through banks or other lenders.** FHA loans typically require a 3% down payment, but you must pay a fee equal to 3% of the loan—that's $3,000 on a $100,000 mortgage. FHA-insured loans are usually limited to $67,500, but can go up to $151,572 in high-cost areas like New York City and Los Angeles. **Borrow from family members for the down payment.** If your relatives have deep pockets and big hearts consider Fannie Mae's so-called 3/2 loan. You put down 3%; Mom, Dad, or any relative contributes the other 2%. Anytime you borrow from your parents, treat the loan as a business transaction. There should be a note specifying an interest rate and repayment schedule. Interest should be set according to market rates. If a family member offers to cover part of the down payment, be sure to get a note from that person stating that he or she is giving you the money as a gift. Otherwise, your lender will suspect that you received a loan and the debt may hinder your ability to borrow as much as you need.
You don't have the cash for the up-front cost of mortgage insurance	**Finance the insurance.** Several mortgage insurers, including GE Capital Mortgage Insurance and Mortgage Guaranty Insurance, let you pay your first year's premiums in monthly installments—which would come to about $50 a month on a $100,000 home. Insurance with this feature costs a bit more, but if the lower up-front payment helps you afford the loan, the financing is worth the price.

HELP FOR FIRST-TIME MORTGAGE BORROWERS

PROBLEM	SOLUTION
Your credit record is flawed	**Come clean and offer a good explanation.** Most lenders won't reject you because of two or three 30-days-late payments on your credit report. If you have had numerous 30-days-late payments, have been late 60 days or more on any payments, or have defaulted on a loan within the past two years, you'll have some serious explaining to do. By volunteering the information and a reasonable explanation, you may be able to convince a lender that you're actually a good risk. If that fails, a mortgage broker who specializes in helping bad credit risks might be a possibility. For a list of mortgage brokers in your area, call the National Association of Mortgage Brokers (602-992-6181).

Mortgage Loan Discrimination

Some mortgage seekers face a special hurdle: bias. According to studies by the Federal Reserve and others, minority mortgage applicants are turned down two to four times more often than whites. The Fed has also discovered that lenders sometimes discriminate against single women and young people.

Discrimination can be tough to spot. It may take the form of an unhelpful loan officer or one who tries to steer you to an-

other bank. For a rundown of your rights, call for the Federal Reserve's free booklet *Home Mortgages: Understanding the Process and Your Right to Fair Lending* (202-452-3245). If you feel you have been treated unjustly, call the discrimination hot line at the U.S. Department of Housing and Urban Development (800-669-9777). There are several other steps you can take to protect yourself:

■ **When you apply, find out how long you can expect to wait for a decision.** Then call the lender if you haven't heard by the promised date. Some banks may simply delay action, hoping you'll

153

give up. Demonstrating that you intend to stand up for your rights may improve your chances of qualifying for a loan.

■ **If the bank turns down your loan request, ask for an explanation of its underwriting standards.** This information may help you learn whether the institution rejects all loan applicants with credentials like yours.

■ **Watch out for lowball appraisals.** If the stated reason for your rejection is that the home you want to buy is worth less than the purchase price, ask to see a copy of the lender's appraisal report. Then, if the appraisal seems unreasonably low, take it to a fair lending expert such as one at the U.S. Department of Housing and Urban Development. This kind of pro may be able to spot evidence of bias in the subjective information that's often part of an appraisal—comments about the quality of neighboring houses, for example.

Working with a Mortgage Lender

Once you have been approved for a loan, take a shot at predicting which way mortgage rates are headed over the next few months. If you think rates will rise, lock in a rate at application. Some lenders let you lock in for 60 days or longer at no charge. Others charge a fee equal to 1% of the loan's amount. Be sure you'll be able to close before the lock-in period ends. Otherwise, if rates have risen, the lender can boost your rate, too.

You can chop weeks off the loan-processing period by dealing with a lender who follows alternative documentation guidelines. This procedure streamlines the mortgage application routine. For example, instead of requiring a letter from your employer confirming that you have a job, the lender will accept W-2 forms from the past two years and a current payroll stub.

Another way to close on a house more quickly is to get your loan application preapproved. Even before you've found the house you plan to buy, many lenders will approve you for a mortgage of a specific amount. Then, all a lender has to do after you find a house is have it appraised and assure that the seller can legally transfer title to you.

Lenders typically charge fees known as **points** for granting mortgages. One point equals 1% of the loan amount. Often a lender will charge between one and three points; that works out to $1,000 to $3,000 on a $100,000 mortgage. With most lenders you can lower your interest rate by agreeing to pay more in points. For instance, you may be offered an 8% rate with no points, 7.7% with one point, and 7.6% with two points. How do you decide which is best? By figuring out how long you plan to stay in your home.

Let's say you can get a $100,000 fixed-rate 30-year mortgage at the terms just described. The monthly payment on the no-point loan would be $734; on the two-point loan, it would be $706. It would take you 72 months, or six years, before the $28-a-month savings would fully offset the two points ($2,000/$28 = 72). So, in this example, paying points now in exchange for a lower rate would make sense if you plan to stay in your home at least six years. If you expect to move again sooner, it won't be worth it to pay the points.

In addition to points, borrowers may be asked to come up with numerous other costs at the closing, not to mention the price of hiring a mover. For a list and description of these assorted expenses, see the following table:

YOUR MORTGAGE FEES

TYPE OF COST	CHARGE	WHAT IT IS
Application fee	$75–$300	A lender's charge to cover the initial costs of processing your loan request and checking your credit report. Generally not refundable.
Appraisal	$150–$400	An estimate of the property's value.
Survey	$125–$300	An inspection of the boundaries of a property and any improvements on it.
Homeowners insurance	$300–$600	Protection against loss from fire and other natural hazards. You may be required to carry flood insurance, too.
Lender's attorney's review fee	$75–$200	What the lender pays the lawyer or company conducting the closing on its behalf.
Title search and title insurance	$450–$600	An examination to confirm ownership of the real estate plus insurance against any loss caused by discrepancies to property's title.
Home inspection	$175–$350	A written review of the structure.
Loan origination fee	1% of loan	Charge for the lender's work evaluating and preparing your mortgage.

YOUR MORTGAGE FEES (continued)

TYPE OF COST	CHARGE	WHAT IT IS
Mortgage insurance	0.5%–1% of the loan	Protection for the lender in case you default. Generally required only when you make a down payment of less than 20%.
Points	1%–3% of the loan	Prepaid interest charged by the lender.
Your attorney's fee	$500 to $1,500	The cost of hiring a lawyer to look out for you when negotiating a contract to buy a home.

Always attempt to negotiate a lender's fees. This is easiest to do when your local housing market is in the dumps and lenders have trouble bringing in mortgage borrowers. Consider the savings scored by one man who took out a several-hundred-thousand-dollar mortgage at a New York City area thrift in 1994. The bank offered to lock in its 4.85% rate on a one-year ARM for 60 days. He asked the bank to extend its lock to 90 days free of charge and got it. That saved him roughly $2,100. In addition, he avoided having to borrow at a slightly higher 5.65% when interest rates rose. By insisting that the bank waive all fees except those that he was legally required to pay, he was also able to get the bank to cover its own attorney's fee ($450), the mortgage underwriting fee ($100), the application fee ($125), and the appraisal fee ($275). His total savings: about $2,496 in interest for the loan's first year plus more than $3,000 in up-front fees.

Chances are your lender will one day sell your loan to another lender while you are still paying it off. Before that happens, you should get a letter from your lender, known as a **sign-off letter,** explaining its plans and where to send your payment. If you get such a letter, but something about it looks fishy, call your original lender to verify that the letter wasn't written by a scamster who got his hands on your name and address. Never send your mortgage payment to another firm if you haven't gotten this sign-off from your original lender. When you get the first statement from the new lender, review it carefully to be sure the institution got everything right.

Homeowners with adjustable-rate mortgages, unfortunately, need to check to see that their lenders aren't overcharging them. Lenders frequently come up with the wrong figures when they recalculate ARM payments—either by honest goofs or by unscrupulous greed. Lawrence Powers, president of the nonprofit Consumer Loan Advocates (655 Rockland Rd., Suite 106, Lake Bluff, Ill. 60044), believes that 33% of ARM borrowers are overcharged. You can figure out if you're one of them by following the steps in his group's $20 book, *ARM Aid*.

Should You Refinance Your Mortgage?

If you already have a mortgage, you might want to **refinance** it—swap the loan for a different one—to get a lower interest rate, snag a lower monthly payment, unload the loan faster, or pull some money out. Refinancing also is sometimes a smart idea for homeowners who want to get out of an ARM and into a fixed-rate loan in order to know exactly what the mortgage payment will be for the life of the loan. You will encounter the same procedure and often the same types of costs as you did when you got your first mortgage, though some lenders waive some fees for refinancers. Plan on spending an average of 3% to 6% of the outstanding principal in refinancing costs, plus any prepayment penalties on your first mortgage.

For many years the general rule of thumb was that you should refinance only if the interest rate on your current mortgage was at least two percentage points higher than the prevailing market rate. Say, for example, you had a five-year-old fixed-rate loan with a 10% rate and $100,000 balance. If interest rates on new 30-year fixed-rate loans had dropped to 8%, you could refinance and lower your monthly payments from $878 to $733. Instead you might choose to refinance with a 15-year fixed-rate loan at, say, 7.5%. Your monthly payments would be $927—higher than they were before the refinance—but you'd pay off the entire mortgage in just 15 years. You'd also save a bundle: you'd pay just $66,861 in interest on the new 15-year loan, compared with $164,149 had you chosen to refinance with a 30-year fixed loan.

In many ways, however, this two-percentage-point rule is too simplistic. Lowering your interest rate by as little as a quarter of a point can save you money in the long run. What's more, the rule was invented at a time when lenders charged a lot to refinance. In slow housing markets, some lenders waive their application fees and pay your closing costs. The crucial question for anyone considering a refinancing is, How long will I stay in my home? If you plan to remain well beyond the time it would take to recoup your closing costs through lower monthly payments, it makes sense to refinance.

When balancing the cost of refinancing against your savings, you'll need to figure out this break-even point. To do this, subtract the monthly payment on your current mortgage. Then add up the costs of refinancing, including points, closing fees, and taxes. Then divide your costs by your monthly savings. For instance, if your current loan is 10% and you can refinance to a 9% mortgage with $1,500 in assorted expenses, it will take you 21 months before you start saving. Some lenders, however, levy no points or closing costs to refinance but charge an interest rate that is one point higher than if you had paid the points up front. With a no-closing-cost, no-point loan, you break even immediately as long as your new rate is lower than your old one.

Shop the deals offered by a half dozen or so lenders before applying for a mortgage refinance. Be sure to check with the lender who holds your current mortgage. The firm may be willing to waive some of the closing costs to keep your business.

Shopping for a Home-Equity Loan or Credit Line

Home-equity loans (or **second mortgages**) and **home-equity lines of credit** let you borrow against the value of the equity you've accrued. They're hot—with rates that easily consign such rival sources of cash as credit cards to their rightful place in credit inferno. Factor in the deductibility of home-equity interest payments on loans up to $100,000 and the deal gets even better. To figure the after-tax cost of a home-equity loan, subtract your marginal tax rate from 1 (to find your tax rate, see Chapter 4); multiply the result by the loan's interest rate. So for someone in the 28% bracket, the after-tax rate on an 11% home-equity loan is 7.9% (0.72 x 11%).

A home-equity loan can be taken all at once; a credit line lets you draw against it over time. With both home-equity lines and loans, the maximum amount you can borrow depends on the value of your home, as determined by the lender's appraisal. You frequently can borrow as much as 75% to 80% of the house's value, minus the balance on your mortgage. You must typically repay a lump-sum loan within 10 to 20 years. Credit lines generally must be paid off within two to 15 years. Just remember: If you default, you could lose your home.

Home-equity loans can have either fixed rates (typically about the prime rate) or variable rates. Home-equity credit lines generally have interest rates that fluctuate monthly. In most cases, the variable-rate loans and lines are set at 1.5 to 2 percentage points above prime. When shopping for a variable-rate home-equity deal, look for interest rate caps that will prevent the rate from rising more than two percentage points annually and five or six points over the life of the loan.

Which is better, a home-equity loan or a line? Go with a line if you'll be using the debt for recurring expenses like a child's college tuition or if you're not sure how much you'll need to borrow. Just avoid borrowing more money than you can pay back in three to four years—a hedge against an unexpected zoom in interest rates. A fixed-rate loan is best if you don't want to be faced with the prospect of rising payments due to rising rates.

These days it's fairly easy to find a lender willing to waive part or all of a home-equity's up-front points and fees, saving you $200 to $1,500 in closing costs. But beware: Some lenders are pushing home-equity loans hard, with deceptive come-ons or exorbitant costs. Don't sign up unless you clearly understand the loan agreement.

For example, be sure your monthly payments will cover a portion of both your loan's interest and principal. Some home-equity loans look inexpensive because you pay only the interest each month. Their true cost is clear, however, when the loan is due and you must come up with the balance to pay off the principal.

Reserve your home-equity debt for big-ticket bills such as college tuition or home renovation. Indeed, home-equity loans and lines now are the most common form of borrowing to finance a college education, according to the Student Loan Marketing Association. Nearly 40% of borrowing for educational purposes was through home-equity lines and loans, accounting for a full $2.4 billion in debt in 1994.

Believe it or not, a growing number of banks are encouraging their customers to use home-equity loans to cover ordinary expenses. Many lenders now issue credit cards that let cardholders draw on the equity in their home, even permitting customers to draw on their home equity via their ATMs. Prudence argues against using these cards. If you're determined to play with them, however, follow these two tips:

■ **Shun any home-equity deal that can sap all—or even more than all—your equity.** A home-equity loan or line that lets you borrow more than 80% of the value of your home minus outstanding debt carries a big potential pitfall: Should home prices fall and you wish to sell, you might have to come up with more money than you can get from the sale to repay the mortgage and home-equity debt. Today, some lenders even let you borrow as much as 25% more than your home is worth.

■ **Don't borrow more than $100,000.** Interest is deductible on home-equity loans over $100,000 only if the money is used for home improvements, business expenses, and income-generating investments. If you use your cards for other purchases beyond the $100,000 limit, you won't get any tax breaks.

Shopping for a Personal Loan

A personal loan from a bank, S&L, or credit union is about the most expensive way you can borrow, short of a cash advance on a credit card or going to a loan shark. Typically, such **unsecured personal debt**—so named because the loans are not backed by an asset such as a home or a car—comes in the form of a loan with a term of one to five years or a line of credit that you draw upon as you need it. Personal loans come with a rate that is typically pegged to the prime rate—*way* above the prime rate. The average rate at banks and S&Ls recently: 17.75%, or 10

percentage points above prime. Typically, credit unions have the lowest rates on unsecured personal loans.

Paying Off Student Loans

One of the biggest debt albatrosses around is surely the student loan. Fortunately, there are ways to lower the cost of paying off your student loan forever. Many banks, credit unions, and the Student Loan Marketing Association (800-643-0040) offer debt consolidation plans. You can also call the U.S. Department of Education (800-455-5889) for information about its direct loan consolidation program. This arrangement lets you merge all your school loans into one loan at one interest rate—recently 7.43%. That interest rate can fluctuate but cannot exceed 8.25%. You can choose from four repayment options:

1. The standard plan, which requires you to repay the loan over 10 years.
2. The extended plan, which lets you make lower monthly payments by giving you 12 to 30 years to pay off the loan. Of course, by extending the loan, you wind up paying more in interest. That's why this option is really best only if you have no other way to pay back your loan. If

you go with the extended option and your income rises, tell the government you want to switch and shorten your loan's term.

3. The graduated plan, which lets you start out making low payments that rise every two years. You can pay off this loan in 12 to 30 years. It's a worthy choice for young doctors, lawyers, and anyone else who feels pretty sure that his or her income will climb.

4. The income contingent plan, which lets your payments go up or down along with your income. You pay off the loan in 12 to 25 years. Consider this deal if your income fluctuates a lot from year to year.

Sources of Emergency Cash

If you're in a bind and need to borrow cash fast, check out the following:

■ **Retirement plans at work.** The tax law prohibits withdrawals from 401(k)-type plans except in narrowly defined emergencies. However, most employers will let you borrow from your 401(k), 403(b), profit-sharing, or thrift plan. The interest is not deductible, however. These loans generally have a maximum term of five years (sometimes up to 10 years if you use the funds to buy or renovate your home), a rate that is often as low as the prime rate or prime plus one percentage point, and a fixed-repayment schedule through payroll deduction. The most you can borrow is 50% of your account's value, up to $50,000. You usually can get your loan in a matter of days, and you won't be subjected to a credit check.

One of the seeming advantages of borrowing this way is that you are paying interest to yourself on the amount that you borrow. In other words, the interest you pay goes right back into your plan's account. In truth, however, that's not as terrific as it seems. After all, the money in your account would be growing tax-deferred along with its investments if you didn't take it out for a loan. One clear drawback with these loans: If you're fired or quit your job and have an outstanding balance on one, you will have to repay it quickly. Otherwise you'll owe taxes on the amount still due plus a 10% early withdrawal penalty if you're younger than age 59½. The bottom line: Don't borrow against your 401(k) or other employer plan until you've exhausted other alternatives such as student loans and home-equity loans.

■ **Margin loans.** Getting this kind of loan from your stockbroker by putting up stocks, bonds, and mutual funds as collateral is fairly popular these days. That's understandable, considering that a margin loan lets you borrow at a rate near or below prime; the rate is roughly the same as the home-equity rate. When you take out a margin loan, the interest you owe accumulates in your account, so you can repay whenever you want or wait until you sell the securities you've put up as collateral.

Before you call your broker for a loan, make sure you understand these three main drawbacks:

1. Interest on margin loans is tax-deductible—but only if you invest the dough and not if you borrow to buy tax-free bonds or muni bond funds. There is another tax limitation. You can generally deduct margin interest only up to the amount of interest and dividend income you receive in a year.
2. Your broker may have to sell your securities. If the value of your stocks and bonds drops, you can get a **margin call** requiring you to put up more cash or securities as collateral. If you don't ante up, the broker may have to sell some of your investments to reduce your balance. To play it safe, avoid borrowing more than 20% of your portfolio.
3. A margin loan creates leverage, making your investments riskier. Borrowing to buy stocks and bonds magnifies your losses if the value of your securities declines.

■ **Cash-value life insurance loans.** Borrowing against your life insurance policy can sometimes provide easy money at low rates. But pay it back quickly or you will diminish the value of the policy for your survivors. That's because if you die with a loan outstanding, the death benefit of your policy will be reduced by the loan's balance.

If you bought your life insurance policy during the 1960s or before, you might be able to secure a loan against its cash value for a rate as low as 4.5%. If you purchased your policy more recently, you'll probably pay around 8% or a floating rate that is roughly prime plus one percentage point. Actually, the true cost of borrowing against your cash value is usually slightly higher since the portion of the cash value you have borrowed against will grow more slowly than if you had left the money in your policy. Your agent or a company representative should be able to figure out your true borrowing cost.

Seven Ways to Be a Smart Borrower

Now that you're familiar with the borrowing basics, you're ready to follow these seven strategies:

1. Borrow for long-term goals, not short-term pleasures. Try to take out loans only for purchases that will pay long-term returns, like a house, a home remodeling, a college education, or a car, and not for a better wardrobe or a European vacation. One useful rule of thumb: Never take out a loan that will last longer than what you're buying.

2. Apply for the shortest-term loan you can afford. Stretch to make the larger monthly payments that come with shortening a loan's term. By doing so, you'll pay less in interest over the life of the loan. Consider your choices for a $20,000 car loan at 9.5%. If you select a five-year loan, you'd pay just $420 a month but spend $5,200 on interest, bringing your total payments to $25,200. Opt for a three-year term, however, and although your monthly payments would rise to about $640, you'd pay just $3,060 in total interest or $23,060 in total over three years. By biting the bullet and taking on the higher monthly payment, you could save $2,140 in interest costs.

3. Pay as much as you can up front. When you finance a purchase, put down as much as you can—and don't go by lenders' guidelines. Double or triple the minimum down payment the lender demands, if possible. If you can make one or two large payments during the loan's first months without incurring a prepayment penalty, do it. This strategy, known as front-loading, can shave months off your loan.

4. Consolidate high-rate credit-card debts with a lower-rate card or home-equity loan. If you carry a balance on several credit cards, you may be able to merge them into one balance on a single low-rate card. Many credit cards will send you a balance transfer form or so-called convenience checks that you can use to pay off your balances on other cards. Be sure to ask your issuer to describe its terms on a balance transfer first: some treat transfers as cash advances and thus may impose a transaction fee of up to $10 or charge higher interest on the amount you transfer. If your debt is large enough and the rate is low enough, however, you can still come out ahead. For example, if you transfer your $5,000 balance from a card that charges 18% interest to a card that charges 13% interest, you could save $125 in interest over just the first six months.

Another option is to scoop up debts into a home-equity loan, assuming you're a homeowner. Say you're in the 28% federal income tax bracket and transfer $10,000 from credit cards that charge 18% interest into a 9% home-equity loan. You'll save about $2,700 in interest payments over five years, plus another $750 or so in federal income taxes, since the home-equity interest is tax-deductible.

5. Shop around for the best borrowing deal. The most recent issue of

MONEY or perhaps your local newspaper are good places to start. You can find lists of the best credit cards, as well as the best deals on mortgages, home-equity loans, and car loans in your area.

Be sure to call at least half a dozen lenders before taking out a new loan. Two options you should always check out: credit unions and the bank where you have your savings. On average, credit unions offer loan rates that are one to 2.5 percentage points lower than those available at banks and S&Ls. What's more, they have become increasingly flexible about their membership; call the Credit Union National Association (800-358-5710) to find out if there is one in your area that you can join. Also, ask a loan officer where you keep your checking and savings accounts whether depositors get special breaks on loans. You can sometimes get a quarter-point discount on the interest rate by having payments deducted automatically from your account each month.

6. Review your credit report before applying for a loan. Credit-reporting agencies keep data on your debt payment history and the amount of credit you already have. They then sell this information to lenders, merchants, and other credit issuers, who use it to target you as a potential borrower and to decide whether to grant you more credit. You can get a copy of your credit report by calling each of the major agencies: Exper-

ian (800-353-0809), Trans Union (800-680-7293), and Equifax (800-556-1111). Equifax and Trans Union charge about $8 for the reports, and Experian will send you one free copy each year. If you have been denied credit, a credit bureau must give you a free copy of your report.

7. Negotiate rates and fees. Though lenders don't like to admit it, with a little arm twisting many today will cut their credit-card interest rates and fees, as well as lower costs on all kinds of loans. You can score potential savings simply by asking for a better deal and, if necessary, threatening to take your business elsewhere.

Recently, a team of 28 **MONEY** reporters (who didn't identify themselves as such) with MasterCards, Visas, or Discover cards called their card's issuing bank and asked for better terms. Result: Of the 38 banks called (some reporters owned more than one card and called more than one bank), 84% waived their annual fee, lowered their interest rate, or did both. As an example of the difference that dialing for dollars can make, Signet Bank responded to one reporter's call by ditching the $18 fee on her MasterCard and lowering her 19.8% interest rate to a reasonable 13.9%.

You can also save beaucoup bucks by asking lenders for lower interest rates and fees on car loans, home-equity loans, and mortgages. Most banks have an official rate for each type of loan they make. But if you are an existing customer or have a good credit rating, it's not difficult to convince the bank to lend to you at a lower rate.

How can you cut yourself such a deal? First, get a copy of your credit report two months before you plan to borrow money, so you can correct any errors before you meet with lenders. Second, compare rates and fees from a bunch of institutions and ask the two or three with the best deals to beat each other's offers. Finally, prepare to offer the lender something in return for its largesse: many banks will shave as much as a full percentage point off the interest rate on your car loan, for example, if you arrange to have your loan payments deducted automatically from your checking account.

What to Do When You've Been Turned Down

If you apply for a loan or a credit card and get turned down, demand a copy of your credit report from the three big credit bureaus: Equifax, Trans Union, and Experian. Carefully review your reports for mistakes. According to one recent survey, about 30% of would-be borrowers said they were denied credit because of an error in their credit reports, and close to half who checked their credit reports reported finding errors.

Here are some other common causes for credit rejection and how to avoid them:

■ **A recent move.** Credit-card issuers prefer people who have lived at the same address and had the same job for at least a year or two. Attach an explanatory note to your application if you've moved or changed jobs within the past two years.

■ **Too many credit inquiries.** Every time a lender checks your credit history, that inquiry shows up on your record. Trouble is, several recent inquiries—and shopping for a car loan might generate half a dozen—can make a credit-card issuer worry that you are about to take on too much debt. If you think your credit report will show more than five inquiries in the past six months, attach a letter that explains the reason.

■ **Too much debt.** Card issuers want evidence that you can handle credit, such as having made prompt payments for at least a year on one or two credit cards, store accounts, or car loans. You risk rejection, however, if you owe 80% of your credit limits on two or more cards or if you owe anything at all on four or more cards. This rule can snag credit-card gamers who transfer their balances from card to card in search of super-low rates. If you don't cancel your old accounts, you'll risk being hamstrung by credit overload when you apply for a loan or a new card.

Even people with pristine credit histories who pay their balances in full each month can be rejected because of a pocket full of plastic. Prospective lenders almost always scrutinize the amount of unsecured credit available to you as shown in your credit report. If they notice that you have, say, five credit cards with a credit limit of $5,000 each, they may be reluctant to lend to you.

When canceling a card, scissors don't cut it. You'll need to write or notify your card issuer and ask that it notify the credit bureaus that your account has been "in good standing and closed by the borrower." Insist, too, that the card company send you a copy of this letter.

Maybe there's a legitimate reason for your credit problems—a job loss or a serious illness, for instance. Then, send a letter of explanation to each credit bureau and let each know that those problems are behind you. This way, prospective creditors will be able to read that letter in your file, making them perhaps more understanding than they would have been.

If your credit-card issuers have taken away all your cards, apply for a secured card. This will help you establish your creditworthiness. You'll automatically qualify for the card, as long as you agree to keep a savings account with the card issuer and keep an amount equal to your credit line in the account. You are likely to find that after a year and a half of paying your secured card bills on time, you can switch to an unsecured card with a lower rate.

Credit Counseling and Bankruptcy

If you're unable to pay lenders on time, be up front with them. Tell your creditors what the problem is and the amount you think you can pay per month to get rid of the debts. Each creditor probably has repayment guidelines for customers in distress. So if you lose your job, for example, you might be able to negotiate a breathing spell that will temporarily cut monthly charge-card payments by 25%. Some lenders let you waive paying interest charges for up to six months if you can demonstrate that you'll have no problem paying your bills in full when that time is up. One other possibility: See if your lender will let you refinance your loan at a lower interest rate. It's a long shot, but your lender may go along if it appears that this move can prevent the institution from taking more drastic action against you and get some money back, too.

When a creditor refuses to negotiate further, seek outside help. Head for the nearest nonprofit **credit counseling service,** which you can find by calling the Consumer Credit Counseling Service (800-388-2227). A credit counselor will first review your debts and your ability to pay them, then set up a supervised payment plan. The initial consultation is often free. After that, you'll be charged according to your ability to pay. The average fee is $9 a month; some people aren't charged at all.

Credit counselors typically create a two-year or three-year schedule for liquidating your debts. Then they notify your lenders to get them off your back. Each month you write a check to the counseling agency for the specified payment amount, and counselors mail out separate checks to your creditors. About 60% of the people who go to CCCS for assistance find that within 3½ years, they've wiped their debt clean.

Do not confuse these legitimate counseling programs with so-called **credit repair services,** a/k/a credit doctors or credit clinics. These operators promise to remove adverse data from your credit report and even get you a credit card for a fee of as much as $500. Although some of these firms are legit, most charge excessive fees and do nothing that you can't do

yourself or with the help of a less expensive nonprofit counseling service.

If all else fails, you may have to file for **bankruptcy.** The time to weigh this desperate measure is when creditors threaten to seize part of your wages through a court process called **garnishment.** Bankruptcy stops creditors from hounding you by putting you under the protection of U.S. Bankruptcy Court. Of course bankruptcy has its price. First, you'll have to liquidate most of your assets, probably including your house if you have one. Then, a record of the bankruptcy will show up on your credit bureau files for as long as a decade. You may be sentenced to a long term of paying cash for practically everything. Getting a mortgage or a car loan is likely to be nearly impossible for seven years.

There are two forms of personal bankruptcy: the **wage-earner plan** and **straight bankruptcy.** Under the wage-earner plan, called **Chapter 13,** a court trustee supervises the full or partial repayment of your debts, usually over three to five years. Under a straight, or **Chapter 7,** bankruptcy, the court apportions most of your assets among creditors. Federal law, unless overruled by stricter state limits, lets you keep up to $7,500 of home equity, all household goods worth less than $200 apiece, $1,200 in auto equity, and $400 in other assets. Those amounts are doubled for couples filing jointly. In addition, creditors cannot touch life insurance policies or accrued pension benefits. By and large, the balance of your debts then gets wiped out. Some exceptions include alimony, child support, three years' back taxes, and some government-subsidized student loans. The trustee is supposed to sell the remaining assets and distribute the proceeds to creditors, keeping as his fee a percentage that varies with the assets' value—3% on amounts over $300,000, for example.

Today, 37 states have laws that supersede the federal bankruptcy code, while the remaining 13 (Connecticut, Hawaii, Massachusetts, Michigan, Minnesota, New Jersey, New Mexico, Pennsylvania, Rhode Island, Texas, Vermont, Washington, and Wisconsin) and the District of Columbia allow bankrupts to choose between state and federal rules. Some states make Uncle Sam seem downright parsimonious because they allow bankrupts to hang on to so much. For example, in Texas, bankrupts may retain up to 200 acres in a rural area plus any dwelling on the land. Florida exempts a principal residence of any value on as many as 160 acres outside of a municipality plus certain annuities, retirement benefit plans, and deferred compensation programs.

CHAPTER 7

Smart Strategies for Buying a House, Condo, or Co-op

Home ownership isn't merely the American dream, it's really the American way. More than 60 million Americans own their own homes, and nearly nine out of 10 persons who've yet to buy a home say attaining ownership status is their top financial goal. That ringing endorsement for owning a home is well founded. Beyond the personal satisfaction of owning your own property—which no one can really put a value on—there are two compelling financial reasons to own a home.

First, over long periods of five to 10 years, home values on average appreciate at a rate that has outpaced the annual inflation rate. While housing experts and economists don't expect rapid home price appreciation in the future, there is near

unanimous agreement that home values will continue to appreciate at a rate that at least matches inflation or exceeds it by a percentage point or so a year. In 1997 home prices rose 4% on average, while inflation increased by under 3%. Of course, what happens in your neighborhood depends on your local economy. During 1997, for instance, while home prices were going up by 4% on average, they were rising far more in certain places and falling elsewhere. Even when a few down years curtail or reverse house price appreciation, however, the trend over longer periods is that home values rise.

In addition to the fact that it's an asset that will grow in value, your home is the best tax deduction you've got. That's because the federal government has (so far, at least) left intact the deductibility of mortgage interest, while it has gutted other write-offs such as interest paid on consumer loans and credit cards. Currently, homeowners can deduct 100% of their mortgage interest payments—up to a $1 million maximum—provided the loan is used to finance either a primary residence or a vacation home. Property taxes are also deductible. Your home can also be a source of tax-advantaged lending to yourself: as Chapter 6 explained in detail, you can use your equity in a home (the appraised value of the home minus the outstanding balance of the mortgage) as collateral to get a home-equity line or loan. Rates on these loans are generally five percentage points below what you would pay for a general personal loan, and the first $100,000 of interest is tax-deductible.

While the financial and personal reasons for owning your own home are no doubt compelling, it is critical for any potential home buyer—whether a first-timer or a repeat buyer—to develop an astute strategy. The main reason is pretty simple: Homes are expensive. According to the National Association of Realtors, the median-priced home now costs $126,600; in high-priced metropolitan areas such as San Francisco and New York City, typical prices can be double that amount. Unless you plan on acquiring a stable of Ferraris, buying a home

will undoubtedly be the single biggest purchase of your life. What's more, with home prices likely to appreciate at an annual rate that matches or slightly exceeds the rate of inflation, generally 3% to 4% a year, if you overpay by 10% or more when you purchase your house, it will take at least a few years to recoup the cost of that misstep. Then, when you sell your home you may well pay a real estate sales commission of about 6%, which would work out to another two years' appreciation that you won't be able to pocket. So any chance of breaking even will probably take at least five years if you overpay and at least two years even if you pay a fair price.

To make sure you get the most house, condo, or co-op for your money, this chapter covers the rules and tools you need to construct a winning game plan. Follow this step-by-step guide to maneuvering through the home-buying process and you'll emerge with a place you love that's also a solid financial investment. One quick note to potential first-time buyers who haven't been able to save enough for the down payment on a home: Get smart! Flip back to Chapter 5 and read up on how to construct a painless savings plan. You'll be surprised how quickly you can amass the $10,000 or so you'll need for the down payment.

Renting Versus Buying

While owning a home is a wise financial move for the vast majority of Americans, there are a few scenarios where it is probably better to rent than own. For instance, if you plan on moving within three to five years, it's smarter to rent. That's because of the forecast of slow appreciation combined with the costs of selling a home. If you have the bad luck of buying right before your part of the country downshifts into an economic slowdown, home prices in your area could slide or stagnate for a couple of years. Once you add in the 8% or so cost of the real estate agent's sales commission and your moving expenses, you could easily be out by more than 10% if you try to sell your home a few years after moving in.

You might also consider renting rather than owning if rents in your community are too cheap to pass up. As a rule of thumb, consider being a tenant if the rent on a place you like equals about 65% or less of the monthly mortgage costs—including property taxes and homeowners insurance—that you would pay to own a comparable dwelling. You can run on your home computer a detailed analysis that compares the after-tax costs of owning and renting, using programs such as *Buying Your Home* from Home Equity

Software of Mountain View, Calif. ($49.95).

Keep in mind, however, that even though renting can cost less *now*, the long-term cost of renting could soon outstrip today's cost of a fixed-rate mortgage. For example, let's say you set out to purchase a house with a price tag at the national median of $126,600. At an 8.9% interest rate, a 30-year fixed-rate loan with a 10% down payment will cost about $680 a month. Annual property taxes and homeowners insurance would probably add up to about 3% of the purchase price. So in this example, your total monthly cost of home ownership would come to about $950. Remember, though, that you can deduct both the mortgage interest and your property taxes on your tax return. So for someone in the 31% federal tax bracket, the after-tax cost drops to $650. While the tax benefits will decline in the latter stages of your loan as your mortgage payments are earmarked to pay down more principal than interest, your property taxes will remain fully deductible.

Now consider what happens if you decided to rent at a cost of just $600 a month, including the annual premium for a renters insurance policy. That's $340 less a month out of pocket than if you had bought, and still about $50 cheaper on an after-tax basis. Unless you have a landlord who moonlights as an angel, however, the rent will undoubtedly rise.

Let's say the rent increases at a rate of 4% a year on average, which is about in line with the historical long-term rate of inflation. After five years the rent will hit $729, and in the 10th year you'll be forking over $888 a month to the landlord. In the 20th year your rent would be in the neighborhood of $1,315. Some expensive neighborhood! Now, remember that 30-year fixed-rate mortgage? It doesn't budge. So after 20 years you'd still be paying just $675 a month. Sure, your taxes and insurance premiums will probably increase. However, the bulk of your housing cost—the mortgage—won't rise one penny, and those property taxes will remain fully deductible (unless Congress changes the law). Most important, while you get nothing in return for your rent apart from the right to live there for another month, your mortgage payments are helping you build up equity and your net worth. Eventually you can tap that equity to take out a loan or, when you sell, either keep the cash or use it to buy a more expensive residence.

Of course, there are other costs of ownership that renters don't have to worry about, such as maintenance. Fortunately, major outlays that are actually improvements—say, replacing the heating system—can be added to the original price you paid for the home, thereby increasing what's known as your **cost basis**. That means when you sell the home, any taxable gain (your sales price minus your cost basis) will be lower than it would otherwise be. For a full description of the tax angles when you sell your home, turn to Chapter 8.

Scoping Out the Right Home for You

Everyone's heard that the key to a successful real estate deal is location, location, location. Even more important to home buyers is plan, plan, plan. Think of your job finding and buying a home as though you are an architect. The success of your project will come from all the time and effort you put into building and executing a solid strategy. Much of your important planning work should occur before you even meet a real estate agent.

The key to the home-buying process is knowing what you can afford to buy. More precisely, it's knowing what a mortgage lender *says* you can afford to buy. So the first step is to turn to Chapter 6 and read up on how lenders compute the amount of money they are willing to lend to you for a mortgage. You'll need to come up with quite a bit of cash just to get the loan—the down payment plus a bushelful of closing costs. When you get a mortgage, your lender will give you a helpful brochure called *Settlement Costs*, produced by the U.S. Department of Housing and Urban Development (HUD), that estimates the up-front costs you'll have to pay when you buy the home.

This is a good time to get your down payment squared away. You'll generally need to make a 10% down payment, though anything under 20% will require buying private mortgage insurance that, for homes in the $100,000 price range, can add $450 to your purchase cost plus a monthly premium charge of about $25. Some lenders will pay the premiums in return for a slightly higher interest rate.

If you have the down payment money stashed away, great. You may instead plan on supplementing your down payment savings with a gift from family members. In that case, ask them to transfer the money to you now, rather than waiting until you're ready to take out the loan. Here's why: Lenders won't give you the loan—or will give you only a smaller loan amount—if the bulk of your down payment is a gift or loan from your parents or in-laws. However, if that money is

deposited in your bank account months before you begin shopping for the mortgage, the lender will consider it as your personal asset, not a gift or loan.

You know what you can afford to buy. Now you need to determine what you want to get with that money. If you will be buying the house with a companion or spouse, you need to be sure you're both in agreement on what you're looking for in shelter. Equally important, you'll want to decide which items you would be willing to compromise on, since no home will have everything you want in exactly the way you dreamed it would. The following checklist will help you sort out your housing "needs" from your housing "prefers."

YOUR HOME-HUNTING CHECKLIST

Mark in the checklist below which are absolute necessities **(CRUCIAL)**, potential deal breakers **(IMPORTANT)**, ones you can be flexible about **(WOULD BE NICE)**, and ones you can pass on **(NOT IMPORTANT)**:

	CRUCIAL	IMPORTANT	WOULD BE NICE	NOT IMPORTANT
STYLE				
Spanking new				
Less than 50 years old				
More than 50 years old				
Colonial				
Split-level				
Ranch				
EXTERIOR				
Stucco				
Brick				
Wood				
Siding				
Yard				
Garden				
INTERIOR SPACE				
1 bedroom				
2 bedrooms				
3 bedrooms				
4 bedrooms				
More than 4 bedrooms				
1 full bathroom				
2 full bathrooms				
3 full bathrooms				
More than 3 bathrooms				
Master bed/bath				
Family room/den				
First-floor family room				
Eat-in kitchen				
Separate dining room				
Home-office space				

	CRUCIAL	IMPORTANT	WOULD BE NICE	NOT IMPORTANT
Attic basement storage				
Central air-conditioning				
Gas heat				
Oil heat				
Electric heat				
Fireplace				
More than 1 fireplace				
1-car garage				
2-car garage				
3-car garage				
LOCATION				
Neighborhood with children				
Can walk to school				
Can walk to town				
Can walk to transportation				

Once you've created your imaginary home in your mind, you next want to research the local housing market. A real estate agent will certainly be able to help you understand the market (more about agents in a moment), but there's no substitute for doing your own legwork. It will give you firsthand knowledge of what's happening in your area. Plus, when you are ready to hook up with an agent, your market knowledge will prove that you mean business and will let you get a quick lead on whether the agent's pitch about market conditions sounds accurate.

If you are moving to a new and unfamiliar area, head to the library of the town (or towns) you are interested in. Almost every local paper will have a real estate section where you can get an idea of recent sales. In addition to listing the sales prices of recent home deals, many newspapers also list how long the homes were on the market and the owners' original asking price. Quite often you will also find a small table that lists the typical or average sales price from a year or two ago. If not, create your own time-line going back a year or so and track the typical monthly sales price, the original asking price, and how long the home was on the market. This will help you get a feel for whether homes are selling quickly at a price very close to the asking price (a hot housing market) or if they are sitting on the market for more than, say, three months and selling for more than 10% below the asking price (a cold housing market). If the local paper does not furnish this information, call the local Board of Realtors; many publish a monthly or quarterly report on market activity.

While you are at the library, check out the recent economic activity in the area. Specifically, you want to know if the local job growth rate is rising or falling. A handy guideline: If the rate of growth has fallen by more than 50% in one year—say, from 2% to 1%—home prices are likely to remain stagnant in the near future. Where there is no job growth—that is, the rate has turned negative—prices are likely to decline. Conversely, if the job growth rate is increasing, you can expect home prices to follow suit. You can find job growth statistics for nearly 300 metropolitan areas in *Employment and Earnings*, a monthly publication of the U.S. Bureau of Labor Statistics.

Even if an area has strong job growth, be mindful if most of that growth is in one industry or if the entire economic base of the region is dependent on one industry. If the fortunes of that industry decline, the local economy can be devastated. Most recently that's been painfully clear in places dependent on defense spending—spanning from Connecticut over to southern California—where post–cold war downsizing has devastated local economies and sent home prices plummeting 20% from their levels in the mid-1980s. In the 1970s the Oil Patch region, including Texas and Oklahoma, saw home prices plummet along with the fall in oil prices. If you are moving to a one-industry town, try to ascertain the prospects for that industry. The research librarian can surely help you collect recent articles on the region's economic future. You can also check forecasts for housing price appreciation across the country published in **MONEY** and *USA Today*.

Working with a Top-Notch Real Estate Agent

Now it's time to hire a real estate agent to help you on your hunt—probably. While there's no law that says you must work with a real estate pro, you will almost certainly put yourself at a disadvantage if you try to house hunt on your own. True, you could go on your own from house to house advertised in the paper. You might even subscribe to an on-line computer service that can direct you to homes for sale in your area. By going solo, however, you won't have access to the **Multiple Listing Service (MLS),** a compendium of all the homes in a local region that are for sale. Bypassing the MLS means missing out on the majority of homes that are for sale, since only a small fraction of them are listed in the newspaper.

A real estate agent is also a great time-saver: it's up to her (generally it is a "her") to make all the arrangements with the seller and the seller's agent for you to visit a home. Plus, a savvy real estate pro provides valuable advice on the attributes and drawbacks of certain neighborhoods (the schools aren't so hot; it's a quiet complex; traffic is a problem . . .), as well as information on recent market sales. Finally, a real estate agent can help you determine both how much home you can afford and which mortgage lender to use. Increasingly, real estate brokers are hooking up to computerized services that let them scan mortgage terms of a variety of lenders in the area. A brief clarification about job titles: Don't feel that you have to work with someone called a real estate "broker." The broker's employees—associate brokers or sales agents—are fine, as long as you are working with someone motivated and knowledgeable.

Finding the best real estate agent takes a bit of work. If you have friends who live in the area you're moving to, ask them for names of agents they or their friends have used. When you don't know anyone in the area, a trip to the library again will be helpful. You can check out recent advertisements and announcements of home sales in the newspaper to give you a lead on the names of the locally productive agents. If the newspaper lists only the name of the brokerage firm that handled the sale, call the firm and make an appointment to meet with the head of the office to discuss which employee is suited to your needs.

Meet with several agents or brokers and ask the following four questions to size them up:

1. Do you work at this job full-time? Your main job is finding out how dedicated the agent will be in finding you a home. Sure, that Broker of the Year plaque on the office wall looks impressive, but is it from 1997 or 1977? You want someone hungry and aggressive who is willing to push for you. If she has recently scaled back and now works just a few days a week, she's probably not the agent you want.

2. How many homes have you listed and sold in the past year? There's no magic number here, but once you interview a few agents, you'll get a pretty good idea which ones are the pluggers and which are the plodders.

3. Which neighborhoods or towns or what price ranges of homes do you

work in primarily? Real estate agents tend to specialize in particular places or types of homes. You want to find an agent who really knows the landscape in the area you're searching. If you want to live in East Platte and she says she really knows Platte, North Platte, and South Platte, keep on looking. It's also important to find an agent who specializes in homes within your price range. If you want a home costing about $150,000, you won't get much attention from an agent who specializes in luxury homes in the $500,000-and-up price category.

4. How long have you lived in the area? Newcomers aren't necessarily bad—they often are the most motivated—but if you are new to an area, you're probably best off working with an agent who can really give you the inside poop.

Theoretically you can work with as many agents as you want, but give serious thought to working with just one. If your agent knows you are working with other agents, she is probably going to lose a bit of enthusiasm in working with you since there's a good chance you won't be buying the house with her assistance. So tell one agent that you are willing to work just with her, and because of your fidelity you expect her to make your house hunt a priority. Of course, if you are unsatisfied with your agent after a few weeks, you can then branch out to your second and third choices.

No matter how much you like your agent—and she you—don't forget this is a business deal. And guess what? Real estate agents work for the seller, not you. After all, that's who pays the agent. Here's how the real estate brokerage compensation system works: The seller pays a percentage of the sales price, typically 6%, to his agent, who then shares that commission with the agent who was working with you, the buyer. You aren't going to pay the agent one penny, no matter how many hours the two of you work together. Because your agent's compensation will come from the seller, you've got a troubling conflict of interest when it comes to negotiating your asking price. If you bid $100,000, but tell your agent you are really willing to pay as much as $115,000, the agent must tell the seller that you will go to $115,000. You'll learn more about this arrangement later in the chapter, but for now just keep in back of your head that your agent works for the seller, not you. At least most of the time . . .

Now here's the exception to that rule: There's a relatively new breed of real estate pro known as a **buyer's broker** who will work exclusively for the buyer, not the seller. While buyer brokerage is still a small part of the industry, it is a rapidly growing specialty. The big national real estate brokerage Re/Max recently had more than 2,500 of its agents complete a training course in buyer representation. You can find a buyer's broker by calling the National Association of Real Estate Buyer's Brokers (415-591-5446).

Hiring a so-called buyer's broker or broker's agent can be a smart move if you are house hunting in an unfamiliar area or if you don't have the time or initiative to look at many homes. A good buyer's broker ought to conduct extensive research that will help you be a sharp bidder and price negotiator. For example, a seller's broker will give you a list of recent comparable sales and sales prices in the area, but a buyer's broker will provide you with more important information, such as when the current owners bought the home and the price they paid. The buyer's broker will also spend time researching recent property tax issues. The seller may be paying just $2,000 a year in property taxes, but the buyer's broker can find out now how many years it's been since the house was assessed, when the next reevaluation will be, and what the effect might be on the house's taxes. That way you won't be unpleasantly surprised later to learn that the property taxes will jump to $6,000 when the home is sold and the tax assessor then reevaluates the home.

Because the sole fiduciary responsibility of the buyer's broker is to you and not the seller, you can also expect to have some frank discussions on the pros and cons of one home versus another or one neighborhood over another. Agents who work for sellers often are extremely discreet. Finally, buyer's brokers can be a

godsend for folks who loathe negotiating; they can literally do all your bidding and negotiating. You can also arrange for the broker to help you shop for a mortgage and your homeowners insurance.

Of course, there's a catch: Unlike other buyers who work with real estate brokers, you'll need to pay for this service. Even after paying the buyer's broker, however, your net cost to buy a home may wind up lower than if you opted for the traditional arrangement where the agent works for the seller. That's possible because the buyer's broker should be able to negotiate a lower sales price than if you did the negotiating yourself. In fact, one national firm found that when it used buyer's brokers to assist more than 250 of its relocating employees, the brokers nailed down sales prices that were generally 9% below the initial offer price, compared with a typical 4% discount for buyers who worked with seller's agents. In dollar terms that's a saving of $7,500 on a house listed at $150,000.

Unfortunately, there's no industry standard for how buyer's brokers get paid, so you'll have to discuss the particulars of your arrangement with the brokers you interview. If you can, try to strike a compensation agreement in which you'll pay the buyer's broker a commission equal to 2% to 3% of your *target* price range. This will let you sidestep one major potential conflict of interest: If the buyer's broker is going to be paid a percentage of the final sale price, it raises a reasonable question whether he is sufficiently motivated to negotiate a lower price for you. By agreeing to a commission based on a target range, you are essentially agreeing up front what the broker's fee will be regardless of the exact price of the home you eventually buy.

Say you're looking for homes in the price vicinity of $100,000 to $130,000. The average of that range is $115,000; so you agree that you will pay the broker a 3% commission of $3,450 when you buy your house. Sound high? It isn't really. Assume that the buyer's broker can get you a price that's at least 5% lower than what you could do on your own. In that case, you would save about $6,000 on a house listed at $120,000. So even after paying your buyer, you will still come out ahead. Be skeptical if the buyer's broker insists on being paid a percentage of the final sale price. Ask for at least three recent clients you can speak with to see if they were pleased with the agent's service and the compensation agreement. These referrals will help you know if the buyer's agent is a pro you'll want.

Home buyers who want negotiating help and nothing more might consider hiring a buyer's broker on an hourly basis. Figure on paying between $60 and $125 per hour. Make sure your real estate agreement includes an upper limit on how much you will ultimately pay. You can arrange for a cap that is equal to 2%

or 3% of the sale price or set a specific dollar limit.

To find a competent buyer's broker, nothing beats a word-of-mouth referral. Otherwise call the local Board of Realtors and ask if they have a list of local agents who either work part-time or exclusively as buyer reps. If you strike out this way, check the local Yellow Pages for listings of buyer agents. You'll want to interview several buyer's brokers to find the right one for you, just as you would with a traditional broker.

Once you choose a buyer's broker, give her a reasonable period of time to help you; an agreement that covers two to three months is sufficient. Don't sign an **exclusive rights agreement,** forcing you to pay the agent an agreed-upon fee or commission even if she doesn't help you find the house you eventually buy. Instead, ask for an **open agreement,** in which you'll pay the agent only if she helps you land the house.

Add a Lawyer to Your Home-Buying Team

In most parts of the country, you've got one last job before you start to actually look for homes: hire a lawyer. You'll want the lawyer to make any necessary changes to the real estate purchase contract and help you through the closing process, to be sure all the legal mumbo-jumbo is completed. Once again, word of mouth is the best way to shop. In addition to checking with friends, your agent will surely have names of two or three local lawyers who either specialize in residential real estate transactions or spend a sizable amount of time working on these deals. Be sure to stick with a lawyer who knows local real estate customs and has experience in reviewing and drawing up real estate contracts. While your cousin Ned's brother-in-law may be a terrific lawyer, he isn't going to be all that helpful if he specializes in corporate takeovers.

You'll want to meet with the lawyer now—or at least have a short phone conversation—to tell him you're about to launch into a house hunt and that you expect you'll need his assistance sometime within the next few months. By taking this step early, you'll ensure quick access to your lawyer when you're ready to make a bid on a home. If you wait until that point to find a lawyer to review your offer to purchase, you will waste a crucial day or two—which could mean losing out to another more organized bidder. Plan on paying the lawyer an hourly fee of anywhere from $75 to $200. Depending on where you live and the complexity of your contract, the lawyer's

charge could run between $500 and $1,500 or so.

Shopping for Your Home (Finally!)

Now on to the real job: finding your future house, condo, or co-op. There are always homes on the market, so you can house hunt any time of the year. If you can be flexible, though, consider shopping during the off-season; that's wintertime in many parts of the country. (The most active house-buying season is typically spring.) By shopping during the off-season, chances are you'll find an agent who isn't very busy and can devote plenty of time to you. You also might have the good luck to be the only interested buyer a home seller has seen in weeks—or months. While that doesn't mean the seller will be desperate, you may find he's quite amenable to negotiations.

No matter how good a memory you've got, after a few hours of house hunting, you'll be hard-pressed to remember if the master bedroom with the skylight and Jacuzzi was in the three-bedroom contemporary ranch or in the 75-year-old farmhouse with the new addition. To help you keep it all straight, bring along a camera. Ideally you want to pack a Polaroid so you can make any notations right on the back of the photo. You might instead want to bring along a camcorder. The idea is to have a record of what you saw so you'll have a visual reference later on when reviewing all your potential future homes. An etiquette tip: Make sure you ask the agent to check if the homeowners object to having you take a few shots.

You will also need a notebook to mark down any particulars of the house. While your agent should give you an information sheet on the house that includes the price the owners are asking, the lot size, and a current property tax assessment, you'll want to jot down additional information. For example, if you're house hunting in the Northeast, you'll no doubt want to find out what the typical monthly heating bill is in the winter. In southern states you'll need to know how much air-conditioning adds to the electric bill during the sultry months.

You'll also want to bring along your poker face. The goal, after all, is to negotiate the best deal you can get. So even if you've just walked into your dream house and your heart is pumping, look as dispassionate as possible. One item you want to leave at home: the kids. Regardless of how well behaved or cute they are, house hunting is serious business; you want to spend all your time checking out the house, not chasing after your kid.

While surveying a house, see if you can get any information from the agent—or the homeowners if they're present—about why the home is on the market. If it's part of an estate sale or if the owners have to move across the country to a new job in a month, you may be dealing with a very motivated seller. That could mean a steal for you. Or your antennae might pick up that the sellers have been living in the house for 20-odd years. If that's the case, they're probably in the position of selling the home for a lot more than they originally paid. A longtime owner may not be as reticent to shave a few thousand dollars off the sales price as someone who moved in just a few years ago. The short-term owner will be hard-pressed to break even, given the modest appreciation rates and even price declines during the past few years in many regions. Ask the agent, too, if any appliances or furnishings are included in the sale price. Don't assume that, for example, the custom-built unit that houses all the electronics in the den is automatically part of the deal.

Try to limit your search to four houses a day. Otherwise you'll find yourself dazed, confused, and exhausted. Don't forget to check out the **For Sale by Owner (FSBO)** listings in the newspaper. In these instances the seller isn't using an agent. While you can find some great deals in so-called Fizbos, be sure to use a lawyer to handle the transaction. The seller may not have a clue about the way that the closing process is supposed to go.

Tips for New Home, Co-op, and Condo Shoppers

No doubt about it: new homes can be enticing. Not only is everything bright, shiny, and in great condition, but you can probably even get to customize the home. You can opt for the standard model home, or you might choose the builder's option to add skylights in the bedrooms or to finish the basement so it can be converted into a home office. It's essential, however, to make sure the builder has a reputation for doing quality work; these days builders sometimes cut corners to finish the jobs more quickly and build in more profit. Ask for the names of three buyers who moved into one of the builder's homes within the past three years or so. Talk to these homeowners about how well the builder finished the customizing work and if they have had any major problems with the structure since they moved in.

Be cautious about buying a home that's part of a large project still in its early development stages. If less than 50% or so of the development has been sold,

you run the risk of moving into a lemon: unless most of the homes in the development eventually sell, your home's value will have little chance of appreciating. Plus, many developments advertise common areas, such as tennis courts or a swimming pool facility. These areas are typically the last part of a development to be completed, though. If the housing complex is not successful, the builder may never finish constructing the amenities that enticed you in the first place.

Value-conscious shoppers who are attracted to new homes shouldn't automatically give the cold shoulder to existing homes. According to the National Association of Home Builders, the median price for a new home is just over $130,000, somewhat more than the cost of the median-priced existing home. You'll also have a tough time negotiating price concessions with the builder. That tactic works best during economic recessions, when demand is low and builders are more inclined to bend a bit to get their homes sold.

Condominiums can be a terrific opportunity for first-time buyers or anyone shopping for a home in an expensive housing market, since condo prices are usually 15% to 20% below the cost of comparable single-family detached homes. Condos are either apartments or town houses; while each owner has absolute control over his own unit, all the condominium owners share some common areas. Each condominium owner must make a periodic payment—usually monthly—to cover common charges for the upkeep of areas such as hallways and lobbies and for maintenance of the roof and grounds.

If you're looking at a condo in a new development, make sure you do all the research mentioned above for new homes. One added risk is that you have no idea if the common charge is actually enough to cover costs or if the actual costs will cause a hike in the common charge. Home buyers looking at existing condo developments, however, can learn if the development has been able to maintain the property without frequently imposing big increases in the common charge. Ask your real estate agent to get information on the amount of the common charge for the past five years or so.

The best way to nail down value in a condominium is to concentrate on developments where most units serve as the primary residence for the owner, rather than as rental real estate investments. The live-in owners have a bigger stake in the upkeep and appreciation of their properties. Also, be wary about buying if the condo development is near an area where a number of new complexes are being constructed. Overbuilding means there could soon be more supply than demand, and that will make it extremely tough for condominium values to rise.

Cooperatives, or **co-ops,** are a rather small and arcane corner of the residential real estate world. Generally limited to New York City and a few other large metro areas, co-op apartments and town houses are essentially corporations where each owner of a unit within the building or development is a shareholder. All the shareholders wield veto control over the corporation's activities: you can't buy, sell, or rent a co-op unit without the approval of a co-op board. You'll be interviewed by the board before you buy, so use that experience as an opportunity to size up your neighbors. Will they let you rent out the unit if you later decide to move and have trouble selling? How many units have been for sale in each of the past few years? How long were they on the market? Did the board deny any prospective buyers—and if so, why?

In addition to getting a feel for your fellow shareholders, prospective co-op owners need to assess the financial strength of the corporation. That's because the co-op owns one collective mortgage; if the couple in apartment 3B misses two months of payments, the rest of the co-op's shareholders will need to cover the payments. Generally that comes out of the co-op's cash reserves. Your lawyer can help you determine the health of the co-op's reserves and find out whether shareholders have been hit with hefty special assessments to cover the cost of major repairs, such as replacing the heating system or roof.

What You Should Expect from the Seller

Will the seller tell you if something is wrong with his home? That all depends. Seller disclosure about significant defects in their homes is mandatory in 25 states: Alaska, California, Delaware, Hawaii, Idaho, Illinois, Indiana, Iowa, Kentucky, Maine, Maryland, Michigan, Mississippi, Nebraska, New Hampshire, Ohio, Oklahoma, Oregon, Rhode Island, South Dakota, Tennessee, Texas, Virginia, Washington, and West Virginia. While seller disclosure is voluntary in the other states, most real estate agents encourage—and even require—their clients to complete a disclosure form for prospective buyers. So in those states, always ask if there is a recently completed disclosure report; be wary of any prospective homeowner or agent who says no.

Typically, the seller-disclosure form includes a laundry list of all the operating systems and amenities in the home, including items such as the air conditioner, sump pump, intercom, rain gutter, and garbage disposal. The seller is required to report if he is *aware of* any significant defects or malfunctions in those items and must also note any problems with the electrical or plumbing systems. Where forms are mandatory, sellers must also let prospective buyers know of any environ-mental hazards, such as the existence of radon or lead paint in the house. Many disclosure forms also demand the seller report if he made any alterations or additions to the house without obtaining the proper permits.

While you will eventually hire a professional home inspector to assess the condition of any home you intend to buy, obtaining a seller-disclosure form is a helpful first step in learning the state of the house. The information on the form can also be useful during your negotiations; if you know ahead of time that there's asbestos in the basement, you may ask that your purchase be contingent on the asbestos being removed before you make a deal.

Making a Bid on a Home

Once you find the home you want, it's time to make a bid. If you are working with a buyer's broker, you'll get all the help you need in determining the best initial offer and overall negotiating strategy. However, if you are working with the seller's agent, you need to bear down and be a smart player. The seller's agent should give you data on at least three comparable homes that have sold within the past few months. You'll want to compare the original list price and final sales price of the homes. Then pull out the calculator and see the difference. If the final sales price is 5% lower than the asking price, you can make your bid at least 5% less than the asking price. In fact, you'll want to give yourself some negotiating room, so consider a bid that is 8% to 10% below the list price. It's essential, however, to be sure you're assessing the pace of recent home sales and prices. If homes are selling 5% below list today, but were selling 10% below a few months ago, that's a sign that the market is improving for sellers. Conversely, if homes that now sell at a 5% discount were selling right at their asking price a few months ago, that's a tip-off that the market is improving for buyers.

While you don't want to overpay for your home, you also want to avoid committing the big mistake of getting greedy and making a lowball bid. If homes are generally selling at 5% below list and you have determined that the house you want is fairly priced, offer 8% to 10% below the list price, not 20%. While you may think that a 20% bid is a smart opening salvo that will help you negotiate a lower price, the seller will more than likely interpret it as an insult—and may refuse to negotiate with you at all.

Once you choose the amount of your initial offer price, the agent will write up the **offer to purchase,** which your lawyer should review. In addition to the price, your offer will also include a closing date (generally 45 to 60 days from the time you and the seller agree to the deal), plus a few contingency clauses that your lawyer will work out with you. Typically, you want the deal to be contingent on (1) your obtaining a mortgage; (2) a home inspection that shows the house has no significant defects; and (3) a guarantee that you may conduct a walk-through inspection 24 hours before the official closing. Don't write down a specific date, since the actual closing date may need to be changed. This last clause is important: you want to make sure everything is up to snuff before you become the owner. If the sellers have already started packing and tore out a light fixture that created a gaping hole in the ceiling, you'll want to agree about repair costs before buying the house.

You'll also need to offer the seller a **good-faith deposit,** which is also known as **earnest money.** Basically you're making a deposit on the purchase of the house; the typical deposit amount ranges between 1% and 3% of the purchase price. Ask your agent or lawyer to deposit the earnest money in an escrow account; the seller will get the cash upon the successful completion of the deal. You don't want to test the good faith of the seller by giving him the check directly before any deal has been closed.

Negotiating with the Seller

If you use a real estate agent, she will pass along your initial bid to the seller. After that, you need to stay near a phone as the negotiation begins. Expect the seller to give the agent a counteroffer that will be somewhere between his original price and your bid. You can make a counter to his counter, but if his offer is what you had set in your mind as a fair price to pay, tell the agent you've got a deal. However, if it's still too steep a price, you can make a second bid.

By all means, consider other negotiating tactics. For instance, you could tell the seller you'll agree to his counteroffer if the washer and dryer are thrown into the deal. Be creative: if you learned during your house hunt that the sellers are having trouble finding their next house, tell them you're willing to delay the closing date for an additional month if the price comes down. The seller may want that extra breathing room enough to cut the sale price by the $2,000 you had been anticipating. Keep in mind that the amount of room you'll have to negotiate will depend a lot on the pace of your local housing market. You have far more leverage if homes aren't selling than if you're competing with other bidders for the same house.

After Your Offer Is Accepted

Once the seller has agreed to take your offer, you've got some more chores to take care of before he'll hand over the keys. Your biggest job is landing an acceptable mortgage. If you have a buyer's agent, you can enlist her help scouring local lenders for deals. Whether you use an agent or not, make sure you do some of your own legwork. The mortgage business has become extremely competitive, so lenders in the same town can offer very different deals. See Chapter 6 for advice on how to shop for the best deal.

To help you with your mortgage shopping, consider hiring a **mortgage broker** to do the searching for you. This expert is a kind of intermediary between lenders and consumers. The mortgage broker has access to many different lenders and their mortgages and will help find the kind of loan you want. If you haven't been in the mortgage market for a while, you might be thinking that mortgage brokers are just for desperate folks who get turned down at banks. Well, times have changed. Not only have mortgage brokers become lenders of first resort, they are now responsible for almost half of the 700,000 or so mortgages issued each month. Mortgage brokers can be especially helpful if you are not an ideal candidate for a loan—for instance, you can afford to make only a 5% down payment or you were out of work within the past year. In such cases a mortgage broker can help find you a lender who is willing to work with your unconventional situation.

You won't really pay more out of pocket by using a mortgage broker, since generally the mortgage he obtains for you will be a wholesale price that doesn't include origination fees and closing costs, which typically can add to up 2% of the loan amount. The broker makes his living by adding on such fees for his services. Using a broker makes financial sense as long as those fees will be less than what you would pay if you worked directly with a lender. Ask a lender to estimate loan origination costs for your situation and then compare those costs to what a mortgage broker says he will charge you. If you decide to use a mortgage broker, the only fees you need to pay up front are the $40 to $60 for a credit check and $150 to $300 for a house appraisal. All other fees should be paid once you have the loan and the broker's job is done.

To find a worthy mortgage broker, ask your agent or lawyer for recommendations; state licensing is pretty worthless. In addition to word of mouth, contact the National Association of Mortgage Brokers (706 E. Bell Rd., Phoenix, Ariz. 85022; 602-992-6181) for a list of mortgage brokers in your area. You're looking for a broker who can cast his net wide and let you select a loan from a variety of lenders. So when you interview several mortgage brokers, ask them how many mortgage lenders they deal with and the range of options available. You want to be sure that the broker doesn't have a sweetheart deal with one lender who'll wind up charging you a higher mortgage rate or fees than the competition. If you're really diligent, you'll also ask for three recent clients you can contact to see if they were satisfied with the broker's service.

You'll need to get a **homeowners insurance policy,** of course. Don't slough off this job. Buy a lemon and you'll be stuck without sufficient coverage to pay for costs of repairing or rebuilding your home in the event it is damaged or destroyed. (For details about shopping for the right homeowners policy, see Chapter 2.) Plan on spending between $400 and $1,000 a year for solid coverage. If you currently own a home, you obviously already have a relationship with an insurance agent. If not, ask your real estate agent, friends, or lawyer for recommendations. Some insurance agents represent just one insurer while others, called independent agents, can sell policies of different companies. The bottom line: You want your policy to be with an insurer on solid financial footing. The last thing you need is an insurance company that could be stretched beyond its financial limits.

Your lender will require you to pay for

a professional home appraisal to make sure the house is worth what you are paying (or, more to the point, the amount the lender is loaning you). In addition to the appraisal, you want to hire a professional **home inspector.** Again, your real estate agent or your lawyer can give you some names of local inspectors; so can friends who have bought homes in the area recently. Be sure to talk to clients of inspectors before you agree to hire one of these pros. The home inspection business is something of a racket; just about anyone can call himself an inspector, and just about anyone does. At the very least, work with an inspector who has been trained and certified according to the standards of the American Society of Home Inspectors. That's no guarantee that your inspector won't turn out to be an Inspector Clouseau, but it will help you weed out the fly-by-nighters.

The home inspection will cost about $200 and takes an hour or two to complete. Schedule the inspection so you can tag along; you'll be amazed what you can learn about the house. Not only will the inspector point out whether, say, the electrical system or gutter needs to be repaired or upgraded, but you'll also learn about the overall condition of the house and the quality of its construction materials. If you're new to the area, the inspector can recommend local contractors for future repair work. If the inspector discovers a major problem—like the gut-

ters need replacing—have your lawyer discuss the matter with the seller. You'll want the seller to either fix the problem before you move in or deduct the cost of the repair from the final sales price.

Closing on the Home

The actual process of taking possession of the house, condo, or co-op from the seller is a ritual with some regional differences. Some areas refer to it as settlement; others call it close of escrow. The players also vary. In some markets the lawyers handle the festivities, while escrow companies are in charge in other regions. Regardless of how it works in your neck of the woods—and your agent will tell you what's common if you are new to the area—all closings have the same outcome: the buyer takes possession of the deed to the house.

To get to this happy moment, you will first need to sign a slew of checks to cover all sorts of closing costs. At least 24 hours before the actual closing ceremonies, the lender will give you a final HUD Settlement Statement that will list all the charges you will be expected to pay at the closing. Review this statement carefully with your lawyer. The two big-ticket items in the statement will be the

loan origination fee and the **loan discount cost**—more commonly known as points. (For more information on points see Chapter 6.)

You'll also find a charge of $40 to $60 or so for a credit report and an **appraisal** charge of $150 to $300. Ask the lender for a copy of the appraisal. It contains detailed information on the particulars of your home's structure as well as the appraiser's evaluation of its market value based on comparable homes that have recently been sold. Since you pay for the appraisal, you are entitled to a copy. However, you may have to make the request in writing since some lenders don't like sharing this info.

Title insurance is another expense you'll incur. While your lawyer will conduct a title search to make sure no one else has a claim to your home or property, the lender will want to protect itself from any future title concerns by making you buy a policy that will protect you and the lender in case any questions arise in the future. Plan on paying about $200 for a policy on a $100,000 house.

The lender will probably also require you to establish an **escrow account** that it can tap if you fall behind on your mortgage and property tax payments. (If you're borrowing less than 80% of the home's value, the lender may let you get away without an escrow account. You'll have to ask for this waiver, though.) Thanks to regulations introduced by the

U.S. Department of Housing and Urban Development in late 1994, the lender can now ask for an escrow deposit that covers only two months' worth of payments. In the past, lenders made borrowers deposit up to six or even eight months of mortgage costs. The changes should cut the size of a typical new escrow account by as much as $250.

Make sure your up-front settlement fees don't include a charge for hazard insurance; your own insurance policy will cover that, so there's no reason to pay the lender. To avoid any confusion, ask the lender what specific documentation it will require at the closing to confirm that you have secured the necessary homeowners insurance.

Once you pay all the settlement charges—including a transfer tax and deed recording fee charged by the county or municipality—your lender will have you sign a bond or note that commits you to repaying your loan. Next the lender will have you sign the mortgage. Then the lender will write you a check for the amount of the loan (you'll be very rich for about 60 seconds), which you will quickly endorse and pass to the seller. Once the seller accepts the check, he'll hand over the deed to the house along with the keys. You now own your home. One last bit of work before you begin celebrating: Make sure whoever oversees the closing takes the deed to the county clerk's office to be recorded.

Taxes and Home Ownership

As mentioned earlier in the chapter, your home is a great tax haven. The biggest break is the deductibility of mortgage interest payments made for a primary or second home, up to a maximum of $1 million. At the end of each year, your lender or the mortgage service firm that handles your loan will send you Form 1098, which lists the amount of interest you paid for the year.

Uncle Sam also gives you a nice homewarming gift the year you buy your home: The points you pay on your mortgage are fully deductible, as long as you claim the deduction in the year you paid the points. If fact, even if the seller pays your points, you can deduct them. The same Form 1098 will include an accounting of your point costs. Other home-buying fees, including the cost of an appraisal, title insurance, attorney's fees, and transfer taxes, aren't deductible, but they'll save you on taxes in the future. You'll wind up adding them to the cost of your home, which will reduce any taxes you'll pay on the eventual gain after you sell the place someday.

The 1997 tax law also gave welcome relief to home sellers, especially those sitting on a lot of built-up appreciation. For home sales after May 7, 1997, you won't owe any taxes on gains of up to $250,000 if you're single or up to $500,000 if you're married and filing jointly. But you must have owned the home as your principal residence for two out of the last five years. You don't have to buy a new home to get this exclusion and—best of all—you can keep taking this exclusion as many times as you want so long as you meet the two-year ownership rule. If your home-sale profits top the exclusions—lucky you!—taxes will be due on the excess gain.

If you move to take a new job, you may be eligible for a handful of tax deductions available by filing IRS Form 3903. The general rule is that your new job must be full-time (at least 39 weeks in the first year, or 78 weeks over the first two years for self-employed individuals), and the job must have spurred a move that is at least 50 miles from your current home. If you meet those stipulations, go ahead and deduct the entire cost of moving your belongings and your family to the new house. You don't have to itemize to get these write-offs; they show up as an adjustment to income on your 1040 long form. One caveat: The cost of meals during your family's trek to the new home is no longer deductible, thanks to a 1994 change in the federal tax code.

Buying a Vacation Home

This could be an excellent time to buy a vacation home, if you can afford to do it. The aging baby boomer brigade is expected to spur strong demand for second homes within the next decade. That's because most boomers will be moving into their peak earning years, when they can begin to contemplate buying and owning a vacation home; the oldest boomers will be reaching their mid-50s when thoughts of retirement havens begin to form. Consequently, housing experts anticipate that values for vacation homes could rise sharply in the coming years. The last time boomers made a concerted housing move was during the mid- and late 1970s, when their rush for first homes set off a surge in residential real estate prices around the country. The growth in the number of telecommuting workers is also expected to buoy vacation home prices. Second homes once relegated to weekends are now increasingly used as offices one or two days a week, as computers and faxes make it possible to work away from the traditional office.

While the prospects for vacation home appreciation are strong, prospective second-home buyers need to be extremely careful when hunting for their Shangri-las. In addition to following the strategies outlined in this chapter and understanding the tax rules for vacation home owners (see Chapter 16), you'll increase your chances of landing a great second-home deal by following a few additional rules:

■ **Rent for at least one season before buying.** Get familiar with the area before committing to a home purchase there. While you're renting you can investigate different neighborhoods or sections of a development and decide where you would like to live.

■ **Shop during the off-season.** It's best to do your house hunting when the area isn't at the peak of popularity. You'll get more attention from agents during the off-season, when they aren't dealing with the usual deluge of in-season renters who are considering making a purchase. There's a good chance you'll get a better price in the off-season, too, since you'll be talking to sellers who won't have many prospects and will be more open to negotiating. You may also find it easier to be more businesslike during the off-season; shopping for a beach house when it's 30° and a storm is brewing off the coast is a lot different from house hunting when the area looks like a picture postcard.

■ **Make sure the vacation home is within three hours of a major city.** The demand for vacation homes near a major metropolis will likely remain strong, since there is a built-in pool of prospective buyers to tap into when you decide to sell. City folk will continue to clamor for getaways within weekend commuting distance. If you plan on renting the home, the same pool of urbanites will provide a strong supply of prospective tenants. The more remote the location, the harder it will be for you to find a buyer when you want to sell someday.

■ **Look for a two-, three-, or four-season home if you plan to rent out the place.** You can generate far more rental income if your vacation home is attractive to renters during different seasons. While a beach house may be ideal for summer, a home that attracts renters in two or more seasons will increase your rental opportunities.

■ **Plan on paying more for a vacation home mortgage.** Lenders get a bit nervous when offering mortgages for a second home. After all, if you run into financial trouble, chances are you'll unload your second home—and pay off the loan—before you consider selling your primary residence. So expect a hefty down payment requirement of at least 20%. You'll also be charged a mortgage interest rate that is as much as a quarter of a percentage point higher than if the mortgage was for a primary residence.

■ **Factor in all maintenance costs.** Many vacation home developments include a homeowners association that levies annual fees. Before you buy, find out what costs the association usually covers and ask for a five-year record of how the fee has increased. You may also need to hire a local contractor to keep an eye on the house during the seasons you're not using the property. Your real estate agent will be able to estimate the typical fees for this out-of-season service.

■ **Deal with the issue of homeowners insurance before you buy the house.** Make sure you understand the availability and cost of insurance for vacation homes in the area. This advice is especially important in areas where flood and storm damage are frequent threats. Talk to an insurance agent familiar with the area in advance of your house hunt. You'll get an idea of what typical premiums are for local vacation homes, and the agent may be able to tip you off to certain spots that are especially prone to flooding or storm damage. This crucial information will keep you from buying a property that could get clobbered—both by the elements and financially.

CHAPTER 8

How to Get the Most Out of Your House, Condo, or Co-op

House-itis. It can strike at any time, regardless of whether you moved into your home two years or two decades ago. There's just no predicting when a once happy homeowner suddenly gets that itch for a bigger, better, or just simply different home. Maybe it's the imminent arrival of (another) child that's got you contemplating adding on an extra room or moving to more spacious digs. Conversely, once all the kids have moved out (finally!), the house could simply seem too big. Or a job relocation could be the culprit. Alternatively, if you are now part of the growing contingent of work-at-home types, altering your quarters may be necessary to make room for office space.

In this chapter you'll get all the information you need to cure your house-itis.

First you'll see whether some remodeling or renovations might be the antidote to your house problems. If you plan to become one of the millions of homeowners who annually spend a total of more than $100 billion to upgrade their homes, you'll find advice on how to spend your remodeling money wisely. If you need to make a move, you'll learn how to make yourself a successful home seller. These days a smart sales strategy is crucial. With about three million homes on the market each year, there's plenty of competition among homeowners. So you need to equip yourself with the competitive edge that will distinguish your home from all the others.

Plus, in many regions of the country, home values have been stuck in pause—

or even jammed in reverse—in recent years. So if you bought your house within the past five years you could be faced with a rather depressing housing reality: even if your house will sell for the same price you paid, you'll still come out thousands of dollars in the red. That's because you'll probably end up spending about 8% or so of the sales price to cover the real estate agent's commission and the cost of physically moving your family and your stuff to the new home. Given that grim reality of real estate, it is imperative to get the most out of all your housing moves.

What to Know about Remodeling

Just because your current house doesn't provide all the room and amenities you and your family want doesn't necessarily mean you should move. For starters, there are plenty of compelling emotional and economic reasons to stay right where you are. Chances are you still really like the house—it's just that you need space. Maybe your parents are going to move in and to assure everyone's sanity you'd like to provide them with a bedroom and bathroom apart from the main living

quarters to give them and you enough privacy. Perhaps you have teenagers and would like a little breathing room in the house. Then there are the compelling economic reasons to stay ensconced where you are.

For instance, let's say you paid $110,000 for your home in 1989. Now, after the 1990–91 recession and corporate downsizing, your metropolitan area still isn't experiencing the type of economic growth necessary to spur home price increases. So you figure you would be lucky to get $105,000 if you tried to sell the house today. That's a 5% loss right there. Then you'll need to pay a commission of 6% to a real estate agent who sells the house. After spending another 2% or so of the sales price for moving costs, you'll be lucky to pocket $97,000. Even if you could put together enough money to cover the down payment on a new home, you could have a tough time qualifying for the new mortgage, thanks to rising interest rates.

Here's the deal: Let's assume you bought a new home or refinanced your existing mortgage of $100,000 in early 1997, and locked in a rate of 7.5% on a 30-year fixed-rate mortgage. The monthly payment on that loan works out to about $700 before taxes and insurance. Now, let's assume that the new house you've got your eye on is going to cost $150,000 and that you'll make a 10% down payment. In other words, you're facing a $135,000 mortgage. Even if interest rates hadn't budged an iota, your monthly mortgage cost on your new home would climb about $240, to $940 a month. But if rates have risen to, say, 9.8%, you'll be facing a rather ugly monthly mortgage payment of $1,165, which is two-thirds more than the cost of your current mortgage.

One final economic reality to face up to: You aren't the only one who finds today's high rates depressing. When interest rates rise sharply, more and more prospective home buyers are forced to put their housing plans on hold. So even if you are determined to make a move, you will have to deal with a dearth of prospective buyers. And when supply (of houses for sale) exceeds demand (prospective buyers), the supply side has to lower its price to entice the buyers to consider their commodity. Making a profit in such a buyer's market will be extremely tough.

So whether your reasons are emotional or economical, there are always plenty of reasons *not* to make a move. But that doesn't mean you must resign yourself to living in a house that no longer fits your lifestyle. You can renovate or remodel your existing home to better meet your current needs or create more space by building an addition.

If you're interested in remodeling, join the crowd. A nationwide poll found that less than 40% of homeowners are pleased with their current residences. Renovating and remodeling your home is one sure way to deal with that discontentment, but you'll make yourself disconsolate if you fail to approach the task with a well-thought-out plan—a financial blueprint, if you will.

Your first job is to be realistic. The day will eventually arrive when you or your heirs will want to sell the house. When this time comes, the goal will be to recoup as much of the cost of your renovation projects in the sale price of the home. That will be especially difficult if your previous remodeling and renovations have upgraded your house far beyond the value of other homes in your neighborhood. If you create a Tara in a Levittown neighborhood, there's little chance that a home shopper will be willing to pay you top dollar. After all, if the buyer is going to pay for Tara, he will no doubt expect to be living in a neighborhood with Taras all around.

As a general rule, then, you'll want to avoid upgrading your home to a level that exceeds the median price of neighborhood homes by 15% to 20%. Of course, there's no law against improving your house to make it the standout gem of the neighborhood. But just go into the project knowing that you can't expect to fully recoup the cost of the upgrade.

It's a good idea to understand the types of remodeling projects that tend to offer the best paybacks when you eventually sell your home. That may help you decide which type of project to undertake or which to do first. According to *Remodeling* magazine's annual survey, adding a bathroom and upgrading a kitchen offer the best payback potential. On average, homeowners are able to recoup about 98% of the cost of adding a second bathroom and 95% of renovating a kitchen when they sell their house. (These percentages assume you have a contractor to do the work and sell the home within a year of completing the job.) Adding a master bedroom and bath is also a high-payback undertaking, with an average recoup rate of 91%. And building a family room gets you 88% back, on average. But if your plan is to just build a deck, the payback rate will be about 72¢ for every dollar spent on the bathroom upgrade.

When you choose to remodel or renovate, you can tap into a rare tax break offered by Uncle Sam. To finance your project, you can borrow against the equity in your home and deduct 100% of the interest payments on this home-equity line or loan, up to a maximum value of $100,000. In today's competitive bank-lending environment, these loans are available at rates typically about one percentage point above the prime rate, which is well below the typical rates charged for personal loans. For details on how to shop for the best home-equity deal, see Chapter 6. An alternative way to finance the job is by taking out a loan against your 401(k) plan, if your employer offers this privilege. Typically, you can borrow up to half of your balance and pay back the loan into your own account over a period of up to five years or so. The interest rate is generally about one percentage point over the prime rate.

If you decide to remodel rather than move in a soft market, here's some really good news that will turn your half-empty glass to half full. When the home-buying market is so slow that it keeps you on the sidelines, it also means that home builders aren't feeling too great, either. So they've got plenty of time on their hands to handle your remodeling project. In fact, you'll find that the slow sales market translates into a competitive market for contractors. You'll get plenty of bids from top-rate contractors, and they won't dare tack on the 10% or so premiums they are known to add on when the home-building market is booming and folks are banging on their door for help. Plus, the slow market means that contractors can probably jump into your project right now rather than making you wait your turn for a few months.

Labor costs account for about two-thirds of the price of any renovation project. To reduce the bills for your remodeling job, you could do a lot of the work yourself, but that assumes you have both the expertise and time. Therefore you'll probably need to hire a professional contractor to do much of the work.

If you are working with an architect or designer, this pro can provide you with names of reliable contractors who've done a good job on other projects. Alternatively, you can check in with friends who have had work done that you admire. No matter how highly an architect or friend may recommend a general contractor, make sure you ask for additional references. You want to get a few different opinions on the quality of the contractor's work, how well he stuck to the timetable, and his willingness to repair or alter any parts of the project that didn't meet your expectations. You should also put in a call to the local Better Business Bureau or your local government's consumer affairs department to make sure there are no outstanding complaints against the contractor. For a large project, ask prospective contractors whether they have their own crew to perform all the jobs or whether subcontractors will be hired. If you will be dealing with subcontractors, you'll need to go see their work to check that it's also up to your standards.

Tell all the contractors that you will only consider written bids and that all bids must include a breakdown of all costs as well as a detailed description of the materials that will be used on the project. Once you have a bid, do not fall for any pressure tactics such as being told that this offer is good only for 48 hours. Simply tell the contractor that you will call him within a week. If you decide to accept the bid, all the specifics need to be spelled out in a written contract. Include the date when the project will begin, the materials that will be used, and what sort of guarantee the contractor will give on his work. A decent contractor should have no problem with a one-year guarantee.

You also need to work out a payment schedule and have it spelled out in the contract. This is the trickiest step. Pay too much up front and you may be left in the lurch. Pay nothing and you may never see him again. The ideal arrangement is to have as many payments as possible. If the project will last eight weeks, pay 20% at the end of every two weeks, with the stipulation that the final payment will not be made until 30 days after the work is completed. This will insure that the work *is* completed, and it also allows you some time to live with the new construction and see if any problems need to be ironed out. One final job before you sign the contract: Make sure the contractor has a workmen's compensation insurance policy that covers his employees, as well as a liability insurance policy to cover himself and his crew while they are on the job. Ask that a copy of these insurance policies be attached to the contract.

When You Want to Sell Your Home

You've decided that rather than fix up your house, you'd rather just move into a different one. Or you want to relocate for work. Although you can put your house up for sale any time of the year, if you're not in a terrific rush, try a bit of strategic timing. That is, put it on the market when you will be competing with a smaller pool of homes. In most regions of the country this means wintertime. Not only will you probably find agents clamoring to represent you, but any prospective buyers will give your home more attention than usual since it may be one of just a handful on the market. That's quite an advantage compared with the spring and summer markets, when dozens or even hundreds of homes are for sale.

Be prepared for your home to stay on the market for between three and six months. Of course this varies with market conditions. If there is plenty of buyer demand in your town and you have set a fair price (more on both later in the chapter), you'll probably be able to make a deal quickly. However, if sales are sluggish, you'll need to be patient. And strategic . . .

To sell your house wisely, you need to devise a strategy that takes into account the current market conditions, the competition from other seller wanna-bes, and the general economic outlook in your area. Get started on scripting your winning plan by spending some time studying the local newspaper. Keep an eye on the real estate section for a month or so to get a feel for prices in various neighborhoods. Many papers now print both the selling price and the original list price. Calculate the difference between the two and keep a ledger of the typical gap.

If you've got the time and initiative, head to the library and pull out the newspaper from six months and 12 months ago and do the same calculation. This will give you an idea of the trend of home sale prices—whether they are going up or down and if there is a pattern about how close the sales prices are to the original asking prices. All this data will be crucial to help you set the price for your home and even later when you begin negotiating with a potential buyer. For instance, if you found that most homes were selling at 10% below list price a year ago, but are now typically selling at list price or just 3% below list, that's a great sign for you. It indicates that sellers aren't having to take low bids from buyers. In other words, you are in the enviable position of putting your home on the market during a seller's market. Another positive sign: If homes were taking an average of, say, nine weeks to sell a year ago but now are on the market for less than six weeks, you've got more confirmation that sellers are gaining momentum. Conversely, if either the gap between list and sales prices or the time on market is getting larger, then you must prepare for a tough sales environment.

Before getting to the next logical step—hiring a real estate agent—it's worth discussing the most enticing but most misunderstood part of the home sale process: selling your home without professional assistance. Trying to go the **for sale by owner** (**FSBO** or, as it's sometimes called, **FIZBO**) route is no doubt attractive, since you'll avoid paying an agent's commission, which typically runs about 6% of the sale price of the home. With the median-priced existing home now selling for roughly $106,000, that commission works out to a hefty $6,360. And given that you are lucky if your housing market is appreciating at a 3% clip, the commission is essentially the equivalent of roughly two years' worth of appreciation.

Be careful, though. The FIZBO route can be a great example of being penny wise and pound foolish, especially in a slow housing market. Here's the big problem with going it alone when homes in your area aren't moving: At a time when others are struggling to get their homes sold, you would have a better shot of getting a lot of buyer attention if you have a

pro hustling for you. If you don't hire an agent, your home will not be included in the Multiple Listing Service (MLS) run by the local Board of Realtors. And that MLS is the single greatest marketing tool available to homeowners who want to become home sellers. All agents in a local area tap into this computerized listing of prospective homes to produce a roster of homes that fit the specifications of their home-buying clients. Shut yourself out of the MLS and making the sale can become one tough challenge.

Time is another major consideration. If you try to sell FIZBO, you'll need to spend time writing and placing ads in newspapers, screening all callers, and arranging times when you will be available to show the house. In today's world of two-income households, that's a lot to ask of yourself or your spouse. But if you think you have the time and gumption to pull off a FIZBO, make sure you position yourself as ideally as possible.

Your first job as a FIZBO is to hire a lawyer. This is crucial. Since you won't have a real estate agent helping you deal with bidding and contracts, you *need* a lawyer to represent you from the get-go. And just because you're going it on your own, don't slam the door or phone on any broker who inquires about the house. You haven't signed any listing agreement, so you have no financial obligation to the broker. Just listen to what the broker has to offer. It could be that she is working as a buyer's broker and being paid by the buyer, so you won't lose any money by having her show your house. Or you can just tell the broker that she is welcome to let her clients see your house, but that you have no intention of paying her one penny. Remember: If you ultimately find selling your home is too difficult, you may eventually want to hire one of the brokers you've met.

Any seller who tries FIZBO must work very hard to establish credibility with prospective buyers. So it's essential to establish that your price is fair. Hire an appraiser (cost: $250 or so) to get a fair value for your home. You will base your asking price on this appraisal and can also show the document to prospective buyers as proof that you are being reasonable.

Working with a Real Estate Agent

There are plenty of compelling reasons to hire a real estate agent and get professional assistance. Since hiring an agent is the only way to gain access to the Multiple Listing Service, you'll effectively open your home's doors to many more prospects. In addition to getting your house in the MLS, a skillful agent will provide a variety of other services, such as making sure that only financially qualified buyers are shown your home, helping you get the best price, and ushering you through the closing process.

The real estate agent's first job is to help you determine the price you will ask prospective buyers to pay. This is called the **original list price,** or **asking price.** To determine this price, the agent ought to present you with at least three recent sales in your area to show how long the homes were on the market, their original list price, and the final sales price for each. This market analysis will also include the agent's assessment of whether recent activity is improving or slowing down.

Agents are also responsible for placing ads in newspapers and local real estate inserts distributed at grocery stores and shopping malls. The agent may also arrange for one or more open houses, in which other agents will be invited to see your home before it goes on the market. This technique serves as a pre-market screening to generate enthusiasm among local real estate agents for the new listing. Prospective buyers who want to see your house will be filtered through your agent's office to make sure they have enough income to purchase your home. Your agent will also assist you during the negotiating process when you and the buyer try to work out a deal. Home buyers don't always remember, but you should: When a real estate agent shows your house to someone shopping for a home, the agent is working for *you* and trying to get you the best price.

Choosing the right real estate agent may be the most important decision you make when selling your home. If the agent who initially sold you the house is still in business and you were pleased with that deal, by all means ask the same agent to help you sell the house. The next-best idea: Ask for references from friends who've sold their homes recently. Otherwise, check the newspaper for firms that seem to be most prominent not just in advertising, but also in the listings of homes that have recently sold. Make an appointment with the head broker at a few of these agencies. Tell each broker your specific needs and then ask which agent in the office is best qualified to sell your house. Don't simply accept anyone who is offered up. You want to make sure the agent is successful and motivated. Ask how many sales the agent completed during the past year, whether the agent works full-time or part-time, and if the agent has expertise in selling homes in your price range. The idea here is pretty simple. You want an agent who has already proven to be quite successful at getting homes like yours sold. And don't be shy about asking the agent for a few references—then calling them.

Once you find an agent, the next step is to formalize your relationship by sign-ing a **listing agreement.** This document lays out the specifics of your arrangement, including how long you will let the agent represent you to prospective sellers as well as the amount of the agent's compensation when she engineers a sale. In most cases you will need to sign an **exclusive listing,** in which you agree that the agent will receive a commission regardless of whether she is actually responsible for finding the person who ultimately buys your house. The common commission fee for exclusive listings is 6% of the final sale price of the home. (Just so you know how this works: Your agent doesn't pocket the entire 6%; typically the agent's firm keeps 3%, and the other 3% belongs to the firm whose agent brought you your buyer.) The only time exclusives aren't required is when there is no MLS, which usually occurs only in rural areas. In these situations the buyer doesn't sign up with any one agent. Rather, all interested agents take a shot at making the sale, and the agent and the firm that get the deal done receive the entire commission. Because the real estate agent in a non-exclusive listing won't be splitting the commission, the seller using her should not agree to a commission above 3% or so.

When you sign on with an agent, be willing to commit to a three-month hitch, but no longer. If your house is still unsold after 90 days but you are pleased with the agent's efforts, you can simply renew the agreement. What you *don't* want is to be locked into a four-, five-, or six-month agreement and find out after the first two months that your agent isn't terribly motivated. Then you're stuck.

At the point when you and the agent are reviewing the listing agreement, ask about some peripheral issues. If you are uncomfortable with a For Sale sign being posted in your front lawn, tell the agent now. You should also alert the agent to any stipulations that are important to you. The agent should be quite amenable to what you want, but it's only fair to lay out your requirements up front rather than run into difficulties once the agent gets down to work. For example, if you don't want the agent bringing strangers into the house when you are at work and the kids are home with a sitter, just lay out your schedule ahead of time.

A tip: While the 6% commission is common, it is not written in indelible ink. All commissions are negotiable. So if you have a very expensive home, talk to the agent about reducing the commission to 5% or even less. After all, a 6% commission on a $150,000 home is $9,000 while a 5% commission for a $400,000 home is a stunning $20,000. When you bring up the idea of a lower commission, ask the agent how it will affect the marketing of the home. A hungry agent probably won't flinch, since she is still in line to make a tidy sum when the house sells. But if you have an agent who tells you a lower commission won't work because she'll be able to offer the buyer's agents only 2.5% rather than 3%, then you've got a big decision to make. One option is to talk to some other agents. Another is to work out a deal with the agent by agreeing to a higher commission if the home sells at least for its original list price, but 5% if the final sale is at least 5% or more beneath your original asking price.

A bit of counterintuitive thinking will pay off if you are about to put your home up for sale in a tough selling market. Rather than scrimp on the commission, offer a *bonus* of one percentage point or so for any agent who pulls off the sale within 95% of your list price. That incentive will certainly keep your house in the thoughts of all agents in the area, who will no doubt be interested in the possibility of bringing in a 3.5% commission rather than the typical 3%.

One big red light that needs flashing: Do not agree to a **net listing,** in which the seller agrees to hand the agent all proceeds that exceed a predetermined sale price. For example, if you set a $100,000 price and the home sells for $115,000, the agent would keep the $15,000, or a whopping 13%. These setups are illegal in half the states. If you live in a state in the other half, just say "No, thank you."

Between the world of FIZBOs and full-service agents, there is a viable middle ground known as **discount brokers.**

You can find these fee-for-service real estate agents in the Yellow Pages. They operate sort of like self-service gas stations. A discount agent will supply you with what you need, but you have to get out and do some of the work yourself. For instance, you can hire a discount broker for a flat rate or a commission of 2% or so. Because you are getting a cut rate, you won't get all the help of a full-service agent. So you will have to work out with the discounter what jobs you will take on, such as placing ads in the newspaper, or showing the home to prospective buyers. One warning here: By working with a discount broker, you won't be listed in the MLS system, since the agent isn't about to split such a low flat fee or commission. That may not be a terrible problem if you are in a hot housing market. But in slower markets, ask the discount agent what you can do if the discount route doesn't work after, say, three months or so. In most cases your discounter is a member of the local Board of Realtors. So if you ultimately decide you need to have your house listed on the MLS, you can agree to pay a 3% commission to a buyer's broker who finds your house via the MLS.

Once you've chosen an agent or decided to sell your house yourself, it's time to check in with your lawyer to tell him you're getting ready to put the house on the market. All you want to do at this point is effectively put the lawyer on no-tice that you'll need his assistance within the next few weeks or months to review all bids and contracts. The reason for this preliminary call is so you will be assured of quick access to your lawyer once you finally receive a written bid. If you wait until then to call, you may have to wait a few days before the lawyer gets moving on your request. And don't think you can save a few bucks by working without a lawyer. An attorney familiar with real estate contracts will be invaluable in reviewing the buyer's request for contingency clauses in the contract, as well as in doing the research and paperwork to prove you have full title to the house.

Preparing the House for Sale

You wouldn't wear a rumpled and dirty shirt to an important job interview, right? Well, consider putting your home up for sale the equivalent of a *very* important job interview. In this case you want to impress buyers, so you need to dress up your house in the most impressive way possible. That means sprucing up the exterior. So if the house is in dire need of painting, do it. It may cost a couple of thousand dollars, but the first impression is crucial and a neat exterior can be the difference between getting the home sold and having it sit on the market for a few more months. Also, weather permitting, fill the front yard with shrubs and flowers. At the very least, purchase a few planters and fill them with inviting colorful plants at the front door and by the driveway. If your lawn and garden area is looking, well, a bit mangy, consider hiring a gardener for a one- or two-day massive clean-up job: give the lawn a professional mowing, trim the shrubs, and remove any dead and ungainly plants.

Your next job is to stand outside your front door. Pretend you are house hunting. Now open the door and step into the entrance of the house. Quick, what's the first thing you see? And the second? Okay, now your job is to make those first and second impressions clean and inviting. So if your front entrance is a vestibule, fill it with flowers, a nice coat rack . . . you get the idea. Make a really good first impression.

You should also go through each room and remove as much clutter as possible. Think about it: everyone is shopping for as much space as they can afford. So make your rooms feel big and roomy by stashing all unnecessary furniture and "stuff" up in the attic or the basement. And clean about your closets, since everyone craves closet space. You can make your closets appear bigger than they really are by removing all those extra

shoes and boxes. And here's one other tip: Even though it is still your house, realize that absolute strangers will be walking through it and trying to envision themselves living in those rooms. So you don't want the place to be full of religious symbols, personal artifacts, or imposing artworks that may not be in the buyer's taste. Consider toning down some of the rooms a bit. After all, you aren't trying to sell the buyers on the way you live; you just want to sell them on the structure.

Caveat emptor is a goner when it comes to selling a home. Now, half the states require that all sellers complete a disclosure form that lists all *known* structural and operational problems, from a leaky roof to a garbage disposal that is on the fritz. And in the states that still don't mandate disclosure, wise real estate agents require their sellers to present prospective buyers with a rundown of the condition of the home's structure and operational systems.

Savvy sellers won't see disclosure as just a necessary evil. Rather, you can turn it into a nifty selling tool. Add as much detail as you can think of, such as the year you had major systems repaired or overhauled. And provide the name of the contractor who did the work. A detailed—and honest—rundown of every aspect of the house will impress all home shoppers. You can also go a step farther and make available copies of your utility bills in each season, as well as a copy of your most recent property tax bill. If you live in a condominium or cooperative apartment, make sure all shoppers are presented right off the bat with the documents listing the maintenance fee and common charges; don't make the prospective buyer ask for the detailed information. That sort of candor telegraphs how eager you are to make a deal and what a decent person you are. You'd be surprised how many people buy homes these days just because they like the sellers.

How to Set a Price That's Right

Select an asking price that is too low and you'll undoubtedly get a buyer, but also needlessly forfeit thousands of dollars. Set the price too high and you will live the seller's nightmare of spending months on the market without many buyers stopping by, let alone making a bid on your home. To get the best price for your house, condo, or co-op and sell it promptly, you need to make sure you settle on a competitive and alluring initial list price.

Here's where your agent starts to really earn her commission. She should auto-matically present you with a detailed market analysis that shows the key elements of recent sales in the neighborhood that are most like your place. That includes a breakdown of the original asking prices, the final sales prices, and the number of weeks or months the houses were on the market.

These "comparables" are really the only factors you should use in determining the general price range for your home. Accept the fact that the price you paid when you bought the home is irrelevant. That's right: irrelevant. Just because you paid $120,000 for your home at the market peak a few years ago doesn't mean a prospective buyer will automatically match or exceed that amount. If comparable homes now sell for $110,000, that's what you can expect to receive for your home.

A renovation or remodeling job will no doubt affect the value of your house, but you won't receive a 100% payback. For example, the fact that you added a third bathroom may well increase the value of the home, and your agent will be careful to use three-bathroom homes for your comparables. But at no time will the actual cost of your project come into play. Just because you paid $25,000 for the renovation project doesn't mean you can increase your asking price by $25,000. Fortunately, you'll be able to get some additional payback on the project after you've sold the house. That's because the

IRS lets you add the cost of all actual improvements to the price you originally paid for the house. This **adjusted cost basis** is the base amount that you will then use to calculate the taxable capital gain. Because you have effectively raised the purchase price, you will therefore have a smaller taxable gain to report.

Once your agent has provided the market analysis of comparable sales in the area and you know the ballpark you'll be playing in, your job is to pull out the research you did at the library and sit down with the agent to talk pricing strategy. If you determine that the recent trend is that homes are taking longer to sell and that the gap between list price and sale price is widening, you are in a slowing sales market. So should you need to make a move quickly, you'll have to make the price of your home extra enticing to attract attention. Consider setting the asking price of your home 5% or so below its market value. Advertising that sort of value will get you the kind of buyer action you need.

You should also consider a strategic approach to putting your house on the MLS system. Most of these real estate listing systems segregate homes into price categories of $10,000. Therefore, if you set your asking price at $151,000, your home will be included in the $150,000-and-above screens. But if you instead set the asking price at $149,000 you will also capture all the prospective buyers whose

upper limit is the $140,000 to $149,000 level. So while you've started $2,000 lower, you've greatly increased your number of possible buyers, which is a savvy move in slow sales markets.

If you are in the enviable position of selling your home during a local real estate boom—lucky you!—then you can afford to add a bit to your home's current market value when setting an asking price. For example, let's say $120,000 is the market value, but you and your agent have determined that homes are selling within just a couple of weeks of landing on the market and are getting snapped up right at the asking price. If your comparables are from a month or two ago, they may slightly understate the strength of the market since those sales occurred. With your agent's input, think about adding 2% or so to the market value. But be careful about getting greedy. If you set the price at too high a premium, your home will not get enough attention from shoppers. Then, chances are, no one will make you a reasonable offer.

Don't assume you can simply lower the price in a few weeks if you aren't getting any serious buyer attention. It's tough to shift the focus on your home once the agents and buyers have moved on. The critical time for any home is the first few weeks it arrives on the market. That's when agents and buyers will give it their closest attention. You can't be assured the buzz will return in a month when you lower the price. By then, some other houses have come on the market and they're drawing the interest of agents and buyers.

Consider taking what might be called the Goldilocks approach: If the housing market is neither too hot nor too cold where you live, be realistic and set the price in line with the comparables. But leave yourself a bit of negotiating room; that means tacking on a bit to the market value. Everybody does it. Remember your research that showed homes were selling 3% below their original list price? Well, then add that 3% or so to your list price. This becomes your negotiating cushion. If a potential buyer makes a bid that's 5% below list price, you can then make a counteroffer that is 3% lower. That may mollify the buyer and you've got a deal—right at the price you determined was the home's true market value. Of course, the process of determining your home's asking price is far from a science, so talk to your agent about how the bidding process usually works in your area and where a comfortable cushion would be for your list price.

Showing Your House

This is another area where the agent earns her commission. Your best bet is to leave this job completely to the agent and not be present when a prospective buyer comes by to see your home. Go out for a long drive or use the time to start checking out homes you might want to bid on. If you happen to be at home, try to be as invisible as possible. You don't want to be drawn into a conversation with the buyer that tips your hand too much. For example, you might offer up the seemingly innocuous tidbit that you and your family have been happy in the house for the past 20 years. A sharp shopper will store that information away; when he makes a bid he will know that you've got a lot of years of appreciation and may be more amenable to reducing the price than someone who bought three years ago at the market top. Similarly, you don't want to let on that you have to sell the house within a few weeks. If you do, the buyer may decide you're desperate and then make you a lowball offer. While all market-wise home shoppers will ask their agent for this information, you at least want to make sure that they ask rather than have it volunteered to them.

If you are present and a buyer makes an oral bid, do not show any emotion. Simply tell the buyer you will consider any written bid. Once you have a written bid, your agent and your lawyer can review the offer.

Renting Out Your Home

If you live in a very slow market and can't make a sale but must make a move, don't resign yourself to being house stuck. You can at least cover your mortgage costs by renting out the house temporarily. If you can find renters who are interested in buying when they have more savings, you may be able to work out a deal where you lease the house to the renters and give them the option of buying the home within a specific period—say, two years. To help sweeten the deal, you can agree to credit 10% or so of their rent payments toward the purchase price of the house. While this arrangement can be a lifesaver if you must relocate to a new area, it does have a few drawbacks. You will not only still own the home and be responsible for its upkeep, you'll also become a landlord. Plus, you probably won't be able to qualify for a mortgage to buy a home in your new town until you are able to sell this home and pay back the loan. So if you are renting out your home, chances are you'll become a renter, too, temporarily.

If the renters ultimately decide not to buy the house, you can either extend your rental agreement with them or put the house back on the market. With luck, the local economy will have improved enough so that you can now find a buyer willing to pay a fair price for the home. But if the market is still sluggish, you may be able to take advantage of an IRS rule that will let you deduct the loss from the sale if you have rented out the property for the two years prior to the sale.

Negotiating with a Potential Buyer

Congratulations, you have a bid on your home. Even if it's lower than you expected, do not be discouraged. At least the ball is in play. Now huddle with your agent and figure out your next move. If the bid was just 5% below your asking price, it looks like you'll be able to make a deal. Make a counteroffer that gives back the cushion you worked in—say 3%—and tell the prospective buyer you've got a deal, but no more negotiating. Chances are very good that the home shopper wants this process to be over with, too.

However, if you get a bid that is 10% or more below your asking price, you have a few choices. Ask your agent to help you assess the buyer's approach. It may be that the person making the bid just likes to negotiate. Some people do. If so, make a counteroffer that is 2% or 3% lower and see what offer you get next. Otherwise, you can just have your agent convey that you have set a fair asking price and that you will not entertain a bid that is so far below it. What you're doing here is forcing the buyer essentially to raise his initial bid before the negotiating begins. Of course, there's the risk that the buyer will simply refuse and walk away from the house. But if you are pretty confident that you've set a fair price and that the buyer was trying to take advantage of you, then you need to be willing to let such a lowball bidder walk.

Another approach is to give in a bit on the price and then add in some barter. For instance, if you have a terrific gardener and your landscaping is part of the home's charm, tell the bidder that you'll pay for the first six months of the gardener's bill when he moves in. Or if the dishwasher and other appliances weren't originally part of the sale, you can now offer to throw in one or two of the appliances.

In addition to deciding how to deal with the bidder's offer, you also need your lawyer to review the contingency clauses that the bidder has included in the bid. Unless you are totally desperate to make a sale, do not agree to a clause that states the deal goes through only if the buyer is able to sell his current home. That's *his* problem; don't make it yours. If you agree to that clause, you could be stuck waiting, while being unable to entertain offers from other buyers.

Your lawyer should also make sure that each acceptable contingency is given a specific time frame in which it must be completed. For example, it is perfectly reasonable for the buyer to make the deal contingent on the house passing a home inspection. But you want to make sure that the inspection is done within a week of signing the contract. The same is true of the closing date. Make the buyer commit to a reasonable date; don't leave it hanging in the air.

If you and the prospective buyer can't agree on the price and your bartering didn't help close the deal, you might consider helping the buyer by offering to pay some of his mortgage financing costs. **Seller financing** can be especially enticing to first-time buyers who are typically a bit cash strapped to come up with the down payment, let alone cover all the mortgage and closing costs.

If you have a government-insured loan, you may be sitting on your best marketing tool. All loans insured by the Federal Housing Administration before December 15, 1989, and all Veterans Administration loans issued before March 1988 are what's known as fully **assumable loans.** That means you can transfer the mortgage to the buyer, who then takes control of the payments without having to qualify for the loan. For all government loans issued after these dates, the buyer will have to meet the lender's qualifying criteria. (For more about government loans, see this book's Appendix.)

Another seller financing tool is to **buy down** the buyer's mortgage rate by agreeing to pay an extra point or two in the closing costs. In general, every point the seller pays will reduce the interest rate on the buyer's mortgage by an eighth of a percentage point. That not only helps lower the buyer's monthly mortgage costs, but the new lower rate will also make it easier for him or her to pass the lender's financial qualification screen. In addition to helping get the deal done, you get a nice tax break, too. Uncle Sam lets you add the cost of these buy-down points to your cost basis, thereby reducing the size of the taxable gain you will have to report to the government. But don't get too excited. Unlike the points that you paid when you bought your house, these points can't be claimed as a deduction on your federal tax return.

Once you and the bidder have an agreement, you'll both sign the contract and the buyer will make an **earnest money** deposit with the agent or lawyer. This good faith financial gesture is typically equal to 1% to 3% of the sale price and will be credited to the down payment at the actual closing.

Speaking of the closing, your job is to show up—generally with your lawyer—and have the deed to the house ready to pass along to the new owner. One of the contingencies you probably agreed to was allowing the buyer a final walk-through inspection of the house a day before the closing. This should just be a formality, so the buyer can make sure there isn't any confusion about which appliances and fixtures stay with the house.

At the closing, you and the buyer will write each other a few checks to settle some shared payments. For instance, if you already paid the entire property tax bill for the year, but you're moving after just six months, then the buyer must reimburse you for half of the payment. Or if you haven't yet been billed for the property tax, you'll need to write the buyer a check for the six months you were the owner.

After the buyer writes a slew of checks to his lender, he will sign over a check to you for the agreed-upon sale price. You then write a check to your lender to cover the remaining principal balance on your mortgage. Then you give the buyer the deed to the house and the deal is done. You have officially sold your home. Now just remember to give the new owner the keys.

Taxes and Home Selling

If you sell your home at a taxable profit or a loss, the sale must be reported to the Internal Revenue Service. Your lender will report the transaction by filing Form 1099 with the IRS. And as the seller, *you* must report the sale by filing Form 2119 with the IRS and showing the gain or loss on Schedule D of your federal tax return; if the gain is tax-free, you need not file this form. To help you wade through these forms and procedures, call the IRS at 800-829-3676 and ask for a copy of Publication 523: *Tax Information on Selling Your House*.

While the federal government may be interested in taxing your capital gain on the house, you won't be expected simply to subtract the sale price from your original purchase price and consider that the taxable gain, before figuring whether you'll qualify for the new exclusion. In one of its rare shows of magnanimity, the tax code lets you add to the original pur-

chase price a bunch of costs you paid during the time you lived in the house. You can tack on only the costs for actual improvements, such as replacing the roof, installing central air-conditioning, or adding a bathroom. Basic maintenance and repairs such as cleaning the gutters or painting the exterior are not considered to be improvements. In addition to the cost of improvements, you'll also be able to add on a variety of fees you paid in the process of selling the home, such as the sales commission you paid to the agent. The sum of all additional costs are added to the original purchase price, and the total is called the **adjusted cost basis.** You subtract this final adjusted cost basis from the sale price to determine any capital gain. Below, a worksheet to help:

DETERMINING YOUR TAXABLE GAIN OR LOSS

1. Price you paid for the house $_____
(If you inherited the house, use the appraised value of
the house at the time of the inheritance, known as the
stepped-up basis)
2. Price of improvements

_____ $_____

_____ $_____

_____ $_____

_____ $_____

_____ $_____

_____ $_____

                    TOTAL COST OF IMPROVEMENTS $_____

3. Add Line 1 and total from Line 2 $_____

4. Your selling expenses:
   Real estate agent commission $_____
   Points you paid for the buyer $_____
   Legal fees $_____
   Advertising expenses $_____
                                         TOTAL $_____

5. Add Line 3 and total from Line 4 $_____

6. Value of energy credits you received $_____
   Value of insurance losses deducted $_____
   Deferred capital gain from previous sale(s) $_____
                                         TOTAL $_____

7. Subtract Line 6 from Line 5 $_____
                              (YOUR ADJUSTED COST BASIS)

8. Subtract Line 7 from your sale price $_____
                              YOUR CAPITAL GAIN (OR LOSS) BEFORE
                              FACTORING IN THE $250,000 OR $500,000
                              EXCLUSION

If you work out of your home, you need to have your accountant or tax preparer help you with this next exclusion, since only the portion of the house that was used solely for residential purposes can be deferred. You must add to your gain amounts you depreciated for your home office. And that total is subject to a 25% "depreciation recapture" tax.

CHAPTER 9

Getting the Most Out of Your Career and Benefits

Okay. You've got an office, a respectable paycheck, and a stack of engraved business cards—maybe even complete with your personal e-mail address. Are these the trappings of a hot-rod career or a plain old job? The answer depends on what you make of your own unique career journey. Savvy career climbers know that any single job may help them advance to the next rung on the ladder, but long term, a successful work life is much more complex than simply getting the next job. It's having and taking advantage of benefits from your employer. It's balancing your work life with your life away from work. It's parlaying your skills to get more money and more enjoyment from your job.

By the way, you probably will have many jobs at lots of places over your working years, perhaps more than you'd like. For better or worse, paternalistic corporations and the decades-long careers they fostered have gone the way of disco dancing. In 1953 the average American professional changed jobs just three times over the course of a career. Today that number is up to seven jobs. As the year 2000 approaches, career footwork will be even fancier, with competition keener for the best, high-paying gigs. Even as companies renege on their promises of 30 years and a gold watch, however, don't expect them to demand less of whom they hire. Quite the contrary. Employers of the twenty-first century will require their fast-trackers to be superspecialists—adaptable types equipped to juggle several skills and tasks.

While you may not be able to control

your entries and exits through corporate America's doors as much as in the past, don't let news of layoffs discourage you. At the same time companies are slicing layers of management in one part of their business, they may be ushering in a new set of employees with a completely different set of skills in another. Here's proof: Despite job bloodletting throughout America from 1989 through 1994, the nation's 50 largest firms actually posted a net *increase* of nearly 460,000 jobs during that period.

Don't assume you're stuck in the field you've chosen, either. Thousands of people chuck one field for another every year, and plenty of others dream about doing it. In fact, a recent **MONEY** survey asked respondents, "If you could start again, would you choose the same career?" A striking 42% said they'd take a different route today, with more women (50%) than men (35%) ready to choose a different path.

Four Keys to a Successful Career

Worried that you might not have what it takes to make it on the job in the future? You're not alone. In a survey of 100 personnel managers by the Cambridge Human Resource Group, a consulting firm, more

than 40% said that their firms' employees worry about what talents and abilities will be expected of them in the future.

Take it easy. This chapter will lay out the details of getting ahead in the workplace of today and tomorrow. Before zeroing in on the details, though, here are four broad themes to remember for improving your odds of on-the-job success:

1. Further your education. Consider these telling statistics: For every dollar earned by a college graduate, the average high school grad makes about 57¢. Holders of doctorate and professional degrees take home roughly twice as much as those who have B.A.'s.

A fast-tracker's learning curve shouldn't end with any particular degree. By building up new skills at work, you stand to enhance both your career and salary. Among the abilities most sought after in corporate America today? Computer know-how, for starters. Workers who use PCs to ply their trade, for instance, earn roughly 10% to 15% more than those who don't. Other top talents include technical writing ability and managerial wizardry. Regardless of your line of work, in our global economy foreign languages can give you added leverage. As a banker, think of the edge you'll have with a fluency in Spanish; if you're a corporate lawyer, think of the punch you'll pack with crack Japanese.

Luckily there are plenty of places that can help keep your skills competitive.

Hundreds of colleges and universities nationwide offer executive education seminars and short courses. For a quick tune-up in a specific area, say, negotiating prowess, don't forget community colleges and professional associations; many offer a wide range of career classes. Both new and seasoned managers might want to consider comprehensive training available through the American Management Association (AMA) in New York. For $160 per year, members have access to dozens of business classes, videos, and AMA publications. Held in half a dozen major cities, classes range in duration from one to five days and cost between $750 and $6,000. For more information, write to the AMA at 135 W. 50th St., New York, N.Y. 10020, or call 212-586-8100.

2. Don't thumb your nose at lateral moves. "Up" would seem the only logical career climber's destination. As corporations continue to strip away management layers, however, you can count on more job openings to be sideways moves. In fact, over the next decade roughly half of all job moves are expected to be lateral ones, not vertical.

Such career zigzags can carry you farther than you might think. By testing out new opportunities in other departments and divisions at your current employer, you may gain valuable experience, not to mention great networking contacts and a better view of how the overall firm functions. Although your pay and prestige probably won't spike right away, such experiences can help stem job boredom, broaden your career prospects, and eventually help you to move vertically. So if you're in a rut and don't see much chance for a step up at work, ask your boss for a lateral transfer.

3. Job-hop judiciously. Recent college grads can afford to surf from post to post for the first two to four years out of school. It's a great way to find your way in the working world. In midcareer, though, you should carefully orchestrate your voluntary job switches.

Good reasons to switch jobs include scaling perceived hurdles in your current post (such as low pay or failing to get credit for your work) or simply forging ahead in a field like fashion or entertainment that lends itself to movement. Otherwise, however, playing job hopscotch might only trip you up. Too many entries on a résumé may cause a prospective employer to wonder if you're focused enough on your own career goals or may raise doubts about your ability to get along with other workers. Don't make a switch before asking yourself the following three questions:

■ Would the new post move you in a career direction that's in keeping with your overall goals?
■ Are you thinking about accepting the new job not because you think it's a worthy one, but merely because your current job is a bummer?
■ If the new position is from an em-

ployer trying to lure you, would you be so eager to move if you weren't being hotly pursued?

If your answers to these questions reveal that you're thinking of making a job-hop just for convenience or because you're flattered to get an offer, stop! You're making a mistake.

4. Feel free to make a career switch.

No matter how old you are, it's never too late to make a 180° turn and plunge into a new career. Just try to pick a new career that melds your passion with the skills you've aced in a previous one. Let's face it: Very few of us could easily make the switch from, say, corporate accountant to French chef. However, a journalist who is a sideline musician, for instance, might find satisfaction working in public relations at the local symphony. A lawyer with a love of film might hop on the Hollywood bandwagon by chasing a legal affairs gig at an independent film company on the rise. To get help making a radical move, see a career counselor for advice. A one-on-one could cost you upward of $100 per hour, but check out community colleges and universities in your area. They may offer these services for a much lower cost.

Another way to make the transition smooth is to find out what fast-growth fields have a need for your talents. You may be surprised by some of the categories in which the U.S. Bureau of Labor statistics predicts high growth over the next decade: education, travel, advertising, and management consulting, to name just four. An outplacement specialist or career counselor can help show you how you might retool your skills to suit a new field.

One clever way to gain experience in a new field is by taking an apprenticeship, a part-time job, or an internship doing something you love, even if the pay isn't great. Write to the human resources offices of companies you admire and see if they'll take you on. If no obvious opportunities present themselves, be creative. For example, you could take a weekend clerk's job at a computer store to learn about electronics marketing or apprentice at a gallery to see how artists are groomed.

REALITY CHECKLIST: 10 TIPS TO ACCOMPLISH YOUR CAREER GOALS

1. Do what you enjoy and seek financial rewards later.
2. Define what job satisfaction means to you and apply the criteria in each job you land.
3. Always have a Plan B. If something doesn't work out where you are, know your next move.
4. When leaving a job, do so with as much grace as you can. Burning bridges is a bad idea.

5. Be flexible about your hours. Dolly Parton's song about working 9 to 5 won't cut it anymore. In this techno-age, you may be on call round the clock via fax, beeper, and computer.

6. Spot the hardest-working person where you work and use him or her as the standard to outperform.

7. Look for new challenges. Ask your boss for new and different assignments.

8. Don't be afraid of failure. Risk takers usually reap rich rewards.

9. Take time to appraise what you've learned or could have learned from each job.

10. Turn workplace changes to your advantage. For instance, a streamlined department in your office could give you a greater chance to excel.

How to Search for a Job

You know the old saying "Look before you leap." Oddly, many people don't heed this crucial advice when seeking a new job. Make sure you do. Just think: Many employers hiring today are likely to put job candidates through interview paces not once, but three or four times. Why shouldn't you check them out as thoroughly as they do you? A proper search takes time. Specifically, job hunters who've already been in the workforce can today count on spending an average of one month on the interview circuit for

every $10,000 they formerly earned. Remember these tips the next time you're ready to survey the employment terrain:

■ **Tap your network of friends and associates to meet people working at companies that interest you.** Reach out to everyone possible for "insider information" about the companies you're keen on. Career counselors figure that as many as 70% of all managerial or white-collar jobs are filled through the corporate grapevine, so it truly does pay to broadcast your situation to as many people as possible. Even if you're looking for an accountant's job, someone working in, say, public relations or marketing at that office can give you a valuable tutorial. Find out about a company's corporate culture, job satisfaction rate, and general workload. Are the managers flexible and open to new ideas or entrenched in their old ways? Such queries can also clue you in about a company's long-range business plans—which just might include a need for someone with your skills.

WHERE THE JOBS WILL BE

According to Woods & Poole, a respected economics research firm in Washington, D.C., the following ten metropolitan areas (listed alphabetically) stand to offer some of the best job opportunities over the next decade. In these places, job openings are slated to increase faster than the national average of 1% annually (yes, even in financially strapped Orange County, Calif.):

Metropolitan Area	Great Job Prospects For . . .	Metropolitan Area	Great Job Prospects For . . .
1. Albany, N.Y.	Home health aides, child care workers, registered nurses, systems analysts	6. Orange County, Calif.	Registered nurses, accountants, auditors, financial managers, bank tellers, computer programmers, carpenters, fire fighters, systems analysts
2. Atlanta	Top executives, systems analysts, secondary and elementary school teachers, child care workers, labor relations specialists	7. Orlando, Fla.	Computer engineers, systems analysts, physical therapists, customer service reps, teachers, paralegals, flight attendants, private investigators
3. Dallas	Surgical and radiological technicians, home health aides, paralegals, occupational therapists and chiropractors	8. Phoenix–Mesa	Accounting and auditing clerks, registered nurses, secondary school teachers, financial managers, carpenters and electrical engineers
4. Houston	Surgical and radiological technicians, home health aides and chiropractors	9. Raleigh–Durham, N.C.	Computer engineers, occupational therapists, systems analysts, dental hygienists, paralegals, special ed teachers, home health aides, detectives
5. Las Vegas	Registered nurses, gaming supervisors, executives, retail salesmen, carpenters, bartenders, cooks	10. San Diego	Registered nurses, general managers, top executives, computer programmers, auto mechanics, physicians, advertising managers, financial managers, systems analysts

■ **Visit your local library and the Internet.** Curious about general job prospects in your field? Want referrals to organizations that can give you further job-seeking information? Maybe you're an unemployed recent college grad and are searching for detailed job descriptions in a particular field. No matter where you are in your work life, if you're looking for a job, head to your library's stacks and page through the thick *Occupational Outlook Handbook*, published annually by the Department of U.S. Labor. This publication contains job growth forecasts in hundreds of job categories through the year 2005.

Ask your librarian also to help you cull newspaper and magazine stories about particular employers you're researching. Assuming the business or organization is large enough or based in your area, you'll find a treasure trove of information. Articles will tell you things like whether there have been layoffs lately and if so what kinds of severance packages were offered; who has been promoted recently; the quality of the top management; and if there have been any major scandals or success stories. Publicly traded companies will also have earnings reports and sales histories on record.

Increasingly, companies post job openings on the Web too. In fact, there are more than 3,500 Web sites with job postings. The three most comprehensive are *Online Career Center* (www.occ.com), *Monster Board* (www.monster.com), and *E-Span* (www.espan.com), which have between 10,000 and 50,000 listings apiece and are updated daily.

Once you've selected a potential company, visit its Web page. You can find it by entering the company's name in a search engine like *Yahoo!* (www.yahoo.com) or *Lycos* (www.lycos.com). For a more critical look at employers, read the latest news reports on them at sites like *Wall Street Research Net* (www.wsrn.com) and *Business Wire* (www.businesswire.com). You can also find chat rooms and discussion groups on the Net where you can talk with current and former employees about the companies.

■ **Look for work at a local small employer.** Finding a job in a small business or nonprofit is a little more difficult than finding one at a big place. For one thing, there's usually no personnel or human resources office. For another, job openings are less frequent and often get filled faster. That said, small companies remain the biggest employers in America, a trend that's likely to continue. Over the next decade, according to the U.S. Bureau of Labor Statistics, job openings will increase by 26.4 million, and 93% of these jobs will be offered not by large industrial behemoths like GM, but by service companies with fewer than 500 employees. This shift from an industrial job market to a service-based one bodes well for folks like public relations managers, marketing managers, and other problem solvers.

Before you start daydreaming about open-door bosses and offices brimming with creative types, however, do your homework. Besides checking out the pay and benefits, determine the prospects for the place—and for you. Does the business or nonprofit group have a unique product or service? Is management experienced? Is the location an appropriate one? If you can confidently answer yes to these questions, you'll have a better shot at gliding through calm waters than making an icy splash to the ranks of unemployment.

■ **Investigate where a specific job may lead.** To get a better glimpse of whether the job opening is a dead end or an entry to even bigger and better things, seek out people who've previously held the position you're after. This type of one-on-one can provide valuable information. Ask them why they left, what they're doing now, and whether they think the position helped them move forward in their career. You can often locate these people by asking their co-workers who are still on the job how to find them. At the very least, be sure to ask your interviewer about the fate of the person you stand to replace.

■ **Check out your chances for advancement.** You won't find a road map to success in the employee handbook. By being a keen observer of the office scene when you go for an interview, however, you can get a pretty fair indication of your own chances for advancement. If you're a woman or a minority, for instance, take a look around. Are there senior females or people of color working in a senior capacity? If so, try to speak with them. Was it especially difficult for them to get ahead? If you find no one in the upper ranks who even remotely resembles you, this may be a topic to broach in an interview.

Education is another point to consider. Are you equipped with the same training, skills, and degrees as the company's stars? If you have your sights on a management position and most of the firm's honchos have advanced degrees from prestigious schools, for instance, this may be an indication that the employer is more likely to propel the careers of those types.

■ **Find out if you'll be entitled to an employment contract.** The corporate cutbacks of the '80s and '90s have made professionals more wary—and more savvy—about jumping into new job situations. While there is no way to assure job security, you may be able to get a safety net in the form of an employment contract. Drawn up by your prospective employer, this document articulates your job title, duties, and salary as well as any benefits, such as vacation pay, bonuses, and severance arrangements. These contracts, usually reserved for executive types, specify a length of employment, anywhere from a year to three years.

Remember: Although employment contracts protect you in many ways, they also serve the needs of your employer. For this reason, be sure to review the contract language carefully, searching for any clauses that might be restrictive or nebulous. For instance, most contracts will spell out grounds for termination. Here's where to watch out for vague wording such as "incompetence" and "uncooperative." Also, be on the lookout for limits on what you could do after you leave the firm. For instance, with companies zealously guarding corporate secrets, many have inserted contract clauses barring certain managers from accepting future employment with direct competitors. Once you have a firm offer in hand and an employment contract is presented, take your time with it. Ask your lawyer to review it to be certain it serves your interests.

RÉSUMÉ DOS AND DON'TS

It's no fun to draft a résumé—laying out your life history on a single sheet of paper. Coming up with just the right résumé is tough, too. After all, this is a document that requires you to be assertive but not pleading, impressive yet not pompous, a calling card that can land you in the interview chair, not the reject pile. It's quite appropriate, incidentally, to brag when you have something to brag about. If your smarts saved the company $50,000 last year, say so. If your negotiating skills made it possible to keep a valuable client, fess up. You ought to highlight anything that distinguishes you as someone who gets results. For more help in crafting a winning résumé, heed these dos and don'ts:

Do	Don't
1. Pay attention to presentation. Avoid offbeat typefaces and use heavy bond white or cream paper. Be brief and use active words to describe your previous duties.	**1. Simply prepare a list of your past jobs or education.** Instead, flaunt your responsibilities and what you learned from each job.
2. Include all your educational credentials, including any courses or seminars you've taken recently to upgrade your skills.	**2. Include your salary history.** You may over- or underprice yourself before getting a foot in the door.
3. Double- and triple-check for grammar and spelling errors. Nothing irks a manager more than reading about someone's stint at General Mothors.	**3. Dust off an old résumé and slap your latest job on top.** Take the time to tailor your pitch to the work you're seeking.

From Résumé to Job

Once you've polished your résumé, you need to circulate it effectively. At first, you'll probably be best off narrowing your focus to the few employers suited to your search. If you're an unemployed manager who has either been looking for work for a while or is open to the idea of moving, you may want to let an **executive recruiting firm**—a/k/a a headhunter—flaunt your credentials far and wide. Approximately one in five midlevel managers land new positions with the help of headhunters. To locate reputable firms, browse through *The Directory of Executive Recruiters* in your library. Make a note of those who specialize in your field plus local ones. The service of a headhunter doesn't come cheaply, however. Expect to pay upward of $4 per résumé and cover letter. If you're paying that kind of dough, the firm should have a policy of checking addresses and resending any mail that comes back undelivered.

As a rule, you should bypass so-called **retainer firms.** These are recruiters who charge employers a fee for their services—whether their efforts result in a job placement or not. Instead, check out **contingency search** firms. Because these firms make a buck only when their applicants land a job, they tend to be more motivated in locating and selling top talent.

Most recruitment firms won't charge *you* a fee unless they perform a specific service, like mass résumé mailings, as mentioned above. Reputable ones that do charge might demand about 10% of your first year's salary, but only after you've started your new job. If you are thinking about going with a firm that charges a fee, first call your local Better Business Bureau to see if any recent complaints have been levied against the firm. Should you wind up going with a fee-based firm, be sure to get a signed contract that clearly specifies all costs and services up front.

When looking for a job, don't forget investigating **temporary work.** Think temping is a blot on your résumé? Get a new attitude. The ranks of temporary workers have swelled since the 1980s, with over 1.5 million Americans collecting temp paychecks in 1994—more than a threefold increase over 1982. These aren't just secretaries or file clerks, either. One in four temps today are highly skilled professional types, ranging from lawyers and nurses to accountants and pharmacists.

You may be surprised to learn just how rewarding temp work can be. For starters, the pay is often decent. Generally, temps earn hourly wages that are on par with full-time jobs in their fields. Some temp jobs even provide workers with health insurance and vacation pay. Even more encouraging: Roughly a third of all temporary positions now blossom into full-time gigs. The best way to up the odds of getting hired is showing the company how it can save money.

With over 7,000 temporary employment services nationwide, there are plenty of places to hunt for work. Aside from reading the classifieds, try calling personnel managers at companies where you'd like to work and ask for recommendations of whom they use. Incidentally, you'll find temp agencies in the Yellow Pages under "Employment Contractors—Temporary Help."

If you are one of the millions who tap away ferociously on such **on-line services** as CompuServe or America On-line, broaden your job hunt by surfing the various bulletin boards. There's no solid research on how effective this mode of job searching is, but recruiters are watching cyberspace carefully for possibilities. You should, too. For fees of anywhere from $10 to $50, some employment agencies will post your résumé on one of several electronic databases seen by recruiters nationwide. Or, you can do it yourself. Plugged-in types can now zap their vitae over the wires via services such as the Internet's Online Career Center, which on any given day is clogged with 30,000 résumés.

John Guare's play and film *Six Degrees of Separation* carries a tantalizing theory:

For every person on this earth, there are but six individuals who separate us. Meaning your aunt in Milwaukee, by some labyrinth measuring no more than six folks, has some connection to the pope. Well, in corporate America this rule applies doubly. And that's why **networking** is a great way to land a job. Far from the mere drudgery of attending industry conventions and collecting a Rolodex of business cards, however, serious networking requires careful orchestration. It's one thing to meet someone who may help advance your career. It's quite another to find ways of compelling that person to remember you and help you when you need assistance getting a job.

Successful networking is like a pyramid game—each person you elect into your circle gives you access to a completely new set of job contacts. There are several ways to network like a pro:

■ **Join professional associations on the local level.** You may feel lost at a trade group's national get-together, but moving in on the regional scene gives you a terrific chance to get to know key players in your field. Increase your visibility by joining a committee or helping to organize career workshops and networking get-togethers.

■ **Check out your college alumni network.** In the past few years, many colleges and universities have stepped up their alumni programs. There may now be a local chapter of your alma mater in your area. Or your college might now have an electronic résumé service for its graduates. Call your school's alumni office to see what kind of job placement is available to alums.

■ **Sweat the details.** After you've met someone you'd like to include in your network, keep up the relationship with small gestures. Thank-you notes after a lunch date are de rigueur. You'll stand out even more by sending a new contact things like relevant newspaper clippings, the names of other people in the field, or reminders of upcoming events.

Acing a Job Interview

If you haven't been on a job interview in a while—or ever—you may be surprised at the kinds of questions being asked these days. For instance, you might be asked to write an essay on the spot about your past successes and failures. Or you could be asked for an example of something that would make you a useful addition to the staff during your first year on the job. You might even be given a psychological test to see if you're the kind of person that the hirer is looking for.

So how do you sell yourself properly?

The key is to show the potential employer that you know a great deal about what the firm needs, that you have what it takes to get the job done, and that you'll fit in well with the current workforce there. Here's where having done your library research will really pay off. And if you know someone who now works for the place, or did recently, all the better. Pump that person for information about what the interview will be like, whom you're likely to see, and what you might do to prepare. The more you know going in, the better you'll be once you're in the interview.

Although you want to demonstrate to the employer how great you are, there's a wrong way and a right way to do this. The wrong way is to just keep talking about what a terrific person you are and how people like you. The right way is to impress on the interviewer how your qualities and skills will benefit the firm. Try to give at least one example of something you did at your last job that would be helpful at this job.

Also, show the quizzer that you've given a lot of thought to the interview and the job by asking dazzling questions of your own. By getting a conversation going, you'll raise the chances that the interviewer will remember you as someone smart and thoughtful. Don't be shy about asking key questions such as how many people will report to you, how often you'll be expected to travel, what kind of savings and pension plan is available, what kind of health, life, and disability insurance coverage you would receive, and so on.

Getting the Pay You Deserve

Here's a bit of good news: Wages for virtually all workers are on the upswing. So don't sell yourself short. Before you go into the job interview, however, you should have a pretty good idea of what the job will pay and what the competition is paying. Want ads in trade journals and local newspapers will help you establish this figure. Better still, a contact at the firm or a competitor could clue you in.

Try to get the company to make you an offer before you reveal your most recent salary. If you're asked first, however, take a few minutes to spout all the responsibilities the job entails. Really build it up. Then, put on a poker face and cite a figure that's in the high end of your range. You may wind up negotiating from there.

If the interviewer hits you with a pay offer that is downright chintzy, you have a few options:

■ **Hedge.** Explain to your prospective boss that while the job sure feels like the right fit, you're still weighing a few other opportunities (even if you aren't).

■ **Try to get the money in a more circuitous way.** Ask if part of the money you're requesting could come from a bonus pool. Or see if you can get the firm to commit to giving you a raise of a specified amount of money in six months if you meet certain goals laid out in advance.

■ **If you're in the upper rungs of management or know that you'd be quite a catch, ask for a signing bonus.** Even if the firm can't offer you a fat salary for starters, it might be able to sweeten the pot with a signing bonus—cash paid simply for your walking in the door. If so, you may want to negotiate further, say, taking a $5,000 signing bonus and tacking on another $5,000 to your salary vs. accepting a $10,000 up-front bonus. This way your annual pay increases are assured to be larger.

■ **Walk away.** Granted, this strategy takes guts, especially if you've been offered an alluring job. One possible advantage here: By sticking to your guns, you'll be giving the employer a taste of your convictions. That may cause the firm to pony up the money you want after all.

Tips for Four Types of Job Seekers

Smart career strategies depend on where you are in your career. Here's advice for the four different types of people who look for work:

1. **If you already have a job.** If the new job bug bites while you're still gainfully employed, congrats. You've got a leg up on the competition. Surveys show that roughly 70% of all new hires are freshly plucked from another job rather than rescued from the unemployment ranks. Do what you can to beef up your title and responsibilities at work before you start interviewing around. You might even bargain for a better job title in lieu of a raise. But pay attention to timing. If you're expecting a large Christmas bonus, perhaps you should postpone your job search until you've earned the money.

   Be cautious about sharing your new-job aspirations at the office. True, some bosses may appreciate your candor and welcome the news that you're ready for a fresh challenge. Before letting your superior in on your plans, though, be sure your boss is as progressive as you think. Otherwise you could be out the door sooner than you'd like. Also, keep in mind that using company resources to check out a job or interviewing on company time can easily cost you your current job—before you've safely landed another.

   You may want to join the estimated 100,000 Americans who hire personal career coaches each year. The nation's 4,000 coaches typically charge $200 to $500 a month to help you determine your top skills, figure out your goals, and devise a plan to get where you want to be in your career. You can get free referrals from the International Coach Federation (888-236-9262; www.coachfederation.org) or the Professional and Personal Coaches Association (415-522-8789; www.ppca.com). One word of warning: Anyone can call himself a career coach. So before you hire one, ask the prospect what qualifies him or her to coach you and how this coach would handle your particular situation.

2. **If you're unemployed when your search begins.** Millions of Americans will seek to enter the workforce this year. Prime candidates: women who took time off to raise their children and middle managers who have fallen victim to the corporate ax. Dreading the job search, and how you'll have to explain away any gaps in your résumé while on the interview trail? Well, take heart. Career counselors emphasize

227

that bows in and out of the workplace are now commonplace in today's zigzag economy, and there's no need to apologize. Furthermore, workers who've had decade-long careers with one company have a valuable track record under their belts, often giving them an edge. If you've had some black holes in your work life, try to mask them by charting your jobs year by year, rather than by month. And if you were laid off, ask your former employer for out-placement assistance. Don't assume headhunters will pass you by.

3. **If you're over 40.** Recent surveys have confirmed that age discrimination is alive and well in the work-place. This especially applies when trying to get in the door. In 1993, 700,000 people over age 50 were out of work and on the job trail. During that same year, complaints filed with state and federal regulators about age-bias soared to 30,000—up nearly 30% since 1990.

Forty-something workers can get a boost from an organization called **Forty-Plus.** That's not a suit size, but a nonprofit outplacement group with more than 20 chapters located in 13 states plus Washington, D.C., provid-ing great networking opportunities and job search seminars. Call 202-386-1582 for more information. An-other excellent resource, limited to

job hunters who are over 50, however, is the **American Association of Retired Persons (AARP),** which sponsors an eight-session job primer called AARP Works. AARP also has a free publication, *Age Discrimination on the Job,* which gives 20 pages of useful legal facts, plus addresses and phone numbers for the Equal Employment Opportunity Commission's 50 field offices nationwide. To get a copy, write for publication D12386, AARP, P.O. Box 22976, Long Beach, Calif. 90801.

4. **If you want to create your own job.** The dream of becoming an entre-preneur is a common one today. Before you make that pledge of inde-pendence, however, consider the fol-lowing brief tutorial on starting your own business. Here are five key rules for would-be Bill Gateses:

■ **Make sure you're motivated by a good idea, not by bad circum-stances.** You've heard it before, but it bears repeating: Nine out of ten busi-nesses fail within five years after opening. So you really need to consider what is driving you to strike out on your own. If your entrepreneurial desire springs from general worker malaise, think twice. A start-up requires the patience of Job and the passion of Julio Iglesias. People who are not prepared to face endless hours and potentially years of red ink are poor candidates for being their own boss.

■ **Write a solid business plan.** A business plan clearly outlining your company's raison d'être will help you to define both short- and long-term goals for your business. Researching your plan should also help you focus your concept and even gauge demand for your product or service. Luckily there are many excellent resources for helping you draft a solid plan complete with cash-flow projections. You might take a business-plan writing class at a local college. Another valuable resource is the U.S. Small Business Administration (202-205-7701), whose small business information centers nationwide offer free publications and one-on-one advice sessions on writing plans. Additionally, check your local software supply store for titles to help polish your plan.

■ **Take stock of your financial condition.** It takes time to start earning money from a new business, typically 18 months. Can you survive without a paycheck for that long? Make sure you've gotten enough dough to support yourself and your family for a while before plunging into entrepreneurship.

■ **Ferret out sources for start-up cash.** Franchisors often provide start-up capital for their franchisees. Other owners of fledgling businesses will have a tougher time getting financing, though. The most common source of money for entrepreneurs is friends and family members. After you try tapping your circle, you may want to try your state's economic development office, the Small Business Association (for details, see the Appendix), banks, or even venture capitalists—speculators whom you repay with money, equity in your business, or both. Once you go to serious lenders asking for money, you'll need to have a business plan that sings and the expertise to pull it all off.

■ **Finally, before signing on with a franchise company, check it out.** A franchisor is a business that licenses its concept to many business owners to create a uniform chain of stores or outlets. The most popular examples are food businesses, such as McDonald's and Burger King. These titans typically require a pile of start-up cash, in excess of $500,000. Plenty of other franchisors ask far less, however—sometimes under $25,000. They typically include franchisors of decorating, cleaning, travel, and auto services businesses.

Because they require less start-up capital and the concept is already proven, franchises generally pose less risk than a business started from scratch. But never forget that a franchisor merely provides a foundation for your business; it's no guarantee that your operation will succeed. For a listing of more than 5,000 franchisors nationwide, plus information on how to check out the financial soundness of a franchisor, call the International Franchising Association in Washington, D.C. (800-543-1038) and ask for the *Franchise Opportunities Guide*. For $21, they'll send you a copy.

Holding On to the Job That You Have

Wake up in a cold sweat lately, roused from a nightmare where company cutbacks are mandated and the roulette wheel aims smack in your direction? Welcome to the 1990s job world. For the average worker, job tenure in corporate America has fizzled from a stalwart 12.5 years in 1984 to less than six years today. Unless you're a nimble and willing job-hopper, these statistics will no doubt seem a bit dismal. You can't control how the economy, new technologies, or just plain old back luck will influence your job longevity. On the other hand, savvy employees with an eye on the future can help secure their footing by following a few rules:

■ **Learn to be a master of more than one trade.** You can't make yourself indispensable, but you can make yourself less expendable. The surest method to keep things moving your way is to get comfortable juggling several tasks. Adaptable types—antispecialists, if you will—show employers that they are malleable to change. Your best strategy: Try your hand at several key functions that interest you. A marketing executive, for example, who adds superior purchasing skills to his or her résumé will open far more career doors over the long term. True career champs excel in two or three complementary areas.

■ **Update your skills and stay flexible.** When is the right time to hit the books to keep current? The answer: Don't wait until your colleagues do. Don't delay until a plum position opens up, forcing you to scramble and acquire the skills needed to fit the bill. Instead, scope out positions that pique your interest and assess what tools you'll need to bolster your qualifications. A tip: If you're aware of a course that you think would make you a better worker, tell your boss. Even if tuition reimbursement isn't a part of your benefits package, he or she may be impressed enough to find tuition fees in the department budget.

■ **Understand the corporate culture, and adapt.** "No eating at your desk. Stockings mandatory for women. Docked pay for showing up late." These sorts of work rules may sound old-fashioned, but many companies, particularly small, family-run businesses, abide by them. Whether *you* can is another issue—and one that you should consider before you accept a job where they are strictly enforced.

■ **Cultivate work relationships.** While office gossip may turn you off, office politics is one arena you can't afford to ignore. As with networking outside the office, the onus is on you. Ask colleagues to lunch, those who work both beneath you and above you. You may be surprised how a friendly conversation turns into an invitation to join an important meeting. Don't think your boss isn't watching how you perform on this score: the best managers are able to get along with all types, and the more you can demonstrate this at work, the farther along you're likely to get.

■ **Don't get yourself into trouble.** Sounds obvious, but you'd be amazed how many people sabotage their careers by saying or doing the wrong thing at the wrong time. Be careful of what you zap over your e-mail. Likewise, if your boss is the buttoned-up type, but your off-the-job lifestyle is anything but, keep that part of your life quiet at the office. Alarmingly, workplace privacy rules are so scant that your boss can legally monitor your every on-the-job move. This means everything from searching through your office file cabinets to browsing your "confidential" e-mail to tapping into your phone calls. To be safe, don't send anything over e-mail that you wouldn't want to fall into the hands of your boss. And

unless you have a physical disability that may affect your job duties, use discretion when discussing your medical history with your supervisor. You never know what bias your boss may have against, say, someone seeking psychiatric help or relief from a substance abuse problem.

If all this sounds a bit scary, remember that you do have some rights, and keeping your job may, at some point, depend on your defending them. To find out about the cornucopia of information that may be contained in your employment file (anything from salary history to suspected drug use to your political bent), call your state attorney general's office and ask if your state is one of the 18 that has laws giving you access to your employment files. For more advice on exactly what types of issues your boss can raise on the job, phone the American Civil Liberty Union's National Task Force on Civil Liberties in the Workplace at 212-944-9800. The ACLU can also help you interpret state privacy laws and dispense advice on possible legal actions.

■ **Make the most of the job review process.** Most medium-size and larger employers have formal review policies for their workers, appraising their deeds annually. Yet in the fast-paced workplace of the '90s, where situations change with the blink of a computer screen, a once-a-year report card may be inadequate. Your manager, in fact, may not have a handle on how valuable you've been over the past 12 months—unless you make a point to show him or her. By asking for feedback (and this often means volunteering for extra work), you set yourself up for special notice. You can take control by asking to get together with your boss, say, once every other month to informally discuss your progress, goals, and shortfalls. Consequently, the annual review will hold few surprises and will be far less daunting.

■ **Don't disappoint your boss.** Keep yourself from taking on more work or responsibilities than you can reasonably handle. Otherwise you'll have one unhappy boss. Unfortunately, one bad break can stick in your boss's mind for months or years and could be used against you if he or she needs to lay off staffers.

Getting More Money from Your Boss

In this era of puny or nonexistent raises, it's tough to get extra cash from your boss. It's not impossible, though. The magic word is bonus. More and more, companies around the country are getting rid of annual raises and replacing them with bonuses. About 30% of large and medium-size businesses now award bonuses, and many more are planning to start. The big hitch is that even if your firm has a bonus program, you're not guaranteed to receive a bonus. The size of the bonus—if you get one at all—depends on your performance on the job and your employer's profits. Generally, bonuses range between 2% and 30% of your annual pay. There's one other drawback to a bonus system. Your benefits such as profit sharing, pensions, and life insurance typically are pegged to your base pay. So if you get a juicy bonus, that money won't be included when figuring your bennies. To boost the size of your bonus, do whatever you can to show your boss just how useful you've been in making your employer more profitable, efficient, or both.

Whether or not you get a bonus, you may well want to persuade your boss to give you more money. The subject is no longer taboo. You need to raise the issue gingerly, however. If you can demonstrate to your superior that you're underpaid, simply ask for the money you think you deserve to receive. Sometimes the answer will be "Sorry, everybody gets the same raise this year." In that case, if there's a bonus pool where you work, ask your supervisor what it would take to either start swimming in it or get a larger bonus than you were promised. You might want to set target goals with your boss and then update the list periodically.

Getting the Most from Your Benefits

The difference between a good job and a truly great one may be bundled in a package of perks. A decent benefits package—health coverage, life insurance, one or more retirement plans—may have a value of as much as a third of your pay or more; but many employers offer less. These days a generous benefits package is truly a gem to covet. As corporate America has looked for ways to cut costs, many firms have either cut back on their benefit plans, required employees to pony up more cash for their perks, or both. According to the Employers Council on Flexible Compensation, nearly half of its 480 member corporations slashed benefits in recent years. Moreover, many companies are asking employees to pay larger sums to cover both health premiums and medical deductibles. Businesses are getting especially stingy, too, about giving their retirees health benefits; some are forcing their ex-employees to pick up the entire tab for coverage, while others are eliminating health benefits altogether for seniors.

It's up to you to keep abreast of how your benefits measure up. You ought to pore over the employer's benefits handbook as soon as you accept a job or even while you're interviewing for a position if you can get your hands on it. If you're a new hire, ask for a conference with your benefits counselor or personnel manager to ensure you understand everything you're entitled to receive and when you're eligible to start getting the benefits. At many companies, for instance, health coverage doesn't kick in until several months after you've started.

When your firm passes out new benefits books or memos, be sure to read and keep them. Lurking in these publications may be news of costly changes (higher medical deductibles) or valuable features you may have previously overlooked (free legal counseling). At the very least, you'll want to have a copy of the most current benefits book in case you have questions about how the perks work. A good example: You may not care about how the firm's 401(k) loan rules work today, but six months from now you may need to know them so that you can tap your account to help pay for a home remodeling job.

What follows is a guide to making the best use of the benefits you have at work:

MEDICAL COVERAGE

Be prepared for **managed care** to become a part of your life. (For a detailed discussion of health maintenance organizations, preferred-provider organizations, and how to size them up, see Chapter 2.)

Assuming your employer offers a choice between an HMO and a PPO, take a hard look at the HMO. It just might save you some money. Though your premiums may be slightly higher, HMOs typically carry no deductible and charge patients minimal copayments (as little as $5) for doctor visits. Because they are so affordable, and limit your access to specific medical providers, HMOs are best for workers with average medical needs and for families with young children requiring routine, periodic checkups.

To cut costs in managed-care programs, insurers want you to use the preapproved doctors in their networks. You'll start by selecting a primary-care physician: a general practitioner who will see you for routine checkups. If your doctor is not on the preapproved list, you are going "out of network." Be prepared for limited reimbursement—as little as 50% in some cases. Similarly, when you need a specialist, you generally must seek a formal referral from your primary-care physician. Failing to do so will limit your reimbursement or wipe it out altogether. One tip: Managed-care plans require you to be a card-carrying member, so always carry your ID card. That way, if you have to make an emergency trip to the doctor or the pharmacy, you'll be charged only what the arrangement requires. Without the card, you could be forced to pay in full, up front.

Almost half of large U.S. companies now offer so-called **flexible spending accounts (FSAs),** which let you pay for certain unreimbursable medical costs with pretax dollars. Here's how they work: You decide how much you'd like to place in your FSA during the year (typically between $2,000 and $5,000), and the amount gets zapped from your paychecks in equal installments *before* taxes. When you need access to the funds (for such costs as health deductibles, prescription eyeglasses, even cab rides to your doctor's office), you simply fill out a claim form for reimbursement. Best of all, with an FSA you can withdraw the maximum amount pledged even *before* you've paid in the cash for it. Anyone with significant out-of-pocket medical bills—more than a few hundred dollars a year—definitely ought to consider enrolling in a tax-saving FSA, if one is available. Need proof? A married worker with a $50,000 salary who spends $1,000 on health care can expect to save about $350 in taxes by opening up an FSA. Incidentally, if one spouse makes over $65,400 and both have access to an FSA, the one with the lower income should fund the FSA. Aside from avoiding federal and local taxes, he or she will be able to shield some pay from the 6.2% Social Security tax on incomes up to $63,600.

Now, here's the catch with an FSA: You lose any funds that you pledge but don't use during the year. That's worth repeating. If you tell your employer to put $2,000 into your FSA and then use only $500 of the money, you will never get the other $1,500 of your pay. So before signing up for an FSA, carefully gauge how much you think you'll incur in out-of-pocket medical costs during the year ahead. You might jot down a list of last year's outlays with an eye toward new expenses in the year ahead. Don't forget to include these expenses (if you expect to have them): deductibles for medical plans; transportation costs to and from your medical appointments; prescription eyewear; hearing care and alternative medical treatments, such as acupuncture.

Roughly 90% of large U.S. companies offer **dental plans,** picking up the bills for between 50% and 100% of all work. As firms search for ways to trim the fat from their medical plans, however, dental plans seem a prime spot for drilling. Increasingly, employers are axing their traditional dental plans and replacing them with managed-care options. Often referred to as dental HMOs, these plans charge no deductible (versus $25 to $50 under traditional plans) and limit your choice of dentists to a preapproved list. Although you may have to switch dentists to use one in the plan, a dental HMO can be financially attractive. This type of plan will pay the full cost of many routine services, such as tooth cleanings and fillings, as opposed to 50% to 80% reimbursement for traditional plans. Should your employer offer you a choice

between a standard plan and a dental HMO, you may be served best by an HMO if preventive services such as tooth cleanings are covered free; waits for emergency services are held to under four weeks; and its dentists are members of the American Academy of General Dentistry.

Chances are, if you're married, both you and your spouse have access to health plans at work. Which one is best? To find out, you'll need to comb through the provisions of each to see how you can get the best features for the least amount of money. When scrutinizing plans, consider each of these important factors:

■ **Deductibles.** Count on shelling out anywhere between .3% of your annual salary and 5%. Remember the general rule about these deductibles, however: The higher the deductible, the higher your reimbursement.

■ **Out-of-pocket maximums.** If you anticipate high medical bills, compare the maximum amount each plan requires you to pay before it picks up 100% of the tab.

■ **Choice of providers.** Just because one plan may have more doctors doesn't necessarily make it a better choice. You'll want to make sure that the doctor you'd use in any managed-care network is not oversubscribed. You can find out how harried physicians are by calling the provider or the doctor directly and asking how many patients he or she has. Don't forget to see which hospitals, labs, and pharmacies are affiliated with each plan. If your favorite pharmacy or the hospital you prefer isn't in the group, you may not want to join the managed-care plan.

LIFE AND DISABILITY INSURANCE

Most large corporations dole out free life insurance equal to each employee's annual pay. Anything more, say benefits counselors, is considered munificent indeed. (At Xerox, for instance, workers are entitled to life insurance payouts of up to six years' pay, depending on their age and tenure.) Typical, too, is free long-term disability coverage, which pays you as much as 60% of your salary should you become incapacitated.

Is it wise to sign up for extra life and disability insurance, known as supplemental coverage, which are often available through your company? Perhaps. If you've determined that you do want to beef up your insurance, check the rates and coverage offered by insurers outside your employer, too. Your company's rates may not be the best. For instance, if you are in good health, are a nonsmoker, and are under the age of 45, you can probably buy term life insurance more cheaply from an agent or a low-load life insurer than through your employer.

RETIREMENT PLANS

If you work for a company that will help finance your golden years, consider yourself lucky. Since 1990 nearly 50,000 U.S. firms have axed the traditional, company-paid pension. This benefit is quickly becoming a relic of the past. In 1988 close to 80% of the nation's small- and medium-size companies offered this type of retirement package. That figure is closer to 65% today. Instead, the majority of companies are asking employees to fund their own retirements, most typically with 401(k) accounts; nonprofits often offer similar vehicles, known as 403(b) plans. Named for a section in the tax code, such "defined-contribution" plans let you stash away dollars, before they're taxed, through payroll deductions. The earnings grow in your account tax-deferred. By federal law, employers must offer several places for you to park your 401(k) dough, such as stock and bond funds, money-market funds, and company stock. As a bonus, most employers will match a portion of your contributions, usually 50¢ for every dollar you ante up. (For more detailed advice on the care and feeding of your 401(k), see Chapter 5.)

If your company offers a 401(k) plan, sign up as soon as you're eligible. This may sound about as obvious as "Eat your vegetables," but only 65% of all eligible employees participate. To help make your retirement comfortable, contribute as much as you can afford, as early as you can. Recently, the allowable maximum was roughly $9,500. Generally speaking, however, if your salary falls in the top 20% for all earners at your firm, you can probably contribute no more than 6% to 7% of your pretax salary to the plan. Some plans also let you salt away after-tax dollars.

As you hopscotch from one job to the next, remember that unlike the assets of a traditional pension plan, the money in a 401(k) is fully portable as long as you follow a few rules. In order to escape costly taxes and penalties when you leave company A for company B, you must "roll over" your 401(k) proceeds into an Individual Retirement Account or to your new company's retirement plan. Keep in mind, the clock is ticking. You have just 60 days to do this before the tax man cometh.

To transfer funds properly, *do not* request a check from your old employer. You'd be taking possession of your 401(k) assets, which is a sure way to get slapped with the dreaded 20% federal withholding tax. Instead you'll want to do a "trustee-to-trustee transfer," in which funds go directly into the investment you've selected for your IRA (typically a mutual fund) or from the plan administrator at one job to the next. Before switching jobs, you'll want to discuss

these moves with your benefits department to ensure the transfer goes smoothly. The process may take several months or even up to a year.

OTHER GOODIES

In this age of diminishing corporate givebacks, there *is* some good news. More companies are willing to offer so-called family-friendly benefits—perks that tend to be easy on the corporate coffers and, in turn, raise job satisfaction among employees. Some of these perks may be unwritten, and still others may be up for negotiating. So check out the ones below, and if your employer doesn't offer them, try politely to push for a change in policy:

■ **Flextime.** Not long ago, Jackie O. was one of the few working women who could dictate her job schedule and keep the paychecks coming. But so-called flextime, which lets workers forgo standard hours and put in ones best suited to them, became popular in the early '90s when the number of working mothers zoomed 23% from a decade prior. Because flexible schedules demand increased efficiency of employees, many firms actually view these arrangements as a boon to productivity. If you have only a few years on the job, you probably won't be permitted to work flextime, since management may be skeptical of your ability to pull off such an arrangement. Once you have five or more years under your belt, though, you may be able to strike a deal.

■ **Vacation and comp days.** It's common to start at a new company with two weeks of vacation, more for senior executives. What do you do if you get just two weeks or so but put in dozens of unpaid overtime hours on weekends and holidays? One way to get your due—and to potentially extend your vacation—is to keep a tally of those phantom hours and request time off for those hours worked. You've got nothing to lose by asking.

■ **Referral services.** Need a good lawyer? Want help in sizing up college choices for your teen? Believe it or not, your company may be able to help. Roughly 55% of all Fortune 500 companies now boast referral services that assist employees with everything from finding a reliable baby-sitter to counseling you about spousal abuse. Some firms even have the equivalent of a concierge on their premises, ready to help make your life outside of work a little easier. Depending on where you work, these programs may be formal or informal, offered on or off site. Ask your benefits counselor whether such programs are available. Before spilling private secrets about your life to an employee assistance counselor, however, find out who could ultimately

have access to that information. You may find that getting a little help at work isn't worth the invasion of your privacy.

■ **Child care assistance.** A few years ago, workers at Xerox got what the American rank and file would kill for: child care grants (up to $2,500 per year) for any employee earning under $50,000. Most companies aren't quite so generous, yet fully eight out of 10 today provide some type of help with child care. For example, 12%—more than double the number in 1993—now offer emergency child care facilities. If your regular sitter gets sick at the last minute, for instance, your child could spend the day (or before- and after-school hours) at an on-site company facility. Because these services are either free or low-cost for parents, they are wildly popular, making space extremely limited.

Some employers also offer flexible spending accounts that let employees set aside a specified amount of money, pretax, for child care expenses. A pretax, child care FSA is a great deal, but you can't use it if you claim the child care credit on your tax return. So if you already take the credit, you may need to run some numbers to see if you'll save more on taxes with an FSA or with the credit.

If you feel that your company is behind the curve on the child care score, speak up. Get together with other colleagues who would like to see some sort of child care plan and approach your manager or benefits counselor with a workable arrangement, such as a successful one in use by a nearby firm or competitor.

■ **Financial-planning and legal advice.** A fairly recent trend in the employee benefits field is the offering of financial and legal advice to employees. Often such seminars are free and quite useful. Just be careful that the speaker isn't there to hawk his or her own products or business. Unions sometimes provide such services to their members, too. Members of the United Auto Workers, for instance, are entitled to free legal services, such as the drafting of wills. So even if your boss doesn't pay you what you deserve, you might to able to use his office to learn how to make the dollars you earn stretch farther.

CHAPTER 10

How to Afford Your Child's College Education

Nobody needs to tell you that the cost of college is out of sight—and headed even higher. The College Board estimates that tuition, room, and fees these days average about $7,118 a year at a public college and $18,184 at a private one. And if your child has his eye on one of the elites, such as Princeton or Stanford, make that a wallet-busting $28,000-plus once you add room and board. Worse still, if college costs gallop ahead at a conservative 6% a year, the average price of a four-year college degree in 10 years will range from $66,000 to $135,000—and at an Ivy, nearly half a million bucks.

But don't throw up your hands just yet. Though sobering, the figures aren't quite as daunting as they sound. Don't forget that your income will be rising just as college costs increase. So that fatter paycheck will help cover some of the tuition bills. Also, your child will likely qualify for some financial aid in the form of grants, scholarships, loans, or campus jobs. On average, about 70% of students at four-year colleges cover roughly half their costs through a financial aid package. The average amount of financial aid received: $2,919 a year. Borrowers who get federal loans take out an average of $3,145 a year. And new tax breaks can help soften the blow. Still, there's no question that a chunk of money for college will come directly out of your family budget. So to give your child the widest possible choice of schools when the time comes, you'll need to do two things: start saving for college as early as you can and, as application time approaches, search out all possible sources of financial help.

Figuring How Much You Will Need

Until your child has actually been accepted to a college and secured a financial aid package, it's impossible to know exactly what costs you'll face. After all, your income, the financial aid formulas, and the inflation rate for tuition bills will change over time. As a result, the farther off college is for your child, the more tentative your estimates will have to be. Still, by making some preliminary calculations now—even if your son or daughter is just starting to crawl—you'll gain a firmer sense of the financial challenges that lie ahead.

Virtually every family can get some kind of financial help putting a child through college, if only through a government-guaranteed loan. At the same time, though, virtually every household sending a child to college is expected to kick in its share of college costs, known as the "family contribution," based on its income, family size, and debts. Unfortunately, it will be up to the college and the federal or state government to determine the minimum size of that contribution, not you. As a result, the amount of aid your family qualifies for will be, at best, the difference between that designated contribution and the full cost of the college your child chooses. (A fuller description about negotiating an aid package appears later in this chapter.) If the college your child will go to is financially strapped, the size of his or her aid package may be even less than that. For a rough preview of how much your required family contribution might be today, fill out the worksheet on page 253.

On page 242 you can find out how much money you would need to stockpile now and in the future to fund college for your child. Once you have this approximate number in hand, you may be pleasantly surprised or shocked and appalled at the amount of saving it will take to pay for your son's or daughter's education. Armed with this information, however, you'll be ready to devise a strategy to meet—or at least approach—your goal.

YOUR COLLEGE SAVINGS WORKSHEET

Naturally, you can't know years in advance exactly how expensive a school your child will choose or how fast college costs will rise between now and the time the freshman bells peal. And you don't know what your income will be then or how the financial aid rules will change in the future. That said, the following worksheet will give you a pretty good idea of the amount of money you would need to set aside each year to pay the likely cost of college when the time comes.

The worksheet at right assumes that college costs will rise at an average annual rate of 7% (that may be a mite high, but it's always better to err on the side of caution), that your investments will earn 7% a year, that your child will enter college at age 18, and that you'll continue saving until he or she graduates. Depending on how much of your child's college costs you expect to pay for yourself, you can use one of three assumptions for the figure on line 1: (1) your expected family contribution (from the worksheet on page 253); (2) the full current cost of college (you can either contact specific schools or use rounded-off average figures: $9,000 for public colleges, $18,800 for private ones); or (3) 50% of the figures above, which is the current average family share after financial aid. By choosing the third assumption, for instance, you'll discover that if your child is three years old and headed to a state college, you'll need to set aside $1,413 a year after the first year. If she's 14 and Ivy League bound, make that a whopping $8,626 a year.

1. **Current one-year cost (see note above)** _____
2. **Four-year cost in today's dollars (multiply line 1 times 4)** _____
3. **Amount to invest the first year (line 2 times appropriate age factor from column A on page 243)** _____
4. **Amount to save at beginning of each of the following years (multiply line 3 by the appropriate factor from column B on page 243)** _____

AGE	A	PAYMENT NUMBER	B
Newborn	.0603	2	1.040
1	.0624	3	1.082
2	.0646	4	1.125
3	.0672	5	1.170
4	.0700	6	1.217
5	.0731	7	1.265
6	.0767	8	1.316
7	.0807	9	1.369
8	.0854	10	1.423
9	.0907	11	1.480
10	.0970	12	1.540
11	.1044	13	1.601
12	.1133	14	1.665
13	.1242	15	1.732
14	.1378	16	1.801
15	.1553	17	1.873
16	.1787	18	1.948
17	.2115	19	2.026
		20	2.107
		21	2.192
		22	2.279

A Short Course in Saving for College

No matter what age your kids are right now, there are six basic rules you should follow in creating your college savings plan:

1. Invest in stocks to meet your goal. Stocks are the only investment high–octane enough to power your portfolio past the expected 6% average annual increase in future college costs. You've read this earlier in the book, but it bears repeating: Over the past seven decades or so, returns on blue-chip stocks have clobbered those of Treasury bills and bonds.

2. Use mutual funds as your primary method of investing for college. Mutual funds offer an unbeatable combination of professional management, reinvestment of earnings, and record keeping. What's more, many funds suspend their standard minimum initial investments of $1,000 or more if you sign up for an automatic savings plan that transfers as little as $25 a month from your bank account. Such a savings arrangement is an ideal way to painlessly put away cash for looming college bills. Every month you'll get a statement from the fund company reminding you how brilliant and responsible you are, noting your most recent deposit, and listing the total you've accumulated so far.

One caveat: Don't put all your college cash in just one or two mutual funds. To buffer yourself against picking a lemon—and with more than 3,000 mutual funds out there you can be sure there are lemons aplenty—you ought to select three to five funds with dissimilar portfolios. For example, you could invest in a growth mutual fund, a balanced or growth-and-income fund, a Treasury or municipal bond fund, and an international stock fund. To help make your picks, check the six-month or annual mutual fund performance rankings in magazines such as **Money,** *Forbes*, or *Business Week*.

3. Skip prepaid tuition plans, generally. These "pay now graduate later"

schemes offered by a bunch of states can seem tempting. The pitch: By contracting to pay tuition at today's rates or something close while your child is still years away from enrollment, you sidestep future college-cost inflation. Example: For just under $6,000, you can sign up your two-year-old for four years at any of Florida's nine state university campuses if you live in the Sunshine State; out-of-staters must pay nearly twice that. Twenty other states offer variations on such prepaid plans, up from twelve in 1996.

But prepaid plans really make little sense for most families. You and your child will be committing to a college long before he or she is really ready to choose. If your child goes elsewhere instead, drops out, or skips college altogether, typically all you'll get back is your original cash, with no interest. That's a losing proposition. Contrast this deal with an investment in stock mutual funds. Not only have their returns beat college inflation rates by three to four points a year on average, but your investment pays off, no matter what your child decides to do about college.

All that said, some prepaid plans are more flexible than others. The most flexible—and thus the best—are in Alabama, Florida, Michigan, Mississippi, Ohio, Pennsylvania, Tennessee, Texas, and Virginia. Eight of those will pay an amount equal to the state's average current public-school tuition toward your child's tuition at any college in the U.S. The ninth, Virginia, will do the same only for tuition at a school in the state; but it will return your cash plus compounded interest at average money market rates out of state. Most of these plans will also refund your original payment, often with interest, for any reason at any time.

4. Don't rush into buying long-term zero-coupon bonds, either. These investments—often given a hard sell by stockbrokers who pitch them—can sound as enticing as prepaid tuition plans. The idea behind them is simple. Like other bonds, zero-coupon bonds carry an interest rate that remains fixed if you hold them to maturity. There are zero-coupon Treasury bonds, municipal bonds, and corporate bonds. Unlike most bonds, however, zeros pay their interest not semiannually, but all at once, at maturity. So by buying zeros long before your child reaches college age, you can lock in a large guaranteed payment back to you in the future for a fairly modest investment up front. For instance, in July 1995 you could have invested just $20,000 and bought a zero Treasury bond that would be worth $50,000 upon maturity in August 2009 when your three-year-old would enroll in college.

But zeros present two significant drawbacks. While they provide a guaranteed return if you hang on to them until they mature, they can cost you dearly if you don't. Indeed, long-term zero-coupon bonds are the most volatile of all bonds. Should interest rates rise, the market value of your bond will fall—quite possibly dramatically. If you then need to sell the bond, the amount it brings will be discounted for the lower interest rate it carries, reducing your yield. What's more, even though you won't actually receive any interest until the bond matures or you sell it, you'll have to pay the Internal Revenue Service income taxes on the imputed amount each year. If you're virtually certain that you won't be forced to sell early and the yearly taxes don't daunt you, then consider including zeros in the bond portion of your college portfolio (more on that in the next section). Otherwise, pass them by. You'll lower your zero risks by waiting to invest in the bonds until your child is about 14. Then you can buy short-term zeros.

5. Give Series EE U.S. savings bonds a look. These securities, which can be purchased through banks, brokers, and many employers, offer a federally backed rate of return. Their interest is free from state and local taxes, too. Like zero-coupon bonds, you buy savings bonds at a discount (in this case, 50% of the face value) and get your interest when your bond matures or you sell it. If you hold the bonds for five years or more, you earn a rate equal to 90% of five-year Treasury securities, a figure that is adjusted every May and November. In the mid-'90s that would have worked out to a rate of about 7%. However, if you redeem the bonds before five years, you will lose three months of interest. There's a real advantage for holding on to your savings bonds for at least five years, since six-month Treasuries typically yield less than five-year Treasuries.

While the rate of return on savings bonds may not be spectacular, if you use the bonds for college, you may qualify for a special tax break that effectively increases your yield. Here's how it works: The interest on your savings bonds for college will be fully free from *federal* taxes, too, if you hold the bonds to maturity and your income in the year you redeem them is below a certain threshold—recently $50,850 if you're single and $76,250 if you're married (those figures rise each year with inflation). Above those figures the exclusion begins to phase out, and it disappears completely once your income hits $65,850 or $106,250 if you're married.

6. Take advantage of the new tax breaks for college. As explained in the tax chapter of this book, the 1997 tax law created five new ways to help pay for college.

First, starting in 1998, you can pull money out of an Individual Retirement Account penalty-free before age 59½ if you're using the money to pay for college.

Second, the new Hope scholarship tax credit lets you write off up to $1,500 per student per year in the first two years of college. You can claim 100% of the first $1,000 of tuition costs and 50% of the second $1,000.

Third, the new Lifetime Learning tax credit—for education expenses paid after June 30, 1998—permits you to take off your taxes 20% of up to $5,000 of qualified expenses, including those for acquiring or improving your job skills through a training program (that's a maximum of $1,000). After the year 2001, the credit rises to 20% of $10,000 in expenses, or a maximum of $2,000. Both the Hope and Lifetime Learning credits start to phase out once your adjusted gross income hits $40,000 if you're single and $80,000 if you're married and file jointly. The credit is unavailable if your income is $50,000 or more and you're single, $100,000 or above for joint filers.

Fourth, starting in 1998, you can once again deduct student loan interest. You needn't itemize to claim this writeoff, but the tax break is limited to $1,000 of interest in 1998, $1,500 in 1999, $2,000 in 2000, and $2,500 in 2001.

Finally, you may now be able to open a special nondeductible, tax-deferred Educational IRA account of up to $500 a year. This account is for savings you put away toward college. Again, your ability to take the break depends on your income. The $500 contribution limit gets phased out when your adjusted gross income hits $95,000 if you're single and

$150,000 for joint filers. You cannot open an Educational IRA if you're single and have an AGI over $110,000 or married with an AGI topping $160,000.

The Best Investment Strategy for You

The biggest factor in devising your college savings plan is the age of your kids. The younger they are, the more years you'll have to make your cash grow. If your children are little, you have enough time to weather any short-term setbacks to your progress and can then invest heavily in higher-risk, higher-return securities. Meanwhile, however, inflation will be running alongside you all those years, pushing up the price of the education you're saving for. With older kids, your situation is reversed. A few more years of college inflation won't hurt you too much. But with fewer years to grow your cash, you'll need larger amounts of it to seed your college fund. So keeping your college stash safe will take priority over investing for the fattest returns. Here are the most sensible saving strategies, depending on the age of your child:

■ **If college is eight or more years off.** Your biggest challenge is to outrace

inflation, which can easily double current college costs before your child becomes a freshman. To stay ahead of inflation, you'll need an aggressive portfolio, and that means mostly—or exclusively—stocks. To lessen the odds that a slide in the U.S. stock market will crack your entire college-saving nest egg, keep only 75% or so of your money in U.S. stocks and the rest in international stock funds and bonds—through a conservative bond fund or U.S. savings bonds.

For your U.S. stocks, be sure to diversify among mutual funds that invest with different approaches. For instance, you might balance a growth fund, comprising companies expected to deliver high earnings, with a value fund, comprising companies with stock prices that seem low relative to their assets. Or you could offset a small-cap fund, which buys the stock of companies with less than $500 million in market value, with a large-cap fund, which sticks with $1 billion–plus companies. (For a fuller description of portfolio diversification, see Chapter 13.)

After you select your U.S. mutual funds, check out international offerings. If you're on the conservative side, stick to funds that invest primarily in the established financial markets in Europe and the Pacific, such as Germany, Australia, and Japan. In the past 10 years such diversified international funds have gained an average of more than 18% annually, compared with 15% for the Standard & Poor's index of 500 major U.S. firms. But if you're adventurous, you might venture into mutual funds specializing in more volatile emerging markets such as Brazil, Malaysia, and Turkey, which in recent years have soared as much as 60% (and sometimes stumbled badly, too). Even if investing in developing nations appeals to you, though, don't sink more than half of your overseas investment money in them. They're too risky.

For the bond portion of your college-savings portfolio, you could go the safe savings bonds route. The easiest way to do this is by signing up for a payroll-deduction savings plan at work. That way you'll be buying the bonds on a regular basis without having to think about it. Otherwise you can get the best diversification by investing in a conservative bond fund, such as one buying only U.S. government agency securities or an intermediate-term municipal bond fund that sticks to high-quality, tax-exempt securities. If you're in the 28% tax bracket or higher, tax-exempt municipal bond funds generally can give you better returns than taxable bond funds. Bear in mind, though, that as you lower your risk with bonds, you also lessen the performance potential of your portfolio.

Tax tip: You may be tempted to put college investments in your child's name, to take advantage of the IRS rules that let a child under 14 earn $650 a year tax-free and another $650 at his or her own tax rate, usually 15%. (Assuming your investments earn 8% on average, the portfolio wouldn't throw off that much income until it tops $15,000.) But remember that once the portfolio is earning more than that, it will be taxed at *your* rate until your child is 14. What's more, money in your child's name may limit his financial aid down the road, because standard financial aid formulas require kids to fork over 35% of their assets before qualifying for help. You can retain control of the assets until your child is 18 (or 21 in some states), by investing in his or her name in a Uniform Gift to Minors Act (UGMA) custodial account or by setting up a so-called 2503(c) trust. But after that point, the money in your child's name is *his*, not yours. If he uses it to spring for a Miata rather than college, there's nothing you can do about it. In short, the minor tax advantage of putting college savings in your child's name is almost certainly not worth the disadvantages.

■ **If college is four to seven years off.** With college closing in, you need to back off a bit from full throttle and adjust your portfolio to the possibility that a big downturn in the stock market could badly crimp your savings efforts. So now is the time to start moving 10% to 15% of your aggressive stock holdings each year into more conservative investments, such as total-return mutual funds, which deliver dividends as well as capital gains, and safe bond funds that buy short- to intermediate-term U.S. Treasury securities.

Tax tip: If you know that your family income is way too high to qualify your child for any financial aid, you can safely shift college cash into his name once he turns 14 without worrying that doing so will cut the aid you'll get. Starting at that age, he'll pay all taxes he owes at his own rate—probably 15%—instead of yours, which may be much higher. Similarly, you and your spouse can each hand over as much as $10,000 a year to each of your children without triggering a gift tax.

■ **If college is only one to three years off.** For you, stocks are becoming way too risky to pay those looming tuition bills. So continue cashing out until you've got, at most, 10% of your portfolio invested in a conservative stock fund. Put the rest in short-term bond funds with maturities of four years or less and money-market funds or perhaps short-term zeros.

■ **If college is less than a year away.** As your child begins packing for college, transfer enough cash to a money market fund to see you through his freshman-year bills. Put the rest of your college savings in bank certificates of deposit timed to mature at the beginning of his sophomore, junior, and senior years. By staggering the investment lengths, you'll get maximum returns. If college is right around the corner and you haven't got the money you need, don't panic. But be sure to read the "Emergency Cash for College" section at the end of this chapter.

Snagging the Best Financial Aid Package

There are three elements to most financial aid offers: scholarships or grants, loans, and a campus job. In name, at least, most packages are put together based on a family's financial need. If your income is $50,000 or less and you have few assets beyond your home, your child is certain to qualify for some form of help. Even with an income of $100,000 and few other assets, your family may still receive financial aid if you have two or more children attending college. If you qualify for aid, you can expect to receive between 65% and 100% of your need, according to standard aid formulas. The rest, however, must come from you.

In reality, though, how much aid your child actually receives and what form it takes depends partly on how well you and your student work the financial aid game. To help boost the amount and quality of the financial aid package your child receives, keep the following points in mind:

■ **In the immortal words of bank robber Willie Sutton: Go where the money is.** State schools generally save their greatest subsidies for home-grown students. Private colleges generally have the richest endowment coffers. Before your child decides where he'll send his college applications, do a little homework on how much cash each of the colleges under consideration has to spread around. You can get such information by asking the college financial aid offices directly for the average percent of costs covered by their aid packages and what portion of it is given in grants. Alternatively, you can check college guidebooks, which often list more than 1,000 colleges and contain data about financial aid and scholarships.

■ **Work the financial aid rules to your benefit.** Send for the free Application for Federal Student Aid (call the U.S. Department of Education at 800-433-3243) so you can familiarize yourself with the questions on the standard form used by colleges to calculate federal, and sometimes their own, aid packages. Read each line carefully so you don't wind up shortchanging yourself. For example, 401(k) savings plans from employers or other retirement savings vehicles don't count as current wealth. So don't mistakenly list them under "Assets" and reduce the amount of aid you're legitimately entitled to receive. You can also boost the aid package your child may get by subtracting commuting expenses from your salary when determining your annual income.

One rule worth remembering: Only 5.6% of your assets will be deemed available for college expenses, but up to 47% of your current income will be. By taking those figures into account, you can make some shrewd moves accordingly. For instance, if you're planning to get rid of an appreciated asset to pay for college, do it more than a year before filling out the financial aid form. That way you will avoid having your gain counted as income just when your child is applying for tuition money and thus raise the size of any financial aid package.

Take the same kind of peek at the colleges' own financial aid forms to make sure you understand how the rules compare with the federal forms. While the feds don't count your home equity as an asset, for example, most colleges do. So if you're relying on a home-equity loan to cover any shortfalls in college expenses, get the loan before you apply for aid.

Two more tips: First, apply for every federal financial aid program you hear about and report all rejections in your aid applications to colleges. The reason? A college may be stingy in allocating its financial resources to your child if its financial aid office feels you haven't explored all other opportunities. Second, send in the application forms as early as you can. The size of your total aid package won't change if you're a late applicant, but the best grants and most lucrative campus jobs may be gone as early as December.

■ **Negotiate from your strengths.** All schools want the brightest, most talented, and most interesting students they can find. In the past 20 years, however, the college applicant pool has shrunk by 15% and along with it, the supply of desirable students. Consequently, if your child is blessed with above average qualities academically, athletically, musically, socially, or otherwise, be sure he emphasizes them when filling out his college application.

■ **Don't settle for the first offer you get.** Here's a little secret about financial aid: The package your child is offered isn't necessarily the best he can receive from that college. A bit of negotiating on your part can up the offer. So if your son is accepted at his first-choice school, but the financial aid offer is not to your liking, try testing the school's true interest in him. Call the financial aid office and explain that your child wants to attend the school but you simply can't swing it on the offered package. Mention any information you might have left out of the original application, such as support for your aging parents, high living costs in your area, or any new developments such as a job loss or a recent medical emergency. If another college, equally prestigious but less appealing to your child, offered a better package, use that as a bargaining chip, too.

Don't conclude your argument on the phone. Tell the financial aid office that you'll be following up with a written statement that recapitulates all your points. Then do so. And keep a confident outlook. A recent study by the National Association of College and University Business Offices showed that many small, private schools are willing to bargain down their sticker prices by as much as 30%. There are no guarantees, of course, but neither are there any penalties for asking. A college will not withdraw its acceptance or reduce your aid package simply because you challenge it.

YOUR FINANCIAL AID WORKSHEET

This worksheet, based on the rules that Uncle Sam uses to determine a family's need for federal college aid, will give you a rough idea of the minimum share of your child's educational costs you'll have to shoulder. Individual colleges may have their own, somewhat different, methodology. This worksheet assumes that there are two parents in your family, that the older one is 45 and the younger one is any age. When you add together your expected contribution and your child's contribution, you'll get the key figure: your "expected family contribution." If it turns out that this figure is more than the cost of your kid's chosen college, you probably won't qualify for financial aid based on need. But if it's less, you can most likely expect to be offered a financial aid package.

TABLE I: INCOME PROTECTION ALLOWANCE

Family size (including student)	NUMBER OF FAMILY MEMBERS IN COLLEGE				
	1	2	3	4	5
2	$11,150	$9,240			
3	13,890	11,990	$10,080		
4	17,150	15,240	13,350	$11,440	
5	20,240	18,330	16,430	14,520	$12,620
6	23,670	21,760	19,860	17,960	16,060

TABLE II: PARENTS' CONTRIBUTION

IF LINE A PLUS LINE B EQUALS . . .	THEN THE PARENTS' CONTRIBUTION IS . . .
$3,408 or less	Minus $750
$3,409 to $10,000	22% of line A plus B
$10,001 to $12,500	$2,200 plus 25% of amount over $10,000
$12,501 to $15,100	$2,825 plus 29% of amount over $12,500
$15,101 to $17,600	$3,579 plus 34% of amount over $15,100
$17,601 to $20,100	$4,429 plus 40% of amount over $17,600
$20,101 or more	$5,429 plus 47% of amount over $20,100

Source: College Money, Marlton, N.J.

1. Parents' Income

Enter your adjusted gross income from last year's federal tax return. _____

Subtract any child support you paid last year. _____

Add the sum of all nontaxable income you received. _____

Add back deductions you took for IRA and Keogh contributions. _____

Subtract federal, state, and Social Security taxes you paid. _____

If both parents work, subtract employment expenses:
$2,500 or 35% of the lower salary, whichever is less. _____

Subtract your income protection allowance (from Table I).

If the result is negative, enter "0" on line A. If it's

positive, enter the amount on line A. _____

A. $_____

2. Parents' Assets

If your adjusted gross income is $50,000 or less and you
did not itemize deductions on your tax return, enter "0"
on line B. Otherwise, enter the total value of your
investments, including stocks, bonds, and real estate other
than your principal home. _____

Add the sum of all cash, bank, and money-market accounts. _____

Subtract $38,900. _____

If the result is negative, enter "0" on line B. If it's positive,
multiply by 0.12 and enter the result on line B. _____

B. $_____

3. Parents' Contribution

Enter the total of lines A and B. _____

Use this number to determine the parents' expected
contribution from Table II. Divide this figure by the
number of family members attending college and enter
the result on line C.

C. $_____

4. Student's Contribution

Enter the student's adjusted gross income as reported on
his or her tax return last year. _____

Subtract federal, state, and Social Security taxes paid last year. _____

Subtract the $1,750 income protection allowance.   _____

If the result is negative, enter "0." If it's positive, multiply by 0.5.   _____

Add 35% of the student's investments and savings, and enter

total on line D.

D. $_____

5. Total Family Contribution

Add lines C and D, and enter sum on line E.   _____

E. $_____

Scholarships, Grants, and Other Freebies

The best kind of financial aid, of course, is an outright gift of money that you don't have to pay back. Depending on your family's economic circumstances, your child's brain-power, and your persistence in pursuing all possibilities, you may be able to secure more free cash than you think. Here's where to look:

Nearly $30 million is awarded each year in **college scholarships.** But resist the temptation to sign up for a pricey scholarship search service or buy a book that promises to reveal "little known" sources of scholarship cash. The sad truth is that portable scholarships—the kind you can use at any school of your choice—are generally so small ($500 on average) that your child would need to

earn a half dozen to make a real dent in college costs (for a list of five exceptions, see page 256). Most scholarship awards of any real size come through individual colleges themselves. In fact, about 25% of the money handed out by colleges comes in the form of scholarships; the average award: $4,600. For on-line links to more than a thousand Web sites with scholarship information, visit the Financial Aid Information Page (www.finaid.org).

You may be thinking that your family's income is too high to qualify for a scholarship. Not necessarily. Even if your family is well-off, your child may be able to snag an award if he's a good student. The definition of that will vary according to the academic standards of the college and the high school he graduates from. Generally, though, a good student is someone with at least a B average in high school and a score of 1000 or better on the Scholastic Achievement Test. Your child can improve his chances of getting a scholarship, however, if he targets a school where his academic standing makes him a star. Generally, this means choosing a less prestigious school than he could actually qualify for, a move worth considering only if the college is one that your child can be happy attending.

Your child may also be able to score a scholarship by gaining admission to one of the 436 honors programs at state colleges. He'll need a grade-point average of at least 3.5 and Scholastic Achievement Test scores of 1150 or higher. In addition to getting into special seminars and individual tutorials, plus meeting classmates as smart as he is, he'll become eligible for scholarships that are often the richest the school has to offer. For example, most of the 200 students enrolled in Ohio University's Honors Tutorial College get awards of $1,000 to $1,500 a year, and many also get summer apprenticeships paying $3,000. The perks go a long way toward covering the nearly $8,000 in costs for Ohio residents and much of the $12,000 out-of-staters pay.

Unlike scholarships, which are often given for academic achievement only, **grants** almost always require strong financial need. The size of a family's need is usually defined by a federal formula that is updated each year but similar to the one in the previous worksheet. You must file a supplementary aid application,

however, or your child won't be eligible for grants from a college's coffers.

The federal government sponsors two programs for grants, whose money is provided outright and need not be repaid:

Pell grants (named after the senator who wrote the legislation creating them) are guaranteed to every student who qualifies for the aid. The maximum amount of the grant changes every year, based on funding from Congress, but the award was really $2,400 per year. The amount your child could actually receive depends on your family income, costs at your child's college, and whether he attends full-time and for a full academic year.

Supplemental Educational Opportunity Grants are not guaranteed, however. Colleges get a set amount of money from the federal government and distribute it to qualified, needy kids until the allocation runs out. Currently, students can receive as much as $4,000 in Supplemental Educational Opportunity Grants.

States, too, offer significant grant aid, though some require a student to use that aid at a public, state institution or provide service to the state after graduation. Not always, though. In Georgia, for instance, high school students with financial need plus exceptional academic records can receive up to $1,461 a year from the state to use at any Georgia college, private or public. To find out what kinds of grants might be available in your state, call the state's department of education, generally in the state capital.

What if your child is just not scholarship material and no grant money materializes? Is no-strings-attached cash out of the question? Not necessarily. Schools have their own quirky ways of rewarding loyalty. Because colleges lose an average of 32% of their freshmen before sophomore year, including scholarship holders (even Harvard graduates only 96% of its freshmen), more cash may be available from your child's school to help a hard-pressed sophomore, junior, or senior, even one without star quality. And at least 75 colleges offer discounts for family ties. Indiana's Franklin College, for instance, reserves $2,000 a year for each alumni offspring or grandoffspring. And if your first college kid can't get a grant, at about 70 colleges your second one can. George Washington University in Washington, D.C., cuts its $18,000 cost in half for siblings of current students. Not a bad deal.

Five Scholarships That Really Pay for College

Most scholarships are more like scholar rafts—they pay only enough to keep you above water for a short while. But the five ocean liners listed below will really (or nearly) pay your child's way through college—if he can snare one. None is based on financial need, but competition to get these scholarships is extremely tough. And in the case of the Reserve Officers Training Corps scholarship, the payback may be more than he—or you—are up for. But all are worth a closer look:

1. **National Merit Scholarship program.** Each year, students who score highest in the Preliminary Scholastic Achievement Tests are selected as semifinalists for a Merit Scholarship and invited to submit applications for awards ranging up to $8,000. Final selection is based on academic excellence, test scores, community service, and recommendations. Roughly 6,700 of the one million students who take the PSATs each year get these scholarships; that's about one in 150. To get in the running, simply make sure your child takes the optional PSATs.

2. **Reserve Officers Training Corps (ROTC).** If your child, male or female, is in top physical and academic shape and willing to join the Reserve Officers Training Corps, Uncle Sam may be happy to pay 80% to 100% of his or her college tuition, books, and fees, plus provide a stipend of $100 a month to live on, for four years. In return, however, your

youngster will have to serve an eight-year hitch in the military. Lately, ROTC has handed out about $131 million a year, with an average disbursement of $8,000 per recipient. For more details about this scholarship program, contact your local ROTC unit.

3. Coca-Cola Scholars Foundation. Each year, the soft-drink manufacturer bestows 50 awards of $20,000 each to high school seniors who demonstrate civic responsibility, leadership, and other worthy qualities. Another 100 get $4,000 apiece. For more details, write to Coca-Cola Scholars Foundation, One Buckhead Plaza, Suite 1000, 3060 Peachtree Rd. N.W., Atlanta, Ga. 30305 or call 404-237-1300.

4. Tylenol scholarships. About 25,000 students submit essays and applications each year, and Johnson & Johnson, the pharmaceutical company that makes Tylenol, awards $10,000 to each of the 10 entrants who best demonstrate leadership and academic excellence. For more details, write to Tylenol Scholarship, Mc-Neil Lab, Fort Washington, Pa. 19034 or call 215-233-8505.

5. Westinghouse Science Talent Search. From the thousands of eager science students who crowd high school science fairs each year, 1,500 are chosen by Westinghouse to submit research projects in science, math, or engineering, along with recommendations and transcripts. Of the entrants, 10 are ultimately chosen to receive $10,000 to $40,000 each. A school official must request an application from Westinghouse Science Talent Search Scholarships, Science Service, Inc., 1719 North St. N.W., Washington, D.C. 20036.

How to Borrow Wisely for College

Despite your best efforts, there simply may not be enough money available through your savings, grants, scholarships, or on-campus work to meet the expenses of the school your child finally selects. If so, your only choices are for your child to trade down to a less costly school or for one or both of you to borrow the missing cash. Roughly half of all undergraduates borrow to pay for college.

While it's tempting to rush to the conclusion that your child must go to his first-choice school and the borrowing responsibility will be all yours, don't do it. Consider your own situation as well as your child's. For instance, you almost certainly should be setting aside cash for your retirement. If paying back more debt for college means that saving for retirement will become impossible, consider sending your child to a less expensive school or have him take out some loans himself. Be careful about your child's debt load, too. If you're not careful, your son or daughter could easily graduate college owing more than $10,000 in loans and shelling out over $100 a month in repayments. That's a tough way to start out in the world.

Fortunately, reasonable college loans are available to both of you. In fact, as much as $5 billion in low-interest federal loans go begging each year because families don't know about them, think they're not eligible for them, or don't bother to follow through on the paperwork. (For answers to questions about federal student loan availability, eligibility, and where to get such loans, call 800-433-3243.) To qualify for federal loans, you'll have to fill out the so-called Free Application for Federal Student Aid (FAFSA), which you can get at any high school guidance office or by phoning the number above.

Students with the greatest financial need are eligible for **Perkins loans,** available through colleges. These loans provide up to $3,000 per year of undergraduate study at a rock-bottom 5% interest rate. No interest accumulates while your child is in school, and he'll have up to 10 years to repay the loan, beginning nine months after he graduates (or leaves college). In certain situations the loan can even be forgiven—if your child becomes a teacher or a nurse working with disabled or low-income kids, for example.

If your family demonstrates financial need, your child can also receive a **subsidized Stafford loan.** This means he'll be able to borrow money at low rates for 10 to 30 years and the federal government will pay the interest while he's in college. Both the maximum loan amounts and the interest rate are reset every year. Recently, the largest subsidized Stafford loans ranged from $2,625 to $10,500 (depending on what year of college or grad school your child is in) and the interest rate was capped at 8.25%, with a 4% loan origination fee.

Even without demonstrating need, your son or daughter can get an **unsubsidized Stafford loan** directly from a bank, credit union, or other lender at the same low rate as a subsidized Stafford. With this type of loan, however, interest is not paid by the government while the student is in school.

If your lender sells your Stafford loan to the Student Loan Marketing Association (Sallie Mae), you're eligible for an even better interest rate. After you've paid 48 consecutive installments on time, Sallie Mae will shave two points off your rate. So you might want to ask the financial aid office for lenders in your area that then sell their loans to Sallie Mae. Agree to a direct withdrawal from your bank account for loan repayments and Sallie

Mae will knock off an additional quarter point.

When it comes time for your child to repay his loans, he'll have several options, including a graduated plan, in which the payments start out small but get bigger over time. For example, on a 10-year $10,000 Stafford loan, your child might pay just $67 a month for the first two years, $141 for the next two, and $150 for the final six. A similar plan pegs payments to a fixed percentage of his (hopefully rising) income.

Parents, rather than students, can also secure low-rate college loans through the federal government. As long as you have no loan delinquencies of more than 90 days and your child attends college at least half-time, you can take out a 10-year **Parent Loan to Undergraduate Students (PLUS)** for the difference between the full cost of your child's education and any financial aid he receives. The interest, at a rate that is reset every year, is equal to the one-year rate on Treasury bills plus 3.1%, with a 9% cap. That's a few percentage points lower than what you'd pay for a personal loan from a bank or a home-equity loan. In recent years the PLUS rate has been around 8.7%, with a 4% loan origination fee.

PLUS loans, like unsubsidized Stafford loans, are available through most lenders. Starting in 1995, however, about 500 colleges began making the loans directly through the U.S. Department of Education. Although the feds hope that lending money directly through schools, instead of private lenders, will speed up processing, loans made through schools won't be sold to Sallie Mae. So students getting these direct loans will lose their interest discount for a good payment record.

If you need to borrow more, see if your child's school is one offering **Guaranteed Access to Education (GATE)** loans. The rate—typically 7% to 10%—is fixed and there are no origination fees. Students can make interest-only payments for five years after graduation and pay off the loans in 13 years.

Three more low-cost sources of cash for college are **your home, your company savings plan,** and **your cash-value life insurance policy.** With a home-equity line of credit, you can borrow up to 80% of your equity, drawing out cash as needed for college bills. The rate generally fluctuates and is tied to the prime bank rate. Typically, the home-equity line rate is the prime rate plus between one and two percentage points. That has put the rate at about 10% or so in recent years. Since home-equity interest is tax-deductible, unlike most other types of interest, the after-tax cost of such loans makes them just a bit higher than that of government-backed college loans. But be careful. If you can't meet the payments, your house is at risk.

What's more, some lenders and brokerage firms charge steep fees to take out home-equity lines, so be sure to compare the cost of the offerings before signing up for any.

Company savings plans, such as 401(k)s, generally allow you to borrow an amount equal to up to half your account balance or $50,000 (whichever is less) at reasonable interest rates—often 1% or so over prime. The rate is fairly low because your loan is secured by the savings in your 401(k) account. However, if you don't pay the money back within the set time period—typically five years—it will be treated as a withdrawal and subject to income taxes and a 10% tax penalty.

You might also look into borrowing against the cash value in your life insurance policy. The insurer will charge annual interest of 6% to 8% and let you borrow up to the full cash value in your policy. Although you don't have to pay back the money, if you die and have a policy loan outstanding, your beneficiaries will suffer; they'll get just the insurance policy's face value minus the unpaid balance of the loan.

If you can't snag a low-interest loan, there are a handful of commercial lenders that offer college loans for all, or nearly all, college expenses (minus financial aid), with long repayment schedules at fairly attractive rates. In the mid-'90s, these lenders were charging between 10% and 13% to borrow. Five examples:

1. The New England Loan Marketing Association (Nellie Mae) will lend up to the entire cost of your child's education through its EXCEL loan. These loans can run as long as 20 years and are available at both fixed- and variable-interest rates. Cost: generally 2% to 4% over prime, plus a onetime fee of 5% of the loan amount. For more information, call Nellie Mae at 800-634-9308.

2. The College Board sponsors the Extra Credit Loan, which covers room, board, tuition, and fees. Interest is tied to the 90-day Treasury bill rate plus 4.5%, and you can borrow for up to 10 years. For more information, call 800-874-9390.

3. Knight Insurance, a private firm, has loans similar to the Extra Credit Loan. For details, call Knight at 800-225-6783 (Massachusetts residents, call 617-267-1500).

4. Plato lets you borrow up to $25,000, with 15 years to repay. The interest rate is variable, set at 4.85% above the previous month's rate on commercial debt. For more information, call 800-467-5286.

5. The Education Resource Institute, another private lender, lets you borrow up to the entire cost of education and stretch out loan payments as long as 25 years. The interest rate can be as low as 1% to 2% over prime. Specific terms are set by the sponsors—primarily banks—that offer the program. For a list of lenders in your area, call 800-255-8374.

Working for College Cash

You might want your son or daughter to help foot the college bills by **working part-time during high school.** After-school employment not only helps make college more affordable, it also teaches your child a little about the real working world. Plus, when your son or daughter puts at least some of the earnings in the bank or in a mutual fund, he or she will get an education in the world of personal finance. Just don't let your kid work so much that he won't have enough time to devote to his studies, causing his grades to suffer. For a fuller discussion about kids and money, see Chapter 20.

Your child's financial aid package may also include a **college job,** generally 10 or so hours a week of light work on campus for which he'll be paid roughly the minimum wage. Don't worry that limited part-time work during the school year will spoil your child's college experience or lower his grade-point average. A **MONEY** survey of 1,000 undergraduates showed that working up to 10 hours a week did not diminish either satisfaction

or academic achievement. Above 10 hours, however, both dropped markedly. So if your child must earn a large share of his college expenses, it's best for him to do so primarily through well-paid summer jobs.

Another way for your child to pick up some cash to pay for college is through a **co-op education program.** About 1,000 two- and four-year colleges offer opportunities for students to earn as much as $8,000 a year *plus* college credits by working part-time in their anticipated fields. Co-op education works only for students who are fairly certain about their future career, however, since you must pick an area of study in advance and then look for a related co-op opportunity. A school may offer a co-op program in accounting, for instance, but not in health sciences. To locate co-op education programs in the private sector, write to the Center for Co-operative Education, Northeastern University, 503 Stearns, Boston, Mass. 02115. For co-op programs offered by the federal government, contact one of the six regional Federal Job Information Centers, listed under "Federal Government" in your Yellow Pages.

One new way for your child to earn pay for his education is through **Ameri-Corps,** the national service program initiated by President Bill Clinton soon after he took office. In 1997 25,000 young volunteers gave nine months to community programs such as home care for the aged, outreach to the homeless, and playground building. For their efforts, volunteers receive a living allowance of $7,500 and another $4,725 toward college costs or payment of student loans. For more information, call 800-942-2677 or visit the Web site at www.Americorps.org.

Emergency Cash for College

Crisis time: the deadline for paying your child's college bills is looming, and despite all your best efforts, you simply don't have the needed cash. What to do? Look into two loan programs made just for parents in your situation:

■ **Academic Management Services (AMS)** will charge you a $45 fee to set up a budget and installment schedule with your child's college that will let you pay the upcoming tuition money over a period of 10 months. But the college must be affiliated with AMS, as about 1,000 schools are. To find out more, call 800-635-0121.

■ **The Education Credit Line** will lend you up to $50,000 at interest rates as low as the prime rate plus 2.5%, depending on your other debts—as long as your

credit is good. (That rate worked out to about 11.5% in the mid-'90s.) There is a 3% application fee, and a repayment of 2% of the outstanding balance per month or $100-a-month minimum must begin within 45 days. For more information, call 800-477-4977.

Smart Ways to Cut College Costs

No matter how much you need to shell out for your child's college, chances are you wouldn't mind paying less. Here are four ways you or your son or daughter may be able to shave those tuition bills:

1. Have your child zip through college. Not only will you save a year's tuition if your son or daughter graduates in three years rather than four, your kid will get an extra year of lifetime earnings. Total savings, including room and board: as much as $20,000. But getting through college in three years requires more discipline than many kids have, so don't even think about it unless you believe your child can pull it off. Most colleges let students take extra courses to graduate sooner, but nearly 200 now have formal three-year bachelor degree programs.

2. Sacrifice selectivity for scholarship cash. Increasingly, colleges others than those in the Ivy League and a few other hoity-toity institutions are giving out handsome Merit Scholarships to smart students, whether or not their parents can demonstrate financial need.

3. Join the community. Let's say your child goes to one of the nation's 1,000 or so community colleges for two years and then transfers to a four-year institution. Talk about savings! Many community colleges charge only $200 to $2,000 for tuition, far less than the cost at four-year schools.

4. Stick around your home. Nearly two dozen states dangle juicy financial incentives to good students who stay in-state for college. In some cases, however, you may need to demonstrate financial need and your child may have to keep up his grades in college. Your state's department of education can tell you if there are deals like this where you live.

CHAPTER 11

How to Retire Comfortably

It's time for a little perspective. In the course of your personal financial concerns, you face three main challenges—three mountains of expense that you must scale and conquer to provide yourself and your family a decent life. The first is buying your home (covered in Chapter 7). If you doze off slightly in the ensuing years, you'll be brought up short by the second mountain looming in the middle distance: financing your children's college (Chapter 10). If you haven't been saving for it, you and your kids may be running up considerable debt for years to come. It's a worthwhile investment, though.

Now for the challenge to end all challenges. You don't even have time for a brief nap before this Everest starts staring

you down: financing your retirement. This is the supreme test that will take more energy and attention than the other two peaks combined. Proof: Most retirees today must plan to live for 30 years after the paychecks stop. Do a back-of-the-envelope computation on that one. The rule of thumb is that you'll need 80% of your final year's pay in retirement. If your income at the end will be, say, $80,000 a year, then you'll need $64,000 a year times 30, or $1,920,000. What?! A nest egg of nearly $2 million? How in the name of John D. Rockefeller are you going to come up with that amount of change?

There are actually two answers to that question. They are the essential twin lessons of retirement planning that will be discussed in the rest of this chapter.

First, the frightening figure arrived at—$1,920,000—is grossly misleading. Feel tricked? Don't be angry, be instructed: you should have been aware that it doesn't take into account Social Security, which may be a more substantial part of your nest egg than you may have been led to believe. Really. It also doesn't account for either the earnings you'll get on your investments or inflation. Lesson one: You must find out with reasonable precision the amount of money you'll need to accumulate by retirement, or you will not know how much you need to save. Later in this chapter you'll see how to do just that.

Second, you just have to do a few things right and the supersonic engine of compound interest will do the rest. For example, if starting at age 40 you put $8,000 a year in your 401(k) or other tax-deferred account and you earn an 8% annual return, you would accumulate $880,000 by age 62. But if you were to wait five years longer to start saving, your pot would be worth only $704,000. Lesson two: Your eventual success depends on how early you start building your nest egg, how well you fund it year in and year out, and how well you manage your portfolio over time.

The thread that runs through both of these lessons: you. Because of changes in law and corporate policy, employers and the government will be doing less and less to help you build your secure retirement. Consequently you will have to do more and more yourself. But if you do, the payoff will be spectacular: a comfortable, worry-free retirement.

Why It's All Up to You

For your parents and maybe even your grandparents, retirement was financed largely by Social Security and a company pension. The younger you are today, the more the retirement income scene will change from that traditional one. Take Social Security. As things now stand, it will replace about 42% of wages if your earnings throughout your career average $21,800 a year. But if your average salary is, say, $68,400 a year—the highest amount taxed by Social Security—only about 27% of that figure (or $18,468 a year) will be replaced by Social Security benefits. In addition, as your post-retirement income from other sources grows, count on more and more of your Social Security benefits being taxed. Right now, 85% of Social Security benefits are subject to federal income tax if your total income (including half of Social Security checks) exceeds $44,000 for married couples and $34,000 for singles.

You're increasingly on your own with employer-sponsored retirement benefits, too. About four out of 10 workers today are lucky enough to be accumulating traditional employer-paid pensions. These are the so-called **defined-benefit plans** that pay out a fixed monthly amount for life after you retire. Typically, you get about 30% of your final salary if you have worked 30 years or more at the same company. These plans are still going strong at large corporations, but their years—if not their days—seem numbered. They are tremendously expensive to maintain, partly because the employer does all of the funding and partly because government reporting regulations are complicated and onerous. The number of small- and medium-size companies offering defined-benefit plans has been plummeting, dropping 41% between 1985 and 1990, and there's no reason to think that trend will reverse itself.

Just as typewriters have been swept away by computers, the defined-benefit plan is gradually being replaced as the principal employer-sponsored retirement savings vehicle. Taking its place is what is called the **defined-contribution plan,** such as the 401(k) for private companies or the 403(b) for nonprofit organizations. The significant difference: You, the employee, do most of the funding and *you* take responsibility for deciding how to invest the money. Employers at more than half of companies with 401(k)s match a portion of the money employees kick in, however.

In some ways, these 401(k)–type plans are a perfect match for the rootless work styles of Americans today. If you change jobs, you can take your retirement savings with you. That is a considerable improvement over defined-benefit pensions, which are not portable and aren't worth much unless you stay for decades at one company. While you do become **vested** in a defined-benefit plan after five years of service at a company—that is, you become eligible to receive benefits—you usually have to wait until you're 65 to start receiving checks. So if you leave the company at, say, 40 after 10 years there, the eventual payoff could be minuscule.

On the other hand, a 401(k) is far less secure than a traditional pension, which pays you that monthly check no matter how the stock and bond markets perform. You invest a 401(k) among a selection of mutual fundlike choices. So your account's value when you retire is not guaranteed, but depends on how well you have managed it. All too often, employees invest their 401(k)s too conservatively, producing lower returns than those from old-fashioned pensions. Also, many employees either spend their 401(k) savings when they change jobs or borrow excessively from them, robbing their retirement years. On top of all this, companies generally contribute less to 401(k)s than they do to defined-benefit pensions.

Employee contributions plus matching funds from employers together add up to roughly 7% of pay compared with the 10% or 12% of pay that employers put into the traditional plans.

It should be clear by now that the partnership of Uncle Sam (Social Security) and your employer (pension) isn't enough anymore to ensure a safe and sound retirement. Ask almost any retirement-planning expert and you will be told that the new configuration is a troika: Social Security; your company's contribution, which is more likely to be a 401(k)–type plan than a traditional pension; and your own savings and investments. Finding out just how big this third element needs to be is critical: the earlier you make some rough calculations, the easier it will be to amass what you'll need.

By completing the following two worksheets, you'll know how much you'll need to invest to make your retirement comfortable. But what if you started saving too late or can't set aside such an amount in the years left before retirement? In that case you will have to make up the shortfall in the only other way possible: by working during retirement. Is this the dirty little financial secret of aging? Not at all. The fact is, as many as half of all retirees take on less demanding jobs after they quit their full-time jobs. They do so not only to make up for a savings shortfall, but also to ease the emotional transition from work to full retirement. Besides, the good health that is typical of today's retirees makes the prospect of 30 years with nothing much to do seem less than heavenly.

Figuring Out How Much You'll Need

The moment you decide to get serious about retirement planning, your first act should be figuring out how much you'll need to save each year in order to retire well. You will need to complete the simple eighteen-step worksheet that follows. Don't be put off. It's easy and takes just minutes to complete. A second worksheet on page 271 is optional but helpful. It lets you estimate your likely post-retirement cost of living. If you want to complete this worksheet, you must fill in its lines before filling out the first worksheet. If you don't want to bother, just go by the traditional rule of thumb that retirees need 80% of pre-retirement income in retirement. One caution: For many of today's active retirees, the first decade or so of freedom turns out to be at least as expensive as life was before packing it in. To deal with this phenomenon, the optional worksheet will help you calculate how your retirement spending habits may change in both early (ages 60 to 75) and late (over 75) retirement.

When you finish the worksheet, don't be alarmed if you find that your pension and Social Security together will not equal your expected retirement living expenses. Unless you have been socking away 20% or more of your gross income year after year for two decades or more, you are likely in the same position as most pre-retirees: you need to work on building up your portfolio of taxable investments. You'll also find that higher earnings during your working lifetime mean there is that much more to replace if you are to maintain your living standard. For example, early in this chapter you read that if you had just retired and were earning $68,400, your Social Secu-

rity benefit would have replaced about 27% of that amount. Now let's say you had earned $85,000: that Social Security benefit would have made up only about 19%.

HOW MUCH YOU MUST SAVE FOR RETIREMENT

Use this worksheet to figure how much your retirement life will cost—and how much money you must save to pay for it. For the first 10 lines, estimate your annual expenses in today's dollars. To be conservative, we've assumed that you'll live until 92 and earn a modest 8% annually on your investments. We have also assumed that the inflation rate will be 5% a year.

1. Housing (including insurance, utilities, property taxes, furnishings) _____
2. Food (including meals out) _____
3. Transportation _____
4. Taxes _____
5. Clothing, personal care _____
6. Medical expenses (including health insurance) _____
7. Entertainment, recreation, vacations _____
8. Debt payments (including credit cards) _____
9. Savings _____
10. Other (including life and disability insurance) _____
11. **TOTAL ANNUAL EXPENDITURES IN RETIREMENT**[1]
    (Add lines 1 through 10.) _____
12. Your expected Social Security and pension income (You can
    obtain estimates from the Social Security Administration at
    800-772-1213 and from your employee-benefits office.) _____

13. Annual retirement income you will need from savings and
    investments (Subtract line 12 from line 11.) _____

14. How much you must save by retirement (Multiply line 13
    by factor A below.) _____

15. How much you've already saved (including tax-deferred
    accounts and the total amount you expect your employer
    to add to them before you retire) _____

16. Inflation-adjusted value of your savings at retirement
    (Multiply line 15 by factor B.) _____

17. Total retirement capital you still need to accumulate
    (Subtract line 16 from line 14.) _____

18. **HOW MUCH MONEY YOU MUST SAVE EACH
    YEAR UNTIL RETIREMENT** (Multiply line 17 by factor C.) _____

Age at retirement	55	56	57	58	59	60	61	62	63	64	65	66
Factor A	22.2	21.8	21.5	21.1	20.8	20.4	20.0	19.6	19.2	18.8	18.3	17.9

Years to retirement	3	9	15	20	25	30
Factor B	1.09	1.30	1.56	1.81	2.09	2.43
Factor C	0.324	0.098	0.054	0.037	0.027	0.021

Note: [1]On average, this number constitutes 71% of an affluent retiree's pre-tax, pre-retirement income.
Sources: MONEY poll; Moss Adams in Seattle

Estimating Your Retirement Spending

This optional worksheet will give you a pretty good sense of how much you'll be spending in retirement. That, in turn, will help you figure out how much you'll want to be saving now. The worksheet lets you plug in figures for your early years of retirement and your later ones, since spending levels change as you age. In the "Current" column, write in how much you spend each year on these items today. The total ought to add up to a figure that's close to your present income. In the "Early Retirement" column, you'll insert figures for your estimated outlays if you were newly retired today. The "Late Retirement" column assumes you're retired and over 75. Use today's dollars in all cases, since the previous worksheet factors in inflation.

A few tips: In **Housing,** avoid overestimating the savings you'll enjoy once you get out from under the burden of a mortgage. Homeowners also tend to minimize nonrecurring expenses like major repairs. To be safe, figure that property taxes, homeowners insurance, utilities, and upkeep will cost just as much as they do now, unless you will move to a smaller house or to a lower-cost area. **Food costs** often drop as much as 25% in retirement if you eat out less—largely because you won't be buying lunch at work every day. Many sedentary retirees, however, find themselves eating out *more* just to get out of the house. One clue to your future behavior: If you are a big restaurant-goer now, you are apt to continue the habit later on. **Transportation costs** probably will drop, since you will not be commuting to work anymore. You may also find that you don't need to replace a car as often or to keep two. **Taxes** represent a big saving if you don't work in retirement, since you won't have to pay the 7.65% Social Security and Medicare tax on wages. In addition, certain states exempt from taxes some income from Social Security benefits and pensions. **Medical expenses** are difficult to predict. Assume that since you will have to shoulder a bigger share of health care costs in retirement, those expenses could

be 25% to 30% higher. In addition, early retirees may face higher medical costs until they qualify for Medicare at 65 if they have to buy their own insurance, which can cost a married couple $6,000 a year. **Clothing and personal care items** offer real savings—as much as 40% or more on clothing, for example, if you are going from a dressy office job to jeans and sports clothes. **Recreation and travel** are categories that can add measurably to your budget. Whatever adventures you are planning in this regard, find out how much they will cost and budget for them. **Support of relatives** can run into real money when you want to help grown children buy a home or pay for their children's schooling. If you are a member of the so-called sandwich generation, moreover, you may have to pay for the care of your aged parents. **Loan and credit-card payments** ought to be as close to zero as possible after you retire. **Life insurance costs** generally drop in retirement, and the need for **disability insurance** typically ends when you retire. **Savings and investments** ought to remain active pursuits after you stop working, to ensure that you counteract the effects of inflation. Some experts even advise that you plan to save about 5% to 10% of your income each year in the first five to 10 years after you retire.

EXPENDITURE	CURRENT	EARLY RETIREMENT	LATE RETIREMENT
1. **Housing** (rent, mortgage, utilities, property taxes, upkeep, furnishings, homeowners insurance premiums)	_____	_____	_____
2. **Food** (include alcohol and tobacco)	_____	_____	_____
3. **Transportation** (include car loan payments, insurance, gas, repairs, parking, and commuting costs)	_____	_____	_____
4. **Taxes** (don't include Social Security taxes after you retire unless you expect to work)	_____	_____	_____
5. **Medical and dental** (include insurance premiums, out-of-pocket expenses, prescriptions, and glasses)	_____	_____	_____
6. **Clothing and personal care items**	_____	_____	_____
7. **Recreation and hobbies**	_____	_____	_____
8. **Travel**	_____	_____	_____
9. **Education** (include savings for your child's education)	_____	_____	_____
10. **Support of relatives**	_____	_____	_____
11. **Loan and credit-card payments**	_____	_____	_____
12. **Life and disability insurance**	_____	_____	_____
13. **Savings and investments**	_____	_____	_____
14. **Gifts and contributions**	_____	_____	_____
15. **Other**	_____	_____	_____
TOTAL EXPENDITURES	_____	_____	_____
% OF TODAY'S INCOME NEEDED (divide your total expenditures by your current income and multiply the result by 100)	100%	___ %	___ %

How Retirement Software and the Web Fit In

If you are even marginally computer-literate and have access to an IBM PC or compatible hardware, you can make the task of retirement planning considerably easier, a lot more accurate, and possibly even fun. Just get one of a handful of excellent computer programs or visit some fine Web sites and spend an hour or two playing—and that is the apt word—with them. For this small investment of time, you will gain considerable insight into the art of retirement planning and increased confidence in your ability to home in on how much you will need to finance your later years.

For example, take one of the best of the programs, the *Vanguard Retirement Planner* (800-950-1971; $18). It starts you off with easy-to-follow "what if" scenarios on the income you will need for the duration of your retirement. You can plug in many different assumptions covering all the pertinent variables, then change them if you wish. For instance, you can figure a future inflation rate of anywhere from 0% to 20%. Likewise you can play around with rates of return on your investments, the amount of income you will need each year in retirement, and the number of years your retirement will last. The computer quickly drops each of these variables into your retirement plan and shows you when, or if, your money will run out. You'll be told how much more you will need to save if it turns out that your money won't last as long as you hope. In addition, you can see how different scenarios play out year after year as you draw down income and eventually spend down your principal in the later years of retirement. Unlike most of the other retirement software programs, Vanguard's automatically computes your Social Security benefits. You also can see graphically how much early retirement will cost you in Social Security benefits.

Next, you move from the clear and purposeful first half of your trek (called the Savings Planner) to the Portfolio Planner. Here the quality of the help drops, however. This is partly because the aim of this section is arriving at a recommended asset allocation. To do so with any precision, though, you would require a far more complex and expensive piece of software. The Portfolio Planner does, however, introduce you to the importance of asset allocation (though you're apt to be annoyed at the self-promotion here as the software highlights Vanguard's own funds).

Other worthy retirement software and Internet offerings include *Quicken Financial Planner* (800-446-8848; $39.99) and personal finance programs with retirement calculators like *Quicken Deluxe*

(800-446-8848; $45) and *Microsoft Money 98* (800-426-9400; $34.95).

On the Net, stop by *FinanCenter* (financenter.com) or **MONEY**'s site (Money.com) for a wealth of financial calculators that include how to plan for retirement and figure your retirement living expenses. The retirement area of the *Quicken Financial Network* (www.qfn.com) lets you run the numbers to be sure you'll have enough income to live comfortably in retirement. And Vanguard's retirement planning Web site (www.vanguard.com) is especially useful for helping you determine the most tax-friendly withdrawal strategy for your retirement stash.

Social Security—What You'll Get and When

Given the gloomy press Social Security has received in recent years, you may be wondering why this book includes a discussion of the subject at all. Why hold out false hope for a benefit that will likely not be around for our retirement anyway? After all, a recent survey showed that more adults under 34 believe UFOs exist than think that they'll get Social Security. This pessimism has been advanced largely by two interest groups that may have mixed motives: politicians and financial planners. Politicians have made a habit of accusing their opponents of plotting to cut Social Security benefits, whether this is true or not. So don't look to them to help decide whether there are Social Security checks in your future.

Then there are the financial planners, who generally make a better case, although a flawed one. Planners are responsible for informing their clients of what they need to know for their financial health. Leaving Social Security benefits out of any retirement computations results in a conservative financial plan likely to guarantee that the client never runs out of money but has bought a lot of investments. Suppose your planner is wrong, though. Then you will have sweated unnecessarily, and perhaps you will have bought too many annuities, mutual funds, or other financial products from your planner, giving him or her too many fat commissions along the way.

What's really likely to happen to Social Security in the future? No one knows for sure, of course. But reflect on how the U.S. government has coped with the threat of Social Security deficits in the past:

■ **Your Social Security tax has grown immensely over the years.** In 1997 the tax topped out at $8,110, or 12.4% of wages up to $65,400. Only three decades ago, in 1966, the highest tax amounted to a tiny $382.80, or 5.8% of wages up to $6,600.

■ **Social Security benefits have been taxed somewhat.** For decades these benefits were tax-exempt. Then, up to 50% of benefits became subject to tax. Today as much as 85% of benefits may be taxed, depending on your income.

■ **The age at which you can claim full Social Security benefits has been raised.** While this change hasn't taken effect yet, it's coming. The retirement age will begin moving from 65 to 67 in the year 2003.

In short, while Social Security itself is sacrosanct, the political will to manipulate the rules has always reemerged when emergencies were foreseen. In all probability there will be more tinkering ahead—but not a wholesale junking of the Social Security system. As of today, the Social Security trust funds for retirement and disability benefits will run surpluses until 2013. That's just two years after the oldest baby boomers turn 65, marking the leading edge of potential disaster. As more and more boomers retire, a shrinking younger population will be working to pay for all those benefit checks. This slide is expected to hit bottom in 2029, when the till finally empties. But bank on one thing: Politicians, with armies of boomers snapping at their heels, will long since have succeeded in pushing the problem deeper into the twenty-first century.

Here is what you can reasonably ex-pect in the way of Social Security changes that would affect your retirement:

■ **If you were born before 1938,** you're home free. The only blip on your Social Security screen is the fact that most of your benefits may be taxable now. Despite efforts to turn back the tide, it seems prudent to expect that if your retirement income will exceed $50,000 or $60,000, you will pay tax on your Social Security checks, perhaps even on every penny of them, in the coming years. Currently, as soon as your "provisional" income (your adjusted gross income plus tax-exempt interest and half of your Social Security benefits) inches past $35,000 on a joint return ($25,000 if you're single), 50% of your benefits are taxed. When your provisional income tops $44,000 on a joint return ($34,000 if you're single), up to 85% of your benefit is subject to federal income tax.

■ **If you were born between 1938 and 1959,** you are already heir to a slight delaying of your benefits and you're likely to be the first to see more of your benefits taxed. The normal retirement age for Social Security, now 65, switches to age 66 for people born in 1950. It then gets pushed back a little more each year until it hits 67 in the year 2027 (people born in 1960). The fancy footwork with the retirement age also changes payouts for people who retire before 65. Today, if you retire at age 62, you receive 80% of your full Social Security benefits for the rest of your life. That percentage is scheduled to decline to 75% in 2005.

In addition, many experts believe that starting around the year 2000, Social Security benefits will be taxed more. The current betting is that *all* people earning Social Security checks will pay taxes on some of their benefits and the threshold for paying taxes on 85% of benefits will drop to a lower income level than $44,000 for joint returns and $34,000 for singles.

■ **If you were born from 1960 on,** you'll be fingered the most. In fact, recent studies indicate that workers born after 1960 will get back less from Social Security than they have paid in taxes during their working years. By contrast, according to one estimate, a worker who retired in 1980 got back $63,000 more from Social Security than he put in (calculated in 1985 dollars). You may wind up being able to keep only half of today's scheduled amount of Social Security benefits. The early retirement penalty will get stiffer for you, too. If you were born in 1960 or later, when your normal retirement age would be 67, retiring at 62 will mean you'll get only 70% of your full benefit, down from 80% today.

How much will your Social Security benefit check actually be, under today's rules? Finding out is one of the simplest matters in all of personal finance. Just call the Social Security Administration (800-772-1213) and ask for a projection of your annual benefit. In a few weeks you will get a report laying out how much your check is likely to be, based on your income history and an estimate of your future income. The process has gotten even more convenient: people aged 55 or older have begun receiving an automatic annual accounting of their benefits projections from the Social Security Administration.

You will qualify for Social Security benefits under one of five categories:

- **Your own benefits, based on your work record**
- **Spousal benefits, based on your husband's or wife's work record** (these benefits generally equal half of your spouse's full benefit)
- **Divorced spouse's benefits** (if you were married at least 10 years, your former spouse either is receiving Social Security or is older than 62, you are not remarried, and you have been divorced for at least two years)
- **Widow's or widower's benefits** (if you were married at least nine months and did not remarry before you were 60)
- **Divorced widow's or widower's benefits** (if you were married to your ex-husband or ex-wife at least 10 years, are 60 or older, and married your present spouse before age 60)

To give you a rough idea of the dollar amounts involved, the top monthly Social Security benefit for someone who retired in 1995 at age 65 was roughly $1,200 or about $14,400 a year. If these figures don't impress you, take another look. A couple, each of whom receives the top monthly benefit—and that will likely be more and more typical among two-professional households—would pull down close to $29,000 a year in Social Security at the 1995 pace. You'd need a stash of about $350,000 to generate that much income from assets earning an 8% return.

When should you start taking your Social Security benefits? That depends. If you can afford to delay getting the checks until age 70, you should. That's because you'll get a larger annual benefit by postponing the date the checks start arriving. For each year you hold off retiring past your 65th birthday, until you reach age 70, your Social Security check grows by 4.5%. Put another way, if you wait until 70, you'll get 22.5% more than at 65 and will keep getting that much more as long as you live. Conversely, you're penalized if you start receiving Social Security early; retirement benefits are available beginning at age 62. Start taking Social Security at 62 and you'll get 20% less than you would have by waiting until 65—for the rest of your life. Even so, 62% of men and 73% of women start getting Social Security at age 62.

When you hit 60 or so, determine whether you expect to work after retirement. If you plan to keep working, estimate how much you would be earning. You may find that the amount you'll be pulling in will persuade you to delay getting Social Security checks until at least age 65 or until age 70. You may even find that it won't pay to work. The reason: Social Security benefits for people aged 62 to 64 are reduced by $1 for every $2 earned above $8,640. Social Security recipients aged 65 to 69 lose $1 in benefits for every $3 they earn above $13,500. That means if you qualify for the maximum benefit and you're 62 to 64, you will lose all of it once your employment earnings rise above $37,000 or so. Americans aged 65 to 69 expecting to get the maximum benefit see their Social Security wiped out after their annual earnings exceed about $55,000. Good news: The $13,000 threshold is scheduled to rise to $30,000 by the year 2002.

Your Pension and Its Safety

Perhaps you're counting on getting a decent pension from your employer when you retire. Maybe you will. But keep in mind that two factors will greatly determine how big your employer's pension will be: how long you stay at the same employer and whether your employer is financially capable of making good on its pension promises.

The size of your pension checks will be based on your years of service and your salary over, typically, your three to five highest-paid years on the job. Traditional defined-benefit pensions rarely increase with inflation. Government workers, however, usually receive annual increases in their pension checks to offset inflation, known as **cost-of-living adjustments (COLAs).** That may not be true much longer. Government budget balancers are eyeing COLAs closely, making them especially ripe for cutting.

Job-hopping can sharply reduce the size of your defined-benefit pension, as shown by the following figures from the benefits consulting firm William M. Mercer. Take three people, each of whom has been working for 40 years, started with an initial salary of $14,200, got raises of 5% a year, and was earning $100,000 before retiring at age 65. The person who stayed at the same company for all 40 years might get an annual pension of $72,700. If he had three employers over those years, his total pension would shrink to $44,600. If he had worked at eight employers, however, his pension would be cut to just $36,000—half the size of the one-employer employee.

The other consideration is the safety of your pension. Every year about 100 companies default on their pension plans.

Since 1974 nearly 2,000 plans have gone under. That's a small percentage overall; indeed, about 75% of large-company pension plans are fully funded. But if you were an employee at one of the companies whose pension plans blew up, the effect on your retirement could be considerable. Fortunately, a federal agency known as the Pension Benefit Guaranty Corporation (PBGC) acts as something of a safety net for pensioners. The PBGC has lately paid out about $720 million a year in benefits to more than 174,000 retirees. The PBGC does *not* guarantee 401(k) or other employer-sponsored, defined-contribution savings plans, however. What's more, the PBGC won't necessarily guarantee that you'll receive your full pension even if your defined-pension plan tanks. By law the PBGC pays a maximum benefit—recently it was $2,573.86 a month or $30,886 a year. Worse still, the top payout shrinks for early retirees. If you took early retirement at age 55, the most PBGC will pay is about $1,160 a month or just under $14,000 a year.

Fortunately, the chance that a company will not be able to pay its pension benefits appears to be shrinking. PBGC officials believe pension plans are under-funded to the tune of $71 million, but that the figure will narrow by 70% over the next 15 years. The prime reason: 1994 legislation that, among other things, required underfunded pension plans to pay stiffer premiums to the PBGC.

That legislation also helped send an early warning signal to employees of companies with shaky pension plans. Now, if your firm's plan has less than 90% of its necessary funding, the company must send you a notice. While getting such a memo in your mailbox won't make your day, it will help prevent you from being taken by surprise one day that the plan is kaput.

Anyone whose employer offers a pension plan, however, should do a little homework to learn how safe the plan really is. (You needn't worry about the safety of your employer-sponsored savings plan, since your account is your property.) Ask your employee benefits office for a copy of Form 5500, which companies must file annually with the U.S. Department of Labor. Then read the actuary's report in the back of the form. That independent opinion will clue you in to the soundness of the plan.

The Best Way to Build Your Nest Egg

Now that you know what the government and your employer are likely to give you for retirement, you're ready to get cracking on what you can and should do for yourself. The key words to remember: asset allocation. That's another way of saying diversification, but with one important added feature—you spread your money over just the right mix of stocks, bonds, and other investments. The extra touch is adjusting that mix according to your age so that your investment risks gradually diminish as you get closer to retirement.

Aside from this commonsense reason for adopting asset allocation is the statistical one that has emerged through studies. For example, a 1991 study by money managers Gary P. Brinson and consultant Gilbert Beebower determined that about 92% of investors' returns come from the right combination of assets. The rest comes from their skill in picking securities and from timely buying and selling. Some analysts say that 92% figure overstates the case. But for most middle-income people, commonsense asset allocation means following three basic guidelines:

1. Make stocks your central investment. Fixed-income investments are the ballast of a portfolio, reducing its overall risk. But stocks are the long-term powerhouse and the only way to overcome the ravages of inflation. While stocks can certainly produce nerve-twisting losses in the short term, they have never lost money over every decade since World War II.

2. Take maximum advantage of tax-deferred plans. There is no surer way to a secure retirement than the tax-deferred compounding offered by 401(k) and 403(b) savings plans, IRAs, and Keoghs. For instance, if you contributed $5,000 annually for 30 years to a 401(k) plan, you would wind up with $611,729 before taxes, assuming an 8% rate of return. However, the same investment taxed each year at 28% would leave you with only $288,587.

As you may recall, although every working American under 70½ can invest in an IRA and defer taxes on its earnings until they are withdrawn, only some people can deduct their contributions (in 1998, your income must be under $60,000 if you're married, $40,000 if you're single). The rest can either make nondeductible contributions or—if your income is less than $160,000 and you're married or $110,000 and you're single— nondeductible contributions to a Roth IRA whose withdrawals may be tax-free.

The basic rules on deductibility are as follows: If you have no retirement plan at work, you can write off your entire IRA contribution of up to $2,000 a year. If you are covered by a plan at work, however, the size of your deduction depends on your income. You get a full deduction if your adjusted gross income is less than $30,000 in 1998 and you're single or under $50,000 if you're married and file jointly. You get a partial deduction if your income is less than $40,000 and you're single or $60,000 and you're married.

From 1999 through 2002, those figures will rise annually by $1,000. And beginning in 2003, singles with employer-sponsored retirement plans will be able to write off some or all of their IRA contributions if their incomes are less than $60,000; for married couples, the new limit will be $100,000. One last point: According to the 1997 tax law, if you're not covered by an employer's retirement plan but your spouse is, you can now claim a $2,000 IRA deduction as long as your household's income is under $150,000 and a partial deduction for income up to $160,000.

A nondeductible IRA works the same as a traditional deductible IRA, except you don't get the tax break at the time you invest. Like a deductible IRA, your earnings are taxed as ordinary income when you withdraw them. And if you pull money out of either IRA before age 59½, you'll owe taxes plus a 10% tax penalty on the amount of the distribution. You can pull money out of either IRA without penalty at any age, though, if the cash will be used for college expenses, to buy a first-time home ($10,000 limit), for medical expenses greater than 7.5% of your adjusted gross income, or for a disability. You must begin withdrawals by age 70½.

The Roth IRA, created by the 1997 tax law, is a whole different breed of cat. True, it also limits you to contributions of $2,000 a year per person, and earnings grow tax-deferred while they're in the account. But nearly all the other rules are different. Contributions are never tax-deductible and earnings are fully tax-free if you've held the account for at least five years and are older than 59½ when you withdraw them. You'll be hit with the 10% tax penalty for withdrawals of your earnings before age 59½, but contributions may be withdrawn penalty-free at any time. One other key difference between a Roth IRA and the other two types: You don't have to start pulling money out at age 70½.

So which type of IRA is best for you? In general, a Roth is great for people in their 30s and couples in their 40s with kids (the account can be used as an estate-planning tool to give more money to your children). As a rule, the decision about whether to open a Roth IRA or another type depends on your age and what you expect will happen to your tax rate in retirement. These three rules will help you choose the most appropriate IRA:

■ **A Roth IRA always beats a nondeductible IRA.** If you're married and your adjusted gross income is between $50,000 and $150,000 ($30,000 to $95,000 for singles), a Roth is the best deal. Your income is too high for a deductible IRA and the tax-free earnings on a Roth beat taxable earnings on a nondeductible IRA.

■ **A Roth is better than a deductible IRA if you think your tax bracket will not drop after you retire.** Most people figure that their income will fall in retirement. If you're one of them, then a deductible IRA will probably be wiser than a Roth. But if you believe your income will rise in retirement because of, say, pension proceeds and Social Security benefits, a Roth will be best.

■ **The longer you can wait to withdraw money from your IRA after retirement, the better a Roth looks.** If you're age 70 and earn 7% a year in a Roth IRA, you can double your money by age 80 by leaving it there instead of pulling it out and spending it. Of course, if you're over 70½, have earned income, and want to keep saving, a Roth IRA is your only choice.

The 1997 tax law also lets you convert your old IRA into one of the new Roths if your household's income is $100,000 or less. Although you'll owe taxes on any deductible contributions plus the earnings in the account, all future earnings will be tax-free as long as you hold the account for more than five years and don't withdraw them before age 59½. Converting to a Roth generally makes sense only if you think your tax rate will rise in retirement, you'll hold the money in the account for at least five years, you won't need to tap the IRA to pay the conversion taxes, and converting to a Roth won't mean giving up some tax breaks limited by your income.

3. Concentrate on mutual funds. Asset allocation requires you to spread your investments over a number of categories. For example, you need to be in large-company stocks, midsize-company stocks, small-company stocks, and international stocks as well as bonds. (For the best allocation depending on your age, see the table on page 282.) Unless you have the time and skill to research and track many individual securities, mutual funds are your best option, offering low-cost diversification as well as professional management and convenience. You'll learn more about stocks, bonds, and mutual funds in Chapters 14 and 15. For advice about investing in annuities for retirement, see Chapter 17.

Here are the four model retirement portfolios—for those in their 20s to age 30; 30 to 40; 40 to 50; and 50 to 60:

■ **20s to 30:** Now is the time to put at least 80% of your retirement portfolio into stocks. With 30 to 45 or so years before retirement, there is plenty of time to make up for the sometimes sharp fluctuations that the stock market will inevitably endure. Based on past returns, a portfolio with 80% in stocks and 20% in bonds is likely to grow an average of 9% annually, with a possible expected return as high as 25% in any single year.

When you start out, you may not have enough money to break up your portfolio into the six categories suggested. In that case go for a single mutual fund that buys either **blue chips,** those large companies that offer solid capital appreciation with less volatility than small stocks, or an index fund that mirrors the S&P 500 index. If you're supercautious, you might look for a **balanced** or **asset-allocation fund** instead. These all-in-one funds usually keep about 60% of their assets in stocks and the rest in bonds and other fixed-income investments.

Once you have $10,000 or more to invest, begin putting together a diversified portfolio of funds. A recommended lineup: invest 10% in large-company funds, 15% in **small-cap funds,** 25% in **midcap funds,** and 30% in **international stock funds.** The reason for the tilt toward small stocks is that they have historically outpaced large stocks, with average annual returns of 12.4% versus 10.3% for blue chips. The heavy weighting for international stock funds reflects the consensus conviction among market experts that international equities will command some of the highest returns in the '90s.

To balance out your portfolio with fixed-income holdings, you might stash 15% of your money in high-quality corporate bonds with intermediate maturities of five to 10 years. Studies show that five-year issues produce 96% of the return of 30-year issues with only half the volatility. About 5% of your investments should be in a **convertible bond fund,** which will give you a shot at capital gains, or in a **high-yield fund,** which takes on extra risk for potentially higher

THE BEST PORTFOLIO MIX FOR YOU

The table below provides a quick look at how best to divvy up your retirement portfolio, depending on your age. As you'll see, the older you get, the safer the investments become. "Small-cap" is short for small-capitalization stocks, which are companies whose total value—the number of shares multiplied by the current stock price—is between $50 million and $500 million. "Midcap" stocks are companies whose value is more than $500 million but less than $1 billion. "Large-cap" stands for large-capitalization stocks, representing companies whose total value exceeds $1 billion. High-yield bonds sometimes are known as junk bonds. Munis are tax-exempt municipal bonds.

	PORTFOLIO MIX BY AGE			
	20–30	30–40	40–50	50–60
STOCKS				
SMALL-CAP	15%	10%	10%	5%
INTERNATIONAL	30	25	20	20
MIDCAP	25	25	20	15
LARGE-CAP	10	10	20	20
BONDS				
CORPORATES	15	20	0	0
TREASURY NOTES/MUNIS	0	0	25	40
CONVERTIBLE/ HIGH YIELD	5	0	0	0
INTERNATIONAL	0	10	5	0

yields. Steer clear of bond funds that carry loads or fees that total more than 1% of net assets; managers of such funds are generally unable to achieve performance good enough to overcome high expenses. (You'll find fees listed in every fund's prospectus.)

■ **30 to 40:** You may be inclined to turn down the risk level at this point, particularly if you have little children and big mortgages. Any such impulse should be honored, but not indulged. Since you still have about 25 to 35 years to go before retirement, you should stay with at least 70% of your money in stocks. To do this, you can gradually trim your small-stock allocation to 10% and your international funds to 25% of your portfolio. Then transfer half of the proceeds to your intermediate-term corporate bond holdings, which should now be 20% of your stash. You should also transfer the money in your convertible or high-yield corporate bond fund to an **international bond fund** and add enough money so that it becomes 10% of your portfolio. Since fixed-income markets in the United States and abroad generally move in different directions, you will offset a falling market with one that is on the rise. Past performance suggests that this 70–30 configuration should yield annual average returns of about 8.75%, with a risk of losing no more than 5.75% in any given year and a possibility of gaining as much as 23.25%.

■ **40 to 50:** At this point in your life you have probably reached your peak earning years, but your savings may be held back by your kids' college bills. Considering these factors and the undeniable truth that you are beginning to close in on retirement, tone down your portfolio's risk level. You can do this while keeping a solid 70% of your portfolio in stocks. Simply put more money into large-cap and fixed-income funds, thus limiting your probable risk of loss to 5% and allowing for a possible gain of 21% in any given year. Average annual return: 8%.

Large-caps can expand to 20% of your holdings, and midcaps can drop to 20%. In the fixed-income portion of your portfolio, you might go for added security by slicing

international bonds to 5% and exchanging your intermediate-term corporate bond fund for one that holds U.S. government or tax-free issues. Instead of buying a mutual fund that buys U.S. Treasuries exclusively, you might do just as well by purchasing on your own Treasury notes that mature in two to 10 years. You can buy Treasuries directly from the Federal Reserve Bank with no fee or commission. For details, see Chapters 5 and 15.

■ **50 to 60:** Now that you've made it this far allocating your assets wisely, don't make the mistake so many people do as they approach retirement: don't dump all your stock funds and settle in with safe CDs. In your fifties, you are looking forward to 30 or 40 more years of life, when inflation will be sucking the blood from your assets like the wealth vampire that it is. Even if inflation averages a tame 3% a year, the purchasing power of today's dollar will be cut in half in a dozen years.

Consequently, stay with at least 60% of your money in equities. The recommended portfolio allocation aims to produce average annual returns of 7.5%, with an average risk of loss of 4.5% and a possible gain of 19.5% in any one year. To get this return, pare your midcap-stock allocation to 15% of your portfolio and bring your small stocks down to 5%. On the fixed-income side, you can increase your safety measurably by moving out of international bonds entirely and going big into U.S. government or municipal issues.

Three Critical Decisions about Your Retirement

Wise retirement planning is not all numbers. There is a huge emotional component to it, reflecting the fact that retiring involves one of life's most profound periods of change. No one really knows in advance how he or she will weather the process. That is why some people enter a period of prolonged depression, convinced that once a career ends, useful living stops, too. For others, the transition is so easy that anyone observing them might think such individuals were born to retire.

At any rate, three crucial decisions that many pre-retirees must make vividly display the mix of financial and emotional elements. They are (1) knowing when you should retire; (2) sizing up an early-out offer from your employer; and (3) deciding between taking a lump-sum pension and an annuity.

Decision 1: Knowing When You Should Retire. Recent studies indicate that about 25% of retirees are unhappy, primarily because they had not been ready to retire. For some, the decision had not been theirs to make. But in general, at the end of a long career most people think they are headed for freedom and do not stop to consider whether the free time they'll have will lie heavy on them or be the prolonged

vacation they envision. Retirement planners say that six months or so after quitting work, reality sets in.

To make sure that retirement is a welcome reality, weigh carefully the decision to call it quits. Look for the two prime signals that you are ready to retire: (1) You find it harder and harder to keep your mind on your work; and (2) You view retirement not as a passive vacation, but as an active adventure.

Be honest with yourself and admit just how rigid you might be in your life as it is at present. The more averse you are to change, the more you will have to work on making the transition bearable. If your employer provides retirement-planning seminars, take advantage of them. They are apt to address emotional as well as financial issues. If such seminars are not available, seek them elsewhere, perhaps through community groups. Or you can write for information to the American Association of Retired Persons (601 E St. N.W., Washington, D.C. 20049).

The following quiz, prepared by retirement specialist Helen Dennis at the University of Southern California in Los Angeles, can also help you decide if you are emotionally ready for early retirement. (The questions are designed for people who have worked 20 years or more; younger workers may get a false reading because, for example, they are confident of the availability of jobs.)

ARE YOU READY FOR RETIREMENT?

When completing this early-retirement quiz, circle as many answers to each question as apply to you:

1. **The feeling that I make a difference at work is . . .**
   a. extremely important to me.
   b. somewhat important to me.
   c. of little importance to me.
   d. not at all important to me.

2. **My co-workers . . .**
   a. are like my family.
   b. are my major social contacts.
   c. are rarely seen by me (and my spouse) outside work.
   d. are not very important to me.

3. **At work, I feel . . .**
   a. energized.
   b. extremely important.
   c. underutilized.
   d. overworked and underpaid.

4. **To meet my financial obligations and responsibilities, I am counting on . . .**
   a. my next pay raise.
   b. increasing my savings.
   c. winning the lottery.
   d. my spouse.

5. **Retirement means . . .**
   a. you're over the hill.
   b. you haven't yet peaked.
   c. you are old.
   d. you have new choices.

6. **Power and influence . . .**
   a. are aspects of my work that I thoroughly enjoy.
   b. are an essential part of my work.
   c. apply to others, not me.
   d. are almost impossible to achieve in retirement.

7. **I plan to retire and live . . .**
   a. alone.
   b. with my spouse.
   c. with a friend.
   d. with my mother.

8. **I feel . . .**
   a. attractive.
   b. unattractive.
   c. vigorous.
   d. mentally sharp.

9. **I currently have . . .**
   a. some wonderful hobbies.
   b. at least one volunteer commitment.
   c. few outside interests.
   d. some outside interests I would like to develop.

10. **My spouse (or mate) . . .**
    a. is eager for me to retire.
    b. dreads my retirement.
    c. has my chores planned.
    d. has packed our bags for a trip.

11. I consider myself . . .

  a. a good self-manager.

  b. a planner.

  c. a procrastinator.

  d. one who can advise others, but I have difficulty taking my own advice.

12. Knowing I will have free time in retirement . . .

  a. I have planned how I will use my time.

  b. I don't have a clue about what I will do.

  c. I have a plan, but I don't know if it will be fulfilling.

  d. I think that I am already overcommitted.

13. Most of my friends . . .

  a. are working and plan to continue working.

  b. are retired.

  c. plan to retire soon.

  d. are split among all of the above.

14. I've recently thought about . . .

  a. the losses I might feel when I retire.

  b. how my spouse and I will get along in retirement.

  c. what gives meaning to my life.

  d. none of the above.

Score: Give yourself one point for checking each of the following: 1a, 2a, 2b, 3a, 3b, 4a, 4b, 5a, 5c, 6a, 6b, 6d, 7a, 8b, 9c, 10b, 11c, 11d, 12b, 12c, 13a, 14d. The higher the score, the less emotionally ready you are for early retirement. If you scored **15 to 22 points,** either early retirement isn't right for you or you need to start preparing for it immediately; **9 to 14 points** means you are a possible candidate for early retirement but need a little more emotional preparation; and **8 points or fewer** suggests that you can retire happily tomorrow.

The "RIF" (or reduction in force) accompanied by a "package" or early retirement buyout are becoming bywords of American corporate life. If one comes your way, you should be able to tell how generous the offer is and how much latitude you have in determining whether to accept it. You won't have much time, though. Employers typically demand that employees decide quickly whether to take early-out offers.

Compensation specialists report that such offers are becoming increasingly skimpier. Companies have shed the guilt they used to feel about downsizing their workforces and setting aside lifetime loyalties between them and many of their employees. Moral: If you are offered an early retirement package, you may want to take it if only because the next one will likely be less generous—maybe a lot less.

Corporations generally use two types of buyouts. The first is the **early retirement offer,** usually made to workers age

55 and over. It may include a better pension than you would normally have received retiring early; a bridge that pays you the equivalent of your Social Security benefits between 60 and 62, when you can begin claiming the actual benefits themselves; and a generous continuation of your medical coverage. Because formal early retirement packages tend to be expensive, however, fewer than a third of corporations offer them. The second and more popular type of buyout is the so-called **voluntary-separation package.** It typically amounts to little more than enough to tide a family over for a year at most.

Here are the two considerations that should determine how to evaluate an early-out offer:

■ **What choice you really have.** You can't be forced, under federal law, to take a package. Of course, you can be fired later for poor performance, demoted, or see your job eliminated—without any recourse. If you are inclined to turn down an offer, ascertain if your company wants you to stay. Let's say that your boss seems happy with your work and the offer is companywide. Then, you can probably ignore it if you choose. However, if your boss is not pleased with your performance or the offer is restricted to a specific department, you might be wise to take the money and leave.

Perhaps the offer is generous but you don't feel the pressure to accept it. Then turn it down. Remember that your pension rises with your salary and years of service. If you have been toiling at the same address for a couple of decades, it may be worth your while to carry on there for another few years.

■ **What's in the offer.** The best elements in an early retirement package: adding several years—from two to five—to your age, length of service, or both to fatten your pension payout and a Social Security bridge. The best terms in a separation package: two or three weeks' salary for each year of your service, up to a maximum of a year's pay. A poor package, by contrast, might include only a week of salary for each year of service, or the offer might top out at 26 weeks and give you no health insurance.

Many early retirement offers include lifetime health insurance, but voluntary severance packages typically do not. The prospect of buying private insurance at a cost of as much as $5,000 or more a year may be daunting. If you are not healthy, you may not even be able to obtain coverage. Since health care costs are sometimes the difference between comfort and poverty in retirement, this is no small consideration.

Decision 2: Deciding between a Lump Sum and an Annuity. If an old-fashioned defined-benefit pension is in your future, you probably will be offered a choice when you retire. Take the pension as an annuity and get a monthly check for the rest of your life or take the money in one lump sum and invest it yourself. You also might have a sizable lump sum coming from a 401(k) savings plan account. To lump or not to lump, that is the question.

The question has become even timelier recently because of changes snuck into law by Congress in 1994. The legislation said that companies could change the interest rate assumptions they had been making in calculating the size of their pensions. As a result, retirees taking lump-sum distributions may now get less money than before the law passed. In fact, some people in their thirties and forties could wind up with pensions between 30% and 60% smaller than before.

Many pre-retirees warm to the idea of having a large lump sum. It makes them feel more secure about their future and lets them fantasize about spending it and possibly leaving a big chunk to their children or grandchildren. This kind of daydreaming, however, can lead you to turn one of the most important moves of your retirement planning into a long-term nightmare.

Retirement planners with long experience and their clients' interest at heart often recommend the annuity route for pensions instead. They find it the safer way to go if the client is not ready or able to take on the responsibility for investing such a large amount of money—often $1 million or more for many professionals and middle managers who have been at the same company for decades. If you have both a pension and a 401(k), they reason, the pension can represent the fixed-income part of your overall portfolio. You can then take the 401(k) as a lump sum, investing it in, say, a well-allocated assortment of stock funds for growth and inflation protection. You can even take the 401(k) lump sum and buy an annuity with it from an insurance company. You won't have any growth of principal, but you will have the comfort of knowing that month in, month out, no matter what the stock and bond markets do, your regular check will be in the mail.

What if you are capable of guiding your investments and see it as an interesting way to spend some of your time in retirement? Then, taking the lump *may* be a smart move. You can dip into principal if necessary to meet emergencies, while an annuity can never give you more than the monthly allowance. In addition, while the value of the fixed annuity will inevitably decline because of inflation, you can protect a lump sum against rising prices by putting part of it in blue-chip growth stocks.

The closest thing to a rule of thumb in this complex matter: If your company's effective interest rate on your pension taken as an annuity is lower than the rate of 30-year Treasury bonds, you should take the cash as a lump and buy Treasuries. If the pension's interest rate is higher than the Treasury bond rate, you should take the cash as an annuity. Your company's benefits department can tell you the effective interest rate on your pension if you take it as an annuity.

Here's an example. Let's say the pension's interest rate is 8%. This is the rate you would have to beat if you took the money in a lump sum and then invested it. If Treasury bonds are paying, say, 8.5%, you could take the lump, buy 30-year Treasuries, and lock in a better deal than your company's pension annuity could provide. If T-bonds are paying, say, 7.5%, the annuity would look like a better deal.

The best advice for anyone facing the lump versus annuity decision: Hire a competent tax accountant or retirement planner to help run the numbers and explain the pros and cons of both choices. This is one financial decision you don't want to make alone. You will be dealing with complicated actuarial assumptions, intricate tax regulations, and probably the largest pile of money you've ever had. Here are just a few issues you'll face: whether to take the lump and pay tax on it at a favorable rate through five- or 10-year averaging; whether to roll the money over into an IRA, delaying taxation until you withdraw cash while letting the principal grow untaxed; how long you are likely to live; what rate of return you expect on your investments; and how badly you think inflation will erode your savings.

Anyone planning to take his pension as a lump sum must decide how to handle the taxes on the payout. When you get your lump-sum payment at retirement, the Internal Revenue Service will want its cut immediately unless you roll over the money into an Individual Retirement Account within 60 days of receiving the distribution. (In addition, if you make the rollover yourself instead of letting your employer do it directly, 20% of the payout will be withheld under IRS rules and you will have to claim a credit on your next tax return to get it back.)

By choosing instead to pay the tax now, you may receive a mercifully low tax rate reserved for such lump-sum distributions through a technique known as **averaging.** The rate is calculated as if you paid the taxes over either five or 10 years and can yield after-tax results that are far more favorable than paying up in a single year. However, you can use averaging only if your lump-sum distribution meets four requirements. It must be:

1. From a qualified pension, profit-sharing, stock bonus, or Keogh plan in which you participated for at least five years.
2. The entire balance due you from all your employer's qualified plans.
3. Paid to you within a single tax year. If you retire in May, for instance, and pay income taxes on a calendar-year basis, then you must get your entire balance by December 31.

4. Paid after you turn 59½. (The age test does not apply if you were born before January 1, 1936.)

If you meet all these tests, you can apply averaging to the taxable portion of your lump sum. This includes your employer's contributions to your account and its earnings over the years—but not your own nondeductible contributions. The taxable amount will be listed on the Form 1099-R your employer gives you.

Here is a rare gift from the IRS: If your pension distribution is less than $70,000, part of it is tax-free, thanks to what is called the **minimum-distribution allowance.** This break exempts 50% of the first $20,000 of a lump sum from tax. As the payout rises above that amount, the tax-free portion phases out. At $30,000, $8,000 is tax-free; at $40,000, it's $6,000; at $50,000, it's $4,000; at $60,000, it's $2,000; and at $70,000 or more, it's zero.

Figuring the tax on the rest of the distribution is simple if you'll be using five-year averaging. First, divide the remaining distribution by five. Next, find the tax on the result, using the rates for *single* taxpayers; the rates are listed in the IRS instruction booklet for filing your annual tax return. Finally, multiply that tax by five. For example, if you get a lump-sum distribution of $180,000 that has no nondeductible contributions of your own in it, the entire amount will be taxable. Using five-year averaging, one-fifth of $180,000 is $36,000. Find the tax on that amount and then multiply that figure by five. Without using averaging, the tax could run to double the amount you pay with it.

If you were born before 1936, you may use the even more advantageous **10-year averaging.** It works the same way as the five-year method except that you divide and multiply by 10 instead of five. There's one catch: With 10-year averaging, you must use the higher and more steeply graduated 1986 tax rates for singles, which ranged from 11% to 50%, compared with the current 15% to 39.6%. If you qualify for both five- and 10-year averaging, use Form 4972 to figure your tax both ways and choose the one that results in the lower bill.

You can use averaging only once. If you expect a bigger lump-sum distribution from another qualified plan in the future, you might want to postpone taking advantage of averaging. For instance, maybe you're taking early retirement from your current job and are going to work for another employer with a better savings plan and plenty of years before your next retirement. Odds are you'll do better by using averaging when you retire from your next position.

If you were born before January 1, 1936, and earned retirement benefits before 1974, you may be in line for yet another IRS gift: you may treat part of the payout as a capital gain and pay a flat 20% tax on it. That's a big discount not only from your income tax bracket, but from the top capital-gains rate of 28%.

When you compare taking a lump sum through tax averaging with rolling over the whole caboodle into an IRA, the IRA is typically the winner (see the table below). One exception: If you are going to be in a higher tax bracket when you draw money out of the IRA than you are when you retire, the rollover could be more costly than averaging. In general, however, the rollover wins not only because you are likely to be in a lower bracket later on, but also because the money will continue to compound tax-deferred inside the rollover IRA—a powerful force that often enlarges a nest egg measurably during the early years of retirement.

Decision 3: Choosing a Place to Live. While most retirees don't move out of their communities, each year about 500,000 Americans in their sixties do. What do they look for? According to experts interviewed by **MONEY,** retirees look for these attributes when they relocate, in descending order from most important to least: low crime, mild climate, affordable housing, attractive environ-

THE BEAUTY OF ROLLING OVER TO AN IRA

The following example shows how rolling over a pension to an IRA can leave you with far more than paying taxes on it now, even with averaging. Assume that a new retiree who is 62 gets $250,000 in a lump sum and plans to let the money grow at 6.5% a year in an IRA until age 72, when he'll start withdrawing it over 15 years. He expects to be in the 34% combined federal and state bracket during those years. The $250,000, untouched by taxes, will grow to $440,643 by age 72. With 10-year averaging, his after-tax $205,882 ($250,000 minus an immediate tax of $44,118) will increase to only $300,471. Five-year averaging leaves him with even less.

	IRA ROLLOVER	10-YEAR AVERAGING	5-YEAR AVERAGING
Immediate tax	None	$ 44,118	$ 55,635
Amount available for investment	$250,000	205,882	194,365
Accumulated assets at age 72	440,643	300,471	283,663

ment, proximity to cultural and educational activities, strong economic outlook, and excellent health care. (For 20 places that score well in those departments, see the table that follows.) Your priorities, of course, may differ. When you have chosen a place that seems right, spend six months to a year visiting the area—in as many seasons as possible—before you take the big step of buying a house there. During that time, soak up as much information as you can about the area. Find out about the best neighborhoods, activities for retired people, offerings by local colleges, the quality of municipal services, the cost of living, and so on. This is the only way to make sure that you and the community make a good fit.

20 GREAT PLACES TO RETIRE

MONEY recently had a panel of experts rank the 20 places in America that best met the top characteristics for retirees. Here, as a kind of starter list to get your own fantasies working, is the ranking, with key data on each place from tiny Clayton, Ga. (pop. 1,613), to bustling Las Vegas:

CITY/CHAMBER OF COMMERCE PHONE NUMBER	POPULATION	2-BEDROOM HOUSE/CONDO AVERAGE MONTHLY RENT	AVERAGE COST
1. **Prescott, Ariz.** 602-445-2000	28,211	$800	$115,000
2. **Fairhope, Ala.** 205-928-6387	9,000	$400–$600	$80,000
3. **Mount Dora, Fla.** 904-383-2165	7,500	$400–$600	$65,000–$70,000
4. **Las Vegas** 702-735-1616	920,000	$875–$1,150	$110,000–$115,000
5. **Chapel Hill, N.C.** 919-967-7075	41,524	$800–$900	$100,000–$180,000
6. **Naples, Fla.** 813-262-6141	19,505	$1,100	$80,000 (condo)
7. **Sedona, Ariz.** 602-282-7722	7,898	$1,150–$1,350	$150,000–$200,000 (continued)

CITY/CHAMBER OF COMMERCE PHONE NUMBER	POPULATION	2-BEDROOM HOUSE/CONDO AVERAGE MONTHLY RENT	AVERAGE COST
8. Palm Springs, Calif. 619-325-1577	41,674	$850–$900	$92,000–$103,200 (condo)
9. Aiken, S.C. 803-641-1111	20,534	$400–$850	$40,000–$85,000
10. Fayetteville, Ark. 501-521-1710	42,962	$500	$60,000
11. Kerrville, Texas 210-896-1155	18,068	$750	$60,000–$80,000
12. Brevard, N.C. 800-648-4523	5,476	$350–$500	$68,000–$95,000
13. Durango, Colo. 303-247-0312	13,091	$850	$80,000–$110,000
14. Asheville, N.C. 704-258-3858	63,598	$550–$750	$68,000–$95,000
15. Myrtle Beach, S.C. 800-356-3016	25,656	$450–$650	$70,000–$85,000
16. St. George, Utah 801-628-1658	38,000	$750	$85,000 (condo)
17. Hendersonville, N.C. 704-692-1413	7,403	$400–$500	$68,000–$95,000
18. Sequim, Wash. 206-683-6197	4,075	$800	$120,000
19. Charleston, S.C. 803-577-2510	83,095	$540	$85,000–$110,000
20. Clayton, Ga. 706-782-4812	1,613	$350–$450	$80,000–$87,000

Note: Real estate data provided by Century 21.

One factor in choosing where to live in retirement is the amount of state taxes you'll owe. As it turns out, although every state has special provisions to lower tax liabilities for people age 65 and older, your tax bill can differ dramatically just by crossing state lines. According to the National Conference of State Legislatures, a senior citizen with taxable income of $29,000 would be able to get as much as $635 in elderly tax benefits in New Mexico, but only $20 in special breaks in Arkansas and Kentucky. Other differences:

- **Seven states have no personal income tax:** Alaska, Florida, Nevada, South Dakota, Texas, Washington, and Wyoming.
- **Four states have marginal income tax rates of 10% or higher:** California (11%), Hawaii (10%), Montana (11%), and North Dakota (12%).
- **Five states have no state sales tax:** Alaska, Delaware, Montana, New Hampshire, and Oregon.
- **Two states fully recognize the federal credit for the elderly and disabled:** Rhode Island and Vermont.
- **A few states let seniors exclude from income some dividends and interest on investments:** For instance, Montana residents 65 and older can exclude up to $800 of dividends and interest. In Michigan you can exclude up to $1,000 of dividend and interest income.
- **Half the states and Washington, D.C., fully exclude Social Security benefits from taxation:** Alabama, Arizona, Arkansas, California, Delaware, Georgia, Hawaii, Idaho, Illinois, Indiana, Kentucky, Louisiana, Maine, Maryland, Massachusetts, Michigan, Mississippi, New Jersey, New York, North Carolina, Ohio, Oregon, Pennsylvania, South Carolina, and Virginia.
- **Six states fully exempt private pensions from taxes:** Alabama, Hawaii (noncontributory plans), Illinois, Massachusetts (contributory plans), Mississippi, and Pennsylvania.
- **Some states have much larger personal exemptions, credits, and standard deductions for people 65 or older than others.** For instance, single people 65 or older get a maximum tax break when combining these write-offs of $15,200 in New Mexico, $12,000 in Connecticut, and $10,000 in West Virginia. By contrast, you can only claim $650 plus a small credit in Kentucky and Ohio.

How to Avoid Being a Ripped-off Retiree

It should come as no surprise that if a retirement payout is the most money you will ever get, you are not alone in realizing it. Pension and 401(k) lump-sum distributions ranging from the low six figures to well over $1 million have become so common that a virtual industry has grown up in recent years to help you invest those dollars. Old-fashioned insurance salesmen, plain-vanilla financial planners, and others have been transformed into retirement planners. Some will guide you to the wisest and most fruitful decisions you could ever make and charge you modest fees or commissions to do so. Others, however, will skin you alive and leave you stripped of much of your carefully amassed fortune. Here are the two types of snakes with the deadliest venom and how best to avoid being poisoned by them:

■ **Planners who won't even discuss the pros and cons of taking an annuity instead of a lump-sum distribution.** These schemers, usually earning their keep through commissions, will tell you that lumps are always the better choice and then almost immediately try to sell you anything from mutual funds (always with a load or commission) to fee-laden limited partnerships. These people may well even refuse to discuss how they will be paid. Advice: Walk away as quickly as possible from anyone who appears to be more interested in selling financial products than in finding out your needs.

■ **Life insurance salesmen who want to sell you things you cannot clearly understand.** Retired folks need very little life insurance since life policies are primarily for breadwinners whose loss would cause deep financial misery to their growing families for many years. Yet many insurance salesmen persist in pushing such coverage to retirees and pre-retirees. Recently, some salesmen for one of the giants of the life insurance business were selling life insurance as a retirement investment, largely by masking the fact that they were selling insurance policies. In other instances, pre-retirees get talked into taking their pension as an annuity that covers only their own lifetime and not their spouse's. This yields a bigger monthly check. But the customer then is urged to dip into his annuity payments to buy a costly life policy so his spouse will get its death benefits when he dies. In most cases the retiree would be better off taking an annuity with payments based on the joint life expectancy of both him and his spouse. For most retirees there is only one reason to buy a life insurance policy: to provide your estate's executor with cash to pay off its bills while the family assets await probate.

CHAPTER 12

How to Manage Your Estate

More than any other chapter in this book, the one you're starting now deserves to be launched with a sermonette. Sorry about that, but there's no other way. Estate planning is the one personal finance topic that has a chilling effect on most people. And it shouldn't. When you're in your twenties, you tell yourself it's too early to think about such a grim subject as how to dispose of the worldly goods you haven't even accumulated yet. But that starts a process of putting it off until, ripe and maybe even a bit rich, you find yourself pushing 60. You know you should have looked into estate planing earlier, but the habit of procrastinating is almost as old as you are. Or perhaps you've never done any estate planning because you didn't want to pay a lawyer

to draw up a will or trusts. Here's the truth, short and bittersweet: Everyone—from the moment they are on their own financially—needs to think about estate planning and then do something about it—especially since Congress changed some key estate-law rules in the 1997 tax law. So don't wait a day longer.

Strong words? Yes, but the argument behind them is just as powerful. There are six reasons to embark on estate planning: (1) to make sure that each of your assets goes to precisely the person you want to have it; (2) to prevent estate and death taxes from taking a huge bite out of your assets, leaving a diminished legacy for your heirs; (3) to be sure your children are in good hands after you die; (4) to be prepared in case you can't take care of yourself any longer; (5) to have enough cash available to your heirs after you die in order to cover taxes due and pay your burial expenses; and (6) to be sure your loved ones know what you want them to do if you become incapacitated or die. Here are two examples of why estate planning can really matter.

A freak auto accident ends your life at age 29. You and your live-in lover have been accumulating stuff—furniture, a CD player, silverware—for four years. You may even own a house, condo, or co-op. Together, you've talked about wanting most of these possessions to go to the other in case one of you died. You've also made it clear that certain items of jewelry or art are to go to a brother or sister for sentimental reasons. But since you never bothered to make a will, under the laws of your state everything that you own goes to your *parents.*

Cancer claims your husband at 59, just as he is about to retire. You've been blessed over the years. The house you bought 33 years ago for $35,000 is now mortgage free and worth $450,000. You and your husband have retirement accounts, savings, investments, and personal property that push your net worth to $1.8 million. It turns out that your husband has kept all the assets in his name, however, and also died **intestate,** or without a will. Under the laws of the state where you live, his 90-year-old mother gets one-third of the $1.8 million, you get a third, and your two children split the other third. The fact that you and your husband had agreed that you were supposed to get it all doesn't matter to the state. That's not all. The federal government takes $412,800 in estate taxes, since your husband's estate has fallen into the 45% federal estate tax bracket. It could have been worse, because the estate tax rates run as high as 55%. But it could have been much better: if you and your husband had done your estate planning, you could have eliminated the tax entirely.

End of sermonette.

Drafting a Letter of Instruction

Perhaps the most important estate-planning move you can make is the one that is easiest to ignore: drafting a letter of instructions to your loved ones. By putting down on paper the key things that should be done after you die, you will avoid many possible errors of judgment by your family and also help make the process of handling your final affairs a bit easier. You don't have to hire a lawyer to write this document. Just be sure you include the following: who should be contacted after you die; what kind of burial and funeral you prefer; how to take care of immediate financial matters; where your key financial documents are located; and any views you have about such important personal issues as how you'd like your children to be raised and what to do with your home. Of course, be sure that your family and key financial advisers know where to find this letter of instruction.

How to Own Your Property

Every time you take legal possession of a sizable asset—a house, a mutual fund, a bank account, jewelry, a car—you create a situation that determines how your estate will be distributed and taxed. So here's the first rule of estate planning: Decide how you want to own each important piece of property you acquire. You have a number of choices: **fee simple or sole ownership, joint ownership (also known as joint tenancy with right of survivorship), tenancy in entirety, tenancy in common,** and, in some states, **community property.** Many couples think that holding all their property jointly is always the best way to go. In fact, it isn't.

■ **Fee simple** means that a piece of property is individually owned. You de-

cide who will get it after you die. If, say, a husband's name is the only one that appears on the deed and other documents related to buying the house, he owns it outright and his wife has no part of that ownership. While this arrangement might simplify things if the couple eventually divorce or if his wife's work makes her vulnerable to being sued, it would considerably complicate any surviving spouse's life. That's because the house would have to go through **probate,** a costly and time-consuming court process discussed later in this chapter. (Lawyers' fees and probate court costs cut at least 5% off an estate.) So if you're part of a couple, never hold property as fee simple unless an estate attorney whom you trust advances a powerful reason for doing so.

■ **Joint ownership or joint tenancy with right of survivorship** is designed for couples, married or otherwise. It means that two people share title to an asset and upon the death of one of them the survivor automatically becomes the sole owner. On the other hand, one partner has the right while alive to sell or give away his or her share without consulting the other. Joint tenancy is the easiest way to avoid the legal process of going through probate court. It makes a lot of sense if the value of your estate in 1998 is under $625,000, a figure that will rise each year before hitting $1,000,000 in 2006. Joint ownership isn't necessarily the smartest way to hold assets if your estate's value exceeds $625,000, though, since a surviving spouse's estate worth more than $625,000 would be vulnerable to federal estate tax. (By federal law, every person can pass up to $625,000 tax-free to a beneficiary in 1998.) In addition, if both spouses die simultaneously, the whole estate will immediately become subject to taxes. Another drawback of joint ownership: If one of you becomes incapacitated, the other may need to get permission from a court to sell jointly held assets.

■ **Tenancy in entirety** is a form of joint ownership recognized in 24 states. It differs from joint tenancy with right of survivorship in one important respect: Tenancy in entirety requires a partner, who must be a spouse, to secure the permission of the other before disposing of his or her share in the asset. This provision avoids such unpleasant surprises as when, say, a husband gives valuable assets to his children from an earlier marriage without informing his wife. One drawback: If a couple dies with the entire estate in tenancy in entirety, one spouse will have wasted his or her $625,000 federal estate tax exemption.

■ **Tenancy in common** is when two or more people share ownership in property with the right to bequeath their shares to whomever they wish. In other words, the surviving spouse won't necessarily get all the assets in the estate when his or her spouse dies. Also, tenants in common

don't have to have equal interests in an asset, unlike joint tenants and tenants by the entirety. You could have a 55% interest and the other tenant could have a 45% interest, for example. Tenancy in common often is used by business partners and spouses who plan to leave their valuables to somebody else—say, children from a former marriage.

■ **Community property** is the rule for couples who are residents of Arizona, California, Idaho, Louisiana, Nevada, New Mexico, Texas, Washington, and Wisconsin. In those states all property acquired after a couple gets married is considered to be owned equally by the two partners. All assets owned by one of the partners before the marriage continue to be owned separately. If you live in a community property state, you'll need a prenuptial agreement artfully crafted by a first-rate estate attorney in order to keep separate ownership of property that was acquired after the nuptials.

When confronted with these legal terms, most Americans tend to become instantly befuddled. In fact, most people don't have the vaguest idea how they own their prime possessions. So here's the short of it: If yours is the only name attached to the asset's title, you own it individually (fee simple). If your name and one or more others appear on the title, then you all own the property either in common or as joint tenants, depending on the laws of your state. Your best bet is to ask a lawyer in your state whose judgment you trust and then make sure that from then on you take ownership in the way that best meets your needs.

The Basics of Estate Taxes

To understand estate planning, you need to understand the rules of federal estate tax. The good news is that in recent years the U.S. Congress has not tinkered with the federal estate tax nearly as much as it has with income tax. The bad news is that the good news is destined to change—almost surely by the end of the decade. That's because Congress is ever more desperately looking for revenue, and the constituency for raising estate taxes—those Americans who do not have sizable estates—is larger than the one that favors keeping them where they are. (State death taxes vary tremendously depending on where you live; talk with an estate attorney to find out what you can do now to lower the death taxes when the time comes. For example, if you're about to retire, you might want to move to a state with low death taxes.)

For the moment, then, the cornerstone fact to remember about estate tax is that there is a **unified estate and gift-tax credit** of $625,000 in 1998. This credit represents the maximum amount of your estate ($625,000) that you can pass on free of federal estate taxes during your life or after you die; there's a special larger exclusion for some owners of family-run businesses starting in 1998. Beyond that, any individual may give away to any other individual up to $10,000 a year without incurring any gift tax. This is known as the **annual exclusion from gift tax.** (After 1998, that $10,000 figure rises with inflation as a result of the 1997 tax law.) A couple may bestow joint gifts of up to $20,000 per recipient per year. The $625,000 credit offsets any gift taxes you might otherwise have paid during your lifetime on gifts valued in excess of the $10,000 or $20,000 thresholds. Then, what is left decreases—or wipes out entirely—your ultimate estate tax. (The IRS free Publication 448 provides more details on federal estate and gift taxes.)

The $625,000 figure is actually more generous than it sounds. First, it is calculated after deductions for charitable gifts, debts, funeral expenses, and executor's and attorney's fees. Far more important, all property left to a surviving spouse goes directly to the spouse without tax, thanks to the **unlimited marital deduction.** So, no matter how large an estate is, it isn't taxed by Uncle Sam upon the death of a married individual as long as the assets are left to a surviving spouse who is a U.S. citizen. If the surviving spouse is not a U.S. citizen, he or she receives no such special treatment under the law. The only way to get around this provision is to set up what's known as a **qualified domestic trust** for the survivor. The unlimited deduction is restored, but there may be no distribution of assets to that noncitizen spouse without incurring estate tax. On the other hand, he or she may draw all the income from the trust free of estate tax.

Taxable estates over $625,000, however, are severely whacked by the IRS. The federal tax rate schedule:

TAXABLE ESTATE OF	TAX RATE
$500,000–$750,000	37%
$750,000–$1,000,000	39%
$1,000,000–$1,250,000	41%
$1,250,000–$1,500,000	43%
$1,500,000–$2,000,000	45%
$2,000,000–$2,500,000	49%
$2,500,000–$3,000,000	53%
$3,000,000 and up	55%

It's easy to see from this table how quickly a middle-class family's legacy can become depleted. A house bought decades ago for five figures could easily be worth $500,000 today. Add savings, investments, life insurance, and retirement accounts and a couple's net worth can top $1 million with no problem at all.

An estate of that size would trigger estate tax of $345,800, without savvy planning.

How big an estate do *you* have? To find out, scribble down on a sheet of paper the totals for all of your assets—your bank accounts and CDs, mutual funds, stocks, bonds, real estate, personal property, and the eventual death benefit of your life insurance policy. The sum of these figures gives you the total value of your gross estate. Then, add up your estate's liabilities: the amount left on your mortgage, other loans and debts still outstanding, the estimated cost of your funeral and burial costs, and the cost of settling your estate (figure 5% to 10% of the gross value of the estate). Subtract those liabilities from your gross estate and you'll have a rough idea of the value of your estate, before taxes.

Fortunately there are a multitude of offsetting estate-planning techniques, including two that don't require hiring lawyers or drawing up fancy documents:

■ **Making gifts while you are alive.** The annual $10,000-per-person gift-tax exclusion can be a great way to reduce estate taxes. Let's say you have two children and three grandchildren, a beloved sibling, and a cousin who has not been as fortunate financially as you have been. In a single year you and your spouse could give $20,000 to each of these seven people tax-free, thereby reducing your estate by $140,000 in that year alone. You might also add some bequests to an institution such as your alma mater and to a few favorite charities, moving even more out of the grasp of estate taxes. When making a gift to someone under 18 (or 21 in California), you should put it in a custodial account at a bank, brokerage, or mutual fund. Name a custodian other than yourself. That's because if you don't, the IRS will treat the gift as part of your taxable estate should you die before your child reaches the age of majority.

■ **Leaving your heirs investments that have appreciated.** Another way to substantially decrease the size of your taxable estate is what amounts to perhaps the largest loophole left in federal tax law. Some mordantly call it the "angel of death" provision. It is more formally known as **tax-free step-up in basis.** Translation: Your heirs pay no taxes on any capital gains on investments you leave them when you die. For instance, let's say you had bought $10,000 of Berkshire Hathaway stock years ago and its market value is now $200,000. If you died tomorrow and left that stock to your daughter in your will, she would owe tax only on any capital gain between your death and the date she sold the stock. So your $190,000 in appreciation will not be taxed. Reason: The so-called basis for tax purposes of this asset was stepped up from $10,000 to $200,000 at your death.

This loophole, potentially huge in the case of appreciated stock, is somewhat less roomy when it comes to mutual funds. That's because funds typically make periodic capital-gains distributions and you must pay capital-gains tax on those distributions at the time. So from an estate tax point of view, it may be best to invest in stock mutual funds that have minimal capital-gains distributions. These could be index funds and other stock funds whose managers don't sell shares very often; a fund with a portfolio turnover rate of less than 50% would qualify. One cautionary note: Variable annuities, a popular way of investing in stock mutual funds and deferring income tax, do not qualify for a tax-free step-up in basis.

Why You Need a Will—and Possibly Some Trusts

This chapter began with a sermon. Now here's an order: If you are an adult and have any assets, *get a will!* Without one, you will die intestate and upon your death the distribution of your property will be made according to the laws of the state you lived in. Chances are these laws will not correspond to whatever plans you had in mind for giving away what you've got. For instance, in most states a married parent's assets are apportioned among his or her spouse and children, often with half to two-thirds going to the kids. Then there is the matter of taxes. Writing a will alone will not free your estate from getting taxed. But a will is the proper repository for any trusts you might want to set up to minimize taxes.

In addition, a will lets you name a person or people who will manage your affairs or take care of your children after you die. You'll want to name an **executor**, the person to carry out your instructions for disposing of your property. This way you'll avoid the need for a court-appointed administrator, who would not only likely be expensive, but would not have your best interests at heart, since he or she would not know you or your interests. If you have children, you'll also want to appoint a **guardian.** This person would be responsible for raising your kids and managing their inheritances if they were minors when you died—or, if you're married, when both you and your spouse died. If you fail to name caretakers for your kids, a probate court judge will appoint guardians of his or her own choosing for the children and their assets.

If you're thinking of relying on joint ownership as a worthy substitute for a will, think again. Here's why: Take a childless couple without a will who are in an auto accident in which the wife is killed while the husband survives for a day or so. The wife's half of the couple's joint property would automatically pass to the husband. Because there is no will, however, all of the couple's assets would go to the husband's relatives after his death, leaving her family with nothing.

If you're convinced that you need a will, here's your next order: *Get it right!* Otherwise the will may not do what you want it to do. For instance, if you have heirs who are very young, disabled, or simply disinclined to manage their money well, you will shortchange them if you write only a rudimentary will. What if you and your spouse die and you have left all your assets to your minor children in your will? The guardian of their property named in that will must then report expenditures and investments on the children's behalf to a judge. This gives a judge who is unfamiliar with your financial goals and investment philosophy power over how your legacy is managed and spent.

Be sure your will contains the following: your name, the date, any bequests and the names of the beneficiaries, provisions for any trusts (more about them shortly), the names of any guardians, executors, and trustees, and your signature. You'll need two witnesses who watch you sign the document. If you have changed the will, you'll be adding a **codicil.** Your original will and any codicils must be witnessed and signed. You'll want to update the will at least every three years, and certainly after any momentous event in your life such as the birth of a child, the death of a loved one, your marriage, or your divorce. In addition, it's important to have an estate attorney review your will after Congress or your state passes any major legislation affecting estate or death taxes.

You may have thought that **trusts** are exclusively a way for the rich to pass on money to their kids and save some taxes to boot. If so, it's time to jettison that notion. Actually, trusts are a financial device that anyone can use to own assets, to buy or sell them, or to transfer them. In some cases trusts can save on income taxes or estate taxes. In some cases they help speed up the processing of an estate after the person setting up the trust dies. Depending on the trust, you may or may not have to give up legal ownership of the assets you put into it.

To clear up some confusion about trusts, here are three myths about them that should be exploded right now:

Myth 1: Trusts are expensive. (They actually can cost as little as $250 each.)

Myth 2: Trusts are for old people. (In truth, their primary function is to protect children and preserve their inheritances. It's wise to create a trust in your will to hold your children's inheritances. Among their other advantages, trusts keep money out of children's hands until you think the kids will be mature

enough to manage the cash. If you simply leave assets to your kids in your will, they can claim their inheritances when they reach the age of majority, which is 18 in most states.)

Myth 3: Trusts are too complicated to understand. (The following short course on trusts will show that this is not so.)

It's true that trusts, like any legal documents, have their own jargon. Once you understand the different types of trusts and what they can do, however, you'll see that the world of trusts isn't really all that complicated after all.

The best way to make sense of the different types of trusts is by seeing how they fit into the answers to two key questions:

1. When does the trust kick in? That depends on which of the two types of trusts you're talking about. A **testamentary trust** is part of your will and takes effect upon your death; most trusts are testamentary. This kind of trust can save estate taxes for a married couple after the second spouse dies. However, a testamentary trust will go through probate. A **living trust** isn't part of your will, and it starts to operate during your lifetime. Another useful benefit of a living trust: The assets inside it escape probate.

2. Can you change a trust if you change your mind? Here again, it depends on which of two types of trusts you're talking about. A **revocable trust** means you *can* change its provisions or even terminate it while you are alive. Property in a revocable trust is part of your taxable estate because you controlled it during your lifetime. So there are no estate tax advantages to setting up a revocable trust. A revocable trust won't go through probate, however, and its contents will thus forever remain private. An **irrevocable trust** is one you can't change or alter. Nor can you control its assets. An irrevocable trust can dramatically cut your estate tax since all property in this kind of trust is not included in your estate for the purpose of calculating estate taxes. Confining, yes? But a real money-saver for your heirs. You'll want to put appreciating investments in an irrevocable trust, since their growth in value won't be hit with gift or estate taxes.

There are six basic types of trusts that you might want to consider, depending on your needs and wishes. (A head-to-head comparison appears on page 308.) Here's what they are and how they work:

■ **Bypass trust.** (A living or testamentary, revocable estate tax cutter. Sometimes called an **A/B trust,** a **unified credit trust,** or **credit–shelter trust.**) A bypass trust is the most important trust in estate planning. Couples use reciprocal bypass trusts in order to leave $1.25 million to their heirs free of estate tax—double the standard exclusion. In other words, a bypass trust can raise the amount your heirs will get from you.

Each spouse would set up a separate bypass trust. It can be either testamentary or living; most are now of the living variety, which do not involve the expense and inconvenience of probate court filings, as is the case with testamentary trusts. Say the husband dies or becomes unable to manage his financial affairs. At that point, up to $625,000 of his assets gets placed in his trust. The wife then starts receiving income from the trust and is entitled to as much as 5% or $5,000 of the principal each year, whichever is greater. In addition, the trustee has the right to give the wife whatever part of the principal she needs for general support or to pay her medical bills. After her death she can pass on to her heirs $625,000 thanks to her right to exclude that amount from her taxable estate. On top of that, the $625,000 from the trust goes to the beneficiaries and no estate tax is due on that amount, either. (If the wife dies first, of course, her trust is funded similarly for the husband's benefit.) So the beneficiaries wind up with $1.25 million free and clear.

■ **Life insurance trust.** (A testamentary, irrevocable estate tax cutter.) The death benefits from life insurance policies are often a major part of an estate. Not always, though. With this type of trust, your life insurance proceeds go into the trust instead of into your taxable estate, which reduces the amount of potential estate tax. So if you think your estate will be taxable, you might want to put your life insurance policy into one of these trusts. Typically, your spouse also gets income from the trust for life and can even tap its principal if necessary. After he or she dies, the remaining assets go to the heirs named in your trust agreement. Two catches: First, once you put a cash-value life insurance policy in a trust, you give up the ability to borrow against it. Second, if you die within three years of establishing a life insurance trust, the benefits are *included* in your taxable estate. That's why attorneys often include a clause in this kind of trust agreement stating that should you die within three years, the insurance proceeds would go directly to your spouse or into a trust for his or her benefit. That trust, in turn, is included in his or her estate.

■ **Charitable remainder unitrust.** (A living or testamentary, irrevocable income tax cutter that can also provide income for life.) This type of trust does a variety of useful things: it lets you give assets to a charity while you're alive, for example, and receive tax deductions when you make the donations, and it gives you or members of your family all the trust's income for life. After a specified time period, often upon the death

of your surviving spouse, the trust terminates and the charity gets outright ownership of the assets. A charitable remainder unitrust is either living or testamentary because you can create one while you're alive or write it into your will. In the latter case, the donated property is still considered part of your estate, but a portion of its value is deductible before estate taxes are taken out. If you start a charitable remainder unitrust while you are alive, you'll probably get an income tax deduction in the first year equal to the value of the **remainder interest,** an amount that your lawyer or accountant can calculate using special IRS guidelines. Despite the irrevocability of the unitrust, you can drop the charity you originally named as beneficiary and name another later. Most charitable remainder trusts require at least $50,000.

■ **Charitable lead trust.** (A living or testamentary, irrevocable income tax cutter that preserves assets for your heirs.) This variation on a charitable remainder unitrust assumes a level of affluence beyond most middle-class people. That's because the charity gets all the income from the donated assets until you die. Then your heirs receive the assets. In exchange for forging the trust income, you get larger tax write-offs—in some cases up to the full value of your contribution. IRS tables compute the size of your estate tax deduction for a charitable lead trust based on the amount you contribute, the investment's projected rate of return, and the trust's specified life. For example, let's say you set up a 20-year charitable lead trust with a principal value of $100,000 and a payout rate of 6.5%. The charity gets $6,500 a year for the term of the trust and you get an estate tax deduction of $71,842. The value of the payout is deductible from your income tax only for the year you place the property in the trust. But since in future years the payout is taxed to the giver—*you*—many people decide not to claim any income tax deduction at all; then none of the payout is taxed to you.

■ **Charitable remainder annuity trust.** (A living or testamentary, irrevocable income tax cutter that provides income.) This works much like a charitable remainder unitrust, but the charity pays the donor a fixed amount each year, usually 7% to 9% of principal. Appreciated property producing little or no income makes the best gift for this type of trust. The reason: If you sold the property and reinvested the proceeds for higher income, you would incur a taxable capital gain. If a charitable trust sells the property and then replaces it with an annuity, no capital-gains tax is due, however.

■ **Grantor retained trust.** (A living, irrevocable estate tax cutter that lets you transfer property to your heirs.) There are three types: GRITs (for grantor retained income trusts), GRATs (grantor retained annuity trusts), and GRUTs (grantor retained unitrusts). If you are looking for ways to transfer major assets to your heirs while reducing your exposure to estate tax, one or more of these may be for you—after you have a serious discussion about them with your estate attorney. After you create a GRIT, you keep getting any income from it for a specified period. And a house included in a GRIT would be yours to live in for a specified number of years. After the trust's term elapses, ownership of the property goes to the beneficiary, removing it from your estate. If you die before the trust expires, however, its assets are taxable in your estate.

Many wealthy people use GRITs to avoid estate taxes on such significant assets as houses, artworks, or antiques. GRATs and GRUTs differ from GRITs because the grantor—you—must get a fixed payment from the trustee, even if the trust does not generate enough income. In such a case, the trustee can either sell trust assets to cover the shortfall or borrow the funds.

A HEAD-TO-HEAD LOOK AT TRUSTS

Here are the six major types of trusts. Columns are marked with an "X" when they are an option for the trust.

TYPE OF TRUST	REVOCABLE	IRREVOCABLE	LIVING	TESTAMENTARY	CUTS INCOME TAXES
Bypass (a/b, unified credit, or credit-shelter)	X		X	X	
Life insurance		X		X	
Charitable remainder unitrust		X	X	X	X
Charitable lead		X	X	X	X
Charitable remainder annuity		X	X	X	X
Grantor retained (GRITs, GRATs, GRUTs)		X	X		

A Trust Apart:
The Living Trust

The living trust entered American folk-lore back in the 1960s with the enormously successful publication of Norman Dacey's *How to Avoid Probate*. This volume, a large portion of which consisted of inter vivos (Latin for "among the living") trust forms waiting to be filled out, promoted the living trust as the ideal way to keep your estate out of probate court. All you did was set up an inter vivos or living trust and transfer your assets to it, and the property could pass unimpeded to your chosen heirs. What's more, since a living trust is revocable, you can alter it or even end it while you are alive. The popularity of Dacey's book has since spawned a hard-sell living trust industry hawking seminars, books, do-it-yourself kits, and direct advice from what some scornful lawyers dismiss as "trust mills."

As you might suspect, there's more to estate planning than just setting up a living trust. As a matter of fact, a living trust is *not* advisable for many people. What's more, a living trust doesn't do everything some of its hard-charging advocates claim. Before putting your signature on a living trust document, you'll want to discuss the matter with a first-rate estate attorney, but here are the things you should know before you even start his or her fee clock ticking.

The case for avoiding probate is compelling. As noted in the previous discussion of bypass trusts, not only is the court process expensive, it's time-consuming. Probate courts often take from a few months to two or three years from the time of death until they are finally done with a case. Still another plus: By avoiding probate court, living trusts ensure that your affairs are kept private after you die. Wills and trusts that pass through probate become part of the public record.

On the other hand, since a living trust is revocable, its contents are included in your taxable estate, a stark contrast to the essential function of most of the trusts named above—keeping assets safe from estate taxation. In exchange for taxes, the living trust offers vast flexibility. For instance, you can retain any or all income a living trust produces, act as the trustee, change the trust's provisions, or even terminate it.

Many middle-class people find themselves in just the right niche to benefit from a living trust because their estates are not large enough to be subject to federal estate tax; the value of assets in the estate does not exceed $625,000. If your estate is less than $625,000, you may want to set up a living trust to maintain control of the assets you place in it during your lifetime. When you die, the trust can

remain intact for the benefit of your heirs or it can terminate, with its assets distributed to those same beneficiaries.

Another advantage of the living trust is that it accommodates what for many people is the best form of trusteeship. First, you can act as your own trustee while you are in good health. Should your doctor certify that you are no longer able to handle your own affairs, a successor trustee named by you takes over trust management. The far less pleasant alternative is for your family or friends to ask a judge to declare you incapacitated and name a conservator to handle your investments and pay your bills. A conservatorship's annual fees can equal three-quarters of 1% of your assets. Conservatorships also have an ugly history of political patronage and corruption.

Besides exposure to estate taxes, the biggest disadvantage of a living trust is the inconvenience involved in transferring your assets to it. Title must be meticulously changed on all documents for your stocks, mutual funds, life insurance, bank accounts, and real estate to show that the trust, not you, owns the assets. This is almost always far more tedious and time-consuming than you expect. Do it wrong (or forget to do it, as many people with living trusts have) and the assets will be subject to probate.

If you decide to set up a living trust, have your attorney write a so-called **pour-over will,** in which you can bequeath personal property of limited or sentimental value and, if you wish, name a guardian for your minor children. This is also the place to stipulate that any items that you neglected to put in your living trust should go there after your death. As a result, all of your property will be administered in one place for the security of your beneficiaries. Any such forgotten items will become subject to probate, though.

Your particular situation may have a bearing on whether a living trust is appropriate for you. For instance, gay partners may be particularly well suited for a living trust. Their relationship often is not legally recognized, and their wishes set down in a will may be more easily challenged in court than if they had set up living trusts. A gay partner can be trustee, co-trustee, or successor trustee and take over managing the assets immediately if the other partner is incapacitated.

Picking Executors, Trustees, and Guardians

As outlined earlier in this chapter, these are the three essential players who can carry out your wishes once you are no longer able to do so. An **executor** is the person you name in your will to wrap up your financial affairs and make sure your will is probated. A **trustee** is the person you nominate at the time you set up a trust to administer it. A **guardian** is someone you name in your will to watch over the interests of your heirs—principally young children—once you are gone. Some details and advice for choosing these critical appointees:

The executor of your will sets the value of the assets that are part of your estate. This does not include trusts, life insurance policies, pension plans, and some kinds of jointly owned property, which pass directly to beneficiaries. The executor sometimes must hire an appraiser, lawyers, accountants, and other professionals to identify asset values. Fees for all these pros come out of your estate, as does the executor's fee, which typically can run from 3% to 5% of the estate. (If the executor is a family member or friend, the fee often is waived.) The executor sees that all your remaining debts get paid, files tax returns, and distributes whatever is left to your heirs. He or she must keep careful records and give probate court a detailed account of all money received, spent, or held by your estate.

For estates of modest size (up to $2 million or so), with only a handful of beneficiaries and few complicated assets like a portfolio of volatile stocks, the best choice for an executor is often a spouse or best friend—in short, a beneficiary. For larger estates, two executors may be advisable: someone close to you who will be able to interpret your wishes and another person, perhaps an employee of a bank or another financial institution, who will make business or investment decisions, pay taxes, and keep records. You can spell out their specific responsibilities in your will; otherwise both executors are considered equally responsible for all aspects of the estate. Before you decide on an executor, make that person aware of your choice to ensure that he or she is willing to accept the responsibility. Some people won't want the responsibility that comes with being an executor; you and your heirs will be far better off finding this out before you die. Go over your will with your executor: your intentions must be known so they can be carried out.

Choosing a trustee is even more critical if you have any trusts. While the executor's job lasts at most a year or two, the trustee's can drag on for decades and affect the disposition of most, if not all, of your assets. The trustee typically gets wide discretion to manage your property and distribution income and even principal. That's why a trustee ought to know enough about personal finance to be able to make sound investment judgments either on his own or based on the advice of reliable advisers.

Just as with an executor, it is wise to base the selection of a trustee largely on how tough a job he or she will face. If the trust provides for mandatory distribution of income or trustee discretion regarding just one or two beneficiaries, the task will not be too challenging. But if the trustee will have discretion to distribute income and principal in unequal amounts among several heirs, the job can become hellishly complicated. Just consider all the deliciously gossipy books and magazine articles relating the fights among beneficiaries and the suits brought by heirs against trustees charging mismanagement. If you think that kind of thing can happen only to the Harrimans of the world, you're wrong.

More and more, in fact, middle-class families are turning to independent trustees, for reasons far more mundane and practical than internecine jealousy. In the past, when trusts were used primarily for large estates, the trustee's main role was to preserve assets. That's how the comic-book caricature of the sleepy bank trust department presided over by a dreamy octogenarian came into the language. Increasingly, as middle-class estates have become the order of the day, the demand is growing for trustees who will preserve purchasing power for trusts that may last many years. So the emphasis is moving toward counteracting the effects of inflation.

To find this kind of expertise, you might want to hire a professional trustee, usually a trust company that may be independent or a subsidiary of a bank or investment house. Interview at least three or four trust companies to make sure that you'll get the kind of service you want. Ask about their fees (usually an annual charge of 1% to 1.5% of the value of the assets under management) and their investment philosophy, so you can see if you are comfortable with it. To keep a professional trustee honest, many families name a co-trustee—a friend or relative who will be in a position to monitor the performance of the pros.

If you have minor children, you'll want to name a guardian for them in your will or trust. Choose this person extremely carefully. The best candidates for the job are friends or family members who are not only young enough to cope with children, but have the time and inclination to take up the responsibility. Sound out any prospects beforehand, to test both their will to perform the task and their values, which should be similar to yours. You may even want to appoint two guardians: one to take care of your children's well-being and the other, known as a property guardian, to manage their finances. Splitting the duties is especially worth considering if you don't think the guardian who will be raising your children has enough knowledge to handle your finances well.

Living Wills and Powers of Attorney

Just as trusts are underused because of the mistaken impression that they are only for the rich, **living wills** have long been weighted down with the burden of a bum rap: that they are only for eccentrics obsessed with donating their organs when they die. Recent studies estimate that no more than 20% of Americans have living wills, which are a little like wills and a little like trusts. As the cost of health care for terminal patients becomes better known, however, attitudes seem to be changing.

A living will typically consists of two parts. One states exactly what kind of medical treatment you want—and do not want—in case you have a terminal illness or one from which recovery is deemed medically impossible. (This is the will-like part, where you say what you want done with your bodily assets after you die.) The second part of a living will names the person you authorize to make decisions about your medical treatment in case you are unable to decide for yourself. (This person acts like a trustee, ideally making the judgments you would have if you could.) A living will becomes effective once you sign it with a witness present.

It's easy to see why the living will can

be a critical part of an estate plan. Unsettling as it sounds, a recent study showed that for patients who had left no instructions for their medical treatment, the average in-patient charges for a final hospital stay were more than *triple* the charges for those who had left instructions. Those medical bills, perhaps unwanted, can sorely cost your loved ones.

A variation of a living will is a **durable power of attorney for health care,** also known as a **health care proxy.** A living will covers only terminal patients, giving doctors alone the power to make decisions about their medical treatment. Under a durable power of attorney for health care, which also covers nonterminal cases such as people in comas, you appoint a trusted relative or friend who knows your wishes to tell your doctors how far to go in trying to keep you alive. It's a good idea to have a living will and a durable power of attorney for health care. Both living wills and health care proxies are recognized in 45 states. To get free forms for drawing up a living will plus advice about applicable laws in each state, call Choice in Dying (800-989-9455), a national right-to-die advocacy group.

Just as with a guardian, you should ask the person you want to designate as your proxy whether he or she will agree to take on this role, if necessary. Usually this person will be a close friend, your spouse, or one of your children. It's also essential to be sure that your designated proxy, family, financial advisers, and doctor have a copy of your living will. Bring a copy to a hospital whenever you are admitted, too.

Before moving on to the next section, a word or two about **durable powers of attorney** are in order. A durable power of attorney gives someone you trust the right to manage your financial affairs when you can't. Usually a trusted lawyer is given a power of attorney to act for you and sign documents and checks. But the durable power of attorney normally lapses if you lose your mental capacity. Your lawyer should draft a power of attorney document for you (typical cost: $50 to $150). If you have a living trust and have designated someone to take over your financial affairs if necessary, you won't need a durable power of attorney.

You will want to talk to your estate lawyer about all of these issues because they are complex, require precise execution, and vary from state to state. Also, your lawyer can often tailor aspects of your estate plan to your exact desires. For instance, a power of attorney can be made as broad or narrow as you like, deferred (as with a living will), or otherwise. That is just one reason why selecting a lawyer for your estate plan is critically important.

Choosing and Using an Estate Attorney

Here is a rule that is easy to follow and that, if ignored, could cause catastrophe: All but the simplest estate documents should be drawn up by a competent lawyer. For a simple will, go ahead and spend the $50 to $250 that a lawyer typically will charge. You could, of course, save a few bucks by drawing up the will yourself with the help of a $25 to $50 software package like *WillMaker 6*, which you can buy at any computer store. Trouble is, you might think the issues of law are simpler than they actually are, glossing over a legal thicket that could expose your will to challenge when it is probated. A will program may also not be as precise as you'd like. For instance, the software might give so much discretion to trustees that you can wind up letting the trustee favor one of your children over another. A will needs to be reviewed periodically, and on occasions such as the passage of a major tax law, software is no substitute for a knowledgeable attorney. Even more important, each state has a different set of persnickety formalities you must follow *to the letter* in order to make a will valid. Get any of them wrong and your heirs could face the horror of watching as a court declares your do-it-yourself will invalid and you intestate.

Then the laws of intestacy kick in and distribute your assets according to its provisions, not your desires.

One safe use of a will-writing program: Draw up the document with the software and then take it to a lawyer. By putting so many of the details in order ahead of time, you will incur fewer billable hours of the attorney's time.

When you move beyond a will into the more complicated territory of trusts, it's imperative to find a competent estate attorney. A savvy lawyer will also be an essential ally if you own property in more than one state or have a stepfamily; in both instances estate planning can get tricky. As with any professional, word-of-mouth referrals are the usual way of locating a lawyer. A reliable way to check out any lawyer referral is to go to the public library or a law library and look him or her up in the *Martindale-Hubbell Law Directory*. It lists attorneys throughout the United States and features a rating system based on the judgments of other lawyers in the same community. The two top ratings: **a v** (for excellent legal ability and adherence to ethical standards) and **b v** (for high to very high legal ability and adherence to ethical standards). If the attorney you're vetting has either of these designations, you can be pretty sure of his or her competence. Being absent from *Martindale-Hubbell* or lacking one of its top ratings is not necessarily a negative mark, however, particularly for younger lawyers.

When interviewing estate lawyers, you'll want to find out about their fees and their judgment. Attorneys usually charge by the hour, but that information is of no use to you unless you know how many hours will be involved. As a rough guide, you should expect a simple will and a marital trust to run you from $750 to $1,500 and a pair of living trusts from $1,500 to $3,000. Since your estate attorney will likely be with you for years, through significant changes in your life and those of your loved ones, the advice you get may go far beyond trusts to family relationships. For instance, you may need to rely on your estate lawyer for advice on what to do about a disabled child or your elderly parents. A rule of thumb: If you can say that you have real faith in your attorney's honesty *and* common sense, you can be reasonably sure that you've chosen well.

SECTION THREE

INVESTING YOUR MONEY

CHAPTER 13

How to Invest Wisely

Why should you bother investing at all when your neighborhood bank is a nice, safe place to put your money? The answer: inflation and taxes. If your savings, after taxes, doesn't grow faster than the cost of living, its purchasing power will steadily erode. Put another way, if you don't find a way to put your money to work for you effectively, you'll never be able to reach the financial goals you cherish. In short, after you take care of your emergency savings fund, you need to become an investor.

The following example, which doesn't even account for the take of taxes, will show you why. Had your grandmother stashed $90 under her mattress 50 years ago—the price of a decent-quality, three-piece bedroom set in 1945—that money today would buy little more than a set of sheets. If she had invested that $90 in a bank savings account that kept even with inflation, she could still afford that roomful of furniture. But if she had put her 90 bucks in the stock market, it would have grown to more than $25,000 today: enough not only for that bedroom set, but for a down payment on a second home to put it in. If that story doesn't impress you, here's a scarier one: Investing wisely can mean the difference between retiring to a cushy house on the 18th green or retiring to a state-run oldsters' home.

Saving, while extremely important, is essentially just putting money away for safekeeping. Investing, by contrast, is using your money to produce *more* money. Are you thinking that you need a lot of money to invest? You don't. Many equity mutual funds, which pool money from small investors and use it to buy stocks, accept initial investments as low as $500 or even $250. More than 140 fund families let you in with $100 or less. Most funds also let you invest as little as $50 or $100 a month. You can also see what it's like to be a stock investor by purchasing a single share of a company for, say, $30.

If you haven't invested a dime in your life, you're not alone. Millions of Americans don't own any stocks or mutual funds. Some of them have just decided that they don't know enough to invest intelligently. Others think that investing is too scary and worry about the possibility that they'll lose money. Still others think that investing in stocks and mutual funds is no different from playing the craps tables. The truth is, it isn't hard to learn how to invest, putting money into stocks or stock funds isn't scary, and by investing defensively, you can protect yourself from losing money. As for the craps analogy—it's flat wrong. Winning at dice means having good luck. Winning as an investor means using your brains.

One excuse people often use to explain why they don't invest: "I just don't have any money." Sorry, that alibi won't fly. Everyone can find ways to reduce their spending in order to come up with cash to invest. Maybe it's shopping at a warehouse club and buying in bulk instead of heading to the chichi department store for a similar item. Maybe it's shaving your medical bills by joining an HMO instead of sticking with your employer's expensive health insurance policy. Maybe the next time you purchase a big-ticket item like a car or TV you can buy a less expensive model than planned. Or maybe you might even relocate from an expensive part of the country such as the New York City suburbs or California to a place where the cost of living is lower. One other tip: Cut back on your trips to the automated teller machine for cash withdrawals. You'll be left with more money in the bank, which you can then withdraw to invest.

In this chapter you'll learn about the basics of wise investing—from measuring your risk tolerance to diversifying properly among the three basic building blocks of any investment portfolio: stocks, bonds, and cash. In addition, you'll find out how to invest internationally and, if you're so inclined, how to invest ethically.

Measuring Your Risk Tolerance

Before putting a penny into any investment, you need to come to grips with your risk tolerance—how you'd feel about the possibility of losing money on your investments. Let's say you decide to put some cash into a stock that involves more risk than you're truly comfortable taking. If the stock tanks, you may well lose your nerve and sell. That's usually exactly the wrong move, however. Selling at a low point means not only that you've lost money, but that you will miss any gain that occurs if the investment rebounds. Conversely, if a zigzag-shaped line charting your investment performance won't make you lose any sleep, you may be hobbling your portfolio by stashing all of your cash in investments that are *too* safe.

How much risk is too much for you? How much is not enough? The answer depends largely upon two things:

1. **Your temperament,** or your own psychological appetite for taking risks.
2. **Your time horizon,** or the number of years you have to build your investment before you need to cash out.

First, take your temperament's temperature. To pin down your investing risk threshold, take the following quiz, developed with the help of psychologist John O'Leary, co-director of Lifecycle Testing in New York City:

MEASURING YOUR TEMPERAMENT FOR TAKING INVESTMENT RISKS

1. **When it comes to investing, my luck has been**
   a. rotten.
   b. average.
   c. better than average.
   d. terrific.

2. **Most of the good things that have happened to me have been because**
   a. I planned them.
   b. I was able to exploit opportunities that arose.
   c. I was in the right place at the right time.
   d. God looks out for me.

3. **If a stock doubled in price five months after I bought it, I would**
   a. sell all my shares.
   b. sell half my shares.
   c. sit tight.
   d. buy more shares.

4. **Making investment decisions on my own is something that I**
   a. never do.
   b. do occasionally.
   c. often do.
   d. almost always do.

5. At work, when my boss tells me to do something that I know is a bad idea, I usually
   a. tell him or her that I think it is a mistake.
   b. get co-workers to join me in opposing the idea.
   c. do nothing unless the boss brings it up again.
   d. do it anyway.

6. In order for me to invest 10% of my net worth in a venture that has at least a 75% chance of success, the potential profit would have to be at least
   a. the same as the amount invested.
   b. three times the amount invested.
   c. five times the amount invested.
   d. no amount would be worth the risk.

7. When I watch television and see people involved in such sports as hang gliding or bungee jumping
   a. I think they are idiots.
   b. I admire them but would never participate.
   c. I wish I could try such sports once just to see what they are like.
   d. I think seriously about participating myself.

8. If I held a finalist ticket in a lottery with a one-in-three chance of winning a $50,000 prize, the smallest amount I would be willing to sell my ticket for before the drawing is
   a. $30,000.
   b. $17,000.
   c. $13,000.
   d. $10,000.

9. In the past, I have spent $100 on one or more of the following activities: gambling in a casino; betting on my own recreational activities, such as golf or poker; betting on professional sports. (Circle the statement that best applies.)
   a. I have done two or more of these in the past year.
   b. I have done one of these in the past year.
   c. I have done one of these a few times in my life.
   d. I have never done any of these.

10. If I had to make a critical decision that involved a large amount of money, I would probably do one or more of the following things. (Circle all that apply.)
   a. Delay the decision.
   b. Delegate the decision to someone else.
   c. Ask others to share in the decision.
   d. Plan strategies that would minimize any loss.

Scoring:

For questions 1, 3, and 4: If you answered A, give yourself one point; B, two points; C, three points; and D, four points.
For questions 2, 6, 8, and 9: If you answered A, give yourself four points; B, three points; C, two points; and D, one point.
For questions 5 and 7: No matter what you chose, don't give yourself any points. Moral courage and physical bravery don't have anything to do with your tolerance for investment risk.
For question 10: Subtract from five the number of answers you circled and give yourself the rest.

What Your Score Means:

8–16: You're a conservative investor, willing to take few risks.
17–24: You're a moderate investor, willing to take moderate risks.
25–32: You're an aggressive investor, willing to take greater-than-average risks.

Now that you know your temperament for investment risk, consider your time horizon. Remember this rule: The longer you can keep your money invested, the more risk you should take with it. If you plan to use a chunk of money within a few years to buy a house, for example, you can't afford to take a chance that the stock market will fall during that time period. So you should keep your down payment money in a safe place, such as a money-market fund, a bank CD, or Treasury bills. However, if you won't need the money for a decade or more—say, you're investing for retirement at age 65 and you're now 55—you face a significant risk if you don't invest at least some of it in stocks. The risk is that inflation will eat away at the earnings on your money in the bank. Moreover, a long time period helps compensate for short-term dips in the stock market.

While this rule generally means that older people should play it safer than younger ones—after all, younger people have a longer life-span and therefore more time to recover from any bad investment—the truth is more subtle. Even 60-year-olds can expect to live at least another 20 years or so. So they need to keep in stocks a portion of the money they'll live on during retirement. Conversely, a 45-year-old couple with teenage kids shouldn't keep all their spare cash in the stock market. After all, they'll probably need to be sure they have some money salted away safely for college tuition in a couple of years.

The Five Major Investment Risks

There are more types of investment risks than you probably realize. Here is a guide to the five major ones:

■ **Inflation risk.** The risk that your investments will lose out to inflation is actually the greatest threat to your wealth. Fixed-income investments such as CDs and bonds carry the most inflation risk because their yields are locked in and won't rise even if inflation does. Stocks are the best way to overcome the ravages of inflation. While inflation has averaged more than 3% per year since 1926, stocks have racked up average annual gains of more than 10%. During the same period, bonds rose just 5% a year, on average, and cash equivalents like money-market accounts were up only 3% to 4%, according to Ibbotson Associates, a Chicago investment consulting firm.

■ **Market risk.** The most obvious type of risk, market risk, is the chance that the value of your investment will fall and you might have to sell your holding for less than you paid. Stocks put you at greater market risk than bonds, bank CDs, or money-market funds since they are more volatile. While you can count on your CD to chug along, paying you, say, 3% or 4% a year, a stock may lose 10% in that year—or gain 20%. In a worst-case scenario, if the company whose stock you own goes bust, you may lose the entire value of your investment. Federally insured bank CDs of under $100,000, by contrast, have no market risk, because you are guaranteed to get your principal back.

■ **Default risk.** This type of risk is one that bond investors need to worry about. Default risk is the chance that the issuer of the bond won't be able to make interest payments. One way you can skirt default risk is by purchasing U.S. Treasury bonds or mutual funds that hold such bonds. Because the U.S. government backs the bonds, they're essentially free from the risk of default. But they're still vulnerable to an often more pernicious and less understood risk . . .

■ **Interest rate risk.** When interest rates rise, bonds and bond funds fall in value because bond buyers are less willing to purchase the securities with the lower rates than new issues with current, higher rates (for more on this, see Chapter 15). The longer the duration of a bond, the farther it will fall in value if rates go up. That's why long-term, 30-year bonds are far riskier—from the standpoint of interest rate risk—than, say, intermediate-term, seven-year bonds. Just ask any investor who bought long-term bonds in the late '70s and sold them after rates had risen in the early '80s. Their principal fell by roughly 45%. In a sense, you're taking on interest rate risk whenever you buy a bank certificate of deposit, too. By investing in, say, a five-year CD at 7%, you're taking a risk that interest rates won't rise during the five years you have the bond. If rates go up, you'll be earning a lower interest rate than if you had waited.

■ **Currency risk.** This is one type of risk that you may not encounter, at least not until you become a more experienced investor. Currency risk crops up when you invest in foreign stocks or bonds or the mutual funds that invest in them. Simply put, it's the chance that your investments can lose value thanks to fluctuations in foreign currency. For instance, foreign stocks can lose value if the dollar rises against local currencies. Fortunately, over periods of five years or more, currency swings tend to balance out. So if you plan to hold an international investment for a long time, currency risk shouldn't have a significant impact on your portfolio's performance.

Why Diversification Pays

Diversifying is probably the single best way to reduce the risks of investing. It means, simply, spreading out your money among several investments. That way, if one of them suffers a loss, your entire portfolio won't fall as far as it would if all your money was devoted to that one investment. Diversifying won't guarantee that you'll make money, however. In 1994, for instance, many people lost money in

both stocks and bonds. To diversify properly, take the following steps:

■ **Split your money among the three basic asset classes: stocks (or stock funds), bonds (or bond funds), and cash investments such as money-market funds, money-market bank accounts, and Treasury bills.** Stocks let you profit by becoming a part owner of a company. If the company prospers, your shares typically increase and you'll make money, too. Stocks also are known as **equity** investments because they represent a share, or a piece of equity, in a company. Bonds, which are IOUs issued by corporations, governments, and federal agencies, produce income for you from their regular interest payments. You can also score profits from bonds if you sell them after their prices have risen. Cash investments are supersafe, highly stable, and liquid (which means they can be cashed in easily). Stocks power your portfolio's value forward; bonds provide income and typically a higher return than cash, and cash moderates the volatility of stocks and bonds.

■ **Invest in mutual funds.** This is the easiest way to spread your investments around the asset classes. A mutual fund offers instant diversification since the fund manager pools money from many people like you and invests it in a variety of stocks, bonds, or money-market securities. Mutual funds are also a low-cost way to diversify. That's because it would probably cost an individual investor tens of thousands of dollars to buy as many securities as one mutual fund holds.

There are two main types of mutual funds: **open-end funds,** whose shares are sold directly by the fund companies, stockbrokers, and financial planners; and **closed-end funds,** which are far less common, have a fixed number of shares, trade on stock exchanges, and are sold by brokers. About two-thirds of open-end funds are **load funds.** They carry a commission (or a "load," typically equal to a few percentage points of the amount you invest) and are the kind sold by brokers. By contrast, a **no-load fund** does not have an up-front fee. You buy this type of fund directly from the mutual fund company or from a so-called fee-only financial planner, who makes his or her living by charging clients by the hour for advice. Unless you want professional fund-picking advice, you can save a chunk of money by buying only no-loads. The savings can be substantial: fully $850 on $10,000 invested in a no-load rather than a fund with an 8.5% initial sales fee. You can diversify even further by buying several different types of mutual funds with different investing styles. For more on diversifying in mutual funds, see Chapters 14 and 15.

Asset Allocation

Proper diversification gives you what's known as **asset allocation.** This investing term is based on the fact that each type of investment offers its own trade-off between risk and reward. Stocks, for example, deliver the highest returns over extended periods of time but are subject to occasional losses that can easily hit 15% to 20% over a three-month stretch. Bonds, by contrast, typically return less than stocks but provide steadier income and often rise in value when stocks are falling.

Here's how asset allocation works. Let's say you want to allocate assets based solely on your appetite for risk. If the quiz you took in the previous section told you that you're a **conservative investor,** an appropriate portfolio mix for you might be 50% stocks, 20% bonds, 30% cash. Assuming that markets perform in line with their historical norms, such a portfolio will show a loss of no more than 4% in its worst year.

If you're a **moderate investor** with an average appetite for risk, consider a portfolio of 60% stocks, 20% bonds, 20% cash. That mix figures to return about 7.5% annually, with a worst-year loss of 6%.

If you're an **aggressive investor,** consider 80% stocks, 10% bonds, 10% cash.

That mix is likely to grow an average of 9% annually, with a worst-year loss of 15%.

When choosing your asset allocation, be sure to factor in your investing time horizon. If your primary financial goals are coming up within a few years, invest more than you might otherwise in safe choices such as money-market funds and short-term bonds. If you plan to let your investments ride for more than 10 years, go more heavily in stocks. The longer your investment horizon, the more aggressive you can afford to be in selecting investments.

As you grow older, start a family, and move closer to retirement, your investment goals and taste for risk will change. As a result, your asset allocation should change along with you. Younger people, for example, can aim for high returns with aggressive portfolios, since they have many years to recover from market slumps. As you get closer to retirement, however, you need to shift to a more cautious allocation that will preserve your gains.

When allocating assets, be sure to review your entire portfolio. That includes money you hold in employer-provided savings plans or profit-sharing plans such as 401(k) or 403(b) plans as well as Individual Retirement Accounts and Keogh plans. A large chunk of that cash may be in your employer's stock, so you already may be more heavily invested in stocks than you think.

How and When to Diversify

You shouldn't think of diversifying, much less investing in the stock and bonds markets at all, until you've amassed an emergency fund equal to at least three to six months' worth of living expenses. Once you have more money than that, here's what to do:

■ **If you have less than $5,000 to invest,** the typical mutual fund minimum investment of $1,000 to $5,000 means that to get the broadest selection, you may be limited to just one to three funds. Never fear. You can be well diversified with just one fund—as long as that fund is itself widely diversified. Your best choice: a so-called balanced fund that holds a variety of both stocks and bonds.

■ **As your portfolio grows to $10,000** or so, put the stock and bond portions in separate mutual funds—a strategy that lets you control exactly how much of your portfolio will go to each asset class. If you have enough cash for three different mutual funds, pick one bond fund and two stock funds. The two stock funds should have different investing styles, too.

■ **With $20,000 to invest,** aim to own about four or five mutual funds. Now, you can afford to add to your portfolio a fund that buys small-company stocks. An international stock fund would be another smart choice. If you're looking to beef up your income investments, consider adding a safe bond fund, perhaps a municipal bond fund that buys tax-free securities if you're in one of the higher tax brackets.

■ **With more than $20,000,** you can branch out to 10 funds, if you're so inclined. Don't own more than 10, though. You won't be able to keep track of them (let alone remember their names). Record keeping would be a nightmare, too. The more funds you own, the more specialized your new holdings should be. In this way you'll avoid duplicating investments you already own. You might, for example, add funds that buy so-called midcap stocks (those with market values between $500 million and $1 billion).

For some people, mutual funds eliminate the gamblinglike thrill of picking individual stocks. But individual stock issues carry risks that pertain to their particular companies, making them potentially more volatile than diversified mutual funds. The solution: Build up a portfolio of mostly funds, but set aside a small chunk of your equity allocation to devote to individual stocks. It's a good idea to limit your individual stockholdings to 10% of your overall portfolio and no more than 20% of the equity portion. Here again, don't buy more stocks than you can reasonably follow. You can be adequately diversified with just a dozen issues in different industries, which could cost as little as $25,000.

How and Where to Invest

Now that you know about the importance of proper diversification and asset allocation, you're ready to start following these six golden rules of investing to stay on track:

1. Never invest in anything you don't understand. Avoiding complex limited partnership arrangements would have saved a lot of people in the 1980s a lot of grief. In the past few years, even professional investors from the treasurer of Orange County, Calif., to Barings Bank's Nicholas Leeson were badly burned by derivatives—an investing category so complicated that few of them fully understood what they were getting into. If a stockbroker talks you into an investment you don't truly comprehend, how will you know if the investment goes sour or if the broker is taking you for a ride?

Steer clear of the latest newfangled investment and put your money in plain-vanilla stocks, bonds, and mutual funds.

2. Invest automatically. Thanks to the power of compounding, earnings on regular, periodic investments can grow rapidly. For example, if you put $100 every month into a mutual fund that earns 6% a year, you can accumulate $16,326 in 10 years or $28,830 in 15 years—enough for a down payment on the average home. Better returns can bring bountiful rewards. Invest just $25 a week earning 10%, on average, for 25 years and you'll wind up with a wad worth $103,028. If you put $25 away for 30 years and earned 12% a year, you'd wind up with $378,621.

Automatic investing has another huge advantage: It forces you to **dollar-cost average,** a proven winning technique. This strategy calls for you to invest a fixed dollar amount in a stock or a stock mutual fund at regular intervals whether the market is rising or falling. Consequently you end up purchasing fewer shares when the price of the stock or fund is high and more shares when it's low. A $100 investment in a no-load mutual fund, for example, will buy 10 shares when the fund sells for $10 a share. If the fund declines to $8, your next $100 buys 12.5 shares. Thus, without ever deliberately timing your purchases, you automatically stuff your portfolio with less costly shares.

Sticking to the methodical approach of dollar-cost averaging in both rising and falling markets boosts your eventual gain and, equally important, keeps you from being driven by your emotions during market swings. Best of all, you buy fewer shares when they are up and therefore pricey and more when they are down and therefore cheap.

There are three ways you can invest automatically and painlessly:

Employee-benefit savings plans such as 401(k)s at private companies, 403(b)s at nonprofits, and 457 plans at government agencies let you invest a percentage of your pretax salary in an assortment of funds that grow tax-deferred until you withdraw the money after retirement. Once you sign up, the money comes straight out of every paycheck. For more on the unparalleled benefits of tax-advantaged retirement savings plans, see Chapter 5.

Mutual fund savings and **reinvestment plans** are offered by nearly all fund companies. Here, every month the fund management firm automatically withdraws the amount of money you specify (usually a minimum of $50 or $100) from your checking account or even your paycheck or Social Security check and transfers it into the fund you select. To enroll, you simply fill out a form authorizing the fund to siphon a set amount at regular intervals. You can switch off the flow at any time without penalty by calling the fund.

You can also automatically reinvest the dividends and capital gains paid by the fund. Another bonus: Fund companies often waive minimum investment levels for customers who sign up for automatic investing plans.

Stock dividend-reinvestment plans (known as **DRIPs**) offer a great way to make more money and keep you from running to the bank to deposit that $12.50 dividend check from your stock. Approximately 1,100 publicly traded companies, from Alcoa to Zurn Industries, offer dividend-reinvestment plans. Most of the companies with DRIPs reinvest your dividends for free. About 100 of them even discount their DRIP share prices by 3% to 5%. About 300 companies even let you buy your first shares through them, avoiding brokers and fees; these are called **direct-investment** plans. You shouldn't choose a stock solely because it offers a dividend-reinvestment plan, but a DRIP plan certainly makes a stock you find attractive even more appealing. To find DRIPs, get the *Directory of Companies Offering Dividend Reinvestment Plans* ($32.45 by mail from Evergreen Enterprises, P.O. Box 763, Laurel, Md. 20725), which lists nearly 900 firms.

3. Go for consistency rather than flashy returns. Too often, last year's success story is this year's also-ran. Instead of stuffing money into the latest top-performing mutual fund, choose funds that have regularly outperformed competitors with similar objectives for three to five years. You can often find this kind of information in mutual fund rankings tables in magazines such as **MONEY,** *Business Week, Forbes,* and *Barron's,* as well as the *Wall Street Journal.*

4. Adopt a buy-and-hold strategy. Some investors—often those who fancy themselves so smart that they can predict market movements with great accuracy—indulge in a practice called "timing the market." These market timers move up to 100% of their dough back and forth between stocks and cash in an effort to dodge downturns and profit from market rallies. Over the short term, bright market timers can beat buy-and-hold investors. The truth is, though, that a simple buy-and-hold strategy is the better bet over multiple market cycles.

5. Monitor the performance of each of your investments. The best way to figure out how any of your investments is doing is by calculating its **total return:** a performance measure that combines dividends, interest, distributed capital gains, and price changes in a stock or mutual fund. Total return is expressed as a percentage gain or loss in the investment's value. To figure yours, use the following worksheet:

YOUR INVESTMENT'S TOTAL RETURN

A. Enter the value of your investment at the beginning of the period you are examining.   _____

B. Add up any additional money you put into the investment during the period. From that total, subtract any withdrawals you made. (If you took out more than you put in, the figure will be negative.) Enter the result.   _____

C. Multiply line B by 0.5 and add the result to the figure on line A. (If the figure on line B is negative, you will subtract it.) Enter the result.   _____

D. Enter the value of the investment at the end of the period, plus any interest, dividends, or capital gains that you have taken as cash, rather than reinvested.   _____

E. Multiply line B by 0.5 and subtract the result from line D. (If the figure on line B is negative, you will add it.) Enter the result.   _____

F. Divide line E by line C, then subtract 1 from the result. (If the result is less than 1, your return is negative.) Multiply that number by 100. This is your total return.   _____%

6. Rejigger your holdings annually. The best asset-allocation strategies produce investment recipes you can leave in place for years. However, even a well-constructed portfolio requires periodic readjustment as rising and falling markets gradually alter your mix of assets. Once a year, rebalance your holdings by transferring profits from the parts of your portfolio that have done well to those that haven't. This will bring your portfolio back to your chosen risk level.

As a bonus, it forces you to sell overvalued investments and buy undervalued ones. For example, in 1997 emerging-market stock funds lost about 14% on average. As a result of such declines, these stocks would constitute a smaller percentage of a diversified investor's portfolio than they did at the beginning of 1997. To rebalance a portfolio, you'd sell some profitable stock holdings and then use the proceeds to, perhaps, buy an emerging-market fund.

International Investing

More and more Americans are investing their money overseas—not just in foreign stocks, but in foreign bonds, too. Experts agree that just about everyone with a significant investment portfolio should keep 10% to 30% of it in foreign stocks or stock funds; foreign bond funds are a dicier proposition, as you'll see later. International investing gives you two arrows for your portfolio's quiver: added diversification and the potential for better returns.

Foreign economies don't always move in sync with the U.S. economy, so when U.S. markets sag, foreign markets can soar. As a result, investing in overseas stocks or stock funds lowers the volatility of your portfolio and helps boost your overall return. A study by mutual fund company T. Rowe Price over 11 overlapping 10-year periods ending in 1992 found that a portfolio 30% to 50% invested in foreign stocks created better returns with less risk than a portfolio composed of only a broad cross-section of U.S. stocks.

What's more, companies in many foreign countries have the potential for faster growth than U.S. firms. The giant United States dominates the world but can't grow as fast as less developed competitors. In 1993, for example, the average foreign equity portfolio climbed 38.3%, more than three times as much as the 12.6% return for the average domestic stock fund.

Sure, you'll face some complications that you needn't worry about with domestic investments. Currency risk, for example. And the chance that a particular country's economy will collapse, as happened in Korea in 1997. It's also more difficult to get reliable information about many foreign companies than for U.S. companies because few countries require as much disclosure to investors as ours does.

For most small investors, it makes far more sense to invest in international mutual funds rather than in individual foreign issues. After all, think how hard it is to keep up with developments in foreign companies, let alone understand them. Another advantage of mutual funds: Many use hedging strategies that (in theory, at least) work to lower currency risk.

The first thing a fledgling international investor needs to learn is the difference between **international funds** and **global funds.** International funds hold only foreign stocks. Global funds, however, can invest in the United States as well as overseas; they tend to keep 20% to 50% of their money in U.S. equities. Here's the problem for investors who don't know the difference. Let's say you want to keep 20% of your overall allocation in foreign stocks. You put 20% of your portfolio into a global fund without realizing that its holdings happen to be 50% in the United States and 50% abroad. Your foreign exposure, then, is far less than you wanted: it's really 10%, not 20%.

When leafing through mutual fund performance tables in financial periodicals, you may be impressed with the stellar performances of certain **single-region** or **single-country funds.** These are specialized mutual funds that invest only in one region of the world (say, the Pacific Rim) or in only one country (such as Mexico). Watch out! Single-region funds are more volatile than diversified international funds, and single-country funds are more volatile still. The reason: If one region or country suffers a crisis or an economic blow, many of its stocks are likely to suffer. (The converse is also true, of course.) To lessen the risk of investing around the world, make your first international foray a diversified international—not global—fund whose manager can shift investments as market conditions change. Never keep more than 5% of your total portfolio in single-country funds.

If you would rather buy individual foreign stocks, you'll most likely do so by buying what are called **American Depository Receipts** or **ADRs,** sold on major U.S. stock exchanges. A bank owns the foreign shares and issues ADR certificates that trade in their stead. More than 500 foreign companies, from European banks to Asian utilities, list their shares as ADRs. Stick with the roughly one-third of ADRs sponsored by the foreign companies that issue the stock. That means

you'll get accounting and disclosure comparable to that of U.S. firms. Without such sponsorship, you probably won't get as much information. Most ADRs trade on the New York Stock Exchange, but some of them trade over-the-counter (see Chapter 14). Over-the-counter ADRs are often omitted from newspaper listings, however; you'll have to get their price quotes from your broker.

If you prefer individual stocks to stock mutual funds but don't want to mess with ADRs, consider investing in U.S. companies that do a lot of business overseas. About half the sales of big U.S. companies such as Boeing, Caterpillar, and Mattel come from foreign markets. Most cost-efficient U.S. companies that have access to global markets are also benefiting from GATT, the 1994 law that reduced tariffs and enhanced international copyright protections. Ask your broker for help identifying such stocks.

International bond funds invest in foreign bonds, and just like foreign stocks, foreign bonds can zig when domestic bonds zag. In other words, an international bond fund can help smooth out a portfolio's performance. However, many experts doubt whether foreign bond funds make sense for the average investor. While bonds have a much lower potential for big gains than stocks do, they say, foreign bonds are just as vulnerable as foreign stocks to currency risk and the unpredictable swings in value that accompany that risk. U.S. investors who are still interested in foreign bonds should probably devote no more than 10% of their bond assets to them.

One more thing: Before investing in any foreign stock or bond fund, check the holdings of any U.S. mutual funds you already own. Many domestic funds invest quite a bit in foreign issues, so you may have more foreign exposure than you think.

Socially Conscious Investing

Some people shy away from investing because they think it means they'll have to turn their backs on their social and political ideals in order to make a profit. That's no longer true. In the past decade, so-called socially responsible investing has boomed, led by mutual fund companies looking for stocks of companies that, for example, aim to reduce pollution or employment discrimination and steer clear of companies connected with businesses such as tobacco, gambling, and weapons manufacturing. There are now at least 25 mutual funds that profess to be socially responsible, offered by such fund families as the Calvert Group, Parnassus, and Working Assets.

The argument for so-called green investing is that those companies that violate social screens are the very companies likely to run into financial problems that can drag down their stocks' price. Tobacco companies risk costly lawsuits from former smokers and their families, for example. And companies that don't encourage promotion of women and lack flexible family-leave policies risk losing valuable employees who could be improving the firm's bottom line.

Will you have to give up some potential profits in order to invest with a conscience? The jury's out on this one. Independent studies have shown that portfolios composed exclusively of stocks of socially conscious companies underperform the Standard & Poor's 500 index (a diversified portfolio of stocks) by about one percentage point per year. Analysts who pooh-pooh socially conscious investing maintain that, by definition, you're limiting your returns because you are putting some potential market winners off limits. However, the Socially Responsible Index, a proxy for the S&P 500, beat the S&P by two percentage points in 1993 and 1994. Also, University of Texas at Arlington professor J. David Diltz recently measured returns from 1989 through 1991 for 28 different portfolios comprising stocks of companies with a range of social consciences. Diltz's study determined that the "ethical stocks" did no better or worse than the other ones.

There's one fairly significant drawback with investing in socially conscious mutual funds: the inflexibility of the most rigid funds makes diversification difficult and therefore increases your risk. Some sectors are partially or entirely excluded: alcohol, tobacco, oil, and defense, for example. Since it's often easier for small companies to pass social screens than it is for large ones, green portfolios tend to be heavily weighted with the little guys. That adds to your portfolio's volatility, because small-capitalization stocks are jumpier than large-cap ones.

The tricky part about investing in socially conscious stocks or funds is defining "socially conscious." Your idea of what's ethical and what isn't may differ from your next-door neighbor's. For example, some investors prefer buying shares only in companies with at least two women among their directors—a test passed by just a few dozen of the S&P 500 stocks. Other investors who favor stringent bans on animal testing avoid all drug companies and nearly all consumer-products companies.

Furthermore, even the socially conscious mutual funds don't agree with each other on the definition. Before investing in a socially conscious fund, read the prospectus and see whether its fund manager's ethics match yours. Is environmental responsibility, such as pollution control, hazardous-waste reduction, and energy conservation, most important to you? How about progressive employee policies, such as promotion of women and minorities, action on child care and AIDS, commitment to on-the-job safety, and fair bargaining with unions? Maybe your concern is good corporate citizenship, such as community involvement and charitable giving. Or you might feel strongly about excluding companies involved in nuclear power, animal testing, or alcohol production.

Of course, it's not impossible to invest in stocks of individual companies known for their commitment to socially responsible causes, such as ice-cream maker Ben & Jerry's, or their opposition to animal testing, such as the Body Shop. One advantage of picking individual issues is that you can create and follow your own definition of what companies are socially responsible. These days, many large brokerages offer research or money-management services geared especially to socially responsible investors. You may want guidance, though, from an independent money manager or a newsletter whose views are similar to your own. The Social Investment Forum, a clearinghouse of this kind of information, can be a big help. The group can refer you to an investing newsletter that specializes in the kind of socially conscious concerns that matter to you most. In addition, for $35, you can get the forum's directory of about 300 socially conscious money managers around the country. To get the names of newsletters or the directory, write to the Social Investment Forum, 430 First Ave. N., Minneapolis, Minn. 55401.

CHAPTER 14

How to Make Money in the Market with Stocks and Mutual Funds

When Americans talk about investing, more often than not they mean buying and selling stocks. Almost every TV news program dutifully reports the daily perambulations of the Dow Jones Industrial Average, a courtesy they don't pay to price changes in municipal bonds, Miami Beach condos, baseball card collections, certificates of deposit, or the dozens of other investments people own. For all the exposure it gets, however, the stock market remains a mystery to most ordinary citizens.

From occasional TV glimpses of the New York Stock Exchange, the market seems little more than a raucous bazaar, where millions of dollars of wealth are alternately created and vaporized from one moment to the next for no apparent reason. It's little wonder that most Americans think stocks are far more dangerous than they actually are. In a recent poll conducted by the investment management firm Oppenheimer and Co., more than half the respondents wrongly believed that most stock investors are wiped out at one point in their life.

Whether or not you, too, find the stock market intimidating—or perhaps merely inscrutable—you will need to make its acquaintance if you are serious about reaching your long-term financial goals. The reason is simple: Over periods of a decade or more, a broad selection of stocks or stock mutual funds are odds-on favorites to provide higher returns than any other investment open to the public. That has been the case for the better part of two centuries, and there's no reason to think it will change anytime soon.

Stocks' long-term superiority is not a matter of chance. Unlike other investments, stocks give you an ownership stake in the ultimate source of prosperity in a free enterprise system: the creativity and industriousness of private businesses. To be sure, not every corporation that issues stock is a hotbed of productivity or a builder of profits. Even successful companies see their stocks languish or fall from year to year, too. On the whole, however, American corporations have been astoundingly successful at generating wealth for the shareholders who own the corporations. Since 1972, for example, investors in U.S. stocks have seen their wealth grow ten times over, according to Ibbotson Associates, a Chicago investment research firm.

Even so, investing in stocks requires you to take a certain leap of faith, as does any activity that asks you to wait for your payback. In essence, an investment in stocks today is a gamble that corporate America in the rest of the 1990s and the twenty-first century will still have the resourcefulness to produce the next Microsoft Windows, Barbie doll, or *The Lion King*. If history is any guide, that is one bet you should take.

You'll probably want to get started in the stock market by investing in mutual funds rather than individual stocks. One or more funds will give you instant diversification, plus professional management. While your fund manager is doing the hard work of choosing the stocks to buy or sell, you can be busy learning the basics of analyzing stocks. What follows is a quick course on stocks and the stock market, followed by sections that will help you as an investor in mutual funds.

The ABCs of Stocks

When a corporation needs to raise money, it has three alternatives: It can borrow the funds from a bank or from private investors such as insurance companies; it can borrow from the investing public by issuing bonds; or it can sell ownership interests in the company by issuing stock. When you purchase stock, you become, literally, part owner of a business. You are entitled to a proportionate share of any **dividends** the company generates—and, if the firm liquidates, to a proportionate share of any assets remaining after other creditors have been paid. In short, you participate in the fortunes of the business. You share in the risk that it may not succeed and in the potentially unlimited rewards if it does.

Not every dollar you invest in stock goes straight to the company's treasury, of course. Stock investors only really add funds to corporate coffers when they purchase shares at the so-called **initial public offering** (when the company issues stock for the first time) or at a **secondary offering** (a new issuance of shares by a company that already has stock outstanding). In the vast majority of trades, a current shareholder simply sells his stock to another investor who wants to buy it.

A company can issue two types of stock: **common stock** or **preferred stock.** Common stock is the type most investors buy and sell. Sometimes the stock pays a dividend, sometimes it doesn't. A company that has already issued common stock may choose to issue preferred stock, which in many ways is more like a bond than a stock. The dividends are usually considerably higher per dollar invested on preferred shares than on common shares. Also, if the company goes out of business and there is any money to distribute to investors, you'll be paid off before common stock owners. In addition, your preferred-stock dividends are fixed, just as a bond's interest rate is set by the issuer. So even if your company prospers,

your dividends won't rise. They won't fall if the company stumbles, either. A preferred stock is designated **"pf"** in a newspaper's stock tables.

Occasionally a company that wants to raise money will issue a security known as a **warrant.** By purchasing a warrant, you are essentially making a wager that the price of the stock will rise. For a fee, the warrant gives you a chance to buy the stock at a certain price higher than the current price within a specified time period. If the stock rises beyond the price you've locked in, you can exercise the warrant and buy the shares at a discount. Then you can sell the shares for a quick profit. However, if the stock is selling for less than the specified price when the time period ends, your warrant becomes worthless. The letters **"wt"** in the newspaper stock tables designate a warrant.

Every so often, a company may choose to split its stock. In a 2-for-1 **stock split,** for instance, instead of owning, say, 100 shares at one price, you suddenly own 200, each worth half as much as before. (As a result, a stock split doesn't make your investment any more or less valuable than it was before.) A company splits its stock when the management thinks the share price has risen so high that it now discourages some potential investors. By splitting a $100 stock into, say, a $50 stock, the company thinks small investors may be more tempted to buy shares and thus help bid up the price even higher. A company can split its stock in any combination—2 for 1, 5 for 1, 3 for 2, whatever. You can determine if a stock has split within the past 52 weeks by looking for an **"S"** in the newspaper stock listings.

The ABCs of Stock Mutual Funds

Increasingly, investors who want to take part in the stock market do so not by buying 100 shares of GM, say, or Microsoft, but by investing in a stock mutual fund. According to the Federal Reserve, mutual funds now constitute 7.2% of the average household's financial assets, up from less than 1% in 1980. Over the same time period, direct holdings of stocks have declined from nearly 39% of individuals' financial investments to 21%.

A stock or equity mutual fund is a kind of corporation whose sole business is to pool its shareholders' money and invest it in stocks. (Other kinds of mutual funds invest strictly in short-term money-market securities or in bonds; you can read more about them in Chapters 5 and 15.) The fund's investment strategy is designed and carried out by a professional money-management firm, which spares individual investors the time

and effort of researching, selecting, and keeping track of a portfolio of stocks. The money managers charge generally between 0.5% and 2.5% of the fund's assets per year for their efforts, but millions of investors have clearly decided that the convenience of leaving the investment work to professional managers is worth the cost.

The Historical Return of Stocks

You've probably seen the disclaimer in mutual fund advertisements: "Past performance is no guarantee of future results." That's a good thing to keep in mind when evaluating any individual stock or stock mutual fund, and it's also worth remembering when looking at the historical returns of stocks in general.

Nevertheless, three basic truths about the performance of stocks are worth remembering:

- **Over the long term, stocks outperform other financial assets.**

- **The short-term performance of stocks is a complete toss-up.**

- **The long-term performance of stocks is quite consistent.**

The figures most often cited in discussing historical stock market performance are those compiled by the Chicago investment research firm Ibbotson Associates: Since 1926, the return on stocks works out to an average of 11% a year, compounded annually. That is far superior to the returns on bonds and Treasury bills, which returned only 5.1% and 3.8%, respectively. The difference is stark enough on an annual basis, but get this: Over 30 years, stocks earning 11% annually would have turned a $10,000 investment into $228,305. By contrast, a $10,000 stake in bonds would have grown to just $44,982, and the same $10,000 invested in Treasury bills would have given you only $30,183. Don't forget, the period since 1926 includes a fair number of rough patches for stock investors, including one Great Depression, three major wars, the hyperinflation of the 1970s, and the biggest stock market crash of the century in 1987.

Over short stretches, however, the stock market becomes much more like the roll of the dice that many people think it is. Looking at every one-year period since 1871, for example, it turns out that there was a roughly one-in-three chance that you'd have made more money in a bank savings account than in the stock market in any given year—

sometimes a lot more. In 1931, for example, the Dow lost 52% of its value. The worst recent year was 1974, when the Dow lost more than 27%.

Fortunately, the risk of this kind of loss dissipates quickly if you hold on to stocks. Your one-in-three chance of losing out to a bank account over one year sinks to one in four if you hang on for five years, to one in seven if you wait 10 years, and to less than one in 100 if you hold on for 20 years. In other words, stocks are not the place to invest money that you might need next year. But for long-term financial goals, the odds are excellent that if you just hang on, you'll be richly rewarded.

Where Stocks Trade

On a typical day, some 600 million shares of stock may change hands on the New York Stock Exchange, the American Stock Exchange, and the Nasdaq system. Unless you are dealing in very small stocks that trade over-the-counter (see explanation that follows), your stockbroker can execute trades in all three markets with equal speed and finalize, or settle, a trade in the standard three days. However, the three marketplaces attract different kinds of stocks and function under slightly different rules, which can affect a stock's price.

The granddaddy of exchanges is the New York Stock Exchange, located at the corner of Broad Street and Wall Street in New York City. The roughly 2,600 stocks that trade here include the aristocracy of U.S. industries (known as **blue chips**), such as Exxon, General Electric, General Motors, and Procter & Gamble. Blue-chip stocks normally pay dividends. All 30 stocks that make up the **Dow Jones Industrial Average** trade on the New York Stock Exchange, as do the majority of the 500 stocks in the other widely quoted index of major companies, the **Standard & Poor's 500 stock index.**

A few blocks away is the American Stock Exchange, with about 800 listed stocks. The American exchange arose to serve stocks that were too small to qualify for the New York exchange. In essence it is the largest of several regional exchanges, including the Philadelphia, Chicago, and Pacific exchanges, which list small regional companies and execute trades in major companies that also trade on the NYSE.

Stocks that aren't listed on any exchange are said to trade **over-the-counter,** or **OTC.** The largest 3,400 of these stocks are part of the Nasdaq National Market system, an electronic network that displays on computer screens the prices at which buyers and sellers of any particular stock are willing to do

business. Trades don't have to be routed through brokers on the floor of the exchange; dealers can fill customers' orders directly from their own inventory or trade by computer with dealers acting in their clients' behalf. A group of about 1,350 smaller, less frequently traded companies known as **small-cap stocks** (short for small-capitalization) also trade via Nasdaq. A small-cap stock is one whose total value—the number of shares multiplied by the current stock price—is between $50 million and $500 million. (By contrast, a **midcap or midcapitalization stock** is one whose total value is more than $500 million but less than $1 billion. **Large-cap stocks,** naturally, are ones whose total value exceeds $1 billion; they're typically old, well-known companies.)

Another 11,000 stocks that are too small even for Nasdaq's second tier are quoted in the so-called **pink sheets,** a daily circular that most brokerages get. Shares in some pink sheet stocks may not trade for weeks at a time. Although investors can make profits in the pink sheets, it is hard to get information on these stocks and often harder still to find investors who want to sell their shares or to whom you can sell yours. The pink sheets represent the riskiest fringe of the U.S. stock market.

The chief difference that investors notice between trading stocks on the major exchanges and over-the-counter is pricing. OTC stocks have a wider **spread,** which is the difference between the **ask** or **offer**—what you have to pay to buy a stock—and the **bid**, or what you could get for it if you turned around and sold the stock immediately.

The wider the spread, the harder it is to turn a profit on a trade. For example, if a Nasdaq stock is quoted at 4¾ ask, 5 bid (translation: $4.75 ask, $5.00 bid), it would have to appreciate by 5.25% just for you to break even when you sell, not counting the broker's commissions.

Small Stocks versus Large Stocks

There is a good reason, though, to pay the higher spreads to buy small-company stocks. Small stocks have the best shot at explosive gains. Companies starting from a small base can more easily double or triple their profits in a few years than an established firm, which tends to make their stock price rise more. Also, when a promising company starts to attract attention, demand for the company's relatively few shares from institutional investors such as pension funds and mutual funds can cause the stock's price to skyrocket. The flipside of this potential,

of course, is a greater vulnerability to market downturns. When the stock market as a whole declines, small-company stocks tend to fall an average of 2% farther.

Despite the risks, small stocks have outperformed blue chips by a substantial margin over the long run. If you had invested $100 in a portfolio of small stocks in 1972, your sum would likely have grown to more than $1,900 by the end of 1993, for example; the same amount in large-company stocks would have topped out at just over $1,100.

The little guys' strong performance runs in streaks, however. From 1975 to 1983, for example, small stocks exploded for an annual gain of 35.3%, compared with just 15.9% for the stocks in the S&P 500. They then sprang a leak, gaining just 36% over the next seven years, while the large-company shares climbed by 146%.

How to Size Up a Stock

Your objective in searching for stocks should be the same as it would be in any kind of shopping: to find the best merchandise at the lowest price. Simple enough. The only problem is that the stock market is reasonably efficient. In

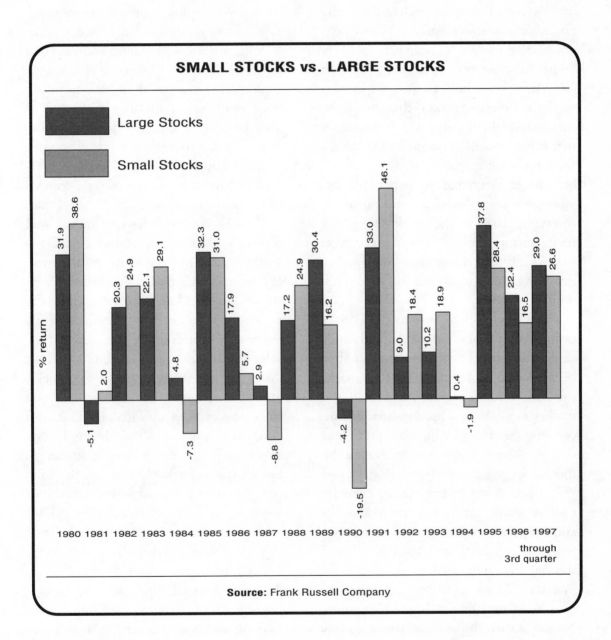

SMALL STOCKS vs. LARGE STOCKS

Large Stocks

Small Stocks

Source: Frank Russell Company

other words, the best merchandise rarely trades at the lowest prices. Conversely, any stock trading at a cheap price is likely to be, in some way, damaged goods. In fact, there is a school of thought known as the **efficient-market theory** or the **random-walk theory,** which maintains that it is practically impossible to outperform the stock market consistently. If you buy the efficient-market theory, you essentially believe that you could do better throwing darts at the stock pages and then buying those stocks than if you hired a professional money manager to invest for you or instead tried to pick winners yourself.

Anyone who chooses individual stocks or buys most types of stock mutual funds can't believe in the efficient-market theory, though. You're trying to find stocks that can turn in higher gains than the market as a whole, which means picking out isolated cases in which the prevailing opinion about a stock—represented by the stock's price—is wrong. Easier said than done. A stock's price represents the sum of all information known about a company, from news, company reports, analysts' opinions, and so on, filtered through the judgment of thousands of investors. Many of those investors are pros, who are likely to have more information at their disposal and more experience than you. So to recognize such situations at the time—and put your money on the line—takes a special willingness to run against the crowd.

Still, small investors have an important advantage over the institutional investors. Unlike the pros, you don't have to justify your stock selections to clients and to your boss every quarter. (You may occasionally need to explain yourself to your spouse, though.) As a result, you can afford to have the courage of your convictions.

Besides, you don't have to outdo Wall Street's wizards to succeed as a stock investor—you just have to match the market's average. After all, doing just that well historically would have given you a better return than nearly any competing investment. Follow the prudent stock selection techniques outlined below, avoid paying inflated prices for stocks, and diversify your holdings so that one stock's unforeseen misfortunes don't ruin you, and you'll do fine. There is one other requirement, though: patience. Stocks pay off reliably only in the long run. If you panic and sell when things look bleak, you'll constantly be selling when prices are lowest—exactly the time you should be buying. To quote Peter Lynch, former manager of the Fidelity Magellan mutual fund and the greatest investor of his generation: "The key to making money in stocks is not to be scared out of them. This cannot be emphasized enough."

What Makes a Stock Cheap

There are two ways to size up a stock: **fundamental analysis** and **technical analysis.** Fundamental analysis is what most amateur and professional investors do. It simply means analyzing the vital signs of a company—its financial shape, the quality of its management, its prospects for the future. When doing fundamental analysis of a stock, you're taking a close look at the company's balance sheet, its debt, and how much its earnings are likely to grow in the future. Technical analysis, by contrast, means studying the historical trends of the price of a company's stock or more broadly, the price trends of stocks in an entire industry or the stock market overall. Technical analysts love to use charts with fever lines that track the performance of stocks. They think past trends can help predict whether a stock or a variety of stocks will rise in the near future.

Determining whether a stock is a bargain or overpriced is not simply a matter of comparing the cost of its shares with another stock. An unprofitable company with high debt and no growth prospects is no bargain at $5 a share. Conversely, a stock that trades for $150 may be a steal.

Instead, the way to judge value in a stock is to compare its trading price to the economic value you derive as a share-holder. These benefits come from the dividends the company generates, growth in the company's assets (which you as an owner have a claim on), and the profits the company earns. These comparisons are expressed in the key **price-to-earnings, price-to-dividend, price-to-book,** and **price-to-earnings growth ratios:**

■ The **price-to-earnings ratio** measures the stock's price against a year's worth of the company's earnings (or profits) per share of stock. **Price/earnings** or **P/E** is the most closely watched and widely cited measure of any stock's inherent value. Profits, after all, are the reason a company is in business, and all the benefits that make a company a worthy investment flow from its earnings. (Since a stock's share price is always several times larger than its **earnings per share,** the P/E ratio is often referred to as the **price/earnings multiple** or, to those in the know, simply the **multiple.**) The higher a stock's P/E, the riskier it is.

You can measure P/E ratios several ways. The ratios printed in stock tables of the *Wall Street Journal* and other newspapers are based on the current stock price and the company's earnings as reported over the previous four quarters. While a P/E based on these so-called **trailing earnings** eliminates guesswork, investors should be most concerned with their stock's price in relation to what analysts expect to happen to the company's earnings over the *next* 12 months. A P/E based on **projected earnings** gives you an insight into whether the stock's potential is factored into its current price. For example, in the winter of 1997 the building supply retailer Home Depot traded at a P/E of 39 based on trailing earnings; on that basis it was quite expensive, compared with the 500 stocks in the Standard & Poor's index, which carried an average trailing P/E of 25. But because analysts expected Home Depot to earn 25% more in 1998 than in 1997, its P/E on its estimated 1998 earnings worked out to a much more reasonable value—assuming, of course, the earnings estimates turn out to be right.

Since, as a rule, the lower the stock's P/E, the better the value, it's not surprising that studies have shown low P/E stocks tend to outperform their high P/E counterparts in the aggregate. Unfortunately it's not all that simple in particular cases. A fast-growing software company like Cisco Systems may be reasonably priced at 32 times next year's earnings, while General Motors may be no bargain at seven times earnings if it turns out that worldwide auto sales are about to slip.

Thus, a stock's P/E alone doesn't tell you what you need to know about its prospects. You also have to compare its current P/E against the overall stock market and its particular industry. Historically, the average P/E of stocks as a whole has been between six and 27; in recent years, it has averaged about 14. If a stock that interests you has a P/E much higher than the market, you should ask yourself: Do the stock's prospects warrant it? If the P/E is lower, could the bad news about the stock be overblown? You should also weigh the P/E against the company's projected growth rate. A company growing at 20% a year whose stock is trading at a P/E of 15 is a steal; a company growing by just 8% with a P/E of 15 may not be. Interest rates also influence the general level of P/E multiples. P/Es tend to rise when interest rates fall, since when rates are low, bonds offer weak competition with stocks for investors' dollars.

■ The **price-to-dividend ratio** of a stock and its even more often cited inverse, the stock's **dividend yield,** measure the share price in relation to the annual cash payout to shareholders. A $50 stock that pays an annual dividend of $2 per share has a price-to-dividend ratio of 25 to one, or a yield of 4%.

Since dividends represent actual cash paid to shareholders out of profits, the yield has historically been a reliable indicator of whether stocks are at bargain price levels or dangerously expensive. A low yield suggests stocks are overpriced and the market is ready for a fall; a high yield means stocks are likely to go up in value. The average price-to-dividend ratio of the stock market since 1926 has been 24 to one, equivalent to a yield of 4.2%. Just before the crash of 1987, however, the average stock's yield sank as low as 2.5%, signaling a market downturn was coming. At the beginning of the 1980s, by contrast, when stocks were poised for one of their greatest runs of all time, the yield had risen to 5.4%. An even more compelling way of putting it: Whenever stocks have yielded less than 3.36%, their return over the subsequent five years was only 1% a year better than inflation. Whenever stocks' yield exceeded 6.6%, their subsequent return beat inflation by a generous 15.7% a year.

As with P/E ratios, the signals sent by price-to-dividend ratios and yield get a bit murky when applied to individual stocks. Many excellent companies pay little or no dividends at all, preferring to reinvest profits back in the business rather than pay out a sizable portion of them to shareholders. In such cases, a tiny or nonexistent yield is not necessarily a reason to rule out a stock. Similarly, an extremely high yield isn't always a sign that the stock is worth purchasing. When Centerior Energy, an Ohio electric utility holding company, traded at a yield of 13.7% in 1987, for example, it didn't mean that Centerior was a screaming buy; it meant only that investors anticipated—correctly, as it turned out—that the company would soon cut its dividend.

Yield, however, can be used for one simple and often successful stock invest-

ing technique: You buy the 10 highest-yielding stocks of the 30 in the Dow Jones Industrial Average on January 1, hold them throughout the year, and then at year end replace those that are no longer the highest yielders with the ones that are. Since 1972 investors following this almost effortless strategy enjoyed an average annual return of 17.1%, compared to 10.9% for the Dow as a whole. By concentrating on the highest-yielding Dow stocks, you automatically wind up with 10 stocks with low Wall Street expectations. If the companies turn their fortunes around—and they usually do—their investors are well rewarded. This strategy doesn't work every year, however. In 1994, for instance, the high-yielding stocks returned 4.1% while the yield for all 30 stocks in the Dow Jones Industrial Average was 4.9%.

■ The **price-to-book ratio** measures a stock against the value of its company's assets minus its liabilities (its net worth). When figuring a stock's price-to-book ratio, you divide its price by the book value per share. Here's an example: If a stock is selling for $20 a share and its book value per share is $10, its price-to-book ratio is two.

In mid-1995 the average stock in the S&P 500 sold for about three times its book value, which is on the high side historically. At the depths of market declines, the price-to-book ratio can be nearly one. A stock with a price-to-book ratio of less than one may be a bargain, because the ratio is telling you that investors overall don't think much of the stock. Of course, that doesn't mean the stock will go up.

Unlike the P/E ratio, there's nothing prospective about the price-to-book ratio. It values companies as they are, without asking the investor to make any prognostications about their future performance. That doesn't mean, however, that savvy investors accept a company's stated book value as gospel. Often, the value assigned to some assets on the company's books understates or overstates their true worth. Companies often carry real estate, for example, at its acquisition cost decades after acquiring it. As a result, a real estate–rich company such as a railroad may have a true net worth far in excess of its stated book value. Book value can also mislead on the high side: inventory may be valued at its wholesale price, even if it's unsellable. That can then make an apparent book-value bargain an expensive mirage.

Such caveats aside, buying stocks with low price-to-book values has proven to be a smart long-term strategy. As the chart on page 349 shows, over the past 25 years the 20% of stocks with the lowest price-to-book ratios substantially outperformed the most expensive 20%. The reason for the low price-to-book strategy's success? Since stocks trade at a low price-to-book because most investors are down on their prospects, low price-to-book stocks have a much greater chance of catching a favorable shift in Wall Street opinion than do high price-to-book stocks.

■ The **price-to-earnings growth (PEG) ratio** is another way to gauge whether a stock is reasonably priced and is likely to go up in price over time. You take the stock's P/E ratio and divide it by the company's expected earnings growth rate. So, for instance, a company growing 25% a year that sells for 25 times earnings has a PEG ratio of 1. When the PEG is less than 1, that's a pretty good clue that the stock is a buy. *The Value Line Investment Survey* publishes both P/E ratios and a stock's three- to five-year estimated growth rate.

Where to Research a Stock

While divining the hidden meaning (if any) in a company's P/E multiple or price-to-book ratio may take a bit of work, laying your hands on the information is remarkably easy. Whatever the shortcomings of the U.S. stock markets, lack of data isn't one of them. Securities laws require companies traded in the United States to reveal more about their finances than stocks traded virtually any-

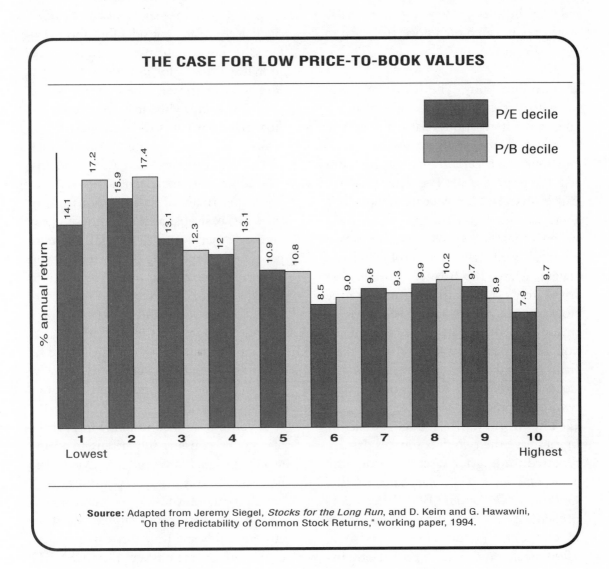

THE CASE FOR LOW PRICE-TO-BOOK VALUES

P/E decile
P/B decile

% annual return

14.1 17.2 15.9 17.4 13.1 12.3 12 13.1 10.9 10.8 8.5 9.0 9.6 9.3 9.9 10.2 9.7 8.9 7.9 9.7

1 — Lowest   2   3   4   5   6   7   8   9   10 — Highest

Source: Adapted from Jeremy Siegel, *Stocks for the Long Run*, and D. Keim and G. Hawawini, "On the Predictability of Common Stock Returns," working paper, 1994.

where else, and hundreds of companies compete to make that information available to investors. Here are the major sources of research on a stock and what to expect from them:

■ **The company.** The firm that issued your stock is the ultimate source of all the financial information related to it, and there's no reason you can't go directly to the source for certain information, just like the professionals. The department to call is **shareholder relations.** Someone there can send you the company's most recent annual report, which contains two essential yardsticks: the profit-and-loss statement and the balance sheet. If you have already done some research into the stock on your own, while you have an investor relations person on the phone, you might probe for more data to confirm or weaken the case made for the stock by brokerage reports or by your own observations.

■ **The library.** Most large public libraries have the two data sources that are required reading for stock investors: the *Value Line Investment Survey* and *Standard & Poor's Stock Reports*. Both offer comprehensive financial data on thousands of companies (Value Line covers some 1,700 stocks and S&P 4,700). Both include an analysis of the company's prospects and a wealth of financial data—including P/Es, yields, and book value—going back a decade in S&P's

case or 15 years in Value Line's. If you prefer, you can subscribe to Value Line at a cost of $525 a year. *Standard & Poor's Stock Reports* are considerably more expensive, but you can order reports on individual stocks for as little as $2.

■ **Your computer.** The power of computers at both delivering and crunching financial data makes them the perfect accessory to the thoroughly modern stock picker. For computer users with modems, getting on-line stock quotes, research reports, and financial data on thousands of stocks is as simple as a few mouse clicks (and as expensive as $10 to $50 or more per month, depending on the service you subscribe to and how often you tap into it). The major commercial on-line services CompuServe and America Online provide instant access to stock quotes, financial data, and research, as do specific financial on-line networks, such as Dow Jones Market Monitor and Reuters Money Network.

If you're interested in following particular stocks, consider subscribing to an Internet financial news service. One of the best is *PointCast* (www.pointcast.com), which updates you on as many as 25 companies. You could instead create a customized home page through an Internet news or search site like MSNBC, CNN, Excite, or Yahoo. Probably the best selection of financial news is at Yahoo (www.my.yahoo.com). Or you may want to sign up with a so-called "push" technology Web service. These companies, such as Closing Bell (www.merc.com), e-mail you the latest price quotes and news about companies—and mutual funds—you want to follow.

The real value of using a computer to help you select stocks, however, is its ability to look through a large database of stocks for desirable characteristics—say, stocks with yields above 2%, price-to-book ratios less than 1.5, and projected earnings growth over the next five years of more than 15% a year. This process is known as doing a **stock screen.** Once you have your screen, you can then subject the stocks that pass it to a more detailed or rigorous analysis.

There are dozens of brands of stock-screening software, including a digital version of the *Value Line Investment Survey* called *Investment Survey for Windows.* The American Association of Individual Investors (312-280-0170), a helpful educational nonprofit group, has chapters across the country devoted to computerized investing and also publishes a newsletter reviewing investment software. The AAII also markets its own stock-screening software, *Stock Investor* and *Stock Investor Pro.*

If you want to screen for stocks via the Internet, check out *MarketPlayer* (www.marketplayer.com). This site covers 3,900 companies and lets you target stocks by extremely precise criteria. Another helpful site, especially if you're re-

searching companies, is *Zack's Investment Research* (www.zacks.com); you'll have to pay about $150 a year for the privilege, though.

Growth, Value, and Income Investors

In shopping for any kind of merchandise, some people believe that quality is the best value in the long run and don't mind paying carriage-trade prices to get it. Others argue that at some price, buyers are paying for reputation and that settling for a less exalted brand name is wiser. Still others identify a specific benefit that they get from a certain brand and will continue to stand by the product as long as it meets their needs.

With only a little stretching of that metaphor, stock investors fall into roughly the same categories. **Growth stock investors** are the quality chasers: in their minds, companies with high, sustainable profit growth are the ones that will serve their shareholders best in the end, almost regardless of how their price stands in relation to their earnings, dividends, or book value. **Value investors,** by contrast, look for companies whose prospects are ambiguous. A cloudy outlook lets their stocks trade relatively inexpensively in relation to their earnings, assets, and dividends. The value investors ultimately make money when the companies improve and other investors bid up their stock prices. Finally, there are **income investors.** They look for stocks with high (or at least rising) dividends that can keep those checks coming and presumably rising for years to come.

While value, growth, and income investors may never agree with each other about a stock, each can make money. Growth stocks typically do better when the economy is slow and investors are willing to pay a premium for the relatively few companies that can sustain solid earnings growth rates. Value investors tend to prosper most during the early stages of a recovery, when stocks that had been ignored often come to life. Income investors often shine when the overall market is flat or falling and a generous dividend can help soothe the pain for shareholders.

How to Buy Growth Stocks

Growth stocks often make for more exciting stories than value or income stocks. Companies that consistently increase earnings faster than the market include not only classic stalwarts such as Coca-Cola, Microsoft, and Wal-Mart, but also small companies with new products in rising, glamorous (often high-tech) businesses, such as Oracle Systems, Advanced Micro Devices, and Micron Technology. Since investor expectations toward such stocks are already fairly high, the shares tend to trade at P/E ratios that are considerably steeper than the market's. A stock whose earnings grow 20% a year, however, should appreciate in value 20% annually as well, as long as the P/E ratio remains constant.

The problem is that few companies can really grow 20% a year indefinitely. Trees don't grow to the sky, and profitable lines of business almost invariably attract competition, squeezing profit margins. If investors lose faith that a stock can grow faster than the market, the stock may tumble back to a P/E more in line with the market average or even lower. The result isn't pretty for shareholders, especially if investors have projected past growth trends to impossible lengths—as they have a tendency to do. Just before the greatest growth stock massacre of all time, the bear market of 1973 and 1974, the so-called Nifty Fifty blue-chip growth companies were selling at outlandish P/Es: McDonald's sported a P/E of 59 and Polaroid traded at an amazing 93. By the time the bear was sated, P/Es had dropped back to earth and many of the stocks had fallen in price by more than 50%.

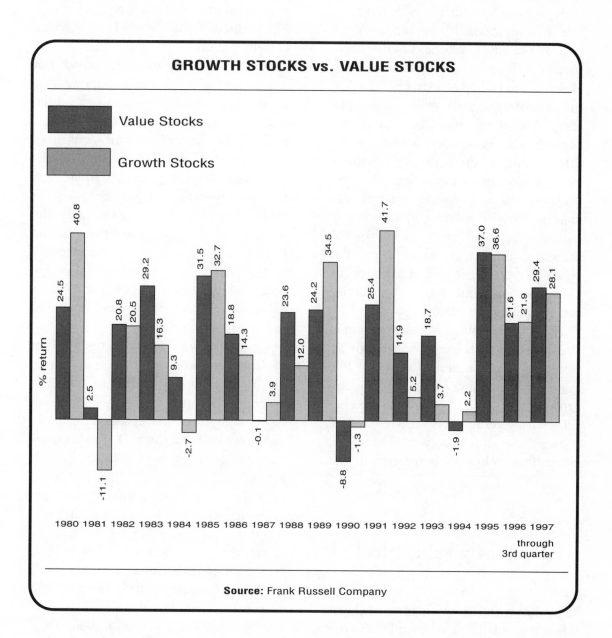

GROWTH STOCKS vs. VALUE STOCKS

Source: Frank Russell Company

As a result, growth investors must answer two questions: Is the company's past growth rate sustainable? and Is the stock's current P/E reasonable, given the firm's likely growth path? The ideal growth company operates in a market where demand is rising, few serious competitors are on the horizon, and its products are so popular that the company can boost profits without losing customers. A classic growth company like Home Depot, for example, can increase sales by building more stores (it currently has a presence in less than half the states). As sales get larger, it can buy goods in even bigger bulk at lower prices, either boosting profit margins or squeezing out competitors—or both.

No stock is an attractive investment if its P/E is too high, however. So growth investors typically measure a stock's P/E against the company's historic or projected growth rate. Stocks of companies are considered dangerously overvalued if their P/E is twice the annual growth rate; they're cheap if the P/E is below the growth rate.

How to Buy Value Stocks

In contrast with growth investors, who select their stocks based mainly on what they believe will happen to corporate earnings in the near future, value investors tend to focus on the present. Trying to predict the future by projecting current trends, they argue, causes investors to be overly optimistic about hot stocks and too pessimistic about ones that are out of favor. Value investors prowl the gloomy reaches of the stock market, looking for basically sound companies that are temporarily on investors' blacklists. Value investing doesn't require you to make any educated guesses about the future except one: that eventually the market will recognize real value. Warren Buffett, one of the greatest value investors of the century, describes the value approach as the belief that "if I can buy a dollar for 50 cents, something good might happen to me."

Value investors tend to be fond of **cyclical stocks,** or companies whose fortunes are closely linked to the economic cycle such as steel companies, heavy equipment makers, mining firms, and paper manufacturers. A classic example would be Stone Container, which makes cardboard boxes. When the economy is strong and manufacturers are shipping lots of products, usually in cardboard boxes, Stone's business explodes. When the economy retreats, Stone's box business suffers. Because profits of cyclical stocks fluctuate sharply from year to year, confirmed growth investors generally want nothing to do with them. During the depths of economic recessions, when the outlook for cyclicals is especially gloomy, neither do most other investors. That's when cyclicals often trade for less than 75% of their previous peak prices and command P/Es that are less than half their former highs. That's exactly the time value investors move in to snap up the shares. When the economy eventually recovers, as it always does, their profits can be enormous.

The risk in this kind of stock is that unrecognized value may remain unrecognized for a long time. Until then, the stock's price will remain flat, at best, and the value investor makes no profits. Nevertheless, value stocks tend to be safer than growth stocks in the long run. That's because big losses tend to occur when companies fall short of shareholders' expectations; however, value investors become interested in stocks mainly after the bad news had become widely known. Whatever surprises occur in value stocks tend to be positive ones.

How to Buy Income Stocks

For some investors, the most intriguing aspect of any stock isn't the prospect for appreciation, but rather the size of the stock's dividend and the prospects for growth in that dividend. Over time, such income stocks tend to have lower returns than growth or value stocks. For investors who need to supplement their income with investment earnings, however, these shares offer a fairly secure stream of income and considerably less risk of loss than other stocks. As a result, income stocks are ideal for retirees and for long-term growth investors looking for a conservative investment to add balance to their portfolios. Why not just buy bonds, which pay steady interest until they mature? Simple. Income stocks can and often do increase their dividends gradually over the years, countering the effect of inflation.

The most popular income stocks are regulated utilities, especially electric companies, which tend to pay out around 85% of their profits in dividends versus 50% or less for stocks in the S&P 500 overall. Utilities tend to be extremely stable investments, in large part because they function as near monopolies in their region. That cozy arrangement has changed somewhat in the past years, though, as regulators have begun to let electrics compete for choice customers outside their normal turf. As a result, many utilities have provided their shareholders with bumpy rides lately. It's important to realize, too, that since utilities are valued almost exclusively for their yields, these stocks are just as sensitive to interest rate fluctuations as bonds. So as interest rates rose during 1994, for example, the Dow Jones Utilities Average plunged by 23%.

Regional telephone companies and a few mature blue-chip stocks, such as drug maker Bristol-Myers Squibb and banker J. P. Morgan, are also popular with income investors who are willing to accept a slightly lower yield than utilities in return for a better shot at capital gains from an increase in their share prices. Another favorite income stock group: real estate investment trusts (REITs), which buy, manage, and develop properties. (For more on REITs, see Chapter 16.)

The first thing to look for in an income stock is evidence that the dividend can at least be sustained and ideally increased by its company over the years. Financial soundness is key: the chance that business problems could force a company to cut its dividend is much higher if the company has a large amount of debt and hence a large interest cost burden. Look for a **financial strength rating** of at least B+ from Standard & Poor's or a rating of 1 for financial strength from Value Line.

Another key factor for income stock investors is the **dividend payout ratio,** or the percentage of earnings (profits) that the company is paying out in dividends each year. You get this percentage by dividing the dividends per share by the earnings per share. If a company is paying out $2 in dividends per share and has earnings per share of $4, it has a dividend

payout ratio of 50%. Less is more here, since a low ratio gives a company plenty of room to absorb a decline in earnings without threatening its dividend. A high dividend payout ratio suggests the company may have to cut its dividend. A payout ratio below 70% is healthy for a utility; below 40% is a promising ratio for an industrial stock.

If you're planning to use income stocks as ballast in a growth portfolio rather than as a source of income, you'll want to reinvest your dividends as they are paid. That can pose a problem, since dividends tend to arrive in small amounts. If you own 1,000 shares with a 6% yield, for example, your quarterly dividend would give you enough cash to buy only 15 more shares. While many brokers reinvest dividends for free, not all do. At a discount broker who charges, a typical minimum commission on such a small trade would eat up as much as 15% of your investment.

The solution to this problem: Invest in stocks with dividend-reinvestment plans (DRIPs). In the previous chapter you can find a fuller description of DRIPs and how to locate firms that have them. Here's a quick refresher course: More than 1,100 companies, many of them utilities, offer these plans, which automatically reinvest your dividends. Instead of paying you a dividend in cash, the company adds shares of stock to your account—including fractions of shares, thus allowing every penny of your dividend to go back to work for you. DRIPs never charge a brokerage commission, although about a third of them levy a nominal transaction fee of $5 or less. Better still, about 100 of the companies with DRIPs award the shares at a 3% to 5% discount to their market price.

If you'd like a comparable break on a regular investment as well as on reinvested dividends, look for companies that extend their DRIP policies to cash investors. In these bonus plans, once you own as little as a single share of the company's stock, you can buy additional shares without a commission and often at a small discount.

Risky Business in the Stock Market

By their nature, stocks carry risks. The value of your investment depends on hundreds or thousands of variables that can affect a company's business outlook or the market's view of its stock. Fortunately there are limits to the downside. A seasoned company bought at a reasonable valuation will not collapse on you overnight. And in the long run, the up-

ward bias of the stock market is a powerful lifting mechanism.

Some variations on traditional stock investing remove or restrict such supports, however, multiplying the risks in the pursuit of higher profits. For instance, buying stock options (as described later in Chapter 17) gives you the chance to make—or lose—a bundle by speculating on the future price of a stock. In general, the three types of investments and strategies about to be discussed are for sophisticated investors who have money to gamble:

■ **American Depository Receipts (ADRs).** Of the four investments discussed here, ADRs are the most like ordinary stocks. Basically, ADRs are chits representing claims on shares of a foreign stock held in trust by the foreign subsidiary of a U.S. bank. They trade on U.S. exchanges or over-the-counter just like domestic shares, subject to the same disclosure requirements as any security registered with the SEC. The advantage to Americans is that it's much simpler and less expensive to buy ADRs than to try to buy the underlying shares on a foreign stock exchange.

Many ADRs represent shares in very solid foreign companies. Sony, Hitachi, Daimler Benz, Nestlé, and Royal Dutch Petroleum, among others, all offer ADRs. However, any form of international investing exposes you to risks you don't face when you buy U.S. shares. Most important, ADRs leave you vulnerable to currency risk, the chance that the currency in which the underlying stock is denominated will depreciate against the dollar, making the shares represented by the ADR less valuable to Americans. In addition, in recent years the bulk of new ADRs has come from emerging economies, especially Southeast Asia and Latin America. However promising these economies may be in the long run, they can inflict growing pains on foreign investors in the short run. For example, when Mexico devalued the peso in late '94, Teléfonos de México and Grupo Televisa, both widely owned ADRs, plunged about 18% in a week.

■ **Initial public offerings (IPOs).** One of the most electrifying dramas on Wall Street plays out when a hot company first issues stock. The company's owners generally make millions by selling their stake to the public; the investment bankers putting together the issue also rake in the dough, as do their favored clients—usually big institutions like pension funds and mutual funds—who are able to reserve shares and quickly unload them at higher prices when the rest of the market gets a chance to buy. After the software company Netscape went public in 1995, for example, its stock price doubled during the first week of public trading.

The only people who don't make much money in these new issues seem to be individual investors. According to a University of Illinois survey of IPOs between 1970 and 1990, an investor who bought on the first day of trading and held on for five years would have earned an average annual return of 5%. Those people who bought existing shares of other companies of the same size the same day and hung on to them for five years earned an average of 12%. Why? Most IPOs are clubby affairs: brokers reserve shares in their most promising IPOs for big-ticket customers. If your broker promises to get you shares in an IPO, chances are it's only because the smart money doesn't want any. For example, the company may be too new to have credible earnings or the offering stock price may be too high.

If you nevertheless are interested in buying IPOs, make sure that before you invest you read the prospectus—the booklet describing the company, its management, and the risks to investors. Check how the company's P/E ratio at the estimated share prices given in the prospectus would stack up against the competition. If those P/Es are not in line with ones of similar companies, find out why not. Watch out, too, if the prospectus notes that insiders are planning to unload more than a small percentage of their privately held shares in the stock offering. This could be a sign that the IPO was designed largely to make its founders rich, not you.

Finally, if you are able to buy shares at the offering price or on the first day of trading, don't hold them too long. IPOs often skyrocket during the first week or month of trading and then start to backslide. This is one area of the market where patient investors sadly often get left holding the bag.

Initial public offerings sometimes trade as **penny stocks.** A penny stock is one whose share price is typically less than $5 a share; in most cases, penny stocks trade over-the-counter. The stock is usually that cheap for an excellent reason—its company's prospects are dicey at best. As a rule, the best advice for investing in penny stocks: Don't.

■ **Short selling.** Often called **shorting,** selling short is a way of profiting from a decline in a particular stock. (Some people consider the very idea of short selling to be un-American.) To sell short, you must open a margin account with your stockbroker, which lets you borrow up to half the value of your account. The interest rate you pay is the broker's call rate, which is typically slightly less than the prime rate that banks charge. In short selling, you are borrowing shares from the accounts of other clients of your broker or other brokerages and then selling them in hopes of replacing them at a lower price. The difference between the price you get when you sell and the (lower, you hope) price when you buy is your profit or loss on the short position.

Selling a stock short is actually riskier than owning it. If you misjudge the stock's prospects and the share price goes up, your losses are theoretically unlimited. (A stock you short, after all, can appreciate 100% or 200% or even more, while one you own can never lose more than 100% of its value.) Investors short only stocks that seem ripe for a fall—those with high P/E multiples, seemingly inflated expectations, and cloudy business prospects. Still, overpriced stocks sometimes only get more overpriced, and when that happens short sellers get pinched.

How to Read the Stock Tables

Trying to make sense of the stock-listing tables in the business pages of the newspaper for the first time can be a bit like visiting a foreign country where you don't speak the language. Once you know the lingo, however, it isn't tough at all. Here's what you need to know to read the stock tables like a pro, using a New York Stock Exchange listing for the stock of BancOne on page 360, as an example:

■ The first two columns (**52 Weeks Hi** and **Lo**) show you the highest price of the stock over the past 52 weeks (in this case $38 a share) and the lowest price (in this case $24.12; stocks trade in eighths of a dollar, from ⅛ to ⅞). If the stock just hit a 52-week high or low, that will be marked by an arrow. As you'll see when you read the rest of the row, BancOne's stock on this day was selling for a price that was near its 52-week low. The bigger the variation between the **Hi** and **Lo** price, the more volatile the stock.

■ The next column (**Stock**) is, of course, the name of the stock. In many cases the actual name of the company is too long to fit into the stock table listing, so you'll see an abbreviated version of it. In the *Wall Street Journal*, the name will be in boldface if the stock's price changed by 5% or more in the previous trading day and its previous closing price was $2 or higher. In some instances the stock's name will be followed by a letter. These are the most common ones and what they mean: **A** or **B** (there are different classes of stock; shareholders of different classes have different voting rights); **dd** (the company showed a loss in the most recent four quarters); **n** (the stock was newly issued during the last 52 weeks); **pf**

(a preferred stock); **s** (there was a stock split, dividend, or cash distribution equal to 10% or more in the past 52 weeks); **vj** (the company is in bankruptcy, receivership, or is being reorganized); **wt** (a warrant); **x** (the stock is trading ex–dividend; that means the company declared a dividend within the past four days and if you buy the stock now, you won't get its dividend until the next one is paid, typically in three months).

■ The next column (**Sym**) is the stock's ticker symbol, in this case ONE. Often, the stock's symbol will be the name of the company or something close, such as an abbreviation. For instance, the symbol for CBS is CBS, for Sears, it's simply S. In other cases, however, the symbol will be something more clever (Tommy Hilfiger is TOM).

■ The next column (**Div**) is the stock's dividend over the past four quarters. If the column is blank, that means the stock doesn't pay a dividend. In this case, Banc-One is expected to pay a dividend of $1.36 a year on each share of its stock. Dividends are normally paid quarterly. The **f** here means that the $1.36 is an annual rate.

| 52 WEEKS | | | | | YLD | | VOL | | | | NET |
HI	LO	STOCK	SYM	DIV	%	PE	100s	HI	LO	CLOSE	CHG
38	24⅛	BancOne	ONE	1.36f	5.0	11	7018	27½	27	27 1.8	–⅛

■ The next column (**Yld %**) represents the stock's dividend as a percentage of its stock price. In this case, BancOne's yield is 5.0%. If the column doesn't show a number, it means there is no yield because there is no dividend.

■ The next column (**PE**) is the price-earnings multiple of the stock, based on the stock's trailing earnings. Here, BancOne sports a price-earnings multiple of 11.

■ The next column (**Vol 100s**) tells you how many shares of the stock were bought and sold in the previous trading day. You generally have to multiply the figure by 100 to get the actual number. If the whole line is underlined, that means the stock had an unusually large change in trading volume in the previous trading day. Typically, this happens because there has been some news about the stock. In this case, 7,018,000 shares of BancOne changed hands in the previous trading day.

■ The next three columns (**Hi Lo Close**) finally tell you what you really want to know: How did the stock do in the previous trading session? The **Hi** shows the most the stock sold for, **Lo** shows the least it sold for, and **Close** shows what it sold for in its last trade of the day. BancOne got as high as $27.50, as low as $27, and finished at $27.125.

■ The last column (**Net Chg**) gives you the bottom line: how much the stock rose or fell in the previous trading day, expressed in dollars and eighths of dollars. BancOne lost ⅛, or 12.5¢ a share.

How to Buy Stocks through a Stockbroker

To an investor, the ideal **full-service stockbroker** is part stock-picking genius, part psychologist, and part father or mother confessor. But to a full-service brokerage firm, such as Merrill Lynch, Paine Webber, or Prudential Securities, the ideal broker is a great salesman. Keep this conflict of job descriptions in mind when you seek advice from a broker. He or she gets paid for convincing you to buy or sell investments. All else being equal, your broker will probably be pleased if you make money on your trade. But he or she and the firm make money whether you do or not. Brokers get about 45% of their income from selling stocks and bonds; they get the rest by selling other financial products from annuities to limited partnerships to mutual funds. The commission you'll pay on actively traded stocks is generally about 2% of the stock price; for thinly traded, over-the-counter stocks, you'll pay a commission of closer to 5%. You'll generally pay a smaller commission by purchasing in groups of 100 shares at a time, known as a **round lot,** than by buying fewer shares (an **odd lot**).

One viable alternative to a full-service broker is a **discount brokerage** firm, such as Charles Schwab, Fidelity, or Quick & Reilly. In return for charging fees up to 70% lower than full-service brokerages, discounters usually drop all pretense of offering advice on your trade. Though discounters aren't the right answer for everyone, they at least make the trade-off clear: If you use a full-commission broker, you're doing so to get advice and information.

Don't expect more advice, however, than a full-service broker can truly deliver. It isn't realistic to expect your stockbroker to know the precise best moment to buy or sell a particular stock or which stock will be the hottest. (If he did, he'd be getting rich trading for his own account and wouldn't have you for a client.) It is realistic, however, to ask your broker to earn his commission by giving you access to information.

Any full-service broker who wants to sell you a stock should be willing to provide you with the company's financial statements, prospectuses, and proxies, as well as the *Value Line* or *S&P* report. It also pays to ask for a copy of a recent report on the stock by the brokerage's own research analysts. (Don't treat these reports as hot tips, however; by the time the brokerage firm makes its company reports available to retail clients such as you, the big institu-

tional clients like pension funds may have known the analysts' opinion for months.) If, in the end, you also want to ask the broker's opinion, fine. But consider him or her to be just one of several sources of stock-picking advice.

Discount brokers were designed for investors who make up their minds without a broker's help. In recent years, however, some have begun to make limited stock research available—but usually at an à la carte fee. (Quick & Reilly, for one, will give you S&P data for free, however.) These amenities, though limited, are still beyond the pale of so-called **deep-discount brokers** such as Kennedy, Cabot and Pacific Brokerage Services, which may charge only half as much as an established discounter like Schwab. However, they provide services to match.

The biggest growth in the brokerage business these days is in electronic trading; that is, buying and selling stocks through your computer. The on-line brokerage biz grew an estimated 50% in 1996, to 1.5 million customers, and growth in 1997 was equally phenomenal. Four reasons: convenience, information, speed, and price. When you trade stocks on-line, you can pad down to your home computer in your pajamas and slippers, read analysts' reports and the latest business news on-line at the broker's site, place your order quickly at any time of the day or night, and pay as little as $9 for the transaction.

This burgeoning field is not problem-free, though. Some investors complain of on-line brokerage systems crashing, price quotes that don't stick, and slow customer service. The last is not too surprising, since one reason the on-line brokers can keep costs down is that their customer amenities are minimal.

To make your on-line experience successful, you need to figure out what you want and then find the broker who offers it. Some on-line brokers are easier to use than others, others are known best for their low commissions, and others provide top-notch customer service. Internet consultant Gomez Advisors of Boston ranked the on-line brokers in different ways and decided PC Financial Network (www.pcfn.com) is best overall as well as easiest to use; Datek (www.datek.com; as little as $9.99 for up to 5,000 shares) has the lowest prices. The study determined Investex (www.investexpress.com) has the best service. You can find the best on-line broker for you at the Choosing a Discount Broker site (www.sonic.net/donaldj).

When you place an order to buy or sell a stock with any kind of broker, you have two choices. You can ask for a **market order,** as most small investors do. This simply means that you want the broker to get you the best price to buy or sell the shares at the moment. Alternatively, you can place a **limit order.** In this case you're giving instructions to your broker about when to buy or sell shares for you. If, for instance, you believe the stock's current

$50-a-share price will fall, you could place a limit order telling the broker not to buy the shares until the stock drops to, say, $45. Conversely, if you own a $50 stock, you could tell your broker to sell the shares whenever the price hits $75. One type of limit order, known as a **stop-loss order,** helps prevent you from losing too much money. With this technique, you instruct your broker to sell your shares if their price ever falls to a specific level; for instance, you could tell the broker to sell if your $50 stock sinks to $40.

One decision you'll need to face when buying stocks is whether to have the shares registered in your own name (and most likely keep the securities in your safe-deposit box) or to register them in what's known as **street name,** the brokerage's name. Both options have advantages and disadvantages. For instance, by keeping the stock in street name, you don't need to worry about your certificates getting lost or stolen. What's more, whenever you want to sell your shares, you can just call your broker and it's a done deal. Also, a number of brokerages now charge a fee of $15 if customers want to receive actual stock certificates.

However, if you keep the stock in street name, you either can't buy shares through the company's dividend-reinvestment (DRIP) program or, if you can, you must pay the broker a full commission. In addition, you could face hassles if you decide to switch brokerages and want to move the securities from your present firm to another one. Some brokerages even slap customers with fees of $50 or so for transferring their accounts.

Most brokerage customers keep their stocks in street name as a convenience. Doing so also cuts down on record-keeping headaches. When your shares are in street name, the brokerage sends you consolidated statements that track your dividends and interest, capital-gains distributions from mutual funds, and all of your purchases and sales. There's another, fairly new, reason to go the street name route. Now that you have to get your broker your certificates within three days of telling him or her to sell your shares, you could be in a fix if you want to sell but can't get the shares to the broker that quickly.

load stocks or **direct-purchase plans** that sell shares directly to the public, ranging from American Recreation Centers to Exxon to Wisconsin Energy. About half of these companies are utilities, and some of them limit this privilege to their own customers. Other firms with no-load stocks, however, include oil companies, banks, and textile makers. You can buy their stocks for an initial investment of $20 to $1,000. About a third of the firms have automatic investing plans, which take a set amount out of your bank account each month and use it to buy shares of stock. To buy a no-load stock, call the company and ask for a registration form. Once you fill it in and send in your check, you can then buy additional shares, reinvest your dividends, and even sell your shares.

Buying Initial Shares without a Broker

You've already read (Chapter 13) about dividend-reinvestment plans, which let you purchase additional shares without paying a brokerage commission. But what if you could buy your initial shares of a stock without using a broker or paying a brokerage fee? Increasingly, you can do just that.

There are now nearly 100 so-called **no-**

Buying Stocks through an Investment Club

Chances are by now you've heard of the Beardstown Ladies. They are that group of women (and best-selling, albeit somewhat discredited, authors) in Beardstown, Ill., who get together and pick stocks for their own investment club. If you are intrigued by the idea of buying stocks routinely with a small group of people, you'll want to join or perhaps even form an investment club, too.

There are now more than 7,500 investment clubs in the country, many with fewer than 15 people in them. Typically, the members get together once a month or so and talk about stocks they think are worth purchasing, plus ones they own that might be worth unloading. As a rule, each member kicks in between $10 and $100 a month. To find out more about such clubs, write or call the National Association of Investment Clubs (1515 East Eleven Mile Rd., Royal Oak, Mich. 48067; 313-543-0612). Once you pay the $32-a-year membership fee, you'll receive information on how to run a club, how to analyze stocks, when to sell stocks, and so forth.

Investing in Stocks through Mutual Funds

Stocks are a necessary part of every long-term investor's portfolio, but selecting and monitoring a collection of them can be daunting at first, even a burden. You may not have the money—$25,000 to $50,000 or so—that it takes to assemble a reasonably diversified portfolio of eight to 10 stocks. You may not be particularly con-

fident in your ability to understand the subtleties of a company's financial statement. You may not feel you have the time to keep track of a company's fortunes, so that you know when to sell.

If any of those descriptions apply to you, then you ought to consider following the example of millions of other individual investors and do your stock market investing through shares of stock or equity mutual funds. When you buy shares in a fund, you become part owner of the fund's stock portfolio, which is likely to hold scores of stocks (if not more) worth tens of millions, if not billions, of dollars. The job of selecting and monitoring the stocks in the portfolio falls to a professional money-management firm. (Usually, but not always, the money manager is the company that sponsors the fund and whose brand—such as American Funds, Dreyfus, Fidelity, or Vanguard—appears in the fund's name.) By owning a fund, you not only leave the hard work to pros, you also indirectly reap the advantages of investing large sums of money. A multimillion-dollar fund, for example, can buy stocks at a lower per-share commission than you can. A fund will also be more diversified than any portfolio you could easily construct on your own.

Investing through funds does not, of course, remove all the work from equity investing. For instance, there's the not so minor matter of choosing the best fund or funds for you. Today, there are more than 1,300 stock funds. They range from relatively safe, income-oriented funds to highly risky small-company stock funds. Many are managed competently, even brilliantly; others are run by under-trained, overworked, distracted, or simply not very bright money managers. Some hold their expenses low, to give fund shareholders every possible advantage. Others carry fees so high that if you invest in them, you're at a disadvantage right from the start. It's up to you to find the equity funds that will match your appetite for risk and give you a respectable return. No easy task.

Unlike stocks, which you usually have to buy through a stockbroker charging a commission, many funds are sold directly by their sponsors with no sales charge—or **load**, as it's known in the fund business. These commission-free funds, called **no-loads,** account for about one-third of the equity funds available to small investors. You buy a no-load fund either by sending a check in the mail, going to a discount brokerage such as Charles Schwab or Fidelity that sells the fund, or, in some cases, by going to the fund company's walk-in office in your city.

The remainder of mutual funds are **load funds,** which are sold by full-service stockbrokers and carry fees of one kind or another. A standard load fund might charge a fee between 4% and 8.5% of the amount you invest. How these commissions are charged has grown more complicated in recent years. You now often have a choice of whether to pay the commission up front all at once or parcel it out over the period you own the shares. The thing to remember, though, is that if you buy a load fund from a stockbroker, you will pay for the privilege of having him or her help you select the fund. If you buy directly from a no-load sponsor, you will pay no sales charge (or only a relatively small one), but you will have to make your choice about whether to buy it and when to sell it without the benefit of a broker's advice.

Where to Find Out about Mutual Funds

The growth in the number of mutual funds has been matched only by the growth in publications purporting to analyze, rank, and allegedly help you pick winning funds. What's more, the funds themselves publish useful descriptions of what they do and how they've done. In addition, software programs and on-line services can assist you. Getting adequate information about funds—at least the biggest and most widely available—is not hard at all. You just need to know where to look.

Your first source of information is the fund's own required disclosure. Every fund publishes a **prospectus,** in which, among other things, it states its investment goal, the sorts of stocks it buys, its past performance, the name of the investment manager, the fees the fund charges, and whether it intends to derive all, some, or none of its return from income. For insight into the actual stocks that a fund currently holds, you can also get the fund's **annual** or **semiannual shareholder report.** Stockbrokers have prospectuses and shareholder reports for all the funds they sell. If you prefer no-loads, call the fund sponsor's toll-free 800 line and ask for a prospectus and shareholder report. Most publications that include full, periodic listings of funds, such as **MONEY**, *Barron's, Business Week, Forbes,* and the *Wall Street Journal*, list the 800 numbers of the funds.

Two publications provide the kind of detailed analysis of mutual funds that the *Value Line Investment Survey* and *Standard & Poor's Stock Reports* provide for stocks: *Morningstar Mutual Funds* ($395 a year; $55 for a three-month trial subscription; 800-735-0700) and the *Value Line Mutual Fund Survey* ($295 a year; $49 for a three-month trial subscription; 800-535-8760). Modeled on the *Value Line* stock reports, both provide a thorough look at the past performance and current portfolio hold-

ings of more than 1,000 funds as well as a description of the fund manager's investing style. You can generally find one or both in large public libraries.

If you prefer to do your investing research electronically, there is some excellent software that can help you pick a fund. For instance, Morningstar's *Principia* ($195 a year with quarterly updates; $495 for the more comprehensive CD-ROM version; 800-735-0700) lets you screen among a universe of mutual funds for ones that meet your specifications. Looking for an international stock fund whose expenses are low and has been in business for at least three years? Just tell it to the disk and you'll get the names you need. You can also use this software to compare a particular fund with others that have the same objectives to see how it fares against its peers. Another fine, less expensive offering is the *Quarterly Low-Load Mutual Fund Update* from the American Association of Individual Investors ($24 a year for members; $30 otherwise; 312-280-0170). You'll be able to look at only 800 funds, but you can at least be certain that they keep their fees down.

The Internet, of course, is chock full of useful stuff for mutual fund investors. If you're looking for news about particular mutual funds or fund investing ideas, visit *CNNfn* (www.cnn.fn.com), the site run by the CNNfn cable network, and *Morningstar.Net* (www.morningstar.net), the on-line area for the Chicago mutual fund rating service. The Morningstar site is also great for taking an in-depth look at your funds or those you're considering buying. When looking to build a mutual fund portfolio, you may want to spring for the $179-a-year cost of the *NetResults* paid Web service (www.isnetwork.com). You list your investing goals and answer some questions. Then NetResults recommends a portfolio consisting of up to eight funds.

While software generally is best for handling mutual fund screens, *StockSmart* (www.stocksmart.com) runs an excellent fund-screening Web site, allowing you to sort through more than 6,000 funds by the criteria you type in.

Understanding the Different Types of Funds

To make sense of the variety of mutual fund choices available, fund analysts break the fund world into different categories, either by the funds' stated investment goals (price appreciation, income, or a combination) or by the fund's investment approach (small stocks, large stocks, growth stocks, value stocks, income stocks, international stocks, or some combination). The table on page 370 describes the characteristics of funds in each of the various categories. Understanding a fund's category based on its investment objective can give you a rough idea of the fund's level of risk and its dividend yield. While there is a great deal of overlap among categories, it's safe to assume that an aggressive growth fund, for example, will be considerably riskier than, say, an equity-income fund. Over time, however, you'd expect the aggressive growth fund to have the higher return. On average, as the table shows, that has been the case over the past three and five years.

Categorizing funds by their investment approach is especially useful in understanding their recent performance. Stock investors tend to favor either growth stocks or value stocks, and mutual fund portfolio managers are no different. As a result, funds with a growth-oriented investor at the helm—such as AIM Weingarten and Meridian—tended to do well in the growth stock booms of 1989 and 1991; those with value hunters in charge—such as Mutual Shares and Gabelli Asset—were on top in the economic recovery years of 1992 and 1993, when cyclical companies had the edge. Similarly, small-stock and large-cap mutual funds largely follow the cycles between big and small companies. Blue-chip funds like Janus and Twentieth Century Growth were giants in the big-cap years of the mid-1980s, while Govett Smaller Companies and PBHG Growth took over in the early 1990s, when small-cap stocks ruled.

Many investors expect a professional money manager to excel in every kind of market. In fact, even the best managers rarely do. Most stick to the investment approach they know best, regardless of the approach that happens to be in style. For that reason, a fund manager's success typically rises and falls with his or her particular investment discipline. Indeed, studies show that investment style accounts for at least 75% of a manager's return. For the ultimate diversified portfolio of mutual funds, therefore, you should own funds that represent all investment approaches—both growth and value, and large- and small-cap versions of each.

One type of fund, known as an **index fund,** doesn't try to beat the market—merely equal it. The fund manager buys a portfolio of stocks that mirrors the ones in a popular index, such as the Standard & Poor's 500 index. There are now more than 125 index funds, and you can find one for just about every type of stock you like: small-cap, midcap, large-cap, or international. In recent years S&P 500 index funds, while performing as well as the market overall, have handily beat the average U.S. stock fund. For instance, the biggest index fund of all, Vanguard Index 500, outperformed more than two-thirds of general stock funds over a recent three-year period and 75% of them over 10 years. Managers of a subset of index funds,

known as **quant funds,** try to beat the indexes, however, through the use of computers. Rather than simply trying to replicate the index, they tilt their portfolios toward industries or specific stocks they think will beat the market.

Should you buy an index fund rather than one with a manager trying to outperform the averages? Perhaps, if you're just looking to invest in the overall stock market. Then, an S&P 500 index fund might be a smart idea. If you'd rather invest in small stocks, value stocks, or international stocks, however, you might start with an S&P 500 indexer and then go with bright mutual fund managers who are likely to beat the averages over the long run.

A HEAD-TO-HEAD LOOK AT STOCK FUND CATEGORIES

Here are 10 broad categories for mutual funds that invest in stocks, listed in order from riskiest to safest; balanced funds also buy bonds. You'll see that two groups—gold and emerging market funds—lost money in 1997. The top performing category in 1997 and over three years was growth and income, while sector funds specializing in a particular industry were best over five years.

FUND TYPE/ TYPICAL INVESTMENT	RISK LEVEL	% COMPOUND ANNUAL RETURN TO JAN. 1, 1998		
		ONE YEAR	THREE YEARS	FIVE YEARS
Gold/stocks of gold-mining companies	**Very High**	–42.0	–14.5	0.3
Emerging Markets/ stocks from lesser-developed countries	**Very High**	–2.4	0.7	6.8
Sector/stocks of one particular industry	**Very High**	26.9	25.6	18.2
Small-Cap/stocks of up-and-coming firms	**Very High**	21.4	23.0	16.5
Growth/companies expecting above average revenue/earnings growth	**High**	25.3	25.1	16.5
Midcap/stocks of mid-size companies	**High**	19.6	22.5	15.2
Growth & Income/stocks with potential growth in price and dividends	**High**	27.7	26.9	17.8
Equity Income/stocks with high dividends	**High**	27.5	25.5	17.0
International/stocks from countries outside U.S.	**High**	4.9	8.4	12.0
Balanced/stocks and bonds that won't lose money	**Medium**	19.0	19.4	13.2
AVERAGE U.S. STOCK FUND	**High**	24.4	25.0	16.9

Source: Lipper Analytical Services

How to Pick a Stock Mutual Fund

Once you've identified the kind of mutual fund you want to buy, your next job is to find a fund that executes that approach with aplomb. Style may account for three-quarters of a typical fund's return, but that still leaves 25% for the individual manager's skill (or lack thereof). It's tempting to assume that the top performing fund over the previous year or five years will repeat in the future. Too bad it rarely works that way, however. Markets can change, a manager's luck can run out, a fund can change its manager, and funds at the top in one time period rarely stay there for long.

A more realistic goal is to try to find managers who are likely to outperform the average fund in their group in the future. That seemingly modest endeavor is more of an art than a science, but you'll improve your chances of success if you look for something more than simply a top performance ranking. Here's what to look for as well:

■ **Consistency.** When checking out a fund's past performance, look for evidence that suggests the returns were consistent and steady year after year rather than erratic flashes of brilliance. For example, both Fidelity Contrafund and MFS Emerging Growth were among the top performing funds in the first half of 1994. Contrafund, however, had outperformed the median growth fund each year since 1991; MFS, by contrast, owed most of its return to an exceptionally strong 1991. In two of the three years since then, in fact, MFS lagged the median in its group.

■ **Bearable risk.** Volatility goes with the territory when you invest in stock funds. But you want to make sure that the fund you choose doesn't dish out more pain during market downturns than you can take. So in your analysis, look for the fund's worst annual return in any of the past five or 10 years and ask yourself whether you could sit through a loss of that magnitude without selling or getting sick to your stomach. Success with mutual funds takes patience and persistence. If a fund's periodic losses would overwhelm both virtues in you, look for one that you can live with, even if its returns are less Olympian. For instance, rather than buying an aggressive growth fund, invest instead in a less volatile income total-return fund. You can also match a fund to your risk tolerance by looking at its manager's investing style, often noted in mutual fund performance rankings. Style, in fund parlance, means whether the fund buys large, medium, or small stocks and whether the manager prefers growth stocks, value stocks, or some combination.

■ **Low expenses.** All else being equal, a no-load fund with annual expenses below the equity fund average of 1.3% will outperform a more costly load fund. Investing in a high-expense fund is like betting on a horse that is carrying a heavier load than the rest of the field: the nag still might win, but the odds are against it. Similarly, shrewd stock picking by a fund manager can more than make up for the burden of extra expenses, but unless you are convinced that the fund really has more promise than its less expensive competition, there's no point in starting out with a handicap. You can find the fund's fees as a percentage of assets in the prospectus, listed as the **expense ratio.** Here, according to Morningstar, are the average expense ratios for the broad categories of funds that buy stocks: aggressive growth (1.75%), growth (1.39%), small-company (1.40%), equity-income (1.30%), growth and income (1.23%), balanced (1.28%), income (1.33%), foreign (1.64%), specialty (1.23% to 1.86%, depending on the specialty), and asset-allocation (1.46%).

■ **Manageable asset size.** Funds with superb returns that win accolades from the financial press can become so popular that they balloon by hundreds of millions of dollars in a few months. A flood of incoming cash can force a manager to modify his investing approach and may even distract the manager from a careful daily monitoring of the fund's stocks. The fund industry is littered with once hot performers that became media darlings, swelled in size, and promptly turned into mediocrities. As a rule, be wary of funds whose sales have more than doubled over the previous year; you can find this information by looking at the year-by-year asset size of the fund in its prospectus. This is especially true of funds that specialize in small-company stocks traded over-the-counter, where big trades are hard to execute quickly and inexpensively. The more conscientious small-cap funds close their doors to new investors when their assets grow too large—say, to $500 million. If a small-cap fund has grown beyond that point and is still accepting new money, you should probably make sure that none of it is yours.

■ **Tax efficiency.** Ever heard the expression "It's not how much you make, it's how much you keep"? This maxim is especially apt for stock fund investors, since a fund's income and capital-gains distributions are taxed by the IRS. Increasingly, annual fund performance rankings in magazines and newspapers list the tax efficiency of the funds, which is the percentage of a fund's total return that an investor in the 28% federal tax bracket would have kept after paying taxes on the income and capital gains distributed by the fund over the past three years. This percentage gives you a truer explanation of how well you would actually have done had you invested in the fund. For instance, if a fund returned 12% on average over three years and its tax efficiency was 87%, your after-tax return in the 28% bracket would be 10.4% (or 87% of 12%). While most fund managers don't concern themselves with their fund's tax-efficiency (their bonuses depend on pre-tax performance), a few funds do expressly attempt to minimize a shareholder's tax burden. So if you're comparing two otherwise identical funds and one has a stated policy of tax-efficient investing, that's the one to choose.

How to Read the Fund Listings

The mutual fund listings in the daily newspaper are easier to comprehend than the stock listings, but not by a whole lot.

Making things even trickier is that different newspapers list funds differently. The following guide to the fund listings in the *Wall Street Journal,* using two Dreyfus funds as examples, will help you see how your funds are doing:

■ **The first column** gives you the fund's name and, if it is part of a fund family, the fund family name in boldface. Generally, the name of the fund will be abbreviated for space. In this case the actual names of the funds are **Dreyfus Growth Opportunity** and **Dreyfus International Equity.** If the fund has various classes of shares, the letter for the class (A, B, C, D) will follow its name. If you see a **p,** this means that the fund levies a so-called **12b-1 fee,** which is an annual charge to shareholders for marketing and distribution. If you see an **r,** that means the fund has a **redemption charge,** which you may owe when you sell your shares.

	INV. OBJ.	NAV	OFFER PRICE	NAV CHG.	—TOTAL RETURN—			R
					YTD	4 WKS	1 YR	
Dreyfus:								
GthOp	GRO	9.06	NL	+0.08	+10.8	+5.5	+4.3	C
InterEq	ITL	13.11	13.11	+0.13	−8.2	+0.3	−12.6	E

■ **The second column (Inv. Obj.)** tells you the investment objective of the fund. In these two instances the objectives are fairly self-explanatory: growth and international. Other objectives you will see are **CAP** (capital appreciation); **G&I** (growth and income; S&P 500 index funds are one type); **EQI** (equity-income); **SML** (small-company growth); **MID** (midcap stocks); **SEC** (a sector or specialty fund); **WOR** (global and small-company global; the abbreviation is short for "world"); and **S&B** (blended funds such as balanced and income funds).

■ **The third column (NAV)** tells you the net asset value of the fund, which is the price of one share of the fund. A fund computes its NAV by dividing the value of the fund by the number of shares. Like stock prices, NAVs can vary enormously for stock funds.

■ **The fourth column (Offer Price)** is the total of the net asset value plus any sales commission. If the fund is a no-load, it will have the NL designation.

■ **The fifth column (NAV Chg.)** is the bottom line for fund investors. It shows how much the fund rose or fell in price in the previous trading day. Dreyfus Growth Opportunity gained 8¢ and Dreyfus International Equity gained 13¢.

■ **The sixth, seventh, and eighth** columns **(Total Return)** are also important. They measure how much the fund has gained or lost on a percentage basis in the year to date, past four weeks, and past 52 weeks, assuming that all dividends have been reinvested. These performance figures are calculated before subtracting sales charges. On different days the *Journal* runs fund performance for the past 13 weeks, 26 weeks, 39 weeks, three years, four years, and five years. Figures for periods longer than a year are annualized returns; that means they represent the average annual return for the funds over that time period. On Mondays the *Journal* replaces these columns with ones showing the maximum initial sales charge and total expense ratio for each fund.

■ **The last column (R)** stands for ranking and shows you how the fund has performed compared with others in its category over the longest time period listed. A fund with an A is in the top 20%; B is the next 20%; C is the middle 20%; D is the next 20%; and E is the bottom 20%. The Dreyfus Growth Opportunity Fund, with its 4.3% one-year return, is thus in the middle 20% of growth funds for the past year. The Dreyfus International Equity fund, with its −12.6% loss, is in the bottom 20% of international funds for the past year.

How to Use a Broker to Buy Mutual Funds

Mutual fund investing is straightforward enough that most enterprising investors can do it without a stockbroker. If you nevertheless feel that a broker's counsel is worth an extra fee, make sure that you get the service you're paying for. Your broker should be able to provide the Morningstar and Value Line report on any fund he or she recommends. You should also ask for the reports on competing funds and ask the broker to explain why his or her choice is best for you. Occasionally a fund company or brokerage firm will promote a particular fund by offering brokers a higher than normal commission. Dean Witter and Prudential, for example, let brokers keep up to five percentage points more commission for selling funds sponsored by their own brokerage instead of other funds. So ask whether the broker stands to make a higher commission on the recommended fund than a comparable one. If so, he'd better have a persuasive case why his fund is better than the competition.

Some funds, typically load funds, come in more than one **class** of shares. Each class has a different fee structure. For instance, one fund company might have the following options: (1) "A" shares, which charge a front-end load of 4.25% and have annual expenses of about 1% a year; (2) "B" shares, with no front-end load but with a fee known as a **back-end load,** which you'll pay when you sell or redeem your shares, plus annual expenses of 2% or so; and (3) "C" shares, with no front-end or back-end fee, but with an annual 1% distribution fee on top of annual expenses of 1% to 2%. If your fund has more than one class of shares, ask the broker to calculate your total commission over the entire period that you plan to own the fund and to tell you what will happen if you decide to sell before then.

Buying Your Funds at the Bank

In the past few years, more than 1,800 banks have started selling mutual funds to customers. Well, it looks that way. Actually, the banks aren't always the ones selling the funds in their lobbies; sometimes independent stockbrokers are doing the selling. Buying your mutual funds at your bank is certainly a convenient way to invest. But is it an intelligent way? Not necessarily.

The trouble is, studies have shown that bank customers are sometimes getting misleading or inaccurate information

375

from the fund salesmen. Sometimes the salesmen don't say that the funds are not FDIC-insured, leaving the impression that they are. In other instances customers are sold funds that are wholly inappropriate for them because the salesmen have failed to ask critical questions about their risk tolerance, income levels, investment goals, and objectives. Worse, many of the funds sold—sometimes pushed—are not as good as ones you could buy elsewhere. One reason: Many banks pay the fund salesmen more to sell customers funds managed by the bank, so-called **proprietary funds.**

Does this mean you shouldn't buy a fund at your bank? Not at all. But you should certainly do every bit as much research checking out the fund as you would if you were buying the fund through the mail or via a stockbroker.

CHAPTER 15

Investing in Bonds and Bond Mutual Funds

There are three main reasons why you ought to give bonds and bond mutual funds a close look. First, bonds can provide a steady stream of income, delivering more than what you would earn if you kept your dollars in a bank account or money-market fund. Second, bonds can help cushion your portfolio against sharp drops in the stock market. Third, some bonds provide tax-free income, often a big advantage if you're in the 28% tax bracket or higher.

To better understand how bonds can fit into your overall portfolio, it helps to take a look at their historic performance. Long-term Treasury bonds that **mature** (or come due) in 20 years have returned an average of 8.9% since 1970. That compares with 11% for large-company stocks,

according to Ibbotson Associates, the Chicago investment research firm. Between 1970 and 1993, investors in mutual funds that buy bonds, commonly called **bond funds,** earned an average of 10.6% a year, according to Morningstar, the Chicago mutual fund research firm. But as with the stock market, the bond market has bad years from time to time—generally when interest rates or inflation shoot up. For instance, bond prices crashed in 1994, saddling investors with an average loss of 4.8%.

While bonds are less lucrative than stocks over the long term, they also can be less volatile. Intermediate-term bonds, which mature in one to 10 years, have lost money for investors just once since 1970, according to Ibbotson Associates. That compares to five losing years for large-company stocks. When stock prices sank by 3.2% in 1990, U.S. government bonds gained 6.2%.

Small investors can buy bonds in three ways:

■ **You can purchase individual bonds through a broker or, in some cases, directly from the federal government.** Although you can buy U.S. Treasury securities with as little as $1,000, it's best to invest at least $25,000 if you want to buy individual issues offered by municipalities (municipal bonds) or corporations (corporate bonds). That way you'll be able to buy enough different bonds to own a diversified portfolio.

■ **You can invest in bonds through a mutual fund.** This strategy makes sense for people who have less than $25,000 to invest in bonds or who don't want to worry about picking individual issues. When you purchase shares of a bond fund, your cash is pooled with money from other people and then professionally managed. Many bond funds require minimum initial investments of $500 to $1,000; some accept amounts as low as $100.

■ **You can buy unit investment trusts (UITs) from stockbrokers.** These are basically baskets of bonds that are held for the trust's lifespan. UITs are usually sold in units of $1,000.

How the Bond Market Works

Before you invest any money in bonds, it will help to understand how the bond market works. Companies and governments issue bonds to finance their day-to-day operations or to fund special projects, like new construction. Because most bond issues are so large, involving hundreds of millions of dollars, issuers usually don't sell their bonds directly to the public. Instead the bonds are marketed through an investment bank known as an **underwriter.** When bonds are issued, they are sold on what is known as the **primary market.** Older bonds can be bought through brokers from other purchasers on what's called the **secondary market.**

Think of a bond as an IOU. When you buy a bond you're loaning money for a set period of time to the issuer—whether it's the city of Chicago, General Motors, or the U.S. Treasury. In exchange for your dough, the borrower promises to pay you interest each year and to return your principal at maturity, when the loan comes due. As a rule, the longer the term of your bond, the higher your yield.

Interest paid on a bond is known as its **coupon,** a name that dates back to the days when bond investors had to clip the coupons on their bonds and send them to a trustee who would mail out interest payments. Today, interest payments are sent automatically to the bond owner's bank or brokerage account. The face value of a bond—the price at the time it was issued—is known as its **par value.** So the **coupon rate** is the bond's percentage yield at par value. For instance, a bond with a $1,000 face value that pays out $70 a year in interest has a coupon rate of 7%. Because a bond's lifespan and the schedule of coupon payments are fixed when a bond is issued, bonds are known as **fixed-income** investments.

When you divide the bond's coupon rate by its current price, you come up with what's known as the bond's **current yield.** This is the amount you would earn if you bought the bond today. Bonds sell at a **discount** if their current market price is lower than their face value. As a discounted bond gets closer to maturity, the discount narrows. At maturity, it vanishes. (If you buy a bond at a discount, you pay taxes on any capital gains from the rise in its price when you sell.) Bonds that sell at a price higher than their face value trade at a **premium.** If the face value and current value are equal, the bond trades at **par.** Another type of bond yield is the **yield to maturity.** This percentage figure accounts for both the interest payments and any capital gain or loss you have when the bond is due.

Some investors mistakenly believe they can't lose money in bonds. But don't let the name "fixed income" fool you. Al-

though the interest payments you'll get from owning a bond are fixed, the return you will earn as a bond investor is not. That's because of the primary rule for investing in bonds: Bond prices move in the opposite direction of interest rates. So when interest rates rise (as they did in 1994), bond prices fall. And when rates fall (as they did in the '80s), bond prices rise. The reason? When rates go up, newer bonds are issued paying the requisite higher interest, which makes older bonds with their lower interest rates less attractive to investors. The prices of these older bonds then fall to make up the difference. Similarly, bond prices rise when interest rates fall because their higher payout becomes more attractive than the lower rates offered by new bonds.

That's why arguably the most important figure to look at when investing in bonds is **total return:** it represents a combination of the bond or bond fund's yield and any capital gains or losses. In fact, according to Ibbotson Associates, of the eight years in the past decade when long-term government bonds had positive total returns, capital appreciation provided the bulk of the returns four times and income delivered most of the returns four times.

To understand what interest rate shifts can mean to you as a bond investor, consider the following example. You pay $1,000 for a 30-year bond issued by Able Shoemaker that carries an 8% coupon. As an

Able bondholder you'll get $80 a year in interest ($1,000 times 8%). Shortly after you make your purchase, however, inflation heats up and interest rates rise. Sunshine Utility decides it needs to raise money, so it starts selling bonds that pay 9%, or $90 on a $1,000 investment. Suddenly your Able bond with its $80 payout doesn't look very attractive. You decide to dump it and use the money to snap up a 9% Sunshine issue. The trouble is nobody wants to give you what you paid for the Able bond with its 8% yield. The only way you can find a buyer is to take a cut in the price of your Able bond. Investors will pay you just $896.80. You take a loss of $103.20.

Here's another, more pleasant example. Let's say that one year passes and interest rates have fallen by one percentage point. Your $1,000 Sunshine bond is paying 9%, while new issues now are paying just 8%. Your bond is now especially alluring to other investors. So if you sell your 9% bond, you'll get $1,113.10. Your $113.10 profit will be taxed as a capital gain. To see what happens to the value of bonds if interest rates rise or fall by different amounts, see the table that follows.

THE EFFECT OF INTEREST RATE MOVES ON BONDS

The table below will show you what would happen to the price of a $100 bond with a coupon rate of 6% if interest rates rise or fall by one or two percentage points. You'll see that the longer the bond's maturity, the more you can gain or lose on an interest rate move.

| TERM OF BOND | Your $100 bond's price if interest rates rise by . . . | | Your $100 bond's price if interest rates fall by . . . | |
	ONE POINT	TWO POINTS	ONE POINT	TWO POINTS
1-year	$99.05	$98.11	$100.96	$101.94
5-year	$95.84	$91.89	$104.38	$108.98
10-year	$92.89	$86.41	$107.79	$116.35
30-year	$87.53	$77.38	$115.45	$134.76

Source: *Thorndike Encyclopedia of Banking and Financial Tables.*

Short-term price fluctuations due to shifting interest rates don't matter much if you plan to hold a bond until maturity. At that time, you'll be repaid the bond's full face value. You could see sharp gains or losses, however, if you decide to sell a bond early or you invest in a bond fund whose manager buys and sells issues routinely.

Even if you're a buy-and-hold bond investor, interest rates can throw a monkey wrench into your financial plans. Let's say you own a Sunshine bond that is paying 9% interest, but rates have plunged to 6%. In that case Sunshine may decide to redeem (or **call**) its bonds before they mature. The company might call in its bonds because it wants to reduce its interest costs and no longer wants to pay the old, higher rate to investors. Although falling rates have pushed the price of your $1,000 bond up to $1,415.10, Sunshine is required to pay you only the par value of $1,000 if it calls in the bond. Not only will you get less than the market price, you'll have to find a place to reinvest the money that's been returned to you. Chances are you'll wind up settling for a new bond that pays 6%, not the 9% you were expecting. Calls can be particularly painful if you're planning to live off your bond income.

Find out whether a bond you're considering can be called before you buy it. Just ask your broker whether the bond contains a **call provision.** If it does, this provision will explain under what conditions a company can buy back its bonds and what price it must pay. Because there's a risk that you won't get the income you expect, callable bonds usually pay a higher interest rate than comparable noncallable bonds. If the bond does have a call provision, ask your broker for the bond's **yield to call**—this is the yield on a bond assuming that the bond will be redeemed by the issuer when it can first be called. This figure is especially relevant when the bond is selling at a premium. When a bond is callable, the lower of the yield to call and the yield to maturity is the rate of return that you're more likely to get.

The Different Types of Bonds

You can choose from a wide array of bonds, which vary both in the potential return they offer and their potential risks. When weighing your alternatives, keep in mind that the highest-yielding issues typically carry the highest risks. The following descriptions will help you sort through the bond buffet:

■ **U.S. Treasuries.** These issues are the safest of all because the payment of interest and principal is guaranteed by the full faith and credit of the U.S. government. Treasuries are sold by the federal government through auctions held weekly, monthly, quarterly, and semiannually. When you buy a Treasury, the interest you earn is exempt from state and local taxes, but not from federal tax. You can buy Treasuries either through a stockbroker or directly from the federal government (see the list of Treasury Direct offices later in this chapter). There are four different types of Treasuries:

Treasury bills are short-term investments issued in terms of 13 weeks, 26 weeks, and one year. You buy so-called T-bills at a discount and get their full face value when the bills come due. The difference between the price you pay and the amount you get back reflects the interest you've earned. To buy individual Treasury bills, you must invest at least $10,000. T-bills can't be called.

Treasury notes mature in two to 10 years. Interest is paid semiannually at a fixed rate and the minimum investment ranges from $1,000 to $5,000, depending on the issue. Treasury notes usually can't be called.

Treasury bonds have the longest maturities—from 10 to 30 years. Like Treasury notes, they pay interest semiannually and usually can't be called. You can buy a Treasury bond for as little as $1,000.

Zero-coupon Treasuries are also known as **strips.** These securities, which cost a minimum of $5,000, are sold by brokers at a deep discount and redeemed at full face value when they mature in six months to 30 years. For instance, you might pay $460 for a $1,000 zero due in 10 years. Zeros pay interest only at maturity; until that point, all the interest your bond accrues is reinvested, letting you earn interest on your interest. Zeros can be especially attractive if you need a fixed amount of money at a certain date, such as the year that you plan to retire.

But zero prices can be highly volatile—25% more volatile than standard bonds—which means you could suffer a sharp loss if you have to redeem early. The reason: These bonds have no coupon, and the smaller a bond's coupon, the more sensitive the bond is to interest rate shifts. The volatility of zeros can work in your favor, too, though. If interest rates fall and you redeem your zeros early, you could profit from a runup in the value of your bonds. For example, if long-term rates fell from 7.5% to 5.5% over two years, your 10-year zero could jump 30% in value. One other drawback with zeros: Even though you don't get their interest until maturity, you have to pay taxes on the interest you've earned each year. There's one exception to this rule. If you keep your zeros in a tax-deferred account such as an IRA or Keogh, you can postpone paying the taxes until the bonds mature.

■ **Corporate bonds.** Interest is fully taxable on these bonds, which are issued by businesses ranging from automakers to utilities. Because their value depends on the creditworthiness of the company offering the bonds, they carry higher yields and higher risks than secure U.S. government issues. Maturities of corporates can range from a few weeks to 100 years, though most have terms of one to 20 years. Unlike Treasuries, these bonds are frequently callable. Most corporate bonds are issued in denominations of $1,000. You can buy zero-coupon corporate bonds, but it's not advisable since the market for those bonds isn't very active. As a result, it's tough to get a fair price when buying corporate zeros.

Top-quality corporate bonds are known as **investment-grade bonds.** Corporate bonds with less than great credit quality are known as **junk bonds,** or **high-yield issues** in polite company. They are rated Ba, BB, or lower for financial soundness by Standard & Poor's or Moody's, the leading bond-rating agencies. Junk bonds typically pay higher yields than other corporate bonds and much higher yields than Treasuries.

■ **Municipal (or muni) bonds.** Munis are issued by state and local governments and agencies, usually for $5,000 and up. Their interest is free from federal taxes. If you live in the state issuing the muni bond, the interest is exempt from federal, state, and possibly local taxes. Munis mature in one to 30 years; they're often callable. You can buy zero-coupon municipal bonds, but as with zero-coupon corporates, these issues don't trade much; so you may not want to buy them unless you're confident that you'll be able to hold the bonds to maturity.

Because munis provide tax savings, they tend to offer lower yields than taxable bonds that are just as creditworthy. To determine whether a muni investment is the better deal, you'll need to compare the yields of munis with taxable bonds on an after-tax basis. You can find out whether munis are right for you once you have two pieces of information. The first is the muni's yield; the second is your tax bracket. Then plug those two numbers into the following simple formula:

$$\text{Tax-equivalent yield} = \frac{\text{muni bond yield}}{(1 - \text{your tax rate})}$$

To see how this works in real life, let's say you're an investor in the 31% tax bracket and you want to compare a muni yielding 6.5% with a Treasury bond yielding 7.8%. You divide the 6.5% muni yield by one minus your 31% tax rate, or .69. The result: a tax-equivalent yield of 9.4%. In this case, since taxable bonds are yielding just 7.8%, the muni would be the better investment.

There are two basic types of munis. So-called **general obligation bonds** (or **GOs**) are issued by states, cities, and counties to finance the building of roads, schools, and sewers and are backed by taxes collected by the issuing government. They have traditionally been considered relatively safe because they are backed by the full faith and credit of the government selling the bond. **Revenue bonds,** on the other hand, are issued by specific institutions, such as an electric utility, a hospital, or a nursing home. These bonds are riskier than general obligation bonds because their payments are secured only by the income of the specific project your money is financing.

Like corporate bonds, municipal issues are rated by Standard & Poor's and Moody's for their credit quality. The highest-quality munis are backed by a bond insurance company, which guarantees the payment of interest and principal regardless of the issuer's health. But you'll pay for the protection: insured bonds and insured bond funds can yield 0.10 to 0.50 percentage points less than comparable bonds that don't carry this protection. However, insurance won't protect you against interest rate risk or the chance that panic selling will drive down your bonds' market value.

Another option for municipal investors looking for maximum safety and high yields is to buy **pre-refunded bonds** backed by U.S. Treasuries. Here, the interest and principal you get is assured because marketable securities, usually Treasury bonds, have been set aside in a special escrow account to meet these payments.

■ **Mortgage-backed bonds.** These bonds—whose minimum investment is usually $25,000—represent an ownership stake in a package of mortgage loans issued or guaranteed by government agencies such as the Government National Mortgage Association (GNMA, sometimes called Ginnie Mae), the Federal Home Loan Mortgage Corporation (Freddie Mac) and the Federal National Mortgage Association (Fannie Mae). The interest on these bonds is not exempt from taxation, and with the exception of Ginnie Maes, these bonds are not backed by the full faith and credit of the U.S. government. They mature in as long as 20 years and are not callable by issuers.

Interest rate shifts are a special concern for investors in mortgage-backed securities. If rates fall, for instance, homeowners may decide to refinance their mortgages, prepay their existing loans, and then take out new mortgages at a lower interest rate. In that case, you the mortgage-backed security owner will have to reinvest your money at a lower interest rate, leaving you with a lower return than you expected. As a result, mortgage-backed bonds don't get as much of a boost from falling rates as other types of issues; in some cases they lose value.

■ **Foreign bonds.** Issued by governments outside the United States to meet their financing needs, these bonds are offered at varying minimums, often $25,000. Because foreign interest rates don't move in lockstep with U.S. rates, the bonds can provide diversification to your portfolio. Foreign bonds subject you to currency risk, however. A small increase or decline in the value of the currency behind the bond could boost or slice the value of your investment. Say you buy a French bond yielding 8%. If the value of the dollar slides 5% against the French franc, you'll be left with just a 3% return. If the dollar strengthens by 5%, though, your total return could jump to 13%.

Understanding Credit Risk

When you buy a bond, the issuer promises that it will repay you both the interest and principal you are due. But can you be sure the issuer will make good on that promise? The answer lies largely in the bond's **credit risk**—the chance that financial troubles will make the borrower late in its payments or unable to meet the payments at all. The level of credit risk you face depends on the type of bond you buy and the issuer's financial health. Bonds, bills, and notes issued by the U.S. government are considered to have no credit risk, since they are backed

by the full faith and credit of the U.S. Treasury. Junk bonds have the highest credit risk.

It's easy to get a feel for the creditworthiness of a particular corporate or municipal bond, since rating agencies such as Standard & Poor's and Moody's evaluate most companies and about 75% of municipalities. Bonds from the strongest issuers carry the rating of Aaa or AAA. The next step down the credit ladder is Aa or AA and then A; all are high-quality bonds. Issues rated below investment grade, Ba or BB or lower, are considered to be speculative investments. The lowest bond rating for a bond that's not in default is C. A slight difference in a bond rating can be quite meaningful. According to Moody's, B-rated bonds are nearly five times more likely to miss making a payment in their first year than slightly better-rated Ba bonds.

There are several reasons why a bond might not be rated. The issuer might decide the underwriting is too small. Or the issuer could view getting a rating as too costly or time-consuming. Alternatively, the issuer might just figure that the rating it will get will be low so it would rather not have one.

Investors generally get rewarded for taking additional credit risk. As a rule, the lower the credit rating, the more the bond yields, since you're increasing the chance that the issuer won't be able to make good on its payments. So, for instance, a 10-

year bond rated C might yield one percentage point more than another rated AAA.

You can find out a bond's rating by checking with your library or broker. In addition, the ratings services maintain phone numbers you can call for ratings information. At Moody's it is 212-553-0377. At Standard & Poor's, it's 212-208-1527. There's no cost for the service except your long-distance charge. You can also contact S&P at its Web site (www.ratings.com).

Keep in mind, however, that a high credit rating when you buy the bond isn't a guarantee that you'll never face any credit risk. For one thing, a bond's credit rating can drop if the issuer's financial health declines. Some money managers also say that rating agencies tend to be backward looking and do a poor job of anticipating potential problems. In 1994, for instance, rating agencies were suddenly forced to downgrade bonds issued by dozens of municipalities in Orange County, Calif., after the county investment pool that held much of their money suffered big losses and was forced to file bankruptcy. One comforting fact: Bond price drops that generally follow ratings downgrades aren't as sharp as those from rises in interest rates, unless there's a real chance that a bond will default.

Keep in mind, too, that defaults generally aren't all that common. Historically, fewer than 1% of munis have ever defaulted, while the default rate for corporate bonds ranges from 1.4% for AAA-rated bonds up to 5.7% for those rated BBB, the lowest grade that is still considered investment quality. Bond defaults were at their peak in 1991 when the economy was weak and many companies took on more debt than they could handle. In other words, they were overleveraged.

Understanding Liquidity Risk

Even if you own a high-quality bond, you can lose money if you want to sell that bond and no one wants to buy it at the price you think is reasonable. **Liquidity risk** is the chance that you or your bond fund won't be able to unload a bond quickly without a stiff penalty. You don't need to worry about liquidity if you buy an individual bond and plan to hold it until maturity, but you should be aware of this risk if you think you might need to draw on your bonds to meet a sudden expense. Liquidity risk is also a concern for bond fund investors, since fund managers regularly add and subtract bonds from their portfolios and may have to dump issues to raise cash if a flood of investors redeem their fund shares and want their money.

The amount of liquidity risk you'll face depends on the type of bond or bond fund you are buying. U.S. Treasury issues are highly liquid. Their pristine credit quality means there's always a ready market for them if you want to sell. By contrast, the markets for bonds sold by municipalities and financially distressed companies can be highly illiquid since many of these issues trade rarely, if at all.

Illiquid markets have punished bond investors several times in the past decade. For instance, in April 1987, when interest rates jumped 1.5 percentage points at the same time many bond fund holders were redeeming shares to raise cash to pay their taxes, investors pulled more than $3 billion out of municipal bond funds. Fund managers were forced to sell bonds to meet redemptions. With few buyers in the market, muni share prices dropped 5% in just five days. Similarly, investors rushed to the exits in 1990 when the junk bond market hit the skids. Shareholders yanked $3.2 billion out of junk bond funds, helping hand junk funds an average loss of 9.7% for the year.

Understanding Derivatives

You've probably heard a fair amount about **derivatives** by now but likely have little understanding about what they are or how they work. Don't worry; you're in good company. Even the sharpies who create and trade in derivatives don't fully understand the securities. Simply put, derivatives are complex financial instruments whose value is based on or derived from another financial product or benchmark, such as long-term interest rates or a commodity price index. Bond fund managers embraced these products in the early 1990s as a way to juice their investment returns. But their efforts often backfired, socking investors with big losses.

Not all derivatives are bad, however. For instance, a mutual fund that invests in foreign bonds might use currency futures—basically a contract to buy a single currency or basket of currencies at a future date—to protect itself against currency fluctuations. That type of strategy can protect bond fund investors against losses due to big currency swings.

But derivatives can also be used for speculation. When these gambles backfire—and they often do—investors can get socked with whopping losses. High-risk derivatives include such arcane securities as **inverse floaters** (financial instruments that increase in value as interest rates decline); **structured notes** (customized bets designed to meet a fund's particular investment objectives); and **collateralized mortgage obligations,** or **CMOs** (created by slicing up pools of government-backed mortgage obligations).

Some of the worst derivative disasters have occurred when bond fund managers used mortgage-based derivatives, which carry names such as **principal-only strips, interest-only strips,** and **inverse floaters,** to bet on falling interest rates. For instance, in the first 10 months of 1994, the Piper Jaffray Institutional Government Income fund posted a stunning 28% loss because of mistaken bets on derivatives created out of pools of mortgages. When interest rates rose, those derivatives fell sharply in value, socking investors with stunning losses. A year earlier, similar bets had helped the Piper Jaffray mutual fund post a 15.6% return, an unusually high gain for a seemingly low-risk short-term government fund.

Reading the Bond Tables

If there's anything harder to read in the newspaper than the stock tables, it must be the bond tables. So here's a plain-English bond Baedeker to the below sample listings for bonds and notes:

The first column (Bonds) tells you first the name of the issuer, in this case IBM; then the bond's coupon rate (ranging here from 6⅜% to 8⅜%); and then the last two digits of the year the bond matures and the principal is paid off (00 means the year 2000). The interest rate is a percentage of the bond's par value, typically $1,000. In other words, the an-

CORPORATE BONDS

BONDS	CUR YLD	VOL	CLOSE	NET CHG.
IBM 8⅜19	8.1	8	102⅞	−¼
IBM 6.4507	6.4	10	100⅜	+¾
IBM 7¼02	7.4	612	98⅝	−⅛
IBM 6⅜00	6.7	133	95⅞	——
IBM 7½13	7.9	234	95	+⅛

nual interest payment on the IBM 7¼02 bond is $72.50 ($70 for the 7% and $2.50 for the ¼). If you see the letters **zr,** that means the bond is a zero-coupon issue; an **s** means nothing more than a space between the rate and the term of the bond; a **vi** means the issuer is in bankruptcy, in receivership, or being reorganized.

The second column (Cur Yld) tells you what interest rate you would earn if you bought the bond today at its current price. When the price is less than par, the yield is higher than the coupon rate, but when the price is above par, the yield is lower than the rate. Here, the first IBM bond has a price above par (102⅞), which is why its current yield is less than the coupon rate. All the other IBM bonds here are trading below par, so their yields exceed their rates.

The third column (Vol) is shorthand for the dollar value of the bonds traded in the previous day, shown in thousands of dollars. You'll see that the IBM 7¼02 had the highest volume, with $612,000 traded. The IBM 8⅜19 had a thin volume of $8,000, most likely because so few people want to lock in an interest rate for roughly 24 years.

The fourth column (Close) shows you the price the bond sold for at the end of the previous business day, in $100 units. This price reveals whether the bond is trading at, above, or below par. You can calculate the value of the bond by multiplying this figure by 10.

The fifth column (Net Chg.) is the bond's gain or loss in the previous trading day. For example, the first IBM bond, which lost ¼, fell in value by $2.50. While the price of this bond was falling, its yield was rising.

The first column (Rate) in the government bonds table is the coupon rate on the U.S. Treasury bond or note. Put another way, it's the percentage of par value that will be paid out as annual interest.

The second column (Maturity Mo/Yr) shows you the month and the last two digits of the year the bond or note matures. An **n** means it's a Treasury note, not a bond.

GOVT. BONDS & NOTES

RATE	MATURITY MO/YR	BID	ASKED	CHG.	ASK YLD.
4¾	Sep98n	99:08	99:10	+2	5.64
9¼	Feb16	118:02	118:04	+1	7.52

The third and fourth columns (Bid and **Asked)** show you the latest market price for the issue. Treasuries are traded over-the-counter, so there are no closing prices per se for them. The bid is the highest price being offered by buyers, and the asked is the lowest price sellers are asking. The difference between the two prices is known as the **spread.** Here, the figures after the colon represent a fraction of a thirty-second of a percentage point. So, 99:10 means 99¹⁰⁄₃₂.

The fifth column (Chg.) is the difference between the bid price and the bid price of the previous trading day. Here, the September 1998 Treasury note gained 2%, while the February 2016 bond gained 1%.

The sixth column (Ask Yld.) tells you the bond's yield to maturity. That's a combination of the bond's current yield and the difference between its current price and its value at redemption when the bond matures. You'll see that in these examples the yield to maturity is higher than the coupon rate for the Treasury note, because this issue is selling at a discount. But the yield to maturity is lower than the coupon rate for the Treasury bond since the bond is selling at a premium.

How to Buy Individual Bonds

Buying individual bonds can make sense if you plan to hold them to maturity and have enough bucks. As a buy-and-hold investor, you won't have to worry about how swings in interest rates will impact the value of your bonds. Buying individual bonds is especially smart if you want to own supersafe Treasuries, which you can purchase from the federal government at no commission through its Treasury Direct program. (The addresses of the Federal Reserve Bank branches that participate in the Treasury Direct program appear in the list on page 393.)

Keep in mind, however, that with the exception of the Treasury Direct program, buying bonds isn't as simple as investing in stocks. Say you want to own 100 shares of General Motors. You can call any broker who can tell you what GM shares last sold for and then buy the stock at the current price. The availability of bonds varies from firm to firm, however. Say you want to pick up a $1,000 bond issued by Chrysler. If your broker's firm doesn't have the bond in its inventory, it will have to go to other dealers to find it.

The price you pay for the bond can also vary. That's because there is no fixed commission schedule for bonds. Instead, the **markup** you'll be charged is set by the dealer. Because dealers typically build their markups into the price of the bond, you won't know how much the firm paid for the bond or how much extra it's charging you unless you ask. Markups typically run between ½% and 2½%, or $5 to $25 on a $1,000 bond. The amount you pay will vary with a number of factors, including the size of your order and the type of issue you're after. On individual muni bonds, commission costs can run as high as 4%.

It's not easy to get price information for particular bonds. Many bonds trade infrequently, if at all, and newspapers provide prices on only a few corporate and municipal issues. In fact, it's often difficult to find the prices of *any* municipal bonds in the paper. Under pressure from the Securities and Exchange Commission, however, the municipal bond industry is trying to provide more price information to small investors. Among the first steps: a table of muni bond yields to be printed in newspapers and other publications and a pilot project that would let investors, for a small fee, check prices on bonds they own or would like to purchase (call Kenny S&P Information & Evaluation Services at 800-266-3463).

Even evaluating the quality of individual bonds on your own can be tricky, especially if you're investing in municipal issues. Municipalities must issue annual financial statements and make public any "material" changes in their financial condition. But issuers don't have to disclose this information directly to individual investors. Instead, the reports are sent to databanks that can be tapped by bond dealers and institutional investors. Getting this information is costly, so ask your broker to retrieve it for you.

Pay attention to two numbers when buying individual bonds: the **bid** (the price a seller would get) and the **ask** (the price a buyer would pay, which is always higher). The difference between these two is the **spread;** it represents the commission on the trade and sometimes extra profits for the brokerage firm.

Because prices vary from dealer to dealer, it pays to shop around for the best bond deals. Call two or three brokers for price quotes by asking each for the spread between the bid and the ask and what you would be paid if you had to sell the bond tomorrow. If you're investing in munis, buy them at the time they are issued. In that case, every buyer pays the same price and the commission is paid by the issuer. Another tip: Work only with a firm that specializes in bonds or a broker with particular expertise selling fixed-income securities to individual investors.

Remember to ask your broker if your bond is protected against a call or find out by reading the bond's **prospectus, or offering document.** If your bond can be called, check the call provision to learn the earliest date this could happen. This way you'll avoid an unpleasant surprise—learning that your bond has been called in years before maturity and forcing you to reinvest the proceeds at the current, lower interest rates. Bonds most likely to be called are ones bought at a premium. Investors whose premium bonds are called can take a real hit, since their bonds are redeemed at face value.

Buying Treasuries Direct

The cheapest and easiest way to invest in bonds is to buy Treasury bills, notes, and bonds directly from the federal government through the Treasury Direct program. You need only $1,000 to invest. Buying your treasuries through this program has three benefits. First, you'll eliminate commission costs, which can otherwise run as high as $50 per bond. Second, you'll earn the same interest rates as institutional investors. And third, interest payments will be direct-deposited into your bank account.

Investors who want to participate in the Treasury Direct program must open up a government account. To do this, you'll need to get a **tender,** or bid form,

from one of the 37 Treasury Direct offices across the country or at the Web site (www.publicdebt.treas.gov). Filling out the one-page form is easy. You'll be asked whether you want to submit a **competitive** or **noncompetitive tender.** Check the box marked "Noncompetitive." That way you'll get the weighted average rate set at the Treasury auction. Otherwise you have to specify the interest rate you'll accept. If you choose a rate that's too high, your bid may not be accepted, and if you pick a rate that ends up being lower than the weighted average rate, you'll get your rate and lose out on potential income. When you fill out the form, tell the government where you want your interest deposited. Then your interest payments will be automatically credited to your account, as will the principal when the bond comes due. There's only one catch: If you decide to sell your Treasuries before they mature, you will have to use a broker.

THE TREASURY DIRECT OFFICES

The addresses below for the Treasury Direct program are mailing addresses. Where two phone numbers are listed, the second is a recording. FRB stands for Federal Reserve Bank.

City/Phone	Address
Atlanta 404-521-8653 404-521-8657	FRB of Atlanta 104 Marietta St. N.W. Atlanta Ga. 30303
Baltimore 410-576-3553 410-576-3500	Baltimore Branch FRB of Richmond P.O. Box 1378 Baltimore, Md. 21203
Birmingham 205-731-8708 205-731-8702	Birmingham Branch FRB of Atlanta P.O. Box 10447 Birmingham, Ala. 35283
Boston 617-973-3810 617-973-3805	FRB Boston P.O. Box 2076 Boston, Mass. 02106
Buffalo 716-849-5079 716-849-5158	FRB of New York P.O. Box 961 Buffalo, N.Y. 14240
Charlotte 704-358-2410 704-358-2424	Charlotte Branch FRB of Richmond P.O. Box 30284 Charlotte, N.C. 28230
Chicago 312-322-5369 312-786-1110	FRB of Chicago P.O. Box 834 Chicago, Ill. 60690
Cincinnati 513-721-4787 (ext. 334)	Cincinnati Branch FRB of Cleveland P.O. Box 999 Cincinnati, Ohio 45201
Cleveland 216-579-2490 216-688-0068	FRB of Cleveland P.O. Box 6387 Cleveland, Ohio 44101

City/Phone	Address
Dallas 214-651-6362 214-651-6177	FRB of Dallas Securities Dept. Station K Dallas, Tex. 75222
Denver 303-572-2470 303-572-2475	Denver Branch FRB of Kansas City P.O. Box 5228 Terminal Annex Denver, Colo. 80217
Detroit 313-964-6157 313-963-4936	Detroit Branch FRB of Chicago P.O. Box 1059 Detroit, Mich. 48231
El Paso 915-544-4730	El Paso Branch FRB of Dallas P.O. Box 100 El Paso, Tex. 79901
Houston 713-659-4433 713-652-1688	Houston Branch FRB of Dallas P.O. Box 2578 Houston, Tex. 77252
Jacksonville 904-632-1179 904-632-1178	Jacksonville Branch FRB of Atlanta P.O. Box 2499 Jacksonville, Fla. 32231
Kansas City 816-881-2783 816-881-2767	FRB of Kansas City Attn. Securities Dept. P.O. Box 419440 Kansas City, Mo. 64141
Little Rock 501-324-8272	Little Rock Branch FRB of St. Louis P.O. Box 1261 Little Rock, Ark. 72203

Los Angeles 213-624-7398 213-688-0068	Los Angeles Branch FRB of San Francisco P.O. Box 2077 Terminal Annex Los Angeles, Calif. 90051	**Oklahoma City** 405-270-8652 405-270-8660	Oklahoma City Branch FRB of Kansas City P.O. Box 25129 Oklahoma City, Okla. 73125
Louisville 502-568-9236 502-568-9240	Louisville Branch FRB of St. Louis P.O. Box 32710 Louisville, Ky. 40232	**Omaha** 402-221-5636 402-221-5638	Omaha Branch FRB of Kansas City P.O. Box 3958 Omaha, Neb. 68102
Memphis 901-523-7171 ext. 622/629 (ext. 641)	Memphis Branch FRB of St. Louis P.O. Box 407 Memphis, Tenn. 38101	**Philadelphia** 215-574-6675 215-574-6580	FRB of Philadelphia P.O. Box 90 Philadelphia, Pa. 19105
Miami 305-471-6497 305-471-6257	Miami Branch FRB of Atlanta P.O. Box 520847 Miami, Fla. 33152	**Pittsburgh** 412-261-7863 412-261-7988	Pittsburgh Branch FRB of Cleveland P.O. Box 867 Pittsburgh, Pa. 15230
Minneapolis 612-340-2075 612-340-2051	FRB of Minneapolis P.O. Box 491 Minneapolis, Minn. 55480	**Portland** 503-221-5932 503-221-5931	Portland Branch FRB of San Francisco P.O. Box 3436 Portland, Oreg. 97208
Nashville 615-251-7100 615-251-7236	Nashville Branch FRB of Atlanta 301 Eighth Ave. N. Nashville, Tenn. 37203	**Richmond** 804-697-8372 804-697-8355	FRB of Richmond P.O. Box 27622 Richmond, Va. 23261
New Orleans 504-593-3200 504-593-3290	New Orleans Branch FRB of Atlanta P.O. Box 61630 New Orleans, La. 70161	**Salt Lake City** 801-322-7944 801-322-7844	Salt Lake City Branch FRB of San Francisco P.O. Box 30780 Salt Lake City, Utah 84130
New York City 212-720-6619 212-720-7773	FRB of New York Federal Reserve P.O. Station New York, N.Y. 10045	**San Antonio** 512-978-1305 512-978-1330	San Antonio Branch FRB of Dallas P.O. Box 1471 San Antonio, Tex. 78295

San Francisco 415-974-2330 415-974-3491	FRB of San Francisco P.O. Box 7702 San Francisco, Calif. 94120
Seattle 206-343-3605 206-343-3615	Seattle Branch FRB of San Francisco P.O. Box 3567 Terminal Annex Seattle, Wash. 98124
St. Louis 314-444-8665 314-444-8602	FRB of St. Louis P.O. Box 442 St. Louis, Mo. 63166
U.S. Treasury 202-874-4000	Bureau of Public Debt Department N Washington, D.C. 20239

Buying Bonds through Mutual Funds

Most small investors buy their bonds through bond funds. The most important reason is diversification. On your own, you might be able to purchase a single bond or a handful of issues. But as a bond fund holder, you'll own a stake in dozens, or even hundreds, of bonds. That gives you greater protection against interest rate fluctuations and the changing financial health of any single issuer. You may also benefit from the expertise of a professional money manager who can anticipate and quickly respond to changes in the economy or in the financial health of bond issuers.

There are other advantages to buying bond funds rather than individual bonds. Funds pay dividends monthly, while individual bonds pay interest only semiannually. That makes funds a better deal if you need a steady stream of income. If you're planning to reinvest your earnings, you'll wind up ahead with a fund because your interest payments are reinvested more quickly, letting you earn interest on interest at a more rapid pace. Bond funds offer instant liquidity, too: you can get your money out any time you want, sometimes by writing a check. You can also add to your bond fund stake at any time.

The main drawback of bond funds is that they don't have a fixed life. Fund managers are constantly adding and subtracting bonds from their portfolios. So there's no such thing as holding to maturity with a bond fund. As a result, you can't count on getting a fixed interest rate or a preset price when you need your money. Instead you'll be paid the current share price of the fund, which is known as its **net asset value,** or **NAV.** A bond mutual fund's NAV varies from day to day, based on market conditions. Consequently, depending on when you decide to dump your find, you may be blessed with a capital gain (if rates have fallen since you invested) or saddled with a loss (if rates have risen).

Like individual bonds, funds fall into a

wide range of categories. These groupings can give you some insight into a fund's strategy and investment objectives; a comparison of their recent returns appears in the table on page 398. But a bond fund's name doesn't always give you a clear picture of its risk level or holdings. Government bond funds, for instance, may hold mostly low-risk U.S. Treasury securities or be loaded with GNMAs, mortgage-backed bonds that are more vulnerable to interest rate shifts. The use of derivatives also has turned some seemingly low-risk bond funds into roaring tigers. Still, the following broad categories will get you started understanding your bond fund options.

■ **Government bond funds** invest in securities issued by the U.S. Treasury and federal agencies. This group includes **short-term U.S. government bond funds,** which have an average maturity of two to five years, **intermediate U.S. government bond funds,** which have an average maturity of five to 10 years, and **long-term U.S. government bond funds,** with an average maturity of 10 years or more. While government bond funds can hold mostly Treasuries or GNMAs, **Treasury bond funds** typically invest at least 80% of their assets in securities issued by the U.S. Treasury; they can keep the rest in bonds from, say, other government agencies. Longer-term bond funds normally offer higher yields than funds that hold intermediate- or short-term securities.

But your total return isn't always higher if you hold a long-term fund. That's because long-term government bond funds are particularly vulnerable to jumps in interest rates. Short-term U.S. Treasury funds are the safest bond funds you can buy and the least volatile in price.

■ **Municipal bond funds** invest in tax-exempt securities. If you're thinking about buying a muni fund, you'll want first to calculate its tax-equivalent yield to see whether you'll earn more with a tax-exempt muni fund or a taxable fund. General muni funds invest in a diversified mix of municipals issued by various states and are exempt from federal taxation. **Single-state funds** buy issues just within a particular state, letting residents earn interest free from federal, state, and sometimes local taxes. However, these funds are less diversified than general muni funds, which makes them especially vulnerable to a natural disaster or a downturn in the state's or region's economy. What's more, single-state funds may need to buy bonds that are less creditworthy than the ones purchased by general municipal bond funds, since the supply of issues they can choose from can be quite limited. As with other government bond funds, there are short-term, intermediate-term, and long-term muni bond funds. (Some companies also sell limited-term muni funds, a close cousin to intermediate-term funds.) Muni bond funds come sliced one other way: by credit quality. You can buy a fund that invests primarily in investment-grade bonds or a high-yield muni fund that buys lower-quality, often junk, muni bonds. The high-yield muni fund may yield more, but it can take you on more of a roller-coaster ride.

You can reduce your risks investing in muni funds by sticking to highly diversified funds that own bonds with maturities of less than 10 years and funds whose cash reserves equal at least 5% of assets. Information about a fund's bond maturities, cash reserves, and credit quality appears in the prospectus. Because cash holdings don't pay as much income as bonds, however, a fund with a cash reserve of 5% or more will yield a few tenths of a percentage point less than one with less cash.

Another way some investors try to reduce their risks with municipal bond funds is by purchasing so-called **insured muni funds.** These are funds whose bonds have private insurance, protecting investors against the possibility of default. Don't bother with such funds, however. The insurance will clip your yield a bit, and you can protect yourself against default just as well by buying a diversified fund that invests in top-grade muni bonds.

■ **Corporate bond funds** invest in securities of corporate issuers, which makes them slightly riskier than government bond funds. **Junk bond funds** or **high-yield funds** are corporate bond funds that invest primarily in the issues of financially troubled companies. Given the high risks of owning individual junk issues, buying a fund is the best way to invest in this sector. The safest junk funds

will have at least 50% of their assets in the highest-quality tier of junk bonds: those rated BB or B. Safer junk funds also hold plenty of actively traded bonds, typically securities issued by companies whose names are easy to recognize. In addition, the best junk funds are well diversified, holding 100 or more securities.

■ **GNMA funds** typically invest at least 80% of their assets in GNMAs and other mortgage-backed securities. They yield more than Treasury funds, and since GNMAs are backed by the full faith and credit of the U.S. government, you don't have to worry much about credit risk. But these funds aren't as risk-free as many investors would expect. Because GNMAs are highly sensitive to changing interest rates, you could lose money if you need to get your cash out after interest rates have risen.

■ **Foreign bond or world-income funds** invest primarily in bonds issued by foreign governments. **Global bond funds** invest in bonds issued both in the United States and abroad. **International bond funds** hold only foreign securities. **Short-term world income** funds stick to bonds with maturities of one to three years, while most other foreign bond funds have average maturities of five to 10 years.

If you want the diversification that comes from investing abroad, foreign bond funds are a better bet than individual issues. Remember, though, that these funds not only carry interest rate risk and credit risk, they are vulnerable to currency risk. Jittery exchange rates can cause gains of as much as 10% in a single month, although the ups and downs tend to even out within about eight years.

Many managers of foreign bond funds try to protect themselves against currency shifts by buying futures and options, a practice known as hedging. Currency hedging is no panacea, though. It can cost 2.5% to 5% of the value of the assets being protected. And even seemingly

foolproof hedges can sometimes backfire, socking investors with unexpected losses.

HOW BOND FUNDS COMPARE

Listed below are the six broad bond fund categories, in order from safest to riskiest. All made money in 1997, and four earned more for investors in 1997 than over the past five years on an annual basis. The top performing group over five years: high-yield corporate or junk bond funds.

BOND FUND TYPE TYPICAL INVESTMENT	RISK LEVEL	% GAIN TO JANUARY 1, 1998	
		12 MONTHS	FIVE YEARS
Investment-grade corporate bonds of firms with high credit ratings	Low	8.6%	6.8%
Mortgage-backed securities Ginnie Maes and other issues backed by mortgages	Low	8.1%	5.9%
U.S. government issues of U.S. Treasury or other federal agencies	Low	8.0%	8.9%
High-yield corporate bonds of firms with low credit ratings; emphasis on maximum yield	Medium	12.8%	11.3%
Tax-exempt bonds issues from municipalities; income is free from federal and sometimes state taxes	Medium	9.3%	6.7%
World income Non–U.S. dollar bonds, other high foreign fixed-income issues	Medium to high	3.7%	6.7%

Notes: Annualized. **Source:** Lipper Analytical Services

What to Know Before Buying a Bond Fund

You can take two different routes if you want to invest in a bond fund. The first is to buy your fund from a broker or financial planner who earns a commission for selling you the fund. The second is to purchase the fund directly from the fund company or through a financial planner who collects a flat fee for his services. As with stock funds sold this way, these bond funds are called **no-loads.**

Before you buy any bond fund, assess your investment needs and determine how much risk you are willing to accept. If you're a conservative investor with a low tolerance for risk and a short time frame, go for a short-term bond fund. Investors looking for a steady stream of retirement income, on the other hand, might consider an intermediate fund. And if you're willing to take on more risk in exchange for a higher yield, you might put as much as 5% to 10% of your portfolio in junk bond funds.

Be wary of bond funds without at least a three-year track record behind them. Mutual fund companies are notorious for creating new and untested products that promise bond investors high yields with little risk but then produce unexpected losses. One big disappointment has been so-called **government-plus bond funds,** which were heavily peddled in the late 1980s. The funds promised above average yields on their Treasury bond portfolios by writing **call options,** basically contracts that give others the right to buy the bonds the funds held at a set price by a fixed date. But the income from the options didn't prove to be enough to offset severe drops in bond prices. These funds also suffered when lower interest rates sent bond prices skyward. The bonds they held were called and had to be replaced with lower-yielding issues.

Another disappointment: **short-term world income funds** that invest in government and high-quality corporate securities with maturities of up to three years. These funds were pushed as a slightly riskier alternative to money-market funds. Trouble was, their fund managers were unable to protect investors against short-term currency swings. In the third quarter of 1992, for instance, the average short-term world income fund lost 3.17%, according to Morningstar.

Selecting a bond fund wisely requires doing a bit of research into the fund's investment style and performance. You can learn a lot about a bond fund and compare it with others by leafing through its **prospectus** and **annual financial report.** Among other things, the prospectus will tell you what the fund's expenses are and how much you'll pay in fees on a $1,000 investment if you hold the fund for one, three, five, and 10 years. The prospectus also provides historical returns, including how much of those returns came from interest income and how much from price changes. If you have additional questions, you can call your broker or your fund company's toll-free 800 number, listed in the fund's prospectus.

Some secondary research sources can help, too. Publications such as **MONEY,** the *Wall Street Journal, Business Week, Forbes,* and *Barron's* run periodic listings of bond fund performance. (For tips on how to read mutual fund tables, see Chapter 14.) The Morningstar and Value Line advisory services also publish excellent data on bond funds. You can probably find their written reports in your public library. Morningstar also sells excellent software that can help you screen bond funds for ones that suit your interest ($95 a year with quarterly updates; 800-735-0700). In addition, the major on-line computer networks provide a great deal of useful bond fund data.

To assist you in sorting through the world of bond funds, here are key factors to assess:

■ **Expenses.** If you buy a bond fund through a broker, you'll pay a **sales load** to cover the cost of his services. Loads come in three basic forms. A **front-end load,** which can run as high as 5¾% of your initial investment, is deducted from

the value of your account at the time you make a purchase. A **back-end load** is collected only if you sell your fund before a preset period of time. This type of charge typically starts at 5% if you sell your fund the year you bought it and then declines by 1% annually, vanishing after year five. Some bond funds charge a **level load,** which is a fixed charge of up to 1% a year. Whether or not your fund levies a sales charge, you'll pay an annual fee to the sponsor for investment management, record keeping, and other services.

When you divide a fund's costs by its total assets, you get a key figure: its **expense ratio.** This is the measure of how much you'll pay each year in fees. Expense ratios for taxable government and corporate bond funds average 1.01%, or $101 a year on a $10,000 investment, according to Morningstar. Investors who buy tax-exempt municipal bond funds pay a little less, about 0.85%, while harder-to-manage international bond funds charge an average of 1.63%.

It's especially important to compare expenses among bond funds. That's because bond funds with similar investment strategies tend to hold similar types of securities. So, apart from taking on more or less risk, the one thing a fund manager can do to stand out from the pack is to keep expenses low. High expenses can also take an enormous bite out of your returns if you're not careful. Say intermediate-term bonds are yielding 7%. If your bond fund charges 0.75% in expenses, it will yield 6.25%, or a full 11% less than the market yield. Be extremely cautious if you find a bond fund yielding one percentage point or more than another fund holding similar bonds if low expenses don't explain the difference.

■ **Yield.** As a bond fund investor, you're likely to come across two types of yield calculations. When bond funds advertise, they must use a figure known as the **SEC yield,** which measures the fund's yield as calculated according to a standard formula mandated by the federal Securities and Exchange Commission. This number is based on the fund's income for the preceding 30 days. It tells you how much you would earn if you stayed in the bond fund for a year and the fund kept paying out interest at its recent rate. It's the best figure to use when comparing bond funds head-to-head.

If you look at newspapers, magazines, and other publications that track mutual funds, you're likely to come across the fund's **12-month average yield.** This figure will tell you what the fund actually paid out to shareholders over the preceding 12 months. While it's no guarantee of future performance, the 12-month average yield is the best proxy for how much income you would have earned over the past year.

Keep in mind that the highest-yielding fund, even within a fund category, may not be the best investment for you. That's because bond funds can boost their yields in only two ways: by lowering fund expenses or by taking on additional risks. Some top-yielding funds later turned out to be disasters for investors. One clue that your bond fund is taking big gambles; its yield is at least one percentage point higher than the average fund in its category and the difference can't be explained by lower operating costs.

■ **Total return.** Bond fund investors are often tempted to pick a fund based wholly on its yield. But yield is only part of the story, of course, since it doesn't reflect capital gains or losses. To find out a bond fund's true return, take a look at its **total return.** This measure combines the income paid out with any changes in the value of the fund's shares. Simply put, total return tells you whether you made or lost money in a fund. Bond fund investors saw this clearly in 1994. Although their funds paid decent yields of 5% to 8% or so, they lost money for investors overall because interest rate hikes produced bond fund price declines. A year earlier, when rates were falling, bond fund investors profited royally, since the price gains added to their returns.

Paying attention to total return also helps you avoid funds that pay high yields at a long-term cost to investors. For instance, many bond funds boost yields by buying **premium bonds**—ones issued when interest rates were high and now trade above their face value. The prices of these bonds decline as they get closer to maturity, however, causing the fund's net asset value to fall. In other words, shareholders get handed a little extra cash in one pocket but wind up paying more out of the other pocket.

In evaluating a fund's total return, don't look just at the preceding three or six months. Instead see how the fund's return has varied over the last one, three, and five years. You can find these figures in publications that track bond fund performance. These numbers will give you an idea of how the fund has weathered the ups and downs of the bond market.

■ **Average maturity.** Because bond funds own a pool of bonds, they have no single maturity. Instead they have what's known as a weighted average maturity, a measure of the maturity of all the bonds a fund currently owns. A fund's weighted average maturity (which you can find in a Morningstar report) will give you some idea of how sensitive it is to shifts in interest rates. The higher the average maturity, the riskier a fund is. That's because it's likely to experience bigger swings when interest rates rise or fall.

■ **Duration.** The **duration** of a bond fund is another, somewhat more precise, indication of how sensitive it is to changes in interest rates. The formula for calculating duration is complicated, but

the basic point is this: The sooner your investment is paid back, the less it will be hurt by changes in interest rates. Don't get put off by the complex mathematics— you can generally get a bond fund's duration from the fund company or a rating service such as Morningstar. Instead pay attention to what duration can tell you about your fund. For starters, duration lets you measure how your bond fund will react to a change in interest rates of one percentage point or less. Take two bond funds, one with a duration of four years and one with a duration of 10 years. Assume that interest rates rise by 1%. In that case, the share price of the fund with the four-year duration will fall by 4%, but the price of the 10-year duration fund will drop by a full 10%.

Duration is an extremely useful yardstick for comparing different funds. A bond fund with a duration of six years, for instance, is twice as volatile as a fund whose duration is three years. If you think interest rates will rise, you'll be best off with a short-duration fund. Because a fund's duration can't be longer than its average maturity, duration can also give you a clue as to whether your fund is taking above average risks. A short-term fund with a duration of six years, for instance, might be boosting its yield through the use of higher-risk securities.

■ **Derivatives.** The use of derivatives can turn a seemingly safe fund into a time bomb. To play it safe, avoid funds that hold more than 5% of their portfolio in complex derivatives. Most bond funds pared back their derivative holdings after 1994's big losses. Still, to make sure you are not exposed to undue risk, avoid funds that have 5% or more of their assets exposed to structured notes, inverse floaters, interest-only strips and principal-only strips, and other exotic derivatives.

Buying Closed-End Bond Funds

Most bond funds are what's known as **open-end.** They have an unlimited number of shares. If new investors come along, the open-end fund manager just takes their money and buys more bonds. If the manager decides he or she doesn't want any more money, the fund is closed to new investors. Another type of bond fund, however, is known as a **closed-end.** This type of fund is, in many ways, more like a stock than a mutual fund. That's because like a stock, a closed-end fund has a finite number of shares and trades on an exchange. You pay a brokerage commission to get in or out of a closed-end fund. Unlike a stock or an individual bond, however, a closed-end bond fund gives you diversification because it contains a basket of bonds. Two common types of closed-end bond funds are **closed-end municipal bond funds** and **closed-end foreign bond funds.**

Closed-end funds can trade at discounts or premiums to their net asset value. In fact, most trade at discounts. That can be a bargain for an investor, since you're buying bonds for less than the market value of their assets. If you invest in a fund with a discount and bond prices rise, that lifts the net asset value of the fund, which tends to close the discount. The combination of a higher net asset value, smaller discount, and yield can produce a terrific total return. New closed-end bond funds often start out trading at premiums to their net asset value and then wind up selling at discounts. That's why it is wise to avoid buying new closed-end bond fund issues—even if they're pushed heavily by your broker—and waiting until the shares trade at a discount. The *Wall Street Journal* and *Barron's* publish weekly performance lists of closed-end bond funds. In addition, Morningstar and Value Line publish data that will tell you about a closed-end fund's holdings, the size of its discount, if any, and how that compares with its historical average. Ideally you'll want to buy a closed-end bond fund when its discount is wider than its historic average.

Buying Unit Investment Trusts

If you like the idea of diversifying among bonds and want to lock in an interest rate and a fixed maturity date, you might want to invest in a unit investment trust. Sometimes called unit trusts or UITs, these investments are packages of eight to 15 bonds put together by brokerage firms and sold in lots of $1,000. Unlike bond funds, UITs are not actively managed. In other words, the trust sponsor usually doesn't buy or sell bonds during the trust's life. Instead, the bonds put into a UIT are left there until the bonds mature and the trust expires, typically in 20 to 30 years. In most cases you get your interest checks monthly, though some trusts pay out quarterly or twice a year. You can sell some or all of your units before the trust expires on the secondary market at the current market price. However, you may incur a capital gain or loss, depending on market values at the time.

These investments have several hitches, however. For one thing, commissions tend to average a hefty 4% of the sales price; there are also annual fees of roughly 0.2% to cover administrative costs. Because these portfolios aren't actively managed, there's no protection against interest rate risk. If interest rates rise, you're stuck with the rate you've got.

Similarly, you have no protection against a decline in the credit quality in the bonds since the UIT manager will hang on to the bonds for the life of the trust. A bond fund manager, by contrast, can buy and sell bonds at will, grabbing new, higher-yielding bonds and unloading issues whose credit rating has slipped. It's not easy to keep an eye on the value of your unit trust, either. Unlike bond funds, whose ups and downs appear daily in the newspaper, unit trust performance is virtually impossible to monitor. One other problem: If any bonds held by your trust are called, you'll get the principal back and then must find somewhere else to invest the money. As a result, you won't earn the yield you thought you would. To learn whether any bonds in a particular UIT are subject to calls, ask your broker or check the trusts prospectus.

How to Reduce Your Risks

Whether you're buying individual bonds, bond funds, or unit trusts, the following investment strategies will help you trim your investment risks:

■ **Stick to intermediates.** The simplest strategy is to invest only in intermediate-term bonds, which have maturities of one to 10 years. Intermediates yield more than short-term issues, which mature in one year or less. However, they are less volatile than long-term bonds, which have maturities of 10 years or more.

■ **Diversify.** Because bond prices can tumble from rising interest rates or an issuer's financial trouble, it's risky to hold a single issue. Instead, diversify by investing in a variety of issues with different maturities. You can get this diversification automatically by buying a bond fund or unit trust. If you would rather own individual corporate or municipal bonds, purchase at least five of them. (You need not worry about diversification with Treasuries, since their credit quality is unmatched.)

■ **Ladder your bonds.** Another way to protect yourself against sudden shifts in interest rates is to build what's known as a **bond ladder.** This means buying bonds with staggered maturities. For example, you might split your bond portfo-

lio among two-year, three-year, five-year, seven-year, and 10-year maturities. By doing this, you get an average maturity of about five years without having to worry whether you timed interest rate moves in the bond market exactly right. Every time one of your bonds comes due, just add another rung to the ladder. So when the two-year bond matures, put the money into a new 10-year issue. By laddering, if rates rise, you'll have new money available to invest at higher rates. And if rates fall, you will have locked in the older, higher rates for a portion of your portfolio.

■ **Don't get carried away by taxes.** While the lure of triple tax exemption may be great, you shouldn't put more than 50% of your bond portfolio in the issues of a single state or in a single-state bond fund. If you keep all your eggs in one basket, you'll be vulnerable to a regional economic decline or a natural disaster.

CHAPTER 16

How to Invest in Real Estate

Many years ago, the humorist Will Rogers said that real estate is the best investment in the world because it is the only thing they're not making anymore. Today, even after a decade of roller-coaster real estate prices, it's easy to see that Will wasn't joking. From 1974 to 1998, real estate values in this country increased more than 15-fold, outpacing both the stock and bond markets. Real estate, however, has more than a limited supply and TV infomercials going for it. In fact, there are at least five reasons why individual investors should consider sinking some cash into real estate once they've built a solid portfolio of stocks and bonds:

■ **Real estate is an inflation hedge.** When overall consumer prices rise, the value of so-called paper investments such as bonds sometimes fails to keep pace. Historically, however, the values of "hard" assets like real estate have kept pace with or outrun inflation. That's because real estate, as a basic necessity, will always maintain its relative value against other assets as their prices rise.

■ **Real estate historically lowers your overall investment risk and raises your returns.** Less risk, but bigger returns? Sounds like a mistake, right? It's not. Earl Osborn at the investment advisory firm Bingham Osborn & Scarborough in San Francisco has done numerous studies showing that real estate actually stabilizes an investment portfolio while increasing returns. For example, an investor who put 80% of his money into stocks and 20% into real estate from 1970 to 1993 would have earned more than 12% a year. Had he stuck solely with stocks, his annualized return would have averaged around 11.5%. What is more important, the portfolio with real estate in the mix actually experienced 6% less volatility. That's a fancy way of saying that his investments didn't bounce up and down as much as the stock-only portfolio. It's worth noting, however, that Osborn defines real estate as shares of real estate investment trusts, a type of stock, which is among the safest ways for individuals to play the real estate game, as you'll read later on in this chapter.

■ **Real estate generates income.** Buildings and apartments can produce significant and reliable cash flows when they are rented out to other people who live or work in them. This is true whether you own the property yourself or invest passively through real estate trusts, mutual funds, or limited partnerships. And reliable income is extremely valuable for investors.

■ **Real estate is stable.** Forget the recent upheavals in home prices. Over the long run, real estate has proven to be quicker to rise in value than to fall. Barring war or natural disaster, real estate holds its value or rises steadily in price over time. You can't say that about all investment alternatives.

■ **Real estate is a core asset.** Companies may rise and fall, but real estate endures. That's why land remains the practical

and emotional foundation of most of the world's great fortunes. It's also why the U.S. government has encouraged home ownership through the deductibility of mortgage interest. (At least it has been for decades. A flat tax could scrap this write-off.)

Despite these advantages, making a profit in real estate is no simple matter. A complicated array of national and local factors affects real estate values and investment returns. These include changes in tax laws, interest rate swings, regional and local economic trends, population shifts, building codes, and supply and demand within individual markets. Adding to the confusion are the numerous and varied ways you can choose to invest in real estate. Today there are seven main ways to put real estate into your portfolio. Three of them—**real estate mutual funds, real estate investment trusts (REITs),** and **real estate limited partnerships**—don't involve owning a piece of land or building by yourself. Rather, investors own shares of one sort or another in legal entities that in turn own the properties. Four others—**rental real estate, vacation homes, time-shares,** and **raw land**—are "real" real estate, if you will—actual land or structures that you can walk through, on, or over and call your own. You can personally increase their value. All seven of these real estate investments are as different from each other as a skyscraper in Manhattan is from 40 acres of Kansas farmland.

Here's how to sort them out, from the most conservative option to the riskiest:

Real Estate Mutual Funds

Given the complexities of investing in real estate, the best choice for most individuals is to buy shares in a mutual fund that specializes in it. Like stock mutual funds (described in Chapter 14), real estate funds pool individuals' money and invest it. Real estate mutual funds invest primarily in the shares of real estate investment trusts (REITs), which develop and manage a diversified portfolio of commercial office buildings, apartment complexes, shopping centers, and other projects. The mutual funds also buy shares of real estate—related companies such as home builders, hotels, and nursing homes. By joining forces with other investors, you enjoy distinct advantages over those lone wolves who venture into the real estate market themselves. Of course, real estate mutual funds, like other stock funds, offer no guaranteed returns. In fact, you could very well lose money in these funds over the course of a year. The average real estate mutual fund lost 10% of its value over the 12 months ending in early 1995. Still, these funds offer substantial returns over the long run. Several, for instance, earned more than 25% over a re-

cent three-year period. Among the most important pluses of investing in real estate mutual funds are the following four:

1. Professional management at an affordable price. Ordinarily, you couldn't interest a money manager in minding your real estate portfolio unless you had at least a six-figure sum to invest. With real estate funds, though, you can ordinarily get in the door for as little as $100. Every fund comes with its own investment management team that can spend the time needed to understand the vagaries of individual real estate investment trusts and real estate–related stocks as well as the far-flung real estate markets that affect them. Some real estate fund managers invest all over the world, not just in the United States. Naturally, this kind of expert management comes at a price, but a reasonable one: The manager typically takes 0.5% to 1.5% of a fund's assets each year as an advisory fee. There may also be an initial up-front sales charge of roughly 4%.
2. Liquidity. You can get into and out of a real estate mutual fund easily, with a call to your stockbroker or the fund itself. You cannot, however, write checks on most real estate mutual funds. Other real estate investments, as you'll see, are not nearly as friendly to buyers or sellers as real estate funds.
2. Diversification. Real estate funds spread your money among a wide variety of regions, industries, and securities.

Consequently, you're not at the mercy of one particular property doing well. Unlike real estate limited partnerships, however, these funds do not invest directly in land or buildings.

4. Income. Because they invest heavily in REITs that pay high dividends, most real estate funds offer investors high yields as well, generally ranging from 3% to 8%.

The process of choosing the right real estate mutual fund is far simpler than choosing a stock fund, since just a handful of funds specialize in real estate. Among them, two stand out as having solid track records: **Cohen & Steers Realty Shares** (800-437-9912) and **Fidelity Real Estate Investment** (800-544-8888). Unlike most real estate funds, those from Evergreen and Templeton invest the bulk of their assets overseas. For ultimate diversification, it's not a bad idea to divide your real estate portfolio between a fund that focuses primarily on U.S. real estate and one dominated by foreign stocks.

Real Estate Investment Trusts (REITs)

Real estate investment trusts (REITs) are publicly traded stocks that invest in office buildings, apartment complexes, industrial facilities, shopping centers, and other commercial spaces. REITs were created for small investors who don't have the money to spend on down payments and mortgages but nonetheless want to own real estate. Each REIT pools the money raised from investors and invests it in a diversified portfolio of real estate assets, similar to the way a stock mutual fund pools shareholders' money to invest in stocks. The trusts, in fact, *are* stocks, and most trade on the major stock exchanges or over-the-counter.

REITs have several advantages and are very popular because of their profit potential: a $1,000 investment in a representative portfolio of REITs in 1972 would have mushroomed to $14,700 by 1993, for a return of better than 1,400%. But REITs can crash, too. In the late 1960s and early 1970s, investors poured their money into REITs because they provided a simple and affordable entrance into a soaring real estate market. This new popularity resulted in a huge growth in REIT assets from just $1 billion in 1968 to about $20 billion five years later. These cash-rich REITs lent much of their money to property developers, who built all sorts of projects. Not surprisingly, the construction boom resulted in a glut of unfilled buildings, which, combined with rising interest rates, sent real estate prices plummeting. Many borrowers couldn't make their loan payments, and some

REITs had to foreclose on properties that turned out to be difficult to unload. The result: a massive shakeout in the REIT industry. Of 216 REITs at the time, nine went bankrupt, dozens flirted with bankruptcy, and more than half cut or eliminated their dividends. In 1973 the NAREIT Equity REIT Index—considered the benchmark for the REIT market the way the Dow Jones Industrial Average reflects the performance of stocks—fell by more than 15%. A year later the NAREIT Index dropped another 21%. The industry bounced back in the late 1970s and early '80s along with the overall real estate market, only to sink again in the latter part of the decade as the real estate market became glutted once again. In 1987 the NAREIT Index fell by more than 3.5%, followed by a nearly 15% decline three years later. Lately REITs have rebounded as tightening rental real estate markets around the country have boosted their share prices.

This brief history is a reminder that the REIT industry has a history of highs and lows, which doesn't negate the fact that over the long run REITs have proven to be a reliable and safe way for individuals to invest in real estate. That's because REITs offer:

■ **Low-cost entry into an expensive business.** REITs let you become a part owner or financier of several pieces of commercial, residential, or industrial real estate. If you bought them directly, each might cost anywhere from $50,000 to several million dollars in down payments alone. You pay only the commissions that a stockbroker would charge if you bought shares in a company like IBM or General Motors. On the other hand, real estate limited partnerships, discussed later in the chapter, are burdened with front-end sales charges and management fees that take a nasty bite out of your long-term profits. REITs are also less picky about their investors, while many partnership deals come with minimum purchase requirements or financial suitability tests that lock out some investors.

■ **Reliable income and capital appreciation over the long term.** By law, REITs must pass along to shareholders 95% of each year's operating profits in regular dividend payments. As a result, REIT shares often yield more than most other types of stocks and provide a predictable income stream—as long as the REIT's underlying properties or mortgages are profitable. REITs also hold out the prospect of capital appreciation, just like any other stock, so you can score a profit when you sell the shares. The flipside of this, of course, is that when the stock market is taking a dive, REIT shares tend to fall, too. As a rule, REIT share prices usually rise and fall in value with the direction of the stock market, not the overall U.S. real estate market. So if you buy only one REIT, you're taking on more risk than if you buy a group of them or a real estate mutual fund.

■ **Easy access to your money.** Another advantage of REITs is that they are easy to get into and out of. Owning real estate directly by being a landlord or investing in a limited partnership usually means tying up your money for many years. When you're ready to sell, you may have to wait a while to get an attractive price. When you want to get your money out of a REIT, you simply call your broker and sell your shares like any other stock.

You can get a list of all publicly traded REITs, as well as other information about the industry, from the National Association of Real Estate Investment Trusts (1129 20th St. N.W., Suite 705, Washington, D.C. 20036; 202-785-8717). The most important thing to know about the subject, however, is that there are three basic types of REITs, but only one—equity REITs—that you need to consider seriously. They are:

1. Equity REITs. These REITs, which typically yield between 4% and 7%, use their money primarily to buy income-producing property—in other words, property with rent-paying tenants. They are generally the best choice for investors who want long-term capital appreciation and current income. They're also the most appropriate form of real estate in-

vesting if you're looking to diversify your portfolio without spending much time. What's more, since real estate values rise over the long run, equity REITs offer a good inflation hedge.

Some equity REITs focus on certain types of properties or invest only in specific regions of the country, while others spread their assets across geographic and industry borders. There are REITs that invest in deals put together by independent developers and REITs that buy, develop, and manage property themselves. Your best bet is to stick with REITs that focus on specific types of real estate or particular regions, as well as those that develop and manage their own properties.

The first step in picking an equity REIT is to get a prospectus or annual report from your stockbroker or the REIT itself. Look at the section that describes what the trust owns and the location of its properties. Make sure you're comfortable owning the types of buildings in the REIT, whether they're shopping centers, nursing homes, apartment buildings, or something else. Make sure, too, that you're content owning them in San Antonio, Los Angeles, Washington, D.C., or wherever the REIT has its holdings. (If the REIT tends to buy real estate in your part of the country and you're optimistic about the economic growth prospects in your area, you may have a winner that you'll also feel comfortable owning.) Be sure that the prospectus says the REIT has been in the business for at least five years. For safety's sake, you don't want to take a chance on a new company or executives without expertise. What's more, if the REIT has been around for a while, you will be able to examine its performance records and its history of dividend increases. Restrict your equity REIT investing to ones whose dividends have been growing and are being paid out from the rental income of the properties in the portfolio. Avoid REITs that come up with the income for their dividends mostly by selling property or using the company's cash reserves.

2. Mortgage REITs. This breed of REIT lends money to developers and buyers and makes its profits from charging interest. More specifically, mortgage REITs originate or buy mortgages on commercial properties. Though they typically offer yields of 6% to 10%, mortgage REITs offer little capital appreciation potential because they don't own much property, if any. Moreover, if its borrowers hit trouble spots or even default, a REIT's share price can plummet. In other words, though the yields of mortgage REITs are generally higher than equity REITs, so are their risks. Also, mortgage REITs tend to behave more like bonds than real estate, so they offer little diversification if you're looking to broaden your portfolio from traditional stock and fixed-income investments.

3. Hybrid REITs. As the name suggests, these REITs are a little bit equity and a little bit mortgage; they own property and make loans. Here again, you are lessening your potential for capital appreciation while exposing yourself to potential mortgage defaults. You do, however, stand a stronger chance of raking in capital gains from hybrid REITs than you do from mortgage REITs.

Real Estate Limited Partnerships

Limited partnerships, which are discussed more generally in Chapter 17, remain a fairly popular way to invest in real estate. The major reason, in all likelihood, is that stockbrokers and financial planners who push high-commission limited partnerships sometimes stress their profit potential and underplay their risks. Luckily that's been getting harder to do, since in recent years newspapers and magazines have been full of stories of pushy brokers and partnerships gone bust. Indeed, over the past few years hundreds of thousands of investors have filed dozens of lawsuits because they believe brokers duped them into investing billions of dollars in dud partnerships.

For as little as $1,000, limited partnerships offer individual investors the chance to invest in high-rise office buildings, apartment houses, medical centers, motels, or shopping malls. Unlike real estate mutual funds and REITs, limited partnerships come with steep commissions and can be extremely difficult to sell. So before you invest in a partnership, consider fully whether you can better meet your goals through mutual funds or REITs. For most investors, limited partnerships are an unnecessarily risky way to diversify into real estate or to generate steady income. Their chief advantage over mutual funds and REITs: tax breaks, though the breaks aren't nearly as great as they were in the early 1980s.

Briefly, a partnership is a business organization comprising a general partner, who runs the limited partnership's daily business, and limited partners, who put up most or all of the money. Limited partners receive income, capital gains, tax benefits, and losses generated by the partnership. You are called a *limited* partner because your liability in the partnership is limited to the amount of money that you invest. You are also protected from legal action against the partnership.

In a **specified partnership,** the general partner explains in advance how the organization will operate and what properties (or at least what types of properties) it will buy. A **blind pool partnership** does not set out its investment strategy.

You must trust the general partner to spend your money wisely. As a rule, blind pools are inadvisable, unless the general partner is, say, your father or someone else you would trust with the keys to your house or combination to your safe.

Now about that advantage of limited partnership: taxes. Unlike many other investments, a limited partnership pays no taxes. Because all income, capital gains and losses, and tax breaks are passed through to the limited partners, you pay taxes only at your own individual rate. By contrast, if you own stock in a corporation that pays dividends, you are, in effect, taxed twice on the company's profits: first when the company is taxed as a corporation and then again when you pay taxes on your dividends.

This tax feature made real estate limited partnerships extremely popular in the early '80s, when they were viewed primarily as tax shelters. At that time individual tax rates were far higher than they are today, so upper-income people desperately sought ways to shield their income from the IRS. Because partnerships pass through all their tax benefits to the partners, investors plowed billions of dollars into limited partnerships to secure write-offs against their regular earned income. The juiciest tax benefits came from real estate depreciation—writing off part of the value of the property each year—and real estate tax credits, which could let people write off more than they invested in the programs. However, many of these deals were unprofitable, and when the Tax Reform Act of 1986 eliminated most of the tax shelters, many partnerships fell apart. Investors wound up holding limited partnership shares that were often barely worth the paper they were printed on, let alone their original price.

Today, two types of real estate limited partnerships can still offer some generous tax goodies. The first is a **low-income housing partnership.** This type of partnership invests in apartment complexes designed specifically for low- to moderate-income residents, as designated by the government. Provided that the partnership meets all the government standards, limited partners can be eligible for tax credits of as much as 9% of their investment for newly built housing projects and 4% for existing properties. A tax credit is much better than a deduction since it directly reduces your tax bill; a $2,000 credit will reduce your tax bill by $2,000. The low-income housing tax credits, however, are limited to investors with adjusted gross incomes of less than $250,000. In addition, if you've ever dealt with government rules and regulations, you know they can be maddening. So it's quite possible that a sponsor of a low-income housing partnership won't meet the government standards and its investors then won't get their anticipated tax benefits. While low-income properties do

generate income, the amount of the rent is generally modest. Capital gains may occur once the partnership liquidates and sells its holdings, generally after 10 years.

The other type of real estate tax shelter is a **historic rehabilitation limited partnership.** Here, the partners put their money to work renovating buildings that the U.S. Department of the Interior has certified as historic. If the partnership's projects meet the government's strict architectural standards—not very easy to do—limited partners qualify for a 20% investment tax credit each year for 10 years. Again, these tax credits are far more valuable than tax deductions, since they reduce your taxes dollar for dollar. There are a few things to keep in mind before scurrying for this shelter, though. First, the historic rehab credits are limited to investors with adjusted gross incomes of less than $200,000. Second, these partnerships don't generate income; however, if the renovated property appreciates during the period the partnership owns it (generally a decade), the limited partners can realize capital gains after the sale of the building.

If you want to invest in a real estate partnership primarily for steady income and possible capital gains, rather than for tax breaks, you ought to invest in a conservative **equity real estate partnership.** This investment pools money from limited partners and buys existing, occupied buildings in the hopes of increasing rents as leases are renewed and then selling the properties for a profit in five to 10 years. For bigger potential capital gains but smaller income and greater risk, you could invest instead in a real estate partnership that will build properties, lease them out, and eventually sell them. Another type of real estate partnership, known as a **mortgage partnership,** loans money to property developers instead of owning buildings outright. The partnership secures a steady source of income for its partners in the form of mortgage payments—presuming that the developers don't default on their mortgages. Like mortgage REITs, these partnerships don't offer you much in the way of capital gains.

Real estate limited partnerships come in two basic forms: **public programs** or **private placement programs.** Public programs typically include thousands of individual investors who hand over as little as $1,000 or so. These public partnerships, which generally last from five to 12 years before they disband, are registered with the Securities and Exchange Commission and state regulatory authorities. They generally invest in numerous projects and are consequently highly diversified. Private placements, on the other hand, are not registered with the SEC, invest in just one or a few properties, and generally cannot be sold to more than a few dozen investors, all wealthy (you need to prove your financial suitability to

a broker or planner in order to get into the private placement). These partnerships, which can last anywhere from three to 20 years, are generally riskier than public programs but offer the potential for greater profits.

One of the major drawbacks of investing in limited partnerships are the fees you will pay, both when you put in your money and throughout the life of the partnership. For starters, the brokerage firms who sell limited partnerships charge up-front commissions that generally range from 8% to 10% of your investment. In addition, most partnerships charge between 3% and 4% of assets each year for management fees. Many partners also levy an incentive fee, often as high as 15%, every time the partnership sells a piece of property. The theory is that the fee provides incentive for the general partner to get the highest sales price possible when selling off the partnership's assets.

Getting your money out of a limited partnership without taking a financial bath can be a struggle, too. First of all, your partnership shares aren't tracked in the paper, unlike the shares of a REIT or a real estate mutual fund, which can be sold immediately after you call to redeem them. From time to time the general partner will estimate the value of the shares and send you its opinion. You won't necessarily get paid this amount if you want to sell your shares before the partnership dissolves, however. Instead you'll receive whatever a buyer is willing to pay for them—assuming you can find a buyer. (There is an exception: **master limited partnerships,** which operate like traditional partnerships except that they trade on exchanges like any other stock.)

If you want to withdraw from a partnership early, you will most likely have to sell your stake in the so-called secondary market. More than a dozen firms buy and sell units of existing partnerships there, often at a large discount to their original value. For a free list of these firms, write to the Investment Partnership Association (Suite 500, 1100 Connecticut Ave. N.W., Washington, D.C. 20036).

Still interested in limited partnerships? Then keep these rules in mind before you write your check:

■ **Be prepared for the risks involved.** That means answering "Yes" to the following questions: Can you afford to potentially lose your entire investment? Can you afford to go without the money you're planning to invest for the entire estimated life of the partnership? Do you fit the investor suitability standards listed in the partnership's offering memorandum? If you answered "No" to any of these questions, you can't afford to invest.

■ **Stick with existing partnerships.** Opt for one that is at least three years old and is on solid financial footing. That means, among other criteria, that the partnership's cash flows are covering its expenses with at least some money left over for income distributions. You can ask the Investment Partnership Association for a list of firms that buy and sell these used units. Alternatively, you could call Partnerline (Shrewsbury, N.J.; 900-786-9600), which offers information on thousands of private and publicly registered partnerships. You can also ask your broker. Be wary if he begins pushing his firm's house-brand partnerships; brokers often get bonuses to sell these products, and that's exactly how many of the recent partnership lawsuits got started.

■ **Go with an experienced general partner.** Before investing in any partnership, get a prospectus laying out the deal. Scour this document closely for information about the general partner—to whom, after all, you will be entrusting your money. Specifically, you want a partner with at least a couple of similar projects already well along. A successful apartment complex developer, for instance, may not know a thing about building or buying shopping malls. By definition, a firm with an experienced general partner has probably been in business for at least five to 10 years—the longer the better.

■ **Stay out of the blind pools.** Evaluating partnerships is tricky enough when you know what properties are owned or are being sought. When you don't know, it's like throwing money down a well and hoping it doesn't get wet.

■ **Avoid highly leveraged partnerships.** Even after they've raised money from investors like you, many partnership sponsors borrow money to finance projects. The advantage in using someone else's money as leverage, like this, is that the potential return on your investment is higher. However, the disadvantage is that a larger cash flow from the properties will be required to make payments on the debt before the limited partners get any returns. These kinds of partnerships are for high-fliers only.

■ **Steer clear of partnerships with high fees.** Above average fees and incentive fees are usually a clue that your general partner does not have your best interest at heart. Ask your broker or planner to show you how this partnership's fees compare with those of similar programs.

■ **Ask an objective pro for advice.** Before investing in a partnership, go over the deal with your lawyer, financial planner, accountant, or ask some other independent, trustworthy adviser to look over the terms and give you objective advice. Don't rely exclusively on the broker or investment adviser selling you the partnership shares, since she'll receive a hefty commission from the sale and won't be completely disinterested.

Rental Property

Now, you're about to enter the realm of dirt-under-the-fingertips real estate investing. With rental properties and the other alternatives that follow, you'll be doing most of the work yourself. You'll also have a chance personally to increase the value of your investment. Of all the hands-on real estate investments, residential rental property is the most attractive for individuals. Raw land doesn't generate rent or go up in value unless someone is willing to develop it. High-rise office buildings and shopping centers typically require more money and expertise than most amateur real estate investors possess. On the other hand, down payments on apartment houses are often within the reach of the average investor.

These days, residential rental real estate offers some of the best tax breaks around, plus the chance to earn 10% or more annually in income and capital gains. However, investing in a rental property is not the same as choosing a house for yourself. First, other people have to live there, so your taste doesn't matter a whit. The prospect for appreciation, which may not matter much to you when buying a home to live in, is an essential factor to consider when shopping for investment property. You must also calculate how much income you can reasonably expect the property to generate and whether that amount will cover your operating costs (mortgage payments, maintenance, and insurance, to name just three).

Investing in rental property is such a hands-on proposition that only people who have plenty of time and energy should consider it. Becoming a landlord means locating the right property, arranging financing, making repairs and improvements (or getting someone to do them), finding tenants, and collecting rent. Don't be discouraged, though. Anyone who takes the time to learn the rules of property investment can make it work and perhaps make a bundle. Here's a quick rundown of those rules.

1. Get the best price you can. Ideally you want to pay no more than 80% of the building's market value. To determine the value, work with an appraiser or a real estate agent who will check recent sales prices of comparable places. You might even consider joining a local real estate club to better familiarize yourself with the market. There are more than 100 of these kinds of groups around the country.
2. Buy property that will be easy to rent. Choose a house or apartment in the best neighborhood within your price range, where the crime rate is low and the nearby properties are clean. Drive through a neighborhood during the day and at night to get a feel for these factors.

You should also check with the local police to assess the level of criminal activity in the area. You generally want to choose a property that has broad rental appeal; unusual, modern-looking structures may appeal to your artistic nature, but not to many others.

You're better off owning property close to home, for two reasons. First, even if you can afford to hire someone to manage your property, you will almost certainly want to visit the place regularly. That's a lot easier to do by car than by plane. Second, you will more likely understand the dynamics of the real estate market in your own backyard than in another region of the country. So stick close to your home turf—say, no more than an hour's drive from your business or home.
3. Buy property that is likely to appreciate. Although real estate appreciation is influenced by such national factors as the level of mortgage rates and the overall economy, the market conditions you really need to understand are those where you want to buy. You can get information on regional and metropolitan prices from the National Association of Realtors (430 N. Michigan Ave., Chicago, Ill. 60611; 800-874-6500). Ask local real estate brokers for more specific information on prices in a given area if you need it.

If your goal is to beat the average appreciation rate in your area, you may want to invest in a property that is a little rundown and fix it up on your own.

Generally, for every dollar of renovation you put into a dump, you can expect to gain $2 to $5 when you sell it as a palace. Make sure, however, that you don't get yourself in too deep. A house that requires a fresh coat of paint, new shutters, or light fixtures is fine, but you'll most likely want to avoid buildings in need of major repairs like a new foundation or a plumbing makeover. Chances are that you won't recoup enough on resale to justify the cost of such major face lifts. It's worth spending the $250 to $2,000 that a building inspector will charge—depending on the size of the structure—to estimate how much work will be needed and how much it will cost. Your real estate broker can tell you if the increased value of the house after you repair it would make the investment worthwhile.

Your chances of selling property at a profit will be greatly improved if you buy it cheap. A smart way to do that is to keep an eye out for sellers in a hurry to unload their buildings. The real estate section of your local newspaper will invariably carry ads with phrases such as "Need to sell in a hurry." You can also ask friends and co-workers if they know of anyone moving to another city who is anxious to sell quickly and cheaply. Another strategy: Search through legal journals for notices of foreclosure sales. You can ask about these sales at your local bank, savings and loan, or credit union, too. Or you can call the Federal National Mort-

gage Association (800-732-6643) for a list of local foreclosed properties that it's selling. In any case, you'll want to be sure you know what a property is really worth. To find a qualified real estate appraiser, check your local Yellow Pages or contact the Appraisal Institute (312-335-4100) and ask for its membership directory.

In addition, ask local real estate agents for a list of the area's communities or neighborhoods that have the shortest resale time for residential properties. Such places are seller's markets that push property values higher. These days, single-family rental houses typically take about three months to sell.

Also, get the area's vacancy rate from a real estate agent. If it's around 5%, you can probably rent your property easily. If it's 7% to 10%, you may have trouble. Above 10%, forget it—unless you're getting a steal and think the neighborhood will turn around. Then buy and cross your fingers.

4. Buy property that is profitable. Your building should ideally produce a rental stream that will throw off income after it covers your mortgage installments, property taxes, maintenance, and insurance expenses. There's a simple formula for figuring this out. Divide the total selling price by the gross annual income and come up with the **rent multiplier.**

$$\text{Rent Multiplier} = \frac{\text{Selling price}}{\text{Gross annual rental}}$$

For example, say a four-unit apartment is selling for $250,000 and generates $25,000 in annual rent. The formula would go like this:

$$\text{Rent Multiplier} = \frac{\$250,000}{\$25,000 = 10}$$

In other words, the building is selling for 10 times the annual gross rental, or has a rent multiplier of 10. Generally, avoid property that is selling for more than seven or eight times gross annual rental. That's because it is more than likely to produce a negative cash flow; put another way, such a property will require you to spend more money than you take in. Worthwhile residential properties are those that generate enough rental income to pay your big operating expenses—mortgage, maintenance, and taxes—while you wait for your investment to appreciate. As a rule, you don't want to buy a building if the carrying costs are more than the income it produces, no matter how little you'll have to pay for it. The exception is if you can afford to pay the difference for as long as it takes the investment to rise in value and you're in a high enough tax bracket to make the wait worthwhile.

For a more detailed way to check out the rental numbers before you buy, after you find a property you like, fill out the following worksheet:

HOW TO CHECK THE RENTAL'S NUMBERS BEFORE YOU BUY

Pay close attention to two figures. On line 11 you'll find the annual return you can expect on the cash you invest, after the building is in rentable condition. You're looking for a figure that's at least double the one-year CD rate. On line 14 you'll get the overall projected return on your investment. If it's 10% or more, buy.

1. a) Annual rents $_____

   b) Allowance for $_____
      vacancies and
      uncollected rents
      (typically 5%)

2. Net rents (line 1a $_____
   minus line 1b)

3. Annual deductible $_____
   operating expenses
   excluding mortgage
   payments—such as
   your repairs and
   maintenance (typically
   10% of net rents),
   property taxes,
   insurance, management
   fees of 7% to 10%

4. Net operating income $_____
   before mortgage
   expense (line 2 minus
   line 3)

5. Annual mortgage $_____
   interest payment

6. Annual pretax cash
flow (line 4 minus
line 5) $\$_____$

7. Annual property
depreciation (cost of
the building, but not
the land, divided by
27.5 years) $\$_____$

8. Tax loss or gain (line
6 minus line 7) $\$_____$

9. Annual tax loss or tax
due (line 8 multiplied
by your combined
federal, state, and city
tax rates) $\$_____$

10. After-tax cash flow
(line 6 plus or minus
line 9) $\$_____$

11. Cash-on-cash return
(line 10 divided by
cash invested) $_____\%$

12. Projected one-year
gain in price (purchase
price multiplied by the
estimated 12-month
percentage increase in
value) $\$_____$

13. Projected total return
for year (line 10 plus
line 12) $\$_____$

14. Return on investment
(line 13 divided by
cash invested) $_____\%$

Source: Michael P. Sampson, professor of taxation at American University and author of *Tax Guide for Residential Real Estate.*

5. Buy property with more than one tenant. As with any investment, diversification is essential with rental property—even if you own only one building. You do not want to be beholden to the whims of one deadbeat hard-luck case. So buy buildings with as many rental units as you can afford. Your income will then be higher, your cost per apartment will be lower, and a vacancy won't wipe out your income. If a small, six-unit dwelling is too expensive, begin with a duplex or triplex, sometimes called a two-family or three-family house. These units generally cost more than single-family houses, but they also generate more income. For example, you might pay $200,000 for a duplex in the same neighborhood where single-family houses cost about $150,000. If you charge each tenant $900 a month per unit and take in $1,800, you'll fare a lot better than if you were getting even $1,200 for a single-family house. By investing 33% more, you have increased your rent by 50%, and if one of your tenants leaves, you would still collect $900 a month.

6. Keep your ownership costs down. Stipulate in the lease, for example, that a tenant pay for utilities or for minor repairs. The best way to hold down costs is to arrange for easy financing terms. You generally can get a better interest rate on your mortgage if *you* live in the property, providing your building has more than one unit and fewer than six. Bankers generally consider any apartment house with six units or more as investment property. This is an important distinction since bankers are likely to insist on tougher terms if you are borrowing for investment than if you are taking out a mortgage on a house you'll occupy. Lenders generally ask for a 10% to 15% larger down payment for investment properties with fewer than six units than they require of home buyers. For larger buildings, a 20% to 25% down payment is standard. It's also likely that if you don't live in the building you will be charged half a percentage point more in mortgage interest and an additional point in loan fees.

If you think you'll be able to raise rents substantially within two to three years of buying a building, you might keep your mortgage payments down initially by negotiating a fixed-rate, graduated-payment loan. Like an adjustable-rate mortgage, this loan will let you make lower monthly payments at the outset than with a standard fixed mortgage. Locking in the rate, however, guarantees that you won't run the risk that carrying costs will rocket skyward if interest rates shoot up in the future. Many real estate pros warn against taking out an adjustable mortgage since it makes it harder for you to project your future expenses. If it's the only mortgage you can qualify for, though, be sure the interest rate can't rise by more than six percentage points over the life of the loan.

You may also be eligible for low-interest or low-down payment loans offered through federal, state, and local governments. For example, you might qualify for a lower mortgage rate if you invest in a marginal neighborhood that is being rehabilitated. Or you might be able to negotiate a smaller down payment than you would get from a bank by purchasing property in a government foreclosure sale. You can find out about federal loan programs from the U.S. Department of Housing and Urban Development (202-708-1400). Your state housing authority will give you information about state and local loan programs.

7. Manage your property yourself. Once you've located the property with the best potential returns, arranged the financing, and closed the deal, you're still left with the chore of managing your investment. You can hire a professional property-management firm, but you'll sacrifice as much as 10% to 15% of your gross rental income for the privilege. Professional management may be worth the cost if your building generates income exceeding your expenses; otherwise, try to manage the property yourself. To find tenants, place an ad in your local newspaper or post a note on the bulletin board of grocery stores and colleges. Be certain to check any potential tenant's employment record and references from previous landlords. Even if you think you've fully vetted your prospects, you may wind up with some who don't pay their rent. Therefore it's smart to budget 2% to 10% of your rental income, depending on the turnover rate in the neighborhood, to cover the costs of deadbeat tenants. Such costs will include not only missing rent, but any potential enforcement or legal action you may choose to take. (Being a landlord can be an ugly business sometimes.) Set aside another 2% to 10% for repairs, and expect the occasional nighttime or weekend call from a frantic tenant, demanding that you fix whatever has just broken.

8. Take advantage of tax breaks. The hassles of owning rental property may not seem worth it until tax time. Then, wow! Becoming a real estate investor can really ax your taxes. Of the assorted tax breaks, depreciation is by far the most valuable. Typically, you could choose the **straight-line depreciation** method, in which you deduct the cost of the building over 27.5 years. Commercial real estate gets written off over 39 years. The IRS publishes standards for different items that make up a building, giving each a minimum number of years over which you could deduct the total value. You can also deduct many of the expenses you incur, including the cost of mortgage interest, property taxes, insurance, maintenance, and transportation to your property.

Middle-income taxpayers get a special break for investing in rental real estate. If your adjusted gross income is less than $100,000, you can write off against your earned income as much as $25,000 a year from your rental real estate losses as long as you actively manage your property (setting rents, choosing your tenants, that sort of thing). This tax break phases out until your adjusted gross income hits $150,000; at that point it vanishes.

Vacation Homes

One of the most enduring fantasies for many American homeowners is to own a vacation home—preferably up in the mountains or near a lake or the ocean. Not only do you have a restful retreat from the pressures of your daily life, but the house pays for itself because you rent it out when you're not using it, generating enough cash to cover your expenses and maybe throw off a little extra income on the side. After a few years the value of your piece of paradise ideally rises enough so that you realize a dandy profit when you decide to sell it.

That's the fantasy, anyway. The reality is often quite different. Many vacation homes never generate enough income to cover their costs, let alone produce profits for owners. What's more, for every vacation property that triples in value over time, there are two that rise no more than the average piece of real estate—and some even lose value.

This does not mean that vacation homes are a bad idea. Indeed, for people with realistic expectations, vacation homes can prove to be among the most enjoyable of investments. You just need to go into this world of real estate with both eyes wide open.

Before buying a second home, it is crucial that you understand the tax consequences. Most of the tax benefits associated with owning your primary residence apply to a vacation home—providing you use it solely for your personal pleasure. You can deduct mortgage interest, property taxes, and, if you're unlucky enough to have them, casualty losses. These deductions, however, are limited to your first and second homes only.

Should you decide to rent out your vacation home for part of the year, however, the tax laws start getting complicated. Now the rules vary according to how long you rent out the property and how much you use it personally.

■ **If you rent out your home for no more than 14 days a year,** you'll owe no taxes on the rental income you get. You can still deduct the mortgage interest and property taxes.

■ **If you rent out the home for more than 14 days during the year,** your rental income is taxed at your regular income tax rate. You will, however, be able to write off expenses that you incurred as a landlord, such as depreciation and oper-

ating costs like advertising for tenants and the upkeep on the property.

■ **If you rent out the home for more than 14 days but also use it *yourself* for more than 14 days or for more than 10% of the number of days you rent the home—whichever is greater** (whew!), you can still treat your vacation home as a second home since the IRS will consider it to be your personal residence. That means mortgage interest and property taxes on the vacation home will be deductible to the extent that the house is for your use and not a rental. Likewise, you can deduct expenses related to the rental portion of the house only up to the amount of the rental income. For example, if you have $10,000 in rental expenses but only $5,000 in rental income, you can deduct only $5,000 in expenses. Fortunately you can carry over any excess write-offs to a future year when you have excess rental income.

■ **If you limit your personal use of the home to 14 days or 10% of the number of days the home is rented, whichever is greater,** then the home will be considered a rental property and not as a residence. As a result, mortgage interest attributable to your personal use of the home is considered consumer interest and thus no longer deductible. However, you may be able to deduct rental expenses in excess of rental income. As noted previously, the IRS may let you deduct up to $25,000 of business losses from your adjusted gross income as long as you actively rent and maintain the property. You qualify for the full $25,000 write-off if your adjusted gross income is less than $100,000; the tax benefit is phased out for incomes of $100,000 to $150,000. If you earn more than $150,000, you can deduct rental business losses only against rental income, but not against regular income from your job or other types of investments. (There's an exception to this limitation for people in the real estate business; they can deduct rental business losses against income regardless of how much they earn.) Rental business losses, by the way, mean your expenses for maintaining the property—which includes depreciation, painting, yard maintenance, repairs, and property taxes. You can also factor in the costs of any trips you take to inspect or repair the property. However, don't try to disguise personal use of your home as inspection trips. Reason: the IRS may not let you claim the house as a rental property if you take advantage of your visitation rights.

Once you understand the thorny tax issues concerning second homes, ask yourself the following questions before you take the plunge and buy a place:

1. Can I afford it? As a rule, your combined mortgage payments, homeowners insurance, and property taxes for your primary and vacation homes should not exceed 33% of your gross annual income. Otherwise you could find yourself un-derwater financially. Moreover, the total payments on all your mortgages and other long-term debts should not exceed 40% of your gross income.

A lender will probably insist you make a down payment of 20% versus as little as 10% for a primary residence. That's because financial institutions believe they're taking on bigger risks by lending money to people who won't be living in, and taking care of, their homes full-time. So they want more equity in the vacation homes from the start. You may even be told to put down 25% if you plan to rent out the property. Expect to pay one-quarter to one-half of a percentage point more for a mortgage on a second home than for the mortgage on a primary residence. Because your hideaway may be off the beaten track and frequently empty, your total homeowners insurance costs may run 50% higher than for a primary residence selling for a similar price. If you rent out the home, expect to pay roughly 20% extra to cover the potential damage while tenants are there.

2. Do I want a house or would I prefer a condominium? Condos are usually cheaper than a detached single-family house, but they are harder to sell. Their prices typically don't rise as much, either. Condos also are generally smaller than single-family houses. The bottom line: Condos are best suited for people who view their second home primarily for personal use.

3. Is the home in a desirable location? There are several factors to consider when answering this question. Resist the temptation to look for a house in a resort area merely because you enjoyed your vacation there this past summer. Take a reality check. For instance, if the trip back and forth from your principal home would be unbearable on a regular basis and you're looking for a place you could escape to any weekend, you need to scout out a more accessible spot. The same reasoning applies even if you're planning to use the home mostly as a rental. Don't figure you can start a new vacation trend by buying in some out-of-the-way spot. You're best off purchasing a place where vacationers want to vacation and one with a proven rental record. Not only will you know that people have chosen to rent the place previously, you'll have a built-in list of potential future renters. You should also pay close attention to location because you'll want a place that repairmen, couriers, gardeners, and rental agents can get to easily. Generally, stick with homes that are within a half day's drive of a major population center.

Before buying a home, it's worth your while to talk with local government officials in an area you're considering. In winter resort areas, for example, a police officer can tell you how often your street or road gets plowed—secluded homes may be left adrift for many days. In a beachfront community, ask city officials about the shore-line's erosion pattern, since you'll want to avoid buying a home that might eventually require an expensive retaining wall.

4. Do I have a reliable real estate and rental agent? Local real estate agents can be helpful in a number of ways. For example, they can clue you in about area real estate trends, the best neighborhoods, and other important factors you may know little about. You'll need a top-notch rental agent if you want to limit your involvement in the day-to-day management of a vacation home. For example, a proficient agent can find renters for you, collect rent from them, clean up between tenants, and even make minor repairs. The agent's commission typically runs between 15% and 25% of the rent, so you'll have to decide how much all of these services are worth.

5. Are the house and its contents in good shape? The same rules that apply when you buy a primary residence hold when you're buying a vacation home— that means a solid foundation and roof, adequate plumbing, and good insulation. A home inspector can give you a complete description of the condition of the home. Remember to consider your potential renters when furnishing the place. Sturdy is important, since many strangers with no investment in the house will be plopping on your chairs, beds, and couches. Stylish counts, too, if you want return business. Just think what *you* would want on vacation, in terms of attractive furnishing, modern appliances, and air-conditioning. Then make sure your place has it.

6. Am I paying the right price? A knowledgeable real estate agent can help you here. Ask the agent for the average number of days houses are on the market—two to four months is typical—and how much the seller has dropped his asking price. Sellers in languishing markets will often accept low bids. Before you make one, though, ask yourself why the market is languishing. The local vacation home market may be whispering to you: "Don't buy here. The place is on the skids!"

Ask your agent about auctions. These sales are common among banks with foreclosed homes, developers with unsold properties, and even homeowners in a hurry to sell (though you ought to ask why they're going this route). Auctioned homes generally sell for 10% to 45% of their list prices. If you plan to buy at auction, bring a certified check, usually ranging from $2,500 to $10,000. Within a week you'll need to come up with any remaining balance that equals 10% to 15% of the purchase price. You will have 45 to 60 days to find a mortgage.

Time-Shares

Buying a time-share generally means plunking down anywhere from $5,000 to $20,000 for a designated chunk of time—typically one week—at a specific place, generally a condo in a resort area. There are two types of time-shares. The most common is a **fee simple plan,** which gives you title to a portion of the property and ownership of your week there year after year. The other kind of time-share, a **right-to-use plan,** grants you the right to occupy your slot only for a specific number of years.

There's something innately alluring about time-shares: the ability to guarantee prepaid vacation accommodations for a week or more annually at a resort you'd enjoy repeatedly or, if you want, trade your week or location for another one. After all, when you have a time-share, you don't have the hassle of making reservations or the disappointment of having to stay at a so-so hotel because the one you wanted was booked. What's more, one day when you decide to sell the place, you can theoretically make a handsome profit. The cost? In addition to the purchase price, you'll owe an annual maintenance fee averaging $300 or so and subject to increase.

There are now more than 1,000 condominium and hotel time-share resorts in the United States and another thousand or so overseas. Millions of Americans have bought time-shares in the past two decades. For many, however, these investments have caused more heartache than happiness. That's because unprincipled fast-buck artists have plagued the time-share industry. Some are hustlers who disappear after being paid. Others are fast-talking marketers who exaggerate or even lie to close the deal. Still others are honest developers who lack the resources or experience to adequately manage time-shares.

Many owners have also learned that the solid initial attraction of time-shares can melt away. You may grow tired of visiting the same resort year after year. Or you may not always be able to schedule your vacation during that same week in August. You may also find that trading your time-share with someone else isn't so easy either. As real estate investments, time-shares often come up short. Though time-shares in some popular resorts have been resold for two or three times the original price, those are the exceptions, not the rule. Indeed, thousands of time-share owners have struggled to find buyers because the time-share salesmen in their resorts have steered potential buyers to *new*, unsold units. It's not unusual to swallow losses of 35% to 60% of your investment when you unload your time-share property. In short, time-shares provide an object lesson of why you should never mix business with pleasure.

If you're still interested in buying a time-share, pay close attention to the following rules:

■ **Proceed with caution.** Don't surrender to a hard sell and buy on the spot. Instead, rent a few times in the develop-ment that appeals to you. Be sure to go during the week you think you'd want to own. These test visits will help you determine if you would really want to spend time there year after year after year.

■ **Buy one- or two-bedroom units.** Smaller or larger ones will be harder to sell later.

■ **Buy time during the peak season in a popular area.** This will enhance your chances of swapping your unit, renting it out, or selling it.

■ **Buy in a place that's easy to reach.** If the location is remote, you may be discouraging potential swappers or buyers.

■ **Don't overpay.** If you are buying a fee simple unit, don't pay more than 10 times the going rate for a comparable week in a local hotel or rental apartment. You can get those figures from newspaper ads or from a real estate agent. For a right-to-use time-share, divide the sales price by the number of years offered. If the amount is less than the cost of the equivalent rental, you're getting a good deal. Before buying from the developer, see whether a time-share resale agent is listing equivalent accommodations at the same project. If so, you may be able to swing a better deal on the price.

■ **Buy from a proven developer.** Stick with experience and you'll be less likely to find your vacation spoiled by poor maintenance, bad management, or unforeseen lawsuits. Big developers—such as Marriott, Hilton, and Disney—are also more likely to run rental or resale offices to help you when you want to sell.

■ **Investigate your ability to swap your time-share before you buy.** For information about time-share trades, call the two biggest exchange services: Resort Condominium International (800–338–7777) and Interval International (800–482–4256).

■ **Carefully check out the time-share and the developer.** Ask the developer for customer references and then interview several of them. Check the firm's reputation further with the attorney general's office or any appropriate state agency that keeps an eye on time-sharing.

Before signing any agreement, take home copies of the proposed contract, schedule of maintenance fees, and, if there is one, the developer's disclosure statement or offering memorandum. Scour the sales contract or other materials for a statement of your rights should the resort run into difficulty. If you're buying a fee simple time-share, you'll want to know when the title will become free of any claims by the property's lenders. In most cases there won't be clear title until you've paid in full and a certain percentage of weeks in your unit is sold. In a right-to-use contract, you will want a nondisturbance clause that ensures that the property's mortgage holder recognizes your occupancy rights in case of a foreclosure on the property. Make sure the same clause is in the time-share's mort-

gage or construction loan. If it isn't, the clause in your sales contract won't hold up.

Be sure that the developer is obligated to reserve a portion of your maintenance fee for major repairs and replacements, too. Otherwise you may face heavy special assessments in later years. The developer should be required to ante up for this fund an amount equal to the number of all unsold time-share weeks.

Have a real estate attorney familiar with the rules of time-sharing review any agreements before you sign. If you don't know of such a pro, ask your attorney to refer you to one. Most states that regulate time-shares—not all do—require the developer to give you at least three days to cancel your contract without penalty, but you'll want to have your lawyer write in such an escape clause if it's not already included.

Raw Land

Who hasn't watched the spread of cities and suburbs in this country and wished he'd had the foresight to buy a chunk of land 20 years ago and wait for developers to start a bidding war over the property? Success stories based on such prescience are common in the world of land speculation. Unfortunately, so are stories of unmitigated failure. Many speculators have bought land only to find that the interstate they were expecting wound up detouring 15 miles to the north. Others have learned that the cost of buying raw land—financing, property taxes, and insurance—were far greater than they had expected. And what about those unsuspecting souls who bought Florida swampland from fast-talking salesmen? So it should come as no surprise to you that raw land is the riskiest of all real estate investments.

Indeed, land speculation is suitable only if you have extra money you can afford to lose and you can wait years for appreciation—typically 10 years or more. Unlike other types of real estate, raw land won't pay you annual income; the payoff, if any, comes only when you sell. Still, if you can afford to tie up your money for years and you invest wisely, the profit potential in buying undeveloped land is huge. Some general rules for land grabbers:

■ **Do the math.** Empty land that seems to be just sitting there is actually busy gobbling up money. When buying a parcel, you'll need to come up with a down payment and then mortgage payments, property taxes, and insurance premiums year after year. So you can't calculate the true profit potential of any land deal until you first determine the costs of owning the land. Start by totaling the preceding expenses and add any other charges you might have to pay, such as environmental studies or swamp drainage. As a rough

rule, land values have to double every four or five years just to keep up with the ongoing costs of ownership. Therefore it's essential to work with a real estate agent to estimate the sort of price appreciation common in the area you're considering.

■ **Know what the land is worth.** Land values vary dramatically from region to region and from year to year. For example, one lot that is suitable for residential development might run anywhere from $10,000 to $100,000. Farmland, on the other hand, is generally cheaper; it typically runs between $1,000 and $5,000 an acre. Whatever your pleasure, have any property appraised before you make a bid. The Appraisal Institute (875 N. Michigan Ave., Suite 2400, Chicago, Ill. 60611; 312-335-4100), an industry trade group, can refer you to an appraiser in your area. Ask the appraiser to tell you not only how much the property is worth today, but its expected future value, given local development and population patterns.

■ **Have plenty of cash on hand.** Banks routinely make loans for purchases of raw land, but they require unusually high down payments to help lessen their risks. Expect to put down a minimum of 25% of the total cost and as much as 40%.

■ **Be wary of out-of-the-way bargains.** There's usually an excellent reason why acres in the middle of nowhere are selling so cheaply: they're in the middle of nowhere. Forgive the cliché, but location is the most important factor to consider when buying undeveloped property. Check with local government authorities to see if the area's population is growing or if there is a shortage of land available for development. Ask these officials, as well as local builders and developers, how long it will take anticipated development to reach your particular plot of land.

■ **Understand the local land-use trends.** It won't do you much good to own land suitable only for industrial use if local developers want property for building apartment houses. So make sure you understand the realistic potential of any parcel you're considering. Also, be certain that the local zoning board agrees with your estimation. If you think your land is perfect for a shopping mall, but the area is zoned for tract houses, you'll be out of luck. Sometimes zoning laws can be changed, however. So if you face a zoning problem, ask town officials whether you could get a rezoning. Remember to factor into your original cost analysis any expenses for lawyers and government fees.

Find out, too, whether any nearby developments might affect your property. Generally, new schools and shopping malls are good neighbors. Nuclear waste dumps and prisons are bad ones.

■ **Seeing is believing.** Never buy land without visiting the property. Brochures, off-site sales presentations, or videotapes are not sufficient. They reveal only what the developer wants prospective buyers to see. You need to walk the property and check out things like the terrain, view, and path of the sun.

■ **There's no place like home.** Playing the land speculation game is tough enough without losing the home-field advantage. So stick to properties in your own region. You'll have a much better shot at figuring out development and population growth trends than if you buy in a place you can barely pronounce.

■ **Turn over rocks.** Not literally, of course. It's nearly as important to know, however, what's under your land as what you might put on it. Get a percolation test to determine how well your property drains. Test the land for environmental hazards such as toxic waste and to determine the property's ability to support buildings. Seemingly solid land can sometimes be little more than quicksand. Expect to pay several thousand dollars for all these tests; it's money well spent, though. When investing in raw land just as with any other type of real estate, early expense and effort can save you from later losses and lament.

CHAPTER 17

How to Invest in Other Ways—If You Dare

This chapter will discuss investments that, for the most part, you ought to avoid. Why bring them up at all? Simple: One day you will probably hear a pitch to invest in some of them from a stockbroker, financial planner, insurance agent, or a commercial. When you hear the spiel, you'll be prepared. To be sure, a smart or lucky investor can make money investing in the likes of pork bellies, vintage Coke bottles, or oil and gas partnerships. Millions have in the past, and millions will in the future. For most individuals, however, a balanced and diversified investment portfolio can be achieved quite easily and satisfactorily with three kinds of assets: stocks, bonds, and cash. You might add a fourth—real estate. In this chapter, however, you will read about investment products and categories that fall outside those classes or represent a potentially unwise way to invest in them.

Three of these—**annuities, futures, and options**—may involve either risks or costs that you might find unacceptable. Two others—**precious metals** and **limited partnerships**—are widely misunderstood and often a drain on the average small investor's portfolio. Still another category—**collectibles**—is great fun and a potential profit maker. It is, however, among the hardest markets to understand or predict. Finally, **lending to relatives or friends** puts not only your money at risk, but your important relationships, too.

Now, these investments sometimes can help you achieve your financial goals and meet legitimate needs. Still, vigilance and skepticism should be foremost in your mind when you consider any of the following investment alternatives.

Annuities

Like most life insurance industry products, annuities can be a bit confusing. Stripped down to its essentials, an annuity is a tax-sheltered investment sponsored by an insurance company that pays you earnings and also has a death benefit. Generally, when you buy an annuity you hand over a lump of money—ranging from $2,000 to $10,000—to a stockbroker, insurance agent, or financial planner. This salesman then passes the money along to a life insurance company, which in turn issues the annuity contract. Some insurers instead let you buy a **flexible-premium retirement annuity** through regular periodic payments, sometimes of as little as $25 a month. In either case, the insurer agrees to pay the holder of the annuity contract a certain amount of money at a certain date; if you die while owning the annuity, the beneficiary you name will receive a death benefit. Just as with an Individual Retirement Account, the income that your money earns grows tax-free until you

make a withdrawal from the annuity. Unlike an IRA, though, your annuity contributions are unlimited.

When you're ready to withdraw your money, you have three options. You can (1) pull all your money out; (2) withdraw a little at a time: or (3) **annuitize.** This latter simply means that you can convert the account's value into a monthly income stream that can run for a period you select, typically the rest of your life. Incidentally, you don't need to annuitize with the same insurance company that sponsored your annuity; you can switch to a different company offering a better deal. However you decide to receive your cash, you'll owe income tax on the earnings when you get them, at whatever tax bracket you happen to be in at the time. If you take the money out of the annuity before you reach age 59½ you'll also have to pay a 10% tax penalty for early withdrawal.

By and large, there are no front-end fees on annuities. The salesman's commission, which ranges from 4% to 7%, is factored into the annuity's interest rate and your payout. In other words, the commission is hidden by tucking it into—or, more accurately, taking it out of—your earnings. Annuities come with hidden annual fees, however, which can easily total 2% a year. That's almost a full percentage point more than the fees on an average mutual fund bought through a tax-sheltered IRA or 401(k). Most annuities also charge you sizable fees for substantial withdrawals. These so-called **surrender charges** are as high as 15% of your accumulated earnings for a withdrawal made in the first year of the contract. After that, the charges drop by about one percentage point each year until they disappear, typically in about seven to 10 years. Many insurance companies, however, let you withdraw 10% of your account's value each year without incurring any penalty (although Uncle Sam will not be as forgiving if you're younger than 59½).

Once you get beyond those basics, things get thorny. For instance, deciding which annuity, if any, is right for you means choosing not only between two payout options—deferred and immediate—but also between two rates of return: fixed or variable. Confused already? Unfortunately, this already daunting investment is made even more difficult to understand by the zealous legions of insurance agents, stockbrokers, and investment advisers who tout annuities as a panacea for virtually every financial need. To hear some hucksters, annuities are the answer to paying for college and funding your retirement, as well as the greatest tax shelter on earth.

The truth is quite different. In fact, there are two very important reasons why you should use extreme caution before buying annuities. First, no annuities are federally insured, even those sold in banks. You might not realize this, given the aggressive marketing of annuities in bank lobbies. It's easy to assume that because an investment is hawked in a bank and because bank CDs have federal insurance, the investment must be insured, too. The second reason for approaching annuities with eyes wide open is that these products generally require a long-term commitment from you. Otherwise you'll wind up paying more in fees than you'll earn on the investment.

These caveats aside, annuities have their merits, and you may want to give them a look. A well-chosen annuity can sometimes be a sensible, tax-deferred way to save for retirement that's at least 10 years away. Alternatively, an annuity can help ensure a reliable, lifelong income stream once you've stopped working.

There are two basic types of annuities, each offering a different schedule of payouts:

■ **Immediate-pay annuities,** sometimes called **lifetime annuities,** are purchased with a lump sum, typically by people in retirement who want to provide a guaranteed stream of income for themselves. You might get the lump sum from your pension plan distribution or from your IRA or Keogh plan. As its name suggests, an immediate-pay annuity begins doling out regular payments as soon as you buy the contract—generally on a monthly basis. Part of the problem with immediate-pay annuities is that by locking in a set amount of income, your earnings can get eaten away by inflation. That is, although the cost of living will keep going up, the size of your monthly checks won't.

■ **Deferred annuities,** which are the type most annuity investors choose, appeal mostly to people in their forties or fifties looking to postpone paying taxes on their investment earnings for years to come, typically in retirement. You don't start receiving their income until you either cash in the contract, make periodic withdrawals, or annuitize. (Consult a financial planner or tax adviser before making any withdrawals, since the rules are complicated.) Think of deferred annuities as tax-sheltered CDs or mutual funds—with higher fees. You can buy them either with a lump sum or on the installment plan.

The amount of income you'll receive depends in large part on a second choice you'll have to make when shopping for an annuity: fixed or variable. If you opt for a **fixed-rate annuity,** the insurer pays a specific, fixed interest rate usually for a year, though some companies lock in rates for as long as 10 years. The earnings are tax-deferred if you go with a deferred annuity. In recent years, fixed-rate annuities have paid 4% to 8% annually. Each year, the insurer announces the fixed return for the year ahead; the rate depends

on the insurer's current investment portfolio. Fixed-rate annuities are generally very conservative investments; they typically buy government and corporate bonds as well as residential mortgages. Since you're locking in an interest rate, however, your fixed-rate annuity won't beat inflation.

Warning: Many fixed-rate annuities pay enticingly high rates in the first year of the contract as a lure. Afterward, your return falls considerably, often by three or more percentage points. One way to assess how an insurer treats its investors after the first year is to ask for the company's interest rate floor—the minimum interest rate you'll receive from the contract. With most fixed-rate contracts, the interest rate is guaranteed to be at least 4.5% a year. If you find one much lower, you can probably do better elsewhere.

The return on a **variable-rate annuity,** by contrast, fluctuates with the stock, bond, and money markets. Consequently, a variable-rate annuity offers the potential for much higher returns than a fixed-rate contract, but at greater risk. Variable annuities are in essence mutual funds wrapped inside insurance contracts; again, the earnings are tax-deferred if you buy a deferred annuity. The insurance usually consists of a guarantee that your heirs will get back what you invested.

The insurer offers an assortment of stock, bond, and money-market funds, called subaccounts in annuity lingo, and gives you the responsibility of choosing among them. Established mutual fund companies such as Dreyfus, Fidelity, and Neuberger & Berman run the subaccount portfolios. The typical annuity offers about seven subaccounts, with a variety of investment objectives. Some annuities, however, boast more than 30 investment options. Within the stock category, you may be offered a selection of aggressive growth, blue-chip, and international funds, among others. Within the bond funds, you might choose among corporate, government, and high-yield portfolios. You can allocate your money as you see fit and switch among subaccounts with no charge, usually by making a telephone call.

With most investments, you do the majority of your research when you put in your money. Annuity investors, however, may have to plan carefully when they are ready to cash out, too. That might be sooner than you think: once surrender charges have expired, you can take your money out of the company that built up your account without penalty and take it to a competing insurer offering better terms. Provided you keep your money in an annuity, you won't have to pay the 10% early withdrawal tax penalty to the IRS. You will, however, have to fill out the IRS's **1035 exchange form,** which your new insurance company will be only too pleased to give you.

Before considering any withdrawal or payout from your annuity, you need to un-derstand annuitizing—turning over the accumulated value of your annuity to an insurer in return for fixed monthly income. Annuitizing has a distinct tax advantage; it lets you further postpone paying taxes on some of the earnings you have accrued. Each check you receive is considered only partly earnings; the rest is your original principal. You pay taxes only on the earnings and only as you receive them. If you want to annuitize for the certainty of getting a specific amount of income each year, you'll have to decide among three more choices:

■ **Life annuity.** By choosing a standard life annuity, you guarantee yourself a lifetime income. Since the payments expire when you die, however, you're also betting on how long you will live. If you die before the insurer thinks you will, you won't get all the annuity income you were entitled to receive. This option may not be appropriate if, say, your spouse will be counting on receiving the annuity income after you die.

■ **Joint-and-survivor annuity.** If you can afford to receive 5% or so less in your monthly checks, you can instruct the insurer to make sure your spouse or another dependent will keep getting paid after you die—for as long as your beneficiary is alive. If you outlive the other person named in the annuity, you'll keep getting checks until you die. A joint-and-survivor annuity is sensible for most couples.

■ **Life-with-certain-period annuity.** This option assures you of a lifetime income while also guaranteeing payments for a set period of time, usually 10 years. If you die within that time, your beneficiary collects the remaining payments.

The other way to pull money out of your annuity is by setting up a **systematic withdrawal plan.** With this method, *you* tell the insurance company how much cash to send you from your account each month. Systematic withdrawal offers flexibility; at any time you can raise, lower, or stop the payments as well as annuitize. However, with this method your account could run out of money someday. What's more, cash paid out in a systematic plan is usually fully taxable until you have drained all your earnings from the annuity account.

You will probably fare better in the long run with a variable annuity than a fixed-rate one, provided you select the right company and that you have at least 10 years to go before you'll need the money. That will give you enough time to ride out any short-term market dips as well as avoid any onerous surrender charges. To start your search for the best annuity for you, get the latest issue of a reliable annuity publication. For information on variable annuities, order Morningstar's *Variable Annuity/Life Performance Report* (800-735-0700) or *Variable Annuity Research & Data Service Large Report* (404-998-5186). For a list of fixed annuities, buy *Comparative Annuity Reports* (916-487-7863). You may be able to find some or all of these publications in your public library.

When selecting an annuity, look for one with:

■ **A solid insurer behind it.** Don't even consider an annuity unless it is offered by an insurer rated at least A+ for financial soundness by A. M. Best, Aa– by Moody's Investors Service, or AA– by Standard & Poor's. Your annuity salesman can provide these ratings, or you can find them in large public libraries.

■ **Proven performance.** To make your first cut in choosing a deferred annuity, compare the record of subaccounts in the contract with the average returns for their investment category over each of the past three years. You can generally find these figures in the *Variable Annuity/Life Performance Report.* If the subaccounts that interest you haven't been around for three years, pass. Similarly, cross off any annuity that doesn't break out its returns this way. Make sure to get performance figures after expenses have been deducted from the results. Any decent insurance agent or stockbroker selling annuities should be glad to help you compare the performance of variable annuity accounts.

■ **Relatively low expenses.** In general, be wary of annuities with total expenses that exceed about 2% annually. That said, you needn't avoid an annuity with a strong investment performance simply because its fees are a bit above this benchmark. Your agent or annuity salesman can show you a breakdown of the contract's annual expenses.

Consider buying an annuity directly from a **low-load insurer** who doesn't use a traditional sales force and thus doesn't have as many selling expenses to pass on to policyholders. A few discount brokerages and mutual fund operators, such as Fidelity, have teamed up with insurance companies in recent years to offer annuities with low or no sales and surrender charges. You can get a list of some of these sold in your area by calling Fee for Service (800-874-5662), an annuity brokerage.

■ **A bailout provision.** Essential for fixed-rate annuity holders, this contract clause gives you one to three months to transfer your money to another annuity without penalty if your interest rate drops by a preset amount, usually one percentage point or more.

Gold and Other Precious Metals

Gold still holds a coveted place in the minds of a considerable number of American investors. No doubt many of these gold bugs can't shake the memory of gold prices rising from $35 an ounce in 1970 to $825 in 1980. They might choose to ignore the fact that prices have ranged between $285 and $400 for most of the past decade, or that precious metals mutual funds, on average, plunged in value by nearly 25% from their mid '94 peak through early '95. Some aficionados can't let go of the notion that gold is an ideal inflation hedge. Yet in the 20 years since Americans could legally own gold, the price of the yellow metal has risen almost exactly in line with inflation. Finally, some diehards see gold and other precious metals such as silver and platinum as the ultimate defense against the collapse of, take your pick: the U.S. economy, the world's financial markets, democracy, or just about any other cataclysmic event that may be lurking around the corner. In reality the price of gold is determined largely by the supply for it and the demand—by jewelers, dentists, some manufacturers, and investors. Silver and platinum, by contrast, tend to fluctuate in price primarily as a result of industrial supply and demands. For instance, silver is bought chiefly for its use in photography, electronics, jewelry, and silverware. Platinum is a key component of catalytic converters for cars and popular in jewelry.

By now you're starting to get an idea of the truth about gold and other precious metals: great for bracelets and rings, not too hot for investors. Still, a fair (though decreasing) number of financial planners and other experts continue to advise some of their clients to put 5% to 10% of a well-diversified portfolio into the stuff. Should you? That depends. If you've got a net worth excluding your home of $500,000 or more, you have enough money to justify the inclusion in your portfolio of assets that guard against catastrophe but pay no dividends or interest. Common folk, on the other hand, don't have the time or luxury to worry about the remote possibilities of currency collapse and hyperinflation. They're more focused on mundane goals like saving for college or retirement, which requires that their investments earn their keep. That means investing in stocks and bonds, which, unlike, say, gold bars in the safe, can consistently earn interest and dividends.

Still determined to own gold or another precious metal? Then you need to decide how to stake your claim. Your choices:

■ **Bullion.** For those who buy gold in preparation for Armageddon, nothing will do but the real physical metal. Gold actually comes in a variety of sizes, ranging from thin wafers up to 400-ounce bars (though the latter are used only by the government). The most convenient way to own gold bullion is by purchasing one-ounce coins. They are easiest to

store, price, and sell. You can take your pick among U.S. American Eagles, Canadian Maple Leafs, and South African Krugerrands. Don't bother with the limited-quantity numismatic coins minted for particular events, since buying them means you need to become a knowledgeable coin collector.

The most sought after one-ounce silver coins are the Australian Kookaburra, the Canadian Silver Maple Leaf, and the U.S. Silver Eagle. Silver sells for much less per ounce than gold—in the '90s, silver has been running about $3.50 to $6.00 an ounce compared with gold's $285 to $425. As a result, silver is a pretty good way to get yourself started in bullion collecting.

Platinum is much rarer than either gold or silver. That's why it sells for a bit more than gold ($350 to $550 an ounce in recent years). When choosing among platinum one-ounce coins, stick with the Australian Koala Bear, the Canadian Platinum Maple Leaf, or the Isle of Man Noble.

Before trading your long greens for gold or any other bright metal, get price quotes from at least three reputable table dealers. Your best bet to find one is calling or writing the Professional Numismatists Guild (3950 Concordia Lane, Fallbrook, Calif. 92028; 619-728-1300) and asking for member dealers in your area. When you query a dealer, ask for the "market" on whatever type of bullion you're seeking, which means you want both the buying and selling price. This way you'll know what you could sell your coins for if you had to unload them immediately. Be sure to ask about commissions, shipping charges, and any other fees. For one-ounce coins, expect to pay a premium of 5% or so over the value of the gold. That covers the cost of minting and distributing the coins, including commissions. There's one more cost to consider: You may want to put your bullion in a safe-deposit box or have a safe installed in your home.

■ **Accounts and certificates.** If you don't need to caress your gold, silver, or platinum cache, some banks, brokerage firms, and coin dealers will sell you a fractional interest in the metals that they hold in a vault. You can buy your stake all at once, for a minimum of $1,000 to $2,000, or you can build up your cache gradually by directing, say, $50 a month in what is known as a so-called **accumulation plan.** Some firms give you a certificate of ownership, while others just send a monthly statement. Shop around among sellers and ask for the total cost of ownership, including application and storage charges. One-half of 1% to 1% of the amount you're storing is standard. Buy only from well-known institutions, and make sure that your metal is in a segregated account, which means that the bank or broker can't use it. Be certain, also, that the gold, silver, or platinum is

insured in case the institution holding the account or certificate fails.

■ **Precious metal stocks.** A more volatile, but potentially more profitable, way to invest in gold, silver, and platinum is to buy shares of publicly traded mining companies. Mining share prices tend to swing more widely than the price of the metals they dig up. That's because their share prices also are influenced by the fluctuations of the stock market and the fortunes of the individual mining company. Shares of North American and Australian gold mining companies are generally less risky than those of South African firms. The South African gold stocks, however, tend to pay higher dividends.

■ **Precious metals mutual funds.** A more conservative way to invest in mining stocks is to buy shares in one of the several dozen gold and precious metals mutual funds that specialize in them (minimum investment: typically $1,000). Since these funds invest in mining stocks, their share prices tend to fluctuate more wildly than the actual price of gold or silver bullion. Because they are highly diversified and often own shares in more than 20 mining companies, however, investing in the funds is safer than choosing just one or two gold stocks. More important, precious metals funds are managed by a professional stock picker who knows the mining business far better than any amateur. Also, these funds can more easily buy shares in foreign mining companies than you could, adding yet another valuable layer of diversification and opportunity. You can compare the returns and investment styles of most gold and precious metals funds in *Morningstar Mutual Funds* and the *Value Line Mutual Fund Survey*; one or both is probably in your local library.

Futures and Options

The first thing you should know about commodity futures and options is that unless you're an extraordinarily confident, knowledgeable, and aggressive investor, you can stop reading right here and jump ahead to the section on limited partnerships. Though the potential for quick and huge profits continues to lure fortune seekers every year (remember Hillary Clinton's lucrative escapade into the cattle futures market?), the even greater chance of losing your shirt makes these investments phenomenally risky at best and downright dangerous at worst. In fact, most brokerage houses require that you meet strict financial suitability tests before they'll even let you start trading in certain futures and options.

Specifically, you'll be asked about your investment experience, net worth, and annual income. Brokerages typically look for investors with annual earnings of more than $50,000 and often a net worth in the hundreds of thousands of dollars. As a rule, when Wall Street hesitates to take your money, you know you are in very deep water. Incidentally, at the same time a broker is sizing you up as a commodities client, you ought to be checking out his credentials, too. Most traditional stockbrokers don't know beans about beans or, for that matter, any type of futures contract.

Before you confuse your discerning palate for orange juice with an ability to predict orange juice concentrate prices in the future, consider this: An estimated three out of every four investors who speculate in commodities lose money. That includes professional traders. Leave out the pros, and the number of amateurs who actually make money could probably fit on one soybean. Nonetheless, this is a full-service book, and those of you who want to venture into the pits ought to know at least how to lose your hard-earned money—or possibly make some.

There are essentially two ways an individual can invest in **commodities.** The first is to open a **commodities account** with a broker, either at a firm that handles commodity transactions exclusively or at a major stock brokerage. The adviser managing your account will decide what to buy and sell. You'll pay a fee equal to roughly 2% of the amount you invest. In addition, many commodities account managers hold on to a percentage of the profits they make—as high as 20%.

If you don't have the inclination or bravado to invest in commodities on your own, you might consider a **commodities fund,** which pools investors' money under the guidance of a professional manager. Public commodities funds actually are limited partnerships. You buy units in the limited partnership through a broker, who receives a commission ranging from 4% to 8%. Generally, you can invest in these funds for as little as $2,500. However, there are several drawbacks to these funds. First, they are generally lousy performers. Studies of public commodities funds have found that, on average, they yield between 4% and 10% annually, depending on the time period and the fund. That's hardly worth the risk. The returns would be a lot higher if not for the second major drawback with the funds: They're expensive. According to one study of commodities funds, investors paid an average of 19% a year off the top to cover management fees, brokerage commissions, and performance fees. By comparison, the average stock mutual fund charges investors less than 2% a year in fees. What's more, it's far rougher to pull your money out of a commodities fund than it is to withdraw from a mutual fund.

What exactly is a futures contract? Simply put, it's a legal obligation to buy or sell a specific quantity of a commodity, financial instrument, or stock index at a particular date in the future for a fixed price. You can buy or sell a futures contract in just about anything: commodities such as corn, wheat, tin, gold, soybeans, stocks, orange juice, gasoline, pork bellies, or oil; or financial instruments such as stocks and stock indexes, which are essentially baskets of stocks. When you buy a futures contract, you're making a bet that the price of, say, wheat will increase by next December.

This expectation of rising prices is called a **long position.** A **short position** is a bet that the price of a given commodity or financial instrument will fall at some point in the future—say, for example, that the price of wheat will fall by next May. How you reach these conclusions is key: if your idea comes from years of research and personal knowledge, you might have a chance of guessing correctly. If your hunch comes from a fast-talking broker on the other end of a cold call, your only sane move is to hang up the phone.

What makes futures trading so tantalizing? Leverage. You need to put up only a small percentage of a contract's value to invest, usually between 5% and 10%. That gives you an opportunity to double your money or do far better, if everything works out. The money you put up is known as **margin**. Here's how it works: Suppose you wanted to control a futures contract for 10,000 bushels of corn at $5 a bushel. For this $50,000 contract, you might have to give your broker only $2,500. As the price of corn rises or falls, the value of your futures contract soars or plunges. For example, if the bushel price of corn jumps just 20% to $6, your profit would be $10,000, or four times your original investment. Now that's leverage. You'd reap this huge profit because the contract you bought that controlled $50,000 worth of corn now controls $60,000 worth. That $10,000 increase is all yours (minus the brokerage commissions you pay, of course).

But here is where it gets interesting. If corn prices fell just 25¢ a bushel, or 5%, you would have lost your entire $2,500 investment. That's because your $50,000 worth of corn is now worth just $47,500—a loss of 5%, or $2,500. If you're starting to get the idea of the potential for loss in the futures market, imagine that corn prices fall $1 per bushel. You would then be out $10,000 and receive a **margin call** from your broker. That's when you're asked—in no uncertain terms—to cough up more money to make up for losses in your contract. So with futures you can lose everything you invested—and more. Now you're seeing the beauty and tragedy of futures: both your profits and your losses can be substantially more than you initially invest. The sky is the theoretical limit on the profit side. On the loss side, however, your theoretical

risk is the entire value of the contract (though it's hardly likely that the price of corn might fall to zero). This is why brokers and dealers want to be sure you have the financial wherewithal to invest in commodities before they accept you as a customer.

If you hold a futures contract until it expires, you will then have to write a check for the cost of whatever commodity or financial instrument you were speculating on. If you had a short position, you'll have to come up with 5,000 bushels of corn or whatever. But don't worry about having a semi pull up to your house and dump 5,000 bushels of corn on your front lawn. Less than 3% of futures contracts are actually carried through. The rest are settled before the delivery date in cash. To close your position, you just buy or sell a similar contract, one representing the opposite of your original position. Most futures investors, in fact, close out their positions months before their contract matures.

It should come as little surprise that disputes frequently arise between commodities clients and their firms, since many investors wind up speculating in futures without sufficient knowledge or direction from their brokers. In some cases they even are egged on inappropriately by brokers. If you feel you've been misled or even cheated by a broker, write to the Commodity Futures Trading Commission (2033 K St. N.W., Washington, D.C. 20581). The federal regulator of all U.S. futures and options markets investigates charges of fraud against dealers. The agency also handles complaints against futures brokers and provides a number of free useful publications. Another avenue of recourse is the National Futures Association (200 W. Madison St., Suite 1600, Chicago, Ill. 60606). Though an industry trade group, the NFA tries to resolve any dispute involving a member firm and also offers an array of free publications.

A somewhat safer way to invest in commodities is through **options.** Though also highly speculative, option contracts lower your risks by limiting your potential losses to the amount you invest. There are two types of options: **calls** and **puts.** When you buy a call option, you receive the right, but not the obligation, to buy a stock, an index, or a futures contract at a set price called the **strike price** for a specific period, typically a few months. (The strike price for stock options appears in the newspaper daily.) A call option, in other words, is a bet that the underlying asset will rise in price. Imagine, for example, that IBM is trading at $50 a share and you think the company has tremendous prospects. You might buy a call option that lets you buy, say, 500 shares of IBM at $52 anytime within two months. If IBM's share price soars to $60 during that time, the investor on the other side of the transaction who

wrote that call option is obligated to sell you—for $52—a stock that is now worth $60. If the price does not rise as you had hoped, you simply choose not to exercise your option. Then, all you've lost is the price of the option, which is considerably less than the cost of buying the underlying shares anticipating that their price might skyrocket.

When you buy a put option, you receive the right, but not the obligation, to sell the underlying security or asset at set price for a specific period of time. In other words, you're betting that the price of the underlying asset or security will fall. Imagine again that IBM is trading at $50 a share. In this instance, however, you think the company will fare poorly in the future. You might buy a put option that lets you sell, say, 500 shares of IBM at $48 in two months. If IBM's share price drops to $40 during that time, the person who wrote you that put option must buy from you at $48 a share the same stock that you can get for $40. As with a call option, if the price of the asset or security doesn't fall, you don't have to exercise the option. Once again, however, you'll then lose your initial investment.

In both of these examples, your apparent profit seems to be $8 a share. However, there are two important costs you must factor into any options calculation. Both will lower your potential gains. First is the commission on the transaction, which generally ranges between one-half of 1% to 5% of the cost of the options contract. That cost, known as the **premium,** is the price you pay for the right to cash in if your options speculation works out. The size of the premium, and thus the cost of the options contract, depends on the particulars of the investment, such as the length of the contract and the volatility of the underlying investment. (The premium per share appears in the options pages of the newspaper.) It's important to remember, however, that you'll need to surpass the strike price on your options contract before you make a profit. So, returning to the previous example, if IBM was trading at $50 and you bought a call option at $52, you would likely *lose* money if the share price rises to just $53, since the commission and premium cost will have eaten up your profits.

Options often are used as a **hedge**—protection against an unwanted move in the price of an underlying security. For example, imagine that you actually own 500 shares of IBM and expect the stock to rise in value. As a hedge against the shares falling in price, you might buy a put option on 500 shares. This is known as **writing a covered option.** Now, if IBM stumbles, at least some of the losses in your stock will be recouped by gains from your options. Conversely, if the stock rises, you'll have sacrificed some of the gains since you will have lost your option investment. For some investors,

however, that's a small price to pay for a little security.

Limited Partnerships

You have quite possibly read a lot about real estate limited partnerships in recent years, since so many of them turned out to be rotten deals for investors, many of whom sued the people who ran the deals. Chapter 16 offers a complete discussion of real estate partnerships. In this chapter you'll read about the other kinds of partnerships—and there are plenty. Broadway plays, computer leasing, motion pictures, cable television, and oil wells are just a few of the varied investments you can make through a limited partnership with a minimum of $5,000 or so. Though some partnerships pay out profits to investors on a monthly basis, most make such distributions (if there are any) just four times a year. The partnerships typically expect investors to stay in for seven to 10 years. For most investors, however, the disadvantages of limited partnerships far outweigh the benefits. You'll soon see why.

A **limited partnership (LP)** is a business organization comprising a general partner, who runs the LP's daily business, and limited partners like yourself, who put up the money. Limited partners receive income, capital gains, and tax benefits generated by the partnership. The *limited* part of the arrangement stems from the fact that your liability in the partnership is limited to the amount of money you invest. If the deal blows up, you can lose your entire investment, but that's all. You also are protected from legal action against the partnership. The general partner, however, has much more exposure to loss and lawsuit should the LP unravel. When you invest in a partnership, you buy what are called **units** or **fractional shares** of units. A **public partnership** is one that is registered with the Securities and Exchange Commission and is open to most investors. A **private partnership** is not registered with the SEC and is generally restricted to affluent investors. Private limited partnerships tend to be far less diversified than public ones; a private partnership might own, for instance, a single medical office building.

There are two basic types of partnerships. A **specified** partnership explains in advance how it will operate and what it will buy. A **blind pool** partnership does not set out its specific investment strategy. You have to assume the general partner will make wise decisions with your money. Three words of advice before you invest a nickel in a blind pool: Just say no.

An LP's edge over many other investments is that the partnership itself does not pay taxes. Because all income and capital gains are passed through to the limited partners, you pay taxes only once—at the individual rate. If, on the other hand, you own stock in a corporation that pays dividends, the firm's profits are taxed twice. The company pays corporate taxes to the government on its profits, and you shell out taxes on your dividends.

You may be wondering, With that tax advantage, why doesn't everybody invest in LPs? For a while it seemed as though everybody did. The salad days of limited partnerships were in the 1980s, when they were viewed primarily as tax shelters. At that time investors plowed billions into LPs, often to legally write off on their tax returns more than the amount they invested. They took advantage of liberal tax benefits such as quick depreciation and tax credits for real estate projects, and intangible drilling costs for oil and gas exploration. Since making money wasn't the chief justification for these partnerships, many deals invested in things (like new office buildings and jojoba beans) that were not necessarily economically promising. The Tax Reform Act of 1986, however, stripped away many partnership tax breaks. Consequently, hundreds if not thousands of partnerships have since unraveled, leaving investors holding the bag. More specifically, they were left holding limited partnership shares selling for as little as 10 cents on the dollar, if they were selling at all.

Given this history, you might think all limited partnerships are bad deals. In fact, for investors who already have a solid foundation of stocks and bonds, a limited partnership can make sense—particularly if you're looking for the chance to reap great profits at great risk. Others might find appeal in the few tax shelters that partnerships still offer, which are discussed next. Some limited partnerships even provide steady income. For most people, though, LPs offer too many risks without enough reward. See for yourself, with the following breakdown of the benefits and liabilities of LPs.

THE BENEFITS OF LIMITED PARTNERSHIPS

■ **Expertise.** Like a mutual fund, a limited partnership can provide you with a level of managerial expertise you otherwise could not afford.

■ **Tax breaks (sometimes).** In addition to the pass-through tax benefit, you can still find shelter from the IRS through some limited partnerships—largely real estate partnerships. For example, limited partnerships that invest in housing designed for low- and moderate-income people, when structured correctly, offer tax credits of as much as 9%. There are also tax credits for investors in limited partnerships that renovate certified historic buildings. Though the major chunk of an LP's payout is generally taxable as income in the year it is received, some of it may be sheltered from taxes. For example, a portion of a real estate LP's distributions may be sheltered by depreciation, while some of an oil and gas drilling partnership's profits may be protected by depletion and depreciation allowances. In certain cases, a portion of the distribution might be treated as a return of your original investment and thus not taxable. Such rules are complicated, of course, and require the expertise of a tax lawyer or accountant.

■ **Diversification.** Successful and well-financed partnerships often invest in multiple projects. In this way they can often provide a dependable income stream to investors even if one or two projects don't pay off.

THE LIABILITIES OF LIMITED PARTNERSHIPS

■ **Income is hardly guaranteed.** It's not uncommon for partnerships, even well-managed ones, to overpay for property or to misjudge the dynamics of an industry. When the underlying businesses or projects can't generate enough cash to cover expenses, the limited partners can find themselves without any income distributions.

■ **Some income is not really income at all.** Some sponsors use investors' capital to make income distributions, especially when the partnership agreement promises a specific return for a specific period of time—say, 8% for the first five years. Often, a partnership sponsor will simply return some or all of an investor's money and call it income.

■ **Partnership fees are often outrageously high.** The brokerage firms who sell limited partnerships charge up-front commissions that generally range from 8% to 10% of the investment. In addition, most partnerships charge management fees of 3% to 4% of assets each year. Some sponsors even levy an incentive fee, often as high as 15%, every time they sell an asset. Ostensibly the fee is to provide an incentive for the general partner to get the highest sales price possible when selling off partnership assets. This presumes, of course, that a responsibility to the limited partners is not incentive enough on its own.

■ **Partnerships will complicate your life.** If you think a mutual fund prospectus is complicated, wait until you see the prospectus and documentation for a limited partnership. A partnership's offering document typically consists of hundreds of pages of fine print, plus tables of projections and fee schedules. Perhaps the most maddening part of being a partner-

ship investor is filling out the IRS's annual **K-1 form,** reporting your partnership income, capital gains, and tax benefits. General partners typically mail out K-1 forms at the last minute, requiring limited partners to request extensions on their own tax returns and pay more to their accountants.

■ **You might not be able to get your money out of the partnership when promised.** Because general partners and sponsors earn big bucks from those annual management fees, they have little incentive to liquidate a money-losing partnership. So when the time comes to sell off assets and distribute the proceeds, they often find reasons to delay. Some general partners opt for a **roll-up,** in which they combine some strong partnerships with some weak ones. They create a new company and issue stock to the limited partners. The company is then listed on a stock exchange or traded over-the-counter (these should not be confused with **master limited partnerships,** which are essentially LPs that start out trading on a public exchange). Though limited partners are given the chance to vote on roll-up proposals, they generally side with the general partner, if only because they perceive they have few options. Voting "No" is often the better choice, since limited partners may end up with more money if the partnership is simply liquidated and its assets sold.

■ **You may also have trouble selling your partnership stake.** If you want to unload your partnership units before the deal is liquidated, you have two choices: sell it back to the broker or sponsor or sell it in what's called the **secondary market.** The first option isn't much of an option, since many brokerages are far less enthusiastic about buying back limited partnerships than they are about selling them initially. They're also rarely willing to pay much for the units, either. Many brokerages list the value of your investment on their monthly statements as its *original cost.* Some artificially raise the value on statements each year. Only when you ask to cash in do you find out how much they really think your investment is worth.

You'll have better luck looking for a buyer in the secondary market. More than a dozen firms buy and sell units of existing partnerships, almost always at a large discount from their original value. For a list of these firms, write to the Investment Partnership Association (Suite 500, 1100 Connecticut Ave. N.W., Washington, D.C. 20036). Be sure to get price quotes from at least several of these outfits, since the values can vary from firm to firm. They also can vary from day to day, so ask each firm how long the price you've been quoted will last.

If you're still determined to invest in a limited partnership, keep these guidelines in mind:

■ **Avoid new partnerships.** Choosing a partnership whose sponsors have a track record is crucial, especially for first-time LP investors. Look for one that is at least three years old and on solid financial footing. That means that the partnership's cash flow covers its expenses, with at least some money left over for income distributions. You can ask the Investment Partnership Association for a list of firms that buy and sell these used units. Alternatively, you can call Partnerline (900-786-9600), a Shrewsbury, N.J., organization that offers information on thousands of private and publicly registered partnerships. They can tell you where a sponsor is located, whether distributions are being made, whether those distributions are real earnings or simply a return of investor capital, and how much real income has been distributed over the life of the partnership. An extra attraction of used partnerships: You can often buy them at significant discounts from their initial prices.

■ **Stay away from partnerships with excessive fees.** Demand that the broker or financial planner trying to sell you the partnership compare the deal and its expenses with others like it. Extraordinarily high fees and incentive fees are usually a tip-off that your general partner does not have your best interest at heart.

■ **Ask the salesman tough questions about the assumptions made by the general partner.** The sponsor or your broker or planner is likely to tell you that the partnership is expected to earn a certain return—say, 9% a year on average. Find out why that return is anticipated. It may be that the general partner is being wildly optimistic about the outlook for real estate or oil prices or the market underlying your investment. If you don't believe the market will do what your sponsor thinks it will, you have no business investing in the deal.

■ **Get advice from a pro.** Before writing out a check and committing yourself to a partnership for seven to 10 years, have a trusted adviser such as your accountant or lawyer look over the partnership terms. Yes, you'll pay a little extra for this service. But if you can afford to invest in a limited partnership, you can afford to check it out first.

Collectibles

The scenario might go something like this: You're watching *Regis & Kathie Lee* one morning when a guest comes on to talk about beer bottles. It seems a lot of collectors out there are willing to pay big bucks for all manner of brew containers, from ancient Budweisers to late-model microbrews. Wait a second, you think. I have some old empties down in the base-

ment that I never got around to throwing away. Maybe they're worth more than a nickel at the recycling center.

Sound familiar? How about if you substitute bottle caps or Barbie dolls or any of a thousand other things you can think of that begin with "B," not to mention every other letter in the alphabet? Face it: America has been transformed into a nation of crazed collectors.

How crazy? In 1991, for example, the price of Persian Gulf War trading cards shot up 7,000% in just three months. Old credit cards—the ones you're supposed to cut up when they've expired—now fetch hundreds, sometimes thousands, of dollars. So do old lunchboxes, famous autographs, antique Shaker furniture, and tacky salt-and-pepper shakers. Not to mention classic collectibles like artwork, stamps, and coins. That's why collecting has gone from the domain of nostalgia and flea markets to deluxe auction houses like Sotheby's and Christie's. In short, collecting has become big business. Unfortunately, it has also become a risky business, especially if you view collecting as an investment activity. So if your interest in knickknacks, souvenirs, and oil paintings goes beyond avocation, pay close attention to the following five rules for smart collecting:

1. Don't buy it unless you're prepared to own it. The market for many collectibles—when there is a market—is volatile and unpredictable. Today's $5,000 Donald Duck watch might be tomorrow's daffy decision when you can't find a buyer willing to pay more than $50. So you can't count on any collectible to make money for you. What's more, when you buy through a dealer, you'll be paying a significant markup. It may be as much as double the price you'd get for the item the minute you walk out of the store.

2. If you must think of collectibles as investments, think of them as portfolio diversification rather than a way to get rich quick. A study by former Marquette University professor David Krause found that collectibles can provide highly competitive rates of return and can actually reduce the risk of an investment portfolio. Moreover, Krause found that collectibles can be decent inflation hedges. Indeed, when inflation is high, people tend to abandon so-called paper investments like stocks and bonds for the relative safety of tangible assets such as real estate, gold, and collectibles. That doesn't mean you should trade in your Treasury bonds for antique furniture when inflation starts heating up, though.

3. Understand the collectibles market. Each area of collecting has its own peculiarities and market cycles. Before you make a serious investment, you need to understand the particulars of your area of interest. Get a sense of the marketplace by visiting a few trade shows, auctions, or flea markets. Start reading collecting magazines and newspapers, such as *Antiques & Collectibles* (619-593-2933). For a general overview of the latest collectible trends and prices, check out *Maloney's Antiques & Collectibles Resource Directory*, available from the Collector's Information Clearinghouse (800-836-2403), or *Kovel's Antiques & Collectibles Price List* (Crown, $13).

Three key variables help determine the value of any collectible: quality, supply, and demand. Mint, or unused, condition is nearly always preferable, even for collectibles whose value comes from having been used by a famous, or infamous, person. Common sense says the fewer there are of a given collectible, the more valuable it is. This is more important with some collectibles than others, however. Important pieces by major artists will always command high prices, but less significant works by a hardworking artist will often fetch a lower price than those of an artist of equal stature who was not as prolific. For collectors of more recently produced—make that mass-produced—Americana, the durability of the collectible should also be considered. Since collector interest in a particular item or category can rise or fall rapidly and without warning, it's important to know how strong demand is for the collectible you want. Conversations with other collectors and articles and advertisements in col-

451

lectible magazines can help you gauge the market. Don't rely on dealers and auctioneers, though; they have a vested interest in keeping demand and prices high.

Depending on the collectible, an auction might be the easiest way to buy or sell an item. General merchandise auctions are held frequently, but specialty auctions might occur only once or twice a year. To find out when auctions are held, ask dealers specializing in your area of collecting interest or call the auction houses in your town. They can also tell you about auctions in other parts of the country. You can try to find buyers for your prized possessions through collector's clubs or through ads in specialized journals and magazines.

4. Beware of fakes. The collecting boom has created a growing counterfeit industry in this country. Fraud and forgery—long staples of the art world—can hit virtually any branch of collecting, from furniture to comic books. Some collectible categories, such as coins, have a well-known system of grading designed to boost buyer confidence in an item's authenticity. Most, however, do not. Your best defense against buying counterfeit goods is dealing with a reputable dealer or auctioneer. For furniture, art, and other classic collectibles, you might also hire an appraiser. Call the Appraisers Association of America (212-867-9775) or the International Society of Appraisers

(312-661-1700) for names of appraisers near you.

5. Don't forget taxes. If you make a profit buying and selling collectibles, you'll owe capital-gains taxes as with any other investment. As a result, be sure to hold on to receipts and other forms of proof that show how much you paid for an item. If your collectible hobby is a bona fide money-making pursuit, you can deduct many related expenses: appraisal fees, insurance premiums, travel expenses to auctions, and subscriptions to related magazines. However, you can deduct these expenses only to offset your income from collecting. To write off hobby losses, you must be able to show the IRS that you were in business to make a profit in three out of five years. A word of warning: Collectible deductions are a red flag to the IRS and may trigger an audit.

Becoming a Lender

Neither a borrower nor a lender be. When Polonius gave that sage advice to his son Laertes, you can bet that Shakespeare was talking about borrowing from—and lending to—friends and relatives. Few things can sour a warm, loving relationship faster than cold, hard cash.

Still, there may come a day when you decide to play banker for a child, sibling, parent, best friend, or co-worker. That decision may spring from a desire to help, say, your kids scrape together enough money for a down payment on a house. Or you might decide that you can improve on the 3% you're earning on your passbook savings. Whatever the scenario, you must treat the loan as a legitimate business transaction and investment. Not only will you be lending real money that would otherwise be earning real interest in the bank, but by formalizing the loan arrangement, you increase the likelihood of getting your money back and remaining on speaking terms with Cousin Jimmy. Here are four guidelines to keep in mind:

1. Don't lend what you can't afford to lose. When loaning to a relative or friend, ask yourself how your relationship would be affected if for some reason you are never paid back.

2. Make the arrangement businesslike. Its best to draw up a formal note or loan agreement. You can find samples at most office supply stores. Be sure any agreement you create includes the amount you're lending, the interest rate (if you're charging interest, that is), the date by which the loan must be repaid, and a description of the collateral (if there is any). If you're making a home loan, file the deed with the county registrar. You might want to hire an attorney to draw up the paperwork. The reason: In the event your relative or friend defaults on the loan, you'll need an enforceable loan document to deduct the loss on your income taxes.

3. If you're lending money as an investment, charge a reasonable rate of interest. What's reasonable? If you lend more than $10,000 or if the borrower has more than $1,000 in investment income a year, the IRS sets a minimum rate of interest that you are required to charge. This so-called **applicable federal rate** fluctuates monthly and in recent years has ranged from around 4% for loans of less than three years to more than 6% for loans of 10 years or more. (For more on this subject, see Chapter 21.) You can charge more than the minimum, of course, and probably should. Go to a nearby bank and ask for its rate on the kind of loan you plan to make. Then set a rate a tad below that.

4. Lend to a specific person. If your son is starting a business with a partner, for example, lend the money to him and not to their company. That way, if the business goes belly up, half your money won't wind up in the hands of a potentially hostile stranger.

SECTION FOUR

YOUR FAMILY FINANCES

CHAPTER 18

How to Get the Best Deals When You Spend Your Money

By now you've learned how to be a savvy saver, a diligent debtor, and an intelligent investor. Now for the fun part: smart spending. Don't worry. You're not about to read a lecture on how to be a tightwad or the importance of buying generic foods. Who wants to live like that? In fact, you'll find out when it makes sense to pay up to 30% *more* for an item. You will also see how to negotiate like a pro and get the best deals when you shell out big bucks. Today, you can negotiate to bring prices down on practically everything. In addition, you'll learn how to give away some of your money to

charities without getting scammed in the process. With so many charity scandals in recent years, that kind of knowledge is essential.

How to Negotiate the Price of Just About Anything

For decades car shoppers have just said "No" to sticker prices. Their battle cry (except at Saturn and other no-dicker showrooms): "Let's make a deal." In the '90s—thanks in part to sluggish retail sales—haggling has become a bit more mainstream, with shoppers cutting deals that would make Bob Barker proud. To profit, you don't need the jabber jaw of an auctioneer. All you need is knowledge. So whether you're in the market for a car, dress, or sofa, it pays to be an informed consumer. Instant recall of competitors' prices is the best ammunition for negotiators. These 11 other strategies can also help you wrangle great deals.

1. Haggle late in the day. That's when cranky store owners and hotel managers are eager to close a deal and make that one last sale.

2. Buy in quantity if you can. A customer who wants three dresses often has more leverage in getting better prices than the shopper buying just one.

3. Paying cash. The green stuff is like music to many merchants, who can lose 6% to 15% on purchases charged with credit cards. Pay the old-fashioned way and ask for a 10% cash rebate.

4. Be polite. Never call the merchandise "inferior." A breezy attitude will win you negotiating points faster than an obnoxious pitch.

5. Be cool. Don't be overly eager to snare a particular item. That's a sure way to squash a deal. If you're dreamy eyed over that antique wall unit, a dealer may fig-

ure you'll eventually break down and pay full price.

6. Offer to buy the floor model or a recently discontinued item. Shoppers at electronic stores often use this technique. With new stereo, TV, and VCR models rolling out every few months, it's smart to consider outmoded floor models. Many stores will sell floor models or recently discontinued items for 15% to 30% off the price of new items. Not a bad deal, considering that floor models are usually in perfectly good condition and typically come with full manufacturer warranties. Just be sure to carefully inspect the item for nicks and scratches so you don't wind up being unpleasantly surprised when you bring it home.

7. Dicker with the big boys, too. No haggling at department stores? These days, that's a myth. You'll have to get past the sales flunky, however. The person with markdown authority is the department manager. Whenever you can summon one (to, say, point out a stain on a sweater), you may succeed in bringing down the price. At the biggies, your best bets for price breaks are on big-ticket items such as overstocked jewelry and furniture; clothes and furnishings that have lingered unsold for months; soiled items; and items with missing buttons or other imperfections.

8. Ask for a layaway policy. What to do if a store manager or shopkeeper flat out declines to accept your lower bid? Try haggling for the next best thing: a layaway plan. Offer to put some cash down for an item (generally 10% to 25%) if the retailer will put aside the goods until you pay them off over several weeks or months. If you find a receptive ear, you can almost always arrange the layaway interest-free. Layaway policies are common at smaller retailers as well as specialty shops such as jewelers and antiques stores.

9. Know when and where to go to bid down big-ticket items. Notice how the price of ski parkas melts when temperatures rise? Many store items have seasonal price fluctuations. You can wrestle down the prices even farther when the weather or retailing climate renders them duds. Some examples:

- Look for end-of-season sales on clothing such as wool coats and cashmere sweaters, which can slice prices by more than 50%.
- Get up to 30% off freezers and refrigerators in January or June.
- Bargain hard for the fur coat of your dreams during March and August.
- Shop for discounted air conditioners in February and September.

10. Negotiate for services, too. Most negotiators vie for *things*. By ignoring costly *services*, however, hagglers win only half the battle. Ask for lower prices or special deals at your dry cleaner, tailor, or hairdresser.

11. Use the Internet to amass key information about product prices and descriptions. For example, *Compare Net's site* (www.compare.net) has a database of more than 10,000 product models in 41 categories, from automobiles to video equipment. Another useful Web site, *Product Review Net* (www.product-reviewnet.com), provides brief reviews from over 150 magazines and other Web sites on more than 60 types of products.

Smart Shopping Tips for Car Buyers

For most people, few shopping experiences are as aggravating and intimidating as buying a car. (Some people get a kick out of trying to outsmart car dealers. Good for them.) Even before stepping into a showroom, a car buyer has to sort out a multitude of issues: Should I buy American? Japanese? European? How big an options package do I really need: Would I be better off leasing? What about buying a used car instead of a new one? How much will insurance set me back? What's the repair record for this model? Which of the nation's 22,000 dealers will give me the best price? Should I just go to a no-dicker dealer or perhaps hire a car-buying service to pay the least? What about automobile financing?

To make matters worse, not all customers are treated alike. A few years ago a national survey confirmed that dealers routinely offer male shoppers better prices than female buyers and that whites pay less than minorities. A former General Motors official reportedly has said that some black dealers maintain they've had more difficulty getting car loans for black customers than white dealers have. Such unlawful discrimination only underscores the value of being a knowledgeable car shopper. Follow these tips to help smooth the bumps on a car-buying journey that's riddled with potholes:

■ **Set a budget.** A hot rod may look tempting. If your budget calls for a mere get-about, though, you won't regret sacrificing form for function. To figure a budget, decide first how much you can shell out for a down payment. As a rule, you should try to put down at least 20%

and finance the rest over as short a term as possible (four years or less is best). Bear in mind that a car is not like a home, which almost always appreciates over time. Rather, it is a depreciating asset that's sure to lose value from the moment you drive it off the lot. In fact, the average new car maintains less than 60% of its value after five years; utility vehicles tend to keep their value best. So to avoid being stuck with a car worth less than the outstanding balance on your loan, you'll want to pay off your note as quickly as possible.

There's another advantage to making a hefty down payment. Your 20% ante will help you win more favorable financing than a down payment of 10% or less—as much as a full percentage point lower at most banks and credit unions. On a four-year loan, that can easily save you several hundred dollars. The following table shows what your monthly payment would be on three- and four-year automobile loans of $15,000 to $25,000 at interest rates between 7.5% and 9%.

YOUR MONTHLY CAR PAYMENT

	INTEREST RATE			
	7.50%	8.00%	8.50%	9.00%
3 YEARS				
$15,000	$467	$470	$474	$477
$20,000	$622	$627	$631	$636
$25,000	$778	$784	$789	$795
4 YEARS				
$15,000	$363	$366	$370	$373
$20,000	$484	$488	$493	$498
$25,000	$605	$611	$617	$622

■ **Get your financing first.** Don't let the tail wag the dog. Shopping for money before price gives you a reality check about how much car you can afford. By doing things in reverse, some drivers may be tempted to fall for a car that's bigger than their wallets, then wind up struggling to find ways to pay for it. When financing your wheels, you have three loan options: your bank, your credit union, or the car dealership. Shop each for the best possible rates and terms. Though credit unions typically undercut banks on rates, auto dealers may surprise you. In partnership with carmakers, many dealers can get you rates well below both banks and credit unions. Rebates and cut-rate dealer financing are harder to find than in the

'80s, but they do exist when manufacturers and dealers are trying to move particular models.

■ **Figure your car's target price and negotiate from there.** At dealers who negotiate, only suckers pay sticker price. Savvy shoppers aim to pay 3% to 4% over the dealer's cost for cars listing for less than $20,000 and 6% to 7% more than invoice for more expensive models. For example, the dealer's cost on a car with a $10,000 sticker price is probably around $9,000. So if you wanted to buy it, you'd set a target price of roughly $9,280. Generally, the pricier the car, the less you're likely to shave off. You can get the dealer's cost of most models from *The Complete Car Cost Guide*, a reference book available

461

at most libraries. Increasingly, on-line services are adding car-buying databases, too. For instance, CompuServe's Automobile Information Center service supplies retail and wholesale car prices. You can also talk to satisfied and unsatisfied car buyers on the CompuServe bulletin board.

■ **Consider no-haggle pricing.** Nearly one in 10 U.S. auto dealers have shifted to take-it-or-leave-it pricing, a tactic that General Motors introduced successfully with its Saturn line. The setup offers option-packed cars at one price, with no room for bargaining. Ostensibly, these vehicles go for 6% over the dealer's invoice, for a savings of half off traditional markups. While buying without dickering won't necessarily yield the best price, you may want to give a little just to save on stress.

■ **Be compulsive about total cost, not monthly payments.** Too often, car shoppers try to determine "How much will I pay each month?" rather than "How much will this car cost me over time?" To drive away with the best deal, however, you'll want to estimate the car's total **five-year ownership cost.** This is how much you'll pay to own and operate the car. Get this: In just five years, the average car costs more to own and operate than its original price. A total ownership figure takes into account projected depreciation plus what you'll pay for financing, insurance, repairs, gas, and registration fees. Stack one simi-

larly priced model against the next and you may well find that the total ownership cost swings greatly. For instance, the 1997 Eagle Talon, with a sticker of $14,059, had a total ownership cost of $26,733, according to IntelliChoice, a California automotive research firm. The Honda Civic LX, a competitor in the same class, was priced a shade higher at $14,650 but had a *lower* total ownership cost of $23,407.

Car shoppers can get data about total ownership costs from several sources. Several publications, including **MONEY** and *Kiplinger's* magazine, publish annual car rankings that feature this important benchmark. You can also call IntelliChoice (800-227-2665) for one of its $19.95 *ArmChair Compare* reports, which lets shoppers compare financial statistics on the two models of their choice. IntelliChoice also has a useful Web site (www.intellichoice.com).

■ **Just say "No" to extended warranties.** Chances are your dealer will push an extended warranty. This contract can cost anywhere from $500 to $2,000 and is designed to cover any repairs you need after your limited factory warranty expires. Dealers love this little invention because it generates huge profits. For drivers, though, the deal isn't so sweet. Most carmakers these days offer excellent basic warranties covering your car repairs, most parts, and roadside assistance for three years or 36,000 miles, whichever comes first. Luxury cars usually cover you for four years and 50,000 miles. So why pay up front for something that won't gear up for three years down the road, if at all? A better idea: Fund your own warranty by keeping spare cash in the bank or a money-market fund.

■ **Get the best price on your old mount.** Before you accept a dealer's offer for any trade-in cars, do your homework. Go to the local newsstand, buy a copy of the quarterly *Edmund's Used Car Prices* ($5.99), and look up your model's average sales price. Then head to a few used-car lots for bids. If your dealer is offering significantly less than the used-car dealers, you might want to sell the car on your own. Sure, it's more work, but the do-it-yourself approach can often bring you 20% more than a trade-in.

■ **Buy at the end of a model year.** Unless you're eyeing a car in heavy demand (in which case you may be forced to pay sticker), it generally pays to buy at the end of a model year. That's when most car dealers clear their lots to make room for newer models and are especially eager to bargain. This rule doesn't apply if you expect to trade in your car after a year. Since your car will quickly be "last year's model," you'll suffer a full year's depreciation in just a few short months. That will be bad news when you sell or trade-in.

■ **Use a buying or shopping service.** You're not up for a showdown in the showroom? There are still ways to get a cut-rate car. **Buying services,** the personal shoppers of the auto world, will hunt down the best price, then order and deliver your vehicle for a fee. More than 30 such services exist nationwide, and their $250 to $500 fees are still low enough to let you drive home a deal. Don't, however, confuse these types with **car brokers.** A broker's allegiance may be questionable, since he or she gets dealer commissions on top of fees paid by you. You can get more information about buying services by writing to the National Association of Buyers' Agents, P.O. Box 513, Kentfield, Calif. 94914.

If you want someone simply to do some price legwork before closing the deal yourself, other services can help. The oldest is Car Bargains (800-475-7283), which for $135 will contact five or more dealers in your area to get rock-bottom price quotes on one or two models.

How to Close a Great Lease Deal

It's easy to get rattled by the decision of whether to buy or lease a car. In the past, leasing almost always proved more costly than buying. These days, however, automakers and dealers are pushing leases like mad and luring many would-be buyers. In some cases their deals can be the cheaper way to go. Trouble is, if you don't know what you're doing, you can get taken for a ride. State attorneys general across the country have been flooded with complaints from customers who think they weren't told the whole truth about leasing from their dealers.

In a typical lease arrangement, you make preset monthly payments over a specific period of time, just as you would on a car loan. Because you're paying for a fraction of the car's value—its value over the time when you lease it—monthly payments are generally lower than comparable car loan payments. At the end of the lease term, you may buy the vehicle for a predetermined price.

Leasing, however, is a tricky proposition, unlike a straight car sale. Dealers often fail to provide shoppers with the underlying financial terms of a lease; instead, they're apt to focus on low monthly payments and little or no money down. Making things more complicated are terms the dealer may toss around, like **capitalized cost** and **residual cost.**

Before getting tangled up in the leasing process, consider whether leasing is really the best move for you. The answer is probably "Yes" if you are a certain type of driver. Strong lease candidates are people who like to trade models every few years, use their cars for business (lessees get deeper tax deductions than owners), drive infrequently (less than 10,000 miles per year), or lack the dough for a sizable cash down payment (at least 20% of the car's price). Drivers planning to keep the same set of wheels for five years or more, however, can almost always save by buying.

Once you decide to lease, cruise the Sunday paper for offers in your area. As you read, remember that the best leases combine several factors: low down payments, a fair selling price, and affordable monthly payments. To cut such a deal, though, you need to be armed with reliable information. You can get the monthly payment and the length of the lease from the ads. Figuring out the crucial money terms—the true interest rate and the car's capitalized cost—will take some dealer prodding and pencil pushing.

The key is to figure your **total lease cost.** Basically, the total cost is the difference between the car's value today (its selling price or capitalized cost) and its value at the end of the lease (its residual value), plus interest. You can't do much about the car's residual value, which you can find as a percentage of list price in *Automotive Lease Guide* ($12.50; Chart Software; 800-418-8450). But you certainly can drive the selling cost south. Do your best to negotiate for a selling price or capitalized cost that's roughly 4% higher than the dealer's cost.

Another money-saving factor is the interest rate on your lease. Oddly, dealers may express your interest rate as some baffling decimal, like .00025. This is known as the **money factor.** Don't be put off by it. Simply multiply this number by 24 to arrive at the real-world annual interest rate (in this example, 6%).

Five other key lease points:

1. Be sure you're comfortable with the term of your lease. If you decide to back out of a lease early, you may (ouch!) be stuck with all remaining payments. In case you're in doubt about how long you'll be needing wheels, go for a shorter rather than longer lease term. Assuming you can afford it, you'll be wise to take a term that's as long as the manufacturer's "bumper-to-bumper warranty"—typically two or three years—in order to avoid paying any hefty repair bills yourself.

2. Reduce pesky up-front costs. Many leases require a trunkload of cash up front. Top siphons: down payments, security deposits, and a check for the first month of your contract. The last one is nonnegotiable. But the amount you're asked to pay for the other two is up for discussion. Just think: By getting your dealer to shave or eliminate the down payment, you can invest that money and make it work for you.

3. Go for a factory-subsidized lease. Cruise for a knock-out deal that's under-

written by the manufacturer. These are almost always superior deals, since carmakers can afford to set interest rates that are way below average. Some manufacturer-subsidized leases are attractive because the carmakers build in a high residual value. These types of leases, typically offered by Japanese carmakers, don't last long, however. Typically, manufacturers tout subsidized leases for three to six months. How can you tell the difference between a subsidized lease and an ordinary one? Check out the residual value against the figure in *Automotive Lease Guide.* If the lease's residual value as a percentage of the list price is five percentage points or higher than the one in the guide, you've got a subsidized lease.

4. Lease early in the model year. Remember the advice for car buyers to shop late in the model year for the best price? With leases you turn that tip on its head. Lease early as opposed to late in the model year. Otherwise you're sure to hit midyear price hikes, which in turn produce higher total costs and monthly payments. The best months to get a lease are October, November, and December, when you can snag next year's model.

5. Drive a hard bargain and read the fine print. Just as you'd dicker with a dealer over a car's sticker price in a purchase, do the same with your lease deal. Once you've chosen a specific model, call or visit at least five or six dealers to comparison shop. Even if you can't manage to get a lower monthly payment, you can always ask the dealer to knock a few hundred dollars off the purchase price, assuming you do intend to buy at lease end, or drop the down payment.

How to Get Great Deals When You Travel

Travelers today have the deck stacked in their favor. Still teetering from the '80s, when travel prices were at their zenith, the industry is working hard to get you to come on board. Consider: The average round-trip domestic airline ticket price recently was $264, down from about $350 in 1990. A flurry of hotel building in the '80s has also widened travelers' choices without expanding their wallets. Add to that no-frills airlines, frequent flier programs, and booming charter deals, and the winner is clearly the consumer. (Service from airlines is another story altogether. A tip: If your flight is canceled, make a beeline to a pay phone and rebook by calling your travel agent's hotline or the airline's 800 reservations number.)

The travel game has grown complicated, however. Airfares seem to change by the minute. Frequent flier deals come with more fine print than an insurance policy. Some airlines don't work with travel agents; others are making travel agents charge their customers for service. Some travel bargains demand that you make some compromises in your plans. You'll navigate your way to the best deals, however, by following these strategies:

■ **Get smart about travel agents.** Whether you travel often or infrequently, a trusty travel agent can be a valuable asset. With the assistance of speedy computer reservations systems, an agent can coordinate your itinerary with speed and skill. What's more, your agent will know your frequent flier memberships, where you like to sit on a plane, whether you prefer no-smoking hotel rooms, if you normally order special airline meals, and what kind of rental car you prefer. In return, your agent typically receives commissions of 5% to 11% from the air carriers, hotels, and car rental companies he or she books.

Though their services have traditionally been free, some agents now charge fees to issue inexpensive airline tickets or create complex trips. Loyal customers, however, may be exempt from these fees. So if you already have a reliable pro, stay put. When shopping around for a new agent (and you *should* try out several), ask him or her to spell out any service charges. Even if the agency charges its customers, you may be able to skirt the fees by presenting yourself as a potential long-term client who will bring in a lot of business. Also, if you are a customer who travels more than once a year and you get hit with a fee, ask the agent for a refund. You just might get it.

■ **Buy a package.** A package that bundles airfares, hotels, and ground transportation is usually the best way to save on a vacation. Available mainly through travel agents and directly through some airlines, these getaways can cost just half of what you'd pay for the pieces separately. Even so, it's smart to comparison shop. That's because agents typically buy packages from wholesalers or tour packagers, many of whom sell nearly identical trips. If you use a travel agent, be sure to get price quotes for the same vacation from several tour packagers. When shopping the airlines yourself by calling their 800 numbers, ask for brochures on any specific area and compare your options. Then head to a travel agent to see if he or she can do better.

■ **Snag the lowest airfare.** Amazingly, the major airline carriers make more than 20,000 fare changes each *day*. So getting the cheapest fare available requires a careful strategy and a bit of luck. To increase the odds that you're landing the best possible rate, ask for price quotes from two or three agencies. Try the computer on-line services and travel Web sites like *Microsoft Expedia* (www.expedia.msn.com) and *The Trip* (www.thetrip.com).

Some of the cheapest fares come from no-frills airlines that save money by limiting their routes, cutting out meals, and, in some cases, eliminating paper tickets. To avoid paying a travel agent's fee for booking these carriers, you'll have to call these carriers yourself to check their prices. After you get the least expensive ticket price from one of these airlines, call the majors or have your travel agent do so. You might be able to match or beat the fare and fly with an airline that will throw in more than a bag of peanuts.

As a rule, reserving two weeks or even five days in advance will get you a better fare than flying last minute. Flexible travelers stand to save even more. The less picky you are about carriers, departure dates, and airports, for instance, the better your chance of flying in a cheap seat. An example: Traveling west to Los Angeles, fliers can save $50 to $150 by routing to nearby John Wayne Airport in Orange County.

Is Paris calling? Maybe Tokyo? Vacationers to foreign destinations shouldn't miss out on the deals from **consolidators.** These companies buy tickets from the airlines at wholesale and sell them to the public at substantial discounts. You can save up to 50% off competing fares by booking with a consolidator, or bucket shop, as they're also called. You'll spot their postage-stamp-size ads in the Sunday paper, or your travel agent can arrange for such a ticket. Once booked, however, these fares are usually non-refundable, with no itinerary changes allowed.

For the truly intrepid, **courier flights** offer some of the best deals around. Prices are at least 50% off regular excursion fares. Here's how it works: You sign up with one of 60 nationwide courier companies, saying where you want to go and roughly when. Then, on a moment's notice, you'll be told which flight to take. As a courier, you transport customs documents for an international shipping company. Although you will travel as a normal passenger, going courier style means giving up the right to check any baggage. The shipping company will use your baggage allotment to rush freight and cargo through customs. You also must travel alone. Be prepared for some other bothers. For instance, you may have to wait at the airport for a few hours while the courier company representative escorts its cargo through customs. You can book up to three months in advance, but prices drop (sometimes to as low as $20!) if the departure date nears and the courier company has no takers. For more information on courier flights and a list of companies, write to the International Association of Air Travel Couriers, International Features, P.O. Box 1349, Lake Worth, Fla. 33460.

When fare wars erupt, play your cards carefully. If a full-page ad trumpeting cheap fares inspires you to pack, don't book right away. Other carriers may soon match the price or undercut it by a notch or two. Wait a day or two after the brouhaha, then shop around.

■ **Book discounted hotel rooms.** Seasoned travelers never pay a hotel's published or "rack" rate. No wonder. In large cities like New York and Los Angeles, standard hotel tarriffs—including eye-popping taxes—can easily push a bill to $200 per night, before minibar. The good news for travelers is that hotels rarely are filled to capacity. On average, U.S. hotels fill only about 60% of their rooms on any given night. This leaves miles of room for negotiating unless you're traveling during peak season or run into a major convention.

Start your hotel rate hunt with your travel agent. Large agencies, especially, often have relationships with specific hotels and can arrange discounts of 20% to 50%. Your next smartest move, assuming you've got a few hotels in mind, is to call each one directly and ask for the best deal in the house. Virtually anyone can qualify for the "corporate rate," which is about 10% less than rack rates. Don't stop at that, though. Deeper discounts for weekends or special promotions may be available for up to 50% off. By calling the hotel directly—as opposed to its centralized, toll-free corporate reservationist in some other city—you may happen upon a manager. If business is slow, he or she may cut you an impromptu deal. No matter what rate you get, though, request a better one when checking in.

To get a decent hotel room at a rock-bottom price, check out a **hotel consolidator.** Like their airline counterparts, hotel wholesalers scoop up room blocks cheaply and pass on to guests the savings—routinely 25% to 65%. The choice of hotels in a given city may be limited, although you're almost always assured of a first-class room. You won't find hotel consolidators widely advertised, however. Two of the oldest and largest hotel wholesalers in the United States: *Hotel Reservations Network* (800-964-6835) and *Express Hotel Reservations* (800-356-1123).

■ **Travel during the off-season to save 40% or more.** In travel, as in comedy, timing is everything. If at all possible, try to vacation when it isn't high season at your destination and rates are at their annual peak. Most areas in the United States, the Caribbean, and Europe have high and low seasons dictated by a number of factors, such as weather, holidays, and visitor traffic. The seasonal difference you'll pay can vary wildly. Consider: When traveling to a Caribbean island, you can save 40% or perhaps a bit more by visiting from March to September. For information on high and low seasons in a particular area, call its department of tourism or the local convention and visitors' bureau.

■ **To set sail, book through a cruise-only agent.** Whether sailing to the Caribbean or Alaska, travelers who book the major cruise lines in advance (as far as a year ahead) can anchor discounts of up to 30%. You can get an even more generous offer by dealing with a cruise-only agent; cruise specialists help passengers get deals of 50% off. As a bonus, they can sometimes upgrade you to a better cabin class. Check for cruise-only agents in the Sunday travel sections of major newspapers.

■ **Join a travel club.** After paying annual fees of $25 to $100, travel club members get access to some tremendous hotel, dining, car rental, cruise, and tour discounts—often up to 50%. There's no fancy footwork or third-party booking involved. Instead, you're likely to get some combination of membership cards, directories, and fat coupon books; it's up to you to provide club credentials when making reservations. Three of the largest travel clubs are *Entertainment Publications* (800-285-5525; for hotels, restaurants, rental cars, and attractions nationwide); *Premier Dining* (800-346-3241; dining only, in 45 cities); and *Travel World Leisure Club* (800-444-8952; restaurants, hotels, rental cars, and cruises).

■ **Haggle for a car rental deal.** Yes, it is often difficult to drive a great bargain off the rental lot. Even when you think you're getting a decent rate—whoops, the fine print proves you wrong. For instance, most car rental companies offer discounted weekend rates, but if you wind up keeping the car into the week, you may jeopardize the deal. Your best strategy, if you have the stomach and patience for it, is to visit the desks of several rental agencies upon landing at an airport even if you've booked ahead. Ask for a lower price and you just might get one, especially if you've lucked into a slow business day. Be sure to mention any discounts you're entitled to receive, such as a corporate rate, a special price for being an AAA member, or a discount for being a senior citizen.

How to Be a Smart Medical Consumer

With corporate employers cutting back on health benefits while the cost of medical care spirals, you need to be an aggressive health consumer these days. Earlier chapters offered advice about choosing among managed-care providers, shopping for health insurance, using your employer's flexible spending account, and getting discounts on prescription drugs. These tips will take you the next step:

■ **Check your hospital bills.** Here's a shocker: as many as nine in 10 hospital bills are inaccurate, with consumers and insurers usually left holding the bag. The errors aren't tiny, either. Overcharges typically run 5% to 7% of most bills, which works out to $500 to $700 on the average $10,000 hospital bill. To avoid a rip-off at the hospital, either you, a friend, or a relative should keep a diary of your daily expenses in the medical center. Begin your tally on the day you check in, noting every charge from each aspirin prescribed to every test you take. Upon checking out, compare your notes with your itemized bill, looking for any suspicious or suspiciously high entries. Among the most frequent errors to watch for: inaccurate charges, such as typos (turning a $5 pill into a $50 one); duplicate charges, where you're charged more than once for the same service or item; and phantom charges for things you simply never received. Hospitals are busy places, and honest billing mistakes happen a lot.

If you find any discrepancies, ask your hospital's billing department for an explanation. If that fails or if you simply want help deciphering your bill, write to the People's Medical Society (462 Walnut St., Allentown, Pa. 18102; annual membership $20). A consumer advocacy group, the society will give you advice on resolving errors and overcharges.

■ **Try ambulatory care.** Too often, Americans use the local emergency room for basic health needs. To avoid getting stuck with a bill your insurer won't pay, treat broken bones and flu symptoms at one of more than 4,000 ambulatory care centers nationwide. These privately run clinics can help you save about 20% on noncritical illnesses and injuries. You can locate a center near you by calling the National Association for Ambulatory Care (612-476-0015).

■ **Question the need for diagnostic tests.** Usually, your doctor knows best. But since many physicians have a financial stake in diagnostic laboratories, they may have a vested interest in a few extra X-rays, too. Of course, no patient should pass up a potentially lifesaving test. Still, it is important to ask your doctor to carefully explain the purpose of any costly tests such as MRIs.

■ **Explore nontraditional therapies.** More and more employee health plans are covering alternative healing methods such as chiropractic adjustments, acupuncture, and vitamin therapy. Clearly, the demand exists for these treatments; roughly one in three Americans has sought such care. Even if therapies such as hypnosis or homeopathy aren't covered by your plan, you may want to check them out—they're relative bargains. Nontraditional healing methods cost an average of about $30 per session versus $75 for the typical M.D.'s bill.

■ **An ounce of prevention . . .** Yes, it does beat a pound of cure. To avoid the need for costly health care, be sure to get regular physical exams and checkups. For women, these include annual pap smears and, if you're over 50, mammograms. Men should get screened for signs of prostate cancer every year starting at age 50.

Finding Furniture Bargains

How would you like to save 30% to 80% off manufacturers' suggested list prices for furniture? It's easier than you think. The secret is shopping the showrooms and stores in central North Carolina towns such as High Point and Hickory. That's where nearly two-thirds of America's furniture is made.

It's best to do your North Carolina furniture shopping in person. After all, that's the only way you can see and test out the furniture. Try not to go in mid-April or mid-October, though. During those periods, the industry holds its biannual home furnishings show in the area and the place is a zoo. Visit in March and September and you'll be able to get some terrific discounts by purchasing last season's items. Bring your checkbook, too. High Point stores typically insist on deposits of 25% to 50% by check or money order. To fly to the High Point area, you'll want to book a flight into Greensboro's Piedmont Triad International Airport or Charlotte International Airport.

You don't have to travel for the bargains, though. Quite a few of the furniture discounters take phone orders. For a directory of the stores, get a copy of *The Fine Furniture and Furnishings Discount Shopping Guide* ($14.95; P.O. Box 973, Bloomfield Hills, Mich. 48303).

When It Pays to Pay More

So far, you've read quite a bit about saving money when you shop. Sometimes, however, it makes sense to pay full retail price—as long as the value is there. For instance, you should be glad to pay top dollar for an item or service you expect will perform for quite a while. A perfect example: mattresses. Scrimp a little now and you could be suffering from back pain for years.

It's also worth paying full freight when the product is far superior to the competition or one of a kind. Case in point—top-of-the-line sports equipment. Custom-made clothing, fine jewelry, and art will set you back a bit, but the quality usually more than compensates for the cost. In fact, the jewelry and art may even appreciate over time.

Finally, safety is almost always worth the price. Sure you'll pay a little more for organic food or lawn care. However, you may sleep better knowing that your fam-

ily will cut its contact with chemicals or pesticides. The same holds for a worthwhile home alarm system.

Checking Out Charities

Perhaps you've dialed in during a charity telethon, sponsored a colleague at work for a walkathon, or simply been torn about dropping a quarter in a homeless person's cup. Americans are fairly generous, in fact, contributing roughly $900 per household annually to good works. Yet with so many seemingly worthy recipients of your dollars, the choices may become blurred. Indeed, some 320,000 new "charities" spring up each year. Just how wisely would each use your donation?

Given the growth of charity scams and frauds in recent years, you'll want to investigate any charitable group thoroughly. During Operation Desert Storm, for instance, phony charities sprang up virtually overnight, purporting to send money, food, and gifts to overseas troops. In 1994 the public learned that United Way—one of the largest and most respected charities in the world—had been ripped off to the tune of $1 million by a few of its former executives.

These general guidelines can help ensure that your dollars end up in deserving hands:

■ **Gather information.** Never agree to make a charitable donation over the phone to a group you don't know. Instead, ask the caller to send you materials about the charity. If the group is legit, you'll receive the mailing. If it isn't, you'll get a song-and-dance over the phone about how the cost of such mailings is prohibitive and why you should make a donation now. Such callers often want little more than to get your credit-card number.

Before giving any of your hard-earned money to a charity, no matter how needy it is, read its brochures, annual reports, or other printed information about the group. They should clearly explain the charity's mission and give you some background on its officers. Before contributing, you'll probably want to make sure you're in tune with a charity's philosophy, political bent, and methods for achieving its goals. The material also should plainly state the group's tax status. This matters, since you can take a charitable write-off for donations only to groups defined as 501c(3)s under the federal tax code—as well as to churches and synagogues. The term "nonprofit" is irrelevant here. Lobbying groups are nonprofits, but unless they also qualify as charitable institutions, any money you give to them is not deductible.

■ **Find out how the group spends its money.** A key barometer of the worthiness of a charity is the percentage of its income spent on actual good works. For instance, according to the *Washington Post*, it was discovered that almost none of the $10 million collected by the otherwise reputable Marine Toys for Tots Foundation went to purchase toys in 1993. Instead the dough wound up supporting the foundation's costly fund-raising efforts. As a giver, you'll want to be sure that at least 70% of a group's total budget goes to the programs it claims to support. With truly well-managed groups, such as the American Red Cross and the Boy Scouts of America, this figure stays fairly consistent from year to year. A smaller charity should be willing to send you data showing exactly how much money it took in during the previous year and how much it spent on programs.

■ **Give appropriately.** If you're inspired to make a gift after checking out a charity, your next task is to do it properly. Avoid scam artists and ensure proper documentation for your tax write-off by writing a check for your donations. (By law, in order to deduct a contribution of more than $250, you must get written documentation from the charity.) Never agree to write your check to an individual, however. Use only the formal name of the group or its fund-raising arm.

■ **Make sure the group can address all of your concerns.** Evasive answers to your questions may signal that something's amiss. Any bona fide charity will cheerfully answer your questions about its programs, donations, fund-raisers, and leadership. If you still have questions or concerns about a charitable group, you may want to contact the watchdog groups that police the charity front. Each keeps tabs on dozens of charities and rates them based on their program spending and administration. They are the National Charities Information Bureau (19 Union Square West, Dept. 399, New York, N.Y. 10003), the Council of Better Business Bureaus Philanthropic Advisory Service (4200 Wilson Blvd., Arlington, Va. 22203), and the AIP Rating Guide and Watchdog Report ($3; 4905 Del Ray Ave., Bethesda, Md. 20814). To investigate local groups, call the Better Business Bureau in your city. This agency can tell you whether consumers have recently filed any complaints about a charity that solicits donations in your area.

Avoiding Other Consumer Scams

Chances are you've recently opened your mailbox and pulled out a suspicious-looking postcard exclaiming:

"CONGRATULATIONS! YOU HAVE BEEN SELECTED FOR A CARIBBEAN CRUISE! TO CLAIM YOUR PRIZE, CALL . . . "

If this sounds familiar to you, count yourself among the millions of Americans who are targeted annually for consumer scams.

Each year, con artists siphon about $100 billion from trusting victims' pockets. Reaching out by mail, phone, and even computer on-line services, rip-off artists creatively spin new ploys daily. Typically, they prey on vulnerable types such as the elderly or people with poor credit. Their games are often more than annoying, they're illegal. Any con artist using the mail system is committing a felony that's punishable with jail time.

Using common sense can help you ferret out the legitimate offers from the scams. For starters, one old saw is still valid: If it sounds too good to be true, it probably is. Never give your credit-card number over the phone to unsolicited callers. Don't dial in on a 900-number ploy, either, no matter what the offer. These lines charge several dollars per minute and often exist to line the pockets of crooks. If you're cautious but get conned anyway, call the National Consumers League's Fraud Information Center (800-876-7060) to find out more about your rights and any recourse you may have.

Among the top consumer scams to avoid:

■ **"Guaranteed" prize offers.** Don't fall for any postcard or phone call alerting you to a "guaranteed" prize. Typically, this is an invitation to *pay* for some inferior product or vacation. Any notice requiring you to put up money or dial a 900 number is only a guarantee that you'll be ripped off.

■ **Credit-card heists.** Fraudulent credit-card purchases cost consumers and issuers $3 billion each year. Many credit cards are simply stolen, but a crook doesn't even need to lift your card to wreak havoc. A credit-card receipt bears your name and number—often that's all the information a thief needs to make purchases in your name. The best defense is to keep an eye on all your cards and credit-card transaction receipts. Request your carbons from salespeople, then tear them up. Destroy all old cards, too. If your monthly credit-card statement fails to arrive on time, don't chalk it up to a postal error. It could have been stolen, so call the card company right away to check.

■ **Phony job opportunities.** Beware anyone touting rich job offers if you merely provide your résumé and a few hundred dollars. Most legitimate employment agencies do not charge a fee, and none should charge a fee for supposed "job listings."

■ **Home repair scams.** Here's a prime example of how con artists prey on the weak. In these scams, the targets often are recent victims of disasters such as earthquakes, fires, or floods. The MO can take various forms. Some "contractors" are phonies who show up, demand a fee, then disappear. Others may be qualified and do actual work—but the work they do winds up being costly and unnecessary.

The best way to check out a contractor is to first make sure that he or she is properly licensed. You can find this out from your state's licensing board. Also, ring up the local Better Business Bureau to check for its record of customer complaints. Next, call several former clients and ask them about the quality of work performed, if the job was completed on time, and if it came in on budget. To make sure a contractor's references are legit, ask if you can drop by to inspect the work yourself. Before proceeding with the job, get at least three different estimates, with the terms of the contract hammered out in writing. In addition to clarifying costs, completion dates, and payment schedules, the contract should be specific about the quality of materials to be used.

■ **Investment muggings.** In the world of investing, there is no such thing as a *sure* thing. Remember this advice the next time you're solicited for some "investment opportunity of the century" hyping sky-high returns and little or no risk. Think

475

you're too smart for that? Maybe. Even sophisticated investors get duped by phony financial offers, though. Indeed, financial fraud costs Americans more than $10 billion each year. Ploys can range from fake high-yielding bonds to worthless stocks, stamps, and real estate deals. Lately, investment scammers have been poaching on the on-line services, trapping unsuspecting users.

Bear in mind, these schemes are often elaborate and can seem quite convincing. Crafty con artists may even send phony performance records for the "investment" you've made. To avoid getting fleeced, take your time making all investment decisions. If the company is unknown to you, gather written information on the opportunity and ask for an annual report or prospectus. You might also ask your banker, broker, and local Better Business Bureau if they know anything about the investment in question. Have doubts about a so-called broker's pitch? Find out if he is licensed or has a complaint record by calling the National Association of Securities Dealers (800-289-9999).

■ **Loan scams.** Consumers with bad credit may get hit with dubious opportunities for loans or credit cards. Your tip-off: The application is not like most others. For instance, most credit-card companies don't charge an application fee. The exceptions are some secured credit cards, which demand collateral. Application fees on loans are fairly common, but watch out for any that sound exorbitant. Also, beware lenders who tout a "guaranteed" acceptance once you've forked over some dough. Another loan ploy involves 900 numbers. If you're asked to dial one for a loan application form, don't. That's just a shady way of charging you for information that may prove useless.

■ **Trips to nowhere.** You probably wouldn't fall for a trip to, say, the Fountain of Youth. Yet there are plenty of bum travel "deals," so you need to be on guard. One common scam beckons newspaper readers to take a cruise or Caribbean vacation. Would-be travelers are asked to fork over a "deposit" by credit card over the phone, then are told to book their trip later. Sometimes callers are promised open-ended tickets. Of course, the trips never materialize. To avoid such trickery, deal only with established agents you know.

What You Can Get for Free and How to Find It

If you relish a mere deal, you'd probably swoon over a freebie. As it happens, these days companies are bending over backward to win customer loyalty, and that means there's a surprising variety of loot for the taking. You just need to know where and how to look. Want advice on the house from a top-notch financial planner? No problem. Free samples of new cosmetics? They're yours. Companies shell out roughly $7 billion a year on freebies. To get your share of free stuff and more, you can:

■ **Be a guinea pig.** Companies and even local stores can be obsessive about testing new products and services. After all, they can't afford flops. To avoid marketing fiascoes, most firms do extensive product research. That's where you can come in. For instance, long-distance carriers have been known to offer cold cash—as much as $100—for trying their services. Hotels and restaurants sometimes pay the tab for ordinary folks to anonymously sample their food and lodging.

Primed to help out with such important work? Then crack open the Yellow Pages for clues. Look under "Market Research," and call the listed firms to ask when they will next need volunteers for surveys, polls, or focus groups. If you're selected, you'll likely receive some good stuff, including cash, free items, and coupons. For those interested in more of a quick fix, you can respond to ads offering everything from soup to aspirin and detergent by reading *Freebies* magazine (call 805-566-1225 for a subscription).

■ **Flaunt your good taste.** Quick, name a product you've recently tried and simply adored. Did you (a) keep your opinion to yourself, (b) recommend it to others, or (c) drop a line to the company brass, letting them in on your new allegiance? If you answered "c," you're catching on. If you responded to both "b" and "c" and mentioned "b" in your letter, give yourself a hand. Companies love repeat customers. Share your feelings about a product or service and you may be richly rewarded.

Hotels, food companies, airlines, and restaurants are particularly flattered to receive fan mail. They sometimes lavish loyal, vocal customers with coupons for free or discounted meals, stays, and flights. So speak up. If the target of your praise is a small store or local hotel, put your compliments in writing to the manager. For the products and services of larger stores and chains, write directly to corporate headquarters, addressing the note to the CEO or to customer service.

■ **Seek out free information.** Believe it or not, you can get an impressive education on somebody else's nickel. Here are just a few examples. Recreational Equipment (REI), the outdoorsman's store and catalog, routinely holds free seminars on rock climbing, camping, and kayaking. Over at Home Depot, the ultimate retailer for house tinkerers, you can learn to build just about anything at the free clinics offered at the firm's 280 stores nationwide. Even at your local video store, there's probably a shelf devoted to titles you can rent for free. These are typically videos focused on public service, ranging from safety for kids to health and family issues.

Professionals like lawyers, financial advisers, and accountants often dispense advice without charge, too. Most, for instance, offer free initial consultations. Others, as a community service, hold free or low-cost seminars at local colleges or libraries.

■ **Celebrate on somebody else.** Got a birthday soon? An anniversary or graduation coming up? Ripe opportunities await those not shy about sharing the news. This doesn't just apply at McDonald's, where anyone presenting proof of his or her birthday can have a free meal on Ronald. (You can find the toll-free numbers of most large companies by di-

aling 1-800-555-1212.) New moms can rack up valuable coupons for diapers, formula, and bottles by dialing up baby-minded companies to share the news—especially upon multiple births. Traveling honeymooners can often get bumped to an airplane's first-class section by informing the gate agent about their recent nuptials. If you loved the place where you stayed as honeymooners, give them a ring. Many hotels will offer you a free night's stay on your anniversary to repeat the experience.

■ **Score points for your loyalty.** Be sure to join any frequent buyer programs that reward your patronage with freebies. The best examples are airline frequent flier programs. Hotels, long-distance carriers, and credit-card companies also offer similar programs. In fact, the list of businesses offering rebates to loyal customers is growing by the day.

CHAPTER 19

Men, Women, and Money

Money is probably the most emotion-laden topic in contemporary life. Only food and sex are close competitors as common carriers of such strong, diverse feelings and strivings. Yet almost from birth, females and males get bombarded by their families and society with very different money messages. David W. Drueger, clinical professor of psychiatry at Baylor College of Medicine, says that women grow up to equate money with safety and security, while men see money as power, enhancing their sense of masculinity and competence. True, these views are changing as society's notion of masculinity and femininity evolves. Still, if teachers and parents think little Janies aren't as good at math as Johnnies, adult Janes can easily wind up feeling they're

incompetent at money management. Making yourself aware of the very different ways men and women view money will help you reduce conflicts with spouses, partners, siblings, colleagues, and friends of the opposite sex. Each sex can benefit by knowing the other's style on such key topics as earning, spending, saving, investing, and borrowing—and then dealing with *la différence*.

Earning Styles of the Sexes

Traditionally, the male has been raised to bring home the bacon. It's a rare female who expects to be the primary breadwinner for her whole life. After aeons of hauling the wild boar caveward, today's male may well even stake his masculinity on being a strong financial provider. Conversely, some women and men believe that financial success will rob a woman of her womanliness. Few women associate having more money with more femininity.

Most working women view compensation as only one measure of their professional achievement, however. A 1993 survey of 2,958 workers by the Families and Work Institute, a New York City research firm, showed that women were 56% more likely than men to consider stimulating work as a key reason for taking their current position. As a result, some women gladly remain in jobs that may not pay very well. The leading women journalists of National Public Radio—including Cokie Roberts, Susan Stamberg, Nina Totenberg, and Linda Wertheimer—have stated publicly that they won their opportunities in part because male competitors left for higher-paying jobs in commercial broadcasting. These women could afford to stay in public radio because they had working husbands and felt less financial pressure.

Unfortunately, one reason women often focus on job aspects other than salary is that they still can't compete dollar for dollar with men. Although females now account for almost half of the labor force, they earn 28% less, on average, than their male counterparts. A pragmatic result: Women generally are much less confident than men about their earning power, which influences many of their financial decisions. In particular, they often are uncomfortable with risk and reluctant to borrow. They tend to prefer supersafe investments to chancy ones because they aren't sure they could replace any lost money—another reflection of insecurity about their earning ability. Veteran financial planners put it this way: Men see money as a flow that keeps on coming, while women see it as a pool that can be drained dry.

The chief breadwinner in married couples (read: the husband, typically) often also expects to be the primary financial decision maker at home. Therapists and financial experts alike deplore this imbalance. They say that whether it's deciding how to invest the Christmas bonus or where to take the August vacation, major money choices ought to be thrashed out by both spouses. Since that idealistic recommendation is often ignored in daily practice, as women make further strides toward salary equality, conflicts with partners are bound to heat up—particularly when a wife makes more than her husband.

Spending Styles of the Sexes

"When the going gets tough, the tough go shopping," say those oversize T-shirts. It's a safe bet you've never seen a man wearing one. Indeed, from Lucy and Ricky Ricardo to Al and Peg Bundy, one of the most enduring American cultural stereotypes features the female rampaging through the stores while her tightfisted spouse tears his hair out over the bills. But the reality is far more complicated than that.

For one thing, women are the designated shoppers in most families, gathering in goods for themselves, their kids, and often their spouses. According to a study by Maritz Marketing Research, while 80% of women buy all their own clothing and toiletries, fewer than half of men do. In short, women are expected to procure the families' needs and then get blamed for their tendency to spend money.

The truth is that neither sex has cornered the market on splurging; each does it in his or her own way. In a survey by Mediamark Research in New York City, the percentage of men and women who describe themselves as impulse buyers was virtually identical—33.6% for men compared with 34.2% for women. The sexes are prone to spend for different reasons and at different stages of their lives, though. Women tend to treat themselves to designer clothing, jewelry, and beauty treatments—items that enhance their value in their own view. They're particularly indulgent in the first few years of their careers, doing so as a declaration of freedom. As they get older, however, women frequently grow more cautious and less whimsical about how they spend.

For men, the cycle is reversed. They sometimes evolve into megashoppers as they grow older and experience financial success. Men tend to have an enduring passion for power toys: pint-size planes, cars, and boats make way for the real thing in adult life. Doubters need only drop by the nearest Alfa Romeo or Porsche dealership and count the number of men driving two-seaters off the lot. Because men are more confident about their earning power, they find it easier than women to shoot for the big purchases. In the Maritz survey, the only categories in which men accounted for more purchasing decision than women were home furnishings and cars. Moreover, psychotherapists report, men are more likely to boast about the amount of money they spend on a car, trip, or house.

Saving Styles of the Sexes

Women, on average, outlive their husbands by six years—if they aren't divorced from them instead, which happens in about half of all marriages. Given this precarious outlook, prudence dictates that women *should* be socking away every dollar they can to provide for their future. That, however, is not the case at all. A Merrill Lynch study shows that women who have begun preparing for retirement save only about half of what men do, on average. What's worse, women start saving later than their male counterparts. The average retirement portfolio: $25,700 for women, $52,500 for men.

There's further evidence that women, especially the unmarried ones, are sabotaging their financial futures. On average, married couples put away 5.4% of their pretax pay, single men stash 3.1%, and single women save only 1.5%. Considering that single women save only about half what single men do even though women earn roughly 70% of men's pay, clearly more than the pay-parity problem is at work. Some women, it seems, still cherish the hope that Prince Charming will someday provide for them. Consider: New York City psychotherapist Annette Lieberman asked 124 women how they planned to take care of themselves after age 65. Few spoke of Individual Retirement Accounts or regular savings plans. Instead their answers ranged from the unlikely to the unimaginable—they would marry a rich man, win the lottery, write the great American novel, even be decimated in World War III and avoid the problem.

Lieberman's advice: Wake up and shoulder the responsibility of paying for your own financial future. (For advice on how to start or increase saving, see Chapters 5 and 11.)

Investing Styles of the Sexes

Too often, this hoary gender stereotype is true: Men really are more willing than women to shoulder investment risk. One reason, mentioned earlier, is men's higher earning power. Another is that many women know less than men about investing, or think they do. In a survey by Oppenheimer Management, the New York City-based investment firm, 41% more men than women said they knew how a mutual fund worked. The gender split starts early and holds true even for younger people. A survey of teenagers by Liberty Financial, a Boston money-management firm, found that male junior high and high school students were almost twice as likely as their female peers to consider themselves very knowledgeable about money and investments. But get this: The study also revealed that actually there was little difference in money and investing knowledge between the female and male students.

Many women, jittery about investing, wind up being overly cautious and keep their cash in bank CDs or Treasury bills rather than in stocks or stock funds. The nervous Nellies see only one dimension of investing risk: the risk of losing money. They totally ignore the second and potentially more devastating risk—that inflation will erode the value of their savings. By contrast, men don't worry as much about the risk of losing a few dollars if there's a probability of a healthy profit someday.

Fortunately for couples, investing is one area in which gender differences can complement each other. While part of every portfolio ought to be invested in stocks or other investments that can outpace inflation, there's also room in your portfolio for CDs and similar safe havens. Indeed, every couple's portfolio needs a balance between risk and caution. So if you're a saver married to an investment risk taker, don't fret. Just remember to view your combined assets as one holistic portfolio.

dox, president of Capital Rose, a Malvern, Pa., company that finances and advises female entrepreneurs, says that a woman tends to borrow only what she needs while a man thinks, *If I can get $250,000, I'll borrow $250,000*. On occasion this restraint by women is admirable. Trouble is, it can also prevent them from starting their dream business, buying their dream home, or otherwise making a financial dream come true.

Men often see a large loan as conferring the same cachet as a luxury car—it's a status symbol, a sign that they have arrived. Such hubris, of course, can get a guy into trouble if he becomes overextended and fails to deal with the problem. In 1993, for example, nearly twice as many single women as men sought help from Budget and Credit Counseling Services, a nonprofit agency in New York City. Yet the average debt load was 24% higher for the males: $3,844 for men versus $3,108 for women.

Borrowing Styles of the Sexes

When it comes to big-ticket borrowing, particularly for a business venture, women are so risk-averse that they may limit their opportunities. Rebecca Mad-

How to Handle Money as a Couple

Love is sticky stuff. It links people; it's the symbol of connection. Money is the opposite. The symbol of separation, money buys us freedom from the control of another person. Yet dealing with money issues during courtship is one of the best ways to cement your relationship, even if the issue is as simple as deciding who pays for pizza. Openness about financial matters early on helps ensure that the two of you won't come to an unhappy parting later, quarreling over assets.

Newlyweds, saving for a sofa or a house down payment, are setting up an economic partnership as well as a family unit. As with any new enterprise, the partners must discuss goals, establish some sort of spending plan, and sort out personal differences. Truth is, embarking on a marital partnership is infinitely more complicated than starting a video store with your mate. Marriage, after all, involves children, parents, and issues of personal intimacy as well as daily issues of getting and spending. In addition, talking about the family's money can bring out tangled feelings about how well or badly you've been treated in the past by those you love.

Even the coolest of couples are likely to encounter some hot money buttons early on. How much is okay to spend on an armchair? A vacation? In the **MONEY** 1994 "Americans and Their Money" survey, couples reported that they usually consult with their partners before buying items that cost more than $134, on average, except for personal clothing and jewelry. They spring for those types of things without asking their significant others.

In the first year of marriage, however, the bride and groom may frequently disagree about what is fair and what is cheap or extravagant. (Just watch an episode of TV's *Mad About You* for proof.) Almost every couple starting out together discovers a wide variance in their beliefs about what they need today and what they ought to put aside for tomorrow. Sometimes these early fights become the stuff of family legend. St. Paul financial consultant Ruth Hayden, who advises couples on how to resolve money differences, recalls the first time her in-laws were coming to dinner, more than two decades ago. She and her new husband, Don, went out to buy glassware. To her horror, Don selected water glasses that cost $16 apiece. Ruth suggested looking at a cut-rate outlet nearby, but her groom swelled with outrage. "You would go to a discount store to buy glasses to serve my parents in?" he stormed. Says Ruth: "I thought he was nuts, and he thought I was kind of trashy."

The truth is that people have different values, and the differences have nothing to do with being trashy, crazy, or cheap. Keep in mind that your partner is different from you. That's probably what drew you together at the beginning, so don't let it make you crazy now.

Differences of opinion, and the compromises you each make to bridge them, become the basis for setting up your financial life. Don't look to financial experts for ironclad rules about whether you should have joint or separate checking accounts, savings that are merged or kept resolutely apart. There are absolutely no absolutes here except one: Do what you and your partner are comfortable doing. In the meantime, while you're working to discover what financial choices please you both, follow two fundamental guidelines to construct the necessary delicate balance:

1. **Give each other some financial space.** Everyone needs a fistful of dollars to use as they please, as long as they remember to cover their necessary expenses. At the very least, you've got to have some cash lying around to surprise your spouse with a birthday gift. Even better, you should be able to afford an occasional personal splurge without having to justify it. Each of you will have an individual money personality and your own tolerance for risk. Make allowances, rather than trying to blot out your differences.

2. **Play fair.** There must be a feeling of mutual trust for any partnership to succeed. Otherwise, expect danger ahead. Let's say the husband is the chief breadwinner and he suspects his wife will overspend uncaringly. He may soon start hiding income from her. She might then detect the deceit and begin to skim cash from the household budget for protection or out of resentment. Even if the relationship survives

such deception, the partners' sense of teamwork is destroyed. The message should be clear: Share information, be honest about your financial downturns or goofs, and be prepared to compromise.

While you must play fair, you and your spouse must also both *play*—that is, be actively involved in your financial affairs. Often, the wife is in a position of ignorance, particularly if she's in her fifties or older. Older women frequently prefer to be left out of decisions about investing and borrowing. In some instances their husbands intentionally conceal information from them. The result is that the wife lands in a disastrous position if she becomes divorced or widowed.

Some aspects of money handling will change as you move into different periods of your life together. While you will be spending, earning, borrowing, saving, and investing continually, the importance of each will shift at different life stages. Early on, in the nest-building stage, you may find borrowing is key as you search for a mortgage and max out on credit cards to furnish your nest or pay for child care. Closer to retirement age, saving and investing are likely to take on new prominence. These shifts don't happen all at once or at specific ages, but represent a gradual evolution in your financial affairs. Following are several smart money-handling strategies for each stage of married life. (Incidentally, although the next part of this chapter talks about married couples, the advice also holds true for unmarried couples living together, both heterosexual and homosexual.)

■ **Newlyweds (ages 25-35).** Getting married usually represents a major change in your financial lifestyle. If you follow the statistical norm and wed in your mid-twenties, your earnings will probably be at their lowest in your adult life—at least until after you retire. You've only recently discovered the fun (and the stress) of being financially free of your parents. Suddenly you have new responsibilities to another person. Chances are you and your sweetheart didn't opt for a prenuptial contract—you have no kids and hardly any possessions to divide, after all. From the start, though, you and your new spouse need to have frank discussions about money. Put all your assets on the table, then portion out joint and separate responsibilities—who will pay the bills, balance the bank statements, and handle the mechanics of saving and investing. Both of you should share in the work. Take into account, however, who has more time, talent, and interest in the tasks.

Choose whether you prefer separate or joint bank accounts, and reserve the right to change your mind later on. Young couples with no assets and little income often live from paycheck to paycheck, pooling nearly all their resources just to make ends meet. When earnings and assets rise, more affluent marrieds may establish both joint and separate savings and investment accounts, perhaps reflecting different risk tolerances, a family inheritance, or simply personal preference. Discuss what works best for both of you.

Establish the habit of setting aside an hour or so every week or two for a regular "business meeting" in which you thrash out ongoing financial issues and new ones that may have arisen. This can be done in your home office, your living room, or at the kitchen table—but best not in the boudoir or as you're heading out the door in the morning. Treat the subject of money with the seriousness it deserves, while treating each other with respect. Such courtesy will go far toward defusing disagreements before they turn into explosive arguments.

As newlyweds, your arguments are likely to revolve around spending and budgeting. In your single days, your spare cash may have disappeared down your throat (for fancy dinners out) or shown up on your back (for designer duds). Now, you and your partner are probably beginning to set long-term goals, like coming up with the down payment for a house. So saving money takes on new importance. Try to sock away 10% of your combined pretax incomes, if you can. Impossible? Then try a strategy of saving 4% to 8% of your gross in your twenties and doubling that percentage when you reach your thirties and forties. Once you have a reasonable emergency fund—say, three to six months' worth of living expenses—start a systematic investment program and be sure to make the most of any tax-advantaged retirement savings plans that your employer may offer.

■ **When baby makes three—or four— and expenses soar (ages 35–45).** Family responsibilities bring new needs for financial protection. Update your will (if you haven't made one, get to it pronto). Check that you have adequate life insurance on the family breadwinner(s). You *don't* need to buy a life insurance policy for your newborn, despite what some pushy life insurance agents insist. The purpose of life insurance is to replace lost income after the policyholder dies.

During this period of your life, your earnings are rising but your expenses are probably mounting even faster. You'll want to start the newborn's college fund, but first you have to pay those rising medical bills and hack away at your credit-card balances. The biggest danger at this point in your life is that you will overuse credit and underplan for future needs. If you're feeling swamped, sit down with your partner and establish some realistic family financial goals—small upcoming ones, if that's all you can manage. Put them down on paper; it makes the commitment stick. Divide difficult, long-term objectives into a series of reachable,

short-term targets. For example, instead of saying "I need to save $100,000 for Max's college tuition in 15 years," say "I need to start investing $250 a month in a mutual fund for Max's future college tuition bills." If you can't afford your heart's desire now, don't cross that goal off your wish list forever. Just downsize a bit or schedule it for a more distant date. Maybe you'll buy that first house in two years, rather than in two months. The important thing is to set your goals and work on meeting them. You can even get the kids involved once they reach age seven or so (see Chapter 20).

■ **College crunch (ages 45–55).** Your earnings are climbing to new peaks, but your kids are in college, you've got a car loan or two, and a mortgage payment, and your property taxes are rising. In short, you have extraordinary expenses. Hang tough. When the tuition bills stop, your borrowing, scrimping, and financial pressure will slacken. At that time (if not earlier), saving and investing become the main financial event. Review your investment plans periodically with your partner and see if you're on track toward a comfortable retirement. A software program could come in handy.

Another possible concern: your aging parents and their financial needs. You can prevent trouble later on by exploring their financial and other concerns now. As you'll see in Chapter 21, it's a smart idea to have an honest discussion with your parents about their current finances and their financial prospects for the rest of their lives. You'll also want to find out from them where they keep their savings and investments, which credit cards and loans they have, and whom they use as financial advisers, in case of an emergency. This way you can help ensure that if their health or mind deteriorates, their debts will be paid and they'll get all their investment, pension, and Social Security checks. Naturally, you and your partner should share with each other the same kind of information about your separate and combined finances.

■ **Peaking earnings (ages 55–65).** This is the time to consolidate your financial assets and nail down your future security. With luck, you're earning more money than you even thought possible 30 years ago. You're considering tax-reduction ideas, new investment opportunities, perhaps even a vacation home that will become a retirement haven. You may be thinking about volunteer work to continue when you retire or contemplating a move to an area with a lower cost of living and warmer climate. The major mistake you can make now is not saving enough to supplement your future pension and Social Security income. A second consideration: Readjust your life insurance. You may need less coverage or even none at all after the kids are on their own.

■ **Preserving assets (after 65).** Making your money last is critical at this stage. Once upon a time, your kids' needs may have dominated your living and spending patterns. Now it's more likely that the health and welfare of you and your partner are pressing considerations in determining your spending, borrowing, investing, and lifestyle. Discuss with your children your wishes for your future living arrangements if you one day can no longer take care of yourself. Would you want to be moved to a nursing home? If so, which one? Would you prefer in-home health care? Would you want to move in with your adult child? Finally, you and your spouse must together face difficult questions of how you will manage—financially and otherwise—after one of you dies. Will your children need to supplement your income? What living arrangements will each of you make? If you have followed the guidelines in this book over the decades, however, and had a modicum of luck to complement your efforts, your reward should be a comfortable self-sufficiency in your final years.

Resolving Money Arguments

He says: "When we first met, she lived from paycheck to paycheck. If she had any money left after paying the bills, she just spent it. That made me nervous.

Being able to save makes me feel happy and financially secure."

She says: "I spend easily, but always within my means. He thinks I'm completely profligate because I occasionally come home with a Gap bag. In angry moments I call him cheap. I will surreptitiously add to the tip he leaves in a restaurant. I will lie about what things cost, even when I'm spending my own money, just to avoid an argument. This behavior is right out of the '50s, and I hate it. I might just as well call him Dagwood."

Perhaps you see traces of yourself or your spouse in the above true-life exchange? Maybe—like this two-income, fortyish New York City couple—you have a lot of money bickering in your own marriage. Perhaps as time goes by, you recognize that you're not getting where you want to be financially. Or maybe you're just steamed about the way your spouse deals with money. If you share some of these symptoms, a cash shortage probably isn't the problem. More likely the fault lies with money beliefs and attitudes. Some likely culprits: disorganization, ill-defined goals, confusion over investment choices, blame over past mistakes, and fear of future insecurity.

The first step toward resolving chronic financial quarrels is identifying patterns that need changing. Couples tend to polarize into opposites: if you're a spender,

chances are you married a saver. If you're a money worrier, most likely you were attracted to a money avoider. Even if you both entered the marriage as worriers, one of you probably became an avoider to get away from the constant worrying. Similarly, if two spenders wed, one often winds up charging like mad while the other feels a need to set limits and becomes the family saver. Washington, D.C., psychotherapist Olivia Mellan teaches contentious couples the process of depolarization—that is, how to bridge their opposing tendencies. The most productive approach, she finds, is to talk about feelings and dynamics first and hard facts afterward. The nub of the process is to practice the nonhabitual: take a half-mile walk in your partner's moccasins, so to speak. How do you do that? Follow these tips:

■ **Pick a nonstressful time to talk, like an afternoon at the beach.** Then, share your early experiences with money. Recall the ways your parents spent, saved, talked, or screamed about money. Confide the financial worries that grip you. 'Fess up to your underlying fear of, say, being a bag lady in your old age. How about spending? Do you go on sprees to cure depression, temper anger, or fight boredom? Do you shop compulsively to compete with your friends? Does your mate save in order to control the household finances or to have power over others? Perhaps one of you works 70 hours a week to make money for the family, while the other denigrates these efforts as being materialistic or a way of avoiding intimacy. In your household, does money represent security? Power? Independence? Dishonesty? Learning to translate the different messages that money sends to each of you can reduce friction.

■ **Describe the financial behaviors you admire in your partner.** Yes, you can share judgments and criticisms of each other, but get past them quickly. Move on to the positive aspects of your mate's behavior and spell them out in detail. Spend roughly three times longer on the redeeming qualities than you did on the criticism. (Your partner, in turn, should lavish similar praise on you. If he or she doesn't, suggest it.)

Mellan favors using opening lines like these: "One of your most endearing qualities about money is . . ." or "One of the things I've learned about money from you is . . ." Spenders might acknowledge that their mate has shown them the value and necessity of saving. They could even confess that their spending makes them feel out of control at times. Risk takers may acknowledge, "I see why you worry. Somebody has to set some limits." After you have established an atmosphere of appreciation and respect, you will be better able to tackle the divisive issues in your money life together.

The aim of this exercise is to break the familiar fight pattern and move both of you toward more centrist positions. Instead of criticizing each other about your differences, own up to your secret envies and appreciations of each other. When each of you feels less attacked, you will feel better able to modify old behaviors. You might even create assignments where you switch roles. Go to the local department store, for example, and let the family saver suggest things to buy while the spender comes up with reasons not to do so. You don't have to spend a penny in the process. The saver might, however, catch a glimmer of the fun of shopping while the spender may begin to see the usefulness of setting limits.

■ **Establish goals—separately.** Better still, each of you should independently set three types of goals. Write up a list of short-, medium-, and long-term goals for yourself and your partner. Then put it aside for at least a week before reviewing it. When each of you has a list, rank the goals in three groups: (1) the ones that are most important; (2) the goals you could live without if necessary; and (3) the items you could relinquish more easily. Set a tentative date for accomplishing each goal. At the same time, put a price tag on each one and figure out how the two of you will earn, save, or otherwise come up with the money necessary to accomplish your goals.

■ **Finally, share your goal lists with your spouse.** If there are major divergences, try to work them out so that both of you can get most of what you want. Ultimately you'll want to meld both wish lists into a set of joint goals. Work out a timetable, put down some preliminary numbers, and start turning those dreams into reality. If a few goals seem unattainable, try slicing them into a series of smaller steps and work on those. If all else fails, discuss how you can scale down an elusive goal to bring it within reach. If you can't own a lakeside cottage, maybe you can rent one. If a full-season vacation rental is an unattainable luxury, go for two weeks or spend a long weekend at a nearby hotel. When you agree on a goal to meet, add it to the joint list, no matter how small or insignificant it appears.

One note of caution: The above guidelines work only if the two of you are functional as a couple—that is, you are committed to the relationship, there is no physical or emotional abuse, and neither of you is addicted to drugs or breaking the monogamous agreement. If the partnership is dysfunctional, the two of you need counseling before you can work out your money differences.

If your mate is what you might call money reckless, you must set firm limits on your partner's behavior as quickly as possible. Pleading, haranguing, or arguing will only wear you out. Instead, state explicitly that you will not cover his or her future bills. In addition, you should re-

duce or eliminate your spouse's access to the money or assets that the two of you hold in common. If possible, drain cash from your joint accounts and put it into an account in your name only. Cancel joint credit or charge cards. In sum, take all possible steps to put brakes on a reckless partner's spending. Then you will be on your way to salvaging both yourself and your net worth from the destructive relationship.

Special Concerns for Unwed Couples

The phrase "unmarried domestic partners" may conjure up memories of hippies in the '60s, but today's reality is quite different: some 3.5 million households are headed by couples who are not married to each other—almost six times as many as in 1970, according to the U.S. Census Bureau. Fully one-third of these homes contain children under age 15. But an estimated 370,000 men and women over 65 live together unmarried. The vast majority of cohabiters are opposite-sex couples, often in their forties and fifties. Many have been married before. A substantial number of the men, in particular, are professionals earning six-figure incomes who feel they were burned in earlier relationships. As a result, they are reluctant to commit themselves a second time, says financial planner Larry Elkin of Hastings on Hudson, N.Y., who has counseled dozens of these walking wounded.

More than most people, young unwed partners are often slow to plan. But this reluctance can boomerang badly, causing serious damage to one or both of the people involved. When things go wrong—illness strikes, you decide to break up, your partner dies—you might not only find yourself having to deal with financial issues for the first time. You will wind up in relatively uncharted legal territory, with few of the protections or financial privileges accorded to married couples.

Certain financial precautions are in order from the start of your live-in relationship. In the early stages, when one or both of you may not be fully committed to coupled, it's best to own little or nothing jointly and to keep most of your cash in separate accounts, to minimize future disputes over joint property. Both of you can contribute equally to a shared checking account for common expenses like the rent or mortgage, food, and utilities. If there's a major income disparity—you make $25,000 a year but your lover brings in $75,000—then chip in proportional amounts.

As the relationship ripens, you and your partner may want to draw up a living-together agreement to avert painful surprises in the future. In this document, address such issues as how you'll own property, if you'll hold income in joint or individual accounts and what will happen if you separate. If your financial lives are comparatively uncomplicated, this could be a homemade document drawn to clarify your arrangements. Once you start building up assets and income, however, you might want to hire a matrimonial or family lawyer. This attorney can draw up a contract stating that all property acquired while you live together, other than that which either of you receives as a gift or inheritance, is to be owned jointly. Any income derived from such property would also be owned jointly. In addition, the agreement could stipulate that should you break up, voluntarily or involuntarily, the property will be sold and the proceeds divided, unless you both agree otherwise at that time.

The apartment you rent or the home you share can be a particular locus of contention if you come to a parting of the ways. The key point to remember is that the property belongs only to the person whose name is on the lease or the deed, regardless of who makes rent or mortgage payments. If the named person leaves, dies, or ends the romance, the partner has no legal right to remain in the home. For mutual protection, both names can go on the lease or deed. Remember, though, that each person will then become legally liable for the entire amount owed if the partner doesn't pay up.

Buying a home can be a disconcerting experience, especially if you are gay. Although it is against the law for a seller to reject an offer or a lender to deny a mortgage because a couple is unmarried or gay, you could face tacit discrimination. Once you find a house, condo, or co-op to buy, you will have to choose between two legal arrangements if you plan to buy the place jointly. **Joint ownership with rights of survivorship** means that you and your lover own the property and one of you will inherit it immediately if the other dies. Ownership as **tenants in common** means that each person owns a half share of the home. If you die, half the property will go to your next of kin unless a will specifies otherwise. Be sure to talk through this issue together to avoid painful future surprises.

In the event that you and your lover split after decades of devotion, the biggest financial pitfall is likely to be the equitable division of retirement assets. "Sometimes a 55-year-old will run off with a 23-year-old," says Elkin, a CPA who has counseled domestic partners of all stripes. "This can happen to a married person, too, of course, but the unmarried one is in a lot more trouble financially because the law doesn't recognize the former lover's claim against the other per-

son's assets." This can be a disaster if you've been paying most of the household bills while your companion has been plumping up his or her retirement account. A carefully drawn living-together contract can go a long way toward protecting both of you, particularly the financially vulnerable partner.

You may also want to grant your partner a **durable power of attorney,** allowing him or her to make financial decisions for you if you become incompetent. Similarly, you probably will want to get a **health care proxy,** a document that permits a nonrelative to make medical decisions for an incapacitated patient. This will also give your lover the right to visit should you end up in a hospital intensive care unit—an entitlement normally limited to close family members. In addition, draw up a will to provide for your companion, since he or she will have no automatic rights of inheritance. If you need a kick to get you to the attorney's office, imagine this scene or a close variation: You own a house that you share with a lover whom your family has never accepted; you die without a will and those relatives automatically inherit the love nest. Not a pretty picture for your beloved.

Wills, trusts, and similar devices are all steps toward getting you the legal protections that a married couple would receive automatically. Because the law doesn't step in to resolve conflicting demands or ensure equitable distribution among un-married couples after separation or death, it is critical that the two of you work to-gether on your financial affairs, perhaps with a lawyer and CPA. The more you settle now, the less chance for confusion later—which is a fine state of affairs for any twosome.

Planning a Divorce

Ending a marriage is almost always a traumatic experience for everyone in-volved except perhaps the lawyers. But contemporary unions are about as likely to end in Splitsville as they are to last. The U.S. Census estimates that during the 1990s, somewhere between four and five out of every 10 marriages will break up, a slight improvement over the 50% rate that prevailed through most of the 1980s.

The financial dependence that comes with wedlock, however, may last well into the next century if there are young children involved. So even if you rend the emotional bonds, you will have to deal with the financial ones—dividing assets you have accumulated and com-mingled over years. The outcome may well be an economic bummer: when couples call it quits, each person typically

has roughly half the assets the pair en-joyed before and, inevitably, a lower in-come and a lower standard of living. Children invariably compare conditions in the new, separate households. Down-ward mobility for them and their mother seems less painful if the father and his new household are enduring similar hardships. The loss is harder to bear if the father continues to live with luxuries that the divorced wife and children can no longer afford.

Some couples who have failed at mar-riage, however, take great pride in their ability to cobble together a fair and equi-table parting. To divorce equitably, says Washington, D.C., psychotherapist Olivia Mellan, don't use guilt or anger to nego-tiate any agreements about money. Your goal is to achieve a full and lasting settle-ment, based on reasonable expecta-tions—not war reparations and revenge. Mellan says she and her first husband achieved "the best divorce anyone could." The most divisive point: four heirloom gold bracelets from her husband's family. "I thought we should divide them two and two, but I gave all four back when I saw how important they were to him. And he was generous in other ways," she acknowledges. One message from Mel-lan's example is that surprising items may emerge as the contentious ones.

If you and your soon-to-be ex become enmeshed in unrelenting quarrels, you might want to seek a professional **di-**

vorce mediator to smooth your parting. Marriage or family therapists, financial planners, even attorneys, may be trained to serve as divorce mediators. Lawyers usually charge their standard hourly fee. Therapists, psychologists, social workers, and ministers generally have lower fees; some even offer sliding scales based on your ability to pay. A simple, budget-priced mediation, limited to financial affairs rather than custody issues, might involved five one- or two-hour sessions at $50 to $150 an hour. The mediator will work with the two of you to carve out a compromise but will not take sides. The result probably will be faster, cheaper, and less rancorous than a solution carved out by warring lawyers. After mediation, use a lawyer to review the agreement you reached and to file the necessary legal papers.

In uncomplicated cases, if you and your ex-partner are equally committed to going through the process with minimum damage, you might consider handling your own divorce. Suitable candidates: couples in their twenties or thirties who have little or no property and either have no children or have agreed on who'll get custody. In some states, such as Arizona, California, and Texas, independent paralegals run thriving businesses handling divorce paperwork for their customers for fees of a few hundred dollars. To find such a service, check the classifieds in your telephone book or local newspaper under the headings "Divorce Assistance" or "Lawyer Alternatives."

Even if you can handle your own divorce, however, it may be wiser not to do so. It's best to seek legal help—either for a limited consultation or for ongoing representation—if you are confused about your legal rights or overwhelmed by the financial complexities. Certainly consult a lawyer if your spouse files legal papers that seem to contradict the facts or spirit of your prior agreements and discussions. If your divorce is complicated because you have hard-to-value assets, are engaged in bankruptcy proceedings, or are disputing ownership of valuable property, don't hesitate to get the specialized help you need from an attorney, accountant, real estate agent, or financial planner.

The traditional "big three" considerations of divorce are alimony, child support, and property settlements. Here are the basics about all of them:

■ **Alimony.** This is the amount of money one ex-spouse is legally bound to give the other under a decree of divorce, separate maintenance, or written separation agreement. In general, alimony is treated as taxable income for the person who gets it, while the one writing the alimony checks can usually deduct the periodic payments. Unrestricted alimony is rarely awarded these days. More likely, a spouse who hasn't worked outside the home (or hasn't done so recently) will get some degree of support for a limited time. The amount and duration of alimony increasingly are determined by each party's earning ability, the length of the marriage, and the recipient's non-monetary contribution to the union. Some counties have adopted financial schedules to help judges determine equitable support levels. But you and your ex-spouse can make your own arrangements outside of court that differ from the guidelines.

■ **Child support.** If you have a child and are divorcing, even though you and your ex cease being husband and wife, your roles as parents continue. Each state sets its own guidelines for determining child support. Two factors are usually paramount: the child's needs and the parent's ability to pay. In order to prevent kids from suffering financially, child support payments must continue until the youngest child is 18 or 21, depending on state law. Child support payments are neither taxable to the recipient nor deductible by the payer.

To compute the amount you or your spouse might be required to pay, get a copy of your state's support formula from a court clerk, attorney, or divorce typing service. Then calculate the income of both parents and the needs of your children that your state factors into its support formula. Your award may differ from the norm if the noncustodial parent has a notably high or low income or if either parent has remarried or has a live-in mate.

When estimating their kids' future expenses, wise parents consider costs that go beyond the scope of the typical formula. By including a cost-of-living adjustment clause in the settlement agreement, for example, parents can ensure that inflation won't erode the buying power of future child support. It may also prevent a return to court to seek an upward adjustment of the amount a few years down the line, with the attendant expense and aggravation. In addition, make sure you and your soon-to-be ex decide who will pay for the following: your children's health insurance; future higher education costs; medical expenses and deductibles not covered by the support formula; and special school expenses such as class trips, activities fees, sports uniforms, and equipment.

Determine, too, how your children's expenses will be met if you or your ex-husband or wife dies or becomes disabled. You may require that one or both parents maintain life insurance and disability coverage at least until the children turn 21 or complete their education.

■ **Property settlements.** These are onetime transfers of cash or other assets upon divorce. You can undoubtedly quickly identify some of your shared property—the house, the car, the checking and savings accounts. To get your fair share of the joint pie, however, consider the less obvious assets: the value of a professional license, the cash value of life insurance, your spouse's businesses or hobbies, the gold coins or savings bonds in the safe-deposit box, even such things as stock options, frequent flier miles, season tickets, and club memberships. One Washington, D.C., couple agreed, after protracted negotiation, that he could continue attending their local church with the children, while she had to seek spiritual solace out of the neighborhood.

When it comes to dividing the assets, state laws consider the nature and duration of the partnership. Equitable distribution is the prevailing concept in 41 states plus the District of Columbia. Under this arrangement, a wife in a marriage of 10 years or more may well receive 50% of the marital assets, even if her husband paid most of the costs while they were living as man and wife. If the union lasted only a few years, she might get 30% of the joint pie, though rulings vary widely depending on the judge and your state. In the community property states (Arizona, California, Idaho, Louisiana, Nevada, New Mexico, Texas, and Washington, with similar legislation in Wisconsin), each spouse is co-owner of any property acquired by either spouse during the marriage if a joint effort was made in acquiring the property. Any gifts or inheritances that one person received during the marriage are usually excluded, but

growth in those assets may be considered joint property if the spouse contributed significantly to the increase. (Community property laws differ among the states, however, so if you are a resident of one, be sure to learn about the specific regulations that apply.)

Remember that you may well have rights to your partner's pension assets as part of the divorce settlement. In community property states, only the portion of the retirement plans earned during the marriage is subject to division. In most other states, a court would consider all retirement benefits in arriving at an equitable distribution of the marital assets.

If both of you have pension plans and Individual Retirement Accounts, the simplest solution is for each of you to keep the accounts that are in your own name. Should the amounts be vastly unequal, you can make up the difference in the way you divvy up other assets. Another option is for each of you to keep a specific portion of the plan (or plans). This choice is a bit more complex, since a lawyer must then draw up something called a **Qualified Domestic Relations Order** (or **QDRO,** pronounced "quadro") for a judge to approve. This is an order from the court to the retirement plan administrator, explaining how the pension plan's benefits are to be assigned to each party in a divorce. The options include an immediate distribution to an IRA owned by the alternate payee;

monthly payments at retirement age; or an immediate full payout, in which case the alternate payee will owe income taxes on the money. You don't need a QDRO to make an immediate transfer from your spouse's IRA to your own, however, or for a payment directly to you. But if you get an IRA distribution and do not roll it over within 60 days, you will owe income tax on the amount you receive plus a 10% premature distribution penalty if you are under age 59½.

As for Social Security, if you were married for 10 years or longer, you will be eligible to collect benefits based on your ex-spouse's earnings record when you reach age 62, assuming you have been divorced for at least two years and have not remarried. Those benefits are equal to half the amount your former spouse is eligible to collect, including the period after your marriage was dissolved. If you have worked for a number of years, your Social Security benefits based on your own earnings record may be greater than the derivative benefit based on your former spouse's earnings. In that case you'll want to collect benefits based on your own record, since you can't get both.

When the divorce agreement has been signed and sealed, you may be ready to take a deep breath—and perhaps a celebratory glass of bubbly. Don't lighten up quite yet, however. While you have scaled the major hurdles, there may still be a few

stumbling blocks to navigate. For instance, you may have to:

■ **Examine your insurance policies.** If your ex-spouse is named beneficiary of your life insurance, change the designation to your children or other heirs. Reconsider the amounts of your life and disability coverage, too. You may need more coverage if you are about to become the sole financial support for your children, or less if the principal aim of the insurance was to provide for your spouse. If you have a car, make sure you have auto insurance in your own name. You may need new homeowners or tenants insurance as well.

■ **Update your will.** You'll probably want to exclude your ex-mate and choose new heirs. At the same time, destroy any powers of attorney or health care proxies you may have given your ex-spouse and decide if you want someone else to have them instead.

■ **Unbundle your joint accounts.** Take your spouse's name off savings, brokerage, and other accounts, according to your property settlement agreement. Similarly, cancel joint credit cards, phone cards, and the like. Otherwise your ex-spouse can continue to use them and you will be financially responsible for paying the bills.

■ **Spread the news.** Friends and relatives probably know already, but you might also want to inform your children's teachers, the pediatrician, your landlord, and perhaps even potential matchmakers.

Reducing Financial Risk in Remarriage

Love may be lovelier the second time around, but it's also more complex. Most of the 1.7 million Americans a year who remarry will bring to the altar their own children and assets, commitments, and obligations—in short, the emotional and financial baggage of adult life. The first marriage is nearly always still exacting some kind of payment from at least one spouse, not to mention the lingering wounds and emotional scars. For all these reasons, don't rush to merge your financial lives too quickly as you pass from courtship to cohabiting and remarriage. Take time to build up trust and deal with problems as they arise.

An honest airing of priorities combined with careful planning, however, can help smooth the choppy passages. Before you exchange new rings, tell each other what you own and what you owe. Discuss your long- and short-term goals and objectives. Before your families blend, lay out each spouse's financial responsibilities. Then, create a plan to ac-

commodate them. If each parent pays only for his or her progeny, for example, you will need to keep separate budgets for everything, plus another set of numbers if you have children with your new mate.

The toughest question is likely to be whether to merge your assets and liabilities completely, partially, or not at all. If you keep financial assets separate, you may need legal advice to ward against the automatic commingling of property under some state laws. The best way to do this is by executing a so-called **property status agreement**—either as part of a premarital agreement or after you're married—noting who owns what and forfeiting any spousal claims to specified assets.

Many financial advisers and attorneys favor prenuptial contracts for their clients who are about to start second marriages. These documents often make sense intellectually, though drafting them may have a chilling effect emotionally. While prenups primarily discuss property arrangements, you can include more mundane topics as well, right down to how you share the housework or who will get custody of Fido if the marriage goes to the dogs. Later, if unforeseen events trigger the need, you and your spouse may decide to draw up a postmarital agreement, dealing with the same sorts of issues.

Whether you and your partner decide on a written agreement before or after

499

the nuptial day, certain rules apply. First, consult an attorney to make sure the document conforms to your state's laws. Second, remember that both parties must enter freely into the agreement—well in advance of the wedding date if it's a prenup, lest it smack of coercion. Finally, full disclosure of the assets, liabilities, and obligations of your financial life is imperative. If the court believes one of you is trying to sell the other a false bill of goods, the judge may well strike down the agreement in the event of divorce.

Estate planning poses particularly delicate problems for blended families, since parents may want to protect their biological offspring without neglecting or offending their new spouse and stepchildren. Even if your new partner has promised to provide for your kids as if they were his or her own, you may still feel queasy. After all, myth makers from the brothers Grimm to Walt Disney have helped create a pretty bad rap for stepparents.

One way to keep your legacy intact is to direct your lawyer to draft a **trust** naming your children as beneficiaries. Upon your death, the assets you've designated will fund the trust, which will be managed by a trustee of your choice. The money can then be parceled out in lump sums when the kids reach the ages you specify. If you want your new spouse to enjoy the benefits of the wealth while he or she is still living, draft a so-called **bypass trust.** After your death, your spouse can get any income thrown off by your legacy and, with the trustee's approval, withdraw part of the principal if he or she needs it to pay for important expenses such as medical bills. When your spouse dies, the assets will then flow directly to your children.

At the same time you're redoing wills, review your life insurance to protect your extended family. Consider changing beneficiary designations on existing policies and retirement plans, just as you did after your divorce. Eyeball other forms of insurance, too, for duplications and omissions in coverage. If your new mate comes equipped with a teenage road devil, for instance, make sure your auto policy reflects the fact.

Keeping your new house in order may involve some unexpected strains. Blended families, bulging with kids from two marriages or more, frequently find themselves squeezed to cover the steep child care costs and other living expenses that accompany large households. Moreover, the two-tiered nature of many blended families—older children from first unions, toddlers from the new marriage—means that parents may face child-rearing expenses over many more years than other households do. In particular, the kids' college costs may well soak up all or most of the money that the parents might have used for their retirement.

If that unhappy choice sounds familiar to you, try cutting your spending by at least 5%. Small economies can make a bigger difference than you think. Even so, many parents will still have to make tough choices between fully funding their own retirement years or bankrolling their kids' education. Only you and your mate can make this decision, of course. From a financial perspective, however, it's much wiser to provide for your retirement. There are plenty of educational compromises you and your teenager can consider, including community colleges, state schools, and loan and grant programs. What's more, the kids will eventually make it on their own if they have the ambition. Your retirement, on the other hand, is ultimately your own responsibility.

CHAPTER 20

Kids and Money

Contemporary kids appear to have a startling financial sophistication: they know that money doesn't grow on trees—it comes from automated teller machines. When parents say they can't afford a toy, credit-wise moppets urge Mom and Dad to charge it.

But for all that, most kids' actual understanding of personal money management runs not much deeper than Bart Simpson's. Parents complain that children spend all their money on junk, don't know the value of a dollar, and cannot save a dime. If you have any doubt that some instruction is in order, consider this: A study by Jerry Mason, associate professor of financial planning at Texas Tech University, found that today's high school students know "dramatically less"

about financial topics than their counterparts did 30 years ago. A survey by the National Council on Economic Education, a private organization to promote the teaching of economics, found "appalling ignorance" of monetary concepts among high school students, two-thirds of whom couldn't even define "profit."

Yet the MTV generation needs to learn financial know-how more than any in recent memory. For one thing, they encounter—or at least covet—serious money sooner than their predecessors did. In the 1960s, youngsters may have wheeled around on no-gear Schwinn bikes costing $50, but their 1990s counterparts often hunger for mountain bikes retailing for $300 or more. Teenagers shell out a totally awesome $99 billion a year or more. Most of it goes for food, clothes, and entertainment, says Teenage Research Unlimited, a market research firm in Northbrook, Ill. Though most teens say they want to salt away funds for college, more than half save nothing at all, except for more expensive purchases.

A few years down the line, these teen spenders will reach adulthood in what forecasters say could be a singularly harsh economy, marked by a brutal job market. Indeed, the unemployment rate for 20-to-24-year-olds has been running around 10%, higher than for any other adult age group. And a hefty 43% of those twenty-somethings are still living in their parents' home, according to the Population Reference Bureau, a Washington, D.C., demographics research firm. Some are there to wait out stormy economic weather; others just aren't ready to make it on their own.

Despite cause for concern, however, you can teach your kids the skills and discipline they need to make the American dream come true for them. The most successful financial training devices are the same four simple strategies that have been deployed by parents since the Ozzie and Harriet era:

1. **Give youngsters an allowance, to prove to them that there are limits to spending power.**
2. **Pay them for out-of-the-ordinary chores, to show that effort produces rewards.**
3. **Encourage them to save, so they become accustomed to delaying gratification.**
4. **Teach them the basics of investing, so they have the opportunity to make their savings grow faster.**

But far and away the most powerful teaching tool is parental example. Even before the tooth fairy leaves a coin under the pillow for that first milk tooth, your child is soaking up money attitudes and values from you. If you give money to your kid grudgingly, that conveys something to your offspring. So, too, if you're in a constant frazzle over your maxed-out credit cards. Whether you donate to charity, return the difference when a cashier hands you too much change, or brag at the dinner table about cleverly cheating on your taxes—these daily choices ram home important messages to your kids on a regular basis. Your off-spring will pay far more attention to what you *practice* than to what you *preach*, so your first task is to set the pattern you want them to follow.

Your second obligation is to draw an honest picture of the family's finances, so your kids understand that the green stuff doesn't grow behind the slots in bank machines. No, you don't have to reveal your precise income or net worth for Junior to trumpet around the schoolyard.

But you should discuss some of the financial choices the family is facing. Example: "We're not getting a new car for a while because we're building a college fund for your sister." Over time, the young ones will develop a sense that there are limits to what they—and the family—can spend.

This process has a beneficial side effect of showing your progeny how you arrive at responsible spending decisions. Early on—through your example—teach them the difference between things the family wants and things the family needs. Older kids—age nine and up—should be invited to express opinions on family financial options presented to them. For instance: Should we take a two-week trip to Mexico or hire cleaning help for the house during the year? If the vacation wins, the younger generation has shared in the decision and therefore must be prepared to accept its corollary—that they will have to shoulder more of the burden of cleaning the household.

The following guidelines will help you enrich your kids' financial education at every age and stage. Be warned, though: the suggestions below require time and attention to implement. Start the education process with your preschooler—children begin to grasp the concept of money as early as age three—and be prepared to keep it up through college and possibly a few years beyond.

Starting Out: Toddlers to Preteens

At this age, your child can start learning basic home economics, money trade-offs, and key financial concepts such as saving money and spending limits. The specifics on what you can do to help:

Teach the basics early. By trusting your own imagination, you can devise simple situations to teach rudimentary money skills to your preschooler. At the supermarket, for instance, he can count apples as he puts them in the plastic bag. Give him the necessary dollars to pay for the apples, get a receipt—then let him keep a few coins in change for himself. Rug rats love to push buttons: let yours punch in the numbers at the ATM, while you explain where the dollars come from. Real-world experience, not merely explanation, increases a child's understanding.

By age five, a child can usually recognize pennies and perhaps nickels, dimes, and other coins. Don't be dismayed if your preschooler thinks a nickel is worth more than a dime, however. A young child almost always thinks that larger coins are worth more than smaller ones. A seven-year-old won't choose the nickel over the dime, can generally name all the coins, and know how many pennies are in each.

Older children begin getting more interested in money, perhaps even saving for a future purchase. Take advantage of this curiosity by involving your child in simple projects. She can help you clip grocery coupons and then track down the items at the store. Give her the cents you save and encourage her to put them in her piggy bank or savings account. If your child asks why you are buying the jar with the red label and not the blue one, explain that yours is cheaper, tastier, thicker, or vitamin enriched. Make use of everyday opportunities—a visit to the mall, a stop at the bank—to give your children a sense of where money comes from, where it goes, and why. Even when you leave for the office in the morning, you can help your preschooler understand that you must work to earn the money needed to help pay for the house, the food—and, yes, her toys.

Give your child a regular allowance. By the time children can count—about age five or six—they are ready for that all-American financial institution, the weekly allowance. Surveys suggest that only a minority of kids get a regular stipend, though child-development experts strongly favor the practice. No-allowance youngsters mainly nag for cash as needed or get haphazard handouts. Parents may be surprised to learn that

kids themselves much prefer a regular income, according to *Zillions*, the kids' magazine published by Consumers Union. In a 1993 survey, youngsters ages nine to 14 told *Zillions* that they were less likely to run out of cash and more likely to save when they had a regular income. They also felt more independent.

Settling on the appropriate sum for the first allowance is the parents' next decision—not an easy one, either. You'll want to consider your child's age, your household income, and the affluence of the community where you live. Some parents start kindergartners with 75¢ or so a week. The amount should be enough for the child to purchase a candy bar or other small treat for himself (under your supervision), with some change left for the piggy bank. To make amounts grow faster, you might offer to match any coins saved and put your money plus his into an interest-bearing savings account.

When your youngster enters first grade, a raise is in order. An easy rule of thumb is to give a dollar a week for each grade a child is in. With the increase, be open and clear about what the extra money is to cover. Decide if the young recipient can spend the whole amount for fun or if she must save part of the money to cover contributions to the church or synagogue or future purchases.

By third grade a child can generally comprehend the difference between fixed and discretionary expenses. Expand the allowance to cover one or two essentials such as school lunch and bus fare but still allow some recreational spending. A reasonable guideline is to grant an allowance that is about twice the amount of the child's fixed expenses. Then if he blows his lunch money on baseball cards, stifle your pity (or annoyance) and show him how to make a peanut-butter sandwich to brown-bag from home. As he gets older, increase the allowance annually—perhaps on a birthday or when the child is promoted to a higher grade. When students reach age 10, parents can start doling out a dollar for each year of a youngster's age. These more princely sums may be expected to cover a wider range of both fun stuff and necessities.

As much as possible, let your children disburse their money as they wish. Setting narrow limits for how they can spend defeats the purpose of the allowance. You, of course, retain veto power over any purchase that's unsafe, unhealthy, or in violation of your family's principles. Apart from that, don't fret if they go a little wild at first. They'll simmer down once they realize that no more money is forthcoming to bail them out. Let them live with their mistakes, rather than shielding them from the disagreeable consequences. Loans should be rare and are best given only to kids who are age nine or older. If you decide to permit advances (all of us come up short occasionally), charge some token interest—a

dime on each dollar, say—so your child learns early that credit carries a price. Alternatively, you could have the child pay you back within a specified time period and owe you a "free" laundry folding or lawn mowing as "interest."

While you should let a child live with his own spending mistakes, take a tougher line when your offspring are careless with expensive stuff that you have provided. If, for example, your daughter forgets to lock her bike and it's stolen, don't replace it immediately. Let her feel the loss for a while—and perhaps buy a cheaper bike next time or let her chip in with part of her allowance. If your son owes $12 for a lost library book, let him pay out of his savings. No savings? Then let him take on extra jobs around the house to earn the $12.

If, in the immortal words of the Berenstain Bears, your child comes down with a bad case of the Gimmes, consider if something else is amiss. Some parents find that when their youngster howls to go to the store because he can't live another minute without the latest video game, what he really wants is the time and attention you spend going there together, the companionship of having a soda on the way. By the time you reach the mall, the game he couldn't live without may be nearly forgotten.

Child psychologists and financial experts generally discourage tying the basic allowance to the performance of routine household chores. Your son or daughter should carry out those tasks as part of ordinary family duty. While experts discourage linking the regular allowance to simple tasks, they almost uniformly applaud paying a child for taking on special projects around the house. Money that is earned is nearly always treated more carefully than cash handouts. The kids like the extra income, of course, and it can be considerable: shoveling the driveway commands from $5 to $25 these days, depending on the length of asphalt and the depth of the snow. More important, however, the youthful workers value the sense of control that comes from choosing their projects, then earning the money for prized objects through their own determined efforts. As employer of first resort, offer your child a chance to do chores you might ordinarily hire somebody to do—mowing the lawn, taking down storm windows, washing the car, or even catering a birthday party for a younger sibling.

Your intuition is probably the best guide as to which tasks are part of being a family member, and therefore done free, and which ones are beyond the call of duty. Some parents pay youngsters for cleaning the bathrooms but not for table setting or walking the dog. Baby-sitting might be done free in the late afternoon, performed for a "family discount" on weeknights, but command full market rate on Saturday nights.

One caveat: Don't be super nitpicky about the way household jobs are performed. You want the work, paid or unpaid, to be a positive experience that your child will be eager to repeat. So if you can't bounce a quarter on the newly made bed, or your daughter missed a few spots when she washed the car, let it be. If the performance was truly substandard, don't withhold pay. Instead, point out what was done wrong and show the child how to correct it.

There is no need, however, to lavish cold cash on your children to reward high marks at school or exemplary behavior. Some things should be done for their own sake; otherwise you're encouraging a young blackmailer-in-training to expect a payoff for every positive action. If your child has made some monumental effort sitting still during the four-hour car trip to Cousin Lulu's house, honor the accomplishment by baking his favorite cake or going to a ball game together.

Don't cut off your child's allowance "earnings" as punishment—that merely encourages the notion that bad behavior is a negotiable item and not simply unacceptable. When your child misbehaves, one appropriate recourse is to banish access to the TV or take away other privileges, rather than cutting the weekly handout. In unusual cases look for creative ways to make the punishment fit the misdemeanor. For example, when their five-year-old daughter did $4,000 worth of damage by drawing with a rock on three neighbors' cars, one New York City couple thought long and hard and discussed with their daughter what further punishment was in order (after an immediate apology to the car owners). First they considered intent: the little girl hadn't damaged the cars willfully; it was raining, and she'd thought the water would erase the marks—and she was terribly contrite. The parents considered taking part of their daughter's 75¢-a-week allowance to help build a fund to repaint the cars, but that would have been a lengthy process with little practical value. Ultimately the couple decided to mete out swifter justice: they canceled their daughter's much-dreamed-of visit to the ballet. Other punishments might have been equally appropriate, but the point is that the parents didn't just rant and rave and then drop the incident. They made it an opportunity for their daughter to learn that things cost money and destructive actions have serious consequences.

Encourage saving. By age six or so, your child is ready (with your help and your signature) to open a savings account. Before marching your youngster downtown, however, check with a bank officer first. Sadly, many commercial institutions no longer accept small deposits even from kids, or they charge punitive fees. If you decide to proceed, ask a bank

representative what identification is required, since the policy varies among institutions. Typically, you will have to provide identification for yourself (a driver's license will do) and a Social Security number for your child. The most relaxed regulations are typically found at credit unions, and many of them welcome small accounts.

If you're willing for your youthful saver to bank by mail, the Young Americans Bank in Denver (250 Steele St., Denver, Colo. 80206; 303-321-2265) is a child-friendly institution that offers savings and checking accounts for anyone up to age 22. Among its more than 16,000 savings customers, the average account holder is nine years old and has a balance of $360. Kids can open accounts in person or by mail with a minimum deposit of $10. If you have a pint-size plutocrat with serious money on hand—say, more than $1,000—you might help her invest in U.S. savings bonds, a certificate of deposit, or a no-load money-market fund to attain a higher return than standard passbook savings accounts provide.

In addition to establishing formal savings accounts for their offspring, many parents attach strings to the weekly allowance to encourage (or enforce) regular thrift. One popular device is the so-called three-jar system, which takes myriad variations among different families. Typically, a chunk of the weekly income is allocated to one container for spending, a second is for charitable donations, and a third (and possibly a fourth) is for savings (which may be divided into short-term and long-term). Plastic soda bottles work quite well for the savings portions, veterans say, since it's easy to get the money in, but—heh, heh—you have to slice off the top to get the funds out.

To soften the sting and make saving more palatable, help establish a savings goal—something the child longs to do or own. It could be a puppy, a leather jacket, or just a small toy that his heart is set on. Once the price (or the child's share of the price) is established, you two can discuss how much might be saved from the allowance each week and how much might be earned from extra chores or outside jobs. Don't expect too much too soon in terms of postponed pleasure: a nine-year-old might save for a few weeks, a teenager for several months. But there are exceptions. If your seventh-grader is truly determined to have a $3,000 car by the time he's a high school junior, show how he might save $10 a week from allowances and gifts in a money-market fund, then increase the amount to $20 a week with jobs in high school.

Thoughtful parents look for small ways to create savings opportunities, to deliberately entice their kids into putting something extra aside. For instance, you might give your campbound daughter $50 for canteen money, then let her keep any remaining funds at summer's end.

The ploy seems to limit mindless consumption of Snickers bars. Or you could agree to match big-money gifts—from grandparents or a bar mitzvah, say—if your son puts them into his long-term savings.

On the sticky question of savings withdrawals, *you* will have to be the referee. Some parents take a hard line and require a strict hands-off policy. Yet for many children, being able to take out the money for a new bike or $120 glow-in-the-dark sneakers provides most of the incentive for saving in the first place. Further, your goal isn't to produce a miniature miser who won't willingly part with a dime. A reasonable compromise is to make a clear distinction at the start between short-term and long-term savings goals—putting some funds aside for a new CD player, say, and reserving other dollars for college expenses. Alternatively, allow children access to a limited percentage of their savings or retain the right to veto purchases that cost more than a certain amount. Sure, the kids are likely to make mistakes and squander some of the money. Undoubtedly their clothing choices will make you wince occasionally. But swallow hard and remind yourself that it's all part of teaching kids to spend responsibly.

Despite your best-laid plans, a bad turn of fortune may force you to shorten the leash on spending. If your family runs into serious financial reverses, such as unemployment for the chief breadwinner, be honest but reassuring in discussing the problem. Otherwise your children may scare themselves with overblown fears. Remember, too, that they probably want to help with the problem. Kids often take touching pride in being able to contribute—by giving up gymnastic lessons, say, or handing over some baby-sitting earnings—if the family is going through a genuinely rough financial patch.

Freer Rein: The Teen Years

This is the time to start edging your youngsters toward financial independence. It's when you should initiate discussions about paying for college education or technical training, allow him or her to take on a part-time job and open a checking account, and get a credit card in her name on your account. Perhaps most important, it's your last chance to keep your kid from developing bad money habits he might later regret. Here's how to set your teen straight about money:

Share your spending decisions. Jut as you talked to your preschooler about simple choices in the supermarket, let adolescents participate in the family's more complex buying decisions. If you decide to

get a new car, for example, read consumer magazines with your kids and discuss what models and options offer true value for money. Talk with them about how you plan to pay for the purchase. If you're getting a car loan, let them see that you're shopping around to compare interest rates and other terms. Similarly, if you are buying a house, keep them abreast of the bidding and counterbidding that go on, even if you shield them from the actual amounts involved. Money is a marker of family values, and teens should learn that the expenditure of big money warrants a big investment of time and thought. Along the way, they'll soak up lessons in how to make smart spending decisions themselves.

Discuss the cost of future education. Sometime in junior high, your child should begin learning about how you plan to pay for his future education—especially if you'll require his help. If you can afford to pay only for the local technical school or community college, say so. That gives teenagers time to earn money if they want to go somewhere else or to boost their grades to qualify for scholarship money.

Begin sharing details of the family budget with your older teen. You'll have to judge whether your kid is mature enough to keep the information confidential, but most adolescents benefit from a dose of reality. When children understand the limits of the family's resources, they are likely to take their studies and their grades more seriously.

Review savings plans that you have in place for your child's education. If there are substantial sums in a savings account that might earn more in a CD or other conservative investment, make the switch. The earlier you and your teen start planning for his future education or training for the real-world job market, the better the chances that your joint efforts will turn dreams into reality.

Expand the allowance. You're virtually certain to pony up more pocket money as your child grows more independent. A 1993 Rand youth poll found that 13-to-15-year-old boys had an average weekly allowance of $16.15 (girls averaged $19.35 a week); 16-to-19-year-old boys got $30.15 (girls: $32.45). Most of the money slips away fast—on food and snacks, clothing, movies, and entertainment. Less than 10% is saved, mainly for more expensive items such as cameras, watches, and videocassettes. Moreover, says Rand, some 70% of teens label themselves and contemporaries "wasteful."

To prevent squandermania at your house, impose some structure on your adolescent's spending. The early teens are a good time to switch from a weekly stipend to a monthly one, so your potentially prodigal son will learn to budget money over longer periods of time. The allowance should be large enough for him to manage most spending for clothes, gifts, fast-food meals, entertainment, and related pleasures. A fringe benefit: This process provides a natural opportunity for kids to sharpen their negotiating skills. If your daughter wants more money than your first offer (and odds are she will), give her the chance to present her case as persuasively as possible, then decide accordingly. Once a spending plan is established, though, make her stick to it. If she blows her budget on designer jeans and can't afford a jacket, let her chill out. She won't make the same mistake twice.

As your teen matures, continue to extend the time between pay periods and further increase the scope of what the allowance covers. For instance, you might exclude clothing from the monthly stipend and instead provide a clothing allowance twice a year, before school starts in the fall and again in the spring. By the mid- to late teens, your child should be managing most of the spending events of his life—just as he signs up for SATs on his own and arranges his social agenda. Managing his money is, after all, essentially a microcosm for managing his life.

To prepare for budgeting during the post–high school years, let your teenager spend a summer or a semester monitoring expenses, either by recording money spent in a small notebook or by using a computer-based personal finance program such as *Quicken* or *Managing Your Money*. Then, with your teen, draw up a list of all the income he has (from allowances, jobs, and gifts) and all the expenses he should shoulder. To bridge the gap between income and outgo, decide together where expenses can be cut and how much income should be raised to bridge the gap. The goal is to have your teen stay on a budget for at least six months without having to ask a parent for financial help before he flies the family nest for college or a job.

Limit your teen's work hours. More than half of high schoolers now troop off to a job in the afternoons and on weekends. And we're talking serious money. A 1993 survey of high school students by the College for Financial Planning in Denver found that about half of working teens earn more than $76 a week, and 24% make more than $100 a week.

But that juicy income can carry hidden costs in terms of academic performance and attention to school activities. A 1993 study of 1,800 high school sophomores and juniors by Temple University psychology professor Laurence Steinberg found that students who worked 20 hours or more after school each week had lower academic achievement and school involvement. They spent less time on homework and cut class more often. Extracurricular activities also suffered, and the kids had higher rates of drug and alcohol abuse.

So don't let your children sacrifice their current education (and possibly their

chances of getting into a good college) just to support a flashy car, a clotheshorse habit—or worse. Be vigilant about hours. High school sophomores can probably handle a 10-hour work week; juniors and seniors can usually manage 15 hours. Remind the new worker, however, that school is his primary responsibility. If grades slip, give him one report card period to bring them back up—or require him to resign from the workplace.

If your teen is dead set on earning money, and many high schoolers are, let him start with a summer job to harvest both money and career-related experience. Or have him start his own summer business (see the list that follows). Such work might also give him a really clear idea of what he *doesn't* want to do for a living. Many students have come off summers toiling in food service or retail sales, making little more than the minimum wage, with a strong determination to prepare for something better than another junk job.

Four Businesses Teens Can Start

If summer jobs have dried up in your area, or if you don't want your future doctor or lawyer to sully her hands flipping burgers or selling sneakers, encourage her to start her own business. Four popular possibilities:

1. Baking. Cookies, muffins, and home-made breads are easy for novices to make and sell to local restaurants and coffee shops. A $200 bread machine might be a good investment, since loaves can be made for under 50¢ apiece.

2. Car care. A simple wash nets $5 to $10, but your young entrepreneur can double or triple that amount by cleaning interiors and waxing.

3. Lawn care. A solid worker gets $10 to $15 an hour, but fuel for the mower can eat up half that amount. Removing garden debris, trimming, and clean-up can increase profits.

4. Tutoring. Math, foreign languages, or English as a second language are likely possibilities. Computer jocks can post signs at retail outlets, offering their services to novice buyers eager to master their new gear. Artistic types can offer crafts classes to younger children for a specific number of weeks over the school break.

If your son or daughter starts making money, offer some guidance on how to handle this newfound affluence. Before the first paycheck arrives, set up an income-allocation plan with your teen. This will force him to manage his salary more seriously. You might, for example, decide that 25% of income should go to a savings account, with the funds earmarked for extra expenses during the college years. Premature prosperity can be a real hazard. If teenage mall rats are permitted to fritter away all their money on clothes and entertainment, while parents pick up the tab for necessities, they can develop unrealistic attitudes about money. Laurence Steinberg's study found that only 11% of working teens used a substantial portion of their monthly earnings to save for their future education. Don't hesitate to ask your future scholar to contribute—he'll take college and his grades more seriously. One caveat, though: Don't eliminate your child's allowance when he takes an outside job. Doing so will only send the message that he was better off accepting your handout without exerting himself.

Taking increased responsibility is the name of the game as the child is finishing high school. When kids hit their late teens, many parents expect them to pay their own way for much of the fun stuff that allowances covered in the earlier years. In a 1993 **MONEY** survey, more than 2,000 poll respondents thought kids over 16 should take substantial responsibility for all social expenses (73%); gasoline, while using the family car (75%); car purchase and expenses for his or her own car (71%); and all personal telephone costs (55%).

Encourage volunteering as an alternative to work. Don't overlook the value in nonpaid extracurricular activities. In particular, don't let your teens waste a summer vacation sitting around the house. By planning ahead, parents and kids can make sure the child does something enriching every summer, something that broadens his or her horizons beyond the local mall.

For more intrinsically rewarding work, consider no- or low-paying projects, such as foreign exchange programs, inner-city volunteer projects, and summer camps. For leads, your child can try the school placement office, churches, and service organizations such as the Lions or Kiwanis or local government officials who administer job training programs. If one of these avenues pays off, you might agree to increase the child's allowance or compensate for the forgone earnings in some other fashion.

Introduce checking accounts and credit cards. Before your child packs off to college, give him practice in handling those two essential tools to adult life: a checking account and a credit card. Let him reconcile the monthly bank statements himself. Keep resources finite, however: don't agree to cover bounced checks or overdraft charges.

If your local bank is averse to handling teenagers' checking needs, accounts are available for customers ages 12-21 at Young Americans Bank, though the applicant needs a "sponsoring adult" until age 18. The minimum opening deposit is $50, plus an initial $6 charge for 50

checks. If the monthly balance is below $150, there is a $2.50 monthly charge and a 25¢-per-check charge after the 10th check written.

Opinions vary on whether a teen needs a credit card, but many parents like the security that plastic provides their child in emergencies. One way to get teens started—under your supervision—is with a secured credit card, where you or your child pays a deposit of $500 or so and then the cardholder can charge only up to that amount. You can also have a card issued in your child's name on the account in which you are the primary cardholder. (His or her expenses will show up on your bill, so it's easy to monitor spending.) If the child has his own credit-card account, review the monthly bill with him. Make sure he purchased everything that is charged on the card, then discuss whether to make a full or partial payment. Many parents insist that the balance be paid in full each month. On rare and special occasions—the skis that he's been dreaming of have finally gone on sale—the limit might be stretched to three months, but let him swallow the finance charges. Well before your teen leaves the nest for college, make sure he understands the meaning of credit-card finance charges, grace periods, minimum payments, and late fees.

Teach basic investing concepts. Some children take to the financial markets at an early age; others don't. But many parents find youngsters get more curious about investing when they reach their teens. If you really want to engage your offspring in the stock market, you're best off using real money, either yours or theirs, once you're assured of their genuine interest. It's hard for anyone to stay interested in a hypothetical portfolio for long.

Smart investors of any age look at things they know, so you can tap into your teen's enthusiasm for fast food, sporting goods, or computers. Let him make his own investment decisions—using 10% to 20% of his savings, say. You will have to do the actual buying and selling, though. Under state laws, a minor isn't legally permitted to trade securities, so you'll have to purchase the shares and hold them in your name as the child's custodian. The securities then legally belong to the youngster, but you are nominally in charge until he reaches the legal age specified under state law (usually 18 or 21).

A few brokers will execute a child's buy and sell orders directly, particularly if they are acquainted with the parents and if the young customer knows what he or she is doing. Some brokers say that kids often are more rational and less emotional about investing decisions than adults are. In particular, they're more willing to cut their losses and admit when they've made a mistake.

Mutual funds might, in truth, make more sense for the fledgling investor, since they offer diversity and professional management. But funds are a tougher concept for teens to get a handle on, since they, as shareholders, don't directly own a piece of an individual company. One mutual fund that works specifically to teach children is SteinRoe Young Investor (call 800-403-KIDS for a prospectus). The fund seeks long-term capital appreciation by investing 60% of its portfolio in companies that kids are familiar with, such as Coca-Cola and McDonald's. the rest of its holdings consist of companies that make products kids enjoy, such as toys or computer software. There is no sales commission, and investors receive an owner's manual full of investing information, a coloring book for younger kids, and teaching materials for parents. The minimum investment is $500, if you agree to have a fixed amount of at least $50 deposited automatically into the fund from a checking account each month.

Alternatively, you can help your kids get into one of the more than 100 stock mutual funds that require initial investments of $500 or less. To locate them, consult the directory of the Investment Company Institute (P.O. Box 27850, Washington, D.C. 20038-7850; $8.50). It lists 4,000 funds, including their initial investment minimums, fee structures, and toll-free numbers.

A tax reminder: Until your son or daughter tuns 14, the first $650 of his or her investment income is tax-free and the next $650 is taxed at the child's rate, usually 15%. But the rest of the money is taxed at your top rate. After the child turns 14 the "kiddie tax" no longer applies, and he or she starts paying federal tax on all income and capital gains at his or her own rate rather than yours.

Cutting Pursestrings: The College Years

Once your child reaches college age, you need to make abundantly clear in advance which expenses you will cover and which are your child's responsibility. And if your son or daughter doesn't know much about credit cards by now, this is the time to explain the rules and the risks of plastic. How to do it right:

■ **Negotiate a realistic spending plan.** The summer before your child heads off to college, begin discussing a budget so your freshman-to-be knows exactly how much is available to spend. Don't just set an overall limit; draw up a list of the types of expenses you will and won't be willing to cover and set spending limits for each category. You might want to segregate certain critical necessi-

ties—textbooks, for example—and agree to pay them separately. That way your young scholar won't be tempted to skimp on buying basic texts because he overspent on pizza and beer. If you can afford it, you may want to foot most or all of the bills yourself and reserve your child's nest egg for graduate school, buying a house, or some other significant milestone. The important point is that you make clear up front how you expect to divide the financial responsibilities.

For convenience, have your child open a checking account in his college town. You can then disburse funds either by wiring the money to his account or by mailing a check for him to deposit. Whatever amount you agree to contribute, parcel out the funds periodically rather than writing a lump-sum check for the year. Fiscal discipline is tough if a student spender has to manage a single payout over many months. You'll be the best judge when your young adult is ready to manage larger amounts paid over a longer duration.

Initially, have your new collegian keep detailed records of where all the money is going. By Christmas break (or earlier, if problems arise), you can check the records to see where the budget needs to be revised—or if Junior's spending habits need reining in. Once the basic budgeting plan is established, it should set the pattern, with only minor modifications, until graduation.

■ **Uses and abuses of credit.** Once kids hit the campus, they're fair game for credit-card issuers. In recent years, Citibank, American Express, Discover, and others have been flooding them with applications for preapproved plastic, some of which carry interest rates of 19% or more. College kids age 18 or older need little more than a student ID to get a card with a credit line of $1,000 and up. Nearly all the credit-issuing standards that apply to adults are waived for collegians—sometimes with dubious results. A 1993 survey by Master-Card International found that 38% of college students had bounced a check, while fully one-third had built credit-card balances to what they described as "an uncomfortable level."

Used judiciously, however, credit cards can help college students build a sound credit history, which will make it easier for them to get a job, rent an apartment, and obtain other kinds of credit after they graduate. In addition, they are convenient, safer than cash, and accepted more readily than checks, particularly if you are away from home. Without one, it's nearly impossible to rent a car or buy an airline ticket.

Consequently, despite the risk of getting carried away with newfound financial freedom, it makes sense for your collegian to have a card of his own and start building his own credit history. But as insurance for yourself, don't co-sign your child's accounts. If you do, his late payments could damage your credit report. (If he is carrying a card on an account where you are the primary cardholder, the bill will be sent to you, which is useful for monitoring his expenses. But you'll have to write the check and then dun him for payment.)

To limit the risk of debt piling up, restrict your child to one card in his own name—two max. Emphasize that credit cards are for limited use—textbooks and airline tickets, for example—or for emergencies. If your kid's in doubt about what qualifies as an emergency, tell him this: Nothing that you can eat, drink, listen to, or wear on your back.

Warn your inexperienced cardholder that the terms of credit-card contracts are growing ever more complex. Many issuers, for example, have introduced so-called tiered rates, in which they commonly charge a lower interest rate for new purchases and a higher one for cash advances. Three other doubtful deals that card issuers have been pushing:

1. Phony no-fee cards. These spare you an annual fee, then sock it to you with other charges such as cash advances at interest rates above 20%.

2. Cards that offer cut rates to big spenders. This is *not* the lesson you want your freshman to be learning. Besides, when you read the fine print, it often turns out that moderate spenders are paying rates that are no deal at all—recently 19.8% on a Discover card.

3. Teaser-rate cards. These advertise rock-bottom interest rates that last only a few months before they're abruptly boosted by 10 percentage points or more.

Your son or daughter also needs to be aware of the harm that a bad credit rating can do. Explain that credit bureaus begin keeping tabs on the balance and payments as soon as a card is issued. Many creditors assess late fees if payment are not received by a certain date each month. This date (which varies among creditors) typically ranges from zero to 10 days beyond the payment due date. And be sure to mention that records of late-payment fees can remain part of your credit history for as long as seven years, hurting your chances of getting an apartment, a mortgage, car or education loans, and sometimes even utilities.

Back Again: Boomerangs

If your son or daughter has decided to move back in with you, it's tempting to fall into the old parent-adolescent roles. Resist this temptation and instead work to treat each other as consenting adults willing to accept financial responsibilities. Households mesh the best when both generations reveal their financial expectations and hash out the areas of disagreement early on. The biggest areas of contention are likely to be your child's contributions to running the household, financial support, and personal relationships.

Some psychologists say it's a compliment if your grown children ask to move back home for a while. It means your kids feel comfortable around you, there's a good enough relationship that they don't find it necessary to reject you. Well, maybe. But that may be small comfort to some parents who find their boomeranger's return a mixed blessing at best. They may resent postponing long planned vacations or depleting their retirement funds because their kids need money. Yet they may also feel guilty if they just snap their checkbooks shut or refuse to let the child reoccupy the bedroom that they so recently turned into a home office.

The boomerang generation—a corps of some 11 million twenty-somethings who have decided to go home and enjoy Mom or Dad's cooking—return (or don't leave) for myriad reasons. Some have lost a job or never found one; others have divorced, can't afford an apartment, or perhaps just want the comforts of home with all the trimmings.

It's men, more than women, who are boomeranging back. Partly that's because men marry at a median age of 26, while women head for the altar two years earlier. Further, the nest is often more comfy for the male: Mom may provide meals, laundry, and maid service, while Dad often permits him a loose leash. Young women typically encounter more nagging from Mom and stricter limits on boyfriends' visits.

Of course, it may all be different at your house: your grown child may be excellent company, and an empty nest may be a lonely prospect for you. Perhaps your young adult child is behaving in a substantially independent and responsible way—she is employed and wants to save the maximum amount possible for a clear-cut goal such as graduate school or a house down payment, for example. Then you may rightly feel that more relaxed rules are appropriate in the situation. But if you have a twenty-something who is earning little or nothing and making a minimal contribution to your household with no clear-cut plans, your job as a parent isn't finished yet. Certainly the urge to nurture your child is natural, but your real job may be to nudge your adult offspring toward financial independence. So consider imposing some boundaries—and incentives to action:

■ **Insist that the young adult earn some income and pay room and board.** This comes hard for many parents; and some just can't bring themselves to do it. But if you want your kids to start

acting like adults, you can't let them just sit around the house without chipping in something. If your boarder is unemployed, require him to perform household services in lieu of rent. But the goal is to find paid work. Expect resistance, particularly if only menial jobs are available. You might permit your son a certain number of weeks to find a job to his liking. After that, make clear the he must sling fast food, ring up groceries, or do whatever else is available—and start paying rent with his earnings. Some parents require their working kids to contribute 25% of their take-home pay to the household kitty; others set a flat sum.

Be prepared for your young adult to argue that you don't need the money, that the bed is sitting there empty, and so on. Don't be swayed. The point is not the money, but that he must begin taking financial responsibility for himself.

A few doting parents set aside the room-and-board money, then return it to their offspring at their departure. If you opt for that choice, keep it a secret from your child. Let the gift be a pleasant going-away surprise when he's poised to exit your nest.

■ **It's your household—but your child must help keep it running.** Before your child returns home—or certainly within the first week back—have a serious conversation about what both sides expect in the new arrangement. Think of this as a kind of Ross Perot "now here's the deal" talk. Set out the basics—this is the amount of time we agree to have you here, this is the rent we will charge, this is how we'll handle meals. Specify what other living costs you will cover—work clothes, transportation, and lunches out, for instance—and which items are your child's responsibility. You may want to draw up a written plan noting the details of the agreement.

In addition, consider the everyday irritants. Kids not only occupy physical space, they take up psychological space and tend to dominate the domestic airspace if you let them. You don't have to endure Pearl Jam if you long for Pavarotti, however. Some parents simply don't permit their child to play the stereo or TV in common areas of the house when they are at home. Others require their child to use headphones. In the same vein, if you can't get your kid off the phone, have a separate line installed in his room and make him pay for it.

Give your child more domestic responsibilities than he had the last time he lived with you. Pay special attention to laundry, cooking, and running errands. A useful litmus test: Ask yourself if a roommate would regularly do these things for your child. If not, then don't you do them, either.

There are other basic financial matters to consider. Add the child to your auto insurance policy, if he or she will drive the family car. The premiums usually won't change unless your child is under 25 (sometimes under 30) or has a bad driving record. If he had his own car, it can be insured with your company at a discount price.

Remember that you can't include your young adult child on your health insurance policy unless he or she is a full-time undergraduate and under age 23 or 25, depending on the policy. But you should get the child health coverage of some kind if you possibly can. Choose an HMO or a major-medical policy with a $1,000 annual deductible, or explore the short-term, six-month policies offered in some states.

As for manners and morals, while your kid is under your roof, he must abide by your rules of behavior. You can set limits about such issues as privacy, drinking, drugs, overnight guests, cleanliness. but give your child input in drawing up the specifics. For example, Mom might agree to stop nagging, at Junior's request, if he will agree to do chores as promptly as he can when asked. (His procrastination is probably what Mom was nagging about in the first place.)

The flipside of setting these rules for your boomeranger is to recognize the limits on *you*. Even as you protect your turf, be fully aware of where your territory ends. You don't have the right anymore to choose your child's friends, set curfews, or tell him to wear galoshes in the rain. And don't forget simple politeness. Would you talk that way to a friend? Would your son or daughter? The same basic courtesy should prevail between parent and child.

■ **Establish a transition plan.** Don't let dependency drag on indefinitely. Set a limit on the time your child can live at home. If she asks for a subsidy when she moves out, lend a hand if you like—but set a maximum limit of, say, six months. That way your daughter will have an incentive to find cheaper lodging, a roommate, or a better-paying job. For your own protection, as well as hers, keep up the health insurance until she can afford to pay for it herself.

While your child struggles for independence, you may be doing some sweating, too, just defending your position and holding your ground. Not to worry. Stiffen your spine and remind yourself that there are good reasons to make life a little uncomfortable for your grownup children. Otherwise, why would they ever leave home?

CHAPTER 21

Your Parents and Money

If you grew up in a financially secure home, you're probably more accustomed to accepting help from your parents than wondering what kind of help they might need from you. No matter how you were brought up, however, the issue of your aging parents' finances is an important one. Even if your mother and father are well off now—and especially if they're not—your parents may need your economic support or advice someday. Figuring out in advance whether your parents are likely to be financially independent for the rest of their lives will not only ease their later years, it will let you anticipate how their needs may affect your own financial future.

Whether or not your parents have plenty of money, you may need to offer other kinds of assistance—with housing, money management, and medical care—as their physical or mental powers wane. Contemplating these needs, too, can save both you and your parents from making the wrong decisions in an emergency.

Helping your parents can be a ticklish task. People who grew up during the Great Depression, as perhaps your parents did, came of age before the word "entitlements" entered our vocabulary and long before family secrets were routinely bared on *Oprah*. As a result, your parents may feel that their financial situation is their problem—and their business. They might also fear that your gentle questioning of their finances is little more than a covert attempt to extract money from them either before they die or after. Your parents could also be reluctant to divulge any information about their financial status, even though you would need details about their income and expenses in order to assess their solvency. In short, helping your parents with their money is as much a psychological exercise for you and them as a financial one.

If possible, you ought to try to discuss your parents' finances with your folks while they are feeling fairly flush and healthy. That's probably when they're in their early sixties. The longer you wait, the more serious the financial problems could become and the harder it may be for you to do much. For instance, if you don't have a talk with your father about money and he develops Alzheimer's, his memory may be too fuzzy to give you the guidance you need to get his finances in order.

How to Know Whether They Need Your Help

Unless your parents ask for your succor or you spot signals that they need it, you'll have to use your own instincts to decide whether to offer a hand. There are some clues that suggest it's time to step in, one way or another. If your normally fastidious parents start leaving their home a mess or you notice deteriorating personal hygiene habits, your mother and father are quietly saying: "I can't or won't take care of myself now." Also, the next time you visit your parents, take a look at their mail stack on the q.t. If you see unopened letters postmarked months ago or second or third billing notices from creditors, that's another strong hint that your services could be needed. One thing you could do to help: Get their mutual fund and dividend checks, Social Security payments, and any pension checks direct deposited into the bank. Pay close attention to any slippage in your parents' health. If you notice that your mother's vision is going, for instance, you may want to hire someone to help her with chores. You might even offer to help write out checks for her bills—with her checks. Be certain, too, that your parents are getting any medication they need and not going without just to save money.

If you're fairly certain that your offer to help will be taken kindly, by all means speak up. Otherwise it's probably better to keep mum until you feel your parents' health or welfare is at stake. Authority and dignity are especially crucial to older people, who often worry about losing both in their later years. By suggesting that *you* can help *them*, remember that you're reversing their role in your life; that's a situation that may provoke their anxieties about the future.

If you raise the subject of money with your parents, but they are unreceptive to the idea of analyzing their situation, drop the subject—for now. Bring it up again in several months, however, after they've had time to think about it. Upon reflection, they may realize that your suggestion is a good one. Remember, however, that the decision is theirs. If they simply will not discuss their circumstances, don't insist.

Talking Things Over

There's no best way to broach the subject of your parents' finances. One hint offered by psychologists: Draw up your own living will (see Chapter 12) and discuss it with your parents. This may ease the offputting implication that they're the only ones who need to think about incapacitation. After they've helped you formalize your intentions, it may be easier to ask if they, too, might want to contemplate the future.

Otherwise, getting the ball rolling depends largely on the relationship between you and your parents. You might be able simply to plunge in, acknowledging your awkwardness but explaining the reasons for your questions. Alternatively, you may be more comfortable hiring a third party,

such as a financial planner, to conduct a family financial discussion lasting two hours or longer. It's unlikely that you'll find one who had extensive experience conducting intergenerational planning sessions, since the concept is still quite new. So if you already work with a financial planner and admire his competence and style, you can ask him to be the discussion leader. If not, locate a planner who specializes in retirement issues; for advice on finding a reputable planner, see Chapter 3. Assuming you can afford one, choose a planner who charges a flat fee for advice and pay the charge yourself. Though the adviser will probably ask for $1,000 to $3,000 to run the session and prepare recommendations, a planner who charges no fee will tend to suggest financial products that carry high sales charges or commissions. After all, the planner has to make a living somehow. Should your parents hire a commission-based planner, they could wind up paying dearly for the advice.

It's best to include all immediate family members in your financial talk with your parents. This way you'll head off possible misunderstandings about the point or nature of the conversation or any resentments about your taking the lead. So invite your spouse, your siblings and their spouses, and, if your parents are divorced and remarried, your parents' present spouses. Don't worry too much if some of these family members choose not to attend the session. You've at least prevented them from blaming you later for plotting behind their back.

To keep this delicate talk on track, draw up a list of the questions you need answered. Start with the least sensitive ones and work up to the toughest ones, as shown below.

Questions to Ask Your Parents

■ **Who are your advisers?** Be sure to get a list of the names and addresses or phone numbers of all the advisers they have, including their lawyer, broker, accountant, primary-care physician, and insurance agents. If they lack financial advisers but could use some, offer to introduce them to yours. Or tell them to read Chapter 3 of this book. You'll want to develop a close relationship to your parents' advisers since you may need to work with them at some point. In addition, you will find out if any of the advisers is in any way hurting your parents financially. One of the best financial moves you can make to help your parents is releasing them from the clutches of un-

scrupulous brokers, financial planners, or insurance agents.

■ **Where are your personal records kept?** You're looking here for the location of your parents' safe-deposit box; insurance policies; will and any trusts; brokerage, bank, and mutual fund statements; and copies of their tax returns. Tell your parents that you're asking not because you want to see these documents right now, but because you may need to review them at sometime in the future. During the course of this conversation, you'll learn if your parents have a will and if they have done any estate planning. Do *not* ask for details about the contents of the will; if your parents want you to know how much you'll get after they die, they'll tell you. Learning about your parents' records will also suggest to you whether your mother and father own unnecessary insurance policies such as duplicate health insurance coverage or a life insurance policy that they can cancel.

■ **What are your monthly expenses?** Tell your folks that you don't need the figures down to the nearest decimal point. You just want to know their rough outlays each month to be sure they have enough income to pay their bills, cover their essential expenses, and have something left over.

■ **What is your income, and what are its sources?** This question could touch a nerve. So make it clear that you aren't looking for their exact gross income, just a rough idea so that you know how they're faring financially. It will help if your parents tell you which stocks, bonds, mutual funds, and real estate investments they own, the rough value of them and why they are holding on to them. You also should find out whose name the investments are in, since there may be some estate-planning implications. If your parents seem to be open about discussing their investments, ask them for the numbers of their brokerage accounts and mutual funds, too; you may need these vital figures someday.

■ **Have you done any estate planning? Would you like to do some?** Here, you're just trying to find out whether your parents want to get their estate in order. If they seem interested but don't have an adviser, you might suggest your lawyer or financial planner. Alternatively, you could ask your parents whom their friends have turned to for estate-planing help. That pro might be someone your parents could hire.

■ **Where would you like to live if you couldn't keep living in your present home?** A section later in this chapter discusses housing alternatives for the elderly and may offer some suggestions.

■ **What life-prolonging measures, if any, would you want taken if you became terminally ill or hopelessly incapacitated?** This topic is critically important. By discussing it, you'll be certain that you'll know your parents' wishes should the occasion arise. (A fuller description of this topic follows.)

■ **What funeral arrangements, if any, have you made?** Grim? Yes. Essential? Absolutely. The more you know now about your parents' funeral arrangements, the easier things will be when the time comes. In times of grief, many people don't think clearly. So if you don't know your parents' burial wishes, you might end up making a colossal mistake. If the thought of bringing up this topic makes you jittery, try turning the tables. Tell your parents about your own funeral arrangements or ask them for advice.

Don't criticize any answers you get from your parents. If you see areas that could use improvement or that your mother and father simply haven't thought about, note that the matter may warrant further consideration in the future. Keep your manner deferential, not bossy. Say, for instance, "I think there are ways to approach this issue that you might want to consider" rather than "Here's what you should do."

Take notes during the discussion or, if no one objects, tape-record it. That way, if any confusion arises, you or any of the other participants can double-check what was said.

Documents That Could Help

If you and your parents foresee a time when you may have to start paying their bills, handling their investments, or possibly even sell their home for them, consider enlisting the help of a lawyer to draw up a document known as a **durable power of attorney.** While many parents simply add an adult child's name to their bank accounts or other assets to facilitate access, doing so is not a great idea. If you're sued or get a divorce, some of your parents' assets ultimately could wind up in the hands of a creditor or your ex-spouse. What's more, if you apply for financial assistance (including college aid), your parents' assets may disqualify you. A durable power of attorney, by contrast, will give you the right to manage your parents' financial affairs while keeping all their assets in their names.

Don't wait to create a durable power of attorney until your parents start failing, though. In order to sign this document, your parents must be of sound mind. If they're reluctant to give you discretion over their affairs while they're still capable, have the lawyer add a "springing" clause, which gives you authority only if a judge in domestic relations court deems them incompetent. Such a clause, however, can create delays and complications, which is exactly what you're trying to avoid.

Virtually any lawyer can draw up a durable power of attorney for you. If you have many questions or special circumstances, however, you may prefer an expert in the fairly new specialty called elder law. For the name of an elder law practitioner, call your state bar association.

In an era when modern medicine can extend the lives of hopelessly ill patients seemingly indefinitely, many older people reject the financial and emotional costs of an artificially prolonged existence. Others, however, covet the full arsenal of care. Whichever camp your parents are in, help assure that their wishes are followed at the end of life by having them sign so-called advance directives such as **living wills** and **health care proxies.** The process is easy, quick, and doesn't require a lawyer. Jacqueline Onassis and Richard Nixon used them, and so have millions of others.

The main difference between the two documents is whom they empower to act for them. A living will, which is for terminally ill patients, gives authority to doctors. A health care proxy, which also covers nonterminal situations such as comas, gives authority to anyone your parents have designated in writing. Both documents are recognized in 45 states. Alabama and Alaska acknowledge only living wills, while Massachusetts, Michigan, and New York recognize just health care proxies. For details on individual state laws plus free forms that fit each state's legal requirements, call Choice in Dying, a national advocacy group (800-989-9455).

Once the advance directives are signed, don't let your parents stow away their only copy in a safe-deposit box or some other place that's hard to reach in an emergency. Have them give copies to their doctor and to you, and suggest they keep a copy handy in their home.

Finances and Money Management

Assuming your parents are strong and healthy, chances are the only help they need, if any, is managing their money. They may not be handling it in a way that best suits their needs, or they simply may not have enough to live on comfortably. Depending on their situation, there may be a lot that you can do to help. You might be able to help them squeeze more from what they've got, offer financial support from your own pocket, or suggest ways the government could assist.

If, like many older people, your parents generally stick to what's safe and familiar in their financial lives, you may find that they haven't created a retirement budget or an investment strategy. Instead they're just doing what they've always done and crossing their fingers. As a result, they may be too liberal in their spending and too conservative in their investing. By reviewing their budget with them, you may discover that your parents are paying for things that may no longer justify their expense, such as a large life insurance policy, a second car, or a pricey country club membership. Naturally they'll have to make all final decisions. Your parents may find, however, that scrutinizing their budget together will produce found money.

Similarly, if you find that your parents are keeping virtually all their cash in safety-first investments such as Treasury bills, bank certificates of deposit, and U.S. savings bonds, there's a lot you can do to help them boost their returns. Taking a few smart investment steps can easily up your parents' income by 10% or more. As a result, they'll be able to worry less about whether their money will last.

Explain to your parents that professional money managers recommend that retirees keep a significant portion of their portfolio in stocks to counteract the diminishing effects of inflation. If they seem unmoved, try this: If inflation grows by 5% a year, their cash will lose half its value in 18 years. Stocks, of course, historically outpace inflation. How much of your parents' money should be in stocks? That depends on how much they have, how much extra income they need, and their risk tolerance. As a rule of thumb, however, the percentage of their portfolio in stocks should be the number you get when you subtract your younger parent's age from 100. For example, for a 70-year-old, the amount would be 30%.

It's wise to steer your parents toward mutual funds for their equity investments, rather than individual stocks that they—or you—will have to actively manage. Ask to borrow the prospectuses of any mutual funds your parents are considering. That way both you and your parents will understand what they're buying. If your parents don't know how to select a mutual fund and don't want to start learning, find out from them what kinds of risks they're willing to take and start hunting for a fund yourself. The mutual fund performance rankings in places like **MONEY**, *Business Week, Barron's*, and the *Wall Street Journal* will help you find funds with strong long-term performance records.

Be sure to consider your parents' tax bracket when you or they choose investments. If they are in a high tax bracket and require extra income, tax-exempt municipal bonds and bond funds may well offer better returns than taxable bonds and CDs. To see whether taxables or tax-frees are better, do this calculation with your parents: 1 - their tax bracket

(0.28 for the 28% bracket, for example) multiplied by the taxable yield they could get today. The result is the percentage yield they'd have to earn tax-free to beat what they could get from a taxable investment. If municipals are yielding more than that, they ought to be in munis.

One major source of extra cash for many retirees is the equity from their homes. According to U.S. Census data, people age 65 to 74 have an average of $48,000 in home equity. If your parents are willing to consider moving, they may be able to generate a considerable cash infusion by selling their home and moving to a smaller house or an apartment. Up to $125,000 of their capital gains will be tax-free under most circumstances.

Even if they're not interested in moving, your mother and father may be able to tap their equity with a so-called **reverse mortgage.** Offered by banks in a handful of states, as well as by some local community agencies, reverse mortgages let your parents keep living in their home while collecting monthly payments generated by a loan secured by up to 100% of their equity. Reverse mortgages can be for a fixed term, say, five or 10 years, or for your parents' lifetime. After the period is up, the loan must be repaid, generally by selling the home. The size of the payments to the homeowner depends on the length of time chosen, the value of the home, closing costs, expected appreciation, and the mortgage interest rate. For instance, at a 10% interest rate, $100,000 in home equity might generate $800 a month for five years, $500 a month for 10 years, and about $350 a month for the rest of the life of a 75-year-old owner. For more information about reverse mortgages, call the National Center for Home Equity Conversion (612-953-4474).

Another way your parents can tap their equity without moving: You buy their home and then rent it back to them. Be careful, though. Purchasing the home presents complicated tax ramifications for you. In general, this arrangement—called a **sale-leaseback**— makes sense for you only if your parents' proceeds on the sale ($125,000 of which will be tax-free if they haven't taken the exclusion previously) can produce more income than you need to charge for rent to cover your expenses. The reason: If you charge too little rent, you may run afoul of IRS regulations requiring investors to charge fair market value for property rentals to qualify for tax deductions. Without write-offs, the transaction probably won't pay for you. Don't base your decision on back-of-an-envelope calculations, either. Be sure to have an accountant figure out the actual cost and benefits of such a deal before you proceed.

Your parents may also be able to get some assistance from federal or state programs for the elderly, depending on their income. For instance, they might qualify for Supplemental Security Income, available to people over 65 with low incomes and assets—assets can't exceed $2,000 for singles and $3,000 for couples, though Social Security excludes homes, personal belongings, and some other holdings. They could also qualify for free Medicaid coverage for medical expenses, prescription drug subsidies, lower utility rates, or home meal delivery. To find out what programs might benefit your parents, call your state department on aging, usually a division of the human services agency. The office is usually listed under "State Government" in your telephone book.

Your Parents and Your Taxes

You can also help your parents extract more income from their assets by sharing the cost of investments with them. With a so-called **split-interest purchase,** you and your parents buy an income-producing investment, such as a bond. They receive all the income while they're alive; after their death you receive any capital gains. The IRS has strict rules governing such transactions, so it's best to check with a tax pro—preferably a tax attorney—before entering into such an agreement with your parents.

If your parents' income is quite low, you may be able to get some sizable tax benefits in exchange for giving them direct financial support. For example, if your father has taxable income of less than roughly $2,500, and you provide more than 50% of his support, you can legally deduct him as a dependent on your own tax return and claim a dependency exemption. What's more, if your dad qualifies as your dependent, you can add any of his medical expenses to yours when determining if you can write off such costs. Normally it's extremely difficult to claim medical deductions since the expenses must exceed 7½% of your adjusted gross income before you can deduct any of them. If you and your siblings jointly support your parents, and each of you contributes at least 10% but no more than 50% to their well-being, you can rotate the annual personal and medical deductions among yourselves; only one person can claim your parents in any year, however. Remember, too, that if your employer offers a dependent-care flexible spending account, you can use the FSA to help support your parents if they meet the dependency qualifications. Check with your company benefits office.

For short-term emergencies, you may want to make a gift or a loan to your parents. A gift is simpler, if you can afford to part with the money. You can give each of your parents up to $10,000 a year without triggering federal gift taxes. It's best to spell out the terms of the gift in writing.

Should you and your parents prefer that you lend them money to be repaid in the future, however, things get a little trickier. If you'll be lending less than $10,000, you can charge as much or as little interest as you choose—even no interest. The written agreement must say when the money will be repaid, though. For larger loans, the IRS demands that you charge at least what's known as the **applicable federal rate.** The government changes the interest rate periodically; you can find the current federal rate in the *Wall Street Journal* around the 20th of the month. Generally, the rate is lowest on loans shorter than three years, a bit higher on loans of three to nine years, and the highest for longer loans. You will also have to pay taxes on the interest you get. To make an interest-free loan of more than $10,000 but less than $100,000, you'll usually have to report as taxable income to the IRS the forgone interest or an amount equal to your parents' investment income, whichever is less.

When you draw up a loan agreement, specify all the terms, including the amount and length of the loan, any collateral, and, if you're charging interest, the interest rate. The advantage of such a formal agreement is that in case your parents become unable to repay the loan, you will be able to deduct up to $3,000 a year of the lost cash as a bad debt on your tax return. If you feel that your parents would be offended by a request to sign this kind of document, however, or that repayment is unlikely, stick with a gift.

Helping with Medical Insurance

Even if your parents don't need money, they may welcome your help finding and managing their medical insurance. They might want to take advantage of a relatively new service: firms that process the filing of health insurance claims for you. Keeping track of all the forms from doctors, insurers, pharmacies, and hospitals can be dizzying. Typically, claims-filing services charge a flat fee of about $200 a year or a percentage of what they collect. You or your parents could check with local senior agencies and groups or the nearest chapter of the American Association of Retired Persons. Make sure your parents don't sign over the right to have checks issued directly to a claims service. One reputable firm in this business is Medical Insurance Claims (800-355-2662), which charges 15% to collect claims totaling $300 or less and 10% for claims over $300. You or your parents could also call the National Organization

of Claims Assistance Professionals (708-963-3500) for names of other similar services.

In general, the medical insurance issues your parents face will depend primarily on their age.

■ **If they're under 65:** Unless your parents have medical coverage from a former employer, the availability and perhaps the cost of health insurance is likely to be a major problem for them. Although a few states have tried to make it easier for older consumers to buy insurance—by requiring, for instance, that insurers offer coverage to anyone who asks—the fact is that people over 50 pay health insurance premiums costing two to four times the cost for people under 30. That can easily come to $5,000 a year or more for a couple. Unfortunately, there's not much your parents can do about cost except to shop carefully for the best deal. One way that they might do this is by paying Quotesmith, a policy shopping service, to search for the best, least expensive coverage (cost: $15; 800-556-9393).

If your parents haven't looked into managed-care plans such as health maintenance organizations (HMOs), encourage them to do so. While premiums may be a bit higher than for traditional plans, the out-of-pocket costs are far lower for those who use a lot of medical services, as older people often do. Unfortunately, only about a third of HMOs accept individual members. In addition, some areas of the country, particularly the central plains, have few HMOs. So if your parents live in one, their choice of plans may be limited. Chapter 2 describes in detail the best ways to check out an HMO generally. Here, though, are two questions your folks should ask before they sign up for an HMO:

1. How good are the doctors in the HMO network? Naturally, it's a good sign if your parents' own trusted physician is on the roster. If their doctor is in the plan, they should ask his opinion of the HMO. Even if they don't get an entirely straight answer, a long pause will be very telling. If your parents' physician isn't listed in the group but you know some doctors who are, you or your parents should ask them the same question. In fact, have your parents ask any medical person they know—from a nurse to their local pharmacist—what they've heard about the quality of care at the HMO. If you and your parents can't find anyone with an opinion, ask the HMO for a few statistics on its doctors. Specifically, inquire about the board-certified percentage (70% is the industry average) and the yearly turnover of doctors (10% is at the high end).

2. How good is the care? Quality doctors can help assure excellent care. Since HMOs monitor the services doctors order, however, you need to be sure your parents will get all the care they need if they join an HMO. One new indicator is

accreditation from the National Committee for Quality Assurance (NCQA), which evaluates HMOs in six vital areas of patient care: quality assessment, physician credentials, preventive services, members' rights, utilization review, and medical record keeping. HMOs can be granted full accreditation, one-year accreditation, or partial accreditation (meaning specified areas are too weak for approval), or they can be denied accreditation. By the end of 1995 nearly half of the country's 550 HMOs will have been evaluated. Though HMOs don't have to submit to evaluation, ask the plan your parents are considering if it has applied for NCQA accreditation (or check yourself by calling 202-662-1885). If the HMO has applied for and received accreditation—even provisionally—you can feel confident that the care is at least reasonably decent. If it applied and flunked, though, you may want to look elsewhere. If it simply hasn't applied, ask if the HMO conducts patient satisfaction surveys you can see. Pass on the plan if no surveys are open to scrutiny.

■ **If they're 65 or older:** Most Americans age 65 or older have federal health coverage through Medicare. As of this writing, part A of Medicare has no premium and pays 100% of hospital bills after a deductible (currently about $720). Medicare Part B pays up to 80% of doctor bills for a monthly premium of roughly

$50. Medicare also offers some coverage for many other medical needs such as lab tests, home health care, convalescent nursing home care, and personal medical equipment. Unfortunately, payment limits are often low. In fact, since its establishment 30 years ago, Medicare's value has eroded. Today the program pays only about a third of beneficiaries' average expenses (for a summary of current benefits, see the Appendix). If your parents—or you—are having trouble understanding their Medicare Beneficiaries Defense Fund (800-333-4114) for free help. This nonprofit group publishes informational pamphlets, answers questions, and occasionally even goes to bat for Medicare recipients.

Your parents could get supplemental coverage by joining a **Medicare-qualified HMO.** Unlike most Medigap policies, many Medicare HMOs provide some coverage for things Medicare won't cover, such as prescription drugs and eyeglasses. They also avoid paperwork and often offer low co-payments and no deductibles. However, despite the term "Medicare-qualified," an HMO open to people over 65 is likely to be no better or worse than another HMO. Here again, it's best to do some investigating before signing up (see previous section). Medicare beneficiaries should go one step farther, however, and seek out HMO members on Medicare to find out if the intensive medical needs of seniors are well met in the plan.

In 14 states, Medicare recipients can purchase "Medicare Select" coverage, which gives them lower premiums or greater benefits if they agree to patronize doctors and other medical providers in a specified managed-care network. Savings differ among states, which run their own networks, but range from 10% to 30% over standard Medicare coverage with its unrestricted choice of providers.

Another way your parents can beef up their Medicare coverage is by purchasing a supplemental health insurance policy known as a **Medigap policy,** described at length in Chapter 2. In 1990 Congress tried to make Medigap policies easier to compare by standardizing them into 10 formats. Insurers were prohibited from selling policies that didn't fit one of the formats or from selling a second Medigap policy to someone who already had one. In 1994, however, Congress amended the law to let insurers sell Medigap policies that don't fit the formats and to sell policies to seniors who already have one. However, the insurers must explain that some benefits may be duplicative and must pay any duplicate claims. The upshot of this reversal is that buyers have to be even more careful than ever when purchasing Medigap policies, which can cost between $600 and $2,000 a year per person.

To help your parents decide among various Medigap alternatives, make sure they or you get a detailed list of benefits included under each offer. Then go over each policy to see which benefits are most desirable to them and their cost. For example, only two of the 10 standard Medigap policies offer coverage for prescription drugs. If your parents take few prescription medications or their yearly cost is less than the policy's deductible, you can cross these policies off the list. However, in the event your mother and father get many prescriptions filled, you'll need to compare the premiums on the two types of policies that cover drugs with the extra reimbursement your parents stand to collect. This way you can make sure the added coverage is worth the extra premium. For a $39 survey of the benefits and premiums of all the Medigap policies sold in your parents' age, call Weiss Research at 800-289-9222.

A key tip: If your parents have significant medical problems and plan to buy a Medigap policy, make sure they sign up for one within six months of turning 65. During this brief window, according to federal law, no one can be turned down for a Medigap policy or charged more than anyone else the same age.

Six Ways Your Parents Can Reduce Their Medical Costs

Health care costs can be a huge expense for your parents. However, they may be able to slice their medical bills by taking some of the following advice:

1. Patronize doctors who agree to accept the amount stipulated by Medicare as their full fee. Even doctors who don't accept Medicare's stipulated fee, however, can charge no more than 15% above it.

2. Seek out free or low-cost medical screenings. Hospitals, state health departments, and other community groups typically offer these services.

3. For savings of 5% to 40% on prescription drugs, look into mail-order purchasing services. The American Association of Retired Persons' AARP Pharmacy Service (800-456-2226; annual AARP membership: $8 a year), Health Care Services (800-758-0555), and Medi-Mail Order (800-331-1458) are three of the biggest mail-order pharmacies.

4. Ask your doctor or pharmacist whether there are generic versions of your prescriptions. Generics can save as much as 70% of the price of brand-name prescription drugs.

5. Comparison shop at local pharmacies. Typically, drugstore chains don't charge as much as independent pharmacies.

6. Use a modest income and the absence of Medigap insurance as bargaining tools to negotiate low rates from hospitals, doctors, and labs.

There's no guarantee that you'll be able to bring down the charges, but it doesn't hurt to ask.

A Guide for Long-Term Care

Neither Medicare nor Medigap covers the cost of non-medical care in a nursing home or at home. Yearly costs for such services can easily top $30,000, potentially impoverishing a spouse or wiping out an inheritance. Medicaid, the government health insurance program for the indigent, pays for long-term care only for individuals whose income and assets put them at poverty levels. As a result, many older people wonder whether they should try to head off this catastrophic expense in one of two ways: either stashing their wealth in so-called **Medicaid trusts** to impoverish themselves, at least on paper, or buying insurance against the cost of long-term care.

For most people, the answer to both questions is probably no. Let's start with the Medicaid trusts. In the past few years Congress has stringently tightened the rules under which people who transfer their assets to others can receive Medicaid. Currently, such transfers must take place at least 36 months before Medicaid qualification begins, and the money in a trust must be so out of reach that its

sponsor is literally, not just legally, impoverished. Under the extreme conditions, few parents are likely to be interested.

Long-term-care (LTC) insurance is a bit more complicated. The cost of premiums for these policies depends on how old you are when you buy the coverage. At age 50, a standard long-term-care policy paying $80 per day in a nursing home and $40 for care at home might run between $500 and $1,000 a year, depending on other features. If you wait until you're 65 to buy that same policy, however, the cost jumps to between $1,000 and $2,200 a year. By age 79, when the possibility of entering a nursing home for a prolonged period starts to increase dramatically, premiums run $4,000 to $7,200 a year. Don't forget, that's per person; if both of your parents are living, they'd double those figures. While sellers of LTC policies argue that starting early is the key to affordability, they ignore the fact that a younger policyholder also pays premiums much longer—for an expense he may never incur.

A more reasonable way to look at the issue is to examine how much money is at stake and what it would cost to protect it. (Keep in mind that as long as one spouse is living in the family home, the other can receive Medicaid without selling the home, provided the Medicaid recipient meets other asset and income qualifications.) For a couple with assets under $100,000, aside from their home, paying hefty premiums indefinitely makes little sense. With assets above $500,000 or so, an elderly person can probably pay his or her long-term-care costs without exhausting the family legacy.

If your parents' assets are somewhere in between $100,000 and $500,000, the issue of buying a long-term-care policy comes down to cash flow. If the yearly cost of one LTC insurance premium or two (one per spouse) would put such a large crimp in your parents' budget that their standard of living would plummet, tell them to forget the inheritance and enjoy themselves. Alternatively, you and your siblings might consider chipping in to pay for the insurance yourselves. By the way, the insurer won't care how old you are if you're buying the policy for your parents. The premium is based on the beneficiary's age.

Should you decide to start shopping for a long-term-care policy for your parents, consider their particular circumstances carefully. For example, most elderly people prefer to remain at home as long as possible, making policies with home care benefits very desirable. If your parent lives in an area without any agencies providing home care or lives alone, however, home care probably will not be much of an option. In that case, paying for a home care benefit is a waste. Similarly, policies with inflation protection that increase benefits periodically are usually a fine idea for buyers under age 75, although they're at least 50% more expensive than policies with flat benefits. After age 75, however, the average life-

span is short enough that inflation becomes a minor threat. Then the extra coverage is not worth the substantial extra cost.

Increasingly, your parents can also buy long-term-care coverage as a benefit offered by a life insurance policy or an annuity. The advantage of this kind of arrangement is that even if they never need long-term care, their premium will provide other benefits, such as a savings fund or a death stipend. These policies also often offer complete discretion on how long-term-care benefits are spent. They merely provide a specified maximum amount per day or month that can be used for nursing home care, home care, retrofitting a private home, or even paying a relative to provide needed services. The drawbacks, however, are that your parents will pay premiums for life insurance they may not want or need, and they'll incur steep withdrawal penalties if they cancel the coverage after only a few years.

Finding Your Parents Housing

Even the most independent seniors may eventually lose the ability or desire to live

537

on their own. As your parents' physical or mental agility flags or they simply begin to feel lonely, they may need to rethink their living arrangements. Depending on their situation, the best choice might be a retirement enclave for active seniors, an elder care community for people needing personal assistance, help in their home or yours, or, in more extreme situations, a nursing home. The best facilities often have waiting lists of three months to two years. So the sooner you and your parents start investigating them, the better. Below, a rundown of the options:

■ **For active seniors.** If your parents need little more than companionship, recreation, and a low-maintenance household, they may be drawn to an **active-adult retirement community** such as Sun City in Arizona or any of the hundreds of similar developments around the country. Bear in mind, however, that these projects offer little for residents needing a lot of personal care or medical attention. Should your parents move into one of these developments and require serious medical attention down the road, they may have to move again. These kinds of facilities may be perfect interim arrangements, though, if you and your siblings plan eventually to move your parents in with one of you. The cost of these types of communities can vary tremendously. Some have no entry fees and charge between $1,000 and $4,000 a

month. Others require an entry fee of $17,000 to nearly $300,000 and charge $500 to $1,000 a month. Part-time living assistance or nursing care may be available, for something like $75 to $150 a day. Otherwise it's best to look farther down the road toward a time when your parents may be less independent than they are now.

A continuing care (or life-care) retirement community (CCRC) is one type of development especially appropriate for active seniors who might like help with daily functions in the future. CCRCs offer a range of services, including independent apartments, personal assistance and medical care, and even nursing home care. A continuing care community is like an insurance policy, since it accepts only seniors who are currently able to live independently but who want to be assured of receiving services if they become dependent later in life. The cost: an admission fee of $15,000 to $500,000, plus a monthly fee of $150 to $3,000.

There are two reasons for the huge range between the least and most expensive continuing care facilities. Some of the communities are far more luxurious than others, offering golf courses, pools, and sometimes even on-site brokerages and banks. Also, some CCRCs include part or all of the projected costs of future services in their fees, while others charge for them only as you use them. Although there are several hundred CCRCs across the country, not all provide value or high-quality services. Many of the best are accredited by the American Association of Homes and Services for the Aging. For a list of accredited communities, plus information on how to evaluate a CCRC, call the association (202-783-2242).

Don't let your parents sign up for a continuing care community until their lawyer or financial adviser fist reviews its financial statements and admittance contract. It's essential to know how much money would be refunded if your parents moved. You'll also want to know what would happen if, sadly, your parents could no longer afford to live there.

Another option is **congregate senior housing.** Here, your parents would have their own apartments. They would eat with other residents in a central dining room. These kinds of facilities push socializing, with dances and trips for their residents. The cost is all over the lot. Some congregate housing arrangements have no entry fee; others charge between $50,000 and $125,000. All charge rent, though, which can range from roughly $600 to $4,000 a month. Many congregate housing developments also offer housekeeping and nursing care.

■ **For seniors needing help with daily activities.** If your parents are not in robust health but don't need the extensive personal and medical services pro-vided in a nursing home, **assisted living facilities** may be the answer. Residents live either in apartments or private rooms and receive meals, housekeeping services, laundry, and professional supervised medical care. As with CCRCs, costs depend on accommodations and the services provided. Assisted living facilities don't require entrance fees, however. Monthly rentals range between $600 and $3,500

Residential care communities are a close cousin to assisted living facilities. Sometimes known as personal care homes or homes for the aged, they can be quite small—the tiniest hold two to 10 people. Residents live in private rooms and pay $350 to $4,000 a month.

Adult foster care sounds like a friendly alternative. Your parents, assuming they're healthy, get taken into someone else's home and pay $500 to $3,000 a month. Trouble is, the adult foster care business is largely unregulated. Be careful here.

■ **For seniors needing continuing medical care.** If your parents are infirm but don't want to move into a nursing home, they may be happiest with **home care.** That home could be theirs or yours. Constructing a downstairs bedroom and bath in their home and bringing in the daily services of a housekeeper and home health care attendant may be just enough to allow your parents to remain in their own home. While such help can easily run $50 to $100 a day, it may be cheaper and less upsetting than a move to another location.

Bringing a parent in to live with you can yield the same advantages, though it can also create major emotional problems for both of you. It's probably best to agree to such an arrangement on a temporary basis rather than risk making your parent feel let down if it doesn't work out.

One way to ease tensions in a multi-generation household is with **adult day care.** Senior centers or for-profit businesses in many areas run programs in which elders get recreation, companionship, meals, and sometimes minor medical attention in a safe setting for eight hours or so a day. Encouraging your parent to have interests and relationships outside your family can enhance everyone's ability to live together. The typical daily cost of adult day care: $20 to $30.

There's no way to make choosing a **nursing home** easy for either you or a parent who needs too much care to remain in his home or yours. You can probably avoid what both of you fear most—poor quality care—by choosing a facility carefully. Time is your best ally. Though most nursing home admissions occur after a medical emergency such as a fall or a stroke, you can foresee many others. If your parent is becoming increasingly frail or is in the throes of worsening Alzheimer's disease, begin your search by asking for recommendations from health care professionals who

work with the elderly. Try to restrict your selection of nursing homes to ones near the home of either a relative or a friend who could drop in from time to time. If a nursing home operator knows that someone might be visiting your mother at any time, you'll raise the chances that your parent will get the attention she so much deserves.

Tour the facilities mentioned. The nursing home should, of course, be clean and the staff cheerful and compassionate. Look for more subtle indicators, though. For instance, most nursing homes will have bedridden and mentally disturbed patients, so if you don't see any, it means they're hidden away. That's a bad sign. Scan menus and activities to make sure they reflect adult tastes and interests—scallopini and chamber music, not spaghetti and construction paper art. Similarly, you will want some to see flexibility in timetables, rather than rigid scheduling.

Though most nursing homes do not openly discriminate against the indigent, it will be easier to get your parent into a quality home if he is paying the bills directly. However, make sure the home accepts Medicaid in case your parents' resources eventually disappear. Nursing homes have no entry fees, and their rates typically range from about $65 to $150 a day.

Where to Go for Help

The following four resources can help you choose an appropriate home for your parents:

■ **A state unit on aging** can provide free information on services for the elderly in the state. For the location of the unit closest to your parents, call the National Association of State Units on Aging (202-898-2578).

■ **The Eldercare Locator,** sponsored by the U.S. Administration on Aging, will direct you to community programs in your parents' area (800-677-1166).

■ *The Consumers' Directory of Continuing Care Retirement Communities,* published by the American Association of Homes and Services for the Aging, has profiles of more than 550 nonprofit CCRCs throughout the United States as well as worksheets and checklists to help prospective residents compare costs and features among facilities ($28.45; 800-508-9442).

■ **The American Association of Retired Persons (AARP)** has free materials on dozens of subjects, including retrofitting a home for an elderly person, evaluating continuing care communities, and buying long-term-care insurance. (For a catalog of publications, write AARP Fulfillment Services, 601 E St. N.W., Washington, D.C. 20049.)

Helping Out When You're Far Away

More than three-quarters of the elderly with adult children live within 50 miles of at least one offspring. If your parents are in the other 25%, however, or in the 5% who are 1,000 miles or more from their nearest child, offering support from a distance can be anything from a strain to a nightmare. Faraway parents can be a source of constant worry and periodic crises. For many families the best solution is having the parents move closer. This can often be accomplished painlessly at the time your parents decide to sell their home for something smaller. By bringing them for a visit and a tour of nearby retirement facilities, you may be able to lure them to your area.

Otherwise you'll have to find someone to look out for your parents on your behalf. If neither you nor they have much spare money, try to enlist either a kindly neighbor or a government or volunteer assistance program to look after them for free or for a small fee. Your best solution is probably a combination of the two.

First, call local government agencies serving the aging to see if they can refer you to home care services supported by government or charitable funds. Then, if there's a neighbor your parents like and trust, consider asking that person to be your eyes and ears to make sure your parents are getting all they need.

If you can afford it, hire a **professional care manager** or a **geriatric care manager** to make sure someone is looking after your parents at all times. You can often find these specialists, generally social workers with training in gerontology, through local agencies that serve the aging. A care manager will secure and supervise all the care your parents need. If necessary, she (most are women) will find a driver or housekeeper for your parents—even someone who will be sure that your parents' bills are paid on time. Professional care managers charge an hourly fee of $60 to $150; the initial, overall long-term-care plan might run $500 or more. Naturally, you need to make sure that the care manager herself is competent and honest. Credentials count; so look for individuals licensed in social work or psychology who have studied gerontology in a recognized academic program and who have experience and references. For the names of professionals in your parents' area who have met these criteria, call the National Association of Professional Geriatric Care Managers (602-881-8008) or the Aging Network Service (301-657-4329). Once you know that your parents are all right, you can then get back to making sure your finances are peachy, too.

What You Can Get from the Government

The federal government provides dozens of benefits to Americans of all ages. By tapping into them, you can—among other things—help pay for your child's education, start or grow a small business, retire more comfortably, and stay healthier. You probably know about some of them. Chances are you don't know about others. The guide that follows spells out the basics about the major benefits and whom to call to find out more. To find out the phone numbers and addresses of other agencies or for more details about specific government programs, call the Federal Information Center at 800-688-9889. If you would rather get your information about government benefits for the middle class through the Internet, get a copy of *The*

Federal Internet Source, which lists 300 sources of federal information on the Net ($18.95; Subscription Services, National Journal, 1501 M St. N.W., Washington, D.C. 20005; you can e-mail an order to fed-order@netweek.com).

Auto Safety Data

Department of Transportation
800-424-9393

Automated hot line with recorded messages explaining everything from how to report a safety problem with your vehicle or child safety seat to how to find out about recalls to getting reports on tire quality grading and vehicle crash tests. You can discuss a safety problem with a hot line representative, too.

College Loans and Grants

Department of Education
800-4FED-AID (financial aid forms and questions about student aid, and information about consolidating federal student loans); 319-337-5665 (information on the status of student aid applications and requests for duplicate student aid reports)

The U.S. Department of Education handles $32 billion of federal student aid each year. Stafford, Perkins, and PLUS loans must be repaid with interest; Pell grants, awarded based on financial need, do not get repaid. (For details about the programs, see Chapter 10.) To qualify for financial aid, you or your child must submit a financial aid application. Maximum amount of aid for undergraduates: $6,625 for the first year, $7,500 the second year, and $10,500 the third and fourth years. Maximum amount for graduate students: $18,500 a year.

U.S. Department of Veterans Affairs
800-827-1000

If you entered active duty after June 30, 1985, and got an honorable discharge, you qualify for education benefits under the Montgomery GI Bill. You may also be eligible for Montgomery GI Bill benefits if you are still entitled under the Vietnam Era

GI Bill. A GI Bill recipient gets as much as $4,860 a year ($404.88 per month) toward education and training by serving for two years on active duty, followed by four years of Selected Reserve service, or by serving continuously for three years of active duty. Enlist and serve for less than three years and you will get $3,948 a year ($328.97 per month). If you participate in the Montgomery GI Bill, your military pay is reduced by $100 per month for the first 12 months of active duty.

Americorps
800-94-ACORPS

This program—targeted for extinction by Republicans—provides education grants of up to $4,725, plus an annual stipend of $7,500 in exchange for doing 1,700 hours of national service work. Among the volunteer jobs: mentoring at-risk youth; working in neighborhood watch groups; providing assistance to homebound elderly, people with AIDS or disabilities; helping to prevent crime through conflict resolution training.

Consumer Protection

Federal Trade Commission
202-326-2222 for a list of FTC free publications

The FTC publishes dozens of free brochures and booklets giving advice on everything from credit and divorce to shopping from home to investment scams. You can also get answers to questions about your consumer rights and FTC regulations.

FHA Mortgages

Federal Housing Administration
202-708-1112
800-733-HOME (for names of Title I lenders)

You can apply for an FHA-insured mortgage through any FHA-approved lender. The maximum mortgage: $152,362. With an FHA loan the mortgage rate is slightly lower than what the lender normally charges and you can make a down payment as small as 3%. FHA charges a mortgage insurance premium of 2% to 2.25% on the mortgage amount.

You also can get an FHA-insured Title I loan for home improvements of up to $25,000 on a single-family home; $12,000 per unit on apartment buildings and two-family houses as long as you do not borrow more than $60,000. This loan is especially attractive to low- and moderate-income homeowners who might otherwise not qualify for a bank loan. You need not have any specified amount of equity (a requirement with a home-equity loan); you qualify for the loan based on your creditworthiness. Also, you can receive the money quicker than with a standard bank loan since you don't have to get an appraisal. Home improvements can include most types of basic construction such as fixing the roof, adding a room, or finishing the basement. Luxury items like swimming pools and outdoor hot tubs are excluded. FHA charges an insurance premium of 0.5%. The interest rate on a Title I loan is a bit higher than on a home-equity loan but less than that of a personal loan.

Investor Protection

Securities and Exchange Commission
800-SEC-0330
703-321-8020 (via modem)

You can call the automated help line at the Securities and Exchange Commission, which regulates stocks, bonds, and mutual funds, for its free pamphlets about investing. You can also call to find out how to file a complaint about your broker or brokerage. If you need to speak to a person, you'll be directed to the SEC Consumer Affairs Office at 202-942-7040. By dialing in through your modem, you'll get access to the SEC's consumer information library and the *SEC News Digest*.

Commodity Futures Trading Commission (CFTC)
800-676-4NFA (hot line)
202-254-8630 (public information office)

Phone the hot line at the federal commodities regulator to check out a commodities broker or his or her firm. If the firm or trader is not registered with the CFTC, call the commission's public information office. For free publications about futures trading, call the order form number and then mail the form to the Commodity Futures Trading Commission, Office of Public Affairs, Brochures, 2033 K St. N.W., Washington, D.C. 20581.

Medicaid

Health Care Financing Administration
Call your state Medicaid office

This is the federal health insurance program for the poor. Administered by the states, Medicaid not only pays medical bills, it also covers nursing home costs. Coverage, costs, and eligibility based on your income and assets vary by the state. Acute care services generally are provided free or nearly free. Typically, you must be 65 and qualify for Social Security's Supplemental Security Income program. So check with your local Medicaid office to see whether you qualify and what benefits you could get.

Medicare

Health Care Financing Administration
800-638-6833

This is the federal program that provides health benefits to most people over 65. You automatically get a Medicare card in the mail if you start collecting Social Security at 65. Otherwise, when turning 65, you can apply for Medicare through your local Social Security office. Medicare has two parts: Part A is hospital insurance, which helps pay for hospital care, skilled nursing facility care, home health care, and hospice care. Part B is medical insurance, which helps pay for doctors' services and many other medical services and supplies that are not covered by Part A.

Part A has out-of-pocket annual deductibles and coinsurance payments, but most people do not have to pay premiums for Part A. Medicare helps pay for 90 days of hospital care in each so-called benefit period. If you need to stay in the hospital longer, you can use some or all of your 60 lifetime "reserve" days. For the first 60 days of hospitalization in a benefit period, Medicare pays for all covered services after you pay the deductible of roughly $720. From days 61 through 90, Medicare pays all but the daily coinsurance, roughly $180. The daily coinsurance payment for reserve days is about $360.

Medicare Part B has deductibles, coinsurance, and monthly premiums that you must pay either yourself or through coverage by another insurance plan. The monthly premium for Medicare Part B costs about $44 for most beneficiaries. The annual deductible is $100, and you or your Medigap insurer must pay up to 20% for most services.

Pension Protection

Pension Benefit Guaranty Corporation (PBGC)
202-326-4000

This federal agency guarantees traditional pension plans, protecting you in case your employer's plan runs out of money. The maximum annual PBGC benefit is roughly $31,000; less if you retire early. The PBGC does not guarantee 401(k) or other employer-sponsored savings plans.

Small-Business Loans

Small Business Administration (SBA)
800-8ASK-SBA
202-205-6673 (for the women's loan program)
800-697-4636 (SBA Online via modem)

This agency guarantees a variety of loans for small businesses; the guarantee is that if a bank or other financial firm makes an SBA loan and the borrower defaults, the SBA will repay up to 90% of the outstanding balance. You often have more time to repay an SBA loan than an ordinary bank loan.

If you want to start a small business or already run one and can't get a loan you can apply for an SBA **7(a) loan** through a commercial bank. The SBA guarantees 70% to 90% of these working capital loans, and the interest rate is comparable to a bank's standard small-business loan rate. Top rate: 2.25% over the prime rate for loans under seven years; 2.75% over prime for longer loans. Maximum loan: $500,000. These loans offer longer repayment schedules than banks normally do—up to seven years.

You may be able to apply for a **Low-Documentation 7(a) Loan** of up to $100,000 and reduce the paperwork. The LowDoc loan program, offered through commercial lenders, has a one-page application and focuses on the strength of your character as well as your credit history. Interest rates generally are similar to those of a 7(a) program, though rates on loans under $50,000 can be two percentage points higher.

If you need to borrow less than $25,000 and want technical assistance, you can apply for funds through the SBA's **Microloan Program.** The SBA targets these loans for start-ups in inner cities and rural areas and firms run by women and minorities.

If the SBA certifies you as "socially and

economically disadvantaged'' because of racial or ethnic prejudice or if cultural bias has kept you from getting loans or capital for your business, you can be eligible for two special types of SBA assistance (as long as your net wroth is under $250,000). The **8(a) program** provides business development assistance and access to federal contracting programs if your business has been running for two years or more. The **7(j) program** is similar to 8(a) but focuses on management and technical assistance.

If you are a woman business owner, you may be able to apply for a preauthorized loan guaranty commitment of up to $250,000 through the SBA's **Women's Prequalification Pilot Loan Program.** The program is available through commercial lenders and nonprofit intermediaries, such as the nation's 900 Small Business Development Centers in 16 parts of the United States.

You can get an SBA credit line of up to $750,000 through the agency's **Greenline program.** The size of the credit line, provided by a local lender, will depend on your inventory and accounts receivable. It's a helpful way to finance short-term working capital needs.

SBA Online offers information on small-business loans, state profiles for small business, courses on developing a business plan, access to other federal bulletin boards such as the one at the U.S. Patent Office, and e-mail access to the SBA's chief counsel. For access to files from the SBA or other government agencies, call 900-463-4636.

Social Security

Social Security Administration
800-772-1213 (to find the nearest office or get a free earnings and benefits estimate statement)

This is the program that pays retirement, survivors, and disability benefits. Each year you earn credits toward future Social Security benefits—a maximum of four credits per year. Most people need 40 credits to qualify for benefits, although younger people need less to qualify for disability or survivor benefits.

Full **Social Security retirement benefits** are payable when you turn 65, but you can start taking Social Security as early as age 62, with benefits reduced by five-ninths of 1% for each full month you get benefits before age 65. If you delay your retirement beyond age 65 you get bigger benefits when you do retire. Your retirement benefits are calculated based on earnings averaged over your lifetime. Call Social Security for an estimate of your future retirement benefit.

After your death, certain family members may be eligible to get **Social Security survivors benefits** if you earned enough credits while you were working. These family members include your widow(er) if he or she is age 60 or over, 50 or over if disabled, or any age if your spouse is caring for a child under age 16; your children if they are unmarried and under age 18, under 19 but still in school, or 18 or older but disabled; and your parents if you were their primary means of support. Social Security may pay a special onetime award of $225 to your spouse or minor children when you die. If you are divorced, your ex-spouse could also be eligible for a widower's benefit on your record.

You can get **Social Security disability benefits** if you have enough Social Security credits and have a severe physical or mental impairment that prevents you from doing substantial work (making more than $500 per month) for a year or more or you have a condition that is fatal. Some family members can get Social Security disability benefits based on your disability, too. They are a spouse who is at least 62 or under 62 but caring for a child under 16; your unmarried children under 18, ones under 19 but still in school, or ones 18 or older but disabled. If you are divorced, your ex-spouse also could be eligible for disability benefits. The maximum Social Security disability payment is roughly $1,400 a month or $16,800 a year.

If your income is low (under approximately $460 per month) and you have few assets, you may be eligible for **Supplemental Security Income (SSI) benefits** at age 65 or older or when you are disabled. The size of these benefits is based on current financial need, not your past employment earnings. The federal government pays a basic rate of up to $458 a month ($5,496 a year), but most states add money to that amount.

Most cities and small towns have one of the 1,300 Social Security walk-in offices generally open weekdays from 9:00 A.M. to 4:30 P.M. Some of the walk-in sites are also open on Saturdays. By calling the 800 number or visiting your local office, you can find out how much you can expect to get from Social Security when you retire and apply for benefits the year before the year you plan to retire.

Tax Information

Internal Revenue Service
800-TAX-FORM (for forms and publications)
800-829-1040 (for tax help; call your local IRS number first)
800-829-4477 (TeleTax)

You can visit one of the hundreds of local IRS offices nationwide or call for tax help if you need answers to questions about taxes. For a comprehensive list of the free IRS services and the agency's 114 free publications, call and ask for the *Guide to Free Tax Services* (Publication 910). The IRS's TeleTax service provides informative recordings on 140 tax topics. IRS reps can't fill out your tax return for you unless you are handicapped and cannot prepare your own return, but they can review your return and tell you how to fix any mistakes.

Travel Alerts

Department of State
202-647-5225
202-647-9225 (via modem)

Here's how to find out if it's safe to travel to a particular country. Call the State Department number and you'll hear about travel warnings, political conditions, and currency regulations. You can get similar information on-line through the Bureau of Consular Affairs' electronic bulletin board.

Unemployment Benefits

Department of Labor
Call your state unemployment office

If you have been employed for at least a year and get laid off or fired, you can apply for and collect federal unemployment benefits one week after you become unemployed. The size of the benefits depends on your state; for instance, Mississippi pays up to $165 a week, but Massachusetts pays as much as $487 a week. The blue pages of your phone book will tell you the location and phone number of the local office administering unemployment insurance.

Most states pay unemployment benefits for a maximum of 26 weeks, 13 extra weeks in periods of very high unemployment. You usually must actively look for a job in order to collect unemployment.

Veterans Benefits

U.S. Department of Veterans Affairs
800-827-1000
800-US1-VETS (via modem)

Eligible military veterans get a variety of free and subsidized medical, disability, pension, and mortgage benefits from the government.

The VA *must* provide **hospital care** to you, regardless of your income, if you are a vet and either get a VA pension; are eligible for Medicaid; have service-connected disabilities; were exposed to herbicides while serving in Vietnam; were exposed to ionizing radiation during atmospheric testing or in the occupation of Hiroshima and Nagasaki; have a condition related to service in the Persian Gulf; are a former prisoner of war or a veteran of the Mexican border period of World War 1; or are a veteran eligible for Medicaid.

If you are a vet who doesn't fit into those categories, you can get health care from the VA if you didn't sustain or aggravate disabilities during military service (a "nonservice-connected veteran") and your income is $20,469 or less (for singles with no dependents) or $24,565 or less (for married or singles with one dependent; the income maximum rises by $1,368 for each additional dependent). You may also be entitled to VA nursing home care if the space and resources are available. If your income is higher than those thresholds, your VA hospital care is considered "discretionary." That means you must pay a deductible equal to what you would have under Medicare (about $720). The VA may provide hospital, outpatient, and nursing home care if space and resources are available. You'll owe an out-of-pocket co-payment equal to the Medicare deductible for the first 90 days of care, including nursing home care, during a 365-day period; half the Medicare deductible for hospital care. Also, you'll owe a co-payment of up to $39 for each outpatient visit, $10 per day for hospital care, and $5 a day for any nursing home care.

You can get monthly **disability benefits** if you are a veteran who was disabled by an injury or disease that happened during (or was aggravated by) active military service in the line of duty and were honorably discharged. If your disabilities are severe, you may be able to receive up to $5,212 per month in nontaxable benefits. You cannot get disability compensation along with military retirement pay.

If your income is limited (less than roughly $8,000 to $9,000 a year) and you are permanently and totally disabled, you may be eligible for a **VA pension.** To qualify, you must have had 90 days or more of active military service, at least one day of which was during a period of war; you must have been honorably discharged; and your disability must not be traceable to military service. You will not get the pension if your assets could provide adequate maintenance. The maximum annual pension: $7,818 for singles; $9,556 for those permanently housebound with no dependents; $10,240 for vets who are married or have a child and for vets married to one another; $11,977 for those permanently housebound with one dependent; $12,504 for those without dependents who need regular aid; and $14,927 for those needing regular aid who have one dependent. Add $1,330 for each additional dependent child.

The VA also guarantees a portion of VA mortgages taken out by vets and their surviving spouses who have not remarried. You get a VA mortgage from a commercial lender; the lender sets the interest rate. If the loan is a graduated-payment mortgage, you must make a 5% down payment. The VA fee of 1.25% to 3% is waived if you are on disability.

Veterans are also entitled to burial benefits in a VA National Cemetery, including headstone and markers, provided at the government's expense. The person making your funeral arrangements will need a copy of your discharged certificate.

The VA's on-line service lets you surf through a Persian Gulf newsletter, read short descriptions of VA benefits and how to apply for them, and learn how to contact some VA staff offices on-line.

Index

552